CITIZEN SOLDIERS

The US Army from the Normandy Beaches to the Surrender of Germany

Stephen E. Ambrose

D0034104

POCKET
BOOKS

TO MOIRA

Contents

Maps

Introduction and Acknowledgments

THIS BOOK is about the citizen soldiers of the U.S. Army and U.S. Army Air Forces in the European Theater of Operations in World War II. It is not a comprehensive history of the campaign in Northwest Europe that began on D-Day and ended with Germany's surrender eleven months later. Although it includes some material on strategy, especially on the Eisenhower-Montgomery relationship and the Bradley-Patton-Hodges-Montgomery competition—enough, I hope, to keep the reader abreast of the big picture—it is not a book about the generals. It is about the GIs, the junior officers and enlisted men of ETO—who they were, how they fought, why they fought, what they endured, how they triumphed.

I make my living by reading other people's mail, listening to their stories, reading their memoirs. My job is to pick out the best and most representative, the ones that illuminate common themes or illustrate typical actions. Long ago my mentors, William B. Hesseltine and T. Harry Williams, taught me to let my characters speak for themselves by quoting them liberally. They were there. I wasn't. They saw with their own eyes, they put their own lives on the line. I didn't. They speak with an authenticity no one else can match. Their phrases, their word choices, their slang are unique—naturally enough, as their experiences were unique.

In his 1997 book *For Cause and Comrades: Why Men Fought*

the Civil War, America's leading Civil War scholar James M. McPherson compares the motivation of Billy Yank and Johnny Reb to that of the GIs. He argues that the Civil War soldiers fought for cause and country even more than they fought for comrades and that it was just the opposite for the GIs. Now it is certainly true that unit cohesion, teamwork, the development of a sense of family in the squad and platoon, are the qualities most World War II combat veterans point to when asked how they survived and won. That is the theme of almost all my writing about the military, from Lewis and Clark to George Armstrong Custer to Eisenhower to D-Day. It is the theme of this book.

But I think unit cohesion was as important to Billy Yank and Johnny Reb as to the GIs. Further, I think cause and country were as critical to the GIs as to the Civil War soldiers. The differences between them were not of feeling, but of expression. Civil War soldiers were accustomed to using words like duty, honor, cause and country. The GIs didn't like to talk about country or flag and were embarrassed by patriotic bombast. They were all American boys, separated by eighty years only—but that separation included World War I. The Great War changed the language. It made patriotic words sound hollow, unacceptable, ridiculous, especially for the next set of young Americans sent to Europe to fight over the same battlefields their fathers had fought over. Nevertheless, as much as the Civil War soldiers, the GIs believed in their cause. They knew they were fighting for decency and democracy and they were proud of it and motivated by it. They just didn't talk or write about it. They speak with their own voices and in their own words.

They were, overwhelmingly, high school or college students when America got into the war. They were drafted or enlisted voluntarily in 1942, 1943, 1944. They entered France beginning on June 6, 1944. From June 7 to September, they came in over Omaha and Utah Beaches; from September to the spring of 1945, they came in at Cherbourg and Le Havre. They came as liberators, not conquerors. Only a tiny percentage of them wanted to be there, but only a small percentage of these men failed to do their duty.

My sources begin with the men of D-Day. As far as possible I follow the GIs quoted in my book on the invasion through to the end of the war, men like Dutch Schultz, Dick Winters, Bob Slaughter, Len Lomell, Sid Salomon, Ken Russell, Jack Barensfeld, and others. In that sense this book is a sequel.

But there are many new voices in this book, of men who came into the campaign from June 7 onward. The Eisenhower Center at the University of New Orleans, under the leadership of Director Doug Brinkley and Assistant Director Ron Drez, has been collecting oral histories and written memoirs from the veterans of ETO on a continuing basis. They now number in the hundreds and they form the base of this book. To every veteran who has contributed his oral history or written memoir to the Eisenhower Center, my heartfelt thanks. It is not possible to quote all of them, but all of them contributed to this book.

In addition, the fiftieth anniversaries of D-Day, the Battle of the Bulge, the crossing of the Rhine, and V-E day brought forth a flood of books by veterans about their own experiences, their squads, their companies. Among the best of these are Bruce Egger and Lee Otts, *G Company's War: Two Personal Accounts of the Campaigns in Europe, 1944–1945;* Harold Leinbaugh and John Campbell, *The Men of Company K: The Autobiography of a World War II Rifle Company;* Paul Fussell, *Doing Battle: The Making of a Skeptic;* John Colby, *War from the Ground Up;* David Kenyon Webster, *Parachute Infantry: An American Paratrooper's Memoir;* and Kurt Gabel, *The Making of a Paratrooper.* There are too many others to name here; they are in the bibliography. The fiftieth anniversaries also prompted the publication of numerous oral history books; among the many that I use, Dorothy Chernitsky, *Voices from the Foxholes* (110th Infantry Regiment, 28th Division) and Gerald Astor, *The Mighty Eighth: The Air War in Europe as Told by the Men Who Fought It* stand out. Of course I used all the standard histories, old and new. As always, Russell Weigley's *Eisenhower's Lieutenants* was my guide and fact checker. I also stole material profitably if shamelessly from Michael Doubler's *Closing with the Enemy: How GIs Fought the War in Europe, 1944–1945,* and Joseph Balkoski's *Beyond the Beachhead: The 29th Infantry Division in Normandy.*

On May 7–8, 1995, the Eisenhower Center (with invaluable support from David Craig) sponsored a conference on the war in Europe. Among those who participated were Andy Rooney, Kurt Vonnegut, and Joe Heller. Rooney gave me a front-line reporter's view of the war; Vonnegut and Heller gave me a novelist's view. The funny thing was, none of these guys was funny when he talked about his personal experiences in the war. They were moving and vivid.

I wanted more German voices for this book than I had in *D-Day*. I wanted to know more about what it was like for them, and even more how they viewed my subject, the GIs. On March 5–8, 1995, my son Hugh and Hans von Luck's son Alexander ("Sasha") joined me, Ken Hechler (author of *The Bridge at Remagen*), some veterans of the U.S. 9th Armored Division, and a group of German veterans who had been at Remagen on March 7, 1945, to talk about what happened there. Afterwards, Hugh and Sasha took off for a two-month tour of Germany, interviewing German soldiers. Sasha's father provided them with names and introductions, as did Captain Dieter Kollmer of the historical section of today's German army. Altogether Hugh and Sasha did sixty oral histories; when he got home to Helena, Montana, Hugh translated and transcribed them for me. Hugh also did the photo research.

Alice Mayhew, Elizabeth Stein, and the entire production team at Simon and Schuster were outstanding, as they always are.

The dedication is to the one I love.

STEPHEN E. AMBROSE
Bay St. Louis, Mississippi
February 13, 1997

Prologue

FIRST LIGHT came to Ste.-Mère-Eglise around 0510. Twenty-four hours earlier, it had been just another Norman village, with more than a millennium behind it. By nightfall of June 6, it was a name known around the world, the village where the invasion began and now headquarters for the 82nd Airborne Division.

At dawn on June 7, Lt. Waverly Wray, executive officer in Company D, 505th Parachute Infantry Regiment (PIR), who had jumped into the night sky over Normandy twenty-eight hours earlier, was on the northwestern outskirts of the village. He peered intently into the lifting gloom. What he couldn't see, he could sense. From the sounds of the movement of personnel and vehicles to the north of Ste.-Mère-Eglise, he could feel and figure that the major German counterattack, the one the Germans counted on to drive the Americans into the sea and the one the paratroopers had been expecting, was coming at Ste.-Mère-Eglise.

It was indeed. Six thousand German soldiers were on the move, with infantry, artillery, tanks, and self-propelled guns—more than a match for the 600 or so lightly armed paratroopers in Ste.-Mère-Eglise. A German breakthrough to the beaches seemed imminent. And Lieutenant Wray was at the point of attack.

Wray was a big man, 250 pounds with "legs like tree trunks." The standard-issue Army parachute wasn't large enough for his weight and he dropped too fast on his jumps, but the men said hell, with his legs he don't need a chute. He was from Batesville, Mississippi, and was an avid woodsman, skilled with rifles and shotguns. He claimed he had never missed a shot in his life. A veteran of the Sicily and Italy campaigns, Wray was—in the words of Col. Ben Vandervoort, commanding the 505th—"as experienced and skilled as an infantry soldier can get and still be alive."[1]

Wray had Deep South religious convictions. A Baptist, each month he sent half his pay home to help build a new church. He never swore. His exclamation when exasperated was, "John Brown!" meaning abolitionist John Brown of Harpers Ferry. He didn't drink, smoke, or chase girls. Some troopers called him "The Deacon," but in an admiring rather than critical way. Vandervoort had something of a father-son relationship with Wray, always calling him by his first name, "Waverly."

On June 7, shortly after dawn, Wray reported to Vandervoort—whose leg, broken in the jump, was now in a cast—on the movements he had spotted, the things he had sensed, where he expected the Germans to attack and in what strength.

Vandervoort took all this in, then ordered Wray to return to the company and have it attack the German flank before the Germans could get their attack started.

"He said 'Yes Sir,' " Vandervoort later wrote, "saluted, about-faced, and moved out like a parade ground Sergeant Major."

Back in the company area, Wray passed on the order. As the company prepared to attack, he took up his M-1, grabbed a half-dozen grenades, and strode out, his Colt .45 on his hip and a silver-plated .38 revolver stuck in his jump boot. He was going to do a one-man reconnaissance to formulate a plan of attack.

Wray was going out into the unknown. He had spent half a year preparing for this moment but he was not trained for it. In one of the greatest intelligence failures of all time, neither G-2 (intelligence) at U.S. First Army nor SHAEF G-2, nor any division S-2 had ever thought to tell the men who were going to fight the battle that the dominant physical feature of the battlefield was the maze of hedgerows that covered the western half of Normandy.

One hundred years before Lieutenant Wray came to Normandy, Honoré de Balzac had described the hedges: "The peasants, from time immemorial, have raised a bank of earth about each field, forming a flat-topped ridge, two meters in height, with beeches, oaks, and chestnut trees growing upon the summit. The ridge or mound, planted in this wise, is called a hedge; and as the long branches of the trees which grow upon it almost always project across the road, they make a great arbor overhead. The roads themselves, shut in by clay banks in this melancholy way, are not unlike the moats of fortresses."[2]

How could the various G-2s have missed such an obvious feature, especially as aerial reconnaissance clearly revealed the hedges? Because the photo interpreters, looking only straight down at them, thought that they were like English hedges, the kind the fox hunters jump over, and they had missed the sunken nature of the roads entirely. "We had been neither informed of them or trained to overcome them," was Captain John Colby's brief comment.[3] The GIs would have to learn by doing, as Wray was doing on the morning of June 7.

Wray and his fellow paratroopers, like the men from the 1st and 29th Divisions at Omaha and the 4th Division at Utah, and all the support groups, had been magnificently trained to launch an amphibious assault. By nightfall of June 6, they had done the real thing successfully, thanks to their training, courage, and dash. But beginning at dawn, June 7, they were fighting in a terrain completely unexpected and unfamiliar to them.

The Germans, meanwhile, had been going through specialized training for fighting in hedgerows. "Coming within thirty meters of the enemy was what we meant by close combat," Pvt. Adolf Rogosch of the 353rd Division recalled. "We trained hard, throwing hand grenades, getting to know the ground. The lines of hedges crisscrossing one another played tricks on your eyes. We trained to fight as individuals; we knew when the attack came we'd probably be cut off from one another. We let them come forward and cross the hedge, then we blew them apart. That was our tactic, to wait until they crossed over the hedge and then shoot."[4]

The Germans also pre-sited mortars and artillery on the single gaps that provided the only entrances into the fields. Behind the hedgerows, they dug rifle pits and tunneled openings for machine-gun positions in each corner.

Wray moved up sunken lanes, crossed an orchard, pushed his way through hedgerows, crawled through a ditch. Along the way he noted concentrations of Germans, in fields and lanes. A man without his woodsman's sense of direction would have gotten lost. He reached a point near the N-13, the main highway coming into Ste.-Mère-Eglise from Cherbourg.

The N-13 was the axis of the German attack. Wray, "moving like the deer stalker he was" (Vandervoort's words), got to a place where he could hear guttural voices on the other side of a hedgerow. They sounded like officers talking about map coordinates. Wray rose up, burst through the obstacle, swung his M-1 to a ready position, and barked in his strong command voice, "Hände hoch!" to the eight German officers gathered around a radio.

Seven instinctively raised their hands. The eighth tried to pull a pistol from his holster; Wray shot him instantly, between the eyes. Two Germans in a slit trench 100 meters to Wray's rear fired bursts from their Schmeisser machine pistols at him. Bullets cut through his jacket; one cut off half of his right ear.

Wray dropped to his knee and began shooting the other seven officers, one at a time as they attempted to run away. When he had used up his clip, Wray jumped into a ditch, put another clip into his M-1, and dropped the German soldiers with the Schmeissers with one shot each.

Wray made his way back to the company area to report on what he had seen. At the command post (CP) he came in with blood down his jacket, a big chunk of his ear gone, holes in his clothing. "Who's got more grenades?" he demanded. He wanted more grenades.

Then he started leading. He put a 60mm mortar crew on the German flank and directed fire into the lanes and hedgerows most densely packed with the enemy. Next he sent D Company into an attack down one of the lanes. The Germans broke and ran. By mid-morning Ste.-Mère-Eglise was secure and the potential for a German breakthrough to the beaches was much diminished.

The next day Vandervoort, Wray, and Sgt. John Rabig went to the spot to examine the German officers Wray had shot. Unforgettably, their bodies were sprinkled with pink and white apple blossom petals from an adjacent orchard. It turned out that they were the commanding officer (CO) and his staff of the 1st Battalion, 158th Grenadier Infantry Regiment. The maps showed that it was leading the way for the counterattack. The German confusion and subsequent retreat were in part due to having been rendered leaderless by Wray.

Vandervoort later recalled that when he saw the blood on Wray's jacket and the missing half-ear, he had remarked, "They've been getting kind of close to you, haven't they Waverly?"

With just a trace of a grin, Wray had replied, "Not as close as I've been getting to them, Sir."

At the scene of the action, Vandervoort noted that every one of the dead Germans, including the two Schmeisser-armed Grenadiers more than 100 meters away, had been killed with a single shot in the head. Wray insisted on burying the bodies. He said he had killed them, and they deserved a decent burial, and it was his responsibility.

Later that day, Sergeant Rabig commented to Vandervoort, "Colonel, aren't you glad Waverly's on our side?"

The next day Rabig wasn't so sure. He and Wray were crouched behind a hedgerow. American artillery was falling into the next field. "I could hear these Germans screaming as they were getting hit. Lieutenant Wray said, 'John, I wish that artillery would stop so we can go in after them.'

"Jesus! I thought, the artillery is doing good enough."

Before the battle was joined, Hitler had been sure his young men would outfight the young Americans. He was certain that the spoiled sons of democracy couldn't stand up to the solid sons of dictatorship. If he had seen Lieutenant Wray in action in the early morning of D-Day Plus One, he might have had some doubts.

Of course, Wray was special. You don't get more than one Wray to a division, or even to an army. Vandervoort compared Wray to a sergeant in the 82nd Division in World War I, also a Southern boy, named Alvin York. Yet if the qualities Wray possessed were unique, others could aspire to them without hoping or expecting to match Wray's spectacular performance. Indeed they would have to if the United States was going to win the war. Victory depended on the junior officers and NCOs on the front lines. That is the spine of this book.

The campaign in Northwest Europe, 1944–45, was a tremendous struggle on a gigantic stage. It was a test of many things, such as how well the Wehrmacht had done in changing its tactics and weapons to defend the empire it had seized in blitzkrieg warfare; how well the assembly lines of the Allies and of the Axis were doing in providing the weapons; the skill of the generals; the proper employment of airplanes on the defense and on the offense; and much more. The test this book looks at is how well General George C. Marshall and that relative handful of professional officers serving in the U.S. Army in 1940 had done in creating an army of citizen soldiers from scratch. Weapon selection and quantities, how many divisions, and a myriad of other problems demanded decisions because of the explosive growth of the Army—from 160,000 in 1939 to over eight million in 1944—and only Marshall and a handful of officers were capable of making those decisions.

All the problems were important, most critical. But the one that mattered above all others was human. America had the numbers of men and could produce the weapons for a mass army, and transport it to Europe, no question about it. But could she provide the leaders that an eight-million-man army required—the leaders at the people level, primarily captains, lieutenants, and sergeants?

Hitler had thought not, and even U.S. Army Chief of Staff George Marshall had his doubts. At the end of the first year of expansion, General Marshall reported that junior officers lacked experience, had little confidence in themselves, and hence failed to assume or discharge their responsibilities.[5] Marshall had put his prodigious talents into an effort to overcome these problems and all the others. He had created the U.S. Army of World War II with a campaign in Northwest Europe in mind. He had designed the Army to take on the Wehrmacht in France, to defeat it in battle, to drive it out of France and destroy it in the process. How well he had done was to be discovered.

The success of D-Day was a good start, but that was yesterday. The Allies had only barely penetrated Germany's outermost defenses and had engaged only a tiny fraction of the German army in France. The Wehrmacht was not the army it had been three years earlier, but it was an army that had refused to die, even after Moscow, Stalingrad, and Kursk.

That the Wehrmacht kept its cohesion through the course of these catastrophes has been attributed to the superior training of its junior officers. They were not only grounded in detail and doctrine, but were encouraged to think and act independently in a battle situation. They also made a critical contribution to the primary bonding—the *Kameradschaft*—that was so strong and traditional in the German army at the squad level.

Could the American junior officers do as well? Could the U.S. Army defeat the German army in France? The answer to the second question depended on the answer to the first.

THE BATTLE FOR FRANCE

On D-Day, the Allies put some 175,000 men ashore in Normandy. Hundreds of thousands in Britain and the States were set to follow. These reinforcements began coming in at dawn on June 7, 1944. This is the story of how they teamed up and overcame determined German resistance to broaden the beachhead, then to overrun Normandy, then to overrun France and drive to the German border.

1

Expanding the Beachhead

June 7–30, 1944

SHORTLY AFTER DAWN on June 7, Lt. Horace Henderson of the Sixth Engineer Special Brigade landed on Omaha Beach. Going in on his Higgins boat,* "I noticed that nothing moved on the beach except one bulldozer. The beach was covered with debris, sunken craft and wrecked vehicles. We saw many bodies in the water. . . . We jumped into chest high water and waded ashore. Then we saw that the beach was literally covered with the bodies of American soldiers wearing the blue and gray patches of the 29th Infantry Division."

Although the fighting had moved inland, sporadic artillery shelling and intermittent sniper fire from Germans still holding their positions on the bluff hampered movement on the beach. Henderson's job was to distribute maps (a critical and never-ending process—eventually in the Normandy campaign, the U.S. First Army passed out 125 million maps), but because the front line was just over the bluff at Omaha, only men, ammunition, weapons, and gasoline were being brought ashore, so he had no maps to hand out. He and his section unloaded jerry cans of gasoline, the first of millions of such cans that would cross that beach.

*Named for its inventor and producer, Andrew Higgins of New Orleans. The Navy designated it Landing Craft Vehicle Personnel (LCVP).

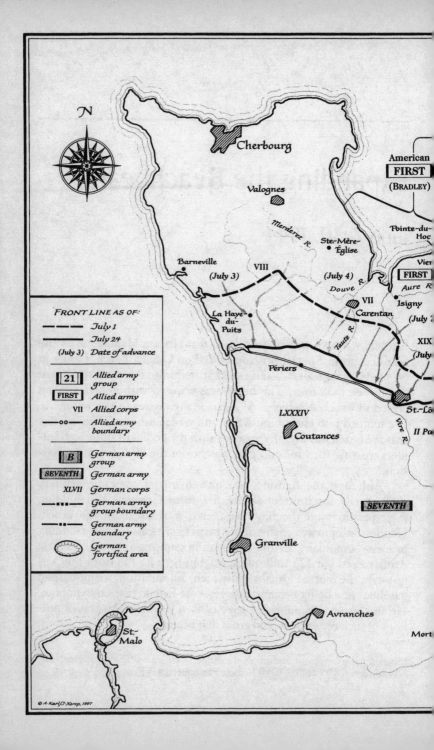

N

Cherbourg

Valognes

Merderet R.

Ste-Mère-
Église

Barneville

VIII

(July 3)

(July 4)

Douve R.

VII

La Haye-
du-
Puits

Carentan

Taute R.

Périers

Pointe-du-
Hoc

Vier

American
FIRST
(BRADLEY)

FIRST

Aure R.

Isigny

(July

XIX

(July

St-Lô

Vire R.

LXXXIV

Coutances

II Pa

SEVENTH

FRONT LINE AS OF:

– – –   July 1

———   July 24

(July 3) Date of advance

21   Allied army
        group

FIRST   Allied army

VII   Allied corps

–oo–   Allied army
        boundary

B   German army
        group

SEVENTH German army

XLVII   German corps

–•••– German army
        group boundary

–••–   German army
        boundary

German
fortified area

Granville

St-
Malo

Avranches

Mort

© A. Karl/J. Kemp, 1997

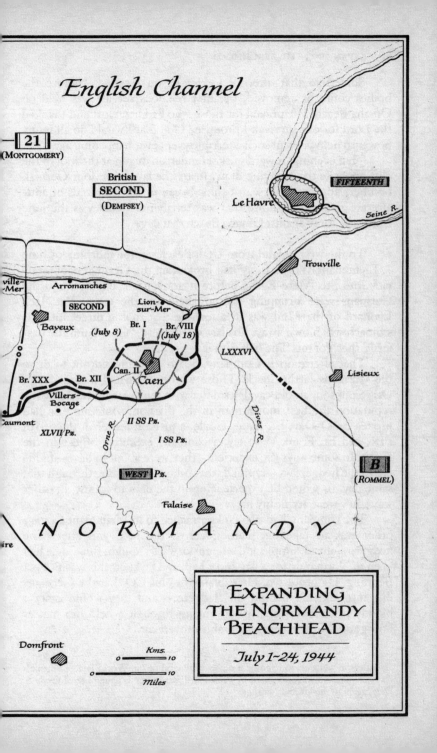

English Channel

21
(MONTGOMERY)

British
SECOND
(DEMPSEY)

FIFTEENTH

Le Havre

Seine R.

Trouville

ville-
Mer

Arromanches

SECOND

Lion-
sur-Mer

Bayeux

(July 8)

Br. I

Br. VIII
(July 18)

LXXXVI

Lisieux

Br. XXX

Br. XII

Can. II
Caen

Villers-
Bocage

Caumont

XLVII Ps.

II SS Ps.

Orne R.

I SS Ps.

Dives R.

B
(ROMMEL)

WEST Ps.

Falaise

N O R M A N D Y

ire

Domfront

EXPANDING
THE NORMANDY
BEACHHEAD

July 1–24, 1944

Kms.
0   10

0   10
Miles

Sometime that afternoon, Henderson recalled, "before the bodies could be removed, the first religious service was held on Omaha Beach. We prayed for those who had been lost and thanked the Lord for our survival. I promised God that I would do all in my power to help prevent such a terrible event ever happening again."*

That evening, toward dusk, Henderson dug in at the foot of the cliff opposite the Vierville draw. Just as he lay down, four German bombers appeared. "A sea of ships began to fire hundreds of anti-aircraft guns with a noise that was terrifying." That was the lone Luftwaffe foray against Omaha Beach that day.[1]

To the west, inland from Utah Beach, on the morning of June 7, Lieutenant Wray's foray had broken up the German counterattack into Ste.-Mère-Eglise before it got started. But by noon the Germans were dropping mortar shells on the town. Pvt. Jack Leonard of the 82nd was in a foxhole that took a direct hit. His stomach was blown away. His last words were, "God damn the bastards, they got me. The hell with it."[2]

That afternoon E Company, 505th PIR, moved out to drive the Germans farther back. Those who participated included Sgt. Otis Sampson, an old cavalry soldier with ten years in the Army, by reputation the best mortarman in the division, something he had proved on D-Day; Lt. James Coyle, a platoon leader in the 505th PIR; and Lt. Frank Woosley, a company executive officer in the 505th. In some ways the experience they were about to have—fighting in the hedgerows—typified what others were going through that same day, or would be experiencing in the days to follow; in other ways they were atypically lucky.

The company had two tanks attached to it. Lieutenant Coyle's order was to take his platoon across the field and attack the hedgerow ahead, simple and straightforward enough. But Coyle had been in Normandy for a day and a half, and he knew this wasn't Fort Benning. He protested. He explained to his CO that the Germans dug into and hid behind the hedgerows and they would exact a bloody price from infantry advancing through a field, no matter how good the men were at fire-and-movement.

*Henderson went on to become a director general of the World Peace Through Law Center, and was appointed by President Eisenhower as a member of the U.S. Delegation to the United Nations.

Coyle figured there had to be a better way. He received permission to explore alternate routes. Lieutenant Woosley accompanied him. Sure enough, Coyle found a route through the sunken lanes that brought the Americans to a point where they were looking down a lane running perpendicular to the one they were on. It was the main German position, inexplicably without cover or observation posts on its flank.

The paratroopers were thus able to observe an unsuspecting German battalion at work. It had only arrived at the position a quarter of an hour earlier (which may explain the unguarded flank) but it already had transformed the lane into a fortress. Communication wires ran up and down. Mortar crews worked their weapons. Sergeants with binoculars leaned against the bank and peered through openings cut in the hedge, directing the mortar fire. Other forward observers had radios and were directing the firing of heavy artillery from the rear. Riflemen at the embankment also had cut holes through which they could aim and fire. At the near and far corners of the lane, the corners of the field, German heavy machine guns were tunneled in, the muzzles of their guns just peeking through a small hole in the embankment, with crews at the ready to send crisscrossing fire into the field in front.

That was the staggering firepower Coyle's platoon would have run into, had he obeyed without question his original orders. Because he had refused and successfully argued his point, he was now on the German flank with his men and two tanks behind him. The tanks did a ninety-degree turn. The men laid down a base of rifle and machine-gun fire, greatly aided by a barrage of mortars from Sergeant Sampson. Then the tanks shot their 75mm cannon down the lane.

Germans fell all around. Sampson fired all his mortar shells, then picked up a BAR. "I was that close I couldn't miss," he remembered. "That road was their death trap. It was so easy I felt ashamed of myself and quit firing. I felt I had bagged my quota."[3]

The German survivors waved a white flag. Coyle told his men to cease fire, stood up, walked down the lane to take the surrender. Two grenades came flying over the hedgerow and landed at his feet. He dove to the side and escaped, and the firing opened up again. The Americans had the Germans trapped in the lane, and after a period of taking casualties without being able to inflict any, the German soldiers began to take off, bursting through the hedgerow and emerging into the field with hands held high, crying "Comrade!"

Soon there were 200 or so men in the field, hands up. Coyle went through the hedgerow, to begin the rounding-up process, and promptly got hit in the thigh by a sniper's bullet, not badly but he was furious with himself for twice not being cautious enough. But he had great self-control, and he got the POWs gathered in and put under guard. He and his men had effectively destroyed an enemy battalion without losing a single man.

It was difficult finding enough men for guard duty, as there was only one GI for every ten captured Germans. The guards therefore took no chances. Corp. Sam Applebee encountered a German officer who refused to move. "I took a bayonet and shoved it into his ass," Applebee recounted, "and then he moved. You should have seen the happy smiles and giggles that escaped the faces of some of the prisoners, to see their Lord and Master made to obey, especially from an enlisted man."[4]

Sergeant Sampson saw another NCO shooting directly down with his BAR. He was the only man shooting. On investigation, Sampson discovered that he was shooting disarmed prisoners who were standing in the ditch, hands up. The GI was blazing away. "There must have been some hate in his heart," Sampson commented.[5]

E Company's experience on June 7 was unique, or nearly so— an unguarded German flank was seldom again to be found. But in another way, what the company went through was to be repeated across Normandy in the weeks that followed. In the German army, the slave troops from conquered Central and Eastern Europe, and Asia, would throw their hands up at the first opportunity, but if they misjudged their situation and their NCO was around, they were likely to get shot in the back. Or the NCOs would keep up the fight even as their enlisted men surrendered, as Coyle discovered.

Lt. Leon Mendel was an interrogation officer with Military Intelligence, attached to the 505th. He did the interrogation of the prisoners Coyle's platoon had taken. "I started off with German," Mendel remembered, "but got no response, so I switched to Russian, asked if they were Russian. 'Yes!' they responded, heads bobbing eagerly. 'We are Russian. We want to go to America!'

"Me too," Mendel said in Russian. "Me too!"[6]

The Wehrmacht in Normandy in June of 1944 was an international army. It had troops from every corner of the vast Soviet empire—Mongolians, Cossacks, Georgians, Muslims, Chinese—plus men from the Soviet Union's neighboring countries, men who had been conscripted into the Red Army, then captured by the Germans in 1941 or 1942. There were some Koreans, captured by the Red Army in the 1939 war with Japan. In Normandy in June 1944, the 29th Division captured enemy troops of so many different nationalities that one GI blurted to his company commander, "Captain, just who the hell *are* we fighting, anyway?"[7]

Ethnic Germans also surrendered. Even veterans of the Eastern Front. Corp. Friedrich Bertenrath of the 2nd Panzer Division explained, "In Russia, I could imagine nothing but fighting to the last man. We knew that going into a prison camp in Russia meant you were dead. In Normandy, one always had in the back of his mind, 'Well, if everything goes to hell, the Americans are human enough that the prospect of becoming their prisoner was attractive to some extent.' "[8]

By no means were all the enlisted German personnel in Normandy reluctant warriors. Many fought effectively; some fought magnificently. At St.-Marcouf, about ten kilometers north of Utah Beach, the Germans had four enormous casements, each housing a 205mm cannon. On D-Day, these guns had gotten into a duel with American battleships. On D-Day Plus One, GIs from the 4th Infantry Division surrounded the casements. To hold them off, the German commander called down fire from another battery of 205 cannon some fifteen kilometers to the north, right on top of his own position. That kept the Americans at bay for more than a week while the German cannon continued to fire sporadically on Utah Beach

The casements took innumerable direct hits, all from big shells. The shells made little more than dents in the concrete. The casements are still there today—they will be there for decades if not centuries, so well built were they—and they bear mute testimony to the steadfastness of the Germans. For eight days the gun crews were confined in their casements—nothing to eat but stale bread, only bad water, no separate place to relieve themselves, the ear-shattering noise, the vibrations, the concussions, the dust shaking loose—through it all they continued to fire. They gave up only when they ran out of ammunition.

Among other elite German outfits in Normandy, there were paratroopers. They were a different proposition altogether from the Polish or Russian troops. The 3rd *Fallschirmjäger* Division came into the battle in Normandy on June 10, arriving by truck after night drives from Brittany. It was a full-strength division, 15,976 men in its ranks, mostly young German volunteers. It was new to combat but it had been organized and trained by a veteran paratroop battalion from the Italian campaign. Training had been rigorous and emphasized initiative and improvisation. The equipment was outstanding.

Indeed, the *Fallschirmjäger* were perhaps the best-armed infantrymen in the world in 1944. The 3rd FJ had 930 light machine guns, eleven times as many as its chief opponent, the U.S. 29th Division. Rifle companies in the FJ had twenty MG 42s and 43 submachine guns; rifle companies in the 29th had two machine guns and nine BARs. At the squad level, the GIs had a single BAR; the German parachute squad had two MG 42s and three submachine guns. The Germans had three times as many mortars as the Americans, and heavier ones. So in any encounter between equal numbers of Americans and *Fallschirmjäger,* the Germans had from six to twenty times as much firepower.[9]

And these German soldiers were ready to fight. A battalion commander in the 29th remarked to an unbelieving counterpart from another regiment, "Those Germans are the best soldiers I ever saw. They're smart and they don't know what the word 'fear' means. They come in and they keep coming until they get their job done or you kill 'em."[10]

These were the men who had to be rooted out of the hedgerows. One by one. There were, on average, fourteen hedgerows to the kilometer in Normandy. The enervating, costly process of gearing up for an attack, making the attack, carrying the attack home, mopping up after the attack, took half a day or more. And at the end of the action, there was the next hedgerow, fifty to a hundred meters or so away. All through the Cotentin Peninsula, from June 7 on, GIs labored at the task. They heaved and pushed and punched and died doing it, for two hedgerows a day.

No terrain in the world was better suited for defensive action with the weapons of the fourth decade of the twentieth century than the Norman hedgerows, and only the lava and coral, caves and tunnels of Iwo Jima and Okinawa were as favorable.

The Norman hedgerows dated back to Roman times. They were mounds of earth to keep cattle in and to mark boundaries. Typically there was only one entry into the small field enclosed by the hedgerows, which were irregular in length as well as height and set at odd angles. On the sunken roads the brush often met overhead, giving the GIs a feeling of being trapped in a leafy tunnel. Wherever they looked the view was blocked by walls of vegetation.

Undertaking an offensive in the hedgerows was risky, costly, time-consuming, fraught with frustration. It was like fighting in a maze. Platoons found themselves completely lost a few minutes after launching an attack. Squads got separated. Just as often, two platoons from the same company could occupy adjacent fields for hours before discovering each other's presence. The small fields limited deployment possibilities; seldom during the first week of battle did a unit as large as a company go into an attack intact.

Where the Americans got lost, the Germans were at home. The 352nd Division had been in Normandy for months, training for this battle. Further, the Germans were geniuses at utilizing the fortification possibilities of the hedgerows. In the early days of the battle, many GIs were killed or wounded because they dashed through the opening into a field, just the kind of aggressive tactics they had been taught, only to be cut down by pre-sited machine-gun fire or mortars (mortars caused three quarters of American casualties in Normandy).

American Army tactical manuals stressed the need for tank-infantry cooperation. But in Normandy, the tankers didn't want to get down on the sunken roads, because of insufficient room to traverse the turret and insufficient visibility to use the long-range firepower of the cannon and machine guns. But staying on the main roads proved impossible; the Germans held the high ground inland and had their 88mm cannon sited to provide long fields of fire along highways. So into the lanes the tanks perforce went. But there they were restricted; they wanted to get out into the fields. But they couldn't. When they appeared at the gap leading into a field, pre-sited mortar fire, plus panzerfausts (handheld antitank weapons), disabled them. Often, in fact, it caused them to "brew up," or start burning—the tankers were discovering that their tanks had a distressing propensity for catching fire.

So tankers tried going over or through the embankments, but the hedgerows were proving to be almost impassable obstacles to the American M4 Sherman tank. Countless attempts were made to break through or climb over, but the Sherman wasn't powerful enough to break through the cementlike base, and when it climbed up the embankment, at the apex it exposed its unarmored belly to German panzerfausts. Further, coordination between tankers and infantry was almost impossible under battle conditions, as they had no easy or reliable way to communicate with one another.

Lt. Sidney Salomon of the 2nd Ranger Battalion, one of the D-Day heroes, found that out on June 7. He was leading the remnants of his battalion, which had come ashore on the right flank at Omaha and been involved in a day-long firefight on D-Day, westward along the coastal road that led to Pointe-du-Hoc. Three companies of the 2nd Rangers had taken the German emplacement there, and destroyed the coastal guns, but they were under severe attack and had taken severe casualties. Salomon was in a hurry to get to them.

But his column, marching in combat formation, began taking well-placed artillery shells. To his right, Salomon could see a Norman church, its steeple the only high point around. He was certain the Germans had an observer spotting for their artillery in that steeple. Behind Salomon a Sherman tank chugged up, the only American tank to be seen. It was buttoned up. Salomon wanted it to elevate its 75mm cannon and blast that steeple, but he couldn't get the crew's attention, not even when he knocked on the side of the tank with the butt of his carbine. "So I ultimately stood in the middle of the road directly in front of the tank, waving my arms, and pointing in the direction of the church. That produced results. After a couple of shots from the cannon and several bursts from the .50-caliber machine gun, the artillery spotter was no more."[11]

Salomon's daring feat notwithstanding, it was obvious that the Army was going to have to work out a better system for tank-infantry communication than having junior officers jump up and down in front of American tanks. Until that was done, the tanks would play a minor supporting role to the infantry, following the GIs into the next field as the infantry overran it.

The U.S. First Army had not produced anything approaching a doctrine for offensive action in the hedgerows. It had expended enormous energy to get tanks by the score into Normandy, but it had no doctrine for the role of tanks in the hedgerows. In peacetime, the Army would have dealt with the problem by setting up commissions and boards, experimenting in maneuvers, testing ideas, before establishing a doctrine. But in Normandy time was a luxury the Army didn't have. So as the infantry lurched forward in the Cotentin, following frontal assaults straight into the enemy's kill zones, the tankers began experimenting with ways to utilize their weapons in the hedgerows.

Beginning at daylight on June 7, each side had begun to rush reinforcements to the front. The Americans came in on a tight schedule, long since worked out, with fresh divisions almost daily. Sgt. Edward "Buddy" Gianelloni, a medic in the 79th Division, came ashore on D-Day Plus Six on Utah Beach. The men marched inland; when they reached Ste.-Mère-Eglise, a paratrooper called out to Gianelloni, "Hey, what outfit is that?"

"This is the 79th Infantry Division," Gianelloni replied.

"Well, that's good," the paratrooper said. "Now if you guys are around this time tomorrow you can consider yourselves veterans."[12]

The Germans came in by bits and pieces, because they were improvising, having been caught with no plans for reinforcing Normandy. Further, the Allied air forces had badly hampered German movement from the start.

The German air force (the Luftwaffe) and the German navy were seldom to be seen, but still the Germans managed to have an effect on Allied landings, through their mines and beach obstacles. The most spectacular German success, the one they had most hoped for, came at dawn on June 7.

The transport USS *Susan B. Anthony* was moving into her off-loading position off Utah Beach. Sgt. Jim Finn was down in the hold, along with hundreds of others in the 90th Infantry Division, set to enter the battle after the ship dropped her anchor. The landing craft began coming alongside, and the men started climbing up out of the hold onto the deck, prepared to descend the rope ladders. Finn and the others were loaded down with rifles, grenades, extra clips, BARs, tripods, mortar bases and tubes, gas masks, leather boots, baggy pants stuffed with cigarettes, toilet articles, helmets, life jackets, and more.

"There was a massive 'Boom!' " Finn recalled. "She shook. All communications were knocked out. All electricity was out. Everything on the ship went black. And here we were, a massive number of troops in confined areas, with tremendous amounts of clothing and gear on, all ready for the invasion, and not knowing what was going on, in total darkness."

The *Susan B. Anthony,* one of the largest transport ships, had hit a mine amidships. She was sinking and burning. Panic in the hold was to be expected, and there was a bit of it, but as Finn recalled, the officers took charge and restored calm. Then, "We were instructed to remove our helmets, remove our impregnated clothing, remove all excess equipment. Many of the fellows took off their shoes." They scrambled onto the deck.

A fire-fighting boat had pulled alongside and was putting streams of water onto the fire. LCVPs began pulling to the side of the sinking ship. Men threw rope ladders over the side, and within two hours all hands were safely off—minutes before the *Susan B. Anthony* sank.

Sergeant Finn and his platoon went into Utah Beach in a Higgins boat, a couple of hours late and barefoot, with no helmets, no rifles, no ammo, no food. But they were there, and by scrounging along the beach they were soon able to equip themselves from dead and wounded men.[13]

Getting the *Susan B. Anthony* was by far the greatest success of the German navy's efforts to disrupt the landing of American reinforcements in Normandy. Thanks to the fire-fighting boat—one of the many specialized craft in the armada—even the loss of the ship hardly slowed the disembarking process. The U.S., Royal, and Canadian Navies ruled the English Channel, which made the uninterrupted flow of men and supplies from England to France possible. The fire-fighting boat that saved the lives of the men on *Susan B. Anthony* showed what a superb job the three navies were doing.

At Omaha, too, reinforcements began coming in to the beach before the sun rose above the horizon. Twenty-year-old Lt. Charles Stockell, a forward observer in the 1st Division, was one of the first to go ashore that day. Stockell kept a diary. He recorded that he came in below Vierville, that the skipper of the LCI (Landing Craft Infantry) feared the underwater beach obstacles and mines and thus forced him to get off in chest-deep water, that he saw equipment littering the beach, and then "The first dead Americans I see are two GIs, one with both feet blown off, arms wrapped about each other in a comradely death embrace." He was struck by the thought that "dead men everywhere look pathetic and lonely. You feel as if you would like them to be alive and the war over."[14]

Stockell didn't get very far inland that morning. The front line, in fact, was less than a quarter of a mile from the edge of the bluff, running along a series of hedgerows outside Colleville. That was as far inland as Capt. Joseph Dawson, CO of G Company, 16th Regiment, 1st Division, had gotten on D-Day—and Dawson had been the first American to reach the top of the bluff at Omaha. On June 7, he was fighting to secure his position outside Colleville, discovering in the process that he had a whole lot to learn about hedgerows.[15]

The 175th Regiment of the 29th Division came in on schedule at 0630, June 7. But it landed two kilometers east of its intended target, the Vierville exit. Orders came to march to the exit. In a loose formation, the regiment began to march, through the debris of the previous day's battle. To Capt. Robert Miller, the beach "looked like something out of Dante's Inferno."[16]

Sniper fire continued to zing down. "But even worse," according to Lt. J. Milnor Roberts, an aide to the corps commander, "they were stepping over the bodies of the guys who had been killed the day before and these guys were wearing that 29th Division patch; the other fellows, brand-new, were walking over the dead bodies. By the time they got down where they were to go inland, they were really spooked."[17]

But so were their opponents. Lt. Col. Fritz Ziegelmann of the 352nd Division staff was one of the first German officers to bring reinforcements into the battle. At about the same time the 175th Regiment was swinging up toward Vierville, Ziegelmann was entering *Widerstandsnest* 76, one of the few surviving resistance nests on Omaha, a kilometer or so west of the Vierville draw. It had done great harm to the 29th Division on D-Day, when the 29th and the 352nd Divisions locked into a death embrace.

"The view from WN 76 will remain in my memory forever," Ziegelmann wrote after the war. "The sea was like a picture of the 'Kiel review of the fleet.' Ships of all sorts stood close together on the beach and in the water, broadly echeloned in depth. And the entire conglomeration remained there intact without any real interference from the German side!"

A runner brought him a set of secret American orders, captured from an officer, that showed the entire Omaha invasion plan, including the follow-up commitment that was taking place in front of Ziegelmann's eyes. "I must say that in my entire military life, I have never been so impressed," he wrote, adding that he knew at that moment that Germany was going to lose this war.[18]

At dawn, all along the plateau above the bluff at Omaha, GIs shook themselves awake, did their business, ate some rations, smoked a cigarette, got into some kind of formation, and prepared to move out to broaden the beachhead. But in the hedgerows, individuals got lost, squads got lost. German sniper fire came from all directions. The Norman farm homes, made of stone and surrounded by stone walls and a stone barn, made excellent fortresses. Probing attacks brought forth a stream of bullets from the Germans, pretty much discouraging further probes.

Brig. Gen. Norman "Dutch" Cota, assistant division commander of the 29th, came on a group of infantry pinned down by some Germans in a farmhouse. He asked the captain in command why his men were making no effort to take the building.

"Sir, the Germans are in there, shooting at us," the captain replied.

"Well, I'll tell you what, captain," said Cota, unbuckling two grenades from his jacket. "You and your men start shooting at them. I'll take a squad of men and you and your men watch carefully. I'll show you how to take a house with Germans in it."

Cota led his squad around a hedge to get as close as possible to the house. Suddenly, he gave a whoop and raced forward, the squad following, yelling like wild men. As they tossed grenades into the windows, Cota and another man kicked in the front door, tossed a couple of grenades inside, waited for the explosions, then dashed into the house. The surviving Germans inside were streaming out the back door, running for their lives.

Cota returned to the captain. "You've seen how to take a house," said the general, still out of breath. "Do you understand? Do you know how to do it now?"

"Yes, sir."

"Well, I won't be around to do it for you again," Cota said. "I can't do it for everybody."[19]

That little story speaks to the training of the U.S. Army for the Battle of Normandy. At first glance, Cota's bravery stands out, along with his sense of the dramatic and his knowledge of tactics. He could be sure the story would get around the division. A lesson would be learned. His own reputation would go even higher, the men would be even more willing to follow him.

But after that first glance, a question emerges. Where had that captain been the last six months? He had been in training to fight the German army. He had been committed to offensive action, trained to it, inspired to it. But no one had thought to show him how to take an occupied house. He knew all about getting ashore from an LCVP, about beach obstacles, about paths up the bluff, about ravines, about amphibious assault techniques. But no one had shown him how to take a house, because there were no standing houses on Omaha Beach, so that wasn't one of his problems.

Not on June 6. But on June 7, it became his number one problem. The same was true for the 200 or so company commanders already ashore and would be for the hundreds of others waiting to enter the battle. As Cota said, he couldn't be there to teach all of them how to take a house. They were going to have to figure it out for themselves.

Normandy was a soldier's battle. It belonged to the riflemen, machine gunners, mortarmen, tankers, and artillerymen who were on the front lines. There was no room for maneuver. There was no opportunity for subtlety. There was a simplicity to the fighting: for the Germans, to hold; for the Americans, to attack.

Where they would hold or attack required no decision-making: it was always the next village or field. The real decision-making came at the battalion, company, and platoon levels: where to place the mines, the barbed wire, the machine-gun pits, where to dig the foxholes—or where and how to attack them.

The direction of the attack had been set by pre-invasion decision-making. For the 1st and 29th Divisions, that meant south from Omaha toward St.-Lô. For the 101st Airborne, that meant east, into Carentan, for a linkup with Omaha. For the 82nd Airborne, that meant west from Ste.-Mère-Eglise, to provide maneuver room in the Cotentin. For the 4th and 90th Divisions, that meant west from Utah, to the Gulf of St.-Malo, to cut off the Germans in Cherbourg.

The objective of all this effort was to secure the port of Cherbourg and to create a beachhead sufficiently large to absorb the incoming stream of American reinforcements and serve as a base for an offensive through France. SHAEF's detailed projections of future activity—where the front lines would be on such-and-such a date—were already wrong on June 7. That was inevitable. What wasn't inevitable was the Allied fixation with Cherbourg—how heavily, for example, the SHAEF projections for August and September were based on having a fully functioning port there. So strong a magnet was Cherbourg that the initial American offensive in Normandy headed west, *away* from Germany.

Eisenhower and his high command were obsessed with ports. Whenever they looked at the figures on supply needs for each division in combat, they blanched. Only a large, operational port could satisfy the logistical needs, or so Eisenhower assumed. Therefore the planning emphasis had been on ports, artificial ones to begin with, Cherbourg and Le Havre next, with the climax coming at Antwerp. Only with all these ports could Eisenhower be assured of the supplies a final fifty-division offensive into Germany would require. Especially Antwerp—without it, an American army could not possibly be sustained in Central Europe.

The Germans had assumed that the Allies could not supply divisions in combat over an open beach. The Allies tended to agree. Experience in the Mediterranean had not been encouraging. Churchill was so certain it couldn't be done he insisted on putting a very large share of the national effort into building two experimental artificial harbors. Russell Weigley has speculated that without the promise of these experiments, Churchill might never have agreed to Overlord.[20] As experiments, the harbors were moderately successful (the American one was destroyed by the storm of June 19; the British one was badly damaged but repaired and soon functioning). But as it turned out, their contribution to the total tonnage unloaded over the Normandy beaches was about 15 percent.

It was the cargo and troop ships, supported by the LST (Landing Ship Tank) and the myriad of specialized landing craft, that did the most carrying and unloading. It was a hodgepodge fleet—a

British crew of old salts on a Higgins boat in the Canadian Navy taking GIs ashore at Utah; LSTs commanded by a twenty-two-year-old American lieutenant carrying British troops to Gold Beach; LSTs at every beach, their great jaws yawning open, disgorging tanks and trucks and jeeps and bulldozers and big guns and small guns and mountains of cases of rations and ammunition, thousands of jerry cans filled with gasoline, crates of radios and telephones, typewriters and forms, and all else that men at war require.

The LSTs at Omaha and Utah and the other beaches provide a symbol for the Alliance. British-designed, American-built, they did what no one had thought possible: they came into open beaches to supply fighting divisions with their needs. The LST was in fact the Allies' secret weapon, far more practical and effective than the secret weapon Hitler put into operation a week after D-Day, the pilotless radio-controlled fighter aircraft carrying a high-explosive bomb, called the V-1 (the V was for Vengeance).

Through June, the Germans continued in the face of all evidence to believe LSTs could not supply the Allied divisions already ashore, and that therefore Overlord was a feint with the real attack scheduled for the Pas-de-Calais later in the summer. A continuing Fortitude deception plan and campaign of misinformation put out by SHAEF reinforced this German fixed idea. So through the month, Hitler kept his panzer divisions north and east of the Seine River.

Hitler had recognized that his only hope for victory lay on the Western Front. His armies could not defeat the Red Army, but they might defeat the British and Americans, so discouraging Stalin that he would make a settlement. But after correctly seeing the critical theater, Hitler completely failed to see the critical battlefield. He continued to look to the Pas-de-Calais as the site where he would drive the invaders back into the sea, and consequently kept his main striking power there. To every plea by the commanders in Normandy for the panzer divisions in northwestern France to come to their aid, Hitler said no. In so saying he sealed his fate. He suffered the worst humiliation of all, the one with the most consequences—he had been outwitted.

The mission of the 101st Airborne Division was to take Carentan and thus link Omaha and Utah into a continuous beachhead. It took an all-out commitment from the airborne infantry. One of the critical actions was led by Lt. Col. Robert Cole, CO of the 3rd Battalion, 502nd PIR.

Cole was twenty-nine years of age, an Army brat and a 1939 West Point graduate, born and trained to lead. On D-Day, he had gathered up seventy-five men, moved out to Utah Beach, shot up some Germans on the way, and was at the dune line to welcome men from the 4th Division coming ashore. From June 7 on he had been involved in the attack on Carentan. The climax came on June 11.

Cole was leading some 250 men down a long, exposed causeway. At the far end was a bridge over the Douve River. Beyond that bridge was the linkup point with units from the 29th Division coming from Omaha. The causeway was a meter or so above the marshes on either side. On the far side of the inland marsh, about 150 meters away, there was a hedgerow, occupied by the Germans.

Once Cole was fully committed along the causeway, the German machine gunners, riflemen, and mortarmen along the hedgerow opened fire. Cole's battalion took a couple of dozen casualties. The survivors huddled against the bank on the far side of the causeway.

They should have kept moving. But the hardest lesson to teach in training, the most difficult rule to follow in combat, is to keep moving when fired on. Every instinct makes a soldier want to hug the ground. Cole's men did, and over the next half hour the Germans dropped mortars on the battalion, causing further casualties. Whenever an American tried to move down the causeway, he drew rifle and machine-gun fire. For yet another half hour, the GIs were pinned down.

Then Cole could take no more and took command. He passed out an order seldom heard in World War II: "Fix bayonets!"

Up and down the line he could hear the click of bayonets being fitted to rifle barrels. Cole's pulse was racing, his adrenaline pumping. He pulled his .45-caliber pistol, jumped onto the causeway, shouted a command in so loud a voice he could be heard above the din of the battle, "Charge!," turned toward the hedgerow, and began plunging through the marsh.

His men watched, fearful, excited, impressed, inspired. First single figures rose and began to follow Cole. Then small groups of two and three. Then whole squads started running forward, flashing the cold steel of their bayonets. The men began to roar as they charged, their own version of the Rebel Yell.

The Germans fired and cut down some, but not enough. Cole's men got to the hedgerow, plunged into the dugouts and trenches, thrusting with their bayonets, drawing blood and screams, causing death. Those Germans who dodged the bayonets ran out the back way and fled to the rear. Paratroopers took them under fire and dropped a dozen or more.

Cole stood there, shaking, exhausted, elated. Around him the men began to cheer. That added to the Civil War atmosphere of the scene. After the cheering subsided, Cole got his men down the causeway to the bridge and over it to the far side of the Douve River. There, the following day, Omaha and Utah linked up.[21]

Cole's victory, memorable in itself, also serves as an example not only of heroism and spirit but also of the many things the Americans were doing wrong. Later in the war, in Holland and Belgium, the 502nd PIR would not have advanced over a causeway crossing a swampy area, with an unsecured hedgerow 150 meters away. It would have found a way to flank the hedgerow. Nor would the experienced 502nd have done what Cole did, make a bayonet charge over open, marshy ground. Not after having seen, too many times, what speeding bullets and hot shrapnel do to the human body. As veterans, the paratroopers would have called in artillery, and fighter aircraft, to blast the German position.

But in June, they didn't have the knowledge nor the communications capability to do any of that. No one had foreseen the need for air-ground communication, pilot to tank commander, infantry captain to forward observer over the radio; as no one had seen the need for the infantry to be able to communicate with tankers when the hatch was down.

Throughout First Army, young men made many discoveries in the first few days of combat, about war, about themselves, about others. They quickly learned such basics as keep down or die—to dig deep and stay quiet—to distinguish incoming from outgoing artillery—to judge when and where a shell or a mortar barrage was going to hit—to recognize that fear is inevitable but can be managed—and many more things they had been told in training but that can only be truly learned by doing. Putting it another way, after a week in combat, infantrymen agreed that there was no way training could have prepared them for the reality of combat.

Capt. John Colby caught one of the essences of combat, the sense of total immediacy: "At this point we had been in combat six days. It seemed like a year. In combat, one lives in the now and does not think much about yesterday or tomorrow."

Colby discovered that there was no telling who would break or when. His regimental CO was "grossly incompetent," his battalion commander had run away from combat in his first day of action, and his company CO was a complete bust. On June 12 the company got caught in a combined mortar-artillery barrage. The men couldn't move forward, they couldn't fall back, and they couldn't stay where they were—or so it appeared to the CO, who therefore had no orders to give, and was speechless.

Colby went up to his CO to ask for orders. The CO shook his head and pointed to his throat. Colby asked him if he could make it back to the aid station on his own, "and he leaped to his feet and took off. I never saw him again."

Another thing Colby learned in his first week in combat was: "Artillery does not fire forever. It just seems like that when you get caught in it. The guns overheat or the ammunition runs low, and it stops. It stops for a while, anyway."

He was amazed to discover how small he could make his body. If you get caught in the open in a shelling, he advised, "the best thing to do is drop to the ground and crawl into your steel helmet. One's body tends to shrink a great deal when shells come in. I am sure I have gotten as much as eighty percent of my body under my helmet when caught under shellfire."

Colby learned about hedgerows. Once he got into a situation where "I had to push through a hedgerow. A submachine-gun emitted a long burst right in front of my face. The gun was a Schmeisser, which had a very high rate of fire that sounded like a piece of cloth being ripped loudly. The bullets went over my head. I fell backward and passed out cold from fright."[22]

About themselves, the most important thing a majority of the GIs discovered was that they were not cowards. They hadn't thought so, they had fervently hoped it would not be so, but they couldn't be sure until tested. After a few days in combat, most of them knew they were good soldiers. They had neither run away nor collapsed into a pathetic mass of quivering Jell-O (their worst fear, even greater than the fear of being afraid).

They were learning about others. A common experience: the guy who talked toughest, bragged most, excelled in maneuvers, everyone's pick to be the top soldier in the company, was the first to break, while the soft-talking kid who was hardly noticed in camp was the standout in combat. These are the clichés of war novels precisely because they are true. They also learned that while combat brought out the best in some men, it unleashed the worst in others—and a further lesson, that the distinction between best and worst wasn't clear.

On June 9, Pvt. Arthur "Dutch" Schultz of the 82nd Airborne was outside Montebourg. That morning he was part of an attack on the town. "I ran by a wounded German soldier lying alongside of a hedgerow. He was obviously in a great deal of pain and crying for help. I stopped running and turned around. A close friend of mine put the muzzle of his rifle between the German's still crying eyes and pulled the trigger. There was no change in my friend's facial expression. I don't believe he even blinked an eye."

Schultz was simultaneously appalled and awed by what he had seen. "There was a part of me that wanted to be just as ruthless as my friend," he commented. Later, he came to realize that "there but for the grace of God go I."[23]

Allied fighter pilots owned the skies over Normandy. On June 15, Eisenhower crossed the Channel by plane to visit Bayeux. Every airplane in the sky was American or British.

Thanks to air supremacy, the Americans were flying little single-seat planes, Piper Cubs, about 300 meters back from the front lines and some 300 meters high. German riflemen fired at them, ineffectively. Still, the bullets worried the pilots. Like all men at war, they feared above all getting hit in the testicles. Ground maintenance men eased their worry by welding steel plates under their seats.

When the Cubs appeared, all German mortar and artillery firing stopped. As Sergeant Sampson described it, "They didn't dare give their positions away, knowing if they fired our pilot would call in and artillery would be coming in on them, pin-point. The results could be devastating."[24]

Sgt. Günter Behr was a radioman with a German artillery battery. Because of spotter planes, two of the guns were blown apart within minutes of the first time the battery shot at Americans. From then on, Behr related, "as soon as we fired our guns, we had to run again, and look for a good place to hide. We were hunted. Always afraid. If you could not run, it was over. Like eagles and rabbits."[25]

Air supremacy also freed Allied fighter-bombers, principally P-47 Thunderbolts, capable of carrying two 500-pound bombs, to strafe and machine-gun and bomb German convoys and concentrations. From D-Day Plus One onward, whenever the weather was suitable for flying, the P-47s forced nighttime movement only on the Germans, at an incalculable cost to their logistical efficiency.

During the day, Germans caught in the open quickly paid. The Jabos would get them. (From the German *"Jäger Bomber,"* or "hunter-bomber.") Fifty years later, in talking about the Jabos, German veterans still have awe in their voice, and glance up over their shoulders as they recall the terror of having one come right at them, all guns blazing. "The Jabos were a burden on our souls," Corp. Helmut Hesse said.[26]

The B-26 Marauders, two-engine bombers, continued their all-out assault on choke points in the German transportation system, principally bridges and highway junctions. Lt. James Delong was a Marauder pilot who had flown in low and hard on D-Day over Utah Beach. On June 7, it was a bridge at Rennes, on the Seine. On the 8th, a railroad junction near Avranches.

These were defended sites. "We were being met with plenty of flak from enemy 88s," Delong recalled. "That Whomp! Whomp! sound just outside with black smoke puffs filling the air was still scary as hell, damaging, and deadly." But there were no Luftwaffe fighters, partly because the B-26s flew tight formations and stayed low, discouraging fighter attacks, but more because most German pilots were on the far side of the Rhine River, trying to defend the homeland from the Allied four-engine bombers, and the Luftwaffe was chronically short on fuel.[27]

Almost exactly four years earlier, following the RAF withdrawal from the Battle of France, the Luftwaffe had ruled the skies over Normandy and all of Europe. Reichsmarschall Hermann Goering's air fleet struck terror in the hearts of its enemies. But in June 1944 it was not even a minor factor in the battle. One German soldier, while being interrogated after being made prisoner, said, "Yah, I saw the Luftwaffe. Seven of them, 7,000 Jabos."[28]

In Normandy in June 1944, German soldiers learned to always look up for danger. GIs seldom had to look up. So total was this dominance that the Germans became experts in camouflage to make themselves invisible from the sky, while the GIs laid out colored panels and otherwise did all they could to make themselves plainly visible from the sky. They wanted any airplane up there to know that they were Americans, because they knew without having to look that the plane they heard was American.

German Gen. Fritz Bayerlein of the Panzer Lehr Division gave an account of how the Jabos worked over his division on June 7: "By noon it was terrible; every vehicle was covered with tree branches and moved along hedges and the edges of woods. Road junctions were bombed and a bridge knocked out. By the end of the day I had lost forty tank trucks carrying fuel, and ninety other vehicles. Five of my tanks were knocked out, and eighty-four half-tracks, prime movers and self-propelled guns." Those were heavy losses, especially for a panzer division that had so far not fired a shot.[29]

Without doubt, the Jabos had a decisive effect on the Battle of Normandy. Without them, the Germans would have been able to move reinforcements into Normandy at a rate three, four, five times better than they actually achieved, in both quantity and speed. Two examples: the 266th Division left Brittany for Normandy on June 10. Unable to use rail transport or major roads, the division marched, at night, averaging less than sixteen kilometers a day. It took more than two weeks to get to the front. The 353rd Division left Brittany on June 14 and finally marched into Normandy on June 30, having advanced to the sound of the guns at a pace slower than a typical Civil War march eighty years earlier.

But airpower could not be decisive alone. The Germans already in Normandy were dug in well enough to survive strafing, rocket, and bombing attacks on their lines. They could move enough men, vehicles, and matériel at night to keep on fighting. Once in Normandy, their mobility was somewhat restored, because they could move along the leaf-covered sunken lanes. The frequently foul weather gave them further respite. Low clouds, drizzle, fog—for the Germans, ideal weather to move reinforcements to the front or to reposition units. And there were more of those days than there were clear ones.[30]

■

Over the first ten days of the battle, the Germans fought so well that the Allies measured their gains in meters. By June 16, the euphoria produced by the D-Day success was giving way to fears that the Germans were imposing a stalemate in Normandy. These fears led to blame and recriminations among the Allies.

The difficulty centered around the taking of Caen. Gen. Bernard Law Montgomery, commanding the ground forces, had said he would take the city on D-Day, but he had not, nor did he do so in the following ten days. Nor was he attacking. The British Second Army had drawn the bulk of the panzers in Normandy to its front. It was at Caen that the Germans were most vulnerable, because a breakthrough at Caen would put British tanks on a straight road through rolling terrain with open fields headed directly for Paris. Therefore the fighting north of Caen was fierce and costly. But there was no all-out British attack.

The Americans, themselves frustrated by their glacial-like progress in the hedgerows, were increasingly critical of Montgomery. Monty sent it right back. He blamed Gen. Omar Bradley, commanding U.S. First Army, for Allied problems, saying that the Americans should have attacked both north toward Cherbourg and south toward Coutances, "but Bradley didn't want to take the risk." Monty added, "I have to take the Americans along quietly and give them time to get ready."[31]

Normandy, the land of fat cattle and fine orchards, and thus of excellent cheese and outstanding cider, had gone from pastoral idyll to battlefield overnight. War came as a shock to the Normans, who had quite accommodated themselves to the German occupation. We get some sense of how it was for the Normans before and during the battle in a top secret report from OSS (Office of Strategic Services) in London direct to President Franklin Roosevelt. Dated June 14, it was based on "an entirely reliable source," an unnamed Frenchman who went into Normandy for a day and interviewed residents.

Highlights: severe gasoline shortages immobilized many German vehicles and even entire units; the general belief among both Frenchmen and Germans was that the Normandy landing was but the first of a series and the next one would be at Pas-de-Calais; people were well fed and clothed; the behavior of the Germans during the four years of occupation had been "extremely correct"; "there is no food shortage apparent in the restaurants, although prices are very high. Source states that the wine cellar of the Lion D'Or hotel is excellent."*

The political gossip had it that "de Gaulle is regarded as a symbol of French resistance, but not liked personally. Pétain is not hated by the majority of persons with whom source spoke; he is regarded merely as a poor, tired, old man. A picture of him in the Mayor's office has been replaced by one of Marshal Foch."32

All over France, citizens were looking at the portrait in their hôtel de ville (city hall), wondering about the right moment to take Marshal Pétain down and put Marshal Foch—or, perhaps, who knows?—General de Gaulle up. Or maybe Stalin. All over France, Gaullist and Communist-dominated resistance groups were wondering about the right moment to strike—against the Germans and in a simultaneous bid for power in France.

At the top, through June, the Allied high command squabbled. At the front, the soldiers fought. They got through to the west coast of the Cotentin on June 18, to Cherbourg on the 20th. It took a week of hard fighting to force a surrender on the 27th, and even then the Germans left the port facilities so badly damaged that it took the engineers six weeks to get them functioning. Meanwhile supplies continued to come in via LSTs.

With Cherbourg captured, Bradley was able to turn U.S. First Army, now composed of the V, VII, VIII, and XIX Corps, in a continuous line facing south. St.-Lô and Coutances were the objectives of this second phase of the Battle of Normandy. To get to them, the GIs had a lot of hedgerows to cross.

To get through the hedgerows, junior officers in the tank units had been experimenting with various techniques and methods. One idea that worked was to bring to the front the specially equipped dozer tanks (tanks with a blade mounted on the front similar to those on commercial bulldozers) used on the beaches on D-Day. They could cut through a hedgerow well enough, but there were too few of them—four per division—to have much impact. A rush

---

*The hotel is in Bayeux. It became Eisenhower's favorite Norman restaurant. Five decades later, it retains an excellent wine cellar, and remains expensive. There is no food shortage.

order back to the States for 278 additional bulldozer blades was put in, but it would take weeks to fill.

In the 747th Tank Battalion, attached to the 29th Division, someone—name unknown—suggested using demolitions to blow gaps in the hedgerows. After some experimenting, the tankers discovered that two fifty-pound explosive charges laid against the bank would blow a hole in a hedgerow big enough for a Sherman tank to drive through. Once on the other side, the tank could fire its cannon into the far corners, using white phosphorus shells, guaranteed to burn out the Germans at the machine-gun pits, and hose down the hedgerow itself with its .50-caliber machine gun. Infantry could follow the tank into the field and mop up what remained when the tanker got done firing.

Good enough, excellent even. But when the planners turned to the logistics of getting the necessary explosives to the tanks, they discovered that each tank company would need seventeen tons of explosives to advance a mile and a half. The explosives were not available in such quantities, and even had they been the transport problems involved in getting them to the front were too great.

An engineer suggested drilling holes in the embankment and placing smaller charges in them. That worked, too—except that it took forever to dig holes large enough and deep enough in the bank because of the vines and roots, and the men doing the digging were exposed to German mortar fire.

A tanker in the 747th suggested welding two pipes of four feet in length and six inches in diameter to the front of a tank, reinforced by angle irons. The tank could ram into a hedgerow and back off, leaving two sizable holes for explosives. The engineers learned to pack their explosives into expended 105mm artillery shell casings, which greatly increased the efficiency of the charges and made transport and handling much easier. Some tankers discovered that if the pipes were bigger, sometimes that was enough to allow a Sherman to plow right on through, at least with the smaller hedgerows.[33] Other experiments were going on, all across Normandy. The U.S. First Army was starting to get a grip on the problem.

It was also growing to its full potential. The buildup in Normandy, slowed but not stopped by the storm of June 19, was proceeding in fine shape. By June 30, the Americans had brought in 71,000 vehicles over the beaches (of a planned 110,000) and 452,000 soldiers (of a planned 579,000). The shortfall in soldiers was felt exclusively in supply and service troops: the combat strength of the First Army was actually greater than originally planned. It had eleven divisions in the battle, as scheduled, plus the 82nd and 101st Airborne, which were to have been withdrawn to England to prepare for the next jump, but which were retained on the Continent and kept in the line through June. The British Second Army also had thirteen divisions ashore, including the 6th Airborne.[34]

The Americans had evacuated 27,000 casualties. About 11,000 GIs had been killed in action or died of their wounds, 1,000 were missing in action, and 3,400 wounded men had been returned to duty. So the total active duty strength of U.S. First Army in Normandy on June 30 was 413,000.[35] German strength on the American front was somewhat less, while German losses against the combined British-Canadian-American forces were 47,500.[36]

That the GIs were there in such numbers, and so well equipped if only partly trained, was the great achievement of the American people and system in the twentieth century and equal to the greatest nineteenth-century achievement, the creation of the Army of the Potomac. In 1864 and again eighty years later the American democracy gathered itself together and although sorely tested by three years of war was able to provide the men and matériel Grant and Eisenhower each needed to carry out a war-ending offensive.

In most cases the GIs were much better equipped than their foe. Some German weapons were superior, others inferior. In vehicles, the United States was far ahead, in both quality and quantity. The Germans could not compete with the American two-and-a-half-ton truck (deuce-and-a-half) or the jeep (the Germans loved to capture working jeeps, but complained that they were gas-guzzlers). The German factories making their vehicles were a few hundred kilometers from Normandy. Their American counterparts were thousands of kilometers from Normandy. Yet the Americans got more and better vehicles to the battlefront than the Germans did, in less time.

Simultaneously, the Americans were on the offensive in Italy and in the Pacific, and were conducting a major air offensive inside Germany. But the Germans were fighting on four fronts, the Eastern, Western, Southern, and Home. They could not possibly win a war of attrition, no matter how much closer to Normandy the German industrial centers were than the American.

The senior German commanders in the West, Field Marshals Gerd von Rundstedt and Erwin Rommel, were perfectly aware of that fact. Having failed to stop the Allied assault on the beaches, having failed to prevent a linkup of the invasion forces, completely lacking any air support and seriously deficient in air defense, chronically short on fuel, sometimes of ammunition, taking heavy casualties, they despaired. On June 28, the two field marshals set off for Hitler's headquarters in Berchtesgaden. On the drive, they talked. Rundstedt had already told Hitler's lackeys to "make peace." Now he said the same to Rommel.

"I agree with you," Rommel replied. "The war must be ended immediately. I shall tell the Führer so, clearly and unequivocally."

Rommel knew what that meant. Hitler had told him, six months earlier, "Nobody will make peace with me." But the failure to stop the landing on the beaches had put victory out of the question. Hitler would have to go, be forced to resign and give himself up, for the good of Germany. And now, at once. Every day the war went on made a terrible situation worse.

The showdown meeting with Hitler came at a full-dress conference attended by the top echelon of the high command: Field Marshals Wilhelm Keitel, Alfred Jodl, and Goering, along with Admiral Karl Dönitz and many lesser lights, were there. Rommel spoke first. He said the moment was critical. He told his Führer, "The whole world stands arrayed against Germany, and this disproportion of strength—"

Hitler cut him off. Would the *Herr Feldmarschall* please concern himself with the military, not the political situation?

Rommel replied that history demanded he deal with the entire situation. Hitler rebuked him again and ordered him to stick to the military situation only. Rommel then gave a most gloomy report.

Hitler took over. He said the critical task was to halt the enemy offensive. This would be accomplished by the Luftwaffe, he declared. He announced that 1,000 new fighters were coming out of the factories and would be in Normandy shortly. He talked about new secret weapons—the V-2—that would turn the tide. He said the Allied communications between Britain and Normandy would be cut by the Kriegsmarine, which would soon be adding a large number of torpedo boats to lay mines in the Channel, and new submarines to operate off the invasion beaches. And large convoys of brand-new trucks would soon be headed west from the Rhine toward Normandy.

This was pure fantasy. Hitler was clearly crazy. The German high command knew it, without question, and should have called for the men with the straitjacket. But nothing was done.

As the meeting broke up, Rommel said he could not leave without speaking directly to Hitler, "about Germany."

Hitler wheeled on him: "Field Marshal, I think you had better leave the room!"[37] Rommel did.

For the Americans, numbers of units and qualities and quantities of equipment helped make victory possible, but it still took men to make it happen. And out in the hedgerows, it wasn't so apparent to the GIs that their side enjoyed great manpower and equipment advantages. Indeed it often looked the other way to them. As, indeed, sometimes it was. Meanwhile all those American vehicles would be idle until the GIs managed to break out of the hedgerows. And that rested on the wits, endurance, and execution of the tankers, artillery, and infantry at the front.

2

Hedgerow Fighting

July 1–24, 1944

WITHIN THREE WEEKS of the great success of D-Day, the ugly word "stalemate" was beginning to be used. "We were stuck," Corp. Bill Preston remembered. "Something dreadful seemed to have happened in terms of the overall plan. Things had gone awry. The whole theory of mobility that we had been taught, of our racing across the battlefield, seemed to have gone up in smoke."[1] And while the American progress was excruciatingly slow, the British and Canadians remained stuck in place outside Caen. Big attacks followed by heavy losses for small or no gains, reminiscent of 1914–18, weighed on every mind.

So did Hitler's vengeance weapon, the V-1. Used for the first time a few days after D-Day, the radio-controlled V-1 pilotless aircraft were coming down by the hundreds on London. They were a haphazard terror weapon of little military value, except to put an enormous new strain on the British public. In June and July, the V-1s killed more than 5,000 people, injured 35,000 more, and destroyed some 30,000 buildings. Worse, Allied intelligence anticipated that the Germans would soon have the V-2s—the world's first medium-range ballistic missiles—in operation.

Naturally there was great pressure on the politicians to "do something" about the V-1s, a pressure that was naturally passed on to the generals. If nothing else, the public had to have a sense that somehow the Allies were hitting back. So big and medium bombers were pulled off other missions to attack the launch sites. Lt. James Delong of the Ninth Air Force, flying a B-26 on a strike against the sites in the Pas-de-Calais area, described his experience: "These were very difficult targets to destroy since they consisted mostly of a strong steel launching ramp. They were difficult to hit since the usual hazy visibility and broken cloud cover made them hard to find, leaving seconds to set the bombsight. They were always well defended; in fact this area was a real hotbed of flak."

The inability to knock out the sites was disheartening to the bomber pilots, because, as Delong put it, "I had been in London many times when the V-1s were coming in and had experienced firsthand their explosions and results. I knew any we destroyed or put temporarily out of action meant lives saved in England."[2]

But they hardly destroyed any and the terror bombings continued. The sites would have to be overrun on the ground to be put out of action. But the Allied armies were a long way from Belgium. Churchill was so desperate that in early July he proposed using poison gas against the launch sites. Eisenhower vetoed that one, emphatically. He said he would refuse to be a party to the use of gas: "Let's, for God's sake, keep our eyes on the ball and use some sense," he said.[3]

According to Eisenhower's chief of staff, Gen. Walter B. Smith, and Deputy Supreme Commander Air Vice Marshal Arthur Tedder, using some sense meant forcing Montgomery to launch an all-out offensive, designed to break through and open the road to Paris. To their dismay, their boss wouldn't push Monty hard enough, at least in their view. When Monty responded to Eisenhower's plea that he get going, he promised a "big show" on July 9 and asked for and got support from the four-engine bombers. The attack, however, failed and on July 10, Monty called it off.

Commander Harry Butcher, Eisenhower's naval aide, reported that the Supreme Commander was "smoldering," as were Tedder and Smith. So was Gen. George S. Patton, Jr., commander of the U.S. Third Army, still in England awaiting its entry into the battle. Patton went to Normandy to observe Monty's attack; when it failed, he commented in his diary, "Ike is bound hand and foot by the

British and does not know it. Poor fool. We actually have no Supreme Commander—no one who can take hold and say that this shall be done and that shall not be done."[4]

At Eisenhower's request, Churchill started putting pressure on Monty "to get on his bicycle and start moving." Monty promised another big attack. On July 12 he told Eisenhower that he was preparing for an offensive in six days, code name Goodwood. "My whole Eastern flank will burst into flames," he said, as he demanded that the full weight of all the air forces be thrown into the battle. Expectations of a breakthrough ran high.

On July 18, Goodwood began with a massive bombardment from the air—7,700 tons of bombs delivered by 1,676 four-engine bombers and 343 mediums, in what Forrest Pogue, the official historian of SHAEF, called "the heaviest and most concentrated air attack in support of ground troops ever attempted."[5]

Goodwood got off to a good start, thanks to the bombardment, but soon ground to a halt. After heavy losses, including 401 tanks and 2,600 casualties, Montgomery called it off. The British Second Army had taken possession of the ruins of Caen, gained a few miles, and inflicted heavy casualties on the Germans, but there had been nothing like a breakthrough.

A Canadian company commander described the German methods: "The enemy's defensive tactics are brilliantly conceived, and carried out with great tenacity by some of the best soldiers in Europe. No rigid defence; under attack, they hold on as long as possible in their excellently concealed slit-trenches, then they withdraw to prepared positions a little farther back. Instantly previously arranged mortar and artillery fire is poured on the positions they've just vacated—even if a few of their own men are still there. The shelling is coordinated with infantry assaults to retake the ground they've lost. Superb tactics."[6]

Montgomery announced that he was satisfied with Goodwood's results. Eisenhower was not. He muttered that it had taken more than 7,000 tons of bombs (seven kilotons, or about half of the explosive power of the Hiroshima bomb) to gain seven miles and that the Allies could hardly hope to go through France paying a price of a thousand tons of bombs per mile. Not to mention sixty tanks and 400 casualties per mile.

Tedder was so angry he wanted Monty sacked. On July 21, the day after Montgomery called off the Goodwood offensive, the Allies learned of the attempt on Hitler's life the previous day. Tedder complained at a SHAEF meeting that "Monty's failure . . . has lost us the opportunity offered by the attempt on Hitler's life." Looking to the future, he insisted that it was imperative that the Allies get to the Pas-de-Calais launching sites quickly. Smith groaned, "We are in fact not going to get there anytime soon."

Tedder snapped, "Then we must change our leaders for men who will get us there."7

But firing Monty was not an option. He was popular with the British press and public, and more important, with the troops and their officers. He had the support of Field Marshal Alan Brooke and to a lesser extent of Churchill. Besides, he had accomplished what he insisted was his objective all along, to pin down German armor on the eastern flank so as to give the Americans an opportunity to break out on the western flank. And it was not his fault that no one knew how to use heavy bombers in an artillery role. Those 7,000 tons of free-falling bombs caused havoc, concussions, misery, and considerable destruction, but after the bombs stopped falling most German soldiers were able to come up out of their dugouts and man their weapons.

Further, it wasn't fair to charge Monty with excessive caution or a refusal to make a full commitment, at least in Goodwood. I've gone over the field of Goodwood with Col. Hans von Luck many times. Luck was in the center of the action, commanding the 121st Panzer Regiment of the 21st Panzer Division. Standing on a low hill that looks over the wheat fields, he described to me the apple orchard that had been on the hill in 1944. Among those trees, he explained, he had placed a four-gun battery of 88s. No bombs fell on them. He was there when the British tanks came forward, in column, through the wheat. He fired at the lead tanks, to halt the column, then at the tanks in the rear, to immobilize the remainder, then proceeded to disable forty tanks, one by one. Then he sent his own tanks into action, with further success.

In other words, the trouble with Goodwood was not a lack of commitment by the British and certainly not a lack of courage. The commitment was there, and so was the will; it was the planning and tactics that were deficient. The biggest error was leading the attack with tanks inadequately supported by infantry (Luck had no infantry around the 88 battery and could have been driven off easily by British infantry).

Goodwood showed that there would be no breakthrough on Monty's front. It was too heavily defended, by a too-skillful and well-armed and numerous enemy. As that also appeared to be the case on the American front, every Allied leader was depressed and irritable. After seven weeks of fighting, the deepest Allied penetrations were some forty-five to fifty kilometers inland, on a front of only fifteen kilometers or so, hardly enough room to maneuver or to bring in the U.S. Third Army from England. The V-1s continued to bombard London.

For those who had inaugurated the battle a month earlier, there was good news. The paratroopers had been told just prior to D-Day that they should fight with fury for three days, after which they would be returned to England to prepare for the next air drop. But they were so badly needed in Normandy the three days stretched to four weeks of hard fighting. The 82nd and 101st Airborne Divisions took heavy casualties, close to 50 percent overall, and higher among their junior officers. In the first week of July, when the 30th Division relieved the 82nd, Lt. Sidney Eichen reported that he and his men stared in shock and awe at the paratroopers.

"We asked them: 'Where are your officers?', and they answered: 'All dead.' We asked, 'Who's in charge, then?', and some sergeant said, 'I am.' I looked at the unshaven, red-eyed GIs, the dirty clothes and the droop in their walk, and I wondered: is this how we are going to look after a few days of combat?"[8]

When the 101st got back to its barracks in England, Sgt. John Martin looked around and said to Sgt. Bill Guarnere, "Jesus, Bill, here we've got only a half a hut full of guys, and we aren't even started in the war yet. We don't have a Chinaman's chance of ever getting out of this thing."

"We lost half the barracks in one goddamn little maneuver in Normandy," Guarnere replied. "Forget it, we'll never get home."[9]

The paratroopers brought with them back to England priceless experience, which they could pass on to the recruits they would absorb as they rebuilt to full strength for the next jump. Pvt. Fayette Richardson of the 82nd, for example, told a story that contained two lessons from one incident. Early in the campaign, Richardson's squad was squatting behind a hedge when a solitary German tank—a light, prewar French model—appeared in the field. The GIs opened fire with machine guns and rifles and drove it off. They cheered, "like kids at a football game when their team scores."

Minutes later, very accurate mortar fire dropped on them. "Men I had just lain shoulder to shoulder with began screaming in pain, screaming for help, hysterical helpless screams that made my stomach tighten. Because of the apparent protection of the hedgerow and our greenness, we had not realized the necessity of digging in and few of us had holes which would have saved us from all but a direct hit."[10] The other lesson, learned more slowly, was that a favorite German tactic was to drive an armored vehicle in front of the line, to draw fire so as to locate the enemy's position.

The infantry divisions stayed in the line, advancing from hedgerow to hedgerow. They suffered brutally. In the 1st, 4th, 29th, and other divisions the turnover in junior officers in the first month of the battle was almost total.

Pvt. William Craft was a twenty-year-old from the Blue Ridge Mountains of Virginia. When he was drafted at the end of 1942, he had never been out of his home county. His trip to boot camp was his first time on a train. A year later he was in Normandy, a BAR man with the 314th Infantry Regiment. "We fought through those hedgerows a long time," he recalled. For his part, he saw no point to "getting out of my hedgerow to run over and get the German out of his, not when there was artillery around to do that." Like most infantrymen, he wanted to see those big Made-in-the-U.S.A. shells dropping right on the enemy in front of him. One time, however, "an artillery observer came up with us and called in fire 200 yards in front of us. That was too close." Craft's squad took 200 percent casualties. "I believe I was the only one in the entire company to come all the way through Normandy without getting wounded."[11]

Maj. G. S. Johns of the 29th described a typical hedgerow action, "with a machine gun being knocked out here, a man or two being killed or wounded there. Eventually the leader of the stronger force, usually the attackers, may decide that he has weakened his opponents enough to warrant a large concerted assault, preceded by a concentration of all the mortar and artillery support he can get. Or the leader of the weaker force may see that he will be overwhelmed by such an attack and pull back. Thus goes the battle—a rush, a pause, some creeping, a few isolated shots, some artillery fire, some mortars, some smoke, more creeping, another pause, dead silence, more firing, a great concentration of fire followed by a concerted rush. Then the whole process starts all over again."[12]

The Germans were able to inflict heavy casualties because they were on the defensive. When they tried to attack in the hedgerow country, they did no better than the Americans. On July 11, Panzer Lehr Division launched its major counterattack of the campaign. Two U.S. infantry divisions, the 9th and 30th, threw back the Germans at minimum cost to themselves while inflicting 25 percent casualties.

Of course the Germans took advantage of their skill in warfare. Many of the German officers and NCOs were veterans of the Russian front, and nearly all were veterans of some battles, while this was the first for most of the GIs. The Germans were bolstered by a weapons system that was much better suited to hedgerow defense than the American weapons were to attack in such country.

The Germans had more mortars, and heavier ones, than the Americans. Their MG 42 machine guns fired 1,200 rounds a minute, the American counterpart less than half that. The handle on the German "potato masher" hand grenade made it easier to throw farther. German gunpowder produced less flash and smoke. The Germans had the *Nebelwerfer,* a multibarreled projector whose bombs were designed so as to produce a wail when they flew through the air—sixty or seventy virtually simultaneously—that was terrifying. The GIs called them "Moaning Minnies." The Germans called them "Stukas on Wheels." There was no American counterpart.[13]

Then there was the panzerfaust, which was far superior to the American bazooka. It did not have the range of a bazooka, but that hardly mattered in the hedgerow country. It was operated by a single soldier and was so simple no special training was required, while the bazooka required a trained two-man team. The panzerfaust launched a bomb that was bigger and better designed than the bazooka's, with greater penetrating power. It was an ideal weapon for the hedgerows.

In heavy artillery, the Americans generally outgunned the Germans in quantity and in amounts of ammunition, but long-range gunnery wasn't effective in the close quarters imposed by the hedgerows. The German 88, without doubt the best artillery piece of the war, in the opinion of every GI, was a high-velocity, flat-trajectory weapon that could fire armor-piercing shells down the lanes and roads of Normandy, or be elevated and fire high-explosive airburst shells against Allied bombers. The shell traveled faster than the speed of sound; one heard it explode before one heard it coming.

But the American .50-caliber machine gun, mounted on tanks, had no equal in penetrating power, and the American M-1 Garand was the best all-purpose military rifle in the world. Overall, however, Americans in Normandy gladly would have traded weapons with the Germans. Especially the tankers. There was a barely suppressed fury among American tankers about the inferiority of the Sherman tank (thirty-two tons) to the latest German models, the Panther (forty-three tons) and the Tiger (fifty-six tons). German tanks had heavier armor, too heavy for the Sherman's 75mm cannon to penetrate, while the Panther and Tiger, armed with 88s, easily penetrated the Sherman. The discrepancy was so great it has led military historian Max Hastings to wonder how in the world "could American and British industries produce a host of superb aircraft, an astonishing variety of radar equipment, the proximity fuse, the DUKW [amphibious vehicle], the jeep [not to mention the atomic bomb and Ultra] yet still ask their armies to join battle against the Wehrmacht equipped with a range of tanks utterly inferior in armor and killing power?"[14]

Lt. Paul Fussell, a platoon leader in the 103rd Division who went on to become one of America's leading literary scholars, was bitter on the same point. Referring to the 88s, Fussell wrote, "The allies had nothing as good, despite one of them designating itself The World's Greatest Industrial Power."[15]

The Sherman was universally denounced by anyone who had to fight in one against a Panther or Tiger. But one thing about the Shermans—there were a lot more of them than there were Panthers or Tigers. Quantity over quality and size was General Marshall's deliberate choice. He wanted more, faster (and thus lighter) tanks, in accord with American doctrine, which held that tanks should exploit a breakthrough, not fight other tanks.

Marshall's first problem was that American tanks had to cross the Atlantic to get to the battle, and the number one strategic shortage of the Allies was shipping. Experiment showed that you could get two Shermans into the space required by one larger tank on an LST. Of course that equation didn't work out if one Tiger could destroy four Shermans, which sometimes happened. But not often, because there were so few Tigers compared to the number of Shermans.

By the end of 1944 German industry would produce 24,630 tanks, only a handful of them Tigers. The British would be at 24,843. But the Americans would by then have turned out the staggering total of 88,410 tanks, mainly Shermans.

For all their shortcomings, the Shermans were a triumph of American mass-production techniques. First of all, they were wonderfully reliable, in sharp contrast to the Panthers and Tigers. In addition, GIs were far more experienced in the workings of the internal combustion engine than were their opposite numbers. The Americans were also infinitely better at recovering damaged tanks and patching them up to go back into action; the Germans had nothing like the American maintenance battalions.

Indeed no army in the world had such a capability. Within two days of being put out of action by German shells, about half the damaged Shermans had been repaired by maintenance battalions and were back on the line. Kids who had been working at gas stations and body shops two years earlier had brought their mechanical skills to Normandy, where they replaced damaged tank tracks, welded patches on the armor, and repaired engines. Even the tanks beyond repair were dragged back to the maintenance depot by the Americans and stripped for parts. The Germans just left theirs where they were.[16]

The Red Army had its own tanks, the T-34s (American-designed, and perhaps the best tank of the war). What it needed was trucks. The American Lend-Lease program supplied thousands of Studebaker trucks (surely a capitalist plot!). When the spark plugs clogged, as they quickly did on the dirt roads, the Russians just walked away from the trucks. The American armored division maintenance crews had men who worked day and night sand-blasting plugs. When they ran out of blasting sand they sent men to the beach to get more. It had to be dried and sifted before it could be used, but it did the job.

Nearly all this work was done as if the crews were back in the States, rebuilding damaged cars and trucks—that is, the men on the shop floor made their own decisions, got out their tools, and got after the job. One of their officers, Capt. Belton Cooper, commented, "I began to realize something about the American Army I had never thought possible before. Although it is highly regimented and bureaucratic under garrison conditions, when the Army gets in the field, it relaxes and the individual initiative comes forward and does what has to be done. This type of flexibility was one of the great strengths of the American Army in World War II."[17]

Thanks to American productivity and ingenuity, there were many more Shermans in action than Panthers or Tigers (in fact, about half the Wehrmacht's tanks in Normandy were Mark IVs, twenty-six tons). Besides numbers, the Shermans had other advantages. They used less than half the gasoline of the larger tanks. They were faster and more maneuverable, with double and more the range. A Sherman's tracks lasted for 2,500 miles; the Panther's and Tiger's more like 500. The Sherman's turret turned much faster than that of the Panther or Tiger. In addition, the narrower track of the Sherman made it a much superior road vehicle. But the wider track of the Panther and Tiger made them more suited to soft terrain.

And so it went. For every advantage of the German heavy tanks, there was a disadvantage, as for the American medium tanks. The trouble in Normandy was that the German tanks were better designed for hedgerow fighting. If and when the battle ever became a mobile one, the situation would reverse. Then the much-despised Sherman could show its stuff.

American transport and utility vehicles were far superior to the German counterpart. For example, the jeep and the deuce-and-a-half truck had four-wheel-drive capability, and they were more reliable than the German vehicles. But again like the Sherman, their advantages did not show in the hedgerows, where squad-size actions predominated and the mass movement of large numbers of troops over long distances was irrelevant.

With any weapon, design differences lead to losses as well as gains. The German potato masher, for example, could be thrown farther in part because it was lighter. It had less than half the explosive power of the American grenade. The GIs said it made more noise than damage.

One other point about weapons. Over four decades of interviewing former GIs, I've been struck by how often they tell stories about duds, generally about shells falling near their foxholes and failing to explode. Lt. George Wilson said that after one shelling near St.-Lô, "I counted eight duds sticking in the ground within thirty yards of my foxhole."[18] There are no statistics available on this phenomenon, nor is there any evidence on why, but I've never heard a German talk about American duds. The shells fired by the GIs were made by free American labor; the shells fired by the Wehrmacht were made by slave labor from Poland, France, and throughout the German empire. And at least some of the slaves must have mastered the art of turning out shells that passed examination but were nevertheless sabotaged effectively.

A major shortcoming of the Sherman for hedgerow fighting was its unarmored underbelly, which made it particularly vulnerable to the panzerfaust when it tried to climb a hedgerow. British tanks without infantry support had been unable to make significant progress at Caen; American infantry without tank support was unable to take St.-Lô, the key crossroads city in lower Normandy. Lt. Col. Ziegelmann of the 352 Division attributed the German success in holding St.-Lô to "the surprising lack of tanks. Had tanks supported the American infantry on June 16, St. Lo would not have been in German hands any longer that evening."[19]

Another reason St.-Lô wasn't in American hands: Normandy had its wettest July in forty years. One Marauder unit, the 323rd Group, had seventeen straight missions scrubbed during the first two and a half weeks of July. Others fared little better. Perhaps more than any other single factor, this bad weather explains the relative German success in Normandy in the early summer of 1944. Rain and fog made it possible for them to move reinforcements and supplies to the front.[20]

There was nothing the Americans could do about the weather, but they could go after their problems in getting tanks into the hedgerow fighting. In so doing, they showed their mechanical ability and talents, and their ingenuity and resourcefulness. Rommel was impressed by the effort and results, saying that he thought the Americans "showed themselves to be very advanced in the tactical handling of their forces" and that they "profited much more than the British from their experiences."[21]

Experiments involved welding pipes or steel teeth onto the front of the Sherman tank. Lt. Charles Green, a tanker in the 29th Division, devised a bumper that was made from salvaged railroad tracks that Rommel had used as beach obstacles. It was incredibly strong and permitted the Shermans to bull their way through the thickest hedgerows. In the 2nd Armored Division Sgt. Curtis Culin, a cab driver from Chicago, designed and supervised the construction of a hedgerow-cutting device made from scrap iron pulled from a German roadblock. The blades gave the tank a resemblance to a rhinoceros, so Shermans equipped with Culin's invention were known as rhino tanks.[22]

Another big improvement was in communications. After a series of experiments with telephones placed on the back of the tank, the solution that worked best was to have an interphone box on the tank, into which the infantryman could plug a radio handset. The handset's long cord permitted the GI to lie down behind or underneath the tank while talking to the tank crew, which, when buttoned down, was all but blind. Many, perhaps a majority, of the tank commanders killed in action had been standing in the open turret, so as to see. Now, at least in some situations, the tank could stay buttoned up while the GI on the phone acted as a forward artillery observer.

These improvements, and others, have prompted Michael Doubler to write in his prize-winning *Closing with the Enemy: How GIs Fought the War in Europe,* "In its search for solutions to the difficulties of hedgerow combat, the American army encouraged the free flow of ideas and the entrepreneurial spirit. Coming from a wide variety of sources, ideas generally flowed upward from the men actually engaged in battle."[23]

They were learning by doing. Back in England, the 101st and 82nd Airborne Divisions were evaluating their performance in Normandy, absorbing lessons learned, making required changes, training. But in Normandy, First Army got no relief.

First Army worked on developing a doctrine as well as new weapons for offensive warfare in the hedgerows. At the forefront of the effort was the 29th Division. In late June it held a full rehearsal of the technique it proposed. In briefest form, it was as follows:

Attack teams consisted of one tank, an engineer team, a squad of riflemen, plus a light machine gun and a 60mm mortar. The Sherman opened the action. It plowed its pipe devices into the hedgerow, stuck the cannon through, and opened fire with a white phosphorus round into the corners of the opposite hedgerow, intended to knock out German dug-in machine-gun pits.

White phosphorus was horror. Lt. Robert Weiss got caught in a rare German barrage of white phosphorus shells (rare because the

German supply was insufficient). He recalled the bursting of the shell, followed by "a snowstorm of small, white particles that floated down upon us. We looked in amazement, and eyes filled with instant terror. Where the particles landed on shirts and trousers they sizzled and burned. White phosphorus! We brushed our clothing frantically, pushed shirt collars up. If any of the stuff touched the skin, it could inflict a horrible burn, increasing in intensity as it burrowed into a man's flesh. . . .

"Another shell. Another missile from hell. Fiery snow! I remember thinking that if the shelling kept up for long it would be more than most men could endure. There was nowhere to hide, no place that was safe." Fortunately, that was the last.[24]

The American tankers loved white phosphorus. They quickly learned that one or two shells fired into a German position meant you didn't have to worry about that machine gun any longer.

After firing the shells, the tank put systematic .50-caliber machine-gun fire along the entire base of the enemy hedgerow. The mortar team lobbed shells into the field directly behind the German position. The infantry squad moved forward behind the Sherman, deployed on line and advanced across the open field using standard methods of fire and movement, throwing themselves to the ground, getting up and dashing forward, firing, moving. As they got close to the enemy's hedgerow, they tossed grenades over to the enemy side. The tank, meanwhile, came on through the hedgerow, either on its own power or after backing out and placing explosives in the holes. Infantrymen could plug into the phone and spot for the tank crew as it fired cannon and machine-gun fire at resistance points.[25]

The tactics developed by the 29th worked and were far less costly in casualties, and were soon adopted, with numerous variations, throughout ETO (European Theater of Operations).

The enemy was fighting with the desperation of a cornered, wounded animal. The German infantry was stretched thin. The front-line divisions were getting one replacement for every eleven casualties. By mid-July, the Wehrmacht in Normandy had lost 117,000 men and received 10,000 replacements.

At the beginning of July, two million soldiers were pitted against one another on a front of 150 kilometers. By the end of July, there were more than 800,000 Americans in Normandy, facing 750,000 or so Germans. The Germans had more men, and many more tanks, facing the British around Caen. (The British and Canadians numbered about 600,000.)

For the Germans, rations and ammunition flows were adequate, if barely, but medical supplies were gone, artillery shells were severely limited. More and more, they had to concentrate their dwindling resources on the front line because they did not have the manpower to create a defense in depth. Knowing that if the Americans broke through there was nothing between them and the German border, the Germans dug even deeper, fought even harder.

Veterans of the hedgerow fighting, on either side, can often recall close encounters of a most serious kind. Lt. Walter Padberg was a newsman in the Wehrmacht who had lost his camera equipment when a Jabo hit his truck, so when he joined Grenadier Regiment 957 he lost his position as a reporter ("I don't really have a lot for a reporter to do," his CO had told him when he arrived) and went into the line as a platoon leader.

A few days later, he was lying behind a hedge. There was silence—no mortars, no artillery, no machine-gun fire. Padberg strained to hear if there were Americans on the other side of his hedge. He could hear nothing. He thought it safe to take a good look. He struggled through the vines to the top of the mound, then leaped forward to the far side.

"I landed almost directly upon the Americans' front line," he recalled. "I landed with my legs spread and in a panic the Americans lying there shot through my legs. I jumped back over the hedge and allowed us both to recover from the shock.

"That was my greatest heroic deed, for which I received the Close Combat Medal. It was given to those who had stared the enemy in the eyes."[26]

Rommel's despair deepened. He was a man with a strong sense of duty who could hardly tell where his duty lay. To Germany? To the Wehrmacht? To Hitler? He continued to direct the battle with his unique touch, even as he went over and over in his mind a search for some way to convince Hitler to step aside so that the war could be concluded while Germany still had some conquered territory to bargain with (as in 1918) and before Germany herself was destroyed.

What he came up with wasn't much, but at least he was trying, something more than could be said for most of the other German generals. On July 16 Rommel sent Field Marshal Günter von Kluge (who had replaced Rundstedt) what Rommel called an "ultimatum," for Kluge to pass on to Hitler. Kluge did, and in a covering letter said Rommel "was unfortunately right."

It was a two-and-a-half-page document. Rommel opened by observing that the ultimate crisis was coming soon in Normandy. The American strength in tanks and artillery grew each day. Meanwhile Seventh Army was not getting replacements for its hideous losses. The replacements who were arriving were inexperienced and poorly trained, which made them particularly likely to panic when the Jabos appeared.

Rommel concluded the document with a handwritten sentence: "It is necessary to draw the political conclusions from this situation." His aides argued that he should cross out the word "political." He did, and signed.[27]

The next day, the Jabos got him. A British fighter shot up his staff car and Rommel had a serious head injury. Two days later, on July 20, a group of conspirators tried without success to kill Hitler. Rommel went home to recover; three months later he was forced to commit suicide because of the assassination plot, even though he had not been directly involved.

The conspiracy, and Hitler's retaliation against the officer corps, put a severe strain on the German army. But, amazingly, it was not split asunder. Rolf Pauls, who had a distinguished career in diplomatic service for the West German republic, was a major in an infantry regiment. He described what happened after July 20 in Normandy: "Many generals disappeared. Many of us were afraid of what was going to happen next. I was a good friend of Gen. Hans Speidel [Rommel's chief of staff] so I was not completely uninformed. I heard the news at division HQ. But we still had to do our job. The war went on."[28]

Throughout the Nazi empire, stretching from central Italy to northernmost Norway, from Normandy to Ukraine, officers of the Wehrmacht did their duty, despite the turmoil and temptation created by the assassination attempt. And they acceded to the demand made by the Nazi Party that henceforth the salute would be given with an extended arm and a "Heil Hitler," rather than bringing the hand up to the brim of the cap.[29]

Corp. Adolf Hohenstein of the 276th Division later said that the enlisted men convinced themselves that the shortages of supplies and ammunition and the breakdowns of administration were the fruits of treachery by their own officers. Actually, it was the Jabos. There is no evidence that during the Battle of Normandy any German officer of whatever rank gave less than his full ability to sustain the men in the line.

They needed it. Corporal Hohenstein watched morale ebb in his squad: "The lack of any success at all affected the men very badly. You could feel the sheer fear growing. We would throw ourselves to the ground at the slightest sound, and many men were saying that we should never leave Normandy alive."[30]

Beyond the physical demands, the German soldier suffered from the awful feeling that in doing his duty he was sacrificing his country. Rommel spoke for every German in Normandy when, on July 13, he told his naval aide Adm. Friedrich Ruge, "We must fight to the very end, all the time knowing that it's far more vital to stop the Russians than the Anglo-Americans from overrunning Germany."[31]

As if the Jabos were not effective enough as it was, the Americans were constantly improving their ground-to-air communications system. There was plenty of room for improvement. Close air support (CAS) was a poor third in Army Air Force fighter-bomber doctrine in mid-1944, far behind the first mission—taking and maintaining air superiority—and the second, blasting the enemy line of communications. Further, doctrine held that airpower should not be squandered as "flying artillery."

But in Normandy, where the big guns hardly dared to fire on the enemy front line because of its proximity to the GIs' line, fighter-bomber CAS provided a way to get high explosives on or near the enemy. Various systems of identification were tried, including colored panels stretched on the ground or smoke signals, but none were satisfactory. P-47s flying at 300 miles per hour missed far more panels and smoke signals than they found.

Solutions came because of Maj. Gen. Elwood "Pete" Quesada, CO of Ninth Tactical Air Force. The casualties in Normandy and the slowness of the advance convinced him that his fighter-bombers had to make a more direct contribution to the battle. He went to Bradley to explore new methods. For example, Quesada said, artillery units have forward observers who radio target information to the gunners. Why don't we equip the planes and artillery units with VHF radios so that they can spot for and talk to each other? Why not, indeed. They tried and it worked.

"This man Quesada is a jewel," Bradley told the CO of the Army Air Forces, Gen. Henry "Hap" Arnold. Bradley later wrote that Quesada was "unlike most airmen who viewed ground support as a bothersome diversion to war in the sky. Quesada approached it as a vast new frontier waiting to be explored."[32]

Why not put radio sets in tanks so the tankers could talk to the pilots? Quesada wondered. Why not, indeed. This too worked. The system worked so well, in fact, that by late July the radiomen on the ground could bring aircraft in as close as 500 meters. And it was an awesome amount of explosive a P-47 carried: two five-inch-by-four-foot missiles under each wing, plus two 500-pound bombs, plus 6,400 rounds of .50-caliber ammunition.

Maj. Gerhard Lemcke of the 12th Panzer Division testified to the effectiveness of the American improvements in ground-to-air and tank-to-infantry communication. He had kept his radio team in a bunker for much of July, but after the pounding on it rose to the unbearable point the men "decided it was better to stay out in the open and be blown into the sky than to stay inside and be buried in a cellar." So out they came, only to discover that the Americans had taken control of the battlefield, thanks to their communications abilities.

"Whenever a German soldier fired his panzerfaust," Lemcke complained, "all of the American tanks, artillery, mortars and planes in the area concentrated their fire upon him. They would keep it up until his position was pulverized."[33]

In July, the 2nd Panzer Division reported on the problems it faced: "The incredibly heavy artillery and mortar fire of the enemy is something new for seasoned veterans as much as for the new arrivals. . . . Any assembly of our troops is spotted immediately by enemy reconnaissance aircraft and bombs and artillery directed from the air . . . and by such dense artillery and mortar fire that heavy casualties ensue. . . . Our soldiers enter the battle in low spirits at the thought of the enemy's enormous superiority of material. The feeling of helplessness against enemy aircraft operating without hindrance has a paralysing effect; and during the barrage the effect on the inexperienced men is literally soul-shattering."[34]

The U.S. Army air-ground team in ETO continued to improve through to the end of the war. Its communication system was vastly superior to anything the Germans ever developed. Meanwhile, the Eighth Air Force B-17s continued to pound away at communications targets in France, particularly bridges and railroads, as did the Marauders of Ninth Air Force. But weather continued through July to hamper the effectiveness of the Allied air forces. Fifty percent of the missions in July, for all planes in England and France, had to be scrubbed because of weather.

The Luftwaffe in Normandy was pathetic. The sole contribution Field Marshal Goering's pilots made to the battle came at night, when one, two, or sometimes a dozen Luftwaffe bombers flew over the beaches, dropped bombs at random, and got out of there as soon as possible. The Americans called the night visitors "Bedcheck Charlies." Every weapon on the beach was fired at the bombers. The tracers made such a dazzling array the Germans named the beaches "Golden City." The Luftwaffe did little damage, except to nerves.[35]

On the ground the Americans continued to advance, slowly but all along the front, except at St.-Lô. Outside St.-Lô, more or less stuck in place for nearly a month, despite many attacks, was the 29th Division. Since D-Day, it had been locked in a mortal embrace with the 352nd Division. But in each division there was scarcely a man present for duty who had been there on D-Day. The 352nd, in fact, had virtually disappeared. In the 29th, Gen. Charles Gerhardt, the CO, was referred to as a corps commander rather than a division commander. "He has a division in the field, a division in the hospital, and a division in the cemetery."[36]

The historian of the 29th, Joseph Balkoski, has a well-deserved tribute to the soldiers of the Blue and Gray Division: "The 29ers were humble men caught up in a war of immeasurable complexity. Most 29ers had done what they were told to do, even when orders made little sense. On the deadly battlefields from Omaha Beach to St. Lo, these simple acts of obedience reflected astounding personal courage. Any soldier who could bring himself to leap over a hedgerow upon command and race, hunchbacked, across a grassy field while bullets snapped over his head like cracking whips, was a brave man indeed."[37]

■

Some of the fiercest fighting was taking place outside St.-Lô. To its defense the Germans devoted much of their strength, as Maj. Randall Bryant of the 9th Division discovered in mid-July when he was walking across an orchard with his closest friend, Capt. Charles Minton, beside him. The Germans laid on a TOT—time on target, an artillery shoot carefully coordinated to concentrate the fire of an entire battery or regiment on one spot at a precise moment. Bryant and Minton happened to be at the spot.

"Suddenly everything was exploding," Bryant related. "There was blood all over me, and a helmet on the ground with a head inside it. It was Minton's. Three young 2nd lieutenants had just joined us, straight from the beach and Fort Benning. I had told them to sit down and wait to be assigned to companies. They were dead, along with six others killed and 33 wounded in a shoot that lasted only a matter of seconds."[38]

Gerhardt was under great pressure from Bradley to take St.-Lô. So far he had already lost more men outside St.-Lô than he had on Omaha Beach on D-Day. His medics were measuring gains by morphine units dispensed. One of them commented that he figured it took thirty-two grains of morphine per hedgerow.[39] The 29th's rifle companies were close to 100 percent replacements. But Gerhardt figured the Germans were in worse condition and ordered a general assault to take St.-Lô, putting all his strength into it: no reserves.

Maj. Tom Howie, a mild-mannered teacher of English literature before the war, led the 3rd Battalion of the 116th Regiment in the 29th. Linked to the 2nd Battalion, he was to drive right on into St.-Lô. On July 17, an hour before dawn, the attack began. Howie told his men to keep going, no matter what. He limited each platoon to two men firing their rifles, and then only in emergency. The others were to use their bayonets and hand grenades.

The idea was to achieve surprise. The tactics had been developed by the star-crossed 90th Division, which had been unlucky in its COs (three had already been relieved by Bradley)* and had suf-

---

*One of them was D-Day hero Gen. Teddy Roosevelt, Jr. On July 13 Bradley replaced the CO of the 90th with Roosevelt, but Roosevelt died that night of a heart attack.

fered, by this time, 100 percent casualties among its enlisted men and 150 percent among its officers. One regiment had been losing its platoon leaders at the rate of 48 percent a week. To cut the losses, the 90th had gone over to night attacks, infiltrating by squads independently, without artillery preparation. This worked; as one 90th Division GI put it, "We learned to prefer the night infiltration attack. It was a lot better to fight the German by surprise than to carry out the normal daylight assault."[40]

In the predawn July 17 attack, the infantry from the 29th broke through or passed through the German line and took the high ground just one kilometer from St.-Lô. The road into the city was open. Howie called the company commanders to a conference and to give them their objectives. "We had just finished the meeting," Capt. William Puntenney, Howie's executive officer, recalled. "The COs had been dismissed and before they could get back to their companies, the Germans began dropping a mortar barrage around our ears. Before taking cover in one of the foxholes, Major Howie turned to take a last look to be sure all his men had their heads down. Without warning, one of the shells hit a few yards away. A fragment struck the major in the back and pierced his lung.

" 'My God, I'm hit,' he murmured, and I saw he was bleeding at the mouth. As he fell, I caught him. He was dead in two minutes."[41]

Captain Puntenney took over, just as a counterattack from the *Fallschirmjäger* hit the battalion. Using the new communications techniques, the 29th called in artillery and a fighter-bomber strike. It broke up the attack and restored the spirits of Howie's men. They began the charge into St.-Lô. In the opinion of Captain Cooper, "It was an almost perfect use of combined arms of air, armor, infantry and artillery working in joint optimum support of each other."[42]

As they crested the hill and started the descent into the town, the Americans were shocked by what they saw. St.-Lô had been hit by B-17s on D-Day, and every clear day thereafter. The center of the place was a lifeless pile of rubble in which roads and sidewalks could scarcely be distinguished. As they moved into the fringe of town, they began to draw German fire from some *Fallschirmjäger* in a cemetery. A macabre battle ensued, rifle and machine-gun bullets smashing into headstones. Rhino tanks that had busted through the hedgerow came up in support, fired their cannons and machine guns, and drove the Germans off. The men of the 29th dashed into the town, guns blazing. There was still hard fighting to go before the town was completely cleared of the enemy, but finally St.-Lô was in American hands.

At Gerhardt's insistence, Howie's body was put on a jeep and driven into the town. Men from the 3rd Battalion draped the body with the Stars and Stripes and hoisted it on top of a huge pile of stones that had once been a wall in the Saint Croix church, a block from the cemetery. Howie's body remained on display through the next day, July 19. GIs and some of the few civilians remaining in the town adorned the site with flowers. "It was simple and direct, no fanfare or otherwise," Lt. Edward Jones recollected.[43]

The story caught on with the press. *Life* magazine featured "The Major of St. Lo." Howie was famous, too late to do him any good. But what he, and the other officers and men of the 29th, had done was far more important than good publicity for the Army: they had captured the town, and with it the high ground in that part of Normandy, thereby putting First Army in a position to launch an offensive designed to break through the German line and out of the hedgerow country.

For that offensive, Bradley was making plans to use the Allies' greatest single asset, airpower. Undaunted by what had happened in Goodwood, he was preparing to use every bomber and fighter-bomber that could fly in a crushing bombardment that would blast a hole in the German line.

3

Breakout and Encirclement

July 25–August 25, 1944

ON JULY 24, seven weeks after D-Day, U.S. First Army was holding an east–west line that ran from Caumont to St.-Lô to Lessay on the Channel. Pre-D-Day projections had put the Americans on this line on D Plus Five.

Disappointing as that was, Bradley could see opportunities for his army. The enemy, although nearly equal in number of fighting men, was sadly deficient in supplies and badly worn down. One of Bradley's chief problems was he had not enough room to bring the well-trained and equipped divisions waiting in England into the battle—not to mention General Patton. For the Germans, the problem was the opposite—no significant reinforcements were available. Another favorable factor for Bradley: six of the eight German panzer divisions in Normandy faced the British and Canadians around Caen.

Bradley was also encouraged by two sets of photographs shown to him by General Quesada. One showed the area behind the German lines. The roads were empty. The other showed the area behind American lines. The roads were nose-to-tail armor and transport convoys, or marching troops. Huge supply dumps dotted the fields, with no need for camouflage. These were among the fruits of air superiority.[1]

The Ninth Tactical Air Force had a dozen airstrips in Nor-

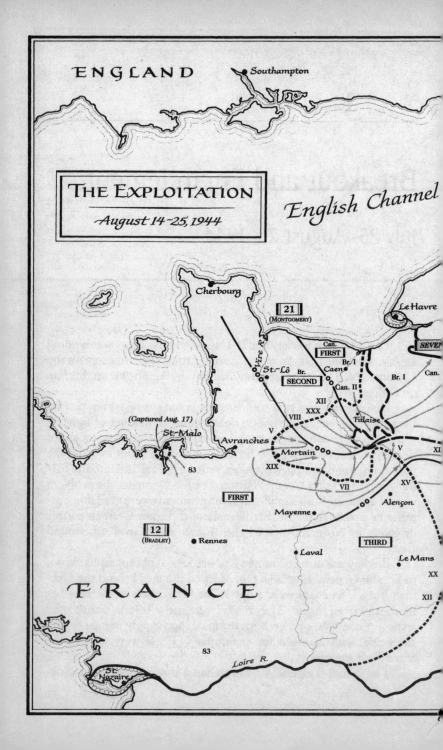

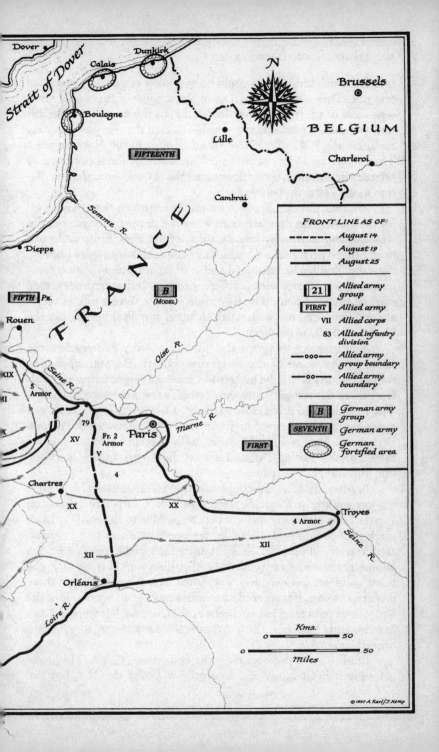

mandy by this time. Pilots could be over their targets in a matter of minutes. They were daredevil youngsters, some of them only nineteen years of age (it was generally felt that by the time he reached his mid-twenties, a man was too sensible to take the chances routinely required of a P-47 pilot). They lived in tents in the Norman mud. They made up to five sorties per day, some of them only twenty minutes in duration. They dominated the sky and brought destruction to the Germans below.

Another plus for Bradley: his men were much better equipped for the battle than they had been when the campaign began both in weapons and tactics. By July 24, three of five First Army tanks had been fitted with a rhino. Ground-air communications were improving daily. Bradley had ruthlessly relieved incompetent division commanders, sometimes with indifferent results, but sometimes seeing marked improvement. The front-line soldiers were a mix of veterans and replacements, with relatively good morale although, like the Germans, badly worn down.

A heartening thing for the GIs: First Army had reached the limits of the worst of the hedgerow country. Beyond lay fertile, rolling countryside. The hedgerows enclosed larger pastures; roads were more numerous, many were tarred, a few were even four-lane. The front line ran on or close to the St.-Lô–Périers road, which was a straight east–west paved highway, the N 800. Between St.-Lô and Périers, the Panzer Lehr Division, badly used up, held the line for the Germans. Facing Panzer Lehr on the American side were the 9th, 4th, and 30th Divisions.

Bradley decided he could use the St.-Lô–Périers road as a marker for the strategic air forces and lay a carpet of bombs on Panzer Lehr by having the bombers fly parallel to the road—a landmark they couldn't miss, Bradley reasoned. The area to be obliterated was six kilometers long (running along the road) and two kilometers south of the road. Massed artillery would come after the bombardment, followed by a combined tank-infantry assault three divisions strong. If it worked, the Americans would break out of the hedgerow country and uncover the entire German left wing in Normandy, with Patton's Third Army ready to come in to exploit a breakthrough.[2]

Bradley gave the operation the code name Cobra. He began planning it in mid-July and was ready to go by the 21st, but bad weather caused delays. Meanwhile there was a dispute over how close to the road the attacking units of the American divisions ought to be placed. Bradley wanted them within 800 meters of the road serving as a bomb line. The airmen wanted a buffer zone of three kilometers. Eventually they compromised at 1,200 meters. That caused a number of infantry units to have to pull back from the road, giving up ground won at such a cost, something they hated to do.

On July 21 Eisenhower flew in a heavy rain from London to Normandy to be present for the attack. Bradley met him and said the attack had been called off. Then he dressed Eisenhower down for flying in such weather. Eisenhower tossed away his soggy cigarette, grinned, and said his only pleasure in being Supreme Commander was that nobody could ground him.

"When I die," he added, looking at the steady rain, "they ought to hold my body for a rainy day and then bury me out in the middle of a storm. This damned weather is going to be the death of me yet."[3]

On July 24 the weather appeared acceptable and an order to go went out to the airfields, only to be rescinded after a third of the force had taken off. By the time the recall signal had gone out to the bombers, one flight of B-17s had crossed the coast and released its load of 500-pound bombs through cloud cover. Most of the bombs fell short, causing casualties in the 30th Division and leaving the infantrymen madder than hell.

Worse, the bombers had come in perpendicular to the line, not on a parallel course. The airmen argued that they couldn't funnel all the bombers involved through the narrow corridor created by using a single marker and flying along it—it would take hours for them all to pass over the target, all the time exposed to anti-aircraft fire from the 88s. By coming in perpendicular, spread out, the bombers would cause a much greater shock on the German side and only be taking flak during the seconds it took to cross the line and drop the bombs. Bradley still wanted a parallel approach, but the airmen convinced him that it was too late to change the plan.

July 25 was clear. At 0938, some 550 fighter-bombers appeared. They were being guided by radio messages from forward air controllers riding in tanks at the head of armored columns. The FACs could talk simultaneously to ground units, P-47s, higher headquarters, and supporting artillery batteries.

The P-47s fired rockets and machine guns on the German positions just south of the road, and dropped 500-pound bombs that were much more powerful than even 240mm howitzers, and could be placed by the pilots within 300 meters of the American lines (most GIs feared artillery preparation closer than 500 meters).

Reporter Ernie Pyle wrote, "The dive bombers hit it just right. We stood in the barnyard of a French farm and watched them barrel nearly straight down out of the sky. They were bombing less than a half-a-mile ahead of where we stood.

"They came in groups, diving from every direction, perfectly timed, one right after another. Everywhere you looked separate groups of planes were on the way down, or on the way back up, or slanting over for a dive."

After twenty minutes, the P-47s gave way to 1,800 B-17s.

Their appearance left men groping for words to describe it. Pyle did it this way: "A new sound gradually droned into our ears— a gigantic far-away surge of doomlike sound. It was the heavies. They came from directly behind us. They came on in flights of twelve, three flights to a group and in groups stretched out across the sky. . . . Their march across the sky was slow and studied. I've never known anything that had about it the aura of such a ghastly relentlessness. You had the feeling that even had God appeared beseechingly before them in the sky with palms outward to persuade them to turn back they would not have had within them the power to turn off their irresistible course."[4]

They were 12,000 feet high. Gen. Fritz Bayerlein compared the flight to a conveyor belt. Lt. James Delong, a pilot in a B-26 coming behind the B-17s, had been on sixty-six missions. He declared flatly, "I have never seen so many planes all together strung out across the sky. Smoke rose from the bomb explosions high into the sky. Loud and frequent commands came over the radio not to drop short of the smoke line."[5]

Capt. Belton Cooper was on the ground. "Once they started it was like some giant prehistoric dragon snake forming a long great continuum across the sky with its tail extended over the horizon. I was reminded of Leonidas in the battle of Thermopylae, when he was told that the Persian arrows were so numerous they would darken the sky. He said, 'Good, so much the better, we can fight in the shade.' "6

The B-17s were overhead for a full hour. Their strike saturated the area just south of the road to a depth of 2,500 meters. The results for the Germans were near-catastrophic. The bombed area looked like the surface of the moon. Craters had overlapped each other in many areas. Entire hedgerows were blasted away. General Bayerlein reported that he lost "at least 70 percent of my troops, out of action—dead, wounded, crazed, or numbed."7

During the second half hour of the bombardment, the bomb line—as seen from 11,000 feet—moved north. The dust and debris raised by the first waves was drifting on a south wind. The CO of Company B, 8th Infantry, 4th Division, described what happened: "The dive bombers came in beautifully, dropped their bombs right in front of us just where they belonged. Then the first group of heavies dropped theirs . . . the next wave came in closer, the next one closer, still closer. . . . Then they came right on top of us. . . . The shock was awful. . . . I called battalion and told them I was in no condition to move out, that everything was completely disorganized and it would take me some time to get my men back together, and asked for a delay."8

There were 111 GIs killed and 490 wounded by the shorts. Among the dead was Gen. Lesley McNair, chief of the Army Ground Forces, who was in the front line to witness the attack.

Ernie Pyle wrote that it was impossible to describe what anyone under those bombs felt or thought: "I believe a person's feelings at such times are kaleidoscopic and uncatalogable. You just wait, that's all. You do remember an inhuman tenseness of muscle and nerves." Pyle was stiff and sore for days after, because of "muscles tensing themselves too tight for too long."9

This bombardment was supplemented by artillery fire, 1,000 guns in all. The gunners' initial task was to suppress all German anti-aircraft fire. When the first wave of bombers appeared, 88s knocked three of them out of the sky. But little Piper Cubs were flying near enough to the German lines to spot the flashes and call in the German battery's positions to American artillery.

Medic Edward "Buddy" Gianelloni was struck by the sight. "The funniest thing I ever saw was those Piper Cubs. They were spotting for the artillery so the 88s couldn't hit our bombers. Little bitsy Piper Cub protecting these great big sons of bitches way up there with the bombs."[10]

When the shells started coming down on them, the German artillerymen dove into their bunkers and the 88 anti-aircraft fire ceased. Bayerlein estimated he lost half his 88s.[11] Then in a general hour-long barrage, the GIs fired 50,000 artillery shells.

Overhead, as the B-17s departed, 350 P-47s swooped in for another twenty-minute strike against the narrow strip just south of the road, dropping napalm-filled drums on the target. Their departure from the area was the signal for the infantry and tanks to begin the ground attack. As they did so, 396 Marauders hit the rear of the German front line.

Altogether some 16,000 tons of bombs hit the Germans, supplemented by the artillery barrage. It was the greatest expenditure of explosives for a single attack in the Army's history.

The effect on the Germans was not far short of disaster. Pvt. Herbert Meier, a radioman, recalled "so many planes over so little space . . . and the bombs rained down." He was ordered to carry a message to an artillery commander in a bunker. "Getting out of my hole I saw the bombs being released, and the way they shone in the sun for a moment, then fell to earth so fast that one could not see them. The explosions sent great geysers of earth into the air. I ran from hole to hole like a rabbit, then into the bunker and delivered my message."[12]

Everywhere there was death and destruction. Men not hit by shrapnel were bleeding from the nose, ears, mouth. The world seemed to be coming to an end. For Major Joachim Barth, CO of an antitank battalion in Bayerlein's division, it almost had. "When the shelling finally stopped," he recalled, "I looked out of my bunker. The world had changed. There were no leaves on the trees. It was much harder to get around. We had wounded, we needed medics, but no ambulances could come forward. Our big guns had been tipped over."[13]

The Americans had suffered, too, and when Bradley got the news of the shorts, he wrote that at his headquarters "dejection settled over us like a wet fog."[14] But he remained determined to take immediate advantage of the shock to the Germans. He sent his energy down the line: Let's Go!

The company CO of the 4th Division who had asked for a delay before jumping off, so that he could reorganize his shattered troops, was told, "No. Push off. Jump off immediately."[15]

Lt. Sidney Eichen of the 30th Division had a similar experience. "My outfit was decimated," he reported, "our anti-tank guns blown apart. I saw one of our truck drivers, Jesse Ivy, lying split down the middle. Captain Bell was buried in a crater." But his division CO, Gen. William Harrison, put the pressure on Eichen's regimental commander: "Colonel, the attack goes ahead as scheduled. Even if you have only two or three men, the attack is to be made." The colonel ran from company to company, shouting "You've gotta get going, get going!" So, Eichen said, "half-heartedly, we started to move."[16]

On the German side, Major Barth remembered that as the shelling stopped, he told his men, "Get ready! Get ready!" They were "digging people out, digging out the guns and righting them. Get ready! Get ready! Prepare your positions, they'll soon be here. And then finally the release: They're coming! They're coming!

"Everyone knew what he had to do. There were no orders to be given. It was our lance corporals who supplied the nerve, they are the ones I admire, they knew their duty and did it. We old soldiers always said the lance corporals were the backbone of the army."[17]

The first advancing GIs passed disabled German vehicles, shattered corpses, and stunned and disoriented survivors—but they also found veterans of Panzer Lehr, "doing business at the same old stand with the same old merchandise—dug-in tanks and infantry."[18] Pvt. Günter Feldmann of Panzer Lehr, later a POW who learned English, recalled that "the first words I heard from an American were, 'Goddamn it all, the bastards are still there!' He meant my division."[19]

German artillery fire on the GIs was also heavy, as some at least of the dug-in German artillery survived.[20] As darkness came on July 25, little or no gain had resulted from the air strike. Cobra looked to be another Goodwood.

But if the GIs and their generals were discouraged, General Bayerlein was in despair. When a staff officer came from army headquarters, conveying Field Marshal von Kluge's order that the St.-Lô–Périers line must be held, that not a single man should leave his position, Bayerlein replied, "Out in front every one is holding out. Every one. My grenadiers and my engineers and my tank crews—they're all holding their ground. Not a single man is leaving his post. They are lying silent in their foxholes for they are dead. You may report to the Field-Marshal that the Panzer Lehr Division is annihilated."[21]

July 26 was a day of suspense. The Americans attacked, throwing divisions scheduled for exploitation into the battle to break through. The Germans held nonetheless. The break came on July 27. The thin crust of Panzer Lehr disintegrated. Sgt. Hans Strober noted that "the Americans had learned how to break through, ignoring their flanks and pushing through to occupy crossroads and set up blocking positions so that our vehicles and heavy weapons could not get through."[22]

The breakthrough was a great feat of arms. First Army had accomplished something that had been nearly impossible in 1914–18, and not achieved by the British in front of Caen in June–July 1944. First Army had accomplished something that it had not been trained or equipped to do, in the process developing an air-ground team unmatched in the world. Now, along with Third Army, it was finally going to get into a campaign for which it had been trained and equipped.

The dean of American military historians, Russell Weigley, referring to the flow of GIs that poured around the German open flank, wrote in his classic study *Eisenhower's Lieutenants*, "This virtual road march was war such as the American army was designed for, especially the American armored divisions. Appealing also to the passion for moving on that is so much a part of the American character and heritage, it brought out the best in the troops, their energy and mechanical resourcefulness. . . .

"Now that Cobra had achieved the breakout, the most mobile army in the world for the first time since D-Day could capitalize on its mobility." Weigley further notes that with the hard-won mobility, "the issues confronting the army became for the first time in Europe strategic rather than tactical. The soldiers' battle of Normandy was about to become the generals' battle of France."[23]

■

With the German left flank in the air, and the Allies facing an open road to Paris, Patton was activated and all his pent-up energy turned loose. He had come over in time for Cobra, to familiarize himself with the situation and to set up Third Army headquarters. He took command of one of the corps already in Normandy and had other divisions coming in from England.* By August 1, he had divisions attacking in four directions. Meanwhile First Army pressed forward to the south as German resistance collapsed.

As the general German retreat began, the American air-ground team pounded the enemy. The Wehrmacht was out of the hedgerows, out in the open, trying desperately to move by day to get away. Patton's tanks mauled them, the Jabos terrorized them.

"I had seen the first retreat from Moscow," Sgt. Helmut Gunther of the 17th SS Panzer Grenadiers recalled, "which was terrible enough, but at least units were still intact. Here, we had become a cluster of individuals. We were not a battleworthy company any longer. All that we had going for us was that we knew each other very well."[24]

The P-47s responded to calls from the tankers and infantry over the radio, descended on their targets, and hit them with napalm, 500-pound bombs, rockets, and .50-caliber machine-gun fire. Destroyed German tanks, trucks, scout cars, wagons, and artillery pieces, along with dead and wounded horses and men, covered the landscape.

Captain Cooper described the Allied teamwork. When two Panther tanks threatened his maintenance company from across a hedgerow, the liaison officer in a Sherman got on its radio to give the coordinates to any Jabos in the area. "Within less than 45 seconds, two P-47's appeared right over the tree tops traveling like hell at 300 feet." They let go their bombs a thousand feet short of Cooper's location: "It seemed like the bombs were going to land square in the middle of our area." He and his men dove into their foxholes.

The bombs went screaming over. The P-47s came screaming in right behind them, firing their eight .50-caliber machine guns. The bombs hit a German ammunition dump. "The blast was awe-

*When Third Army was activated, Gen. Courtney Hodges succeeded Bradley as First Army commander while Bradley moved up to command Twelfth Army Group (First and Third Armies).

some; flames and debris shot some 500 ft. into the air. There were bogie wheels, tank tracks, helmets, backpacks and rifles flying in all directions. The hedgerow between us and the German tanks protected us from the major direct effects of the blast, however, the tops of trees were sheared off and a tremendous amount of debris came down on us."[25]

"I have been to two church socials and a county fair," said one P-47 pilot, "but I never saw anything like this before!"[26]

The Jabos were merciless. The constant attacks inevitably broke up German units, which had a terrible effect on morale. A theme that always comes up when interviewing German veterans is comradeship. So, too, with American veterans, of course, but there is an intensity about the Germans on the subject that is unique. One reason is that generally German squads were made up of men from the same town or region, so the men had known each other as children. Another is the experience of being caught in a debacle—Jabos overhead, artillery raining down, tanks firing from the rear.

Corporal Bertenrath spoke to the point: "The worst thing that could happen to a soldier was to be thrown into some group in which he knew no one. In our unit, we would never abandon each other. We had fought in Russia together. We were comrades, and always came to the rescue. We protected our comrades so they could go home to their wives, children, and parents. That was our motivation. The idea that we would conquer the world had fallen long ago."[27]

Lt. Walter Padberg of Grenadier Regiment 959 was appalled: "Everything was chaos. Allied artillery and airplanes were everywhere." Then, the worst possible happened: "I did not know any of the people around me."[28] Padberg continued fleeing, essentially on his own even though in the midst of others. The retreat was turning into a rout.

A historic opportunity presented itself. As the British and Canadians picked up the attack on their front, Patton had open roads ahead of him, inviting his fast-moving armored columns to cut across the rear of the Germans—whose horse-drawn artillery and transport precluded rapid movement—encircle them and destroy the German army in France, then end the war with a triumphal unopposed march across the Rhine and on to Berlin.

Patton lusted to seize that opportunity. He had trained and equipped Third Army for just this moment. Straight east to Paris, then northwest along the Seine to seize the crossings, and the Allies would complete an encirclement that would lead to a bag of prisoners bigger than North Africa or Stalingrad. More important, it would leave the Germans defenseless in the west, because Patton could cut off the German divisions in northern France, Belgium, and Holland as he drove for the Rhine.

That was the big solution. Obviously risky, if successful it promised the kind of big encirclements the Wehrmacht had achieved in 1940 in France and 1941 in the Soviet Union. But neither Eisenhower nor Bradley were bold enough to take it. They worried about Patton's flanks—he insisted that the Jabos could protect them. They worried about Patton's fuel and other supply—he insisted that in an emergency they could be airlifted to him.

Arguing over the merits of different generals is a favorite pastime of many military history buffs. It is harmless and often instructive. And we all have the right to pass judgment; that right comes from the act of participation. The American people had provided Generals Eisenhower and Bradley with a fabulous amount of weaponry and equipment, and some two million of their young men. There has to be an accounting of how well they used these assets to bring about the common goal. And how well means, Did they achieve the victory at the lowest cost in the shortest time? Were they prudent where prudence was appropriate? More important, given their superiority over the enemy, did they take appropriate risks that utilized the greatest assets their country had given them, airpower and mobility?

In Normandy, in August, the answer is no. Ike and Bradley picked the safer alternative, the small solution. Thus was a great opportunity missed. But of course we know now that the risk was worth taking, because we know the cost of finally overrunning Germany; in July 1944 Eisenhower and Bradley didn't.

They were also responding to their obsession with ports. They wanted the small ports of Brittany, such as St.-Malo, and the one big port, Brest. So they insisted that Patton stay with the pre D-Day plan, with modifications. It had called for Patton to turn the whole of Third Army into Brittany; when he protested that being wedded to plans was a mistake and insisted that he wanted to attack toward

Germany, not away from it, Eisenhower and Bradley relented to the extent that they gave him permission to reduce the Brittany attack to one corps, leaving two corps to head east.

Eisenhower had often said that in war, plans are everything before the battle begins, but once the shooting started plans were worthless. And back in 1926, when he had graduated first in his class at the Command and General Staff School at Fort Leavenworth, Patton had written to congratulate him, then to warn him to put all that Leavenworth stuff out of his mind from now on. "Victory in the next war," Patton had declared, "will depend on EXECUTION not PLANS."[29]

To Patton, it was outrageous that his superiors wouldn't turn him loose. "I am also nauseated," he grumbled, "by the fact that Hodges and Bradley state that all human virtue depends on knowing infantry tactics." Patton thought that "Omar the tent maker," as he called Bradley, was never audacious enough. "Bradley and Hodges are such nothings," he wrote. "Their one virtue is that they get along by doing nothing. . . . They try to push all along the front and have no power anywhere."[30]

Monty agreed with Patton. He, too, wanted to abandon the plan to overrun Brittany. He pointed out the obvious: "The main business lies to the East."[31] He pointed out the not-so-obvious: if the Allies seized the opportunity before them, Brest and St.-Malo would not be needed. And indeed, in the event, St.-Malo held out to the end of the war—Hitler's orders—and Brest until late September. German destruction of the port facilities was so effective that it never made a significant contribution to the supply situation.

An entire corps of well-trained, well-equipped tankers, infantrymen, and artillery had been wasted at a critical moment. In the boxing analogy, Patton wanted to throw a roundhouse right and get the bout over; his superiors ordered him to throw a short right hook to knock the enemy off balance. But the enemy already was staggering. He should have been knocked out.

Although he was downcast by his superiors' orders, Patton was exhilarated as his Third Army drove across France. He was at the front, in a jeep, escorted by an armored car, pushing, prodding, yelling, straightening out traffic jams, always demanding more. "Advance and keep on advancing," was his order.

He was attacking in all four directions at once. "We are having one of the loveliest battles you ever saw," he wrote an old friend. "It is a typical cavalry action in which, to quote the words of the old story, 'The soldier went out and charged in all directions at the same time, with a pistol in each hand, and a saber in the other.' "[32]

Still he seethed. Attacking in every direction at once was fun, but he knew it was a fatal diminution of strength. The objective lay to the east, not north, west, or south.

Hitler knew his army was staggering. Should it fall back? Get out of Normandy and across the Seine while the getting was good? That was what his generals wanted to do, because it made obvious military sense. But Hitler hated to retreat and loved to take risks. Where his generals saw the jaws of a trap closing on them, he saw a once-only opportunity to go for the American jugular.

As Patton began his short right hook, swinging his divisions north toward Argentan, a glance at the map showed Hitler that the corridor through which Third Army received its supplies was exceedingly narrow (about thirty kilometers) and thus vulnerable. By bringing down more of the infantry and tankers of Fifteenth Army from north of the Seine, Hitler told Kluge that he would have ample troops to cut that corridor. The process of bringing troops and tanks south of the Seine had been well started already, as Fortitude was wearing a bit thin by now. The tanks crossed the Seine by ferry after dark; it took the 116th Panzer Division four nights to complete the crossing.

With these fresh troops, Hitler told Kluge, he could mount a full-scale counteroffensive, one designed to cut the Third Army supply line. It would start at Mortain, objective Avranches. Once the line had been cut, Patton could be destroyed in place and the line restored. With luck, the Germans could force the fighting back into the hedgerow country, perhaps even drive the Americans back into the sea.

Kluge and every soldier involved thought it madness. Beyond the problems of the Jabos and American artillery, these new divisions were not well equipped—few Panthers or Tigers—they had fuel shortages, and anyway they were not "fresh troops." Maj. Heinz-Günter Guderian, son of the colonel-general, was with the 116th Panzer Division. He recalled, "Most of our people were old soldiers from the Eastern Front. Many of our wounded had returned. We also received parts of a training division, teenagers who had just been inducted and were not trained."

Guderian went on, dryly, "To begin an attack with the idea that it is without hope is not a good idea. We did not have this hope."[33] Hitler ordered it done.

Because Hitler mistrusted his generals, he took control of the battle, which forced him to use the radio, allowing Ultra—the British deciphering device—to reveal both the general plan and some of the specific details. So on August 5, Eisenhower knew what was coming—six German armored divisions. Between them and Avranches stood one American infantry division, the 30th.

Despite the numbers no one in the American high command doubted that the 30th, supported by P-47 Thunderbolts and British Typhoons and American artillery, could hold. Far from telling Patton to stop, much less pull back, Eisenhower told him to keep moving. In Eisenhower's view, the Germans were sticking their heads in a noose. On the morning of August 7, he flew to Normandy and set up an advance command post in Normandy, a tented headquarters in an apple orchard near Granville, where he had a grand view of Mont-St.-Michel. He met with Bradley, who immediately agreed to hold Mortain with minimal forces while rushing every available division south, through the corridor and out into the interior.

At the same moment, the German attack raced around and through Mortain. It had begun before dawn, tanks rolling forward through the night without the warning of an artillery preparation. It had achieved tactical surprise and by noon was in Mortain. But the Germans could not dislodge the 700 men of the 2nd Battalion, 120th Infantry Regiment, 30th Division, from an isolated rocky bluff, Hill 317, just east of the town. The GIs on the hill had a perfect view of the surrounding countryside and forward observers with a radio communications system that allowed them to call in artillery and Jabos. The Germans had to take that hill before driving on to the coast.

In their initial thrust, the two SS panzer divisions overran the 2nd Battalion CP and made the CO and his staff prisoner. Command on the hill reverted to Capt. Reynold Erichson. As he got his men dug in, the forward observers worked their radios. Before dawn on the second day, August 8, one of the observers—Lt. Robert Weiss—heard more than he saw a concentration of German tanks milling around at a roadblock set up by the GIs the previous night. He had the coordinates already fixed and called in a barrage. "That kept them away," Weiss reported, "except for one tank which came through into our company territory, sniffing the dark like a near-sighted dragon. No other tanks followed. Our guys lay motionless, not a breath, not a sound. In the dark the tank found nobody to fight. It turned and went back to its lair."[34]

With daylight, German 88s from their Panthers and anti-aircraft batteries began shelling the hill. At the top there was a rocky ridgeline. Weiss crawled up to it and lifted his head. He had a panoramic view, but there was the great danger that the Germans would spot him as he spotted them, especially as the sun was coming up in his face and there was a reflection off his binoculars. But he also figured that the concept of "range probable error" would work in his favor. With all the variables involved—wind, elevation, distance (1,500 to 2,000 meters)—it was highly unlikely that the Germans could hit a target as small as a helmet. An 88, after all, was not a rifle.

Of course artillery shells don't have to score direct hits to kill, but Weiss further figured that shells hitting short of him would send their explosive power to the sides and over his head, while those that were long would fly overhead, miss the hill altogether, and hit at the base, and thus among the German troops down there.

So Weiss sucked in his breath, called his radio operator forward, picked up his binoculars, and started crawling to the top of the crag. "We had to be quick," Weiss said. "The fire missions had to come with almost the speed of the shooting in a quick-draw western—and with comparable accuracy."

Sgt. Armon Sasser, tucked into the reverse slope, his antenna up, had his radio set up. "Ready, lieutenant."

Weiss called Sgt. John Corn to move up beside him before scrambling up the precipice to the top. The sun glared. Head low, body flattened, elbows stretched far apart and resting on the ground, binoculars up to his face, just below his eyes, Weiss searched and waited.

The Germans began firing, 88s and mortars. Weiss put his glasses to his eyes. "Smoke from the muzzles of the German guns wreathed their position like smoke rings from a cigar," Weiss remembered. He called out to Sergeant Corn, *"Fire Mission*. Enemy battery," and gave the coordinates. Corn passed it on down to Sasser, who turned on his radio: "Crow, this is Crow Baker 3. *Fire Mission,"* and repeated the coordinates.

Weiss could only wait, in apprehension. Who would fire first? "I watched the enemy guns through my binoculars, now a gun sight."

Sasser called up softly, "On the way."

"A freight train roared by from the left side," Weiss said. "Almost instantly clouds of smoke broke near the German position. I shouted an adjusting command to Corn who passed it quickly to Sasser and on to battalion. The next salvos were right on target." That German battery was out of action.

Shells came in from the left from six enemy self-propelled guns. Weiss repeated the sequence, with similar satisfactory results. Then a single tank and yet another battery fired on Hill 317. The tank was to the south, the battery to the north. Weiss called in a barrage on the tank that set it ablaze, then turned his attention to the battery.

"Fire Mission. Enemy battery. Six guns. Last concentration is 500 right, 300 short."

The American shells fired in response came in on line but way short. Weiss shouted an adjustment over the noise of the enemy shells bursting around him. Corn passed it on: "Tinkers-to-Evers-to-Chance," as Weiss put it. The follow-up rounds were on target. "The enemy," Weiss noted with satisfaction, "had been neutralized."[35]

Weiss called for some thirty fire missions during the course of the day, scrambling up the edge of the ridge each time the Germans began firing. Some half dozen other observers were doing similar work that day.

Even as the Mortain offensive began, Patton's forces had overrun Le Mans. The road to Paris, some 160 kilometers to the northeast, was a good one and was undefended. But instead of plunging ahead to Paris, the Americans turned to the northwest, toward Argentan, in pursuit of the short envelopment of the German armies in Normandy. Montgomery and Bradley agreed that the Americans should halt outside Argentan to await the Canadians (with the Polish 1st Armored Division in the lead) coming down from Falaise.

When they met, the entire German army in Normandy—still attacking in the wrong direction at Hill 317—would be encircled.

This decision has been much written about, lucidly and in detail in Weigley's *Eisenhower's Lieutenants,* and in Max Hastings's *Overlord,* along with many others. Weigley sees a great opportunity lost by the Allies, Hastings sees a great victory won. The debate will continue. How it worked out for the GIs is the concern here.

For the men of the 2nd Battalion of the 30th Division, it worked out that they were on their own. This of course encouraged the Germans to keep attacking in the wrong direction. By not reinforcing Hill 317, Bradley tempted the Germans to keep on pushing west. Of course Hitler's orders to do so were explicit. How long could the men on the hill hold out?

For five days the hill was surrounded. While the Americans and Canadians were closing the envelopment behind them, the Germans continued the offensive. They threw tank columns into the attack on the hill; American artillery, responding to Lieutenant Weiss and the other observers, broke them up. On the second day, August 9, something new: bicycle troops. To Weiss, it was surrealistic, "Innocence itself, the Krauts on bikes, rifles across their backs, pedaling along the country road as if on an outing." Then the American shells roared down on them, stopping that thrust.

German light tanks tried again. Altogether there were five attacks in the first hour that morning. Weiss, who had not eaten or slept for forty-eight hours, was operating on adrenaline. He was twenty-one years old and filled with the wonderful feeling that he was making a difference in a crucial battle. The frantic activity, shooting up tanks, troops, guns, and vehicles—even bicycles—cut through his fatigue and masked it. He was excited, even exhilarated. On the third day, still without rest, after shooting up yet another enemy column, he sent this message: "As sleepy, tired and hungry as I am, I never felt so good as I feel right now."[36]

The Germans could not just bypass Hill 317 because the observers were calling up to P-47s and British Typhoons whenever they saw tanks on the road. On the shoulders of their penetration, meanwhile, elements of the 4th, 9th, and 35th Divisions hammered the German flanks. As on Hill 317, forward observers on high ground called in fire missions. Eighteen-year-old Pvt. Robert Baldridge was in the 34th Field Artillery Battalion, 9th Division. He recalled, "The visibility from the top of this hill was excellent. What a change it was from the narrow confines of the hedgerows. We saw some twenty miles distant the outskirts of the city of Avranches, and even the spires of Mont St. Michel." Through the course of the five-day battle, his team worked with the artillery to pound the enemy. "From our height we could see many of our shells descending from the sky above as they whistled down."

That was a new experience. "The sounds were all different, too." With nightly German probes and attacks, "we got to the point that we could quickly identify many different types of German vehicles. We knew which tanks were theirs, and which ones were ours, at any distance."[37]

That day the leading elements of the American forces got into Alençon. Argentan was but twenty kilometers to the northeast. But the GIs were meeting stouter German resistance because they were running into divisions on the march for Mortain, and because the Germans were awakening to their danger. Maj. Charles Cawthorn, an infantry battalion CO in Patton's army, recalled that this was not "a game of Allied hounds coursing the German hare," as the press was reporting it, but rather the hunt after "a wounded tiger into the bush; the tiger turning now and again to slash at its tormentors, each slash drawing blood."[38] The Canadians were still short of Falaise. Kluge, meanwhile, was pleading with Hitler to allow him to retreat to the east while the gap was still open.

On Hill 317, the position was precarious. No food, small-arms ammunition running low, and worst of all, the batteries were dying. Without those radios, Weiss and his comrades were doomed. Sergeant Sasser began retrieving discarded batteries. During the day, he set them out on rocks. The hot sun warmed them up and restored some life. He switched batteries several times a day, restoring one set while using another, never using one for so long that it got run down to the point of no return. Even so, by the end of the fourth day it was doubtful that he could keep them going.

The battalion was out of rations. The GIs had long since cleaned out the chicken coops and rabbit pens around the half dozen farms on the hill, along with the fruit and vegetable cellars, and were eating raw vegetables gathered from the gardens—when they got anything to eat. Medical supplies had long since run out. The artillery tried taking the explosives out of 105mm shells and replacing them with morphine and penicillin, then firing them onto the hill for the men of the 2nd Battalion to retrieve. It didn't work; everything got smashed when the shells hit. Airdrops of food, water, and ammunition were also a bust, as most of the supplies dropped by parachute came down behind the encircling enemy.

After the fourth day, Weiss reported, "We could see no end." Incoming radio messages told the 2nd Battalion to hold on, help was coming. But when?

The fourth night was the longest. Artillery and mortar fire came down from all directions. Around 0300, a German light tank started up the ridge, stopping less than fifty meters from the top. The GIs crouched low, scarcely breathing, rifles at the ready, not moving one inch. The tank fired once, twice. The muzzle blasts lit up the sky. Shrapnel and rocks flew through the air.

The German tank commander lifted his turret, pushed his head through the opening, and called out in good English, "Surrender or die!"

No one moved. He called again. One GI threw down his rifle, ran to the tank, and climbed on. Everyone else stood fast. After a few minutes, the turret clanged shut, the tank backed off, and the disgusted and angry German faded into the darkness, carrying his sole prisoner.

Lt. Ralph Kerley commanded E Company of the 2nd. After four days and nights of fighting off the Germans, he was exhausted. But he kept at his work. At mid-morning of the fifth day, studying the panorama below him through his binoculars, he spotted a German mortar crew served by a half dozen men.

"Sergeant," he called out to the leader of his own mortar team, "how many rounds do you have left?"

"One, sir."

Kerley paused, thought about what relief it would bring if he could put that mortar out of action, thought about the danger he would be in if he was out of shells.

"Do you think you can hit the son-of-a-bitch?"

"Yes, sir. I reckon I can."

"Then blow his ass off."

The redheaded sergeant gathered up his crew and brought the 60mm mortar barrel, the base plate, and the rest of the assembly forward. Kerley watched the enemy mortar crew. He saw them loafing, lying around, sunbathing, laughing. Occasionally one man would stroll back into the bushes and emerge with a shell, drop it down the tube, and shortly thereafter the shell would explode to the right or left, showering Kerley with rocks and dirt.

Kerley studied his map, turned to the sergeant, pointed, and said, "Put it right here."

The sergeant nodded, made his own survey with his binoculars, made the adjustments. A private, his M-1 rifle slung across his back, clutched the sole remaining mortar shell for dear life against his belly. Another consultation. Kerley and the sergeant talked quietly about wind, distance, elevation. More adjustments on the elevating screw. One last consultation, one final minor adjustment.

Satisfied, the sergeant nodded to Kerley, who nodded back. The sergeant turned to the rifleman with the mortar shell and held out his hands. The private, with great care, stretched his hands out to the sergeant as if passing off a newborn baby. The sergeant took the shell, kissed it, lifted it to the end of the barrel, dropped it in, ducked, and called out, "On the way."

Kerley steadied his glasses, peering intently, holding his breath. He watched the gray-green-uniformed enemy soldiers loafing around.

"Klaboom!" The shell exploded less than ten meters from the enemy mortar team. Two of the men leapt up and ran away. Another tried to get up, fell down, rose again, and staggered away. Two others dashed out from the bushes, grabbed their mortar and ran. Kerley started breathing again. "Nice work, sergeant," he called out.[39]

On August 11, Kluge finally got Hitler's permission to break off the attack at Mortain and begin the retreat through the Falaise gap. It was a momentous, if inevitable, decision (it cost Kluge his job and shortly thereafter his life, at his own hand; his replacement was Field Marshal Walter Model), because once the retreat began, there was no place to stop, turn, and defend short of the Siegfried Line at the German border. The line of the Seine could not be defended; there were too many bends in the river, too many potential crossing places to defend. Once the retreat began, the Battle of France had been won (in fact did not even have to be fought) thanks to the Battle of Normandy.

In assessing the failure of the Mortain attack, Major Heinz-Günter Guderian said in an interview, "It was due to airpower—we were very impressed by the American air force—by artillery and by the excellent fighting of the infantry, which surprised us—there is no doubt about that."[40]

At 1430 on the fifth day of the siege of Hill 317, August 12, the 35th Division broke through the German lines even as the enemy was making preparation to withdraw, and relieved the 2nd Battalion on Hill 317. Of the 700 GIs on the hill, some 300 were dead (including Sergeant Corn) or wounded. Lieutenant Weiss had called in 193 fire missions while the battalion had been surrounded. After eating and getting some sleep, he wrote his after-action report on a typewriter, hunting and pecking, striking over. It was ten pages long.

On the last morning, Weiss concluded, there was a lot of movement below him and "we commenced firing in earnest." Still the enemy attacked, but it "never attained momentum because of the devastating artillery fire. He seemed to have vacated the area by the time the dust cleared. For hours after we could see smoke in the draw to the front from burning vehicles and the east–west road was strewn with wreckage."

Summing up what he had learned from his five-day ordeal, Weiss wrote: "Although quite often beat back and silenced, at the slightest carelessness in exposing ourselves thereafter, the enemy would strike back at us. He doesn't quit. His aggressiveness demands a 24 hour observation, whether by sight or sound." That observation should have been printed up and distributed to all troops. But it wasn't.

Then Weiss wrote a letter to his father: "Not much to write about from here."[41]

The spectacular performance by 2nd Battalion, aided by the remainder of the 30th Division, had stopped the German thrust to the coast. Maj. Helmut Ritgen of Panzer Regiment 130 remembered putting twenty-two tanks into the Mortain attack. By August 12 he had three left. Not all were destroyed by American artillery and Jabos; nearly half were lost through mechanical failures. The war was turning mobile, which should have helped the Germans, Ritgen figured, "because we had experience in mobile warfare in Poland, Russia, everywhere. But now our tanks were worn. We had no supplies.

We got no replacements, no spare parts, so our spine was broken."[42]

Altogether the Germans lost more than 80 percent of the tanks and vehicles they had thrown into the Mortain attack. Now their entire army in Normandy was threatened. The rush to get out, to get over the Seine and back to Germany, was on.

By no means did all the Germans participate. Slackers, defeatists, realists, men too old or boys too young to be in such a pickle, seized their opportunity to surrender safely to the Americans. This was in complete contrast to the German experience on the Eastern Front, where no member of the Wehrmacht ever surrendered voluntarily. The men in retreat could hardly keep thoughts of the retreat from Moscow (in 1812 as well as 1942) out of their minds, but they had the option of just quitting on this one, depending on it that becoming a POW in British or American hands was their best chance of survival.

Beyond those who yearned to spend the rest of the war picking beets in Colorado rather than manning a pillbox on the Siegfried Line, many others were left behind as their units reversed course from west to east and began moving out. Armored vehicles pushed the horse-drawn wagons and the infantry off the road, as they could not keep up. For the most part, the ones left behind just settled down to watch for a good chance to surrender.

Captain Colby remembered "one dark night we pulled off the road. One of our guys lay down to sleep beside an already sleeping German soldier who had become separated from his comrades and had lain down here for the night. When the German awoke the next morning he shook the American to arouse him and then surrendered to him."[43]

Twenty-one-year-old Lt. Charles Stockell found an abandoned farmhouse to sleep in. "The next morning when I am lacing my boots on the front porch, I see a pair of German boots. As I look up, a German officer, a big smile on his face and his hands on his head, bows and says, 'kamerad?' " Inside, he found a two-man crew setting up an MG-42 at the window. They happily surrendered.[44]

But by no means were all the Germans surrendering. The toughest units and the most fanatical Nazis—panzer and Waffen SS troops—were determined to get out so as to fight another day.

Eisenhower wanted them captured. On August 14 he issued a rare Order of the Day (he sent out only ten in the course of the war), exhorting the Allied soldiers: "The Opportunity may be grasped only through the utmost in zeal, determination and speedy action. . . . If everyone does his job, we can make this week a momentous one in the history of this war—a brilliant and fruitful week for us, a fateful one for the ambitions of the Nazi tyrants." The Order of the Day was broadcast over the BBC and distributed to the troops in mimeographed form.[45]

The following day, Eisenhower held a press conference. There was the greatest excitement among the reporters, who had earlier been too gloomy about the stalemate in Normandy and were now too optimistic about what lay ahead, as evidenced by the first question Eisenhower received: "How many weeks to the end of the war?"

The reporter, like everyone else, was thinking of October–November 1918, when the Germans finally had been driven from their trenches and were in full retreat eastward. At that time, they had signed the Armistice. This time, however, it was going to be unconditional surrender, a much different proposition, just as Hitler was a much different proposition from the weak-willed kaiser.

Eisenhower was much disturbed by the excessive optimism. Around this time he wrote his wife, Mamie, "Every victory is sweet—but the end of the war will come only with complete destruction of the Hun forces. . . . There is still a lot of suffering to go through. God, I hate the Germans!"

So when asked how many weeks to the end, he exploded. He said such thoughts were "crazy." The Germans were not going to collapse as in 1918, he said, not so long as Hitler was alive. He predicted that the end would come only when Hitler hanged himself, but warned that before he did he would "fight to the bitter end," and most of his troops would fight with him.[46]

If not most, enough. The Canadians did not get to Falaise until August 17 (a prize Montgomery had held out as a possibility on D-Day) and then failed to close the gap between Falaise and Argentan. The desperate Patton called ever-calm Bradley on the telephone, pleading for a change in the boundary line so that he could go north from Argentan to Falaise. "Let me go on to Falaise and we'll drive the British back into the sea for another Dunkirk," he said.[47]

Bradley said no. He feared the onrushing Germans would trample over the relatively thin line Patton could establish. Besides, why bother? The Germans were caught in a giant kettle, with the Americans on the rim. With the forward observers, accompanying the infantry or in Piper Cubs, plus the radiomen in the Shermans, the Americans could put a devastating fire, from artillery and Jabos, on the enemy.

So instead of letting Patton close the gap, Bradley had him turn east again, toward Paris, in search of the big envelopment Patton had advocated earlier. Having started the short right hook, Bradley dropped it in mid-swing to try a roundhouse—too late. Either starting with the roundhouse, or completing the right hook, might have led to a Stalingrad-like surrender.

As it was, the German army still had an escape route open, albeit one under constant fire.

For sheer ghastliness in World War II, nothing exceeded the experience of the Germans caught in the Falaise gap. Feelings of helplessness waved over them. They were in a state of total fear day and night. They seldom slept. They dodged from bomb crater to bomb crater. "It was complete chaos," Pvt. Herbert Meier remembered. "That's when I thought, This is the end of the world."[48]

The word "chaos" was used by every survivor of the retreat interviewed for this book. German army, corps, and division headquarters got out first and were on the far side of the Seine, headed toward the Siegfried Line. In the pocket, most junior officers felt like the enlisted men, it was every man for himself.

The farmhouses were abandoned; rations consisted of whatever one could find in the cellars. "It was terrible," Lt. Günter Materne recalled, "especially for those lying there in pain. It was terrible to see men screaming, 'Mother!' or 'Take me with you, don't leave me here! I have a wife and child at home. I'm bleeding to death!'"[49]

Lt. Walter Padberg explained: "Honestly said, you did not stop to consider whether you could help this person when you were running for your life. One thought only of oneself."[50]

Private Meier recalled "one of the officers from the occupation, who had had a nice life in France, tried to get through in a troop truck filled with goodies and his French girlfriend. With wounded men lying right there. So we stopped him, threw him and his girlfriend out, along with all of their things, and laid the wounded in the truck.

"It was terrible," Meier went on. "I began to think everyone was crazy. I came across an airfield, the Luftwaffe had long since gone, all of the ground troops there were drunk."[51]

"All shared a single idea," according to Corp. Friedrich Bertenrath of the 2nd Panzer Division: "Out! Out! Out!"[52]

All this time the 1,000-pound bombs, the 500-pound bombs, the rockets, the 105s and the 155s, the 75s on the Shermans, the mortars, and the .50-caliber machine-gun fire came down on the Germans. Along the roads and in the fields, dead cows, horses, and soldiers swelled in the hot August sun, their mouths agape, filled with flies. Maggots crawled through their wounds. Tanks drove over men in the way—dead or alive. Human and animal intestines made the roads slippery. Maj. William Falvey of the 90th Division recalled seeing "six horses hitched to a large artillery gun. Four horses were dead and two were still alive. The driver was dead but still had the reins in his hands."[53] Those few men, German or American, who had not thrown away their gas masks had them on, to the envy of all the others. The stench was such that even pilots in the Piper Cubs threw up.

Lt. George Wilson of the 4th Division saw "dead German soldiers and dead and wounded horses and wrecked wagons scattered all along the road." He was astonished to discover that the Wehrmacht was a horse-drawn army, but impressed by the equipment. He had been raised on a farm and "I was amazed at such superb draft horses and accouterments. The harness work was by far the finest I had ever seen. The leather was highly polished, and all the brass rivets and hardware shone brightly. The horses had been groomed, with tails bobbed, as though for a parade." His men mercifully shot the wounded animals.[54]

By August 18, a week after the lead American elements had reached Argentan, the 1st Polish Armored Division moved south, almost to the point of linking up with the U.S. 90th Division, finally released for a northward drive to close the gap. Still Germans escaped. One of them was Major Guderian, who recalled driving past the Poles, only 100 meters away, in the rain, in the night, out of the pocket. He and his driver would go for two or three minutes, then stop for ten to listen. They made it out.

Lieutenant Padberg did, too. "When we made it out of the pocket," he recalled, "we were of the opinion that we had left hell behind us." He quickly discovered that the boundaries of hell were not so constricted. Once beyond the gap, Padberg ran into an SS colonel.

"Line up!" he bellowed. "Everyone is now under my command! We are going to launch a counterattack." There were twenty or so men in the area, none known to Padberg. He had a pistol only. The others shuffled into something like a line, Padberg said, "but unfortunately, I had to go behind a bush to relieve myself and missed joining the group behind the colonel."[55]

Lt. Walter Kaspers got out, thanks to some unexpected help. "I moved only at night," he remembered. "By myself. I became dog tired. I came to a small farmhouse. I knocked and asked the girl if I could sleep in the barn. I pointed to the east and said that I was heading that way. She told me not to worry, allowed me to stay and even brought me a jug of milk and a few pieces of bread. I thanked her and pushed on the next day."

After telling the little story, Lieutenant Kaspers smiled and added, "Women are always better in these situations in war. They have a feeling for people in need."[56]

Three German soldiers who got out had similar experiences. French farm wives fed them. In each case, the women explained that their sons were POWs in Germany and that they hoped some German mother was feeding their boys.

Even in the bloody chaos of Falaise, a humane spirit could come over these young men so far from home. Lt. Hans-Heinrich Dibbern, of Panzer Grenadier Regiment 902, set up a roadblock outside Argentan. "From the direction of the American line came an ambulance driving toward us," he remembered. "The driver was obviously lost. When he noticed that he was behind German lines, he slammed on the brakes." Dibbern went to the ambulance. "The driver's face was completely white. He had wounded men he was responsible for. But we told him, 'Back out of here and get going—we don't attack the Red Cross.' He quickly disappeared."

An hour or so later, "here comes another Red Cross truck. It pulls up right in front of us. The driver got out, opened the back, and took out a crate. He set it down on the street and drove away. We feared a bomb, but nothing happened and we were curious. We opened the box and it was filled with Chesterfield cigarettes."[57]

On August 20, at Chambois, the linkup of the Americans and Polish troops finally occurred. Capt. Laughlin Waters was the first to shake hands with a Pole, Major W. Zgorzelski of the 10th Polish Dragoons. Zgorzelski had a good sense of history. Waters recorded: "He pronounced that our meeting was the first time American and Polish soldiers had ever met on the field of battle."

Over the next couple of days, Waters wrote, "the Germans attacked with all of the fury they could bring to bear, fueled by their desperation to escape." Others were trying to surrender, many of them successfully. Too many, in fact. Neither the Poles nor the Americans had the facilities to deal with them. Waters established a POW pen in Chambois, but it was badly overcrowded. Still, one morning a Polish captain brought in some 200 additional POWs, to turn over to the Americans.

Polish captain: "Here are your prisoners."

Waters: "I don't want them."

Polish captain: "But I must leave them with you. Those are my orders."

Waters: "I still don't want them. Get them out of here." (Waters's orders were to accept them, but he had been told to expect 1,500; in fact there were only a couple of hundred.)

Polish captain: "But I must still leave them with you."

Waters: "Well, you were supposed to have 1,500 prisoners. Where are they?"

Polish captain: "They are dead. We shot them. These are all that are left."

Waters: "Then why don't you shoot these, too?" A pause, then Waters corrected himself: "No, you can't do that."

Polish captain: "Oh, yes we can. They shot my countrymen." He took Waters by the arm and escorted him away from the others. Then he said, "Captain, we can't shoot them. We are out of ammunition."[58]

On August 23 the SHAEF G-2 summary declared, "The August battles have done it and the enemy in the West has had it. Two and a half months of bitter fighting have brought the end of the war in Europe within sight, almost within reach."[59] Two days later American forces liberated Paris. General de Gaulle was already there, along with elements of the French 2nd Armored Division, but he and they were worried about Communists in the Resistance and Germans remaining in the city. At de Gaulle's direct request, Eisenhower agreed to have the 4th Division move through the city on its route east, and the 28th Division parade down the Champs-Elysées, also on its way to battle. This show of force quieted any hotheads in the city. Paris was overrun by reporters, led by Ernest Hemingway, and over the next few days had one of the great parties of the war.

The Battle of Normandy was over. It had lasted seventy-five days. It had cost the Allies 209,672 casualties, 39,976 dead. Two-thirds of the losses were American. It cost the Germans around 450,000 men, 240,000 of them killed or wounded. Of the approximately 1,500 tanks committed to Normandy by the Wehrmacht, a total of sixty-seven got out, and only twenty-four of these got across the Seine. The Germans left behind 3,500 artillery pieces and 20,000 vehicles.[60]

But between 20,000 and 40,000 Wehrmacht and SS soldiers got out. They had but a single thought: get home. Home meant Germany, prepared defensive positions in the Siegfried Line, fresh supplies, reinforcements, a chance to sort out the badly mixed troops into fighting units. They had taken a terrible pounding, but they were not as sure as SHAEF G-2 that they had "had it."

4

To the Siegfried Line

August 26–September 30, 1944

THE LAST WEEK of August and the first week of September 1944 were among the most dramatic of the war. The Allied Expeditionary Force swept through France, covering in hours ground that had taken months—years, really—and cost hundreds of thousands of casualties to take in World War I. As the sons of the soldiers of the Great War drove north and east, they crossed rivers and liberated towns whose names resonated with the Tommies and Doughboys— the Marne, the Somme, Ypres, Meuse-Argonne, Verdun, the Aisne, Cambrai, St.-Mihiel, and the others. As the Yanks, Brits, and Canadians passed the cemeteries, in some cases men were passing the graves of their uncles. In a few cases, their fathers.

Romania surrendered to the Soviets, then declared war on Germany. Finland signed a truce with the Soviet Union. Bulgaria tried to surrender. The Germans pulled out of Greece. The Red Army's summer offensive liberated Estonia, Latvia, and Lithuania, eastern Poland, and reached Yugoslavia's eastern border. It destroyed twelve German divisions and inflicted 700,000 casualties.

American and French troops had landed in the south of France on August 15 and were driving up the Rhône Valley against scant opposition (they called it the "Champagne Campaign"). American reinforcements continued to come from England to France, enough for the creation of yet another army, the U.S. Ninth, commanded

N

ENGLAND

London

Southampton

English Channel

Cherbourg

(Captured Sept. 12)
Le Havre

Dieppe

Rouen

Caen

Can.
FIRST

VIII

Brest

St-Malo

21
(MONTGOMERY)

Br.
SECOND

XIX

V

NINTH

Par

Lorient

SHAEF
(EISENHOWER)

FIRST

VI

St-Nazaire

12
(BRADLEY)

FIRST

THIR

Loire R.

FRANCE

Bay
of
Biscay

Gironde R.

FRONT LINE AS OF:

- - - - - August 26
- - - - September 3
———— September 14

21   Allied army group

FIRST   Allied army

VII   Allied corps

—ooo—   Allied army group boundary

—oo—   Allied army boundary

B   German army group

SEVENTH   German army

—▪▪▪—   German army group boundary

   Siegfried Line

   German fortified area

* Supreme Headquarters Allied Expeditionary Force
** Oberbefehlshaber (Supreme Commander) West

Kms.
0   75

0   75
Miles

© A. Karl / J. Kemp, 1997

THE PURSUIT TO
THE SIEGFRIED LINE

August 26–September 14, 1944

North Sea

Berlin ⊚

Hanover

Amsterdam

(Captured Sept. 4)

Arnhem

NETHERLANDS

FIFTEENTH

FIRST

B
(MODEL)

Para.

Düsseldorf

Antwerp

Brussels

Cologne

Aachen

Namur

XIX

BELGIUM

VII

SEVENTH

OB WEST ••
(RUNDSTEDT)

V

V

LUT.

G
(BLASKOWITZ)

Mainz

GERMANY

Sedan

Reims

Verdun

XX

Metz

FIRST

Nancy

Strasbourg

XII

FIFTH

Ps.

Épinal

XV

XV

NINETEENTH

Danube R.

Rhine R.

Munich

Dijon

VI

AUSTRIA

Fr. II

Fr. I

Bern ⊚

SWITZERLAND

Fr.
B

chy

Milan

ITALY

SOUTH-
WEST
(KESSELRING)

VI

SEVENTH

Marseilles

Toulon

Fr. II

Florence

Mediterranean
Sea

15
(ALEXANDER)

(Captured Aug. 28)

by Lt. Gen. William Simpson. British, Polish, and American paratroopers—five divisions strong—in England were organized into the First Allied Airborne Army and constituted a highly mobile reserve, capable of striking wherever and whenever needed. So far, however, they weren't needed; more than a dozen operations that had been laid on during the pursuit across France had to be canceled at the last minute because the AEF on the ground in France had already overrun the drop zone.

The end of the war did indeed seem at hand. Thoughts of November 1918 were in everyone's mind. Airborne planners went to work on Operation Rankin. Its mission was to drop Allied paratroopers into Berlin, in the event of a sudden German collapse, before the Red Army got there. In late August, General Marshall sent a message to all his commanders on the subject of redeployment of U.S. Army forces from Europe to the Pacific. His message began, "While cessation of hostilities in the war against Germany may occur at any time, it is assumed that in fact it will extend over a period commencing . . . between September 1 and November 1, 1944."[1] General Bradley issued instructions to store the winter clothing that was coming in at Le Havre and over the beaches, in order to use the space saved on the trucks bringing supplies to the front for ammunition and gasoline. He figured the war would be over before winter clothing was needed.

The German army in retreat was a sad spectacle. Occasionally a battery of 88s, or a couple of Panthers, or what was left of a company of riflemen and machine gunners would try to throw up a roadblock, but when they did a tremendous barrage from American artillery, shell, and machine-gun fire from Shermans, rockets, and bombs from the Jabos, and small-arms fire would quickly overwhelm them. Then it was every man for himself, with the wounded left behind.

"Making it home is the motor of the old soldier," Pvt. Paul-Alfred Stoob, a driver of a Panther, observed. Their tank shot out from under them, Stoob and the crew commandeered a truck and took off for Belgium. "We had no supplies. We had used up our field rations long ago," Stoob recalled. "We had to scavenge for food . . . here a dog without a master, there a few eggs in a chicken coop . . . the houses were mostly empty. We found a field bakery.

One room was packed to the ceiling with bread. So we filled our truck with bread and moved on."

That bread was only one tiny part of the vast amount of supplies the Germans were leaving behind. Stoob and his crew came across a staff headquarters the next day. There they found cognac, wine, sausage, cheese, fruit, and vegetables. They stuffed every corner of their truck with the food. Then their luck ran out. Shermans rolled up to them and opened fire. Badly wounded in the head and leg, Stoob tried to escape through a church cemetery. "Suddenly, I heard someone yelling in French behind me, '*Mon Dieu, Mon Dieu.*' It was a French Father. He lay me down in the grass and went and got an American medic. In ten minutes, along came two medics. They took me to an aid station, then to a field hospital. And that was the end of the war for me."

Stoob was sent to the States. He got back to Germany in 1947. There he discovered that he had been wounded in the same small French village as had his father in 1914—also in the head and leg.[2]

Corp. Günter Mollenhoff, a grenadier, was on foot. In Cambrai, site of the 1917 battle where the British had employed tanks for the first time, he and his companions found an abandoned supply depot. It was filled with cases of French cognac and tins of meat and lard. The soldiers found a horse-drawn wagon and filled it with goods, stole two horses and some tack, hitched them up, and headed east with their loot.[3]

The Americans were close behind. On August 28, Captain Cooper of the 3rd Armored Division reached Soissons, some eighty kilometers north of Paris and site of a 1915 French-German battle. There he saw a working train about to pull out of the station, loaded with armored cars, a German tank, and a company of infantry. American Shermans, half-tracks, machine gunners, and mortarmen opened up. "Although the 37mm antitank shells bounded harmlessly off the tank, like ping pong balls," Cooper recalled, the small-arms fire kept the Germans from getting into the tank. "This encounter turned out to be a real debacle for the Germans. Many soldiers were killed and wounded. The few that escaped into the woods were soon rounded up by the French underground."

Cooper examined the wreckage in the train and was surprised to find that invaluable space had been taken up with women's lingerie, lipstick, and perfume, instead of desperately needed ammunition and food. "The Germans apparently had done a good job of looting all the boutiques in Paris when they pulled out."[4]

The German rout was so complete that not only did the retreating troops not carry supplies out with them, they didn't even take the time to destroy the supply dumps. Elements of Patton's Third Army captured tons of grain, flour, sugar, and rice, along with hundreds of carloads of coal, all of which the GIs distributed to the French civilian population. At another dump, Patton's men captured 2.6 million pounds of frozen beef and 500,000 pounds of canned beef, which was distributed to the troops.[5]

The GIs were getting all mixed up in their pell-mell pursuit. Sergeant Gianelloni remembered trucks going up and down the road, jeeps, tanks, half-tracks, and other combat vehicles headed toward the front. He came up on a battalion of African-American soldiers. "What outfit are you?" he asked.

"Artillery," was the reply. "What outfit are you guys?"

"The 79th Infantry."

According to Gianelloni, "This black guy, he almost turned white. He said, 'The boss done fucked up, he has got us here ahead of the infantry.' They had so many artillery battalions lined up there they was gun to gun."[6]

In the 4th Infantry Division, Lt. George Wilson felt he was engaging in "a wild, mad, exciting race to see which army could gain the most ground in a single day."[7] To the men of the 743rd Tank Battalion, 2nd Armored Division, it was "holiday warfare." There was a little shooting at occasional crossroads, but no casualties. Mainly this was because they had warning of trouble ahead—if the villages were bedecked with flowers and the people were lining the streets, holding out food and bottles of wine, the Germans had pulled out; if there was no reception committee, the Germans were still there.

At dusk on September 2, Shermans from the 743rd got to the crest of a hill overlooking Tournai, Belgium. They sat there looking, instead of moving down to be the first to cross the border, because they were out of gasoline. More Shermans came up; they had just enough fuel to get into town.[8] Then they too were immobilized. The great supply crisis in ETO had hit the 743rd.

■

The crisis was inevitable. It had been foreseen. It could not have been avoided. Too many vehicles were driving too far away from the ports and beaches. The Red Ball Express, an improvised truck transport system that got started in late August, made every effort to get the fuel, food, and ammunition to the front lines. Drivers, mainly blacks in the Service of Supply, were on the road twenty hours a day, driving without lights at night. The deuce-and-a-half trucks were bumper to bumper on the one-way roads. Between August 29 and September 15, 6,000 trucks carried 135,000 tons of supplies on two highways running from St.-Lô to a supply dump near Chartres. At the dump the supplies were picked up by other drivers and taken to the front. But the front line continued to move east and north, and the system just couldn't keep up. From Le Havre and the Normandy beaches it was getting close to 500 kilometers to the front. It took a lot of gasoline just to get the trucks back and forth.

To ease the burden, SHAEF was putting into place an extension onto PLUTO ("pipe line under the ocean," running from England to Omaha Beach), to move gasoline forward by pipe to Chartres. But it didn't get into operation until September 13. Even then it didn't help much. At Chartres, it was put into jerry cans, which were loaded onto trucks that carried the fuel forward to the front-line vehicles. But among other crises in supply, ETO was short on the five-gallon jerry cans, because too many GIs just threw them away after filling their tanks instead of putting them back on the truck.[*]

In the case of the 743rd, the battalion stayed in Tournai for four days, waiting for fuel. On September 7, the battalion filled its vehicles and took off. In one day it made 105 kilometers, to an area south of Brussels. The next day, forty-four kilometers. On September 9, a day-long pause to wait for fuel. On September 10, another leap forward, to Fort Eben Emael close to the Dutch border. According to the battalion history, "it was a swashbuckling, almost skylarking campaign. There was no fighting and the job was to keep moving, looking for a fight."

The GIs got a wild welcome in the Belgian villages. "They cheered, and waved, and risked their lives to crowd up to the tanks

---

[*]All across France today, those jerry cans are still there, serving innumerable purposes.

in motion and in all the demonstrative ways of a happy people they showed their enthusiastic thanks." On September 12 the leading platoon of Charlie Company in the 743rd crossed the border into Holland, the first Americans to reach that country. The German border was but a few kilometers away.[9]

Now there was opposition. German artillery boomed. Panzerfaust shells disabled a couple of Shermans. The other Shermans could still fire, but not move. Their fuel tanks were empty. And the Germans had gotten into the Siegfried Line. They had fuel problems, too, but as they were on the defensive they could dig their tanks in and use them as fortified batteries. Their supply lines had grown shorter—Aachen was just to the south, Düsseldorf and Cologne were just to the east.

They had reached home. Men who saw no point to fighting to retain Hitler's conquests in France were ready to fight to defend the homeland. The German officer corps began taking the terrified survivors of the rout in France and organizing them into squads, platoons, companies, battalions, divisions—and suddenly what had been a chaotic mob became an army again. Slave labor, meanwhile, worked on improving the neglected Siegfried Line. The Germans later called the transformation in their army and in the defensive works the Miracle of the West.

From the Rhône to the Channel, the armies of the AEF were coming to a halt. On September 2, Third Army requested 750,000 gallons of gasoline and got 25,390. The next day, it was 590,000 with 49,930 received. For the following two days, Patton got about half the quantity he demanded; after September 7, he got a trickle only. A handful of advance patrols had gotten across the Moselle River north and south of Nancy, but Third Army was caught up in a terrible battle for the ancient fortresses of Metz, which were practically impervious to artillery shells or bombs. Patton's men were still far short of the Rhine River and the Siegfried Line protecting it.

On September 12, the 4th Division, First Army, to the north, managed to get through the Siegfried Line. Lt. George Wilson led a reconnaissance platoon into the defenses. He saw a German soldier emerge from a mound of earth not 100 meters away. "I got a slight chill as I realized I might well be the first American to set eyes on a pillbox in the famous Siegfried Line." He was east of St.-Vith in the Ardennes.

Looking around, he saw mounds of earth everywhere, each of them a concealed machine-gun emplacement, with cement walls one meter thick and roofs from three to four meters thick. They had large iron doors at the rear, which Wilson's investigation revealed were mostly rusted and off their hinges. Almost all were unoccupied. The 4th Division could drive right on through the Siegfried Line, at least at this spot.[10]

By the 14th, elements of the division had done so and were fanning out on top of the Schnee Eifel, a heavily wooded, rough country that was an eastward extension of the Ardennes. But the division was badly stretched, with a twenty-eight-kilometer front and a ten-kilometer gap on its right and another of forty kilometers on its left. It was almost out of gasoline. It had to pull back.[11]

Another problem: crossing Northwest Europe's many rivers was causing delays. The Germans had not mounted any defense at all on the east bank of the Seine, but that left the Meuse, Moselle, Roer, Saar, Waal, and Rhine Rivers and their tributaries to go. And the closer the Germans got to home, the more they drew on their last bit of strength and their experience. The Wehrmacht knew more about how to defend a river crossing than anyone else, something the officers learned in the long retreat from Russia.

Along the Moselle the Germans mounted an effective defense. It fell to the 80th Infantry Division to defeat it. By September 11, other divisions in Patton's army had crossed to the north and south of the 80th's position, but were unable to expand the bridgeheads. The 80th prepared to force its own crossing, utilizing to the full the combined-arms team that had developed since D-Day. The site was near the village of Dieulouard.

The leading companies of the division began the crossing shortly after midnight. Nine battalions of artillery began shelling the 3rd Panzer Grenadier Division. Tracer bullets from more than fifty .50-caliber machine guns arched through the night sky, giving protection to the men of the 3rd Battalion crossing in rubber-and-plywood assault boats. Resistance was spotty and ineffective. That afternoon, September 12, engineers began building a pontoon bridge. They completed the work just before midnight.

At 0100 September 13, three battalions of German infantry, supported by fifteen tanks and ten assault guns, launched a counterattack. By daybreak, the Germans had driven the GIs back to within

100 meters of the crossing site. Engineers threw down their tools, took up M-1s and machine guns, and joined the fight to defend their bridge. The battle reached its height at 0600. The Americans stood fast. The Germans were too bloodied and tired to press on. A stalemate ensued.

On the west bank, an improbable scene in World War II—a council of war held by four generals on a high bank in sight of the enemy. Also present were Col. Bruce Clarke, commanding Combat Command A of the 4th Armored Division, and Lt. Col. Creighton Abrams, commanding the 37th Tank Battalion. Abrams was a 1936 graduate of West Point; he was two days short of his thirtieth birthday.

The generals were worried about sending Abrams's tanks over the pontoon bridge. The bridge might be destroyed by German artillery, as the Germans now had good observation on it. The tanks could be cut off. Besides, the bridgehead was so constricted the Shermans wouldn't be able to maneuver. And the tanks were short on fuel. Finally, the generals asked Clarke and Abrams for their opinion.

"Well," Clarke replied, "I can't fight the Germans on this side of the river."

Pointing to the high ground on the other side of the river, Abrams told his superiors, "That is the shortest way home."

Go for it, the generals replied. At 0800 Abrams led the way for the Shermans. They rumbled over the bridge, deployed into fighting formation, and began blasting the Germans with their cannon and machine guns. As the enemy fell back, infantry from the 80th Division crossed and joined the attack. By nightfall, they had regained the position held the previous day.

But this was a different German army from the one that had pulled out of France so ignominiously. By the afternoon of September 13 six German battalions were on the march toward Dieulouard. Over the next three nights they counterattacked. Michael Doubler writes, "Between 14–16 September some of the most bitter fighting in the ETO took place as the Germans tried to push the 80th Division back into the Moselle."[12] The Americans fought back with infantry, tanks, artillery, and fighter-bombers. Throughout the ordeal they held their ground, but they could not expand the bridgehead.

Capt. Joseph Dawson, G Company, 16th Infantry, 1st Division, had been the first company commander to get his men up the bluff at Omaha on D-Day. By mid-September he had been in battle for 100 days. He had learned to fight in the hedgerows, how to work with tanks and planes in the attack on St.-Lô, how to pursue a defeated enemy in the dash across France. He was thirty-one years old, son of a Waco, Texas, Baptist preacher. He had lost twenty-five pounds off his already thin six-foot two-inch frame.

On September 14, Dawson led his company into the border town of Eilendorf, southeast of Aachen. Although it was inside the Siegfried Line, the town was deserted, the fortifications unoccupied. The town was on a ridge, 300 meters high, 130 meters long, which gave it excellent observation to the east and north. Dawson's company was on the far side of a railroad embankment that divided the town, with access only through a tunnel under the railroad. Dawson had his men dig in and mount outposts. The expected German counterattack came after midnight and was repulsed.

In the morning, Dawson looked east. He could see Germans moving up in the woods in one direction, in an orchard in another, and digging in. In the afternoon, a shelling from artillery and mortars hit G Company, followed by a two-company attack. "The intensity of the attack carried the enemy into my positions," Dawson later told reporter W. C. Heinz of the *New York Sun*. "I lost men. They weren't wounded. They weren't taken prisoners. They were killed. But we piled up the Krauts."[13]

But it was the Germans who were attacking, the Americans who were dug in. Dawson was short on ammunition, out of food. His supporting tanks were out of gasoline. The artillery behind him was limited to a few shells a day. If he was going to go anywhere, it would be to the rear. The U.S. Army's days of all-out pursuit were over.

That was a conclusion hard to accept, and hardly accepted. On September 15, Bradley's aide Maj. Chester Hanson wrote in his diary, "Brad and Patton agree neither will be too surprised if we are on the Rhine in a week. Prepared the general's map for the next phase of operations which extends from Rhine to the city of Berlin. General anxious to slam on through to Berlin. Marked bullseye on Berlin."[14]

■

The weakened Allied thrust and the stiffening German resistance forced the Allied high command to make some difficult choices. Up to September 10 or so, it had been a case of go-go-go until you run out of gas—and then keep going forward on foot. Every commander, not just Patton, urged his men forward. But on a front that stretched from the Swiss border to the English Channel, dependent on ports now hundreds of kilometers to the rear, it just wasn't possible to continue to advance on a broad front.

So Patton said to Eisenhower, Stop Monty where he is, give me all the fuel coming into the Continent, and I'll be in Berlin before Thanksgiving. Monty said to Eisenhower, Stop Patton where he is, give me all the fuel coming into the Continent, and I'll be in Berlin before the end of October.

There was a third choice. The British had taken the town and docks of Antwerp, Europe's largest port. With Antwerp at work, the supply problem would end. But the Schelde Estuary leading to the port, nearly 100 kilometers long, was in German hands, so no ships could get to Antwerp. If Eisenhower stopped both Patton and Montgomery and put the major effort into opening Antwerp, he would have a stable supply situation for a winter campaign. But although he was the least optimistic of all the Allied generals, Eisenhower nevertheless felt there was a chance to end the war before winter set in. If that happened, he wouldn't need Antwerp. For that to happen, some risks had to be run.

They seemed justified. The German army had not yet ended a retreat that had begun six weeks earlier and turned into a rout. Everything in the situation cried out for one last major effort to finish off the enemy. Antwerp wouldn't do that; a narrow thrust to get over the Rhine would. Should it be by Montgomery, north of the Ardennes, or Patton, to the south?

Eisenhower had moved SHAEF headquarters to the Continent and taken control of the land battle. The decision was his to make. He told Montgomery to go ahead with Operation Market-Garden.

Market-Garden was Montgomery's idea, enthusiastically backed by Eisenhower, who told me two decades after the event that "I not only approved of Market-Garden, I insisted on it."[15] In addition to the irresistible impulse to keep attacking, Eisenhower had the German secret weapons in mind. On September 8 the first of the long-dreaded V-2 rockets hit London. They had been launched from Holland. The only way to stop them was to overrun the sites.

Montgomery's plan was to utilize the Airborne Army—the Allies' greatest unused asset—in a complex, daring, and dangerous but potentially decisive operation to get across the Lower Rhine River in Holland. The plan called for the Guards Armored Division to lead the way for the British Second Army across the Rhine on a line Eindhoven–Son–Veghel–Grave–Nijmegen–Arnhem. The British tanks would move north along a single road, following a carpet laid down by the American and British paratroopers, who would seize and hold the many bridges between the start line, in Belgium, and Arnhem.

The British 1st Airborne Division, reinforced by a brigade of Polish paratroopers, would jump into Holland at the far end of the proposed line of advance, at Arnhem. The U.S. 82nd Airborne would take and hold Nijmegen. The U.S. 101st's task was to jump north of Eindhoven, with the objective of capturing that town and the various bridges in the area.

It was a brilliant but complicated plan. Success would depend on execution of almost split-second timing, achieving surprise, hard fighting, and luck, especially with the weather. If everything worked, the payoff would be British armored forces on the north German plain, on the far side of the Rhine, with an open road to Berlin. It could well lead to a quick and complete German collapse. But if the operation failed, the cost would be the squandering of the asset of the Airborne Army, failure to open the port of Antwerp, a consequent supply crisis throughout ETO, and a dragging out of the war through the winter of 1944–45.

In addition to putting off the opening of Antwerp, Eisenhower had to stop Patton around Nancy and Metz to get sufficient fuel for the British Second Army to mount Market-Garden. In short, the operation was a roll of the dice, with the Allies putting all their chips into the bet.

On August 17 the 101st Airborne had been alerted for a jump into Chartres, packed up, went to the airfield—and sat around, waiting. Pvt. Ken Webster, talking to the subdued veterans, noticed that "the boys aren't as enthusiastic or anxious to get it over with as they were before Normandy. Nobody wants to fight anymore." News came over the radio: Third Army tanks had just taken the Drop Zone (DZ) at Chartres. The jump was canceled. The paratroopers cheered, laughed, praised General Patton and his tankers, and went back to the barracks.[16]

A month later, on September 17, it was back to the airfield. This time there was no possibility of cancellation. Sergeant Sampson was in Lt. James Coyle's platoon in the 505th PIR, 82nd Airborne. The platoon had made a critical contribution to stopping a German counterattack at Ste.-Mère-Eglise on D-Day, then led an American attack on June 7 that disrupted the Germans' plans, then fought in and around Carentan for a month before returning to England.

At the airfield, Sergeant Sampson talked with his men and found that attitudes varied widely. Corp. Tom Burke told him, "Sergeant, I have a lot of respect for you and I'll do anything you tell me to, but when it's done, I'm going out on my own, for I'm in it now to win medals." Sampson nodded. "There was no need to answer him," Sampson said later, "for his mind was made up."

Another trooper pulled Sampson aside. "I have made three combat jumps for my country," he said [North Africa, Sicily, Normandy], "and I feel I have done my part, this time I'm going to do my best to stay out of the fight; I feel I owe the rest of my life to my family back home."

"I don't see it that way at all," Sampson replied. "The job isn't finished and I for one look forward to getting back in there till the end, one way or the other." He later commented, "I know many of the troopers felt as I did by their actions and speech."

But not all. Sgt. Benjamin Popilski was leader of the 2nd Squad. He was gloomy, not in fear of what was coming but in despair over what had happened. He explained to Sampson: "I met a British girl and fell in love, but some lying S.O.B. told her I was a Jew and now she won't go out with me." He shook his head and said, quietly, "I hope this jump straightens it all out."

Another man shot his toe off. He said he had been cleaning his rifle and it went off, accidentally. Sampson told him to get ready anyway, he was going to jump.

"I was told I wouldn't have to!"

"To hell you won't! You're jumping." But the doctor ordered the private to the hospital, and Sampson could do nothing about it.[17]

■

September 17 was a beautiful end-of-summer day, with a bright blue sky and no wind. No resident of the British Isles who was below the line of flight of the hundreds of C-47s carrying three divisions into combat ever forgot the sight. Nor did the paratroopers. Pvt. Dutch Schultz of the 82nd was jump master for his stick; he stood in the open door as his plane formed up and headed east. "In spite of my anxiety about the jump and subsequent danger," he recalled, "it was exhilarating to see thousands of people on the ground waving to us as we flew over the British villages and towns." It was even more reassuring to see the fighter planes join the formation.[18]

When the air armada got over Holland, Schultz could see a tranquil countryside. It was Sunday. Not many people were on the roads. Cows grazed in the fields. The Luftwaffe wasn't to be seen. There was some anti-aircraft fire, which intensified five minutes from the DZ, but there was no breaking of formation or evasive action by the pilots as there had been over Normandy. The jump was a dream. A sunny midday. Little or no opposition on the ground. Plowed fields that were "soft as a mattress."

Gen. James Gavin led the way for the 82nd. His landing wasn't so soft; he hit a pavement and damaged his back. Some days later a doctor checked him out, looked Gavin in the eye, and said, "There is nothing wrong with your back." Five years later at Walter Reed Hospital Gavin was told that he had two broken disks. It was too late to do anything; Gavin's comment was, "Now I have one heel higher than the other to account for the curvation in my back."[19]

To indulge in a generalization, one based on four decades of interviewing former GIs but supported by no statistical data, Jim Gavin was the most beloved division commander in ETO. Some veterans can't remember their division commanders' names because there were so many of them, or because they never saw them; others don't want to remember. But veterans of the 82nd get tongue-tied when I ask them how they feel about General Gavin, then burst into a torrent of words—bold, courageous, fair, smart as hell, a man's man, trusted, a leader, beloved.

Gavin (USMA 1929) was thirty-seven years old, the youngest general in the U.S. Army since George Custer's day. His athletic grace and build combined with his boyish looks to earn him the affectionate nickname of "Slim Jim."

Dutch Schultz wasn't necessarily the best soldier in the 82nd, but he was one of the most insightful. After landing in Holland, Schultz saw Gavin come down, struggle to his feet in obvious pain, sling his M-1, and move out for his command post. "From my perspective," Schultz wrote, "it was crucial to my development as a combat soldier seeing my Commanding General carrying his rifle right up on the front line. This concept of leadership was displayed by our regiment, battalion, and company grade officers so often that we normally expected this hands-on leadership from all our officers. It not only inspired us but saved many lives."[20]

There were but a handful of enemy troops in the DZ area. Lieutenant Coyle recalled, "I saw a single German soldier on the spot where I thought I was going to land. I drew my .45 pistol and tried to get a shot at him but my parachute was oscillating. I was aiming at the sky as often as I was aiming at the ground. When I landed I struggled to my knees and aimed my pistol. The German was no more than 15 feet away, running. Just as I was about to shoot him he threw away his rifle, then his helmet and I saw he was a kid of about seventeen years old, and completely panicked. He just ran past me without looking at me. I didn't have the heart to shoot him."[21]

Sgt. D. Zane Schlemmer of the 82nd had developed a "soft spot in my heart" for the cows of Normandy because whenever he saw them grazing in a hedgerow-enclosed field, he knew there were no land mines in it. In Holland, he had another bovine experience. His landing was good, right where he wanted to be. He gathered up his men and after recovering the 81mm mortars, ammunition, and equipment, set out for his objective in Nijmegen. He spotted two cows. He had plenty of rope. So "we commandeered the cows and hung our mortars and equipment on them. They were very docile and plodded right along with us.

"As we neared Nijmegen, the Dutch people welcomed us. But while pleased and happy to be liberated, they were quite shocked to see paratroopers leading two cows. The first questions were, 'Where are your tanks?' We were not their idea of American military invincibility, mobility and power. We could only tell them, 'The tanks are coming.' We hoped it was true."[22]

The Germans had been caught by surprise, but were waking

up. They got units to the various bridges, to defend them or blow them if necessary. The GIs, moving into Nijmegen and Eindhoven and their other objectives, started taking casualties.

Sergeant Popilski of Coyle's platoon, who had just lost his British girlfriend, was shot in the head. A trooper reported it to Sergeant Sampson. "I just happened to be looking his way," the trooper told Sampson. "He turned white before he was hit, as if he knew it was coming." Sampson recalled Popilski's last words back in England, "I hope this jump straightens it all out," and thought, He got his wish.[23]

As the troopers moved toward their assigned objectives, gliders bearing soldiers and equipment began coming into the DZs.

One crash-landed on the edge of a wooded area and was under German small-arms fire coming from the tree line. Capt. Anthony Stefanich (Captain Stef to the men) called out to Private Schultz and others to follow him, and headed toward the German positions.

Stefanich was one of those officers brought up by General Gavin. Schultz remembered him as a man "who led through example rather than virtue of rank. He was what I wanted to be when I finally grew up."

Stefanich got hit in the upper torso by rifle fire, which set afire a smoke grenade he was carrying. Lt. Gerald Johnson jumped on him to put the fire out, then carried the wounded captain back to the assembly point, where an aid station had been set up. Bending over his captain, Schultz's mind went back to his mother. She had taught him that if he said three Hail Marys daily he would never go to hell. Then he thought of his teachers, all nuns, "who taught me about the power of the rosary, and that if I really wanted something from Jesus Christ I should use our Blessed Mother as my emissary. That made sense, because more than once I had used my mother as an intermediary in trying to get my Dad to change his mind."

So he prayed to the Blessed Mother for Captain Stef's life.

But it was too late. Just before he died, Stefanich whispered to Lieutenant Johnson, "We have come a long way—tell the boys to do a good job." The medic, a Polish boy from Chicago, stood up beside the body. He was crying and calling out, "He's gone, he's gone. I couldn't help him." It was, Schultz said, "a devastating loss. It was the only time in combat that I broke down and wept."[24]

■

By the end of September 17, the Americans had achieved most of their objectives. The British 1st Airborne Division, meanwhile, had landed on the far side of the Rhine, north of Arnhem, and secured the area for reinforcements to come in the next day. One battalion, led by Col. John Frost, went into Arnhem via a little-used river road and took the east end of the bridge. The British Second Army failed to reach its objectives but it had made progress. Not a spectacular but still a good start.

On September 18, however, almost everything went wrong. German 88s, quickly assembled in woods on either side of the single, raised road the British tanks and vehicles were using, began firing with devastating effectiveness. It was easy shooting, looking up at the tanks against the skyline. Soon disabled vehicles blocked the road, causing gigantic traffic jams. The weather in England turned bad—rain, fog, mist—grounding all airplanes. There would be no reinforcements, no supply drops coming from England.

Over the Continent the weather was good enough for the Jabos to fly. Colonel Cole, commanding the 3rd Battalion of the 502nd PIR, got on the radio. A pilot asked him to put some orange identification panels in front of his position. Cole decided to do it himself. As he was placing a panel on the ground, a German sniper shot and killed him. Two weeks later, the Army awarded him the Medal of Honor for his bayonet charge near Carentan on June 11. His widow accepted his posthumous award on the parade ground at Fort Sam Houston, where Cole had played as a child. In Mrs. Cole's arms was the eighteen-month-old son Cole had never seen.[25]

On September 19, the British Second Army struggled forward, passing through the 101st in Eindhoven and linking up with the 82nd outside Nijmegen. In Arnhem, Colonel Frost held his isolated position at the bridge, despite fierce German attacks, but his situation was desperate. He had counted on the first British tanks reaching the other end of the bridge on the second day. Now he was going into a third day, most of the men in his battalion wounded (as was he), under attack from German tanks with nothing but small arms to fight back with, out of food and medicine.

To get to Frost, the Guards Armored Division had to get across the Waal River. Before that could happen, Gavin had to take possession of the railroad and highway bridges that ran parallel and close to each other. The 82nd had taken much of the city, but the approaches to the bridges were still well defended by German tanks, artillery, and infantry.

On September 19 Lt. Waverly Wray, the man who had broken up the German counterattack on the morning of June 7 at Ste.-Mère-Eglise, and killed ten Germans with a single shot to the head of each, led an assault on the bridge. "The last I saw of him," one trooper reported, "he was headed for the Germans with a grenade in one hand and a tommy gun in the other." As Wray raised his head over the railroad track embankment, a German sniper firing from a signal tower killed him with a single shot in the middle of his head.[26]

On the afternoon of September 19, Gavin met with Lt. Gen. Brian Horrocks, commanding the Guards. Horrocks said he could provide tank support for an attack on the bridges, and that he could have trucks bring forward assault boats for a crossing of the river downstream from the bridges. Gavin decided to hit the western ends with Lt. Col. Ben Vandervoort's 2nd Battalion, 505th PIR, and to give the task of crossing the river in the boats to Maj. Julian Cook's 3rd Battalion, 504th PIR.

Cook wanted to cross under cover of darkness, but he was helpless until the trucks carrying the boats came up. They were promised for late that afternoon, but were delayed because the Germans were putting heavy fire on the single road running back to the start point in Belgium. So effective were these attacks that the GIs were calling the road "Hell's Highway." Bulldozers and tanks were assigned to roam its length, pushing wrecks out of the way. Traffic jams ran for miles and took hours to unsnag. Hitler authorized one of the Luftwaffe's final mass raids on the clogged road—200 bombers hit Eindhoven, while another 200 fighter-bombers went after the troops and vehicles jamming Hell's Highway—Jabos in reverse.[27]

At 1530 of September 19, Gavin flung Vandervoort's battalion at the bridges. The boats had not come up, but Gavin hoped the combination of British tanks (all Shermans) and parachute infantry could break through Nijmegen and take the bridges.

Vandervoort's men rode into the attack on the backs of more than forty British armored vehicles. They got to the center of the city without much difficulty. There Vandervoort split the regiment, sending half for the railroad bridge and the other half for the highway span. Both attacks met fierce opposition from 88s, self-propelled guns, mortars, and well-placed machine guns.

Lieutenant Coyle and Sergeant Sampson's platoon led the assault. "On approaching the last houses before the open area in front of the railway bridge," Coyle recalled, "the lead tank began firing its cannon. The roar was deafening. I was moving up alongside the third tank in the column. When I cleared the last house and could see the bridge, I got quite a shock. I didn't expect it to be so large. I learnt after the war that it was the largest single-span bridge in Europe."

As the two Shermans in front of Coyle moved across the traffic circle, two hidden 57mm antitank guns fired. The tanks shook, stopped, began to flare up. The tank beside Coyle went into reverse and backed into a street leading to the traffic circle. Coyle had his platoon retreat into houses on the outer ring, then take up positions on the second floor.

From there, the GIs could see Germans on foot and bicycle coming across the bridge. The men wanted to set up their machine guns in the windows and fire at the enemy, but Coyle ordered them to stay back, because he didn't want the Germans to know he was there, at least not until those antitank guns had been found and knocked out. He was passing this order on to Sergeant Sampson when Sampson saw a German running through the street not twenty yards away. Instinctively, Sampson raised his tommy gun and stepped toward the window. Coyle pushed the weapon aside.

"Not yet," Coyle whispered.

Looking out, he saw the Germans manhandling an antitank gun from behind some bushes in the park and bringing it forward to a spot ten meters in front, pointing it up the street. The Germans were unaware of his presence.

Just at that moment Vandervoort came into the room. Coyle explained the situation, showed him the German gun, and said he wanted to coordinate an attack with the British tanks. Vandervoort agreed. He told Coyle to open up in five minutes; then he dashed downstairs to find the British tanks and put them into the attack. But before Vandervoort could get the tankers organized, someone opened fire from a building adjacent to Coyle. The Germans started firing back. Coyle motioned Pvt. John Keller forward. He fired a rifle grenade at the antitank gun in the street and knocked it out.

"Kla-boom!" as Coyle remembered it. There was a terrific explosion in the room. Another 57mm had fired; the shell went through one wall and exploded against the other. Then another, and another. Coyle pulled his platoon out of the house and occupied the cellar of another. By now dark had come on. Coyle got orders to button down and wait for morning.[28]

Dawn, September 20. One mile downstream from the bridges, Major Cook's battalion waited. The men were ready to go but the assault boats had not arrived. Through the morning, they waited. Vandervoort's battalion, meanwhile, was unable to drive the Germans out of the park, despite great effort (Sergeant Sampson was badly wounded that morning by shell fire).

Vandervoort described the fighting: "The troopers fought over roof tops, in the attics, up alleys, out of bedroom windows, through a maze of backyards and buildings. . . . Where feasible, tanks served as bulldozers, smashing through garden walls, etc. A tank cannon thrust through a kitchen door really stimulates exodus. In the labyrinth of houses and brick-walled gardens, the fighting deteriorated into confusing face-to-face, kill or be killed show downs."[29]

Meanwhile, Cook's battalion waited for the boats. Cook went to the top of a tower at a nearby power station to survey the opposite bank of the Waal. A young captain with Cook, Henry Keep, wrote in a letter home, "We had a glimpse of a scene which is indelibly imprinted on my mind. What greeted our eyes was a broad flat plain void of all cover or concealment . . . some 300 meters, where there was a built-up highway [where] we would get our first opportunity to get some protection and be able to reorganize. . . . We could see all along the Kraut side of the river strong defensive positions, a formidable line both in length as well as in depth—pillboxes, machine gun emplacements. . . ."

Cook had support; ten British tanks and an artillery battery were lined up along the river to give covering fire when he crossed. But not until 1500 did the trucks arrive. What they brought wasn't much. There were only twenty-six assault boats, instead of the thirty-three that had been promised. And they were the frailest of tiny craft, six meters long, of canvas with a reinforced plywood bottom. And there were only three paddles per boat. The Waal was almost 400 meters wide, with a swift current of about ten kilometers an hour.

The paratroopers dragged the boats to the shore, pushed off

into deep water, climbed in (thirteen men to a boat, plus three British engineers with the paddles) and tried to use their rifle butts as paddles. But as they got out into the current, some of the boats started whirling in circles. The tanks and artillery fired away. A smoke screen was laid down—but the wind blew it away. As the boats got straightened out and headed for the far bank, the Germans opened fire.

Cook and Keep were in the first boat. That was not where the battalion commander ought to have been, but Cook had been brought up by Gavin.

"It was a horrible picture, this river crossing," Captain Keep wrote his mother, "set to the deafening roar of omnipresent firing. It was fiendish and dreadful. . . . Defenseless, frail canvas boats jammed to overflowing with humanity, all striving desperately to cross the Waal as quickly as possible, and get to a place where at least they could fight."[30]

Some boats took direct hits, leaving nothing but flotsam. Small-arms fire ripped through the boats. The flotilla seemed to scatter. Yet it came on. Only eleven of the twenty-six boats made it to the far shore, but when they did the paratroopers who had survived the ordeal had their blood up. They were not going to be denied.

"Nobody paused," a British tank officer wrote. "Men got out and began running toward the embankment. My God what a courageous sight it was!"

Cook led the way. Captain Keep commented, "Many times I have seen troops who are driven to a fever pitch—troops who, for a brief interval of combat, are lifted out of themselves—fanatics rendered crazy by rage and the lust for killing—men who forget temporarily the meaning of fear. However, I have never witnessed this human metamorphosis so acutely displayed as on this day. The men were beside themselves. They continued to cross that field in spite of all the Kraut could do, cursing savagely, their guns spitting fire."[31]

In less than a half hour, Cook and his men had reached the top of the highway embankment and driven the Germans out. The engineers, meanwhile, had paddled back to the west bank and returned with a second wave. Altogether it took six crossings to get Cook's battalion over.

As those crossings were being made, Cook led the first wave in an assault on the bridges. His men came on fast. Meanwhile Vandervoort's people on the west side had finally overrun the park and were starting onto the bridges. The Germans scrambled frantically for the plungers to set off the explosives in place on the bridges, but Cook's men did what they had been trained to do—wherever they saw wires on the ground they cut them. The German engineers hit the plungers, and nothing happened.

Cook's men set up defensive positions at the bridges, facing east. As the British tanks with Vandervoort started across the highway bridge, their crews saw the Stars and Stripes go up on the other end. Cook had lost forty men killed, a hundred wounded, but he had the bridges. There were 267 German dead on the railroad bridge alone, plus many hundreds wounded and captured, plus no one could guess how many had fallen into the river. It was one of the great feats of arms of World War II. Lt. Gen. Miles Dempsey, commanding the British Second Army, came up to shake Gavin's hand. "I am proud to meet the commander of the greatest division in the world today," he said.[32]

It was 1910 hours. Darkness was descending. Arnhem was but eleven kilometers away. Frost's battalion was still holding the eastern end of the bridge, but barely. General Horrocks decided to set up defensive positions for the night. When that was done, the Guards began to brew up their tea.

Cook's men were enraged. They yelled and swore at the Brits, told them those were their countrymen in Arnhem and they needed help, now. Horrocks commented, "This operation of Cook's was the best and most gallant attack I have ever seen carried out in my life. No wonder the leading paratroopers were furious that we did not push straight on for Arnhem. They felt they had risked their lives for nothing, but it was impossible, owing to the confusion which existed in Nijmegen, with houses burning and the British and U.S. forces all mixed up."[33]

In the morning (September 21), the tanks moved out, only to be stopped halfway to Arnhem by two enemy battalions, including one of SS troopers, with tanks and 88s. There were Jabos overhead, but the radio sets in the RAF ground liaison car would not work (neither would the radios with the British 6th Airborne in Arnhem). That afternoon, the 9th SS Panzer Division in Arnhem overwhelmed the last survivors of Frost's battalion. Some days later the survivors of 1st Airborne crossed the Rhine to safety. The division had gone into Arnhem 10,005 men strong. It came out with 2,163 live soldiers.

Lt. Col. John Frost put the blame on the Guards Armored Division. Standing on the bridge on the fortieth anniversary of the event, he looked west, as he had so often, so fruitlessly, four decades earlier, and got to talking about the Guards brewing up their tea, and then on to the relatively light casualties the Guards suffered as compared to the 1st Airborne, and on to the magnificent performance of the 82nd.

His face blackened. As I watched, mesmerized, he shook his fist and roared a question into the air, a question for the Guards: "Do you call that fighting?"

Over the next six months, the front line in Holland hardly moved. For the 82nd and 101st, that meant two months of misery. They couldn't move by day, because the Germans held the high ground to the east and had enough 88 shells to expend at a single soldier whenever one was visible. They were on British rations, much inferior in their opinion. They were supported by British artillery and tanks, which often caused confusion. They made no offensive move but had to send out nightly patrols.

The American airborne troops had been trained as a light infantry assault outfit, with the emphasis on quick movement, daring maneuvers, and small-arms fire. They had been utilized in that way in Normandy and during the first week in Holland. But now they were involved in a static warfare that was more reminiscent of World War I than World War II. And as in the Great War, the casualties were heaviest among the junior officers.

One of them was Lt. Willis Utecht. He had led a gliderborne platoon into Holland. On October 2 he was killed. His body was put into a shallow grave on the edge of a wood. For whatever reason, Graves Registration never found him. In 1994, a half-century later, a Dutch farmer plowed the outermost edge of his field and turned up some of Utecht's bones, a boot, and pieces of clothing. The farmer notified the U.S. Army; a team recovered the body and Utecht's dog tags. Until then, Utecht was one of 45,000 Missing in Action from World War II.[34]

Stefanich gone, Utecht gone, Cole gone, Wray gone, so many others gone. Reflecting on the losses, Dutch Schultz commented, "By the end in Holland, most of the officers trained by General

Gavin had become battlefield casualties." And, he added slowly, "Their replacements had no experience with Gavin's style of leadership."[35] The pain of the loss of these good men was compounded by the knowledge that nothing had been gained.

At the beginning of September the Allied armies were streaming across France, driving a dispirited, disorganized army before it. Thoughts of being home for Christmas were in the air. At the end of the month, Patton's Third Army was stuck. So was Hodges's First Army. The supply crisis was worse than ever. Antwerp wasn't open. And Market-Garden had failed. What would be the consequences?

5

The Siegfried Line

October 1944

As the Americans reached the German border from Luxembourg north, they were entering country that had been fought over since Caesar's time. It was interlaced with ancient, walled cities, and villages that made natural strong points, plus the extensive Siegfried and Maginot Line fortifications.

The Germans had men for those fortifications. They had reconstituted the divisions that had fled from France, and created new ones, to the point that they had more men on the Western Front than did the Allies. Some of their armored and SS divisions were outstanding, but the ordinary infantry divisions were composed of teenagers, limited-service veterans missing an arm or an eye, and old men of forty and even fifty years of age. Still, most of them could fire a machine gun or a panzerfaust from the protection of a bunker made of steel-reinforced concrete.

As against this, Eisenhower commanded three army groups— the Twenty-first, under Montgomery, the Twelfth, under Bradley, and the Sixth, under Lt. Gen. Jacob Devers (on the southern flank). The Allies had eight field armies in the field, with fifty-five divisions. Twenty-eight of these divisions were American (twenty infantry, six armored, two airborne), eighteen were British and Canadian, eight were French, and one was Polish.

In firepower, the Allies had a tremendous advantage. It was two and a half to one in artillery (but the supply crisis had hit hard on shells, so that most American batteries were limited to a few rounds only per day), twenty to one in tanks. In the air, the Allies had 5,059 American bombers, 3,728 American fighters, and 5,104 RAF planes. The Germans on the Western Front had 573 planes. The entire Luftwaffe consisted of 4,507 planes, spread across the Continent.

A considerable part of the American firepower, however, could not be brought to bear on the Germans because of the acute gasoline shortage. "There is no point in reaching the German border," Eisenhower had told Marshall in early September, "unless we are in a position to exploit that position."[1] But that was exactly what had happened. And there would not be sufficient fuel to support a drive into Germany, or even to get through the Siegfried Line and other defenses, until Antwerp was open and functioning.

Lorraine is south of Luxembourg. Since the beginning of European civilization, it has been a battlefield. It was an invasion route for the Germanic tribes coming from Central Europe into France. The terrain—a plateau with elevations ranging from 200 to 450 meters—is not so favorable for offensives going west to east, but still usable. Over the centuries there have been many fortifications in the area—which is bounded on the east by the Saar River, on the north by Luxembourg, to the south by the Vosges Mountains, and on the west by the Moselle River.

Metz is on the Moselle, forty-five kilometers north of Nancy, the historic ruling city of Lorraine. Nancy has never been heavily fortified because it is covered to the east by a bastion of scarps and buttes. By contrast, Metz is perhaps the most heavily fortified city in Europe, in the most heavily fortified part of Europe. The first set of modern fortifications was built in the seventeenth century by the famous French military engineer Vauban. There were fifteen of them, close around the city. The Prussians came through Metz in 1870 nevertheless. When Bismarck created modern Germany after the Franco-Prussian War, he incorporated Lorraine into the new nation, and the German army constructed a second, outer belt of twenty-eight forts, mainly north and west of the city. In 1918 Lorraine returned to France; soon the French army was building the Maginot Line some twenty kilometers east and north of Metz, while the Germans built the Siegfried Line another twenty kilometers to the east, along the line of the Saar River, the prewar border.

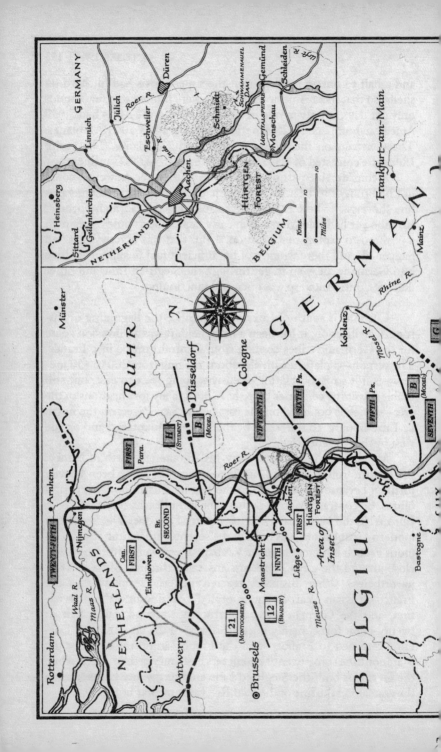

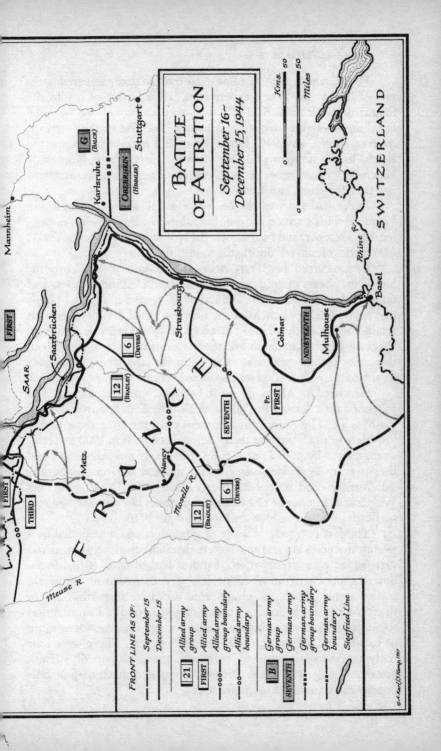

Hitler, whose faith in reinforced cement never wavered, a result of his World War I experiences, poured a lot of it into the Siegfried in this area. By 1940, the strongest part of the Siegfried faced the strongest part of the Maginot Line. When the Germans overran France in 1940, Hitler brought Lorraine back into the Reich. In the summer of 1944, when the retreat from Normandy began, he poured more cement, put more guns into the Siegfried and the Metz forts, and waited.[2]

Hitler had the weather on his side. Fall is the wet season in Lorraine, with an average monthly rainfall of three inches in September, October, and November. (In November 1944 he got lucky: 6.95 inches of rain fell during the month.)[3]

Patton cursed. His Third Army's mission was to take Lorraine, but in the sheets of cold rain, with the mud clinging to boots and tank treads and the Moselle at flood stage, he couldn't do it. "I hope that in the final settlement of the war, you insist that the Germans retain Lorraine," he wrote Secretary of War Henry L. Stimson, "because I can imagine no greater burden than to be the owner of this nasty country where it rains every day and where the whole wealth of the people consists in assorted manure piles."[4]

He lusted for Metz. To get it, he had to take Fort Driant. The fort stood on a dominating hill, with clear fields of fire up and down the Moselle. The Americans could not cross the river above or below Metz until Driant was theirs. It had been built in 1902 and later strengthened by both French and Germans. In size, thickness, and firepower it was greater even than the monster at Douaumont outside Verdun, and indeed had been renamed by the French after World War I in honor of Lieutenant Colonel Driant, who had met his death in gallant fashion at Douaumont in 1916.

The fort covered 355 acres of ground. It was surrounded by a twenty-meters-wide and ten-meters-deep moat, which in turn was surrounded by a twenty-meter band of barbed wire. It had living quarters for a garrison of 2,000. Its big guns rose from the earth, sniffed around, fired, and disappeared back into the earth. Most of the fortification was underground, along with food and ammunition supplies, aid stations and radio rooms, enough for a month or more of battle. The only way in was over a causeway. There were four outlying casement batteries, each with three 100mm or 105mm guns, and a detached fifth battery. Concealed machine-gun pillboxes were scattered through the area.

On September 27 Third Army had made its first attempt to take Driant. The Americans had assumed that the fort would be lightly garrisoned by inferior troops. Although they had only a vague idea of the fort's works and surrounding terrain, they figured that a pre–World War I fortress system couldn't possibly stand up to the pounding of modern artillery, much less air-dropped bombs of 500 to 1,000 pounds, not to mention napalm. From dawn to 1415 hours, the Americans hit the fort with all the high explosives in their arsenal. The men of the 11th Infantry Regiment, who led the assault, were confident that nothing could have survived inside the fort.

At 1415 the infantry began to move in on the fort. To their astonishment, when they reached the barbed wire surrounding the moat, Germans rose up from pillboxes to their front, sides, and rear and opened fire. Shermans came forward to blast the pillboxes, but their 75mm shells hardly chipped or scarred the thick concrete. The infantry went to the ground, and ignominiously withdrew under cover of darkness.[5]

With that withdrawal, Third Army's advance came to a halt. It now faced a new problem in its experience, but the oldest tactical/engineering problem in warfare, how to overcome a fortified position. Like First Army to the north, Third Army began thinking and got started on the challenge of Driant by adopting some new techniques and weapons. It helped considerably that the Americans finally got their hands on the blueprints of the fort, which showed a warren's den of tunnels.

No amount of high explosive was going to knock it down. Infantry would have to get inside the fort, kill the German defenders who resisted, and take possession. To do that, the 11th Regiment would have to get over the causeway. To do that, there were a few new weapons. One was the tankdozer, another was a "snake," a longer version of the bangalore torpedo. The dozer would clear away rubble, the snake would blast a path through the barbed wire. A third new weapon was the flamethrower. Company A got four of them.

On October 3, the second assault on Driant began. The snakes got shoved under the wire, but they broke and were useless. The tankdozers had mechanical failures. Only one of the four flamethrowers worked. Company B, nevertheless, was able to get into the fort. Capt. Harry Anderson led the way, tossing grenades into German bunkers as he ran across the causeway, inspiring his men to follow him into Driant, where he established a position alongside one of the casements.

An intense firefight ensued. Germans popped out of their holes like prairie dogs, fired, and dropped back. They called in their own artillery from other forts in the area. Some American engineers got forward with TNT, to blast a hole in the casement so that the GIs could enter the fortress system. But the heavy walls were as impervious to TNT as to shells and bombs.

On top of the casement, Pvt. Robert Holmlund found a ventilator shaft. Despite enemy fire, he managed to open the shaft's cover and dropped several bangalore torpedoes down the opening. Germans who survived evacuated the area, and Captain Anderson led the first Americans inside the fort. The room they had taken turned out to be a barracks. They quickly took an adjacent one.

The Germans counterattacked. The ensuing firefight was a new dimension of combat. It shattered nerves, ears, and lives. One small firecracker set off in the bowels of one of the old forts is guaranteed to startle a tour group, and cause ringing ears; no one who has not been there can imagine the assault on the ears by machine-gun fire and hand grenade explosions reverberating in the tunnels enclosed by those thick, dripping masonry walls.

The air was virtually unbreathable; men in the barracks room had to take turns at gulping some fresh air from firing slits. The stench was a mixture of gunpowder, gas fumes, and excrement. Wounded could not be treated properly. Fresh water was nonexistent.

B Company was stuck there. It had neither the equipment nor the manpower to fight its way through the maze of tunnels. It couldn't go back; being on top of the fort was more dangerous than being in it. At dark American reinforcements, accompanied by a half dozen Shermans, crossed the causeway and assaulted another casement, but they were badly shot up and forced to withdraw when the Germans came up from the tunnels and filtered into their rear. These small, local counterattacks could be devastating. Four of the Shermans were knocked out by panzerfaust shells.

Capt. Jack Gerrie, CO of G Company, 11th Infantry, led the reinforcements. He had no illusions about the enemy. He had been in on the September 27 attack. "Watch out for these birds," he had told another company commander. "They are plenty tough. I've never run across guys like these before, they are new, something you read about."[6]

On October 4, Gerrie tried to knock down the steel doors at the rear of the fort. Direct cannon fire couldn't do it and protruding grillwork made it impossible to put TNT charges against the doors themselves. The Germans again called down fire on Driant, which forced G Company to scatter to abandoned pillboxes, ditches, shell holes, and open bunkers, anywhere they could find shelter. That evening Gerrie tried to reorganize his company, but his efforts were hampered by the Germans, who came out of the underground tunnels, here, there, everywhere, fired and retreated, causing confusion and further disorganization in G Company. Gerrie could count about half the men he had led to the fort the previous evening.

At dawn on October 5, German artillery commenced firing at Driant. After hours of this, Gerrie wrote a report for his battalion commander: "The situation is critical[;] a couple more barrages and another counterattack and we are sunk. We have no men, our equipment is shot and we just can't go on. . . . We cannot advance. We may be able to hold till dark but if anything happens this afternoon I can make no predictions. The enemy artillery is butchering these troops. . . . We cannot get out to get our wounded and there is a hell of a lot of dead and missing. . . . There is only one answer the way things stand. First either to withdraw and saturate it with heavy bombers or reinforce with a hell of a strong force, but eventually they'll get it by artillery too. They have all of these places zeroed in by artillery. . . . This is just a suggestion but if we want this dammed fort let's get the stuff required to take it and then go. Right now you haven't got it."[7]

Written from a shell hole, under fire, by a man who hadn't slept in two days, nor had a hot meal, it is a remarkable report, accurate, precise, and rightly critical of the fools who had got him into this predicament. It was so compelling it moved right up to the corps commander, who showed it to Patton and said the battalion commander wanted to withdraw.

Never, Patton replied. He ordered that Driant be seized "if it took every man in the XX Corps, but he could not allow an attack by this Army to fail."[8]

Over the next three days, Third Army ignored Gerrie's advice. It threw one more regiment into the attack, with similar ghastly results. The men on top of the fort were the ones under siege. The lowliest private among them could see perfectly clearly what Patton could not, that this fort had to be bypassed and neutralized, because it was never going to be taken.

Patton finally relented. Still, not until October 13 were the GIs withdrawn. About half as many returned as went up. This was Third Army's first defeat in battle.

The only good thing about a defeat is that it teaches lessons. The Driant debacle caused a badly needed deflation of Patton's—and Third Army's—hubris. That led to a recognition of the need to plan more thoroughly, to get proper equipment, to take units out of the line to integrate their replacements, and to conduct courses and exercises on the use of explosives in an assault on a fortress. The next time, Third Army was going to get it right.

North of Luxembourg, at Eilendorf, just outside Aachen, Captain Dawson's G Company was holding its position on the ridge astride the Siegfried Line. The Germans needed to restore the integrity of their line, so they kept counterattacking. By October 4, G Company had repulsed three German counterattacks, and endured 500 shells per day from 105s. Then the Germans came on in division strength, but again Dawson's company beat them back, with help from the artillery and air. "We had constant shelling for eight hours," Dawson remembered. "We had twelve direct hits on what was our command post." Then the German infantry came on. "When they stopped coming we could count 350 that we ourselves had killed—not those killed by our artillery or planes, but just by the one lousy little old company all by itself."[9]

An officer in headquarters company in Dawson's battalion, Lt. Fred Hall, wrote his mother on October 6, "This action is as rough as I have seen. Still the hardships are borne with little complaint." Back at 12th Army Group hq, Bradley might be circling Berlin on the map, but outside Aachen there was more realism. Hall told his mother, "In the lower echelons of command, faced with the realities of the situation, the feeling is that the war will not be over before the spring of 1945 at the earliest."[10]

The fighter-bombers were not always, or even regularly, available, because of the weather. Planes could not fly, tanks could not maneuver, soldiers marched only with the greatest difficulty. Patton was stuck. To his right (south) the Sixth Army Group made only limited gains and could not reduce the Colmar Pocket outside Strasbourg.

Antwerp was what Eisenhower wanted, but Montgomery failed to open it. According to reports coming to Eisenhower, the Canadians trying to overrun the Schelde Estuary were short on ammunition, because Montgomery persisted in trying to widen the Market-Garden salient in Holland and therefore had given priority in supplies to the British Second Army. Montgomery denied this, charged that Market-Garden had failed because the American First Army didn't support it, and demanded that he be given sole command of the ground forces in Europe.

Eisenhower replied: "The Antwerp operation does not involve the question of command in any slightest degree." He said he would never turn Twelfth Army Group over to Montgomery. He ordered Montgomery to put his full effort into opening the Schelde. And he concluded with an ultimate threat: if Montgomery did not agree and act, "then indeed we have an issue that must be settled. If you, as the senior Commander in this Theater of one of the great Allies, feel that my conceptions and directives are such as to endanger the success of operations, it is our duty to refer the matter to higher authority for any action they may choose to take, however drastic."

Montgomery immediately wrote back to Eisenhower to promise an all-out effort to open Antwerp, and to further promise "You will hear no more on the subject of command from me. Your very devoted and loyal subordinate, Monty."

But not until October 16 did Montgomery give up on operations in Holland and give priority to the Canadians. Not until November 8 were they able to drive the Germans out of the estuary. Then the mines had to be cleared and the facilities repaired. Not until November 28 did the first Allied convoy reach Antwerp's docks.[11] By then the weather precluded major operations.

Under the post–Market-Garden circumstances, an obvious strategy would have been to abandon any offensive moves, create defensive positions facing the German border, go into winter camp, and wait for the supply situation to improve and the roads to dry and the weather to clear. That is what Napoleon would have done in his time, or Grant in his.

But there would be no winter quarters in this war. Eisenhower gave no thought to the possibility. With the V-2s coming down on

London, he could not. With thousands dying daily in the German concentration camps, he could not. With Hitler asking the German people to hold on just a bit longer, until the new weapons, including jet airplanes, could be mass-produced, he could not. With the Red Army pushing into Central Europe, with the unknown factor of how the race for an atomic bomb was progressing, he could not.

Eisenhower urged his subordinates to offensive action. All responded to the best of their ability. It was a war of attrition. Like Grant in 1864–65, Eisenhower could afford to continue to attack because his overall resources were superior to those of the Germans. In his memoirs, he wrote that attrition "was profitable to us only where the daily calculations showed that enemy losses were double our own." But calculations were seldom as favorable as two to one— they were more like one to one. Eisenhower kept attacking. At no other time in the war did he so resemble Haig or Joffre in World War I, or Grant in the Wilderness.

Like Grant, Eisenhower justified what many critics considered a sterile, cold-blooded strategy on the grounds that in the long run "this policy would result in shortening the war and therefore in the saving of thousands of Allied lives." And he was quite cold-blooded about the need to kill Germans. "People of the strength and warlike tendencies of the Germans do not give in," he told a critic. "They must be beaten to the ground."[12]

The campaign that resulted was the least glamorous, yet one of the toughest, of the war. There wasn't much strategy involved: the idea was just to attack to the east. The terrain in the center of the American line—the Eifel Mountains and the rugged Ardennes and Hurtgen Forests—dictated that the main efforts would take place to the north and south of these obstacles. To the north, First and Ninth armies would head toward the Rhine River along the axis Maastricht–Aachen–Cologne. The major obstacles were the Siegfried Line, the city of Aachen, and the northern part of the Hurtgen. To the south, Third Army would continue to attack through Lorraine and advance toward the Saar River.

To carry out those missions, the American Army needed to learn new forms of warfare, 1944-style. These would be set-piece attacks, like D-Day but in different terrain—cities, villages, forts, and forests. As in the Norman hedgerows, the Army would have to develop new tactics to overcome the enemy.

Problems there were aplenty. For the first time since early August, when they had fled the hedgerow country, the Germans had prepared positions to defend. One of the first tasks they accomplished as they manned the Siegfried Line was to put S-mines, Bouncing Betties, that sprang when triggered by a trip wire or foot pressure a meter or so into the air before exploding, in front of their positions. Thousands of them. The canister contained 360 steel balls or small pieces of scrap steel. They were capable of tearing off a leg above the knee, or inflicting the wound that above all others terrified the soldiers.

Lt. George Wilson had joined the 4th Division as a replacement at the time of St.-Lô. By early October he had been in combat for nine weeks, but he had not yet seen an S-mine. On October 10, when he led a reconnaissance platoon into the Siegfried Line straight east of Malmédy, Belgium, suddenly they were everywhere. "By now I had gone through aerial bombing, artillery and mortar shelling, open combat, direct rifle and machine gun firing, night patrolling and ambush. Against all of this we had some kind of chance; against mines we had none. The only defense was to not move at all."

Engineers came forward, to clear the mines and use white tape to mark paths through the fields. They took every precaution, but one of the engineers lost his leg at the knee to an S-mine, so they set to probing every inch of ground with trench knives, gently working the knives in at an angle, hoping to hit only the sides of the mines. They began uncovering—and sometimes exploding—devilish little handmade mines, in pottery crocks, set just below the ground. The only metal was the detonator, too small to be picked up by mine detectors. They blew off hands.

A squad to Wilson's right got caught in a minefield. The lieutenant leading it had a leg blown off. Four men who came to help him set off mines, and each lost a leg. Wilson started over to help, but the lieutenant yelled at him to stay back. Then the lieutenant began talking, calmly, to the wounded men around him. One by one, he directed them back over the path they had taken into the minefield. One by one, on hands and knee, dragging a stump, they got out. Then the lieutenant dragged himself out.

Wilson had seen a lot, but this was "horribly gruesome. Five young men lying there each missing a leg." Wilson stayed in the war to the end. He saw every weapon the Wehrmacht had, in action. After the war, he flatly declared that the S-mine was "the most fright-ening weapon of the war, the one that made us sick with fear."[13]

Behind the minefields were the dragon's teeth. They rested on a concrete mat between ten and thirty meters wide, sunk a meter or two into the ground (to prevent any attempt to tunnel underneath them and place explosive charges). On top of the mat were the teeth themselves, truncated pyramids of reinforced concrete about a me-ter in height in the front row, to two meters high in the back. They were staggered and spaced in such a manner that a tank could not drive through. Interspersed among the teeth were minefields, barbed wire, and pillboxes that were virtually impenetrable by ar-tillery and set in such a way as to give the Germans crossing fire across the entire front. The only way to take those pillboxes was for infantry to get behind them and attack the rear entry. But behind the first row of pillboxes and dragon's teeth, there was a second, and often a third, sometimes a fourth.

"The Siegfried Line was undoubtedly the most formidable man-made defense ever contrived," according to Captain Cooper. "Its intricate series of dragon's teeth, pillboxes, interconnected communication trenches, gun pits and foxholes in depth supported by an excellent road net and backed up by a major autobahn system that ran back to Cologne, Düsseldorf and other manufacturing sites less than 50 kilometers to the east, provided the Germans with not only an excellent defense system but also a base from which to launch a major offensive."[14]

Cooper was describing the Siegfried Line as it faced Belgium. Farther south, on the Franco-German border, it was more formida-ble, with major fortifications holding heavy artillery. The pillboxes were more numerous and better constructed. They were half under-ground, with cannon and machine guns and ammunition storage rooms and living quarters for the defenders, typically about fifteen soldiers. Throughout the length of the Siegfried Line, villages along the border were incorporated into the system. The houses, churches, and public buildings in these villages were built of stone and brick. The second floors of the buildings and the belfries on the churches provided excellent observation.

German officers had learned in Russia not to put their MLR (main line of resistance) along the edge of a village—that simply ex-posed the men to direct enemy fire. Instead, they ran the MLR through the middle of the town, where the streets were jumbled and tanks had difficulty maneuvering, where mortar crews had a fix on each crossroad, and riflemen and machine gunners on the second floors had crisscrossing fields of fire. The Germans had a saying: "The MLR is the defender's shield, the reserves are his sword." They kept their best troops in reserve in the center of town, prepared to counterattack where needed.[15]

The U.S. Army had no preparation, no training for attacking the Siegfried Line or driving Germans out of villages. It was going to have to learn by doing, such basic things as the first rule of street fighting—stay out of the streets—and the second rule: a systematic, patient approach works, while audacity and risk-taking don't. Those weren't going to be easy lessons to learn for men who had just raced through France.

In the 1st Division, the officers had come to realize that sweat expended during preparations saved blood in combat and won battles. They had spent much of the last two weeks in September doing weapons training—essential, as by then more than 70 percent of the men were replacements—and practice assaults. Rifle companies had tanks assigned to them, along with flamethrowers and radios that could reach the fighter pilots overhead and the artillery to the rear. By the beginning of October, the combined arms team was ready to go.

The technique for village fighting departed from the manual, most of all by bringing tanks into the streets to blast holes in the sides of buildings, through which infantry could move from one building into the next without exposing themselves in the street. Practice exercises showed that the way to take the buildings was to hit them with mortar, artillery, and if possible fighter-bomber shells, then use flamethrowers and/or grenades tossed through a window or door, dash into the room right after the explosion, spray it with automatic fire, take the second floor, then use grenades and/or verbal persuasion to induce the Germans in the cellars to surrender. And the Americans learned that it was best done one building at a time.

Reconnaissance pilots, meanwhile, had taken tens of thousands of photographs, developing an intelligence picture almost as complete and accurate as that developed for the Normandy beaches. Company commanders were given maps that plotted all known strong points in their area, enough to give each squad leader a map. And the engineers built sand tables for the officers and men to study.

First Army's mission was to break through the Siegfried Line. The route would be along the narrow Aachen corridor, between the fens of Holland to the north and the Hurtgen Forest and Ardennes to the south. After fighting through the Siegfried Line, First Army would drive east and close to the Rhine from Düsseldorf to Bonn. To avoid getting caught up in the urban congestion of Aachen, the breakthroughs would take place north and south of the city. When the two wings linked to the east, Aachen would be enveloped and could be neutralized by a relatively small force, while the bulk of First Army pushed east.

Aachen had little military value. As it was on the border with Belgium, rather than France, it had relatively few fortifications, nothing to compare with Metz. It was more a trading center than a manufacturing site. Its prewar population was 166,000. It had not been heavily bombed.

Aachen's psychological value, however, was immense. It was the first German city to be threatened, symbolic enough by itself, and a city central to German and Western civilization. The Romans had medicinal spring baths there, the Aquisgranum. It was the city where Charlemagne was born and crowned. It was the seat of the Holy Roman Empire—what Hitler called the First Reich.

In early September, thousands of German troops retreated through Aachen. Lt. Wenzel Andreas Borgert, commanding an antitank battalion, arrived with his unit intact. "I was afraid, as we entered Aachen, that we would be regarded badly by its inhabitants," he related. "But I was very surprised to find out how happy they were to see us. I asked one of the civilians, 'How come, when we've been beaten?'

" 'Yes,' he said, 'but you're the first German soldiers who have come back here in an orderly fashion.' "

Borgert put up some makeshift defenses on the main road coming into the city, "and I can tell you, though I'd rather not, what kind of group I gathered from the streets to man that barricade."

Borgert's panzer division wore black uniforms. The French people, and the GIs, confused them with SS uniforms. Borgert was

France, Summer 1944

Carentan, June 12. Men of the 101st Airborne Division watch a jeep tow a light artillery piece through town. Here the men from Omaha Beach linked up with the men from Utah.

Hedgerow country, July. Unidentified American troops moving into the battle. This is not particularly heavy growth; in many cases the treetops met over the sunken lanes.

All photos are courtesy U.S. Army Signal Corps unless otherwise noted.

Normandy, July 6. A captured German sits on the side of his vehicle, practically ignored by the GIs, who are more interested in the intricacies of his machine pistol.

July 8. American infantry and tanks advance through St. Fromond, Normandy.

The first lesson for infantrymen was to learn to love the ground. *Above:* As his buddies keep firing, a GI takes a break to wolf down his K rations—biscuits and cheese. *Center right:* Two GIs from the 4th Division, in combat since D-Day, catch some rest. They have the necessities of war surrounding their hole: ammo clips, hand grenades, water, rations, and bandages in their musette bags. *Bottom right:* A mortar crew from the 35th Infantry at work. The GI on the phone is calling out the adjustments from a forward observer.

Normandy suffered terribly. *Above:* Cerisy-la-Salle, July 25. The girl was the only person in the village. Sgt. David Weiss appears to be telling her that everything will be okay. *Left:* The cathedral of St.-Lô, July 26. A GI patrol searches for booby traps and watches for snipers.

Right: Sgt. Curtis Culin, of Cranford, N.J., in Normandy, July 30. Culin exemplified the citizen soldier; a prewar mechanic, he was one of the men responsible for the "Rhino" equipment that, when welded to the front of his Sherman tank, made it possible for armor to operate in the hedgerow country.

Below: GIs outside the German placement office in Argentan, France, August 20, celebrate putting it out of business.

Above: August 20, Mantes-Gassicourt, France. A black artillery crew is firing at German barges crossing the Seine River. The shell carries the message "From Harlem to Hitler."

Left: Aftermath of the Falaise Gap: destroyed German vehicles and dead horses along the road, August 22. The driver of the lead wagon escaped on foot.

Bottom left: Men from the 3507th Ordnance Maintenance replace a damaged transmission on a jeep, August 25. The Americans beat every other army in the world in getting damaged or worn-out vehicles back into service.

Right: Paris, August 26. Sgt. Kenneth Averill of the 4th Division gets a welcome. The old folks approve.

Below: Hotel Majestic, Paris, August 26. The hotel had been a German occupation headquarters; now it was a temporary POW cage.

In the Hurtgen Forest, November 11, Pvt. Maurice Berzon, Sgt. Bernard Spurr, and Sgt. Harold Glessler take a break.

A GI from the 9th Division talks to a German soldier captured during the Hurtgen battle, December 12.

The Faces
of Men at War

Right: Sgt. Carl Butler, 1st Division, Belgium, December 22. His armored car is snowed in.

Center right: Two GIs man a machine gun in Belgium, December 23.

Left: An unidentified GI finds something to smile about on Christmas morning in Belgium.

Right: Two GIs ham it up with their cold rations for the photographer, Soy, Belgium, December 26.

Left: Sgt. Joseph Arnaldo, an infantry squad leader, comes off the line after ten days in the Ardennes, December 30.

Below: Sgt. William Howard, 79th Division, in the Scheibenhardt area, January 2.

Right: Fosse, Belgium, January 4. One of the lucky ones, a front-line German soldier who has made it safely into POW status. *Below:* A machine-gun crew of the 84th Division, Odrimont, Belgium, January 6.

Right: Sgt. Joseph Holmes, 35th Division, Belgium, January 10.

Below: Pvt. Morton Frenberg, 8th Division, February 24, Germany, waits out a German shelling.

OPPOSITE:
The U.S. Army's medical team was outstanding, beginning with the nurses and medics. *Top:* July 15, Southampton, England. U.S. Army WACs board a troop transport that will take them to France, where the wounded so badly need them. *Center:* Medics at work. In training camp, the medics were derided. In combat, they were called "Doc" and were universally admired for their bravery. *Bottom:* The medical team worked twenty-hour days, which is evident on the face of this Red Cross volunteer cutting bandages.

Medics

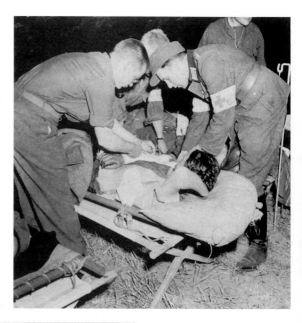

Above: Both sides put captured doctors to work. Here, on August 18, a German medical officer helps American medics treat a wounded German soldier.

Left: On their way to the aid station with a wounded buddy. The GIs were convinced there was an Army regulation against dying if you made it alive to the aid station. The GI on the left has all the look of a just-arrived replacement.

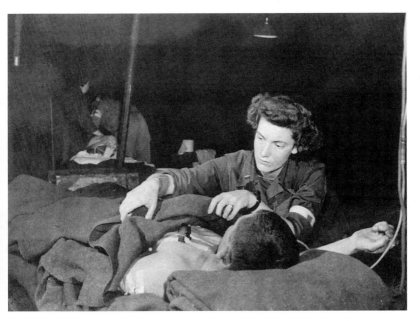

Chances for survival went up to 98 percent if a wounded man made it to a field or evacuation hospital. Here, July 3, Lt. Arm Rowe tends a GI with a chest wound.

August 31, near Chambois, France. A German half-track with a crew of German medics, working on the American side of the lines, picking up wounded to take to an American aid station.

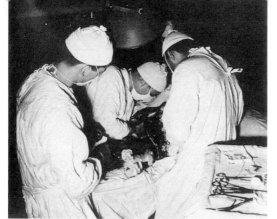

Left: A surgical team of the 49th Field Hospital has just amputated an arm and is engaged in clamping the arteries with hemostats.

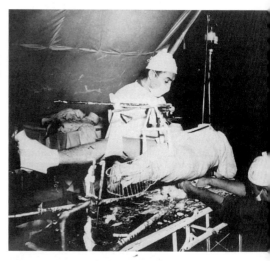

Right: Capt. Jack Gurwitz operates on a patient suffering from a compound fracture of the right thigh and injuries to blood vessels. The patient's lower left leg had to be amputated because of gangrene of the foot.

Below: Operations in progress in the 102nd Evacuation Hospital, January 6, 1945. The lights were reflected by the five gallon cans hung by cable stretched across the room.

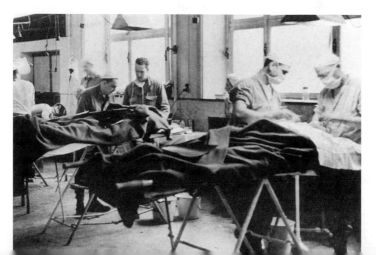

therefore delighted to be back on German soil: "Suddenly we were no longer the Nazis, we were German soldiers."[16]

The Nazis did no good for their reputation in Aachen. In mid-September, when the 1st Division closed on the city, the local Nazi commander deemed the cause lost. Corp. Friedrich Bertenrath of the 2nd Panzer Division described what happened: "The Party men completely failed. They ordered Aachen evacuated. The people, naturally, did not want this. The Party people—and there were a lot of them—set off the air raid siren, went down to the main train station, took over a train, and beat it. People wandered everywhere with no idea where to go. The train was gone, the Party was gone, the police were gone. The city's entire government had left. The civilians sat there."[17]

Hitler ordered the Nazi officials stripped of all rank and sent to the Eastern Front as privates. He was determined to hold the city, and to do so sent in the 246th Volksgrenadier Division, about 5,000 boys and old men with a small assortment of tanks, assault guns, and artillery pieces. He ordered a fanatical, house-to-house "last stand." Evacuation was out of the question. Hitler ordered the CO, Col. Gerhard Wilck, to hold the city "to the last man, and if necessary, allow himself to be buried under its ruins."[18]

The Americans, meanwhile, in Corporal Bertenrath's view, "really loused up the opportunity to capture the city. It would have been so easy. If they had but closed their hand, they could have had Aachen."[19]

First Army's attack on the Siegfried Line north of Aachen was reminiscent of its attack on Omaha Beach four months earlier. It had put to use what it had learned; practice exercises had been realistic and extensive, as the men were trained in assault tactics specific to the Siegfried Line.

For six days prior to jump-off, the heavy artillery pounded forty-five known German pillboxes in the immediate front of the 30th Division. This stripped away camouflage from the pillboxes, ripped up the barbed-wire obstacles, set off hundreds of mines, and forced the Germans to take cover. Otherwise it had little effect, except to let the Germans know where the attack was coming.

H-Hour was set for 1100, October 2. At 0900 hours, the American artillery shifted targets from the German front to anti-aircraft batteries in the rear. It was effective, not only in suppressing flak but also in sending up clouds of black smoke that hampered German visibility. Unfortunately, it also hampered American visibility. The 360 medium bombers and seventy-two fighter-bombers committed to the pre-assault bombing of German front-line positions went astray. Only a half dozen bombs fell in the target area. The air attack had been almost a total failure.

As the planes left, the artillery shifted targets back to the pill-boxes. Mortarmen rushed to their positions; in the next couple of hours they fired 18,696 shells from 372 tubes. As the infantry moved forward, tanks accompanied them. They put direct .50-caliber machine-gun and 75mm cannon fire on the pillboxes, to prevent German gunners from manning their weapons. An infantry lieu-tenant gave his account of combined arms in action: "We had real tank-infantry cooperation. The tanks just machine-gunned the Jer-ries in their holes and when the infantry came up it was mass mur-der."[20] Infantry platoons accompanied by engineer teams maneuvered their way behind the pillboxes, where the engineers blew the rear doors with satchel charges, bangalore torpedoes, and bazookas.

As at Omaha, the Germans tended to fight well from their fir-ing posts, so long as the action was in front of them, but as soon as troops appeared to their rear, they surrendered. The Americans found they needed an average of thirty minutes to capture a single pillbox. The GIs also learned that they had to resist the temptation to occupy the pillboxes and catch their breath. If they did not keep moving forward, they were certain to catch a downpour of German artillery and mortar fire, to be followed by a counterattack.[21]

By the end of the day, the 30th Division had breached the first line of pillboxes. The next day, the 2nd Armored joined the attack. It took three more days, but by October 7 the Americans had made a clean break through the Siegfried Line north of Aachen. The 1st Division, meanwhile, broke through to the south. On October 10, the two wings hooked up, and Aachen was surrounded. This was blitzkrieg warfare: a rupture of the enemy's MLR, bypassing a city considered an obstacle rather than an objective, and an exploitation deep into the enemy's rear area. First Army was on the verge of a classic victory.

But doubts and hesitations set in, and minds were changed. The German resistance was stronger than anticipated, the German ability to counterattack had not been fully appreciated. Without Aachen cleared, it would be impossible to maintain supply lines to support the divisions heading for the Rhine. First Army decided that Aachen would have to be taken after all, before any exploitation to the east could begin.

On October 10, First Army sent Colonel Wilck an ultimatum. When he rejected it, the 1st Division prepared to take the city. Thus were the GIs committed to exactly the kind of action the brass had wanted to avoid in the first place, street fighting.

It fell to Lt. Col. Derrill Daniel, CO of the 2nd Battalion of the 26th Infantry, 1st Division, to lead the attack. His position was just north of Dawson's G Company. Dawson was facing outward, defending against German attacks; Daniel faced inward, toward Aachen. He would be attacking from east to west. He had three days to study the defenses and make plans. He got three Shermans, two towed antitank guns, and other weapons to support his rifle companies. He issued maps and gave individual platoons specific missions. He held exercises. The battalion adopted a motto, "Knock 'em all down," that expressed its readiness to destroy Aachen with American high explosives.[22]

H-Hour was 0930, October 13. The jump-off line was a high railroad embankment, with the German lines just on the other side. At 0930, every soldier in the battalion heaved a hand grenade over the embankment. Daniel's men came after the explosions, shouting and firing. Resistance was light. Using the techniques learned in training, the tanks punched holes in the buildings for the infantry to use. The battalion was nearing the city center as night came on.

In the morning, German resistance stiffened. The battle grew desperate. The GIs brought wheeled artillery into the city, and were able to fire parallel to the front, dropping their shells just beyond the noses of the American infantry. Forward observers learned to call for delayed fuses, so that shells penetrated several floors and exploded right among the enemy rather than detonating on rooftops. Building by building, Daniel's men advanced.

Colonel Wilck's men fought back, from every conceivable hiding place. They used the city sewer system to mount local counterattacks from the rear so effectively that the Americans had to locate and block every manhole to prevent further infiltration. This was the closest the Americans in ETO came to experiencing a Stalingrad-like battle.

■

For Captain Dawson and G Company, the task wasn't to attack but defend. This too was new. State-side training had emphasized offensive tactics, while in France the GIs had done far more attacking than defending. But Dawson and his men were holding high ground east of Aachen, which gave them observation posts to call in targets to the gunners and pilots. The Germans were desperate to get him off that ridge, which reporter W. C. Heinz had taken to calling in his dateline "Dawson Ridge, Germany." The Germans needed the ridge to restore their line and relieve the pressure on Aachen. So Dawson was going to have to defend.

At 2300 hours, October 15, an SS panzer division hit G Company. The first shots came as a surprise because the leading tank in the column was a captured Sherman, with American markings on it. The battle that was thus joined went on for forty-eight hours. There was hand-to-hand fighting, with rifle butts and bayonets. It was surreal, almost slow-motion, because the mud was ankle deep. Dawson called in artillery to within ten meters of his position. At one foxhole a German toppled dead over the barrel of an American machine gun, while in another a wounded American waited until the German who had shot him came up and looked down on him, then emptied his Tommy gun in the German's face. The two men died, at the bottom of the hole, in a macabre embrace.[23]

The American battalion commander cracked. He all but disappeared, or as Lieutenant Hall put it, "he became less and less interested in the conduct of the war." The officers conferred among themselves, then persuaded the battalion executive officer to talk to the regimental commander. He did, and the CO was reassigned.[24] The battalion held its position.

On October 17, a German attack overran Dawson's antitank gun position. He set out to retake it. Lieutenant Hall, battalion S-3, sent a report to regimental S-3 that evening: "I just talked to Dawson and he says that he has position restored where gun was. The gun was knocked out. He was not able to take the house. Said he would get it tomorrow. . . . Dawson's men killed 17 Jerries including five from the crew of a tank which was in back of the house. . . . His men have had no food for 24 hours. Their last hot meal was the night before last. Possibly we can get them a hot meal tomorrow."[25]

■

Inside Aachen the battle raged. The Germans fell back to the center of the city, charging a price for every building abandoned. The rubble in the streets grew to monstrous proportions. In the center, the old buildings, made of masonry and stone, were almost impervious to tank cannon fire, so Colonel Daniel brought a self-propelled 155mm artillery piece into the city, using a bulldozer to clear a path. Daniel reported that its effects were "quite spectacular and satisfying."[26]

On October 16, the battalion ran into a strong German position in the city's main theater building. Daniel brought the 155 forward and wheeled it into the line side by side with the infantry. It fired more than a dozen shells, point-blank, into the theater. The theater survived but its defenders, dazed, surrendered.

Still the fighting continued. For another four days and nights the Germans and Americans pounded each other while they destroyed Aachen. Finally, on October 21, Daniel's men secured the downtown area. Colonel Wilck dared to disobey Hitler and surrendered his 3,473 survivors. At his interrogation he protested bitterly against the use of the 155 in Aachen, calling it "barbarous" and claiming it should be outlawed.

American losses were heavy, over 5,000. The 30th and 1st Divisions were badly depleted, exhausted, used up. They were in no condition to make a dash to the Rhine. German losses were heavier, 5,000 casualties and 5,600 prisoners of war. Aachen was destroyed, with the exception of the cathedral, which housed Charlemagne's coronation chair. It escaped major damage.*

Outside Aachen, Dawson's company continued to hold. After Aachen fell there were fewer, less vigorous German attacks. On October 22, reporter W. C. Heinz of the *New York Sun* got to Dawson's headquarters to do an interview. Dawson summarized the action simply, directly: "This is the worst I've ever seen. Nobody will ever know what this has been like up here."

Heinz wanted to know, as best he could, and arranged to stay

---

*The standing cathedral surrounded by ruin and rubble was common after World War II. Five and more decades later, you can see the phenomenon in London, where St. Paul's stands surrounded by post-1945 buildings, or in Cologne, Aachen, Reims, and elsewhere. Thank God—and thank those medieval craftsmen and architects.

with Dawson for a few days to find out. The dispatches he filed beginning October 24 give a vivid portrait of a rifle company commander in action in World War II. Of course Dawson was special, but not so special that what he was going through was that much different from what his fellow COs were experiencing. Of them it can be truly said that they held the most dangerous and difficult job in the world.

Dawson's hq was in a cellar in the village. There was a candle and a kerosene lamp, a table and some chairs, a radio playing classical music. There were a couple of lieutenants in the room, and a radioman, and Dawson's dachshund, Freda. Heinz got Dawson talking about what it had been like.

"And the kid says to me," Dawson related, " 'I'll take that water to that platoon.' And he starts out. He is about fifty yards from this door-way and I'm watching him. He is running fast; then I can see this 88 hit right where he is, and, in front of my eyes, he is blown apart."

Dawson spoke of other strains. "I had a kid come up and say, 'I can't take it anymore.' What could I do? If I lose that man, I lose a squad. So I grab him by the shirt, and I say: 'You will, you will. There ain't any going back from this hill except dead.' And he goes back and he is dead."

Dawson sighed. "He doesn't know why, and I don't know why, and you don't know why. But I have got to answer those guys."

He looked Heinz in the eye. "But I have got to answer those guys," he repeated, "because I wear bars. I've got the responsibility and I don't know whether I'm big enough for the job." He continued to fix his eyes on Heinz. "But I can't break now. I've taken this for the thirty-nine days we've held this ridge and I'm in the middle of the Siegfried Line and you want to know what I think? I think it stinks."

Dawson began to shed tears. Then he jerked his head up. "Turn it up," he said to a lieutenant by the radio. "That's Puccini. I want to hear it."

Two GIs came into the room. They were apprehensive, because Captain Dawson had sent for them. But it was good news. "I'm sending you to Paris," Dawson announced. "For six days. How do you like that?"

"Thanks," one replied, reluctantly.

"Well, you had better like it," Dawson said, "and you had better stay out of trouble, but have a good time and bless your hearts." The men mumbled thanks and left.

"Two of the best boys I've got," Dawson told Heinz. "Wire boys. They've had to run new lines every day because the old ones get chopped up. One day they laid heavy wire for 200 yards and by the time they got to the end and worked back, the wire had been cut in three places by shellfire."

Dawson told Heinz that he had men who had been wounded in mid-September, when he first occupied the ridge, who returned four weeks later. They had gone AWOL from the field hospital and made their way back "and the first thing I know they show up again here and they're grinning from ear to ear. I know it must sound absolutely crazy that anyone would want to come back to this, but it is true."

The following morning, one of the lieutenants told Dawson, "Captain, those wire men, they say they don't want to go to Paris."

"All right," Dawson sighed. "Get two other guys—if you can."[27]

The Battle of Aachen benefited no one. The Americans never should have attacked. The Germans never should have defended. Neither side had a choice. This was war at its worst, wanton destruction for no purpose.

In the fall of 1944, Ernie Pyle left ETO. He needed a break. "For me," he wrote in explanation, "war has become a flat, black depression without highlights, a revulsion of the mind and an exhaustion of the spirit." He carried with him a conviction: "In the emergency of war our nation's powers are unbelievable." And then he noted, "I have heard soldiers say a thousand times, 'If only we could have created all this energy for something good.' But we rise above our normal powers only in times of destruction."[28]

There was one perverse satisfaction for the Americans. William Walton commented on it in a piece for Life magazine. He was there when "the people of Aachen began streaming out into the smoky sunshine. Heavy with weariness, with fear, and with the bulging bundles of their last possessions, they plodded in double files. For almost ten days they had lived in the basements. They blinked in the sunlight.

"Leaning against the wall beside me, Sgt. Eldridge Benefield said, 'I hope I never live to see anything like this happen in America.

But sometimes I wish people over there could at least see it. Some-times I think they don't quite understand what it's like.' "

They watched for an hour as the weary refugees plodded along. Walton felt he had just "witnessed an historic turning point in World War II. For the first time the people of Germany were join-ing the long lines of Europe's refugees along the road over which they had forced so many other peoples before them."[29]

Lt. Col. John C. Harrison (who later became a justice of the Montana Supreme Court) was a thirty-one-year-old Montana State University graduate with an ROTC commission. He was a liaison officer with corps headquarters. On October 22 he went into Aachen to report on the damage. He wrote in his diary, "If every German city that we pass thru looks like this one the Hun is going to be busy for centuries rebuilding his country. The city is as dead as a Roman ruin, but unlike a ruin it has none of the grace of gradual decay."

Harrison saw not one undamaged building. The streets were impassable. It made him feel good. "I thought how odd it is that I would feel good at seeing human misery but I did feel that way, for here was the war being brought to the German in all of its destruc-tive horror. . . . The war has truly come to Germany and pictures of these terrible scenes should be dropped over the entire country to show them what is in store for them if they continue."[30]

Part Two

AT THE
GERMAN BORDER

*The glorious victories of July, August, and September
came to an end in October. In November and December
1944, the U.S. Army was unable to advance farther, and
in mid-December it was thrown back. The ensuing Battle of the Bulge was, like Gettysburg for the Civil War,
the most famous battle of the war. Also like Gettysburg,
it was a victory for the U.S. Army, but only a defensive
victory, and wars are not won by fighting on the defensive.*

6

Metz and the Hurtgen Forest

November 1–December 15, 1944

NORTHWEST EUROPE in November and December was a miserable place. A mixture of sleet, snow, rain, cold, fog, short days and long nights cried out for winter camp, for shelter and indoor occupations. Rivers were at flood stage. The already poor roads were churned into quagmires by military vehicles; veterans speak of the mud as knee-deep and insist that it is true.

In the center of the American line, in the Ardennes, portions of First Army did go into something like winter camp. It was a lightly held, quiet area, where divisions just coming into the line could be placed to give them some front-line experience. Eisenhower and Bradley figured the terrain made it the least likely area the Germans might counterattack. All was quiet there.

But north and south of the Ardennes, First and Third Armies were on the offensive, the weather be damned. There was no strategy involved. The rain and mud made rapid movement impossible and there was insufficient gasoline to supply deep thrusts into the enemy rear. Once the generals made the decision to continue the offensive, the war in the fall of 1944 became once again what it had been in the hedgerows of Normandy, a junior officer and NCO battle of attrition.

■

157

A steady flow of replacements coming from England allowed the generals to build companies up to full strength after a few days on the line, even when casualties had run as high as 90 percent. Eisenhower was prepared for this. In early November, he sent out a teletype to all headquarters:

COMBAT UNITS ARE AUTHORIZED TO BASE DAILY REPLACEMENT REQUISITIONS ON ANTICIPATED LOSSES FORTY EIGHT HOURS IN ADVANCE TO EXPEDITE DELIVERY OF REPLACEMENTS PD TO AVOID BUILDING UP OVERSTRENGTH ESTIMATES SHOULD BE MADE WITH CARE PD SIGNED EISENHOWER.[1]

The replacement flow added to the sense of strength—surely the Germans couldn't keep up. At higher headquarters the feeling was, just one more push here, or another there, and we'll be through the Siegfried Line and up to and across the Rhine.

In addition to individual replacements, new divisions were coming onto the line in a steady stream. These high-number divisions were made up of the high school classes of 1942, 1943, and 1944. The training these young men had gone through at Fort Benning and the other State-side posts was rigorous physically but severely short on the tactical and leadership challenges the junior officers would have to meet.

Paul Fussell was a twenty-year-old lieutenant in command of a rifle platoon in the 103rd Division. He found the six months' training period in the States to be repetitious and unrealistic. He was struck by "the futility and waste of training and re-training and finding some work to do for the expendables awaiting their moment to be expended." In the field, "Our stock-in-trade was the elementary fire-and-flank maneuver hammered into us over and over at Benning. It was very simple. With half your platoon, you establish a firing line to keep your enemy's heads down while you lead the other half around to the enemy's flank for a sudden surprise assault, preferably with bayonets and shouting."

Fire-and-movement had been the doctrine developed by General Marshall when he was at Benning in the 1920s. Marshall had reasoned that in the next war, the Army would expand rapidly and therefore needed to "develop a technique and methods so simple and so brief that the citizen officer of good common sense can readily grasp the idea."

"We all did grasp the idea," Fussell remembered, "but in combat it had one signal defect, namely the difficulty, usually the impossibility, of knowing where your enemy's flank *is*. If you get up and go looking for it, you'll be killed." Nevertheless, Fussell saw the positive benefit to doing fire-and-movement over and over: "Perhaps its function was rather to raise our morale and confidence than to work as defined. It did have the effect of persuading us that such an attack could be led successfully and that we were the people who could do it. That was good for our self-respect and our courage, and perhaps that was the point."[2] This was distressingly close to the Duke of Wellington's sole requirement for his lieutenants, that they be brave.

Fussell was a rich kid from Southern California who had a couple of years of college and some professional journalism behind him. He had blown the lid off the IQ test. Had he been born two years earlier and brought into the Army in 1941 or 1942, he would have gone into the Army Air Force, or intelligence, or onto somebody's staff, or sent back to college for more education. But he was one of those American males born in 1924 or 1925 to whom fell the duty, as rifle platoon leaders, to bear the brunt of the Battle of Northwest Europe, after their older brothers and friends, born in 1922 or 1923, had driven the enemy back to his border.

There were hundreds of young officers like Fussell, lieutenants who came into Europe in the fall of 1944 to take up the fighting. Rich kids. Bright kids. The quarterback on the championship high school football team. The president of his class. The chess champion. The lead in the class play. The solo in the spring concert. The wizard in the chemistry class. America was throwing her finest young men at the Germans.

Among the fresh divisions was the 84th Infantry. It had gone through its training cycle in mid-1944, then sailed for Europe. It came into France at Omaha Beach on November 2 and moved by truck to the front. Bradley assigned it to the new U.S. Ninth Army (Gen. William Simpson was the CO), which had taken over a narrow part of the front, with U.S. First Army on its right and the Twenty-first Army Group on its left. The 84th's left flank tied in with the British right. K Company, 333rd Regiment, was on the extreme left, outside Geilenkirchen, some twenty kilometers north of Aachen.

"K Company was an American mass-production item," one of

its officers remarked, "fresh off the assembly line."[3] It certainly was representative. There were men who could neither read nor write, along with privates from Yale and Harvard (class of 1946) and sergeants with college degrees. They came from all sections of the country and every major ethnic group save African-American and Japanese-American.

One of the sergeants, Franklin Brewer, was different in many ways from the other NCOs, especially age. He was thirty-seven years old, so the men referred to him as Father Brewer, or sometimes as Mother Brewer. He came from a Philadelphia Main Line family and had a Harvard degree. He was fluent in French and German. He had traveled extensively in Europe before the war, moving in the highest literary circles. He referred to his friend Gertrude Stein as Miss Stein; she made him a central character in her book *Brewsie and Willie*. And here he was a sergeant in a rifle company on the front line, because he wanted it that way.

So K Company may have been mass-produced, but it had a right to think of itself as unique, with its own personality and character. It was special, too, because Capt. Harold Leinbaugh, a platoon leader and then CO, and Lt. John Campbell, a platoon leader, wrote the company's autobiography, *The Men of Company K*. It is one of the finest small-unit histories of World War II.

K Company's first offensive was Operation Clipper. The 84th's mission was to seize the high ground east of Geilenkirchen along the Siegfried, in conjunction with a British offensive to the left (north). For Clipper, the 84th was under the operation command of the British XXX Corps, commanded by Gen. Brian Horrocks. To K Company what that meant, mostly, was a daily rum ration, about half a canteen cup.

For the first three days of Clipper, K Company was in support. It did the mopping up in Geilenkirchen, taking 100 prisoners with no casualties. It was easy. The company congratulated itself and relaxed. "Someone was playing a piano," Pvt. Jim Sterner remembered. He looked into a house and found a half dozen men and his CO, Capt. George Gieszl, playing the piano with a British lieutenant. The song was "Lili Marlene," and "our guys were laughing and singing along with him. What I remember most is a feeling of total exhilaration. Boy, this is really great—the way a war ought to be."[4]

On November 21, it was K Company's turn to lead the attack.

The men got their rum ration with their breakfast. Sherman tanks with British crews showed up to support the GIs. From a low hill behind the line of departure, First Sgt. Dempsey Keller watched the men climb out of foxholes and form up. These were the men he had trained and worried over for many months. "They were the finest men in the world, the very best. I choked up with pride, but I felt cold chills not knowing what was out there waiting for them. It was the one single moment of the war I can never forget."[5]

The company advanced. It took possession of a château the Germans had been using as an observation post but had not tried to defend. It moved forward again, but was soon held up by artillery fire. Sgt. Keith Lance led his mortar squad forward to provide support. But as he approached, "we started taking machine-gun and rifle fire from a stone farm building off to our right." Lance spread his men out and returned fire, but he couldn't use the mortars and had only four M-1s and a couple of pistols.

Lance heard a voice asking if he could use a bit of help. "It was a goddam British officer—standing up in the middle of a firefight without a helmet. He had climbed out of his tank and walked across the field behind us. I told him, 'Lordy Jesus, yes, we need some help.' " The British officer ran back to his tank and gave the farmhouses three quick rounds from his 75, one in each window. Thirty to forty Germans poured out waving white flags.[6]

The rifle platoons, meanwhile, were taking a pounding. Leinbaugh and Campbell describe it: "The concentration of German firepower was absolutely overwhelming with its violence, surprise, and intensity. Artillery fire, 88s and 75s from hidden tanks, and 120 mortars with apparently limitless supplies of ammunition hit us. Machine-gun fire whipping in from pillboxes seemed almost an afterthought. The noise, the shock, the sensation of total helplessness and bewilderment, the loss of control, the sudden loss of every familiar assumption—nothing in civilian life or training offered an experience remotely comparable. . . . Our new-boy illusions of the past two days dissolved in a moment."[7]

It was K Company's welcome to the Western Front. Every rifle company coming on the line that November had a similar experience and drew the same conclusion: there was no way training could prepare a man for combat. Combat could only be experienced, not played at. Training was critical to getting the men into physical condition, to obey orders, to use their weapons, to work effectively with hand signals and radios, and more. It could not teach men how to lie helpless under a shower of shrapnel in a field crisscrossed by machine-gun fire. They just had to do it, and in doing it they joined a unique group of men who have experienced what the rest of us cannot imagine.

At Metz, Patton remained steadfast for advance. The CO of XII Corps, Maj. Gen. Manton Eddy, was scheduled to send his divisions into Metz on November 8. Patton boasted that he would reach the Siegfried Line, sixty-five kilometers east, "in not to exceed D plus 2 days." But the downpours, which prevented any air support, the mud, which was so bad even tracked vehicles found it almost impossible to move, and the swollen rivers, which could not be bridged by the engineers, combined to demand postponement of the offensive. Eddy so informed Patton, who invited him to name his successor. The attack went off on schedule.[8]

It had a different objective than the earlier attack on Driant. No one was ready to attack the fortresses head-on. Instead of attempting to surround and reduce the Metz fortresses, Third Army adopted a new policy: "The primary mission of all troops is the destruction or capture of the Metz garrison, without the investiture or siege of the Metz Forts."[9]

The plan was to have the 5th Division attack to the northeast of Metz, while the 90th Division would break through the German lines to the south of the city. The two divisions would link up east of Metz, isolating it. Meanwhile the 95th Division would push into the city itself, supported by the 10th Armored Division.

Torrential rains and stiff German resistance held up the 5th and 90th Divisions for a week, but some progress was made and by November 15 the encirclement was almost complete. Farther south, meanwhile, other elements of Third Army were pushing eastward. Metz, Patton's goal for two months, was finally within his grasp.

As new infantry divisions arrived, Patton put them into the line and told their commanders to attack east. The 26th Division was one of these. It included G Company, 328th Regiment, and that company included Sgt. Bruce Egger and Lt. Lee Otts, who collaborated to write *G Company's War,* a vivid account of a rifle company in ETO.

On November 11, G Company went into action east of Nancy.

"It occurred to me that this was Armistice Day," Egger wrote, "and wouldn't it be nice if history repeated itself?" Eerily, he heard church bells, and it wasn't Sunday. Then he figured out it was the local French churches observing the end of World War I.[10]

Over the following three days, the company attacked. Nothing fancy, just a skirmish line advancing until it met resistance, then fire-and-movement. "Most of the time we fired from the hip," Egger said, "as we could not see anything but trees." Sometimes they made good progress, as much as a kilometer. At other times they were stopped by mortar shells and machine-gun fire.

Conditions were bad. The mud made movement difficult at best. The air could supply little help. If the FOs (forward observers) brought in the supporting artillery close enough to do any good against the Germans, there were sure to be some shorts causing casualties. Mines were a horror. So was the rain. Egger described the way he spent the second night: "We stopped along the road in a grove of pine trees. We were soaking wet; it had rained all day and we had been making our way through wet brush. Our bedrolls could not be brought up to us, so we spent the night as best we could by digging a hole and covering the bottom with pine boughs. . . . We slept through the storm, which put down about six inches of snow during the night. We were wet, muddy, and shivering from the cold. A barrage of 88s greeted us at daylight." Then it was back to forming a skirmish line and moving out.[11]

Nothing spectacular happened. G Company gained a little more ground. After three days of this, Egger's platoon was down to six men. Of the 525 men in the battalion who had gone into the battle three days earlier, 150 were left. It was pulled out of the line to rest and receive replacements. After a week, it moved back into the line. "I dreaded going into combat again," Egger confessed. "The past two weeks indicated that my chances of getting through the war unharmed were close to zero—though the odds of coming out of it alive were about four to one."[12]

It fell to Col. Robert Bacon to take Metz. He organized Task Force Bacon, composed of two battalions of infantry of the 95th Division, plus three companies of tanks, artillery, and engineers. On November 16, at 0700 hours, he began the drive to the city, advancing in two columns, with tanks at the head. When one column met resistance, Bacon moved the other to hit the German flank, throwing sharp jabs and short hooks, moving forward. By dusk the next day, the columns came together near Fort St. Julien, four kilometers from the city center.

St. Julien was one of the old Vauban forts. It sat on dominating terrain and commanded the two main roads leading into Metz from the north. Surrounded by a moat twelve meters deep and twelve meters wide, with high thick walls and a covered causeway, it had a garrison of 362 Germans. They had no heavy weapons, but with their machine guns and rifles they could prevent American movement on the main roads. St. Julien was the one fort that had to be taken.

The assault began at dawn, November 18, in the fog. By noon Task Force Bacon had fought its way to the moat. For the next hour, the 75mm cannon on the Shermans, plus the 155mm self-propelled cannon, supported by 240mm howitzers from behind, pounded the fort.

At 1300, the infantry jumped off and began to dash across the causeway. The Germans stopped them with heavy small-arms fire. Two Shermans moved forward to spray enemy firing slits with their .50-caliber machine guns, and a second attempt by the infantry was successful. But then the GIs ran into an iron door that blocked access to St. Julien's interior. The Shermans crossed the causeway and fired point-blank at it, but the 75mm shells just bounced off. A tank destroyer with a 90mm gun drove up. It fired six rounds at a range of less than fifty yards. They had no effect. With the machine-gun fire from the Shermans keeping the Germans back from the firing slits, a 155mm howitzer was wheeled into place. The big gun slammed ten rounds into the door, but still it held. That Vauban was some builder.

The Americans decided that if they couldn't blow the door down, they could destroy its stone facing. The 155mm gun slammed twenty rounds into the door's mounts. Finally, the door collapsed inward with a mighty crash. Infantry moved though the opening, bayonets fixed. They were met by Germans with their hands up.[13]

The 155mm had taken the place of the battering ram. This was an altogether new use of the self-propelled artillery. It was part of what was becoming the essence of American tactics in ETO—whenever possible, use high explosives. German veterans, when asked to comment on the Americans as soldiers, invariably begin with a criticism: that whenever GIs ran up against opposition, they hunkered down and called in the artillery. In the German army, the infantry solved its own problems. But most GIs would consider their use of high explosives something to praise, not criticize.

With the fall of St. Julien, the 95th Division began to move to the center of Metz. It bypassed and isolated the other Vauban forts. On November 22, Metz was secured—except that six forts around the city were still defiant. The Americans made no attempt to overrun them, and soon enough they began to surrender. The last to give up was Fort Driant, which finally capitulated on December 8.

Patton had taken Metz, at a cost of 2,189 casualties in the 95th Division, but in the process inflicting twice that price on the German defenders, plus a bag of 6,000 prisoners.

In August, Third Army had advanced almost 600 kilometers, from Normandy to the Moselle River. From September 1 to mid-December, it advanced thirty-five kilometers east of the Moselle. The Siegfried Line, which Patton had said he would reach on November 10, was still a dozen or so kilometers to the east. In crossing the Moselle and taking Metz, Third Army had suffered 47,039 battle casualties.[14]

Up north of Aachen, K Company continued to attack, side by side with the British. General Horrocks surprised the GIs by showing up on the front lines to see conditions. He was a sympathetic yet critical observer. The 84th struck him as "an impressive product of American training methods which turned out division after division complete, fully equipped." The division "was composed of splendid, very brave, tough young men." But he thought it a bit much to ask of a green division that it penetrate the Siegfried Line, then stand up to counterattacks from two first-class divisions, the 15th Panzer and the 10th SS. And he was disturbed by the failure of American division and corps commanders and their staffs to *ever* visit the front lines. He was greatly concerned to find that the men were not getting hot meals brought up from the rear, in contrast to the forward units in the British line. He gave the GIs "my most experienced armoured regiment, the Sherwood Rangers Yeomanry," told the American battalion and division commanders to get up front, and returned to his headquarters.[15]

The problem Horrocks saw was becoming endemic in the U.S. Army in ETO. Not even battalion commanders were going to the front. From the Swiss border north to Geilenkirchen, the Americans were attacking. SHAEF put the pressure on Twelfth Army Group; Bradley passed it on to First, Third, and Ninth Armies; Hodges, Patton, and Simpson told their corps commanders to get results; by the time the pressure reached the battalion COs, it was intense. They raised it even higher as they set objectives for the rifle company COs. The trouble with all this pressure was that the senior officers and their staffs didn't know what they were ordering the rifle companies to do. They had seen neither the terrain nor the enemy. They did their work from maps and over radios and telephones. And unlike the company and platoon leaders, who had to be replaced every few weeks at best, and every few days at worst, the staff officers took few casualties, so the same men stayed at the same job, doing it badly.

In the First World War, a British staff officer from General Haig's headquarters visited the Somme battlefield, a week or so after the battle. The orders had been to attack, with objectives drawn up back at headquarters. The attacks had gone forward, through barbed wire, mud, mines, mortar, and machine-gun fire, fallen back with appalling loss, only to be ordered forward again. This had gone on for weeks. And the officer looked at the sea of mud and was shocked by his own ignorance. He cried out, "My God! Did we really send men to fight in this?"[16]

In the Second World War, the U.S. Army in ETO was getting disturbingly close to the British model of the earlier war. When the chase across France was on, senior commanders (although seldom their staffs) were often at the front, urging the men forward. But when the line became stationary, headquarters personnel from battalion on up to corps and army found themselves good billets and seldom strayed. Of course there were notable exceptions, but in general the American officers handing down the orders to attack and assigning the objective had no idea what it was like at the front. Any answer to why this happened would have to be a guess, and I have no statistics on front-line visits, but from what combat veterans from the fall campaigns have told me, it was only on the rarest of occasions that any officer above the rank of captain or officer from the staff was seen by them.

This was inexcusable. It was humiliating that a British general would have to order American staff officers and their COs to go see for themselves. It was costly to a heartbreaking degree. Tens of thousands of young Americans and Germans died in battles that November, battles that did little to hasten the end of the war and should have been avoided. If there was anything positive to these battles, it was that they gave the American commanders, from Eisenhower on down, the feeling that with all this pressure coming down on them, the Germans surely didn't have the resources to build a reserve for an offensive thrust.

Just south of Aachen lay the Hurtgen Forest. Roughly fifty square miles, it sat along the German-Belgian border, within a triangle outlined by Aachen, Monschau, and Düren. It was densely wooded, with fir trees twenty to thirty meters tall. They blocked the sun, so the forest floor was dark, damp, devoid of underbrush. The firs interlocked their lower limbs at less than two meters, so everyone had to stoop, all the time. It was like a green cave, always dripping water, low-roofed and forbidding. The terrain is rugged, a series of ridges and deep gorges formed by the numerous streams and rivers.

The Roer River ran along the eastern edge of the Hurtgen. Beyond it was the Rhine. First Army wanted to close to the Rhine, which General Hodges decided required driving the Germans out of the forest. Neither he nor his staff noted the obvious point that the Germans controlled the dams upstream on the Roer. If the Americans ever got down into the river valley, the Germans could release the dammed-up water and flood the valley. The forest could have been bypassed to the south, with the dams as the objective. The forest without the dams was worthless; the dams without the forest were priceless. But the generals got it backward, and went for the forest. Thus did the Battle of Hurtgen get started on the basis of a plan that was grossly, even criminally stupid.

It was fought under conditions as bad as American soldiers ever had to face, even including the Wilderness and the Meuse-Argonne. Sgt. George Morgan of the 4th Division described it: "The forest was a helluva eerie place to fight. You can't get protection. You can't see. You can't get fields of fire. Artillery slashes the trees like a scythe. Everything is tangled. You can scarcely walk. Everybody is cold and wet, and the mixture of cold rain and sleet keeps falling. They jump off again, and soon there is only a handful of the old men left."[17]

On September 19, the 3rd Armored Division and the 9th Infantry Division began the attack. The lieutenants and captains quickly learned that control of formations larger than platoons was nearly impossible. Troops more than a few feet apart couldn't see each other. There were no clearings, only narrow firebreaks and trails. Maps were almost useless. When the Germans, secure in their bunkers, saw the GIs coming forward, they called down presighted artillery fire, using shells with fuses designed to explode on contact with the treetops. When men dove to the ground for cover, as they had been trained to do and as instinct dictated, they exposed themselves to a rain of hot metal and wood splinters. They learned that to survive a shelling in the Hurtgen, hug a tree. That way they exposed only their steel helmets.

Tanks could barely move on the few roads, as they were too muddy, too heavily mined, too narrow. The tanks could not move at all off the roads. Airplanes couldn't fly. The artillery could shoot, but not very effectively, as FOs couldn't see ten meters to the front. The Americans could not use their assets—air, artillery, mobility. They were committed to a fight of mud and mines, carried out by infantry skirmish lines plunging ever deeper into the forest, with machine guns and light mortars their only support.

For the Germans, it was equally horrible. One enemy commander, Gen. Hans Schmidt of the 275th Infantry Division, called the forest a "weird and wild" place, where "the dark pine trees and the dense tree-tops give the forest even in the daytime a somber appearance which is apt to cast gloom upon sensitive people."[18] Gen. Paul Mahlmann, commanding the 353d Infantry Division, said his troops "were fighting in deplorable conditions, exposed to incessant enemy fire, fighting daily without relief, receiving little support from their own artillery, drenched by frequent rain, and without the possibility of changing clothes." He went on, "Forsaken as they were they had no choice but to hold out in hopeless resignation."[19]

For the GIs, it was a calamity. In their September action, the 9th and 2nd Armored lost up to 80 percent of their front-line troops, and gained almost nothing. In October, the 9th—reinforced—tried again, but by mid-month it was dead in the water and had suffered terribly. Casualties were around 4,500 for an advance of 3,000 meters. German losses were somewhat less, around 3,300.

Staff officers were learning, if slowly. On the last day of October, the staff of the 9th Division issued a five-page report, "Notes on Woods Fighting." Troops already in the line and still alive knew what the lessons were, but the report was valuable to new units and replacements being fed into the forest. It urged training in forest fighting prior to commitment, said to press against a tree when the shelling began, advised that night operations were physically impossible, suggested never traveling in the woods without a compass, and advised never sending reinforcements forward in the midst of a battle or shelling.[20]

Call it off! That's what the GIs wanted to tell the generals, but the generals shook their heads and said, Attack. On November 2, the 28th Infantry Division took it up. Maj. Gen. Norman Cota, one of the heroes of D-Day, was the CO. The 28th was the Pennsylvania National Guard and was called the "Keystone Division." Referring to the red keystone shoulder patch, the Germans took to calling it the "Bloody Bucket Division."

It tried to move forward, but it was like walking into hell. From their bunkers, the Germans sent forth a hail of machine-gun and rifle fire, and mortars. The GIs were caught in thick minefields. Everything was mud and fir trees. The attack stalled.

"The days were so terrible that I would pray for darkness," Pvt. Clarence Blakeslee recalled, "and the nights were so bad I would pray for daylight."[21] Lt. John Forsell, K Company, 110th Infantry, 28th Division, had a macabre day-night experience. He was outside the village of Schmidt, which was no-man's-land. "Daily we would check the houses," he explained. "The Germans patrolled the same town at night. One morning our patrol came into town and found a G.I. hung on the Crucifixion Cross. We cut him down. We stayed in town and hid in a few houses waiting for the Germans. A German patrol came in, we had a gunfight, they were caught by surprise. A few of the patrol got away but we took three Germans and hung them on three crosses. That ended that little fanfare for both sides in Schmidt."[22]

For two weeks, the 28th kept attacking, as ordered. On November 5, division sent down orders to move tanks down a road called the Kall trail. But no staff officer had gone forward to assess the situation in person, and in fact the "trail" was all mud and anyway blocked by felled trees and disabled tanks. The attack led only to loss.

There were men who broke under the strain, and there were heroes. On November 5, the Germans counterattacked. An unknown GI dashed out of his foxhole, took a bazooka from a dead soldier, and engaged two German tanks. He fired from a range of twenty-five meters and put one tank out of action. He was never seen again.

On November 6, an entire company passed the breaking point. An all-night shelling had caused numerous casualties. At dawn, a German counterattack began. When the small-arms fire erupted from the woods, the men could endure no more. First one, then another, then two and three together, began to run to the rear. Capt. Joe Pruden was sympathetic: "They had just had too much. Their endurance could stand no more." But he knew he had to stop them, get them to turn and face the enemy. Along with other officers at the CP, he tried. But the men were "pushing, shoving, throwing away equipment, trying to outrun the artillery and each other in a frantic effort to escape. They were all scared." He saw badly wounded men lying where they fell, crying out for medics, being ignored.[23]

The 28th's lieutenants kept leading. By November 13 all the officers in the rifle companies had been killed or wounded. Most of them were within a year of their twentieth birthday. Overall in the Hurtgen, the 28th Division suffered 6,184 combat casualties, plus 738 cases of trench foot and 620 battle fatigue cases. Those figures mean that virtually every front-line soldier was a casualty.

Col. Ralph Ingersoll of First Army staff met with lieutenants who had just come out of the Hurtgen: "They did not talk; they just sat across the table or on the edge of your cot and looked at you very straight and unblinking with absolutely no expression in their faces, which were neither tense nor relaxed but completely apathetic. They looked, unblinking."[24]

Bradley and Hodges remained resolute to take the Hurtgen. They put in the 4th Infantry Division. It had led the way onto Utah Beach on June 6, and gone through a score of battles since. Not many D-Day veterans were still with the division—most were dead or badly wounded. In the Hurtgen, the division poured out its lifeblood once again.

Lt. George Wilson was in the battle. He described German methods. Whenever they pulled back under pressure, they called down shelling on the positions they had just left as they occupied prepared bunkers a few hundred meters to the rear. "Their new line usually gave them command of everything in front, being perhaps on an upward slope or near the lip of a ravine. Their bunkers were made of thick logs with a few feet of dirt on top. They were almost immune to artillery. They might as well have been concrete. There was no chance of our tanks getting anywhere near them for direct fire." Therefore, Wilson realized, "the infantry had to take them the hard way, going in after them one at a time, through barbed wire."

Lieutenant Wilson had become company CO through attrition. His orders were to attack. He tried. His men managed to knock out a machine gun. Then he got on the radio to talk to Lt. Col. Thomas Kenan at battalion. Wilson carefully explained his situation: all his officers were gone, he had many wounded who needed evacuation, his ammunition was almost gone. "I said I didn't see how we could continue in this condition against such a formidable enemy defense. It seemed to me I was completely objective, simply listing the plain facts, and that my assessment was correct."

Colonel Kenan replied, "Wilson, ammo is on the way over now. I know what you're up against, and I know *you can and will* continue to advance and take that line of defense." And hung up.

The ammo arrived. Wilson attacked. His company managed to advance about 500 meters. The Germans fell back to their next MLR. Wilson commented, "It was extremely costly yardage, possibly the most expensive real estate in the world, and we never could have gone the other 1,500 yards to the original objective" set by Kenan.[25]

Between November 7 and December 3, the 4th Division lost over 7,000 men, or about ten per company per day. "Replacements flowed in to compensate for the losses," Michael Doubler comments, "but the Hurtgen's voracious appetite for casualties was greater than the army's ability to provide new troops."[26] Lieutenant Wilson recorded his company losses at 167 percent for enlisted men. "We had started with a full company of about 162 men and had lost about 287."[27]

Sgt. Mack Morris was there with the 4th: "Hurtgen had its firebreaks, only wide enough to allow two jeeps to pass, and they were mined and interdicted by machine-gun fire. There was a Teller mine every eight paces for three miles. Hurtgen's roads were blocked. The Germans cut roadblocks from trees. They cut them down so they interlocked as they fell. Then they mined and booby trapped them. Finally they registered their artillery on them, and the mortars, and at the sound of men clearing them they opened fire. Their strong points were constructed carefully, and inside them were neat bunks built of forest wood, and the walls of the bunkers were panelled with wood. These sheltered the defenders. Outside the bunkers were their defensive positions."[28]

First Army put the 8th Infantry Division into the attack. On November 27, it closed to the town of Hurtgen, the original objective of the offensive when it began in mid-September. It fell to Lt. Paul Boesch, Company G, 121st Infantry, to take the town. At dawn on November 28, Boesch put one of his lieutenants to the left side of the road leading to town, while he took the other platoon to the other side. Boesch ran from man to man, explaining what the company was about to do. When he gave the signal, they charged. "It was sheer pandemonium," he recalled. Once out of that damned forest, the men went mad with battle lust.

Boesch described it as "a wild, terrible, awe-inspiring thing. We dashed, struggled from one building to another shooting, bayoneting, clubbing. Hand grenades roared, fires cracked, buildings to the left and right burned with acrid smoke. Dust, smoke, and powder filled our lungs, making us cough, spit. Automatic weapons chattered while heavier throats of mortars and artillery disgorged deafening explosions. The wounded and dead—men in the uniforms of both sides—lay in grotesque positions at every turn."

American tanks supported Boesch's company. He remembered that they would first spray the buildings with their .50-calibers, then use their 75s to blow holes for use by the infantry. "We hurled ourselves through the holes or through windows or splintered doors. Then it became a battle from floor to floor—from room to room." The company took nearly 300 prisoners.

As the battle sputtered to a close, Boesch "started to shake, and it wasn't the cold. I realized that I had not been afraid during that whole day. Not once did I feel afraid. I was busy as hell, and that occupied my mind. But when I shook, visibly, on that floor with a roof at least two feet thick over my head, I was hoping that I would not forget to be afraid because that was the best way to stay alive, to not make careless moves." He was wounded later that night by a German shell and was sent to a hospital in the States.[29]

The 8th Division didn't get far beyond Hurtgen. By December 3, it was used up. A staff officer from regiment was shocked when he visited the front that day. He reported, "The men of this battalion are physically exhausted. The spirit and will to fight are there; the ability to continue is gone. These men have been fighting without rest or sleep for four days and last night had to lie unprotected from the weather in an open field. They are shivering with cold, and their hands are so numb that they have to help one another on with their equipment. I firmly believe that every man up there should be evacuated through medical channels."[30] Many had trench foot, all had bad colds or worse, plus diarrhea.

In late November the 2nd Ranger Battalion entered the forest. Following its heavy losses at Pointe-du-Hoc and Omaha Beach on D-Day, and an equally costly campaign in Normandy, the battalion had gone to Brest, then back to northern France. It had been attached to various divisions and corps, as needed.

Although the battalion had taken more than 100 percent casualties, the core of the force that Lt. Col. James Earl Rudder had led ashore on June 6 was still there. Capt. Sidney Salomon, who had led a platoon onto Omaha Beach, was now CO of B Company. Lt. Len Lomell, who had destroyed the big guns at Pointe-du-Hoc at 0830 on D-Day, had been given a battlefield commission, the first Ranger to be so honored. Lt. James Eikner, who used a World War I signal lamp on D-Day to direct naval gunfire, was in charge of Rudder's communications. Sgt. Leo Lisko, who had operated the lamp (and is today the Ranger historian), was there. Altogether the battalion had 485 enlisted men and twenty-seven officers, less than half the size of a full-strength infantry battalion.[31]

The battalion was assigned to the 28th Division in the Hurtgen. Rudder, Eikner, and the others were disappointed. Eikner explained, "We were a very specialized unit. All volunteers—highly trained in special missions—putting us out on a front line in a defensive position wasn't utilizing our skills and capabilities. The attrition not only from the shelling but also from the weather, the trench foot, just sitting there in those foxholes making a furor every now and then and a little scrap now and then—we were very disappointed about this."[32]

As the battalion moved into the line, it took casualties from mines and artillery. Then the men sat in foxholes and took a pounding. This wasn't the Rangers' idea of war at all.

On December 6, opportunity arrived. Hill 400 (named after its height in meters) was on the eastern edge of the forest, and therefore was the ultimate objective of the campaign. It was the highest point in the area and provided excellent observation of the Roer River less than a kilometer to the east, and of the mixed farmland and forest around it. The Germans had utilized it so effectively that neither GIs nor vehicles moved during the day (as the Rangers replaced a battalion of the 28th, around midnight, they were warned that the slightest movement in the daytime would bring down 88s and mortars). The village of Bergstein huddled at the base of the hill.

First Army had thrown four divisions at Hill 400. Concentrated artillery fire, and when the weather was suitable fighter-bomber attacks, preceded each attempt to drive the Germans off the hill. In every instance the Germans had come up out of their bunkers, manned their weapons, and stopped the slowly advancing line of American skirmishers. Then artillery and mortar fire began exploding among the prostrate GIs, who fell back. Hundreds had been sacrificed, with no gain.

Something new had to be tried. On December 6, the desperate 8th Division commander asked for the Rangers. At the same moment, Ranger leadership was changing. Rudder had been put in command of the 109th Infantry Regiment. His executive officer, Capt. George Williams, was at division headquarters, where the CO had just told him to attack the hill at 0300, December 7. Williams convinced the CO to wait until dawn. The CO wanted to lay in an artillery barrage. Williams indicated that the Rangers would rather have surprise than explosives. He explained that the Rangers had trained to do things a bit differently. As Lieutenant Lomell put it, "Our Rangers tactics seemed to be needed, stealthful and speedy infiltration and surprise assaults where they were not expected at first light. The bigger outfits were too visible. We could sneak into the line."[33] When he returned to Ranger hq, Williams learned that Rudder was leaving. Rudder promoted him to major, talked to him about the upcoming attack, and went on to his new duties.

Shortly after midnight, the Rangers marched to Bergstein. They were shelled by harassing fire on the road. Eikner commented that "it reminded me of one of the old World War I movies that showed units under shell fire at night."[34] As they approached Bergstein, Sgt. Earl Lutz came out from the village to guide them in. "I was told to go to a certain road," Lutz recalled. "I got to the road but there was nothing to be seen, no sound, not even a cricket. I guess I swore a little, and the Rangers raised up all around me."[35]

In town, the Rangers replaced the 47th Armored Infantry Battalion, 8th Division. There was no ceremony. Three Ranger lieutenants showed up at the 47th's CP. "They asked for enemy positions and the road to take; said they were ready to go. We talked the situation over. They stopped and said, 'Let's go, men.' We heard the tommy guns click and, without a word, the Rangers moved out. Our morale went up in a hurry."[36]

By 0300 three companies of Rangers—A, B, and C—had dug in on the edge of a wood, near the base of the hill. Companies D, E, and F took possession of Bergstein and dug in around it. The companies near the hill prepared to charge it at first light. They could hit the hill through open fields of some 100 meters wide, exposing themselves to enemy small-arms and mortar fire, or try a flanking move through known minefields. Major Williams choose the open field. The men fixed bayonets. Sgt. Bill Petty, who had distinguished himself on D-Day, recalled that "tension was building up to the exploding point."[37]

At first light, shouting "Let's go get the bastards!," and firing from the hip, the Rangers charged. They got through the snow-covered field despite the small-arms and mortar fire, and started up the hill. Four machine guns were firing point-blank on the Rangers, who kept moving up the hill, yelling and firing. Sgt. Bud Potratz remembered hollering, "Hi ho, Silver!"[38]

Those who were at Pointe-du-Hoc on D-Day recall Hill 400 as worse. It was not as precipitous, but it was rocky shale, with frost and snow on it, and they had no grappling hooks or ropes. It was hand-over-hand, using the third hand to keep up a stream of fire.

The Germans were caught by surprise. They had good troops on the hill, but not good enough. Ranger small-arms fire kept them pinned down, while other Rangers tossed grenades into the bunkers. Months later, Sgt. Forrest Pogue of the Historical Section interviewed Williams. (It was March 21, 1945, in Germany on the far side of the Rhine. Pogue noted that Williams's statements were "hurried," because he was preparing for a night problem—those Rangers never stopped training.) Williams told Pogue how it was done: "We took the hill by rushing it. One squad of D Co. went over the top of the hill down towards the front. This group didn't have many casualties, although the next group was hard hit."[39]

When Sergeant Petty reached the top of the hill, he "found a situation of turmoil." With another Ranger named Anderson, he approached the main bunker and heard Germans inside. They pushed open the door and tossed in two grenades. Just as they were ready to rush in and spray the room with their BAR, a shell exploded a few feet away—the Germans were firing on their own position. The explosion blew Anderson into Petty's arms. He was dead, killed instantly by a big piece of shrapnel in his heart.

One squad chased the remaining Germans down the hill, almost to the Roer River, then pulled back to the top, where the Rangers were trying to dig in. It was all but impossible on the slippery shale. It was 0830. The shelling intensified. Rangers took shelter in the bunkers and waited for the inevitable counterattack. Petty recovered Anderson's dying brother and "had the dubious distinction of having hold of both brothers while they were in the process of dying within an hour's time."[40]

At 0930, the first of five counterattacks that day began. They came mostly from the south and east, where woods extended to the base of the hill and gave the Germans cover almost all the way, in company-size strength. Major Williams told Pogue, "In some cases Germans were in and around the bunker on the hill before the Rangers were aware of their presence. Once on the hill they attempted to rush the positions. They used machine guns, burp guns, rifles, and threw potato masher grenades. Hand-to-hand fights developed on top of the hill in which some use was made of bayonets."

The Germans simultaneously attacked the town, where Williams had his hq. "They had direct fire of 88s, self-propelled guns, mortars, and artillery, and they attacked from all sides. Five of them got within 100 yards of the church, which was being used as a first aid station." Williams added that he learned that day, "If you want to hold a town, you must stay outside it. Companies A, B, and C stayed outside Bergstein and got very few casualties."[41] (German doctrine was the opposite: hold the center was their idea.)

Through the day and into the night the Germans attacked Hill 400. Field Marshal Model offered Iron Crosses and two weeks' leave to any of his men who could retake the hill. At times, Lieutenant Lomell remembered, "we were outnumbered ten to one. We had no protection, continuous tons of shrapnel falling upon us, hundreds of rounds coming in." At one point, Lomell saw his platoon sergeant, Ed Secor, "a very quiet man, out of ammo and unarmed, seize two machine pistols from wounded Germans and in desperation charge a large German patrol, firing and screaming at them.

His few remaining men rallied to the cause and together they drove the Germans back down the hill."

Lomell is a legend among the Rangers for what he did on D-Day. In 1995 he commented, "June 6, 1944, was not my longest day. December 7th, 1944, was my longest and most miserable day on earth during my past 75 years."[42]

As Ranger numbers dwindled and ammunition began to run out, the American artillery saved the men. The field of vision was such that the forward observer, Lt. Howard Kettlehut from the 56th Armored Field Artillery Battalion, could call in fire all around the hill. The Rangers later said Kettlehut was "the best man we ever worked with." Or as Williams put it to Pogue, "At one point Kettlehut brought down fire from all artillery available in Corps—18 battalions in all; 155s, 75s, self-propelled, 8-inch, and 240mm guns placed a ring of explosive shells around the hill."[43]

During the night, ammo bearers got to the top of the hill, and brought down wounded on litters—terribly difficult on the snow, ice, and rocks. The combined strength of the three companies left on top was five officers and eighty-six men. Lomell was wounded.

Just after daylight, the Germans shelled the town and the hill. On the hill it was "of such intensity that one explosion would cover the sound of the next approaching shell." But when the Germans attacked with infantry, a combination of the shells called in by Kettlehut and the small-arms fire of the Rangers drove them back.

Late on December 8, an infantry regiment and tank destroyer battalion relieved the surviving Rangers. A week and two days later, the Germans retook the hill. Not until February 1945 did the Americans get it back. The Rangers had suffered 90 percent casualties and would once again have to be rebuilt.

With the Battle of Hill 400, the Hurtgen campaign came to a close. The Americans did not have the dams upstream, so they dared not debouch down into the valley. The forest they held, for which they had paid such a high price, was worthless.

The Battle of Hurtgen lasted ninety days. Nine divisions plus supporting units on the American side were involved, more men than Meade had at Gettysburg. The losses were comparable to Gettysburg, too, or the Wilderness. There were more than 24,000 combat casualties, another 9,000 victims of trench foot, disease, or combat exhaustion.

In February 1945 the 82nd Airborne followed a retreating German army through the forest. The 505th PIR got into the town of Schmidt, which had changed hands many times during the battle. The history of the 505th noted that "throughout Sicily, Italy, Normandy and Holland this unit has seen the devastation of war, but never anything to compare with this. There were tanks, tank destroyers, jeeps, 2½ ton trucks, other vehicles and all sorts of GI equipment as well as countless American dead. It was no wonder the men referred to this as death valley."[44]

Gen. Rolf von Gersdorff commented after the war, "I have engaged in the long campaigns in Russia as well as other fronts and I believe the fighting in the Hurtgen was the heaviest I have ever witnessed."[45] Still, the Germans were delighted that the Americans wanted to throw their weight into an attack against dug-in troops in a forest.

What had gone wrong? Not only at Hurtgen but up north, too, where the Ninth Army pounded against the Siegfried Line. Capt. John O'Grady of Ninth Army's Historical Section provided some of the answer. He was at headquarters, 3rd Battalion, 333rd Infantry, in late November. He sent a memorandum back to Ninth Army: "On 23rd November the battalion was attacking a superior German force entrenched on an excellent position. The only thing that higher headquarters contributed to the debacle was pressure, and God only knows where the pressure started, perhaps Corps or perhaps Army. It had the effect of ordering men to die needlessly."

O'Grady was furious: "Tactics and maneuver on battalion or regiment scale were conspicuous by their absence. It never seemed to occur to anyone that the plan might be wrong; but rather the indictment was placed on the small unit commanders and the men who were doing the fighting. The companies went into battle against the formidable Siegfried Line with hand grenades and rifle bullets against pillboxes. The 84th Division walked into the most touted defensive line in modern warfare without so much as the benefit of a briefing by combat officers."[46]

The Americans took the forest but lost the Battle of Hurtgen, and too many good men. The battle did not shorten the war by one minute. For those reasons, it is remembered today by those who were there. The Americans had taken Aachen and Metz, and the Hurtgen, but at such a cost, in time and lives, that for those who were not there these great battles are hard to recall. As Lieutenant

Lomell put it, "The months-long battle of the Hurtgen Forest was a loser that our top brass ever after never seemed to want to talk about."[47]

On December 8, from the OP (observation post) on Hill 400, Lieutenant Eikner remembered "we could see across the Roer River to a town called Nideggen. Trains were puffing in there and bringing in troops and all."[48]

They were heading south. Eikner had cause to feel discouraged; if after all that pounding the Germans were building a reserve somewhere to the south, why then it was the Germans, not the Americans, who had won the battles of attrition in the fall of 1944. The Americans had no reserve at all, save the 82nd and 101st Airborne, which were near Reims being brought up to strength after the Holland campaign. Every other division in ETO was committed to offensive action.

7

The Ardennes

December 16–19, 1944

WHEN THE AMERICANS reached the German border, their best intelligence sources dried up. Inside Germany the Wehrmacht used secure telephone lines rather than radio, which rendered Ultra deaf and blind. Local inquiry in France had given superb intelligence; at the German border, civilians shrugged and shook their heads when asked questions. Early December weather kept the reconnaissance aircraft on the ground. And in the Ardennes, patrols were rare and seldom aggressive, as each side was willing to leave the other alone so long as things stayed quiet.

As a result, the GIs in the Ardennes, like the American intelligence apparatus as a whole, were no better off in the intelligence field than Billy Yank had been eighty years earlier. But owing to complacency and smugness, almost no one worried about it. As Twenty-first Army Group's intelligence summary on December 16, 1944, put it, "The enemy is at present fighting a defensive campaign on all fronts; his situation is such that he cannot stage major offensive operations."[1]

Certainly not in the Ardennes, where the line had been stagnant and the guns mostly quiet for two months. In late October 1944, Lt. Robert Merriman of the Army's Historical Section had been in a jeep headed south along Skyline Drive, a ridgeline on the eastern edge of the Ardennes, just west of the Our River, which was the German-Belgian border. "All was peaceful," he recalled. "Farmers in the fields along the road were plowing their fields for the winter fallow, and some were taking in the last of the summer harvest; cattle were grazing lazily."[2]

A few Americans learned that the pastoral scene was deceiving. P-47 pilot Capt. Jack Barensfeld had flown more than eighty missions between D-Day and mid-December. On the 14th, he flew over the wooded area of the Eifel, on the German side of the Our River. The briefing officer had assured the pilots that the place was benign, but "a great amount of anti-aircraft fire came up. One of our pilots was hit and killed." Barensfeld reported the incident, but no one thought anything of the surprising amount of AA the Germans had in this quiet area.[3]

Capt. Franklin Anderson of the 4th Division was in a wood near St.-Vith, Belgium, on December 14. He went into town to purchase some orange soda at the local bottling plant. There was a crowd of agitated people in the town square. Anderson asked the owner of the plant, who spoke excellent English, "What's going on?"

The man replied, "They think the Germans are going to be back here soon." Anderson asked why. "The Boche always come through the Ardennes. Now there is activity, noise, and so forth over to the east, and they are worried." Anderson reported the conversation to his CO, adding other details: Elise Dele, a Belgian woman who had visited relatives on the German side of the border, reported intense activity. She saw rubber boats, bridging equipment, and more. A patrol brought in a Polish soldier who had been conscripted into the German army, who warned of an impending attack. Anderson's CO sent the information on to battalion, who passed it along to division intelligence. There it died.[4] Human intelligence made little impression on these twentieth-century warriors, who had signal intelligence to keep them apprised of the enemy's order of battle.

Intelligence makes no decisions. The mind-set of the people receiving the information is more important than the intelligence itself. In early December, Eisenhower reviewed the situation on the Western Front with Bradley. His overwhelming goal was to strengthen U.S. First and Ninth Armies to continue the winter offensive north of Aachen. He was preparing to strip divisions from

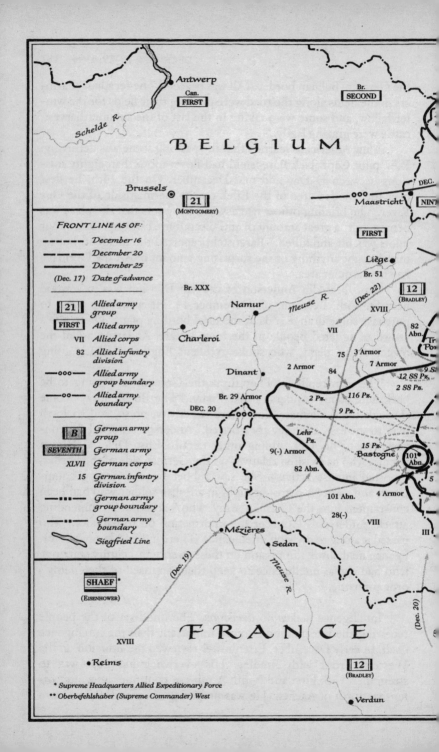

Antwerp

Can.
FIRST

Br.
SECOND

Schelde R.

BELGIUM

Brussels ⊚

21
(MONTGOMERY)

DEC.

○○○

Maastricht

NINT

FRONT LINE AS OF:

- – – – – December 16
- ——— December 20
- ━━━ December 25
- (Dec. 17) Date of advance

21 Allied army group

FIRST Allied army

VII Allied corps

82 Allied infantry division

─○○○─ Allied army group boundary

─○○─ Allied army boundary

B German army group

SEVENTH German army

XLVII German corps

15 German infantry division

─■■■─ German army group boundary

─■■─ German army boundary

⌇⌇⌇ Siegfried Line

FIRST

Liège ●

Br. 51

(Dec. 22)

12
(BRADLEY)

Br. XXX

Namur

Meuse R.

XVIII

VII

Charleroi

75

3 Armor

82
Abn.

Tr
Po

7 Armor

12 SS
2 SS Ps.

Dinant

2 Armor

84

116 Ps.

Br. 29 Armor

2 Ps.

9 Ps.

DEC. 20

○○○

Lehr
Ps.

15 Ps.

Bastogne

101
Abn.

9(-) Armor

82 Abn.

4 Armor

101 Abn.

28(-)

VIII

III

Mézières ●

● Sedan

Meuse R.

SHAEF ●

(EISENHOWER)

(Dec. 19)

(Dec. 20)

XVIII

FRANCE

● Reims

12
(BRADLEY)

* Supreme Headquarters Allied Expeditionary Force

** Oberbefehlshaber (Supreme Commander) West

● Verdun

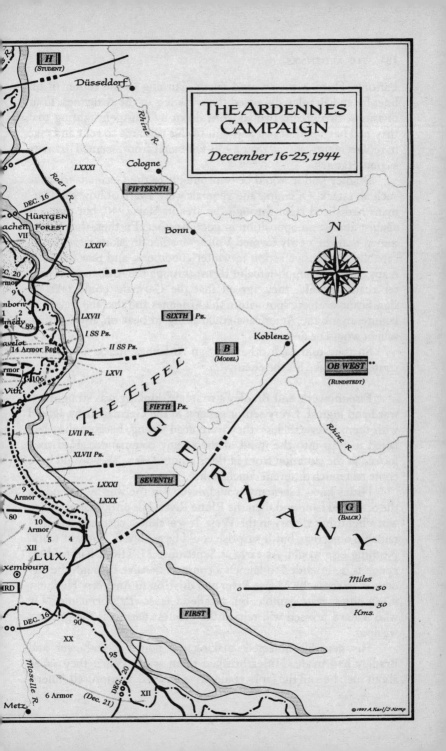

THE ARDENNES CAMPAIGN

December 16–25, 1944

Düsseldorf

H (STUDENT)

Rhine R.

LXXXI

Cologne

FIFTEENTH

Roer R.

DEC. 16

HÜRTGEN FOREST

Aachen

VII

LXXIV

Bonn

N

DEC. 20

Armor

9

nborn

1   2   89

rnedy

avelot

14 Armor Regt

rmor

106

Vith

LXVII

I SS Ps.

II SS Ps.

LXVI

SIXTH Ps.

Koblenz

B (MODEL)

OB WEST **

(RUNDSTEDT)

THE EIFEL

FIFTH Ps.

GERMANY

LVII Ps.

XLVII Ps.

SEVENTH

LXXXI

LXXX

Rhine R.

G (BALCK)

9
Armor

80

10
Armor

5   4

XII

LUX.

xembourg

RD

DEC. 16

90

XX

95

DEC. 20

6 Armor (Dec. 21)   XII

Metz

Moselle R.

FIRST

Miles
0 ———————— 30

Kms.
0 ———————— 30

© 1997 A. Karl / J. Kemp

Patton's Third Army to send north. Turning to the center of his line, he and Bradley discussed the weakness in the Ardennes. Four divisions, two green, two so worn down by Hurtgen fighting that they had been withdrawn and sent to this rest area to refit and take in replacements, spread over a 150-kilometer front, seemed to invite a counterattack.

Bradley said it would be unprofitable to the Germans to make such an attack. Of course the generals were aware of how the Germans had sliced right through the area in May 1940, but that was against almost no opposition in good weather. Further, they determined that the newly formed Volksgrenadier divisions were hardly capable of offensive action in winter conditions, and that the Germans could not supply a major thrust through the Ardennes on winter roads. Finally, they agreed that the Germans could take no significant strategic spot within the Ardennes and that the weight of counterattack the Americans could bring to bear on any German salient would be decisive.

So they told each other that an Ardennes attack would be a strategic mistake for the enemy.[5]

Eisenhower's and Bradley's strategic thinking was straightforward and logical. Every senior general in the German army agreed with them. Nevertheless, they were dead wrong, because they had failed to leap into the mind of the enemy commander. Had they looked at the situation from Hitler's point of view, they would have come to a much different conclusion.

Hitler knew Germany would never win the war by defending the Siegfried Line and then the Rhine River. His only chance was to win a lightning victory in the West. It was almost certainly an unattainable objective, but if surprise could be achieved, it might work. Nothing else would. As early as September 25, Hitler had told his generals he intended to launch a counteroffensive through the Ardennes to cross the Meuse River and drive on to Antwerp. He knew it was a desperate gamble, but recalled Clausewitz's principle: "He who is hard pressed will regard the greatest daring as the greatest wisdom."

His generals objected, making the points Eisenhower and Bradley had made. Hitler brushed them aside. When they asked about fuel, he said the tanks could drive forward on captured American gasoline. He promised new divisions with new equipment, and the biggest gathering of the Luftwaffe in three years.

Hitler said the German onslaught would divide the British and American forces. When the Germans took Antwerp, the British would have to pull another Dunkirk. Then he could take divisions from the West to reinforce the Eastern Front. Seeing all this, Stalin would conclude a peace, based on a division of Eastern Europe, à la 1939. Nazi Germany would not win the war, but it would survive.

Here was the old führer, all full of himself, exploding with energy, barking out orders, threats, questions, back on the offensive. The remembrance of those glorious spring days in May 1940 almost overwhelmed him. It could be done again. It could! It was a matter of will.[6]

To provide the will, Hitler counted on the children. The German soldiers of December 1944 were mostly born between 1925 and 1928. They had been deliberately raised by the Nazis for this moment, and they had that fanatical bravery their führer counted on.

They were well equipped. Hitler brought men, tanks, and planes from the Eastern Front for his offensive, and assigned the greater portion of new weapons to the Ardennes. There were only two-thirds as many panzers on the Eastern Front as in the West. The Luftwaffe managed to gather 1,500 planes (although it never managed to get more than 800 in the air at one time, and usually fewer than sixty per day). Of all the fighting vehicles that came out of German assembly plants in November and December 1944, the best production months of the war for German industry, the Eastern Front got 919 while the Ardennes received 2,277. Manpower climbed in the West from 416,000 on December 1 to 1,322,000 on December 15. Overall the Germans had a three-to-one advantage in the Ardennes, ten-to-one in assault areas.[7]

American aircraft greatly outnumbered the Luftwaffe, not even counting the B-17s. American artillery greatly outnumbered the Wehrmacht. The American road transportation capability was vastly superior to that of the Germans, something partly compensated for by the German rail system, which was highly effective despite frequent bombing raids.

Impressive though the German buildup in the Eifel was, it was not a force capable of reaching its objectives on its own resources. It would depend on achieving surprise, the speed of the advance once through the American lines, a slow American response, captured American stocks, on creating a panic among retreating American troops, and bad weather to neutralize the Allied air forces. That was a long list. Hitler had managed to gather together in the Eifel a force big enough to have the slimmest of chances of achieving the objective. He had also managed to achieve surprise, through a combination of skill, secretiveness, and a too-tight security. Hitler forbade patrols in the final days, for fear of what some captured member might tell the Americans; as a result, the Germans attacked, in Maj. Heinz-Günter Guderian's words, "into the dark."[8] They didn't know, for example, that the 2nd Division had come to the Ardennes front alongside the 99th.

Using many of the same techniques the Allies had used to fool the Germans about the time and place of the cross-Channel attack in June—the creation of fictitious units, false radio traffic, and playing on preconceptions that the German buildup on the Western Front was in support of a counterattack north of Aachen—Hitler gave the Americans a sense of security about the Ardennes. On the eve of the opening action in the greatest battle the U.S. Army has ever fought, not a single soldier in that army had the slightest sense of what was about to happen.

Hitler counted on those soldiers to be green, poorly motivated and poorly trained, recently arrived replacements, cowardly. Despite the pounding the Wehrmacht had taken in France, Hitler remained contemptuous of the American Army. He thought the Allies had won in France only because of overwhelming air and matériel superiority. In Belgium, weather would cancel out the air, and as for matériel the Germans could capture and use American gasoline and the made-in-the-U.S.A. weapons and equipment.

Across from the Eifel the American troops were a mixed lot. The 2nd Infantry Division, in nearly continuous battle since June 7, was moving through the 99th Division on its way to attack the Roer River dams from the south. The 2nd had been in Hurtgen, so it had many more replacements than veterans, but it had a core of experienced company commanders and platoon leaders as well as headquarters personnel. The 99th, and another newly arrived division, the 106th, placed in the line to its right, had few experienced personnel. The 99th had suffered immense turnover at all ranks and grades during the period immediately preceding its movement overseas. There was little or no unit cohesion. And most of the rifle-men were only partially trained. They had been committed to the front line without the benefit of experience gained in maneuvers. But at least the division had spent sufficient time at the front—it had occupied the line from Monschau, Germany, to Losheimergraben since early November—to have toughened up. It ran patrols, made mistakes, learned from them. But the general attitude, as expressed by one soldier, was "The German troops facing us were of low qual-ity and appeared to be of the opinion that if we didn't bother them, they would leave us alone."[9]

The weather was cold, the days dreary and snowy. The men in the foxholes were eating snow because their canteens were empty. They could not build fires, so rations were cold. Clothes were World War I issue and entirely inadequate.

Always hungry, the men of Charlie Company, 395th Regi-ment, tried to supplement their diet with venison. Pvt. Vernon Swanson went after the locally abundant deer with his BAR (a com-mon practice for GIs in Belgium that winter). He dropped one, but the deer was only wounded. "We followed the blood trail for quite a distance into German territory and then discovered the Germans had stolen our deer. Fortunately cooler heads prevailed and we did not send a combat patrol to recover our deer."

But they weren't a bunch of guys out on a camping and hunting trip. The 99th Division took casualties, suffering 187 killed and wounded in November. The weather took a heavier toll—822 hos-pitalized for frostbite, pneumonia, and trench foot. In the front line the night of December 15–16, the men of Charlie Company shiv-ered in their holes as they tried to suppress their coughing. Private Swanson recalled, "During the night we were completely on edge because of a mixture of hunger, cold and fear." The fear was caused by a rumor that German patrols were active. At 2330 hours, a ran-dom barrage of some thirty shells landed in the company area, killing Pvt. Saul Kokotovich.[10]

Capt. Charles Roland was a battalion executive officer in the 99th. Looking out of the headquarters bunker on the afternoon of December 15, he saw "fir forests whose cone-shaped evergreens standing in deep snow and sparkling with crystals formed a scene of marvelous beauty." Going back inside, he read the latest intelligence report from division: "The enemy has only a handful of beaten and demoralized troops in front of us and they are being supported by only two pieces of horse-drawn artillery."

In fact, the 394th Regiment was facing the I SS Panzer Corps, hidden in those beautiful firs. This was an intelligence failure of the first magnitude.[11]

As darkness fell over the Eifel on December 15, a kilometer or so east of Captain Roland, a private in the Waffen SS wrote his daily letter to his sister Ruth. "I write during one of the great hours before an attack—full of unrest, full of expectation for what the next days will bring. Everyone who has been here the last two days and nights (especially nights), who has witnessed hour after hour the assembly of our crack divisions, who has heard the constant rattling of panzers, knows that something is up and we are looking forward to a clear order to reduce the tension. Some believe in big wonders, but that may be shortsighted! It is enough to know we attack and will throw the enemy from our homeland."

Later, just before dawn, he added, "Overhead is the terrific noise of V-1, of artillery—the voice of war. So long now—wish me luck and think of me." He sealed the envelope and was about to hand it in when he added a scribble on the back: "Ruth! Ruth! Ruth! WE MARCH!!!"[12]

The private was in the van of the 1st SS Panzer Division and had cause to feel elated, for he was part of a powerful reinforced armored regiment commanded by Lt. Col. Jochen Peiper. Highly regarded in the German army, Peiper was a veteran of many battles on the Eastern Front. Aggressive and admired, he had no patience with incompetence and was single-minded in his pursuit of victory. When U.S. Army historian Maj. Ken Hechler interviewed him in September 1945, Peiper struck Hechler as "a very arrogant, typical SS man."[13] Hitler counted on him to lead the dash to the Meuse.

The Waffen SS had a mixed reception within the German army. Many veterans say they were always glad to have one of the SS units on their flank. Others resented them because they got first pick on new equipment and recruits (by this stage of the war, the Waffen SS was no longer a strictly volunteer force). Professional officers were sometimes brutal in their remarks. One German division commander said of the SS: "These units—unduly boastful and arrogant anyway—with their total lack of discipline so typical for them, their well-known unreserved ruthlessness, paired with a considerable lack of reason, had a down-right devastating effect and in all cases proved a handicap for any systematic conduct of fighting."[14]

Although designated a regiment, Peiper's force contained some 22,000 men and 250 tanks (many of them right off the assembly line and including sixty Tigers), five anti-aircraft half-tracks, a battalion of 20mm guns, twenty-five self-propelled guns, a battalion of 105 howitzers, and two companies of engineers. As soon as the infantry opened the roads Peiper's force would speed west, toward the Meuse.[15]

Maj. Otto Skorzeny, the most daring commando in the German army, world-famous for his exploits, was accompanying Peiper, along with the 500 men in the 150th Panzer Brigade. They were wearing American and British uniforms. All of them spoke English; most of them had lived for some time in Britain or the United States. They had dog tags taken from corpses and POWs. They had twenty Sherman tanks and thirty deuce-and-a-half trucks. Once a breakthrough had been achieved, they were to drive west as fast as possible. Their mission was twofold: one group would dash ahead to the Meuse to seize bridges, while the other fanned out behind American lines to spread rumors, change signposts, in general accelerate the panic that hits rear-echelon forces when they hear that the front line has broken.

Peiper was excited by the preparations for the attack and proud to have command of such a force. But he had too many worries for the man who would spearhead the greatest German army offensive since 1943. He had only learned of the attack on December 14. He was told he would make eighty kilometers the first day, all the way to the Meuse River. To find out if a tank could make that distance through rough terrain in a day, he made a test run through the Eifel that night. He covered the eighty kilometers, but as he ruefully told Hechler, "Of course with an entire division, that is a different matter." Gasoline had been promised but not delivered. The roads Hitler had assigned him, according to Peiper, "were not for tanks, but for bicycles."

At 0430 on December 16, Peiper briefed his troops. He stressed speed. He forbade firing into small groups of the enemy. He forbade looting. Just keep moving.[16]

German company and battalion commanders gave upbeat briefings. Lt. Günter Materne, an artilleryman, recalled his battalion commander saying, "Now the war is going to be restarted."[17] All along the 100-kilometer front, German soldiers felt similarly elated. For the older officers, going over to the offensive—whatever their reservations—was a heady reminder of the glorious days of 1940. For the enlisted men, striking back at the enemy to drive him from the homeland was exhilarating. Their commanders told them during the briefings that there were many American nurses in the various hospitals in Belgium, and mountains of American supplies. For many of these troops, it sounded like they were about to enjoy the kind of campaign their older brothers, uncles, and even fathers had experienced in 1940.

It was a scene they had seen in the newsreels as students. Everywhere there were new weapons and equipment in great quantity, and thousands of fine-looking troops. They marched smartly, singing lustily. Maj. Gen. Heinz Kokott, commanding the 26th Volksgrenadier Division, scheduled to attack the U.S. 28th Division, was pleased by their attitude: "They were fully conscious of their decisive act, confident in their ability, their strength and the promise of strong air support as well as the effort by the war industries at home. Equipment, organization and armament were up-to-date and good."[18]

The excitement of gathering such a powerful force and going back on the offensive infected even the most realistic Germans. Corp. Friedrich Bertenrath, a radioman with the 2nd Panzer Division, recalled, "We had begun to act like a beaten army. Now, moving forward, the men were extremely happy and filled with enthusiasm. Everywhere there were signs of renewed hope." Still, he added, "I never thought this attack would change the tide of the war. But it was a moment to enjoy."[19]

At 0525 hours, December 16, German officers along a front of eighty kilometers were looking at their watches. There was snow on the ground, a ground fog, and snow-laden clouds at almost ground level, perfect conditions for the Wehrmacht. At 0530 those division commanders who wanted surprise blew whistles and their infantry began to move west, in marching columns down the middle of the road, with no artillery preparation. Elsewhere, in the areas where the commanders wanted a pre-attack artillery preparation, the sky vibrated with the glaring lights of thousands of weapons, from V-1s, howitzers, 88s, 105s, and mortars, being fired simultaneously. As the explosions began to shake the ground, General Kokott was convinced that "the full impact of the shells everywhere reached precisely the designated target areas which were being turned upside down and pulverized by this hail of steel."[20]

At 0530, December 16, Captain Roland of the 99th—which was at the critical point of the attack, as it was there that Hitler had designated the roads he wanted Peiper to use to get to the Meuse—was shaken by "a thunderclap of massed artillery fire amid the blinding mist of the Ardennes winter." The bombardment lasted an hour. When it lifted, waves of infantry, supported by tanks, attacked. "Time appeared to stand still," Roland remembered. "My mind seemed to reject the reality of what was happening, to say it was all make-believe. . . . One of our young lieutenants danced a rubber-legged jig as he twisted slowly, making the bullet hole between his eyes clearly visible. One moment our battalion chaplain and his assistant were kneeling beside their disabled vehicle. The next moment they were headless, decapitated by an exploding shell as if by the stroke of a guillotine." So far as Roland could tell, "the entire division was in peril of destruction."[21]

So inexperienced were the men of the 99th Division that when the German barrage opened at 0530 they thought it was "outgoing mail," as they called American artillery firing on the Germans. They quickly discovered their mistake and jumped into their holes. As the massed firepower came down on them, one battalion executive officer remembered the division intelligence summary he had read the previous evening, especially that part about the enemy having only two horse-drawn artillery pieces opposite them. After an hour of nonstop shelling, he remarked, "They sure worked those horses to death."[22]

In notes that he wrote later, Lt. Robert Dettor of K Company, 393rd Infantry, 99th Division, described what it was like for him: "0540–0640—Artillery concentration on position. 0640–1230—Small arms fire fight. Sent runner to Company CP for reinforcements. Runner returned stating no reinforcements, stay on position and continue fighting. Communications to CP and outposts cut. No contact with men except those in foxholes in immediate vicinity. German troops to rear. Heavy machine gun to front seen captured."

Almost out of ammunition, Dettor ordered all maps and papers burned. "Sgt. Surtorka yelled over grenade being thrown at my foxhole. Hunter hit by grenade. Sgt. Phifer wounded by rifle bullet. Enemy closing in to within 20 feet of foxhole. Took last report of ammunition. Sgt. Phifer had one clip left. I had four rounds. Burp-gun to left rear firing at my foxhole hitting Hunter. Hunter dead. At approximately 1230 position overrun."

Lieutenant Dettor expected to be shot. Instead he was kicked, relieved of his watch and $48 cash, then put to work carrying wounded German soldiers on stretchers. He got to see the German army on the move from the inside, and described it vividly:

"Germans do a great deal of yelling during battle. At least one out of three Germans had automatic weapons, carried a great deal of equipment, wore camouflage suits.

"Had excellent chance to see other side of Siegfried line. Dragon teeth booby trapped. Enemy had excellent prepared covered routes of approach. Pill boxes very well built.

"Could not understand German form of attack. Men came, line upon line through open field on left making them an easy target for flanking fire.

"Many SS troops in vicinity. Pushed around by SS officer. Beautiful observation from enemy position. Firing still going on. Men being ushered into attack. Roads filled with vehicles, ammunition, staff cars, horse and wagons. Staff cars carrying German officer and ammunition trucks draped with large red crosses to disguise them as ambulances. Snow on ground—windy."

The Germans took Dettor's coat, gloves, and shoes, leaving him his overshoes, and put him in a column of POWs marching east. "Roads filled with heavy equipment coming to the front," Dettor noted. "Felt extremely depressed after seeing size of the attack." Then he began to cheer up, as he observed, "German motor vehicles very poor. Much larger than Americans trucks but not as well built. Many vehicles broken down."[23]

Lt. Lyle Bouck commanded the intelligence and reconnaissance (I&R) platoon of the 394th Regiment, 99th Division. He had enlisted before the war, lying about his age. He was commissioned a second lieutenant at age eighteen. Informal in manner, he was sharp, incisive, determined, a leader. The only man younger than he in the platoon was Pvt. William James. The platoon was near Lanzerath. Bouck kept his men up all night, sensing that something was stirring somewhere.

Shortly before dawn, December 16, the sleepy-eyed men saw the sky lit up from the muzzle flashes of 100 pieces of German artillery. In the light of those flashes, Bouck could see great numbers of tanks, self-propelled guns, and other vehicles on the German skyline. He and his men were in deep, covered foxholes, so they survived the hour-long shelling without casualties. Bouck sent a patrol forward to Lanzerath, with orders to climb to a second story and observe. The men came back to report a German infantry column coming toward the village.

Bouck tried to telephone battalion headquarters, but the lines had been cut by the shelling. He got through on the radio. When he reported, the officer at the other end was incredulous.

"Damn it," Bouck hollered. "Don't tell me what I don't see! I have twenty-twenty vision. Bring down some artillery, all the artillery you can, on the road south of Lanzerath. There's a Kraut column coming up from that direction!"

No artillery came. A couple of tanks that had been supporting the I&R platoon had pulled out when the shelling began. The men told Bouck it was time for them to retreat; after all, they had gathered and reported the intelligence, which was their job.

Bouck said no. He started pushing men into their foxholes. Including Bouck, there were eighteen of them. They were on the edge of a wood, looking down on the road leading into Lanzerath. Bouck, Sgt. Bill Slape, and Private James had their foxhole on the edge of village. They were in a perfect position to ambush the enemy, and they had plenty of firepower—a couple of .30-caliber machine guns, a .50-caliber on the jeep, a half dozen BARs, and a number of submachine guns.

The German columns came marching on, one on each side of the road, in close order, weapons slung, no security on either flank. They were teenage paratroopers. The men of the I&R platoon were fingering the triggers of their weapons. Sergeant Slape took aim on the lead German. "Your mother's going to get a telegram for Christmas," he mumbled.

Bouck knocked the rifle aside. "Maybe they don't send telegrams," he said. Then he explained that he wanted to let the lead units pass so as to spring the ambush on the main body. He waited until about 300 men had passed his position and gone into the village. Then he saw his target. Separated from the others, three officers came along, carrying maps and binoculars, with a radioman just behind—obviously the battalion CO and his staff. James rested his M-1 on the edge of his foxhole and took careful aim.

A little blond girl dashed out of the house just down the street. She made a vivid impression on James—later he recalled the red ribbons in her hair—and he held his fire. The girl pointed quickly at the I&R position and ran back inside. James tightened his finger on the trigger. In that split second, the German officer shouted an order and dove into the ditch. So did his men, on each side of the road.

The ambush ruined, the firefight began. Bouck's men had the Germans pinned down. Through the morning, they fired their weapons, including the .50-caliber mounted on the jeep. Without armored support, the German infantry couldn't get at the jeep, nor fire with much effect on the men in the foxholes. By noon, the I&R had taken some casualties but no fatalities.

Private James kept screaming at Bouck to bring in artillery with the new proximity fuse.* Bouck in turn was screaming over the radio. Battalion replied that there were no guns available.

"What shall we do then?" Bouck demanded.

"Hold at all costs."

A second later, a bullet hit and destroyed the radio Bouck had been holding. He was unhurt and passed on the order to hold.

Private James was amazed at the German tactics. Their paratroopers kept coming straight down the road, easy targets. "Whoever's ordering that attack," James said, "must be frantic. Nobody in his right mind would send troops into something like this without more fire support." He kept firing his BAR. The Germans kept coming. He felt a certain sickness as he cut down the tall, good-looking "kids." The range was so close James could see their faces. He tried to imagine himself firing at movement, not at men.

As the Germans, despite their losses, threatened to overrun the position, James dashed to the jeep and got behind the .50-caliber. Three Germans crawled up close enough to toss grenades at Pvt. Risto Milosevich, who was firing his .30-caliber at men in front of him. Unable to swing the .50-caliber fast enough, James brought up the submachine gun he had slung around his neck and cut the three

---

*A fuse that incorporated a tiny transceiver that emitted radio waves after firing, which exploded on the reflection back from the waves when the shell was near the target. Initially it was used only for anti-aircraft fire, but by late 1944 it was being used for bombardment by artillery against Germans caught in the open.

Germans down. In a frenzy, he ran to the bodies and emptied an entire magazine of nineteen rounds into the corpses.

By mid-afternoon there were 400 to 500 bodies in front of the I&R platoon. Only one American had been killed, although half the eighteen men of the platoon were wounded. There was a lull. Bouck said to James, "I want you to take the men who want to go and get out."

"Are you coming?"

"No, I have orders to hold at all costs. I'm staying."

"Then we'll all stay."

An hour later, they were both wounded, the platoon out of ammunition. They surrendered and were taken into a café set up as a first-aid post. James thought he was dying. He thought of the mothers of the boys he had mowed down and of his own mother. He passed out, was treated by a German doctor. When he came to, a German officer tried to interrogate him but gave it up, leaned over James's stretcher, and whispered in English, "*Ami,* you and your comrades are brave men."

At midnight, the cuckoo clock in the café struck. Lt. Lyle Bouck, on his stretcher on the floor, had turned twenty-one years old. "What a hell of a way to become a man," he mumbled to himself.[24]

"The action of the I&R Platoon, 394th Infantry," John Eisenhower wrote in *The Bitter Woods,* his penetrating study of command in the Ardennes, "was remarkable for the contribution that a handful of men was able to make on December 16."[25] Bouck and his men had successfully blocked the Lanzerath road against a full-strength German battalion for a day, inflicting catastrophic casualties of more than 50 percent.

Bouck's heroism and combat effectiveness could not be surpassed. Like Lieutenant Wray on June 7, what he had accomplished could hardly be equaled and seldom approached. But in many ways the I&R platoon's experience was typical.

In the 99th Division alone, there were any number of junior officers, NCOs, and enlisted men who, although new to combat and inadequately trained, stood to their guns, to the dismay of the Germans. At Losheimergraben railroad station Capt. Neil Brown's Company L, 394th Infantry, held through the day. Lt. Dewey

Plankers and his rifle platoon beat off attacks from what should have been an overwhelming force. At one point, when a Tiger tank appeared, Plankers ran up to it and launched an antitank grenade up the bore of the cannon before it could fire. These, and scores of unrecorded actions, were taken independently, as communications between platoons was poor, between companies and regimental headquarters nonexistent.[26]

All along the extended American front, from Monschau in the north down to Echternach in the south, platoons were surprised on the morning of December 16 by German attacks that passed through the extensive gaps in the line and surrounded the American positions. But although surrounded, the Americans in many cases fought back with every weapon available to them—usually just small arms. They stacked up German bodies and held the crossroads, preventing the German tanks from bursting through on their way to the Meuse River.

The German decision to hold the tanks back until the infantry broke through was a major tactical error. With the few German units in which tanks accompanied the infantry, the Americans had much less success. Pvt. Roger Foehringer of the artillery was attached to the 99th, billeted on the outskirts of Büllingen, Belgium. At 0700 on December 16, he was put to work carrying a case of grenades up a hill to a machine-gun pit. With two others he got started. "We were not to the point where we could see over the hill, when down on us came a German Tiger tank." Foehringer jumped into a row of bushes along the road. He lost his rifle and helmet and tore his field jacket, but was untouched by the tank's machine-gun bursts. It moved on, to be followed by another, then a half-track with infantry loaded in back.

"There is no feeling like being alone, being unarmed, and not knowing what to do," Foehringer recalled. Instinct told him to get back to where he came from, the farmhouse on the edge of Büllingen. He took off cross-country and made it, after almost getting blasted by a bazooka round. He found the guy who had fired at one of the German tanks—and missed—and helped him reload. Another shot, but too high again. The tank began to swing its cannon at their position. Foehringer and his buddy ran for the farmhouse. They found two carbines and went up to the second floor, where they broke the windows and began firing at German troops spread across the field.

"It was real easy shooting," Foehringer said, "until we heard the rumble of a tank." As it began to fire, Foehringer ran down to the cellar, where he found a dozen or so GIs, no officers. The men were destroying their weapons. The tank shoved its cannon through the basement window and a voice yelled, *"Raus! Raus!"*

Foehringer and the others gave up. They were marched east. In Honsfeld, Foehringer saw stark evidence of the kind of fight others in the 99th had put up. In the cemetery, "there were frozen corpses behind headstones. You could see that they had fought, one guy at a headstone, another behind a headstone, and there they were frozen just as they had been shot." But in the road, there were uncountable German bodies—uncountable because so many tanks and trucks had run over them. "They were like pancakes. We tried to detour around them but the guards made us march over them."[27]

Major attacks with intense firefights in one area, quiet in another—that was how it was on December 16 for the 99th. In one regiment, men were hardly aware that anything unusual was happening. In the 1st Battalion of the 395th, not until late afternoon did the GIs learn that the firing to their right and left was something more than a local counterattack.

Mainly, however, the story of December 16 was one of thwarted German plans. Although they had infiltrated throughout the American line, nowhere had they taken the crossroads that would allow their tanks to roam free behind the American lines. As night fell, Hitler's timetable was already falling apart, thanks to an unknown squad of GIs here, a platoon over there, fighting although surrounded and fighting until their ammunition gave out.

To the south, in the center of the German attacking line, the situation was similar. The 106th Division was penetrated in numerous places, as was the 28th. The Germans achieved surprise but not a breakthrough, while taking heavy casualties and failing to reach objectives. General Hasso von Manteuffel, commander of the Fifth Panzer Army, later told interviewers that the GIs put up a "tenacious and brave resistance with skillfully fought combat tactics. The roadblocks were the most essential reasons for the slowing up of the attack."[28]

The Army's official historian (and author of the classic book *Company Commander*), Charles MacDonald, writes of one regiment of the 28th Division, "With only two battalions supported for part of the day by two companies of medium tanks, the 110th Infantry had held off four German regiments and had nowhere been routed. That was around two thousand men versus at least ten thousand." That sentence encompasses hundreds of stories of heroism, most of which will never be known. MacDonald gives the highest praise to the 110th: "Considering the odds, nowhere on the first day of the German offensive was there a more remarkable achievement by the American soldier."[29]

General Kokott, whose 26th Division was attacking the U.S. 28th Division, agreed with MacDonald. He told interviewers, "What had not been expected to such an extent was the way the remnants of the beaten units of the 28th did not give up the battle. They stayed put and continued to block the road. Fighting a delaying battle . . . individual groups time and again confronted our assault detachments from dominating heights, defiles, on both sides of gullies and on forest paths. They let the attacking parties run into their fire, engaged them in a fire duel, made evading movements with great skill and speed and then conducted unexpected counterthrusts into flanks and rear." Kokott paid the 28th a fine tribute: "It became evident already during the morning hours that the enemy, after the initial shock and surprise, was beginning to get hold of himself and was making efforts to delay and to stop the German assault with all available means."[30] The GIs—enough of them— were doing what Hitler had been sure they could not.

"We knew more about the Americans now," Major Guderian lamented. "It was an awful feeling, being there at the end of the day. All four of my companies were gone."[31]

Ken Hechler asked Peiper, "Did you honestly expect to reach the Meuse River in one day?" Peiper paused, wrinkled his brow, then said carefully, "If our own infantry had broken through by 0700 as originally planned, my answer is 'yes,' I think we might have reached the Meuse in one day."[32]

Lieutenant Bouck's fight continued to shape the battle. Around midnight, December 16–17, Peiper reached the Lanzerath area. The infantry commanders told him of the strong resistance ahead. They said they had been repelled three times with terrible losses.

Peiper took command. He told his troops to be ready to attack at 0400 hours. He put two Panther tanks in front of the column, followed by a series of armored half-tracks and then another half dozen tanks, with thirty captured American trucks behind them, and sixteen 88s at the rear. At the appointed hour they roared off, only to discover the village was empty.

Peiper was now loose behind American lines. The only Americans in the vicinity were service troops, drivers, medical personnel, and higher headquarters types—nothing to stop an armored column with such firepower. The moment had come to begin the exploitation phase of the operation.

By 0800 Peiper had gassed up his vehicles with captured fuel. Then he roared off, headed west toward Malmédy. This was lucky for the U.S. 99th and 2nd Divisions, because had he turned north he would have cut across their lines of supply, leaving them isolated with little option but to surrender. This was what Rundstedt and the other generals wanted, the "small solution." But Hitler specifically forbade a limited tactical encirclement of two divisions; he was after much bigger game.

By continuing west, Peiper was running parallel to Elsenborn Ridge, the dominant physical feature of that part of the Ardennes. The nature of his thrust, meanwhile, was pushing men of the 99th and 2nd Divisions back toward the ridge. Like Little Round Top on July 2, 1863, the ridge was unoccupied, undefended. Whoever got there first would have the high ground and thus the decisive advantage.

Peiper's breakthrough was one of many that second morning. The sheer weight of German numbers could not be denied. Isolated American groups continued to fight, but without ammunition resupply they couldn't do much. Many surrendered. Two regiments of the 106th surrendered, 7,500 men, the biggest mass surrender in the war against Germany. Everywhere the Skorzeny units began to spread panic, issuing false orders, switching road signs, and otherwise carrying out their missions, but the units assigned to take the Meuse bridges failed in their task.

For the tankers, as Pvt. Karl Drescher recalled, it was "drive, drive, drive. We pushed as fast as possible. We drove at night."[33]

Bradley spent most of December 16 driving from Luxembourg City to Versailles, so he was out of touch. At the Trianon Palace Hotel, Eisenhower's headquarters, he found his boss in a good mood. Eisenhower had just received word of his promotion to the rank of five-star general. At dusk, an intelligence officer arrived with news. There had been an enemy attack that morning in the Ardennes. Bradley dismissed it as of little consequence, just a local spoiling attack designed to disrupt First Army's offensive at the Roer dams. But an hour later, another report came in—there were at least twelve German divisions involved, eight of them not previously identified as being on the Ardennes front.

Bradley still thought it an irritant, nothing major. Eisenhower disagreed. He said this was a counteroffensive, not a counterattack. Studying the map, Eisenhower ordered Bradley to send the 7th Armored Division to St.-Vith on the northern flank and the 12th Armored to Echternach in the south. The 12th was scheduled to attack east of Metz, Bradley reminded Eisenhower, and pointed out that Patton would be furious at having to call off his offensive.

"Tell him," Eisenhower replied, "that Ike is running this damn war."[34]

Hitler had assumed a slow American response because he was certain it would take Eisenhower two or three days to recognize the extent of the threat and that he would not be willing to call off his offensives north and south of the Ardennes until he had checked with Churchill and Roosevelt. Eisenhower had just proved him wrong on both points. It never occurred to Eisenhower to check with Marshall, much less Roosevelt. What he had done was textbook stuff from World War I—the place to hold a penetration is at the shoulders. It is more important to limit the width of the salient than its depth. But if it took no special genius to figure out what to do, it did take a leap into the mind of the enemy commander. Eisenhower made that leap on the night of December 16. He saw what no one else around him saw, that not only was this a major offensive, but that it was the best thing that could happen. The Germans were out of their fixed fortifications, out in the open where American artillery, American tanks, American infantry, American fighter-bombers would be capable of destroying them.

On the morning of December 17, Eisenhower wrote Marshall. He took the blame for the surprise, assured his boss that he had everything in hand, and concluded, "If things go well we should not only stop the thrust but be able to profit from it."[35]

After dictating the report, Eisenhower went back to the maps. He ordered the 101st and 82nd Airborne, then in Reims refitting from their Holland battle, into the battle. He sent the 101st to Bastogne, a crossroads town in the center of the German thrust. He wanted it held at all costs and ordered a combat command team from the 10th Armored Division to join the 101st in Bastogne. He sent the 82nd to the northern flank, near Elsenborn.

Hitler had thought that when Eisenhower was finally aware of what was happening and had permission from his political superiors to act, it would take him some additional days to move reinforcements into the Ardennes. He was wrong about that one, too. The airborne divisions could not go to their assigned position by plane, as the weather continued to be foggy, snowy, cold. But Eisenhower had trucks. He ordered the drivers in the Red Ball Express to drop their loads and use all their resources as troop carriers. The trucks carried the paratroopers into the battle, and much else. On December 17 alone, 11,000 trucks carried 60,000 men, plus ammunition, gasoline, medical supplies, and other matériel into the Ardennes. In the first week of the battle, Eisenhower was able to move 250,000 men and 50,000 vehicles into the fray. This was mobility with a vengeance. It was also an achievement unprecedented in the history of war. Not even in Vietnam, not even in Desert Storm, was the U.S. Army capable of moving so many men and so much equipment so quickly.

Still, it took time to recover from the initial blow and to regroup, reorganize, and redirect the line of advance. Meanwhile hundreds of German tanks were loose behind the front lines, free to move in almost any direction.

The Americans used desperate methods to bolster the defense. Pvt. Kenneth Delaney of the 1st Infantry Division had been in combat from D-Day to November 15, when he was wounded in the Hurtgen. A month later he was recuperating in a hospital in Liège, Belgium.

"On December 17th," he recalled, "the hospital staff informed us that if you can walk or crawl, you will have to go back to your Division as soon as possible. The next morning I left the hospital and with a convoy of soldiers who could not be broken in spirit, started back to the division." That evening he rejoined his regiment, where he traded his walking cane for an M-1 and some hand grenades, and went into the line as a squad leader. Of the eight men in the squad, Delaney was the only veteran. All the others were just-arrived replacements. Four of them were killed that day.[36]

■

On December 17, the sky over Belgium was overcast, but the clouds were at 5,000 feet or more. That day, the Luftwaffe managed its last big offensive mission. German pilots flew between 600 and 700 sorties in support of the ground forces. A thousand and more Allied pilots were there to meet them. Each side had briefed its pilots to rendezvous over St.-Vith. The planes arrived simultaneously and began a day-long dogfight.

Captain Barensfeld was a participant. He led a twelve-plane squadron of P-47s. Each plane carried a 500-pound bomb, napalm, and newly installed five-inch rockets on tracks under the wings, four rockets on each wing, plus the .50-caliber machine guns on each wing. The German planes, for the most part, were armed with 20mm cannon whose shells burst after traveling 4,000 feet. They made a white puff when they exploded. "The sky over St. Vith that day was full of white puffs," Barensfeld remembered.

When Barensfeld arrived on the scene, "I saw two or three fighters on fire, spiralling toward the ground—both sides. I saw a Thunderbolt and a Foche Wolfe [sic] going down in flames. . . . Enemy aircraft all over the place. Our controller, 'Organ,' was calm and calling in a prime target—a pontoon bridge across the River Roer. Many enemy vehicles backed up behind it. We planned our attack to take out the bridge and as many of the vehicles as possible. A great amount of flak coming up. Three or four of our aircraft received battle damage but no one aborted. We used our bombs and rockets on the vehicles and the bridge then set up several strafing passes. There were burning vehicles and some damage to the bridge when we left after about 20 minutes."[37]

On the ground, the Germans made their major breakthrough in the center, in the direction of Bastogne, but the critical threat was to the north. If Peiper could get across the Meuse the roads to Antwerp were open. But the Germans had their own problems. Traffic control and driving discipline were poor. The concentrated power of the armored units flowed to the west not in an even stream but irregularly from traffic jam to traffic jam. The road net in the Ardennes was just as Eisenhower had said it would be if the Germans tried to attack in that area, inadequate. Further, the German infantry marched into battle, as there were insufficient trucks to carry them forward. Worse, much of the German artillery was horse-drawn, which added greatly to the congestion. In the villages, troops milled around, waiting for their officers to get organized, for the roads to clear. Bored infantrymen went shopping in the little Belgian stores, buying Christmas cards and presents.[38]

All through December 17, Peiper continued to drive west, avoiding Elsenborn Ridge, looking for bridges, gasoline dumps, ammunition dumps, isolated American headquarters, avoiding pockets of resistance whenever possible, blasting them out of the way when necessary. Shortly after noon his advance guard ran into an American truck convoy from Battery B, 285th Field Artillery Observation Battalion, just south of Malmédy. Peiper's men shot up the convoy and moved on.

By 1600 hours Peiper, with the left-hand column, had reached the outskirts of Stavelot. The town was clogged with American trucks and other vehicles. He subjected it to a bombardment from his tanks, causing much destruction and confusion. Then he sent his battalion of armored infantry to attack the town. As darkness fell, American small arms repulsed the enemy. Through the night, Peiper watched as the Americans pulled out their trucks: "We observed heavy American traffic all moving westward, without blackout restrictions."

Peiper's success in breaking through was heady stuff to the Germans, panic-inducing to the Americans, but as darkness fell on December 17, he was behind schedule. In May 1940 a German armored column had covered the distance from the Eifel to Stavelot in nine hours and found Stavelot undefended. Peiper had consumed thirty-six hours getting to Stavelot and found it defended.

Still it had been a glorious couple of days. Corporal Bertenrath recalled, "We enjoyed those first days of success, moving forward, taking prisoners and, above all, capturing the wonderful provisions we found in Allied vehicles. We took as much as we could carry: cakes, chocolate, cigarettes." The lowly K-ration of the GIs impressed Bertenrath: "potatoes, vegetables, meat, and even something for dessert. I asked my squad, 'My God, how do they manage such things?' " But being behind American lines also gave Bertenrath a sense of impending doom, because "on one road through the forest were stacks of shells that stretched for, I would guess, two kilometers both left and right—we drove through an alley of shells. I had never seen the like of it. I told my squad, 'My God, their supplies are unlimited!' " He recalled his father-in-law telling him on December 10, 1941, when Hitler declared war on the United States:

"The war is lost. America came in during my war, and it was lost. Second war, America joins, we lose."[39]

At dawn, December 18, Peiper instructed two Panther commanders to charge Stavelot at maximum speed. "They drove around the curve firing rapidly. The first Panther tank was hit, and it burned, but it had so much initial speed that it penetrated the anti-tank obstacle at the curve and damaged two Sherman tanks. The second Panther used this opportunity to drive through and seize a bridge in Stavelot. We followed up with other vehicles, and the Americans evacuated the town."[40]

Not, however, before destroying the gasoline dump at Stavelot. As the evacuation was taking place, Sgt. Jack Mocnik and two others of the 526th Armored Infantry Battalion drove a jeep up the hill to the dump, accompanied by two half-tracks. They saw GIs at the far end, loading gasoline into their vehicles and taking off. Mocnik's party began firing .30- and .50-caliber machine-gun bursts into the cans of gas, but it wouldn't catch fire. The men jumped out of their half-tracks and jeep and started opening the five-gallon jerry cans, spilling the fuel on the ground. Finally they got one to catch fire. As they scrambled away, "the darndest fire you ever saw flared up." Mocnik recalled, "The cans would explode and fly through the air like rockets trailing fire and smoke."[41]

Frustrated, Peiper drove on at top speed in an effort to get to Trois-Ponts ("Three Bridges") in time to seize an intact bridge. Once across the Amblève and Salm Rivers, which flowed together in the village, he would have an open road to the Meuse.

In some American headquarters, at supply dumps, and in the field, there was confusion if not chaos. Men set to burning papers and maps, destroying weapons, throwing other items away and running to the rear. There was a breakdown in discipline, compounded by the breakdown of some of the colonels. Among many, fear drove all rational thought out of their mind. Go west as fast as possible was the only thought.

On December 17, the trickle of frightened men fleeing the battle began to turn into a stream. At 1230 hours, Maj. Donald Boyer of the 7th Armored was trying to open a road for the division's tanks, when "we were hit by a sight that we could not comprehend, at first: a constant stream of traffic hurtling to the rear and nothing going to the front. We realized that this was not a convoy moving to the rear; it was a case of 'every dog for himself.' It wasn't orderly, it wasn't military, it wasn't a pretty sight. We were seeing American soldiers running away."[42]

By December 18 the stream was becoming a flood. The waves of panic rolled westward. In Belgium and northern France, American flags hanging from windows were discreetly pulled inside and hidden. In Paris the whores put away their English language phrase books and retrieved their German versions. In New York the stock market, which had tumbled after the German retreat from France in anticipation of an early peace, became bullish again.

Well it might, as on the third day of the attack, December 19, German armor began to acquire momentum; the greatest gains made by the armored spearhead columns were achieved that day. The U.S. Army, meanwhile, was in an apparent rout, reminiscent of First Bull Run eighty-three years earlier. As the Germans straightened out their traffic jams behind the front, the Americans in retreat were colliding with the reinforcements Eisenhower had sent to the battle, causing a monumental traffic jam of their own.

The U.S. Army in retreat was a sad spectacle. When the 101st Airborne got to Bastogne on December 19, the columns marched down both sides of the road, toward the front. Down the middle of the road came the defeated American troops, fleeing the front in disarray, moblike. Many had thrown away their rifles, their coats, all encumbrances. Some were in a panic, staggering, exhausted, shouting, "Run! Run! They'll murder you! They'll kill you! They've got everything, tanks, machine guns, air power, everything!"

"They were just babbling," Maj. Richard Winters of the 506th PIR recalled. "It was pathetic. We felt ashamed."[43]

The 101st had packed and left Mourmelon in a hurry. The troopers were short of everything, including ammunition. "Where's the ammo? We can't fight without ammo," the men were calling out as they marched through Bastogne to the sound of the guns. The retreating horde supplied some. "Got any ammo?" the paratroopers would ask those who were not victims of panic.

"Sure, buddy, glad to let you have it."

Corp. Walter Gordon noted sardonically that by giving away their ammo, the retreating men relieved themselves of any further obligation to stand and fight.[44] They had long since left behind partly damaged or perfectly good artillery pieces, tanks, half-tracks, trucks, jeeps, food, rations, and more.

Abandonment of equipment was sometimes unavoidable, but often it was inexcusable. Panic was the cause. Guns that should have been towed out of danger were not. When a convoy stalled, drivers and passengers jumped out of their vehicles and headed west on foot.

Panic was costly in every way. Pvt. Ralph Hill of the 99th Division remembered a platoon of infantry who were occupying a deep dugout with a heavy wooden cover. An antitank gun was set up at the nearest crossroads. At 0530, December 16, heavy artillery shells began falling around the position. The gun crew, with no cover, dashed for the dugout. "When they tore off the cover, the 99th Division infantry opened fire from the dugout, thinking they were German. All of the gun crew was killed so the gun was abandoned."[45]

But by no means was everything abandoned. Reporter Jack Belden, who had covered Gen. Joseph Stilwell's retreat from Burma in May 1942, described the retreat as he saw it in the Ardennes on December 17, 1944. There were long convoys of trucks, carrying gasoline, portable bridges, and other equipment headed west, with tanks and other armed vehicles mixed in. "I noticed in myself a feeling that I had not had for some years. It was the feeling of guilt that seems to come over you whenever you retreat. You don't like to look anyone in the eyes. It seems as if you have done something wrong. I perceived this feeling in others too."

Belden went on, "The road was jammed with every conceivable kind of vehicle. An enemy plane came down and bombed and strafed the column, knocking three trucks off the road, shattering trees and causing everyone to flee to ditches." Jabos in reverse. Then came the buzz bombs, or V-1s. "It went on all night. There must have been a buzz bomb or a piloted plane raid somewhere every five minutes."[46]

Belden was right in his perception that others in those apparently endless column fleeing the fight felt guilty. And Major Winters was not alone in feeling ashamed. Pvt. Kurt Vonnegut was a recently arrived replacement in the 106th Division. He was caught up in the retreat before he could be assigned. To his eyes, it was just rout, pure and simple.

His unit surrendered. Vonnegut decided he would take his chances and bolted into the woods, without a rifle or rations, or proper winter clothing. He hooked up with three others who wouldn't surrender and set off hoping to find American lines.[47]

Every man for himself. It was reminiscent of the German retreat through the Falaise Gap. But there were two critical differences. All along the front, scattered groups of men stuck to their guns at crossroads and in villages. They cut the German infantry columns down as a scythe cuts through a wheat field. German losses were catastrophic. The GIs were appalled at how the enemy infantry came on, marching down the middle of a road, their weapons slung, without outposts or reconnaissance of any sort, without armor support, with no idea of where the American strong points were located. The German soldiers scarcely knew how to march or fire their weapons, and knew nothing of infantry tactics.

In launching an offensive, the German army in the first year of the Great War had been better than the German army in the last year of the Second World War. What was happening at the front was exactly what Eisenhower had predicted—the Volksgrenadier divisions were not capable of effective action outside their bunkers. In far too many cases, however, they were attacking eighteen- and nineteen-year-old barely trained Americans. Both sides had been forced to turn to their children to fight the war to a conclusion. In this last winter of World War II, neither army could be said to be a veteran army.

Another difference between the German retreat in August and the American retreat in December was that as the beaten, terrified GIs fled west down the middle of the roads, there were combat troops on each side headed east, reinforcements marching to the sound of the guns.

In May 1940, when German armor drove through the Ardennes, the French high command had thrown up its hands and surrendered, even though the bulk of the French army had yet to even see, much less fire at, a German soldier. In December 1944, when German armor drove through the Ardennes, Eisenhower saw his chance.

At dawn on December 19, as German tanks prepared to surround Bastogne and the 101st marched into the town, Eisenhower met with his senior commanders in a cold, damp squad room in a barracks at Verdun, the site of the greatest battle ever fought. There was but one lone potbellied stove to ease the bitter cold. Eisenhower's lieutenants entered the room glum, depressed, embarrassed, as they should have been, given the magnitude of the intelligence failure and the faulty dispositions of their troops in order to maintain hopeless offensives north and south of the Ardennes. They kept their faces bent over the coffee cups.

Eisenhower walked in, looked disapprovingly at the downcast generals, and boldly declared, "The present situation is to be regarded as one of opportunity for us and not of disaster. There will be only cheerful faces at this conference table."

Patton quickly picked up the theme. "Hell, let's have the guts to let the bastards go all the way to Paris," he said. "Then we'll really cut 'em off and chew 'em up." He had already seen the obvious: the Germans were putting their heads in a noose. By attacking the southern shoulder of the salient with his Third Army, Patton could cut the enemy supply lines, isolate the tanks inside what was already being called "the Bulge," and destroy them. Before leaving Metz for Verdun, he had told his staff to begin the preparations for switching his attack line from east to north. Thus when Eisenhower asked him how long it would take for Third Army to turn two corps facing east to facing north and then attack the German southern flank, Patton boldly replied, "Two days." The other generals laughed—but in fact Patton was already halfway into the movement.[48]

Eisenhower's decisiveness and Patton's boldness were electrifying. Their mood quickly spread through the system. Dispirited men were energized. For those who most needed help, the men on the front line, help was coming, in the form of men like Dick Winters. Ed Cunningham was a reporter for *Yank* magazine. He was in a village where the retreating troops were on one side of the road, the advancing units of an armored column on the other. The civilians on the westbound side were silent, their eyes full of reproach and dread. Those on the eastbound side "are young girls waving and laughing with the Americans in the tanks and half-tracks. Older men and women smile behind their fears and give the V-salute to the men in crash helmets."[49]

From the Supreme Commander down to the lowliest private, men pulled up their socks and went forth to do their duty. It simplifies, but not by much, to say that here, there, everywhere, from top to bottom, the men of the U.S. Army in Northwest Europe shook themselves and made this a defining moment in their own lives, and in the history of the Army. They didn't like retreating, they didn't like getting kicked around, and as individuals, squads, and companies as well as at SHAEF, they decided they were going to make the enemy pay.

That they had the time to adjust and prepare to pound the Germans was thanks to a relatively small number of front-line GIs. The first days of the Battle of the Bulge were a triumph of the soldiers of democracy, marked by innumerable examples of men seizing the initiative, making decisions, leading. Captain Roland of the 99th put it best: "Our accomplishments in this action were largely the result of small, virtually independent and isolated units fighting desperately for survival. They present an almost-unprecedented example of courage, resourcefulness, and tenacity on the part of the enlisted men, noncommissioned officers, and junior-grade commissioned officers of the line companies."[50]

8

The Ardennes

December 20–23, 1944

BY MIDDAY, December 20, Charlie Company, 395th Infantry Regiment, 99th Division, had been retreating for three and a half days, mostly without sleep and water and not enough food, through daytime mud "that was knee deep, so deep that men carrying heavy weapons frequently mired in mud so others had to take their weapons and pull them out. In one area it took 1½ hours to cover a hundred meters." Sgt. Vernon Swanson said that when word came down at 1700 hours that the regiment was withdrawing to Elsenborn Ridge, where it would dig in beside the 2nd Division and where more reinforcements were headed, "It was certainly good news. We felt it was the equivalent of saying we were returning to the United States."

The journey to Elsenborn, however, Swanson remembered "as the worst march of that week," because of the combination of mud, ice, frozen ground, and snow, seemingly all at once and all along the route. A high-pressure system had moved in from the Atlantic on December 18, temporarily opening the skies so that the Allied air forces could fly a few support missions and starting a daytime thaw that slowed German tanks as much as American infantry. After darkness fell on the 20th the ground began to freeze again; on the 21st there was a hodgepodge of snow, blizzards, fog, and sleet. Through this miserable weather, Charlie Company marched.

"We left most of our supplies behind," Swanson said, "but our weapons were always ready. Throughout this entire journey our men made their way, cold, tired, miserable, stumbling, cursing the Army, the weather and the Germans, yet none gave up."

They arrived on the ridge around midnight, and although "we were beyond exhaustion," the men dug in. A good thing, because at dawn a German artillery shelling came down on them. Too late, the Germans had realized the critical importance of Elsenborn. Swanson's company was well dug in, but nevertheless took seven casualties. Four of them were sergeants, "which opened up the field for promotions." One of those hit was Swanson, who got wounded in the neck by shrapnel. "I couldn't make a sound because blood was pouring down my throat." Litter bearers brought him to an aid station, where a chaplain bent over him. "I could dimly make out his collar ornament which was a Star of David. He, in turn, misread my dogtag, thought I was a Catholic and gave me last rites. I remember thinking that I really had all bases covered."[1]

As noted, Elsenborn was the Little Round Top of the Battle of the Bulge. Peiper could have taken it without difficulty on the 17th or 18th, but he stuck with Hitler's orders and moved west rather than north once through the American line. The low ridge lay across the direct line from the Eifel to Antwerp and should have been the main objective of the Germans on the northern flank. But the Americans got there first and dug in. Only a direct frontal assault could oust them from the position.

The Germans tried. "The first night at Elsenborn is unforgettable," Captain Roland of the 99th wrote fifty years later. "The flash and roar of exploding shells was incessant. In all directions the landscape was a Dante's inferno of burning towns and villages." The men of his regiment, the 394th Infantry, dug furiously throughout the night. "We distributed ammunition and field rations, cleaned and oiled weapons, dug foxholes and gun emplacements in the frozen earth, planted antitank mines, strung barbed wire, studied maps and aerial photographs by shielded flashlights, plotted fire zones for machine guns, mortars, and artillery, put in field telephone lines to the various command posts, and set up an aid station to receive a fresh harvest of casualties.

"Everyone was aware that there would be no further withdrawal, whatever the cost. Moreover, I could sense in the demeanor of the troops at all ranks that this resolution was written in their hearts."

Enemy mortar and artillery fire hit the 99th. American artillery fired continuously. At night the temperature fell well below zero on the Fahrenheit scale. No GI had winter clothing. "The wind blew in a gale that drove the pellets of snow almost like shot into our faces. Providing hot food on the front line became impossible, and we were obliged to live exclusively on K rations. Remaining stationary in damp, cold foxholes, with physical activity extremely limited, we began to suffer casualties from trenchfoot. . . . In time the combination of extreme cold, fatigue, boredom, and hazard became maddening. A few men broke under the strain, wetting themselves repeatedly, weeping, vomiting, or showing other physical symptoms." But there was no more retreating.[2]

The fighting was at its most furious in the twin villages of Rocherath and Krinkelt, on the eastern edge of the ridge. There a battalion from the 2nd Infantry Division engaged a German armored division. The Germans and Americans were intermingled in a wild melee that included hand-to-hand combat. American tank crews knew they could not take on the big German tanks toe-to-toe, so they allowed the Panthers and Tigers to close on their positions for an intricate game of cat and mouse among the twin villages' streets and alleys. Shermans remained hidden and quiet behind walls, buildings, and hedgerows, waiting for a German tank to cross their sites. Most engagements took place at ranges of less than twenty-five meters. The 741st Tank Battalion knocked out twenty-seven panzers at a cost of eleven Shermans. The 644th Tank Destroyer Battalion destroyed seventeen enemy tanks at a cost of two of their own vehicles.

The 57mm antitank guns of the Americans were too cumbersome with too little firepower to have much effect; the bazooka, however, was highly effective within the villages, especially after dark, when bazooka teams could work their way close enough to the German tanks to get in a killing shot on the tracks. On December 21 the Germans threatened a battalion command post: the CO and his staff dropped their radios and maps, picked up rifles and bazookas, and joined the fight.[3]

In *Closing with the Enemy*, Michael Doubler wrote, "The fight for the Elsenborn Ridge saw some of the most bitter defensive battles in the ETO."[4] Sgt. Arnold Parish of the 2nd Infantry agreed. He had made the D-Day landing, when he won the Bronze Star, had been wounded on June 9, and had rejoined his unit in August, so he had four months of combat by mid-December. Elsenborn was the toughest. Men who had thought they had seen it all broke under the German shelling. "We were helpless," Parish recalled, "and all alone and there was nothing we could do, so I prayed to God." During the nights, "The time went by very slow as I tried to keep warm but that wasn't possible so I thought about my mother and hoped she didn't know where I was or what I was doing. I was glad I was not married."

Suddenly German floodlights came on, shining against the clouds, and German tanks rolled forward. Parish remembered thinking, Perhaps this is the end of the world. But within seconds he and his platoon were firing back. The Germans were repulsed.[5]

Southwest of Elsenborn, the 82nd Airborne Division was arriving to bolster the northern shoulder and stop Peiper's rush westward. On December 20, Col. Ben Vandervoort's 2nd Battalion, 505th PIR, arrived at Trois-Ponts, where the Salm and Amblève Rivers flowed together. Vandervoort put Company E on the east side of the Salm, while the remainder of the battalion established an MLR among and in the houses along the river on the west bank. Behind the MLR a sheer bluff rose. E Company, on the opposite bluff, had a 57mm gun set up on a shoulder of the road, twenty meters behind the dug-in infantry, who were on the edge of a wood. Lt. William Meddaugh, the CO, put his bazooka teams just ahead and to the left of the infantry. By 0300 hours they were in position to ambush any German force coming from the east. There they waited, no fires, no lights, no smoking, all wide-awake.

German armor—Peiper's—was coming on, accompanied by infantry. Peiper had a twenty-to-one manpower advantage over Vandervoort, and a colossal firepower superiority. The American paratroopers had no tanks, no tank destroyers, no heavy artillery, only that little 57mm antitank gun, six bazookas, and the ultra-light airborne 75mm pack howitzer for artillery support. The 505th PIR was an elite outfit, to be sure, but not all that elite, because after Normandy and Holland it had more replacements who had only just arrived in Europe than it did veterans. But the replacements were volunteers who had qualified with five jumps and had some additional training after joining the 505th.

The 505th had learned new skills and techniques during its time in Holland. It applied one lesson learned even before daylight.

At 0315 hours, an armored German vehicle approached E Company's position. As it rounded a curve on the road as it wound its way down to the river, a bazooka team bushwhacked it. After the German crew fled, the paratroopers moved their minefield to the far side of the burning hulk. At 0400 a second armored vehicle blew itself up on the mines.

At first light, 0800 hours on December 21, Peiper attacked E Company with infantry and five tanks. The bazookas and the antitank gun knocked out the armor; the men in the foxholes drove back the infantry (a few of whom fell into E Company foxholes) with great loss.* From an OP on the high ground on the west bank, the Americans could see Peiper's tanks, self-propelled artillery, and mobile flak batteries maneuvering for another attack.

Vandervoort sent F Company across the river, to support E Company with a flank attack, but it had little effect on Peiper's men and tanks, who were massing for a decisive attack. Vandervoort later remarked that with what amounted to an armored division about to attack an infantry company, "disaster seemed imminent, but not one man of E company left his fighting position." Vandervoort jumped into a jeep and had his driver take him over the bridge and climb to the bluff above the east bank. He arrived at Meddaugh's CP just as the first wave of German infantry attacked. They were supported by tanks firing their cannon and machine guns, spraying the American positions.

Enough, Vandervoort decided. He jumped out of his jeep and ran to Meddaugh. "Pull out," he ordered, "AND DO IT NOW!"

As Meddaugh passed on the word, the Germans began to close in, one of them calling out in English, "Halt Americans! You are surrounded." Meddaugh made no reply. Vandervoort meanwhile began driving down the bluff to the river bank, "urged on by swarms of 9mm rounds from Schmeisser machine pistols." Halfway down the bluff, he passed the antitank gun. It had jackknifed into a ditch and had to be abandoned by its crew.

On the bluff, Meddaugh had his men withdraw using lessons from close-quarter fighting in Holland. In Vandervoort's words, "the men intuitively improvised walking fire in reverse. Moving

---

*Later, Vandervoort's intelligence officer interrogated prisoners. He asked them why they had come straight across open ground shooting and yelling. The POWs replied that that was what they had been doing ever since the start of their offensive and up to then everybody had run away or surrendered.

backward and using the trees for cover, they simply out-shot any pursuer who crowded them too closely."

When the GIs reached the edge of the bluff they had to jump down a sheer cliff, pick themselves up (there were a number of broken bones and many sprained ankles), run a 100-meter gauntlet across a road, cross over a railroad track, and wade the icy river. GIs in the town along the bank, and up on the bluff behind, fired at any German who showed on the opposite bluff. E Company made it to the town, but with 33 percent casualties, all of whom were carried to the battalion aid station in Trois-Ponts. When every man was accounted for, engineers blew the bridge. It was a textbook withdrawal, except that in this case there was no text, as the U.S. Army had not bothered to teach its soldiers how to retreat.

Vandervoort described the E Company survivors as they came into Trois-Ponts: "They were a tired, ragged, rugged looking bunch. But what I saw was beautiful. About one hundred troopers, with weapons and ammunition, still ready to fight."

Peiper brought some Panther tanks to the edge of the bluff. They started to hose down the streets of Trois-Ponts with their machine guns. Then, as Vandervoort recalled, "A Tiger tank appeared on the edge of the bluff road. The menacing white skull-and-cross-bones of the S.S. insignia, and the black-and-white battle cross painted on its armor were clearly visible. It depressed its long-barreled, bulbous muzzle and began firing point-blank down into our houses."

A couple of bazooka rounds hit the Tiger, but only bounced off. Vandervoort called for the mortar platoon to go after the tank. The men selected white phosphorus, to reduce German visibility. "With amazing accuracy," Vandervoort said, "the first round hit the Tiger right in front of the turret. Searing phosphorous globules arched in all directions. Enemy infantry soldiers near the tank scattered like quail. The driver slapped the now-not-so-menacing monster into reverse and accelerated back into the concealment of the woods."

Now another member of the team could go to work. The division artillery observer could spot the German vehicles as they regrouped back from the bluff. He called in fire that forced the enemy to take to the wood, there to spend the remainder of the daylight hours. After dark, German infantry tried to ford the Salm, but were beaten back.[6]

■

The Battle of Trois-Ponts was a subject Peiper didn't much want to talk about in his interview with Ken Hechler. He would say only that after leaving Stavelot, "we proceeded at top speed toward Trois Ponts in an effort to seize the bridge there, but the enemy blew up the bridge in our faces."

Hechler: "What was the importance of the bridge in Trois-Ponts; in other words, what do you think you might have been able to do if you had captured the bridge intact?"

Peiper: "If we had captured the bridge intact and had had enough fuel, it would have been a simple matter to drive through to the Meuse River early that day."

Later, Hechler asked Peiper, "What orders did you receive from headquarters?" Peiper sniffed cynically, then said, "I got one message that I should report immediately the location of my dressing stations for the wounded, and that unless I reported the amount of gas I still had on hand, I could not hope for any additional gasoline."

Peiper went north to find a bridge, but never found one he could take. Trois-Ponts turned out to be his high-water mark. When Hechler asked him what he would have done differently, he spoke not of the battle there but more general subjects: get more gasoline, no artillery preparation, keep the horses off the roads, attack with combined arms, take along bridging units with the point, and, last, "Put a general at each street corner to regulate traffic." Peiper indicated that there were two good reasons for such a move, and one of them was not traffic control.[7]

Peiper's opposite number, General Gavin, rather agreed with Peiper about the quality of German generals, but he put Colonel Peiper in that category, too. Thirty-four years after the battle, Gavin wrote in a letter to Vandervoort, "I have never been able to understand why the Panzer Commander upon reaching the Salm did not bring up all his infantry and make a night assault, establishing a bridgehead during darkness and getting armor across before daylight." Such a combined arms attack would have worked, Gavin felt, and "we had very little behind Trois-Ponts." Gavin denounced Peiper's generalship, calling it "inexcusable." Then he thought about Peiper's problems with the German high command, and couldn't help comparing the mess that existed in the Wehrmacht with the generally smooth-functioning SHAEF. He was struck by another thought: "Sometimes one suspects that some of the senior German officers, figuring the war was lost anyway, did not want to win."[8]

SHAEF made its own mistakes. On December 20 Eisenhower decided to divide command of the battle between Montgomery and Bradley. His reasoning was that the German advance in the center of the Bulge had split the U.S. First and Third Armies and severed Bradley's telephone communications with Hodges. As Bradley's headquarters were on the southern flank, Eisenhower decided to put Montgomery in command of the First and Ninth American Armies on the northern shoulder of the Bulge. Such a command arrangement was what Montgomery had all along been proposing and Eisenhower refusing, which hurt, while the transfer of command at the height of a crisis made it appear as if the Americans had to turn to the British to rescue them, which hurt even more. But Eisenhower insisted it had to be done.

When SHAEF Chief of Staff General Bedell Smith called Bradley on the telephone to inform him of the transfer, Smith pointed out that it was a logical move. Bradley protested at the implied insult, but added, "Bedell, it's hard for me to object. Certainly if Monty's were an American command, I would agree with you entirely."

Eisenhower got on the phone an hour or so later. By then Bradley was set against any change. "By God, Ike," he shouted into the phone, "I cannot be responsible to the American people if you do this. I resign."

Eisenhower, shocked and angry, took a deep breath, then said softly but firmly, "Brad, I—not you—am responsible to the American people. Your resignation therefore means absolutely nothing."

There was a pause, then another protest from Bradley, but this time without any threats. Eisenhower signed off, "Well, Brad, those are my orders."

After hanging up, Eisenhower placed a call to Montgomery to inform him of the command switch. The telephone connection was unfortunately indistinct. Montgomery heard what he wanted to hear and attached his own meaning to the garbled conversation. He told Field Marshal Alan Brooke that Eisenhower "was very excited, and it was difficult to understand what he was talking about; he roared into the telephone, speaking very fast." The only thing Montgomery understood was that Eisenhower was giving him command of U.S. First and Ninth Armies. "This was all I wanted to know. He then went on talking wildly about other things."

Montgomery hung up, got into his jeep, and headed off to visit First and Ninth Army headquarters. A British officer who accompanied him said he strode into Hodges's headquarters "like Christ come to cleanse the temple." According to Montgomery's account, however, Hodges was "delighted to have someone to give him firm orders."9

Montgomery's perceptions were often unusual, sometimes unique. He had an active fantasy life, for example imagining that he had always intended to hold at Caen so Bradley could break out. His fantasies were fed by the adulation of the British public, exacerbated by his sense of how unfair it was that Ike, not he, was the Supreme Commander, topped by his realization that Britain was now a junior partner whose contributions to the AEF were shrinking while those of the Americans were swelling.

His attitude as he met with the American Army commanders was, Well here you have these magnificently equipped men and such mountains of equipment and you've gone and botched it terribly. I predicted all this. But Ike wouldn't listen, so now I'll have to straighten out this mess.

But that, too, was all fantasy. He had not predicted the German counteroffensive, indeed was preparing to go home for Christmas when the blow was struck. Nor did he take control of the battle, as he imagined himself doing.

No one did. Once Eisenhower set the broad objectives—to hold firm along Elsenborn Ridge, to stop the Germans short of the Meuse, and to prepare a coordinated counterattack against the shoulders of the Bulge—this was not a general's battle. At Bastogne, at Elsenborn, at St.-Vith, at Trois-Ponts, it was a battalion commanders' battle, or the company commander's, or the squad leaders'. Putting Monty in command on the northern flank had no effect on the battle, but it was threatening to have a bad effect on the amity of the British-American alliance.

If Hitler made his biggest investment in Peiper, he made his best in Otto Skorzeny's battalion, which had spread out in Peiper's wake. Throughout the Bulge, those 500 or so volunteers in American uniforms were having an impact beyond their numbers. They turned signposts, causing great confusion. They spread panic. Once it was known that the Skorzeny battalion was behind the lines, the word went out with amazing speed—trust no one. The GIs, especially the MPs, questioned everyone, right up to Bradley—who plays center field for the Yankees? Who is Mickey Mouse's wife? What is the capital of Illinois? General Bradley was detained for answering Springfield to the last question; the MP insisted it was Chicago. One general was arrested and held for a few hours because he put the Chicago Cubs in the American League.

By December 21, however, a number of Skorzeny's men had been captured (most of them were shot) and the remainder were trying to get back inside German lines. Sgt. Edgar Lauritsen of the 82nd Airborne had a typical experience. While a German tank was shelling his CP, two jeeploads of soldiers in American uniforms, a captain and eight enlisted men, pulled up in front, got out, and started walking around the other side of the house toward the German lines. Lauritsen hollered to them that they were going the wrong way, but they ignored him. His suspicions aroused, he demanded to know their outfit.

"Ninety-ninth," the captain called over his shoulder.

"What outfit in the 99th?"

"Headquarters," said the captain, but the word tested his English—it came out slightly guttural.

"Halt!" Lauritsen bellowed. The captain and his men started running. Lauritsen shot the captain in the back, but his companions grabbed him and dragged him to the German lines.[10]

Another German in an American officer's uniform drove a jeep to a roadblock, where he was interrogated by a battalion staff officer. The German's speech and identification papers were flawless—too flawless, it turned out. The authentic Adjutant General's Office Identification Card, carried by all GIs, had printed at the top: "Not a Pass—For Indentification Only." With Teutonic exactness, the German forger had corrected the spelling, so that the forged card read "Identification." That missing "n" cost the German officer his life.[11]

One MP at headquarters, 84th Infantry Division, had a bright idea. He asked men he stopped at roadblocks their shirt size, on the assumption that Germans accustomed to the metric system would have trouble remembering a 14½-32 shirt wouldn't fit a big man.[12]

■

Overall, the GIs spent an inordinate amount of time checking on each other. Meanwhile, a rumor started by captured members of Skorzeny's battalion was widely and rapidly circulated—it was that the main mission was to assassinate Eisenhower. Thus everyone at SHAEF became super security-conscious. Insistent guards sealed Eisenhower into his headquarters at the Trianon Palace. Guards with machine guns took up places all around the palace, and when Eisenhower went to Verdun or elsewhere for a meeting he was led and followed by armed guards in jeeps. That kind of security, commonplace around the world a half-century later, was so unusual for SHAEF in 1944 that it left an impression of panic. Stories to that effect were what Montgomery had in mind when he described Eisenhower's telephone conversation to Brooke.

But Eisenhower was far from panicked. On December 21, he expressed his mood and perception in a rare Order of the Day. "We cannot be content with his mere repulse," he said of the Germans. "By rushing out from his fixed defenses the enemy may give us the chance to turn his great gamble into his worst defeat. . . . Let everyone hold before him a single thought—to destroy the enemy on the ground, in the air, everywhere—destroy him!"[13]

His confidence was great because his basic situation was so good. He was rushing reinforcements to the battle to take advantage of the German audacity, men and equipment in great numbers. Maj. John Harrison, at First Army headquarters, wrote his wife on December 22: "There is something quite thrilling about seeing all of the troops and armour moving in on the Kraut. There has been a steady stream for days and tho the Belgians are mighty worried I am sure they are amazed at the sights they see. The armor moves about 25 miles an hour in and out of towns and to see and hear a tank roar thru a fair sized town, turn on one tread and never slow down is quite a sight. The Belgians still line the streets and tho they are not as joyous as when we first moved in, they still wave and show their appreciation."[14]

In the middle of the Bulge, the Germans had made better progress than Peiper had managed, but they had been unable to exploit the breakthrough because the 101st Airborne and elements of the 10th Armored Division got to Bastogne before they did. Although the Germans surrounded the Americans they were denied the use of the roads and flowing around Bastogne was time-consuming. So from December 19 on they tried to overrun the place, with apparently overwhelming strength. Altogether they launched fifteen divisions at Bastogne, four of them armored, supported by heavy artillery.

Inside the perimeter, casualties piled up in the aid stations. Most went untreated, because on December 19 a German party had captured the division's medical supplies and doctors. Nevertheless, spirits stayed strong. Corp. Gordon Carson took some shrapnel in his leg and was brought into town. At the aid station, "I looked around and never saw so many wounded men. I called a medic over and said, 'Hey, how come you got so many wounded people around here? Aren't we evacuating anybody?' "

"Haven't you heard?" the medic replied.

"I haven't heard a damn thing."

"They've got us surrounded—the poor bastards."[15]

As the battle for Bastogne raged, it caught the attention of the world. The inherent drama, the circled-wagons image, the heroic resistance, the daily front-page maps showing Bastogne surrounded, the early identification of the division by PR men in the War Department, combined to make the 101st the most famous American division of the war. As the division history put it, the legend of the 101st was aided by those maps "showing one spot holding out inside the rolling tide of the worst American military debacle of modern times."[16]

But the 101st was not alone inside Bastogne. A combat command team of the 10th Armored was there, along with supporting units from the combat engineers, anti-aircraft units, and more. What stands out about the defense of Bastogne was not so much infantrymen in foxholes holding off the German tanks as the combined-arms approach the GIs used. It was something to learn for the paratroopers, who had in Normandy and Holland fought pretty much on their own.

Now they had tanks around them, but no advanced knowledge of the techniques of infantry fighting with tanks. Even as the battle raged, Col. William Roberts, CO of the 10th Armored team, circulated among the paratroopers, giving them tips on the proper employment of tanks, their capabilities and limits. Roberts's chief criticism of the 101st was that the junior officers tended to use tanks as immobile pillboxes to block roads; Roberts told them to keep the tanks moving and to use them as a mobile reserve.

Inside the thirty-kilometer perimeter encompassing Bastogne, Lt. Col. Harry Kinnard, the 101st's operations officer, organized the four infantry regiments into a combined-arms team, each with its permanent attachment of tanks, TDs (tank destroyers), and anti-tank guns. Each team was responsible for a roadblock, for a cross-roads, or for a mutually supporting position on prominent terrain.[17]

Corp. Robert Bowen, 401st Glider Infantry, 101st, a wounded veteran of Normandy and Holland, was a squad leader on the western sector of the perimeter. At dawn on December 21—following a below-zero night, with ankle-deep snow on the ground—Bowen's CO told him the enemy had slipped through and had established a roadblock between the 101st and Bastogne. "That roadblock has to be taken out, Bowen," the CO said. He gave Bowen two squads and told him to get at it.

"Short, sweet and scary," Bowen characterized the order. He wished the regiment had an officer to put in charge, but it didn't. He met with his men, discussed the situation, and agreed that there had to be a better way than just charging. At that moment, a tank appeared.

"The colonel told me to run down this road and shoot the shit out of those houses," the sergeant in command of the tank said, in a cocky way. Bowen informed him that the Germans in the houses had panzerfausts. "His mood suddenly changed," Bowen remarked, "as he had run into panzerfausts before."

"What've you got in mind, then?"

Bowen proposed that he send his squads down each side of the road, with support from enfilading fire from a squad to the left. But, he lamented, "I don't think we've got enough firepower to drive them out."

"Suppose I take care of the houses with my cannon?" the tanker asked. "My .50-cal can rake those foxholes dug in around them. OK?"

"OK?" Bowen replied. "Man, you've just come from heaven."

They went at it. The tank began to fire, cannon and machine gun. The squad on the left laid down more fire. Bowen's squads moved down the road, using marching fire. Within less than a half hour, some of the Germans were fleeing while others threw up their hands. "It was a textbook attack," Bowen said, "working better than anything we had ever done in practice."

At the roadblock, there were a dozen dead Germans, another score of wounded. "I noted how young they were, nothing but teen-aged boys." The tank sergeant was euphoric. He told Bowen, "I've been in this shit since D plus twelve and seen a lot of things. But I never saw anything like this. You guys are tops in my book."

The threat met and defeated, Bowen went back to his original position. That night the thermometer plunged again. "The night passed like a horrible dream," Bowen remembered. "Nothing I could do could keep me warm. I begged for dawn to come."

When it did, a heavy ground fog reduced visibility to near zero. Germans used the cover to move in on the American positions; their white camouflage cover helped hide them. As Bowen put it, they were "Opaque figures in snow suits emerging from nowhere." A fierce firefight ensued. Bowen looked for the tank that had been so helpful the previous day. He found it, badly damaged. The sergeant had been firing the .50-caliber when an antitank shell hit the turret just under him. His face was horribly cut by shrapnel. Bowen got him to an aid station, then returned to the original position.

Things couldn't have been much worse. Germans were scattered in a semicircle around him, firing at his men in their holes. There were eleven German tanks supporting the infantry. Bowen could do nothing about them because the 57mm antitank gun assigned to his team was useless—its wheels were frozen solid in the ground and it could not be moved. A TD from the 10th Armored had a frozen turret and had no way to thaw it. But at the critical moment, a second TD appeared. Sgt. Chester Sakwinski was in command. He held the enemy tanks at bay, rising from a sunken courtyard to fire at the enemy, then backing down to escape the counterfire.

Other members of the team were becoming fully involved. The heavy weapons platoon sent 81mm mortar fire on the enemy. A forward observer directed artillery—but there wasn't much because of a severe shell shortage in Bastogne. A half-track pulled up, bringing a squad of fighting men forward.

Bowen checked his line. "Some of their wounded lay in the snow, one babbling incoherently and the other screaming. German dead were sprawled in contorted positions." But his own casualties were mounting. An NCO, who had been in jail in Reims on December 16 and volunteered to rejoin the company, got killed. Bowen picked up a bazooka and three shells from the half-track, took careful aim at a Tiger 200 meters distant, fired—and grazed the turret. The Tiger turned its 88mm cannon on Bowen's position. He decided he had better save the remaining two rounds and disappeared into his foxhole. But a mortar shell found him. He was badly wounded and, shortly thereafter, captured. The German doctors treated him, then sent him east, to a POW camp.[18] So it went for the armored troopers and airborne infantry in Bastogne.

Lt. Helmuth Henke was an aide to Gen. Fritz Bayerlein, CO of the Panzer Lehr Division, which had been reconstituted after the pounding it had taken in France in the fall. On December 22, Bayerlein handed him a letter, "From the German Commander to the U.S.A. Commander of the encircled town of Bastogne." It demanded an "honorable surrender to save the encircled U.S.A. troops from total annihilation." Bayerlein told Henke, who spoke good English, to join a colonel from the staff, get a couple of enlisted men and two white flags, approach the American lines, arrange a local truce, and deliver the letter to the American CO.

All went well. The GIs stopped firing when the Germans did and the four-man party waved its white flags. The Germans came into American lines, where Henke told a lieutenant that he had a message for the American CO. The lieutenant blindfolded the Germans, put them in a jeep, and drove to Gen. Anthony McAuliffe's headquarters in Bastogne. A staff officer there asked Henke, "What is your business?" Henke, still blindfolded, handed over Bayerlein's written demand.

As McAuliffe read, his staff officers bombarded Henke with questions: "Why do you shoot prisoners?" "Why are German soldiers fighting in American uniforms?"

Henke replied, "I know nothing of such things and cannot imagine them happening."

Then a new voice said, "Take them back," as the staff officer placed McAuliffe's reply into Henke's hand. The Germans were driven back to the front, where their blindfolds were removed and a brief cease-fire arranged. Henke finally had a chance to read McAuliffe's response. It said, "Nuts."

He looked at his American escort, Col. Joseph Harper. "Nuts?" he asked, in disbelief.

"It means, 'Go to hell,' " Harper replied.

Henke knew what that meant. Before departing for his own lines, "I told the American officer what I told every soldier whom I took prisoner, 'May you make it back to your homeland safe and sound.'"

"Go to hell," was Harper's reply.[19]

Another face-to-face encounter between the enemies went better. German Lt. Gottfried Kischkel, an infantry officer outside Bastogne, was in his foxhole on the afternoon of December 22. An American tank was hit and began burning. Kischkel heard cries for help from the tank. "So I crawled to it. An American was hanging out of the hatch, badly wounded. I pulled him out and dragged him to a ditch, where I applied first aid."

Kischkel looked up from his bandaging and saw several Americans staring down with their M-1s pointed at him. An American lieutenant asked, in German, "What are you doing?"

"He cried for help and I helped," Kischkel replied. The Americans put their heads together. Then the lieutenant asked, "Do you want to be taken prisoner, or do you want to go back to your comrades?"

"I must return to my comrades."

"I expected no other answer," the American said. He told Kischkel to take off.[20]

On December 23 the skies cleared. The Allied air force, grounded for a week, went into action. Medium bombers hit German transport facilities, especially bridges and rail yards around and behind the Eifel. Jabos shot up German vehicles and columns. Capt. Gerd von Fallois, commanding a tank unit outside Bastogne, called it "psychologically fantastic. Airplanes everywhere. Thousands. Shitting all over us. I didn't see a single Luftwaffe plane."[21]

The American transport planes, C-47s, dropped tons of supplies into Bastogne—medicine, food, blankets (although not enough to give one to every man), ammunition, especially artillery shells—with an over 90 percent success rate. The Germans continued to attack—they launched one of their heaviest assaults on Christmas Day—but it was a fool's business. They made no gains for a heavy price against the resupplied men of the 10th Armored and the 101st Airborne. As Captain von Fallois put it, "The Americans were extraordinarily brave. It was amazing what their troops were accomplishing. I knew we wouldn't get any farther than Bastogne."[22]

From the Battle of Trois-Ponts on, Peiper ruefully told Hechler, "events turned rapidly against us."[23] As Major Guderian of the 116th Panzer Division put it, "We started with fuel enough for only fifty kilometers." Captured American fuel gave the Germans enough for another twenty kilometers. Meanwhile behind the German lines, the traffic jams had been straightened out and a supply line established, so more fuel and ammunition could be brought forward (the Germans relied on captured American supplies for food). But by the time the roads cleared, during the night of December 22–23, so did the skies. As Guderian laconically remarked, "We had no defense against air attacks. The columns could no longer come forward."[24]

Peiper's advance ended. That afternoon at 1700 hours he got an order via radio—withdraw. "When I received that message," Peiper told Hechler, "I realized that the only chance was to break out without any vehicles and wounded. Accordingly on 24 December, at 0100, we abandoned all our vehicles and started walking back."[25] For the Germans, the offensive phase of the Battle of the Bulge was over. One of Peiper's privates, Günter Brückner, asked a question to which the answer was obvious: "We were so well equipped, beautiful weapons, but what is the use of having a brandnew tank, but no gas? What is the use of having a machine gun when I have no more ammunition?"[26]

Or, what is the use of having the world's best fighter airplane when there is no fuel to run it? By this stage, the Germans had built hundreds of single-engine jets (Messerschmitt 163) and twin-engine jets (ME 262) and were going into production on a jet bomber. The Americans were not going to have jets until October. The ME 262 was so much better than any propeller-driven plane that some Allied airmen worried that if the war went on the Germans might regain control of the sky by June. But that was unlikely, because the Luftwaffe was without fuel. The all-out strategic bomber assault on German refineries and other oil-related targets had a cumulative effect that was devastating to the German army and air force.

Except for December 17, there was no air war in the first week of the Bulge. But on the 23rd in some areas, the 24th in others, the day broke clear. Captain Barensfeld led his squadron of P-47s on both days. "At last, ah hah! We were off. We knew exactly what to do and where to go. Frustration of the past several days of nothing but bad news manifested itself. Our people pitched in with a zest. Crew chiefs, armament people, everyone worked to put up the maximum amount of missions. We ran almost a shuttle operation to the battle area. There was very little Luftwaffe opposition. Evidently they had 'shot their wad' on the first two days.

"Targets all over the place. Our air controllers zeroed us in on hundreds of fat targets. We caught them out of fuel and exhausted. Hundreds and hundreds of vehicles; tank, trucks, lined up on the road as in a traffic jam."[27]

But the next day brought the frustration of being shut down. That was typical: in the thirty days between mid-December 1944 and mid-January 1945, only eight were sufficiently clear to allow missions to be flown.

For the Wehrmacht, almost everything had gone wrong, all of it predictable—indeed, exactly what Eisenhower had predicted would happen if the Germans launched an offensive in the Ardennes, did happen. It had been madness to attack in the Ardennes, an area with the most difficult terrain and least adequate road system in all of Western Europe, with insufficient fuel.

Of course, Eisenhower had tried to continue the Allied offensive in September and October, when his troops had insufficient fuel. But by December, the Allied supply lines were bringing forward fuel and ammunition in great quantity. The Allies had fuel dumps scattered throughout Belgium and Luxembourg. Peiper's supply officer had a map of the American fuel dumps, but this did Peiper little good, either because GIs defended the dumps successfully, or because they evacuated the dumps (American supply troops successfully removed over three million gallons of gasoline from the Spa-Stavelot area on the northern flank), or because they burned the fuel before Peiper could get to it. The biggest American loss to the enemy was a 400,000-gallon gasoline dump, destroyed on December 17 by a V-1 strike at Liège.[28]

Now it was the Germans' turn to retreat, abandoning their vehicles and heavy weapons, in disarray. Their week of glory was over.

9

The Holiday Season

December 24–31, 1944

DURING CHRISTMAS SEASON of 1944 there were some four million young soldiers on the Western Front, the great majority of them Protestants or Catholics. They said the same prayers when they were being shelled, directed to the same God. They joined in denouncing godless Communism, which was one side's ally and the other side's enemy.

In World War II, no hatred matched that felt by Americans against Japanese, or Russians against Germans, and vice versa. But in Northwest Europe, there was little racial hatred between the Americans and the Germans. How could there be when cousins were fighting cousins? About one-third of the U.S. Army in ETO were German-American in origin.

The Christmas season highlighted the closeness of the foes. Americans and Germans alike put up Christmas trees and used the debris of war—chaff, the tinfoil dropped by bombers to fool radar—to decorate them. Men who would never do such a thing at any other time prepared gifts for other men. On Christmas Eve and Christmas Day the men on both sides of the line had an image of a manger in Bethlehem in their minds. They sang the same carols. The universal favorite was "Silent Night."

But they were there to kill each other. There was no stand-down for Christmas. This chapter contains a series of snapshots of life at the front during the Christmas season. Except for their thoughts, for most of the men Christmas wasn't any different from any other day, so that the snapshots provide a glimpse into the time, place, and living conditions as they were not just in the holidays but throughout the winter campaign.

The scenery was like a Christmas card. It drew oohs and ahs from even the most hardened warrior. One lieutenant said later, "If it hadn't been for the fighting, that would have been . . . the most beautiful Christmas. . . . The rolling hills, the snow-covered fields and mountains, and the tall, majestic pines and firs really made it a Christmas I'll never forget in spite of the fighting."[1]

The towns evoked memories. In Arlon, Belgium, on December 20, Sgt. Bruce Egger of the 26th was amazed: "This area seemed to be untouched by the war, as the city and stores were bedecked with decorations and Christmas trees." Lt. Lee Otts, who was with Egger, remarked that "the streets were crowded with shoppers and people going home from work. . . . Everything had a holiday look about it. It really made us homesick."[2]

Nearly every one of those four million men on the Western Front was homesick. Loneliness was their most shared emotion. Christmas meant family, and reminders of Christmas were all around these men at war. Family and home meant life. The yearning for home was overpowering. Beyond thinking of loved ones, the men in the holes thought of the most ordinary day-to-day activities of civilian life—being able to flick a switch to light a room, no need for blackout curtains, able to smoke at night, hot food on dishes served at a table, cold beer, a bed!, clean sheets, regular showers, changes of clothes, nobody shooting at you!—they thought of these things and could have cried for missing them.

One of the loneliest GIs on the Western Front on Christmas Day was Pvt. Donald Chumley, a replacement assigned to the 90th Division. "I was nineteen, just out of high school—a farm boy with little experience in anything." He was led to his one-man foxhole and told to get in and watch for Germans. Chumley didn't catch the sergeant's name. He couldn't see the men to his right and left. He didn't know what squad, platoon, company, or battalion he was in.[3]

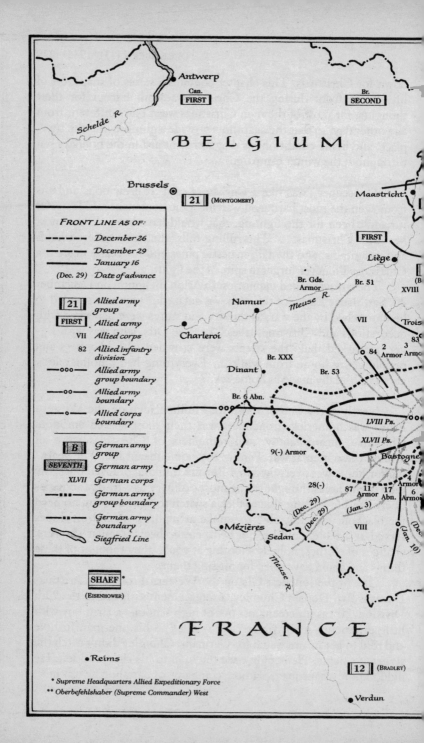

Antwerp

Can.
FIRST

Br.
SECOND

Schelde R.

BELGIUM

Brussels ◉ **21** (MONTGOMERY)

Maastricht

FRONT LINE AS OF:

- - - - - *December 26*
- - - *December 29*
———— *January 16*
(Dec. 29) *Date of advance*

FIRST

Liège

21 *Allied army group*

FIRST *Allied army*

VII *Allied corps*

82 *Allied infantry division*

—○○○— *Allied army group boundary*

—○○— *Allied army boundary*

—○— *Allied corps boundary*

B *German army group*

SEVENTH *German army*

XLVII *German corps*

■-■-■ *German army group boundary*

—■-■— *German army boundary*

〰 *Siegfried Line*

Br. Gds.
Armor

Namur

Br. 51

XVIII

Meuse R.

Trois

VII

83

Charleroi

84   2   3
Armor Armor

Br. XXX

Dinant

Br. 53

Br. 6 Abn.

LVIII Ps.

XLVII Ps.

9(-) Armor

Bastogne

28(-)

87   11   17
Armor Abn.

4
Armor

6
Armor

(Dec. 29)

(Jan. 3)

Mézières

VIII

(Dec. 29)

Sedan

(Jan. 10)

Meuse R.

SHAEF *

(EISENHOWER)

FRANCE

● Reims

* *Supreme Headquarters Allied Expeditionary Force*
** *Oberbefehlshaber (Supreme Commander) West*

12 (BRADLEY)

● Verdun

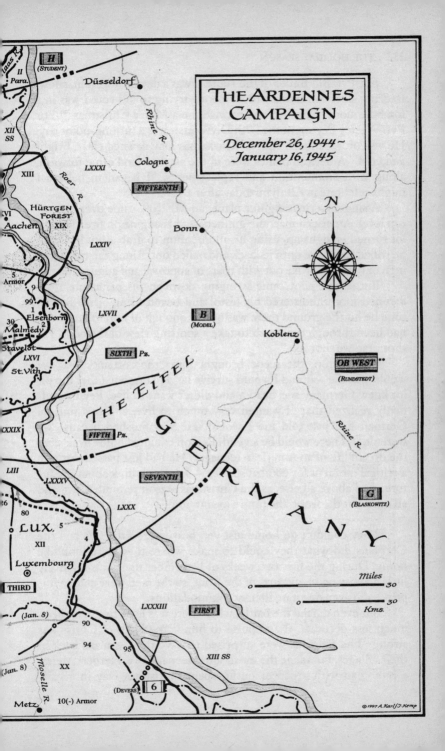

THE ARDENNES CAMPAIGN

December 26, 1944 ~ January 16, 1945

Düsseldorf

Rhine R.

H (STUDENT)

II Para.

Maas R.

XII SS

LXXXI

Cologne

Roer R.

FIFTEENTH

XIII

HÜRTGEN FOREST

Aachen

XIX

Bonn

5 Armor

LXXIV

9

99

1

Elsenborn

2

30

Malmédy

Stavelot

B (MODEL)

LXVII

Koblenz

St. Vith

LXVI

SIXTH Ps.

OB WEST ** (RUNDSTEDT)

THE EIFEL

XXXIX

FIFTH Ps.

SEVENTH

G E R M A N Y

Rhine R.

LIII

LXXXV

G (BLASKOWITZ)

LXXX

86

80

LUX.

5

XII

4

Luxembourg

THIRD

Miles
0 — 30

Kms.
0 — 30

(Jan. 8)

90

LXXXIII

FIRST

94

95

(Jan. 8)

XX

XIII SS

Moselle R.

(DEVERS) **6**

Metz

10(-) Armor

© 1997 A. Karl/J. Kemp

For Pvt. Bill Butler of the 106th it was a day of "fog, rain, snow, freezing sleet combined with someone trying to kill you. I was in a fox hole alone. I had no one to wish me a Merry Christmas."⁴ For Pvt. Wesley Peyton of the 99th Division, it was a turning-point day. He was on Elsenborn Ridge. "Christmas Day dawned clear, bright and cold." American planes were in the air, hot food came forward, along with ammunition and replacements. "I began to believe I might celebrate my 20th birthday after all."

A single German fighter plane, an ME 109, came over at tree-top level. American machine gunners set his engine on fire. The pilot turned straight up, using his momentum to grab altitude. Then he rolled the plane onto its back and bailed out. Along the ridge, the men of the 99th broke out with roars of approval and admiration.

But as the pilot came swinging down in his parachute, "the damned fool unholstered his pistol and began firing at us. By the time he hit the ground there was hardly enough of him to bury. We had been through too much to take a sporting view of the odds. He shot first; we shot last."

For Peyton, the scene brought him "the certainty that we would win the war and I would survive it." He reasoned that the pilot knew Germany was beaten and didn't want to live. Peyton suddenly realized that "I wanted very much to live, and this suicidal German had just told me I would. He was finished because we weren't."⁵ There would be an end. Peyton could go home to take up the dream life of an American teenager. He had just passed through a critical moment for combat soldiers—he could think about the future. And above all else, as the Christmas season reminded him and all others at the front, the future meant home.

They couldn't go home just yet, however, so the GIs and the Germans did what they could to make where they were look like home. During the first two weeks of December there was relatively little activity on many parts of the front, so the men were able to improve and even decorate their accommodations.

But even during the battle, when there was little time to reflect, much less decorate, the impulse to honor the birth of Christ was strong. The Belgians were surprised to have the Germans back in their villages, but made the most of it—teenage Pvt. Herbert Meier, a radioman with a panzer outfit, spent Christmas Day in a half-destroyed village north of Bastogne. He bought a Christmas card to send home to his parents in Bavaria.*

Meier's squad had moved into a cellar in a half-destroyed village north of Bastogne. He cut down a small Christmas tree to decorate the cellar and the squad proceeded to have a party. The highlights were coffee—captured from the Americans, the first coffee Meier had enjoyed since D-Day—and a bottle of schnapps. Fifty years later Meier could not recall the name of the village, but as to the coffee and schnapps, "That I still remember exactly!" He also recalled standing guard in "ice cold weather," and one of his comrades receiving the news that his brother had been killed on the Russian front, which put a damper on the celebration.[6]

A few days earlier the newly arrived 99th Division had taken its position in the Ardennes and gone to work building double-walled log shelters. "We looked forward to spending Christmas secure in our log bunkers," one sergeant wrote, "with a decorated tree, singing carols and enjoying a hot meal."[7]

Many men were in houses. That is where most rear-echelon people lived and slept. Sometimes front-line men, too, but only when the line ran down the middle of a village. But if the houses were within the enemy's artillery range the GIs were staying in the cellars. In many cases the second and first floors had been blown away anyway and if they weren't they made inviting targets. So even in town men lived below ground level.

Almost any civilian walking into one of those cellars would have immediately declared them uninhabitable. The air was a mixture of sweat, brick dust, soot, and cigarette smoke. It could not be breathed. It was too dark to see much more than outlines. It was either too hot or too cold and it had no running water.

Every front-line soldier who walked into one of those cellars thought it the most desirable place in his entire world. The cellars were secure from all but a direct hit. They were dry. There was coffee on the stove. The cooks provided hot food. Sometimes there was

*One of the saddest events of that Christmas season came when General Cota, commanding the 28th Division by this time, ordered the Christmas mail burned so that it would not fall into the hands of the Germans. Over 5,000 letters, cards, and packages were piled in a courtyard near the division CP at Wiltz, Luxembourg, gasoline poured over, and burned. (Chernitsky, *Voices from the Foxholes*, 16.)

a radio and "Axis Sally" playing American music. The exhausted GI could push some straw into a corner, lie down, and plunge into a deep sleep, completely relaxed because he felt secure.

Usually, he was right—he was secure. Even during heavy shellings, direct hits on cellars were rare. Still, they happened. Capt. Günter Materne of the German artillery was in Belgium. "On Christmas Eve of 1944, my men and I were lying in the basement of a corner house. I was lying near the back on some straw. At about 2200 a shell exploded in our cellar. It came through the wall before it exploded." Materne's two radiomen were killed instantly. His sergeant was badly wounded and he had shrapnel in his back. As he was being pulled out the house burned down with the others still inside.[8]

At the beginning of the month, Company K of the 333rd Regiment had been relieved on the line and gone into a Belgian village to spend the night. Pvts. Donald Stauffer and Jim Sterner scouted for cellars. Stauffer found a beauty, big enough to hold a platoon, protected by an arched brick roof. He went looking for Sterner to give him the good news.

Sterner had found a cellar of sorts. He threw himself down. Stauffer found him and said, "Hey, I've found a really great place, let's go."

"Don, I'm so goddam tired I'm not going to move," Sterner groaned. "I don't care if I get killed."

What the hell, Stauffer decided. He stayed with Sterner. Meanwhile another platoon moved into the cellar Stauffer had found. About 0033, there was a terrible explosion. A huge German shell had hit the upper part of the house, blown in the wall, and collapsed the roof of the cellar. Six men were killed, eight wounded. (The battalion's official journal for that day noted the "usual morning mortar fire. Balance of the day quiet except for intermittent mortar fire.") Pulling the living out of the debris was a nightmare. For the wounded men, it was torture. Captain Leinbaugh tried to comfort one man by assuring him that he would be okay, then by remarking on how lucky the soldier was, he would be home for Christmas. The man died within moments.[9]

If the village was under observation, as it almost always was, men didn't dare go outside during the day. Usually the water was off and the sewers were clogged, so the toilets were soon overflowing. Pvt. Gene Amici confessed, "To tell you the goddam truth, I never took a crap outside. I don't believe anybody else did either. We were in the cellars, and we'd shit on the floor upstairs—in the parlor. But [as we advanced] division HQ moved up, and they were finally where we had been in the combat zone. But now it was quiet back there—no need for them to be in the cellars. They could sit in the living room. So they put out a written order. 'There'll be no more shitting in the houses, goddamn it. Use the latrine.' "[10]

If a village had been or was the scene of a battle, its civilian population was usually gone. The first men into a village got first crack at looting, but they couldn't couldn't carry much silver or any paintings or furniture. Besides, the family took its best portable items with it when it fled. But what the combat troops wanted most— food, a change in diet—they often found. Shelves of canned fruits, vegetables, and meats were emptied in a night. It made for some memorable holiday feasts.

Corp. Clair Galdonik of the 90th Division found himself on Christmas Eve in an undestroyed home just inside Germany. His company had occupied the town at dusk. The Germans thought civilians were still there. To keep them fooled, the company CO told the men to build fires. The smoke rising from the homes worked: there was no shelling that night.

But in Galdonik's house, the chimney wasn't drawing. Smoke filled the room. After putting out the fire and clearing the air, Galdonik investigated. He found that the stovepipes were stuffed with smoked hams and sausages that the German family had tried to hide. There was enough to provide his squad with two days of banqueting.[11]

That same Christmas Eve, Pvt. Gottfried Kischkel, a German infantryman, was driving in Belgium. "Look in the trees," someone shouted. There was the improbable sight of two large canned hams with "Hormel" printed on them hanging in a net. How they got there wasn't Kischkel's concern. After retrieving them, he and his crew requested quarters for the night at a Belgian home. It was granted, and on Christmas Day the host family prepared the hams, adding bread, potatoes, fruit salad, and apple liquor of their own. "I can still remember that exactly," Kischkel said in an interview fifty years later.

The Belgian civilians and German soldiers gathered around a

large table. The village, like most of those along Germany's border with France, Belgium, and Holland, was a mix of Germans and Frenchmen, Belgians, or Dutch. In this case the man of the house rose and said in German, "I am the mayor of this little town. Although our countries are at war, I came from German ancestry, as you can hear from my accent. This feast is a friendly gesture to you, as you are all poor young men so unlucky to find yourselves fighting a war on Christmas Day."[12]

There was no general cease-fire anywhere on Christmas Day. Apparently it never occurred to anyone to even suggest it. But the urge to go to church was widely felt. Lieutenant Otts attended services conducted by an American chaplain in a village church. The windows were blown out and "the church was pretty well torn up, but the service was very impressive. The dirty, unshaven men were standing among the ruins of a once beautiful church with the sun pouring in through the holes in the ceiling."[13]

Pvt. George McAvoy of the 9th Armored Division was in Fratin, Belgium, on Christmas Eve. He attended a midnight mass at the village church, along with every man in his company not on duty and most of the town's inhabitants. As the church was jammed, the GIs took seats in the rear. They were in combat dress and armed, which caused considerable embarrassment. Rifles leaned against the pews would slip on the hardwood and crash to the floor. The men put their helmets under the pews in front of them; when people knelt they kicked the helmets and sent them spinning along the floor.

"It was the noisiest service I ever attended," McAvoy wrote. "But the sense of comfort, well-being and safety was amazing."

Throughout the service, McAvoy noted the boys up in the choir stall were giggling. It turned out that one of the squads had gone into the church shortly after dark, thrown their bedrolls down around the altar, and gone to sleep. When the priest arrived he let them sleep. What set the boys to giggling was the sight of one of the GIs suddenly waking up, hearing the organ and seeing the priest, and crying out "I've bought it!"[14]

A custom that was different for the two sides was the Christmas feast. For the GIs, that meant turkey. For the Germans that meant goose or ham. The cooks did their best to get a real Christmas meal up to the front, with varying results. If it got to the foxholes, the turkey or ham was likely to be frozen. At division headquarters level, the feasting could be almost grand. Even the 101st Airborne CO, General McAuliffe, and his staff did fairly well. They sat at a table covered by a cloth, with a centerpiece, and ate turkey and trimmings off real chinaware with silver knives and forks.

McAuliffe was all pumped up. His boys had held, the skies had cleared, help was coming. On Christmas Eve, he somewhere found a printing press and put out a Christmas greeting to his men.

"What's merry about all this, you ask?" was the opening line. "Just this: We have stopped cold everything that has been thrown at us. . . . The Germans surround us. . . . Their Commander demanded our surrender in the following impudent arrogance." There followed the four-paragraph message demanding surrender. Then McAuliffe reprinted his reply: "To the German Commander: NUTS! The American Commander."

McAuliffe concluded: "We are giving our country and our loved ones at home a worthy Christmas present and being privileged to take part in this gallant feat of arms and truly making for ourselves a Merry Christmas."

McAuliffe's men in the foxholes were not so upbeat. Their Christmas Eve dinner consisted of cold white beans. In his company, Captain Winters was last to go for chow. All he got was "five white beans and a cup of cold broth."[15] At least his company didn't get attacked on Christmas Day. On the other side of Bastogne, the Germans launched their heaviest attacks ever to try one last time to break through. They failed.

That was but one of many attacks launched on Christmas Day, by both sides. They were there to kill, holy day or not. On the front, the dead and dying were all around them. Sergeant Egger recalled an attack his company made on a German-occupied village late on the afternoon of Christmas Eve. German machine guns hit the advancing GIs. Two men were wounded, one killed. The platoon dug in. "A wounded man kept crying, 'Mother, Mother! Help me!' as he struggled to rise. Another burst from the machine gun silenced him. That beseeching plea on that clear, cold Christmas night will remain with me for the rest of my life."

Shortly after midnight, the company resumed the attack. It advanced to a frozen ditch beside the road, where it attracted concentrated German machine-gun fire. The men threw themselves into the ditch, where they remained stretched out prone on the frozen snow for six and a half hours. They began to fall asleep. Lieutenant Otts crawled back to them several times, shaking them awake and making them kick their feet and flex their hands and fingers. At dawn the Germans counterattacked. They were repulsed. Then the Americans tried again. "We lost several men that day who would not have been hit if they had been given any infantry training," Otts commented. "One of my men was killed while standing up firing when he should have been lying flat in the snow. I saw him and yelled at him to get down, but he couldn't hear me." It was a Christmas that left Otts and his men "stunned and haunted."[16]

Sgt. D. Zane Schlemmer of the 82nd Airborne recalled a scene of "total black and white; the whiteness of the snowy fields in stark contrast to the darkness of the forests and the long column of troopers struggling under the weight of their total possessions." Through Christmas Eve night and on into Christmas Day, Schlemmer's company was marching to the rear, to take up new positions. The paratroopers hated to give up ground, but they were in a salient and the brass decided to shorten the line. The men were sure the Germans would attempt to attack before they got dug in.

So, when dawn came on, Schlemmer and his buddies were "feverishly grubbing" in the rocky, frozen, root-bound soil. In a near frenzy they set up their weapons, stashed supplies of ammo, placed antitank mines. Snow began to fall, masking the line. Canteens of water froze. The troopers sat in their holes, straining to hear and see.

Darkness came around 1630. The outposts reported that a large force of Germans was approaching. Then, in Schlemmer's words, "Out of the night, through the falling snow, came the German columns trudging in their heavy coats, rifles slung over their shoulders, along the road. Some talking, some smoking, all completely oblivious to the paratroopers dug in mere yards away.

"The wait for the signal to open fire seemed endless; when it came, the firefight was intense and devastating. The falling snow mercifully covered the remains of the two German battalions that, in that short time, ceased to exist."

The American paratroopers went out into the field the next day to retrieve usable weapons. They found a wicker basket, carried on a pole between two German soldiers. It contained a tub of butter.

When they returned to their lines, they found that the cooks had brought up some ice-cold coffee and sliced roast turkey, solidly frozen—their Christmas meal had arrived a day late. They used the butter to heat the turkey over small fires at the bottoms of their foxholes. "No finer Christmas dinner has ever been," Sergeant Schlemmer remarked.[17]

On December 21, Lt. Col. Samuel Hogan's task force of seventeen tanks, two half-tracks, and about 400 men had been cut off in the village of Marcouray, on the northern shoulder of the Bulge. It was a pocket-sized Bastogne. Hogan's parent division, the 3rd Armored, was too hard-pressed to attempt a rescue. Ammunition, rations, medical supplies were short or gone. An attempt to shoot in plasma using artillery shells didn't work. Hogan's men had to endure without fresh supplies or reinforcements for the next two days.

At noon on Christmas Eve, a German jeep approached Marcouray under a white flag. A lieutenant, speaking English, demanded that Hogan surrender. He said resistance was useless, as three panzer divisions surrounded the village, and added that he was authorized to take an American officer on a tour of the German positions.

Hogan replied, "We have orders to hold out to the end. Tell your commander to go to Hell!"

That afternoon, seven C-47 aircraft tried to drop supplies to Task Force Hogan (which by now had caught the reporters' attention and was being called in the newspapers "Hogan's 400"). German 88s got six of the seven, and the supplies that were dropped came down outside the village. The beneficiaries were the Germans and the farmers.

The following day, just as Hogan was finishing his Christmas dinner of cold K-rations, Maj. Gen. Maurice Rose, the much-admired and loved CO of the 3rd Armored, radioed orders to Hogan to destroy his heavy weapons and vehicles and get out on foot. The men set to draining the oil from the engines, then running them until they froze up, putting sugar in the gasoline, and dropping breechblocks into a well. Capt. Louis Spigelmann, the surgeon, and several of his medics volunteered to stay with the wounded. The less seriously wounded guarded the German prisoners knowing that roles would reverse when the German force moved in.

At 1630, small groups began to move out. Hogan was with the last group to leave, at 1830. The American lines were ten miles away, on a straight line. Hogan was wearing fleece-lined British flying boots, not made for walking through snow. To his dismay, he had to stop his group to rest. Not until dawn did the first units reach friends. Hogan was the last to arrive, at 1400 December 26. When he reported to General Rose, Rose wanted to know why he was the last man out. Hogan thought of several heroic answers he might give but decided instead to tell the truth: "My feet hurt."[18]

Pvt. Phillip Stark was a nineteen-year-old machine gunner in the 84th Division. He arrived on Christmas Eve at a position outside the Belgian village of Verdenne on the northern shoulder of the Bulge. His company had been on the offensive for a month and as a result lost 175 out of the original 200 men. Replacements had brought it back to strength. "Upon arrival in this sector," Stark wrote three years later, recording his experiences on paper for fear of forgetting details, "we were told no prisoners. They didn't say, 'Shoot any German who surrenders,' but there was no alternative. Our forces were spread thin. We had no one to take care of those who surrendered or were wounded. Few people back home were aware of or could understand the necessity of the thing."

At twilight, the German troops in Verdenne began to celebrate. "Sounds and songs carried well across the cold clear air." Too well for Stark's safety—officers at regimental level heard the songs and decided to give the Germans a reminder of Washington crossing the Delaware to attack the Hessian troops on Christmas Eve 1776. Stark's platoon was ordered to attack and drive the Germans from the town. That meant going up a hill. In the dark the company got to the top, only to be shelled by American artillery. Stark and his buddy Wib tried to dig in, but below the frozen earth there was rock. They were digging from the prone position and despite frantic efforts, when dawn came "our hole was only about a foot deep and six feet long. Wib was 6'2" and I'm 6'6", but at least we were able to keep ourselves below the all important ground level.

"This is how we spent Christmas Eve in 1944."

Christmas morning, Stark got to talking to Wib about the stories he had heard or read from the First World War, when on Christmas the front-line soldiers would declare a truce. "We longed for a lull, for a day of peace and safety." Instead they got a German barrage, intended to cover the retreat of German vehicles from Verdenne. Stark began cutting down fleeing enemy infantry: "Only on this Christmas Day did I ever find combat to be as pictured in the movies. We blazed away ruthlessly. This action could not be understood or accepted by persons not having combat experience."

At dawn the following day, German infantry and tanks counterattacked. The remainder of the platoon retreated, but Stark stayed with his machine gun, even when Wib took a bullet in the middle of his forehead. "Now I was alone and for the first time I was sure that I too was going to die. But I kept on firing, hoping to keep them off. By now three enemy tanks were very close and firing their machine guns and cannon directly at my position. I was nearing the end of my second box of ammunition." A German bullet ricocheted off his machine gun, broke into bits, and slammed into his left cheek, blinding him in the left eye. He ran to the rear only to bump up against a burning German tank. Then over the hill and back to where he had started three days ago, on Christmas Eve. He had lost an eye and won a Silver Star. In his sector, nothing had been gained by either side in this series of attacks and counterattacks.[19]

One thing about life in a foxhole—you had a front-row seat for the sensory pleasure of seeing the enemy get pounded by American artillery and airplanes. The sights of war are spectacular. Shells bursting, buildings blazing, tracers filling the sky. There is nothing in civilian life to compare.

The infantry were in the front row for aerial battles as well, which could also be spectacular and could catch up the emotions as nothing else. Air battles over the front lines had something of a football game atmosphere—the Germans on the far side cheering their boys overhead, the Americans on their side doing the same—but of course it was not a game.

On Christmas Day, Captain Cooper witnessed considerable air action. It began shortly after dawn. The sky was crystal clear. He could see flight after flight of B-17s flying at 20,000 feet, headed for the enemy rear. "It was indeed a welcome sight. It was St.-Lô all over again. . . . The lead squadron was trailing those long contrails like a series of diamond necklaces in the sky."

German fighters appeared. They went for the lead plane. Cooper was holding his breath. "My fascination turned to horror as suddenly the lead plane literally exploded in midair."

The Germans were armed with rockets. They could stay just far enough behind their target to be out of range of the .50-caliber machine guns of the tail gunner. Cooper thought "the accuracy of these rocket-firing German fighters amazing." Another plane got hit; a bomb in the bay exploded, cutting the plane in half. A third plane lost an entire wing. Two others had engines set on fire "and started spiraling like wounded birds struck with flaming arrows. These spirals became tighter and tighter as the planes plunged headlong down to earth." Cooper didn't want to watch, but the sight was magnetic.

Five out of twelve planes were shot down. All across the sky parachutes began popping open. Cooper counted twenty-five. Debris plummeted downward—landing gears, engines, pieces of wing, parts of the fuselage, and of course the bombs. Even though unarmed, some of the bombs exploded on impact. One B-17, more or less intact, crashed into the ground. "The explosion was unbelievable as the gasoline and the six-ton bomb load went off. A column of flame and debris erupted some thousand feet into the air scattering parts in all directions."

Cooper and others noted a piece of broken wing descending on a parachutist some 500 feet from the ground. The men on the ground screamed and waved frantically to get him to slip his chute to one side, but without luck. The wing sheared the parachute in half and dropped the airman to his death. Another parachutist was headed straight for Cooper's position. A German ME-109 dove at him, his machine guns wide open. Again the guys on the ground screamed and hollered and waved their arms. He saw them and by kicking violently slipped his chute to one side and the pilot missed him. The pilot made a wide turn and came back for another pass. By this time the parachutist was much lower and the pilot was so intent on killing him that he misjudged and crashed into the side of a quarry, killing himself with a terrible explosion. The medics brought in the parachutist: he was a bombardier and was uninjured, except for a frozen foot—he had kicked off his flying boot when he was slipping his chute.[20]

On Christmas Eve, Pvt. Joe Tatman of the 9th Armored found himself with his squad hiding in a hayloft outside Bastogne, well within German lines. They had been trapped there five days and

Above: Piper Cubs could fly in almost any conditions, but this one got defeated by snow. The pilot, Lt. George Kilmer had 250 missions since D-Day. The little spotter planes were invaluable to American artillery and tanks.

The Air War

Right: June 23, Normandy. Sgt. Bernard Janora on the radio with the pilot of a Piper Cub; he will relay the messages to nearby artillery battalions.

Below: The little planes were terribly vulnerable, as they flew so slow and so low. This one was hit by German machinegun fire near Darmstadt, Germany, on March 25. The pilot, although wounded, managed to crash-land successfully, if on his back. He survived.

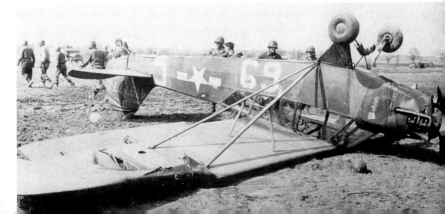

The wreckage of a B-17 burns in a pasture in France. It had been hit while returning from a mission over Germany and managed to make it to France before crashlanding. The crew escaped with only bruises.

The toughness of the B-17 was legendary. Here "Me and My Gal," with three engines gone, managed to make it to Belgium before the crew had to bail out. Eight out of ten crew members escaped. The mark on the hillside in the foreground was from the impact of the pilotless plane, which bounded from this point over the stream and landed on the far hillside, intact.

At Istres Airport near Marseilles, July 15, three crewmen pose beside "Rum Dum," the B-17 that had the record for combat missions at 101. The plane was then put to work flying wounded to England.

The payoff for air superiority: whenever a German soldier heard a plane overhead, he ducked. When a GI heard one, he looked up and smiled.

The Fall Battles

German prisoners being double-timed to a POW cage by their GI captors. Near Maarland, Holland, September 13, 1944.

A 155mm gun mounted on a Sherman tank chassis fires across the Moselle River, September.

The 9th Infantry Division, afoot and riding the back of a tankdozer, passes through the dragons' teeth in the Siegfried line, September.

October 9, Holland. Two American paratroopers on the attack, despite the German barrage, in Operation Market-Garden.

A "Repple Depple" in Luneville, France, October 12. Boredom and a sense of isolation were the dominant mood in these depots.

Aachen, October 15. In a battle that did precious little good for either side, the ancient city was all but destroyed.

Monschau, Germany, October 25. A 60mm mortar team from the 24th Cavalry at work.

American infantry on the attack in the Hurtgen, November 4. In about as unfavorable country as could be for undertaking an offensive, the GIs kept at it.

OPPOSITE:
The Hurtgen was a terrible place to do battle. A major problem was the absence of all-weather roads. *Top:* Engineers work to build one. *Bottom:* Tight turns and severely limited visibility reduced the effectiveness of American tanks.

Right: Sgt. Mike Ala, 4th Infantry Division, on the radio in the Hurtgen Forest, November 18.

Below: Hurtgen, December 9. German prisoners being escorted to the rear by a GI from the 9th Division.

The fall rains made life miserable even without fighting. Here GIs from the 9th Division advance into the Hurtgen, December 12.

Jungersdorf, Germany, December 12. GIs from the 9th Division with a bag of captured Germans. You can distinguish the victors from the vanquished by the smiles on the victors' faces.

Sgt. David Kimmell, 4th Division, in contact with two platoons in the Hurtgen, December 16.

The GIs had no idea what was coming. On December 15, before the snow began, two men from the 5th Armored Division relax in their foxhole.

On December 16, the German army struck out in its last great offensive of the war. The Germans had been retreating since July. Going over to the offensive raised their spirits, as these captured German photographs, all taken on the second day of the Battle of the Bulge, demonstrate.

The GIs were surprised. Some were shocked. But enough stayed to do their duty.
Above: On December 17, GIs from the 2nd Infantry Division crouch in a ditch during a German shelling, ready to fight back when the German infantry began to attack. *Below:* December 20, U.S. tank destroyers attached to the 82nd Airborne Division move up to challenge the German offensive.

Unidentified American infantry move to the front, through the Kinkelter Woods in Belgium, December 20.

The crew of a 57mm gun on their way to Luxembourg, by convoy, December 22.

Movie stars made tours to boost morale, but not many got near the front lines. Marlene Dietrich did. Here she sings for front-line infantry in a barn near Bixieres, France; the town was shelled during her performance.

The Ardennes, December 23. The crew of a 105mm cannon gets ready to send Hitler a Christmas card.

Belgium, December 25. The urge to attend services and pray was overwhelming. Every man in the battle, German or American, who could went to church.

Christmas 1944. In a manger six hundred meters from the German lines, men from the 94th Division dry out and count their blessings.

had run out of food, "but we talked about Christmas and home, never giving up our hopes."

At 1600, the Germans found Tatman's group and forced it to surrender. A captain took charge. He had been a lawyer in New York. He explained that he had returned to his homeland to settle his father's estate and got caught up in the war. He took the prisoners into the kitchen of the farmhouse. His cooks were preparing for a Christmas party. He gave the GIs milk and donuts. He talked and joked about the war. He hoped it would end soon so that everyone could go home.

After they ate, the captain gave the Americans hot water, towels, and shaving materials. He told them to shave and wash up, as he was inviting them to join the Christmas party. The elderly Belgian couple had set a large beautiful table in a decorated dining room, covered with all kinds of food and drinks, including meats. There were plates holding "all brands of American cigarettes." After eating, the two sides joined in singing. The prisoners sang "Silent Night" in English; the captors sang it in German. The captain offered a toast of good luck to the prisoners. He explained that he and his men wanted to give the party because they realized that in the morning, Christmas Day, the GIs "would begin their journey to Hell."[21]

Hell was a German POW camp. By late December they were growing rapidly, as the GIs captured in the first days of the Bulge began to come in. The trip from Belgium to the camps in eastern Germany was Purgatory. Private Vonnegut of the 106th had a typical experience. After his group was forced to surrender, the Germans marched the POWs sixty miles to Limburg. There was no water, food, or sleep. In Limburg they were marched to the railroad yard and loaded into 40-and-8s, French railway cars from World War I designed to hold forty men or eight horses. The Germans crowded 60 men into Vonnegut's car; Pvt. Ian Morrison's car held 100 men. The cars were unventilated and unheated. There were no sanitary accommodations. In Vonnegut's car, half the men had to stand so the other half could lie down to sleep. In Morrison's car no one could lie down. In every car there were any number of men with severe dysentery. There they stayed for four days.

Shortly after dark on Christmas Eve, in Morrison's car "the

only sounds were the moaning of our comrades within our box, and those fore and aft of us."

In one of those cars, a man began singing. "He obviously had a trained voice; he was a superb tenor," Pvt. George Zak recalled. He sang "Silent Night." Soon the others in the car took it up. It spread to the cars up and down the line. The German guards joined in the singing.

Suddenly, the air raid sirens went off. Soon bombs from the RAF were dropping all around the railroad yard. "Let us out!" the POWs screamed as they pounded at the locked siding doors. "For Christ's sake, give us a chance!" But the guards had run off. The thinnest man in the car managed to squeeze through one of the vent windows and removed the wire locking the sliding door. The POWs poured out and ran up and down the track, opening the wire on the other cars. They saw a cavelike gully and ran to it. Some made it, but about 150 got killed or wounded.

When the all-clear sounded the guards returned, rounded up the prisoners and put them back in the cars. It was still dark. Slowly the excited talk died down as the adrenaline drained. Soon it was a silent night.

"Hey," someone called out. "Hey, tenor, give us some more."

A voice from the other end of the car responded, "He ain't here. He got killed."[22]

So it went on the Western Front during the Christmas season, 1944.

Christmas Eve at the Flossenburg POW camp in Bavaria was a macabre experience. A few days earlier, fifteen American paratroopers, captured in Holland in September, had escaped from the camp. But they were caught on December 23 and returned to Flossenburg. There the SS guards held a sadistic "Christmas party" for the inmates, who were compelled to stand in ranks and watch as the guards hanged the recaptured paratroopers.[23]

Out in the English Channel, the transport *Léopoldville,* a converted luxury liner, was headed toward Le Havre, bringing 2,223 replacements for the Battle of the Bulge. The officers were from the Royal Navy, the crew was Belgian, the passengers were Americans, a fine show of Allied unity.

Nineteen-year-old Sgt. Henry Andersen and 150 others went up to the deck just before midnight, to sing Christmas carols. There was a boom. A torpedo fired from a U-boat had hit amidships.

The ship shivered, then began to sink. The officers and crew jumped into the lifeboats—there were only fourteen of them—and took off, leaving the U.S. soldiers to fend for themselves. Andersen managed to jump from *Léopoldville* to the deck of a destroyer that came alongside. Others who tried the same missed and were crushed as big waves pushed the two ships into each other. Still others drowned or succumbed to hypothermia. Altogether, 802 GIs died in the incident, but not one British officer or Belgian seaman died. Bad show for Allied unity. The incident therefore was covered up. There was no investigation, no court-martial.[24]

The *Léopoldville* Christmas Eve disaster was a consequence of the difficulties the Allies had created for themselves with their inadequate replacement policy and of the problems the Germans had caused for them in the Ardennes. The Allies were sending every available man across the Channel on every available boat. The *Léopoldville* was one of them. Built to carry 360 passengers, it held 2,223 troops and a crew of 237 (including 93 natives of the Belgian Congo, with 24 British seamen to man the guns, and a Belgian captain who spoke only Flemish). She was more a ferry than a transport, and was badly run-down. "What a helluva looking boat," Pvt. Leo Zarnosky said. "I don't think we'll make it across, let's swim."[25]

It was early winter, a time when the Channel is always rough and often stormy. The German U-boats posed another threat. On December 23 a troop carrier had been hit by a torpedo in the Channel, outside Cherbourg. But it was a short trip to Cherbourg—half a day—and the troops were needed at the front, immediately.

To speed the process, ordinary precautions were neglected. Lifeboats were not hung over the side, ready for instant use. There were insufficient life jackets, and no instructions on their use were given to those who got one. With men packed into the very bowels of the ship, there were no lifeboat or abandon-ship drills. There were many other screw-ups, most caused by haste. The rescue effort was a disgrace.

As a result, what should have been a minor loss—the

Léopoldville—was the equivalent of losing a full-strength rifle regiment, as the 1,400 or so survivors had to be sent to the hospital rather than the front line when they finally got to Cherbourg.

The survivors don't talk much about it. Lt. Bill Everhard commented, "Along with many others, I have tried for almost 50 years to bury my memories of a night of fear, terror and grief." He adds with some bitterness, "All of us have been helped in this attempt to forget by the governments of the United States, Great Britain, and Belgium." The American cover-up continued until 1959, when the office of the U.S. inspector general released a sanitized summary of its 1945 top secret report. It charged that the Belgian crew were "negligent in performance of their duties. They were not at their posts instructing passengers, reporting condition of the ship, and launching lifeboats. They seemed interested only in themselves."

The report also noted that had an "Abandon Ship" order been given over the loudspeaker system, undoubtedly many would have been saved. Actually, such an order was given—in Flemish. Only the Belgian crew members understood it. The report found no American responsibility and made no mention of the hurry-up, almost frantic nature of the transport system to meet the crisis of the Bulge. The British Admiralty's Board of Inquiry report was released in the 1960s. It exonerated the ship's officers and crew. The Belgian government, in 1992, issued its report, which praised the officers and crew and claimed that the lifeboats were put to sea with GIs aboard.[26]

The incident has never received the attention given to the somewhat similar disaster at Slapton Sands before D-Day, although the loss of life was about the same and although the cover-up was more thorough and lasted longer. The main reason is that three governments are involved, but perhaps in some part it is because of when it happened. It is just too painful to think about.

Asked for his story, Pvt. George Baker, a survivor, replied, "That Christmas Eve, when I with so many others jumped into the sea, filled with oh so many boys crying out to God and Mother, is just something that I do not want to recall."[27]

At the front, Lt. Charles Stockell, a forward artillery observer for the 2nd Division, had two unforgettable experiences on Christmas Day. He was at Elsenborn Ridge. Late on Christmas Eve, he was at a company hq in a cellar. At about 2345 hours, the firing died

DECEMBER 24–31, 1944   247

down. "At the stroke of midnight, without an order or a request, dark figures emerged from the cellars. In the frosty gloom voices were raised in the old familiar Christmas carols. The heavy snowflakes fell softly, covering the weapons and signs of war. The infantry, in their frontline positions, could hear voices 200 yards away in the dark joining them, in German, in the words to 'Silent Night.' It was a time when all men could join in the holy and sacred memories of the story of the Christ Child, and renew a fervent prayer for peace, goodwill toward men!"

Within an hour the shooting started. By daylight, it was going full-blast. The company's position was easily spotted from the air because of panels on the ground at the crossroads, and the sky had cleared. Nevertheless two P-47s came in on strafing runs. No one was hurt. But one pilot turned and made a second run, this time dropping his 100-pound bomb on the mess tent, where 100 men were eating. There were many casualties.

Stockell felt there was no excuse, especially for the second run. Those were his men lying dead and wounded under the bits of canvas. He was infuriated to the point that "I put 75 rounds from a truck-mounted 50 cal. MG through his motor. He went up in flames. He rolled his plane and parachuted. We jumped in a jeep and were fully intent on beating him to death. He came down, fortunately for him, next to the division MPs. We were told he was cashiered."[28]

For that pilot, as for so many others on the Western Front in 1944, it was a Christmas best forgotten.

Patton woke on Christmas morning, looked at the sky, and said to himself, "Lovely weather for killing Germans." But to his disappointment, the spearhead 4th Armored Division for his thrust north to relieve Bastogne failed to break the siege that day. That evening Patton had Christmas dinner with Bradley at Bradley's headquarters in Luxembourg City. Bradley had spent the day with Montgomery, who had told him that Eisenhower's insistence on an immediate counterattack against the base of the German salient was impossible. It would take weeks for U.S. First Army to be able to reorganize itself and prepare an attack. Patton thought Montgomery's statements were "disgusting."[29]

The next morning, 4th Armored moved out, with the 37th Tank Battalion (twenty Shermans strong), commanded by Lt. Col.

Creighton Abrams, in the lead. Jabos—P-47s—preceded them laying bombs into the German lines only a couple of hundred meters ahead of the advancing tanks. Abrams's orders were to go this way, then that, to more or less sneak through the German lines encircling Bastogne, but he took it on himself to seize an opportunity and drive straight ahead. He felt a strong urgency because he could see C-47s dropping supplies into Bastogne taking heavy flak from the German 88s around the circle.

The P-47s hit the village in Abrams's path, finishing up their bombing run just as the first tanks came into the town. Keep moving, Abrams ordered. They did, and at 1650, December 26, Lieutenant Charles Boggess drove the first vehicle from 4th Armored into the lines of the 101st Airborne. He was followed by Capt. William Dwight. "How are you, General?" Dwight asked General McAuliffe, who had driven out to the perimeter to greet him.

"Gee, I am mighty glad to see you," McAuliffe replied.[30]

With the siege of Bastogne broken, with Peiper and the others in retreat, with the bad weather continuing, the week after Christmas was relatively quiet on the front. But to the rear American trucks were rushing reinforcements and supplies forward, preparing for the counterattack. As 1944 drew to an end, the U.S. Army in ETO was getting ready to punish the Germans for coming out of their fortifications.

The Army had come a long way in the second half of 1944, from the English Channel to the German border. Together with the British and Canadian armies, it had taken the beaches in the greatest amphibious assault in history. It had endured the stalemate in the hedgerow fighting, June and July in Normandy; it had swept through France in a lightning campaign in August; it had outstripped its supply and been forced to stop in September; it had engaged in a long, costly, unnecessary, and unsuccessful offensive through November on into December; it had been caught by surprise and pounded badly in the second half of December, but it had recovered, held, and now was preparing the final offensive.

LIFE IN ETO

It is not possible to follow the campaign in Northwest Europe without understanding the conditions under which the GIs fought. As always in war, terrain, weather, and enemy firepower dominated the soldiers' lives, especially at night. These and other factors impacted on them throughout the campaign, whether before the breakout in Normandy or during the race to the German border or while on the defensive in the Ardennes. These factors continued to have an impact through the 1945 fighting, and include such things as: What it was like to spend a night in a foxhole; the universal praise of the GIs for the Army's Medical Corps, from medics in the field to the nurses and doctors in the tented hospitals; how bitterly the GIs resented the replacement and reinforcement policies; the terrors and triumphs of the men who fought the war in the skies; the cost paid by those who did their duty because of the ones who didn't; the experience of being a POW—these are themes that run from June 7, 1944, through May 8, 1945.

LIFE IN ETO

____10_____

Night on the Line

IN THE WINTER CAMPS of 1864–65, Civil War soldiers drilled, marched in closed ranks, built log shelters, repaired equipment, foraged for food. On outpost duty they swapped tobacco, coffee, and insults with the enemy. At night they cooked and ate, sang around the campfire, and retired to bunks. Night was the best time for Johnny Reb and Billy Yank.

It wasn't like that at all in the winter of 1944–45 in Belgium, France, or Luxembourg. Night was the worst time.

The difference between 1864–65 and 1944–45 came about because of technological improvements. Civil War cannon seldom if ever fired at night, as the main body of the enemy was out of range and anyway Civil War gunners could only fire at what they could see—and then inaccurately. World War II gunners could fire much farther, arching high-trajectory shells in with precise accuracy to hit targets on the other side of the ridge, using a variety of exploding shells. Civil War soldiers had only limited, crude mortars. World War II soldiers had a variety of relatively accurate mortars and their small arms were much more accurate, with much greater range and rate of fire. Civil War soldiers at night could light their pipes, cigars, or cigarettes, and gather around a campfire with total security. World War II soldiers hardly dared to have even the smallest fire at the bottom of their foxhole or smoke a cigarette.

In the Civil War, communications between the front line and headquarters were by runner only. World War II communications were by handheld radio and, much better, telephone lines running from the front to the command post. Only the most primitive flares, and only a few of them, were available in the Civil War. In World War II, excellent flares and illuminating shells were readily available. In 1944 small, handheld bombs—grenades—unavailable in any quantity or sophistication in the Civil War, could be thrown across no-man's-land, which was in most cases narrower in 1944–45 than in 1864–65.

The internal combustion engine gave armies a nighttime mobility that was not possible with horses. Tanks and self-propelled artillery provided a nighttime firepower far in excess of anything possible eighty years earlier. Combined, the changes in weapons and equipment made World War II commanders far more aggressive at night than Civil War commanders. The people who paid the price for this aggressiveness were the front-line soldiers.

In this chapter I attempt to give some sense of how it was for those who endured and prevailed in the dangerous environment that was life on the front line at night in World War II.

Sometimes a major or a lieutenant colonel, commanding the battalion; less often a colonel commanding the regiment; very occasionally a brigadier general, commanding the division—these were the only visitors to the front lines. Reporters didn't go there, nor did the two-star generals and above. Neither did the traveling entertainers. "I never saw a USO show," Pvt. William Craft of the 314th Regiment remarked. "I heard they were good, but they didn't come to the front where I was."[1]

The front line belonged to the men who worked there—riflemen and machine gunners, mortarmen, forward artillery observers, communications men, and medics. Its depth varied, depending on the terrain, but generally it was about one half a kilometer. Company CPs were 250 meters or so back from the main line of foxholes and were not considered front-line by the riflemen. Pvt. J. A. "Strawberry" Craft of the 84th Division defined a member of the rear echelon as "any son of a bitch behind my foxhole."[2]

Outposts were anywhere from ten to fifty meters in front of the line of foxholes. The enemy outposts were sometimes almost within touching distance, more often up to fifty meters away. The friendly OPs were the edge of the known world.

Lieutenant Otts remembered a time in March 1945 when his position was closer to the German foxholes than to his buddies in the holes to the left and right. He could hear the Germans talking so distinctly that he was able to take down their names. "They were so close we could hear the clink of the metal and the gurgle of the water as they filled their canteens. . . . Ordinarily we placed two men to a hole, with one standing guard while the other slept, but here with our foxholes so far apart and the Germans so close we found it best to have three men in a hole so two men could be awake at the same time all night."[3]

Most of the time, the principal characteristic of the front line was how quiet it was. Artillery boomed in the distance and the "thump" of mortars sounded sporadically, but otherwise unless the enemy was shelling or attacking there was little noise.

Nor was there much movement. It was as if the earth had swallowed up all the human beings—as indeed it had, because on the front line men lived most of the time below the surface. Life-threatening violence was always present. Thousands of eyes searched their perimeters. Thousands of fingers were ready to pull triggers, thousands of hands were prepared to throw grenades or fire mortars at the slightest motion, or at night at the least noise or the light of a burning cigarette.

In early December, the 84th Division was just inside Germany, near the border with Belgium, at Lindern. Pvt. Chalmers Davis, a mortarman, found an observation post on top of a wrecked house. From it he spotted a haystack moving across an open field. He got on the phone to tell the CP that there was a camouflaged tank out there. Just then a German soldier jumped out of one foxhole and ran to another.

Davis decided to have some fun. "He never should have been out in the daytime," he told his crew, down below behind the house. "He made a mistake."

The crew fired two mortar shells and got a bracket on the foxhole. The third shell was a direct hit. A combination of luck and skill was involved, but whatever the cause the German paid for his mistake with his life. American artillery, meanwhile, got a bracket on the haystack, then knocked out the tank inside.[4]

Thus the first rule of life on the front line: don't move around because someone is watching. Stay in your hole whenever you can.

Depending on the length of the line a rifle company was holding, those holes were anywhere from a few to a hundred meters apart, occasionally even more. In this, World War II was markedly different from World War I. In the 1914–18 conflict, the trench line was continuous. You could walk from the Swiss border to the English Channel without ever showing your head above the earth's surface. The walls were lined with logs. Zigzag trenches ran back from the front to deep in the rear, so food, ammunition, and messages could be brought forward without exposure.

To man those extensive trenches, however, took hundreds of thousands of men, indeed millions. In November 1918, Marshal Foch had commanded three times more men than Eisenhower did in November 1944, on a front of approximately the same length. Hindenburg had commanded three to four times more men than Rundstedt. Necessarily, foxholes replaced trenches.

Soldiers in the Great War didn't know what a foxhole was. For all the terror of their daily existence, they at least had the comfort of being with comrades, seeing men around them, sensing their own power. World War II soldiers didn't know what trenches were. In their foxholes they had one, at most two companions. Otherwise they felt isolated—as in fact in a spread-out company they were.

Compounding the isolation was the unnatural situation of living below the surface of the earth plus the physical misery of digging a hole big enough for your coffin at the end of an exhausting day. But it had to be done, a lesson quickly learned.

Battalions that didn't dig in for the night didn't last long. That should have been learned in training, but it wasn't, so it had to be learned from experience. On June 10, shortly after midnight, the 2nd Battalion of the 29th Division settled in for the night. The men had just marched fifteen miles in the previous twenty hours. Maj. Maurice Clift, the executive officer, picked out a bivouac area, two enclosed pastures. The men moved into them and slumped against the hedgerow embankments, so exhausted they didn't bother to remove their haversacks. Most were asleep immediately. Few paid attention to the sound of engines, and those who did figured they were American vehicles.

But they were German, tanks and trucks from the 352nd Division—the outfit the 29th had been fighting since dawn of D-Day. Unknown to either side, the Germans had been retreating in the wake of the advancing 2nd Battalion. German scouts detected the American movement into the pastures. The German column crept forward and surrounded the fields.

The Germans fired flares. In the eerie light, almost as bright as midday, they fired assault guns over the hedgerows at the sleeping men. Along one hedgerow a full platoon rose up, only to be cut down by a burst of machine-gun fire. Other frantic Americans dashed to and fro looking for an escape route. German riflemen cut them down. German mortar shells exploded all around the pastures. GIs fired their M-1s wildly at the hedgerows, but they were as likely to hit their own men as Germans.

"It was terrible," one survivor reported to General Cota. "We had crawled about 100 yards away from the field when we heard a lot of the guys screaming. I think that the Germans must have been making a bayonet charge."

The CO of the 2nd Battalion, Lt. Col. William Warfield, had his CP in a farmhouse on the roadside. He tried to organize a defense, but it was hopeless. Officers who dashed out of the house to get to the field were cut down. A German called out to the headquarters group, in English, "Surrender! Surrender!"

"Surrender, hell!" Warfield roared back. He tried to lead his small party to the fields where the massacre was taking place, but was immediately killed.

The battle lasted only twenty minutes. The battalion suffered 150 casualties—fifty killed—or more than one-third of its total strength. Shortly before dawn one agonized young lieutenant, reporting the disaster to the division commander, Gen. Charles Gerhardt, fell to his knees and pounded the ground with his fists, sobbing that all his men were dead and that he had let them down.

Gerhardt was enraged. "No security!" he screamed. "They just went into the field and went to bed!"[5]

From June 10 on, every front-line soldier in the 29th dug a foxhole before going to sleep. So did almost all other American infantrymen. Wherever they were. Pvt. Kurt Gabel, 513th PIR, 17th Airborne Division, recalled spending a night in the enormous, beautiful American Meuse-Argonne cemetery, where the dead from the

U.S. Army's biggest World War I battle were buried. It had been meticulously cared for by the Germans during their occupation of France. Gabel and his buddy Jake dug their foxhole between two white marble headstones, as did other members of the 513th. Once the men were in their holes, there was no noise, no movement. "All quiet on the western front," Jake said.[6]

Digging the hole was often arduous, sometimes exhausting. A typical position would be in or on the edge of a wood, which meant many roots, as most of the trees in Belgium were planted in rows, close together. During the second half of December, when the nighttime thermometer began to go down to near or below zero, the ground was frozen to the depth of a foot or more. Pickaxes were hard to come by on the front and even when available they weren't much help. Sometimes it took hours to chip away enough frozen earth to get to unfrozen ground. Men used grenades or satchel charges to blow away the frozen earth.

Often it was just impossible. On the night of December 18–19, near Echternach, Sgt. John Sweeney of the 10th Armored Division tried to dig in, "but the ground was made up of heavy wet clay and our entrenching shovel couldn't dig into it." After penetrating a few inches, he and his buddies gave up. "It was so cold that the rear echelon brought up some overcoats (2 for every 3 soldiers). We placed one overcoat on the ground and three of us lay on it and covered ourselves with the second overcoat. The only one who was warm was the middle guy so we changed places every twenty minutes or so."[7]

The holes were usually rectangular, under the best conditions four or five feet deep, two or three feet wide by six feet long. When the men were in them for more than one night, or if they were veterans, they got them covered.

Sgt. Leo Lick of the 1st Division, a veteran of Sicily (where he won a Silver Star) and the Normandy invasion, moved into the line near Butgenbach at twilight of December 17. He and two buddies worked on their hole for a week. They got some logs which "we put over the hole and then put branches over the logs and then covered that layer with soil and camouflaged the top with snow. We also put six inches of evergreen needles on the bottom of the hole for comfortable sleeping. The opening to the foxhole also served as a warfare trench from which we could shoot or stand guard."[8] (Lick visited the site in 1986 and found the hole still there, an experience I've shared with a number of soldiers who were in the Bulge.)

The cover protected the men from shrapnel and broken branches hurtling down from tree bursts, but there were disadvantages. One night during the opening stages of the Bulge Pvt. Richard Jepsen (who stayed in the Army, got a postwar commission, and retired as a full colonel), of the 30th Infantry Division, was in a well-covered foxhole with a buddy. It got to ten below zero Fahrenheit—and then it started to rain. "Our body heat had risen into the overhead covering and the snow and ice were beginning to melt and drip on us."[9]

During an advance, lucky GIs frequently were able to occupy holes abandoned by the retreating Germans. Nearly always they were deeper and better protected than ones made by Americans. Sometimes this was because the Germans were able to utilize slave labor to dig; more often it was because the Wehrmacht supplied better tools to its men than did the U.S. Army, and because in many cases the German soldiers were more strictly disciplined.

Lieutenant Otts recalled "the best foxhole I ever stayed in. The Germans had dug it about seven-by-five-by-ten feet deep with a covering of six-inch logs, dirt, and snow. . . . It had a little gasoline stove, a candle, and a bottle gas lamp, so we really had most of the comforts of home."[10]

Once the holes were dug, the next task was to secure the area with booby traps, wires stretched across a path or any opening in no-man's-land, attached to grenades. Next the men set out land mines. Between the booby traps and the main line of foxholes, the men dug holes for outposts, to be occupied by sentries. Then they set up communications—"commo"—which meant running telephone lines back to the CP (telephones were more reliable and secure than the handheld radios, and in any case the breath from a man speaking into the radio would condense and freeze on the diaphragms of the radio microphones; on the other hand, telephone lines got cut by enemy shelling).[11]

If at all possible the quartermasters would try to get bedrolls up to the men before full dark, bringing them forward on jeeps. The bedrolls were one half a canvas pup tent which when buttoned to another half became a tent (although seldom did GIs set up a tent on the front, as it was far too conspicuous), wrapped around two wool blankets or a sleeping bag. The bag was much warmer, but more dangerous, because it was harder to get out of if an enemy patrol or attack required instant action.

The cooks would try to get a hot meal up to the front before dark. This could be extremely dangerous, however, especially when taking up a new position, because the enemy might have observation posts. During the third week of December, Private Gabel and the 513th PIR moved into the front line in Belgium. After the foxholes were dug, the booby traps set, and the communications lines strung, Gabel was amazed by two things—how quiet it was, and the sudden unexpected appearance of the cooks with marmite cans and hot food. The men grabbed their mess kits and got into a chow line—"like all the other chow lines from Fort Benning to Neufchateau," Gable noted.

"Get those men spread out," a lieutenant yelled at his NCOs.

But before anyone could move, there was an explosion. Then another. And another. German 88s traveled faster than the speed of sound, so the GIs didn't hear the "whoosh" before the explosion. Cries of "Medic!" intermingled with the lieutenant's order, "Back to your holes. Take cover!" Four more shells exploded before the men reached their holes. The 513th PIR got a quick if expensive lesson in the cost of bunching up when the Germans could be watching.[12]

Mostly, American soldiers stayed in their foxholes where they ate cold C and K rations. Germans had hard black bread and, if lucky, sausage and butter.

Just one night in a foxhole in Belgium in December 1944 was memorable. Ten, twenty, thirty nights was hell. To begin with, night lasted so long in those northern latitudes. Dusk began to come on around 1600 or 1615. By 1645 it was full dark. First light didn't come up for sixteen hours. It was bitterly cold, even for the GIs from Montana or North Dakota. It was frequently below zero and generally damp, with low clouds blowing in from the North Sea and a fog that penetrated everywhere—when it wasn't snowing. Then the wind blew like a gale, driving the pellets of snow into their faces. It was Northern Europe's coldest winter in forty years.

Col. Ralph Ingersoll, the creator of the "Talk of the Town" for the *New Yorker* magazine, was an intelligence officer with First Army. He described the cold: "Riding [in a jeep] through the Ardennes, I wore woolen underwear, a woolen uniform, armored force combat overalls, a sweater, an armored force field jacket with elastic cuffs, a muffler, a heavy lined trenchcoat, two pairs of heavy woolen socks, and combat boots with galoshes over them—and I cannot remember ever being warm."[13]

Ingersoll was lucky. Although it was windy in the open jeep, it was dry, and he was much better dressed for the cold than any GI on the line. The infantrymen's clothing was woefully, even criminally inadequate. As noted, this was because of a command decision General Bradley had made in September. He had decided to keep weapons, ammunition, food, and replacements moving forward at the expense of winter clothing, betting that the campaign would be over before December.[14] As a consequence, the men in the holes had few of the items Ingersoll wore. Their footwear—leather combat boots—was almost worse than useless. Whenever the temperature went above freezing, they were standing in two to twenty inches of water, which the leather soaked up.

There were good boots available in Europe, of the type made popular by L. L. Bean after the war—well-insulated, with leather uppers but rubber bottoms—but to the everlasting disgrace of the quartermasters and all other rear-echelon personnel, who were nearly all wearing them by mid-December, not until late January did the boots get to where they were needed. Maj. Gen. Paul Hawley, the chief surgeon for ETO, commented bluntly, "The plain truth is that the footwear furnished U.S. troops is lousy."[15]

Three days before the Bulge began, Col. Ken Reimers of the 90th Division noted that "every day more men are falling out due to trench foot. Some men are so bad they can't wear shoes and are wearing overshoes over their socks. These men can't walk and are being carried from sheltered pillbox positions at night to firing positions in the day time."[16]

In place of boots, the men got directives on how to prevent trench foot. They were ordered to massage their feet and change their socks every day. Sergeant Lick recalled, "We would remove our wet socks, hang them around our neck to dry, massage our feet and then put on the dry socks from around our neck that we had put there the day before. Then a directive came down stating that anyone getting trench foot would be tried by court martial."

Senior officers threatened court-martial to men who got trench foot, or took disciplinary action against junior officers whose units had a high incidence of the malady, because they suspected the fox-hole dwellers were getting it deliberately. They thought it was almost the equivalent of a self-inflicted wound.

The best way to avoid trench foot was to lace the boots lightly and take them off at night before climbing into the sleeping bag or covering yourself with a blanket. But, Lick said, "we couldn't take our boots off when we slept because they would freeze solid and we couldn't get them on again in the morning." The obvious solution, quickly learned by thousands of men, was to take the boots off but keep them inside the sleeping bag. Still there was another reason for keeping the boots on, the possible need for instant action.[17]

Men wrapped their feet in burlap sacks, when available, but the burlap soaked up the snow, so the boots got soggy, the socks got wet. Sergeant Lick lost all his toenails but through regular massages and a rotation of his socks he avoided trench foot. Thousands of others got it. Trench foot put more men out of action than German 88s, mortars, or machine-gun fire. During the winter of 1944–45, some 45,000 men had to be pulled out of the front line because of trench foot—the equivalent of three full infantry divisions.[18]

First a man lost his toenails. His feet turned white, then purple, finally black. A serious case of trench foot made walking impossible. Many men lost their toes, some had to have their feet amputated. If gangrene set in, the doctors had to amputate the lower leg. It has to be doubted that many men did this deliberately. A shot in the foot was much quicker, less dangerous, and nearly impossible to prove that it hadn't been an accident.

One private in Lieutenant Otts's platoon shot himself in the foot and there was no question of accident. The man had been talking all night to his mate, Pvt. Fonrose LeCrone, about doing it. LeCrone had the flu and was so depressed he just wanted the guy to shut up, so he told him to go ahead and do it. Egger commented: "It was three miles by trail to the aid station. The two medics who went with him made him walk all the way—there was no free ride for those with self-inflicted wounds."[19]

During those long nights, it was impossible to keep out of the mind the thought of how easy it would be to shoot a round into the foot. Sergeant Egger considered it, but "I did not have the nerve to shoot myself. . . . I thought about dropping a case of rations on my foot, but I did not want to live the rest of my life with that on my mind. I decided to stick it out and trust in the Lord."[20] A man in

Lieutenant Leinbaugh's platoon begged his squad leader, "Do me a favor, sergeant, shoot me in the leg."[21]

Captain Roland of the 99th Division recalled, "Men began to wound themselves one way or another in order to get away from the front. Sometimes this was intentional. Sometimes it occurred through a gross negligence born of fear, exhaustion, and misery."[22]

"There were two things in front of you always," Corp. Clair Galdonik of the 90th Division remarked: "the enemy and death. . . . Sometimes morale was so low that you preferred death instead of a day-by-day agonizing existence. When you were wet, cold, hungry, lonely, Death looked very inviting. It was always close at hand and I found myself being envious of a dead comrade. At least he suffered no more physically or mentally."[23]

Pvt. Bert Morphis of the 1st Division remembered that on Christmas Eve he was "on an outpost right in front of the German lines where the choice seemed to be between moving and being shot, or lying perfectly still and freezing to death."[24]

Most of them stuck it out. Dutch Schultz of the 82nd Airborne was one of hundreds who refused to be evacuated because of trench foot. But when he also came down with dysentery and the flu, his CO ordered him to the rear. He commented, "I secretly experienced a great deal of guilt about going to the hospital for anything other than a bona fide wound. Anemia, bronchitis, dysentery, and trench foot seemed to be an easy way out. In hindsight, I understand that if you are sick you don't belong on a battlefield, but when you are an immature kid trying to be a hero it is something of a problem, particularly when you are trying to prove your courage to no one other than yourself."[25]

Getting out of there, honorably, was every man's dream—thus the expression "million-dollar wound." Sgt. John Sabia took five machine-gun bullets in his right thigh. His CO asked if he could make it back to the aid station on his own, as the company couldn't spare a man.

"Hell, yes, I can do it."

Sabia took a limb to use as a crutch and began hopping awkwardly in the snow. After ten meters he stopped, turned around, waved his limb in a gesture of defiance and exuberance, and bellowed at his buddies in their holes, "Hey, you bastards! Clean sheets! Clean sheets!"[26]

Pvt. Donald Schoo of the 80th Infantry Division recalled seeing one of his buddies, named Steehhourst, take a hit from an 88 that blew off his left hand. "He was crying and running around yelling, 'I'm going home! Thank you God, I'm going home!' "27

Steehhourst was lucky, at least according to the standards of the men of the Bulge and specifically to Sgt. Richard Wallace of the 90th Division. After one shelling, Wallace told his squad, "Boys, I'd give my right arm up to here," holding it at his elbow, "if this war would end right now." The shelling resumed. Shrapnel tore into Wallace's face.

"I can't see!" he cried out. "I can't see! Oh, my God, I'm blind." He never saw again and the war was a long way from over.28

Sleep deprivation was a universal experience. Two, three, at the most four hours of fitful sleep was about it. But no matter how sleepy a man was, he lived in constant tension. The men in the front line shivered in their foxholes, attempting to stay alert, straining to see, straining to hear, straining to stay awake. They would chew gum or tobacco. Pvt. Ken Russell of the 82nd Airborne remembered chewing one or the other "very slowly. I didn't want to finish too quickly and have nothing to do but think of the precarious position I was in."29

Lt. Glenn Gray, in his classic book *The Warriors,* calls this "the tyranny of the present." In a foxhole, the past and, more important, the future do not exist. The only thing in the world that matters is the moment. Gray says that there is "more time for thinking and more loneliness in foxholes than [anywhere else] and time is measured in other ways than by clocks and calendars."30

Pvt. Dave Nutt of the 99th Division recalled, "The cold, the snow, and the darkness were enough to set young nerves on edge. The thud of something as innocuous as snow plopping to the ground from a tree branch could be terrifying. Was it snow? Was it maybe a German patrol? Should you fire at the sound and risk giving away your position, or worse hitting one of your own men? But did the Germans have us surrounded?"31

Lieutenant Otts heard a "thud" one night and went out to investigate in the morning. He found a dying German soldier who murmured over and over, "Oh God, I meant no harm, I meant no harm." The boy was unarmed and wore no helmet, so he may well have been coming in to surrender when he set off the booby trap. But the Germans often went on patrols unarmed so if they were captured they could say they were coming in to give up. Otts commented, "I imagine quite a few [Germans] would have surrendered but it was impossible in the daytime, as their own men would shoot them, and at night they were afraid to try to run our gauntlet of booby traps and machine guns."[32]

An experience shared by many foxhole soldiers was the screaming of a wounded man in front of the outposts. Otts recalled "a helluva night. . . . Someone out in front of us was screaming, 'Help! Help! Can't anyone hear me? For God's sake help!' This went on all night. You can't imagine what it does to you to be sitting in a foxhole with the black night all around and someone yelling for help in a mournful voice." Otts knew that there were American wounded out front, but he also know that the Germans used such calls to trick the GIs and would ambush anyone going out to give aid, so he ordered his platoon to stay put.[33]

Tension was at its most pronounced when changing guard. Every two hours the platoon sergeants would get two men from a foxhole and lead them to the outpost position, to relieve the men on duty. "The trip out to the OP was always eerie," Sgt. Burton Christenson of the 101st Airborne remembered of his nights outside Bastogne. "You eyed all silhouettes suspiciously, skeptical of any sound. Reluctantly, you approach the OP. The silhouettes of the men in their positions are not clear. . . . Are they Germans? The suspense is always the same . . . then finally you recognize an American helmet. Feeling a little ridiculous, yet also relieved, you change the guard, turn around and return to the main line, only to repeat the entire process in another two hours."[34]

"You always slept with one eye open," Pvt. Arnold Lindblad of the 104th Medical Battalion recalled. "Unless you were on duty, you hit the hole when it got dark and stayed there till full light. There was no walking around in the dark, no talking from hole to hole. You never got used to it."[35]

On his first night in a foxhole, Pvt. Richard Heuer, a replacement with the 84th Division, was suffering with dysentery. "I didn't want to crap in my helmet," he related, "so I decided I'd crawl outside at night." As he wore two pairs of long johns beneath his wool pants, "it was a real chore getting down to the point where I could do my duty. As I was doing my duty I heard some noises behind me. I thought they were Germans. I jumped into the hole without pulling my drawers up. That really startled my foxhole buddy. I had crapped in the first pair of drawers, so I had to stand there in the middle of the foxhole and cut it out. This wasn't easy, because I had to do the cutting with my bayonet."[36]

Shelling made foxhole living worse. Mortars and artillery could come in at any time. The Germans would watch the GIs take up a position at the end of a day, mark it on their maps, and shell it at night. Pvt. Arnold "Ben" Parish of the 2nd Infantry Division remembered a night during the Bulge when he and a buddy had dug a hole long enough and wide enough to accommodate both men, but only about eight inches deep. As they worked on it, shelling began. "It was raining shells and they were exploding all around our hole. The air was full of shrapnel and spent pieces were hitting us as we laid on our backs with our helmets over our faces. The noise was unbearable and the ground was shaking and we were shaking from fright and cold. We didn't dare raise our heads. It would have been impossible to survive outside of the hole."

Cries of "Medic!" Tree limbs hurtling through the air. The smell of powder. The bangs and flashes and booms and screams, red-hot bits of metal zooming through the air. The only movement you could make was to press ever closer to the ground. Those who endured such a cataclysm were forever scarred by it, even if untouched by shrapnel.

"We were helpless and all alone and there was nothing we could do, so I prayed to God. . . . The time went by very slow. I tried to keep warm but that wasn't possible. I thought about my mother and hoped she didn't know where I was or what I was doing. . . . Maybe this is the end of the world, I thought."[37]

Feelings of helplessness were universal. Corp. Stanley Kalberer, a college student at the beginning of 1944, was by December a replacement in the 84th Division. During the Bulge he, too, got caught in a shelling and described his experience: "I never felt so alone, frightened, forgotten, abused and degraded. . . . I truly believed I would never survive, or if I did I would be maimed by the weather or killed by the enemy, or both."[38]

Private Vonnegut described a shelling during the Bulge with a novelist's insight: "The incredible artificial weather that Earthlings sometimes create for other Earthlings when they don't want those other Earthlings to inhabit Earth any more. Shells . . . bursting in the treetops with terrific bangs . . . showering down knives and needles and razorblades. Little lumps of lead in copper jackets were crisscrossing the woods under the shellbursts, zipping along much faster than sound."[39]

During a January shelling, Lieutenant Otts's platoon was on the verge of breakdown. During a lull, some men were crying, others telling Otts they couldn't stand any more. Otts told them of the system he and his foxhole buddies used to keep from going crazy. "We pretended that the company area was a target as on a rifle range and that our foxhole was the center or bull's eye. We would lie in our hole and score the Heinies on their artillery rounds according to how close they came to our hole—five for a bull's eye and four, three, two, and one as they landed farther away. We gave them a 'Maggie's drawers,' as the red flag on a rifle range is called, for a complete miss." Decades later, Otts commented, "This helped pass the time, but I could think of things I would rather do."[40]

Every man in a foxhole, especially during a shelling, could think of things he would rather do. It seemed it would last forever. It seemed you couldn't possibly survive.

In contrast to the ordeal of shelling, there were endless hours in which nothing happened, but as Sgt. Fred Claesson of the 78th Infantry Division described his experience in the Bulge, "Holding the line didn't mean just sitting in foxholes waiting for something to happen. It meant a continual battle against trench foot and mental depression, sweating out artillery barrages which the enemy habitually sent in at chow time and nights which were lighted with flares and flashes, fighting off enemy patrols . . . [but most of all] it meant hours and days of deadly boredom."[41]

Men talked, softly, to relieve the boredom and the tension. Sgt. Robert Rader and Pvt. Don Hoobler of the 101st Airborne came from the same town on the banks of the Ohio River. "Don and I would talk all night about home, our families, people and places, and what the hell were we doing in a predicament like this," Rader said. Pvt. Ralph Spina of the same company recalled discussing with his foxhole mate "politics, the world's problems, plus our own. Wishing we had a drink or a hot meal, preferably in that order. We talked about what we were going to do when we got home, about a trip to Paris, go to the Follies. Mainly we talked about going home."[42]

"I never observed any loners on the front lines," Sergeant Egger said. "The men automatically paired up. The buddy system worked very well; it provided additional security . . . it provided additional warmth. . . . We were a team, and sharing the adversities of the elements and combat brought us together and created a bond."[43]

Foxhole buddies developed a closeness unknown to all others. They were closer than friends, closer than brothers. Their relationship was different from that of lovers. Their trust in and knowledge of each other was total. They got to know each other's life stories, what they did before they came into the Army, what their parents, brothers, and sisters were like, their teachers, what they liked to eat and drink, what their capabilities were. Sometimes they hated one another; more often they loved one another in a way known only to combat veterans. Without thinking about it, they would share their last bite or last drink of water or a blanket—and they would die for one another.

They also complained, constantly, about the other guy's habits, physical and mental—his farts, his cough, the songs he hummed, his size, his intelligence or lack thereof, his politics, his nationality, his Confederate or Yankee sympathies, his taste in books or comics.

Pvt. Keith Lance of the 84th Division was that rare creature, an atheist in a foxhole. His buddy was "a good Catholic boy from upstate New York." They were being shelled and the buddy " 'Hailed Mary' all night. After taking so many hours of that," Lance commented, he had had enough, so he dashed out of the foxhole to "check on the guys." As he threw himself into the next hole, Lance heard an explosion. He looked, aghast—it had hit his old hole. His buddy was badly wounded and buried in mud.[44]

They were young men with high testosterone levels. As combat infantrymen, they were not having sex for weeks, sometimes months. But homosexual activity in the foxholes was rare to nonexistent. Beyond the danger inherent in forgetting where you were, the U.S. Army in World War II was brutal in its punishment of known homosexuals. They were stripped of all insignia, drummed out of the service, given long sentences in the stockade, disgraced without mercy. They were also beaten up by their fellow soldiers, who were strongly homophobic.

Instead of acting out their sexual needs, the men in the foxholes talked about girls and dreamed about them. One night outside Bastogne, Pvt. Al Vittore and Pvt. Ed "Babe" Heffron of the 101st Airborne managed to catch some sleep. Heffron woke when Vittore threw his heavy leg over his body. When Vittore started to rub Heffron's chest, Heffron gave him a shot with his elbow in his belly.

Vittore woke and demanded to know what the hell was going on. Heffron started to give him hell in return. Vittore grinned and said he had been dreaming about his wife.

"Al," Heffron said, "I can't help you, as I got combat boots, jump pants, and my trench coat on, and they are not coming off."[45]

Pvt. Kurt Gabel of the 17th Airborne dealt with the sexual deprivation problem by talking to his foxhole buddy, Jake, as if they were a married couple. On one of their first nights together, following a shelling at the chow line, Jake commented indignantly, "This is no way for civilized human beings to dine."

They lay down in their hole and tried to get comfortable. Gabel turned, jabbing Jake with his elbow. Jake jabbed back, and issued a warning: "And another thing, dearie, if you thrash around like this habitually, you'll simply have to sleep in the guest room."

"Calm down, dear," Gabel replied. "We'll be moving out of here before long and I just know you'll find us a much nicer and larger place. Now let's kiss and make up, and I'll take you to a fantastic little place for dinner."[46]

Sitting in front-line foxholes was bad, being on OP was worse, going on combat patrol at night was worse than that. Battalion commanders on both sides ordered patrols, sometimes to take prisoners for interrogation, often just to give the men something to do. Such patrols proved that the battalion commander was aggressive. Company commanders and platoon leaders—not to mention the men—hated night patrols.

Lieutenant Otts had his own method of complying with such orders. "I would send a couple of men out to see if the Heinies were still there, telling them to take a look and come right back without drawing any fire. I believed in letting well enough alone. We could have gone over, tossed a few grenades and fired a few shots into their holes, but they would only have come back and done the same thing to us, with nothing gained by either side. I liked everything as it was, nice and peaceful, and couldn't see the sense in stirring up a hive full of sleeping bees. . . . The battalion CO might have known best but he was several thousand yards from the enemy while we were only fifty."[47]

Sometimes on night patrol young Germans passed by young Americans within touching distance. Despite the adrenaline rush, most often each side waited to see what the other would do—which usually was nothing. On at least some occasions, eighteen-year-old GIs and Germans smiled at each other as they passed.

Lts. Harold Leinbaugh and John Campbell of the 84th Division were out one night during the Bulge, feeling their way through the dark, forcing their way through the drifts, stopping frequently to listen for sounds of nearby troops. "We paused," Campbell remembered, "and heard a rustling noise, very close. We dropped to a crouch alongside a narrow trail."

A dozen men passed by, taking care to make as little noise as possible. "They were Germans," Campbell said, "and they weren't lost. They passed so close we could have reached out and tripped each man as he hurried by."[48]

Pvt. Gus Schroeder of Wisconsin grew up speaking German. He was in the 90th Division. A buddy described him as "a big man, incredibly strong and almost a child otherwise." One night on patrol Schroeder fell in with a German patrol "and spoke to them in fluent German. He was brave to the point of being foolhardy." But he personally captured 100 German soldiers.[49]

Lieutenant Colby of the 90th went out on a night patrol in Normandy, to keep an eye on a new squad leader. Colby was in the middle of a string of seven men, following a railroad track. The private in front of him began crawling. Colby asked him why he was crawling.

"Everyone ahead of me is crawling."

They crawled on for fifty meters. Colby bumped into the man in front of him. "Now what's up?"

"I bumped into the man ahead of me."

After another advance, the patrol stopped. "Why have we stopped?" Colby whispered.

"I sent our scout on ahead," the squad leader replied.

After an hour, the scout returned. "Can you see anything?" Colby asked.

"Shit, I think I have seen my whole life pass in front of me," the breathless scout exclaimed. "I have seen every damned thing imaginable out there. I have seen tanks and battleships coming down these tracks right at me."[50]

Later, Colby was promoted to captain and took command of the company. One night in the Bulge he went into a wooded area to check on his overextended outpost line. He bumped into a two-man German patrol. Colby dropped his carbine and put up his hands. The Germans dropped their rifles and put up their hands. The three men talked in broken English and fractured German. The Germans persuaded Colby that as they had him outnumbered, he would have to take them in. They became POWs. Their war was over. Colby's went on.[51]

Much of the time it was pitch black during the Belgian night. Pvt. Gene Amici of the 84th recalled the blackest night of all. "It was raining, no stars, no moon, no nothing. And not knowing where you're going. Everybody hanging on to the guy in front—hanging on to his belt and just walking. You just kept walking. . . . All you'd see was a head up there in front of you."[52]

At Hagenau, Germany, in February 1945, Major Winters of the 101st sent out a patrol that succeeded in bringing back a couple of prisoners. His CO, Col. Robert Sink, was so delighted that he ordered another one for the next night. But that day it snowed, then turned colder. The snow was frozen on top, crunchy, noisy. The cold air had cleared the sky and the moon was shining. Winters thought a patrol under the circumstances was suicidal, so he decided to disobey orders. Sink and a couple of his staff officers came to Winters's CP to "observe." They had a bottle of whiskey with them. Winters said he was going to the line to supervise the patrol. When he got to the foxholes, he told the men to just stay still. With the whiskey working on him, Sink would soon be ready for bed. The "patrol" could report in the morning that it had penetrated the German lines but had been unable to get a live prisoner.[53]

There wasn't anything the colonel could do about it. How do you intimidate a combat infantryman? As every GI in ETO understood, the stockade was infinitely safer than a foxhole on the front line, and far more comfortable.

Being attacked by a German force at night was the worst experience. On the night of December 27, Sgt. Dwayne Burns of the

82nd Airborne had it. He was on outpost duty when at 0115 the Germans attacked. A machine-gun crew to his right put a string of tracers into a haystack 100 meters in front of the line. As it flared up, "all we could see were Germans. They were down on their bellies, crawling toward our lines. 'Good Lord,' I said, 'how did they get there so fast? Another minute and they would have been crawling up into our holes with us!' "

The forward observer called in artillery. The men in their holes started shooting. "I didn't see how anyone could live through it, but the Germans were still coming. . . . They just kept coming, right into our fire. Some of them reached the ditch on the other side of the line. It looked like they would overrun our position just by the sheer strength of numbers." The observer called for American fire right on top of the line.

"I had seen a lot of incoming artillery fire," Burns said, "but nothing like this. It was turning night into day. It was fantastic. I wanted to watch, but I also wanted to be at the bottom of my hole."

The German attackers fell back. The artillery fire died down. Burns got a call on the radio. It was the company CP. The phone line had been cut by a shell. A man had gone out from the CP to find the break and repair it, but he had not come back. Someone had to do the job.

"The someone they were talking about was me," Burns remarked. "Funny how when there is a dangerous job to do they don't call names—just someone had to do it."

Burns slipped out of his hole and started back, holding the wire in one hand and his M-1 in the other. "I took off on a dead run, doubled over to keep low, trying to make a very small target.

"As I ran, ice and snow from the wire would build up in my hand. I would have to stop, shake it off and then start out again. One hundred yards out, I found the break in the wire. I also found the man from the CP. He had found the break but had been killed before he could make the splice.

"I stripped off my gloves, dropped down to one knee and went to work while watching out for Germans at the same time. We had heard about how the Germans would cut our wire, wait for someone to come out to fix it and then take them prisoner. I tied and taped the wire in record time and ran for my hole. I didn't even slow down when I got there, I just went in head first."

In the morning, "we started a count of the dead. We had only one man killed and a few wounded. We could see enemy dead everywhere, some within 20 feet of our line. We counted more than 100 dead Germans."[54]

When men got out of the holes, they looked like slaves coming up from a coal-mine shaft. In February 1945, Company C of the 395th Regiment "was relieved in position by the 69th Division after living in holes in the ground for almost three months. When we popped out of the ground, some of the green 69th Division troops passing by were convinced that they were relieving an all black infantry battalion."[55]

God-awful though the conditions were, men endured and prevailed. How they did so differed with each individual. But all had a sense of fatalism. Pvt. Ken Webster of the 101st Airborne expressed his feelings and insights in a letter to his mother: "I am living on borrowed time. . . . If I don't come back, try not to take it too hard. I wish I could persuade you to regard death as casually as we do over here. In the heat of battle you expect casualties, you expect somebody to be killed and you are not surprised when a friend is machine-gunned in the face. You have to keep going. It's not like civilian life, where sudden death is so unexpected." ("There was no time to mourn the dead," Captain Colby remarked, "even if they were good friends.")

When his mother wrote to express her considerable alarm at this attitude, Webster replied, "Would you prefer for somebody else's son to die in the mud? . . . Somebody has to get in and kill the enemy. Somebody has to be in the infantry and the paratroops. If the country all had your attitude, nobody would fight, everybody would be in the Quartermaster. And what kind of a country would that be?"[56]

Carwood Lipton was a sergeant in the 101st Airborne on D-Day, a lieutenant with a battlefield commission during the Bulge. By the end of the war he had been involved in many different kinds of combat. Asked to comment on how he managed to cope with the challenges of combat, and insofar as he felt he could to speak for others in his answer, Lipton said, "When men are in combat, the inevitability of it takes over. They are there, there is nothing they can do to change that, so they accept it. They immediately become calloused to the smell of death, the bodies, the destruction, the killing, the danger. Enemy bodies and wounded don't affect them.

"Their own wounded and the bodies of their dead friends make only a brief impression, and in that impression is a fleeting feeling of triumph or accomplishment that it was not them. There is still work to be done, a war to be won, and they think about that."

According to Lipton, it is only later, when a man got off the front line, that he had time to think about how buddies were killed or wounded, or about the times when he personally was inches from death. Out of the line, far from combat, "death and destruction are no longer inevitable—the war might end, the missions might be cancelled." Such thoughts made men nervous about going back into the line. But, Lipton insisted, once back in it, all doubts and nervousness disappear. "The callousness, the cold-bloodedness, the calmness return."[57]

Fifty years later, I remarked to Lipton that in December 1944 the stockade was preferable to a foxhole. He turned on me and snapped, "Come on, Steve. No man would choose disgrace. If the stockade was preferable the stockades would have been full, the foxholes empty, and we would have lost the war."

Just there is the point. In the face of conditions scarcely equaled anywhere for fear, degradation, and misery, the great majority of front-line soldiers in ETO in 1944-45 stayed in the line and did their duty, and prevailed.

There are no unwounded foxhole veterans. Sgt. Ed Stewart of the 84th Division commented decades after the war that he had "never known a combat soldier who did not show a residue of war." Stewart's mother told him that he "left Europe but never arrived home." Sgt. George Thompson said that when he came home the sounds of war came with him. Decades later, "when I'm home by myself, at nighttime, it all comes back. I'll hear the noise, the shells exploding. I stay awake thinking about it. I guess it comes from being in a foxhole—the long hours of night time."[58]

11

Replacements and Reinforcements

Fall 1944

FRONT-LINE DIVISIONS in the protracted wars of the nineteenth and twentieth centuries were sooner or later decimated. They were still carried on the roster as divisions when they were no more than two or three companies strong. In World War II the German and British armies withdrew their divisions after they had suffered severe losses, for rest, reinforcements, and reorganization. The U.S. and Red armies kept their divisions, once committed to combat, in the line for the entire war. They were replenished by a steady stream of replacements, to the point that the majority of fighting men in their armies in the campaigns of 1944-45 were individual replacements. Divisions that were in contact with the enemy from Normandy until they reached the German border were well over 100 percent replacements by December (and four—the 1st, 3rd, 4th, and 29th—were over 200 percent by the end of the war, and seven others were over 180 percent). The 90th Division, for example, had more than 35,000 replacements during the course of the campaign, the functional equivalent of three full-strength divisions.

General Marshall made the decision to keep American divisions at full strength through regular infusions of replacements, brought forward not in company or even squad strength, but as individuals. That system seemed to hold great promise. American divisions would be able to stay in the line continuously as they would be drawing in fresh men daily. The replacements would join veteran squads, platoons, companies. They could be integrated into the unit and taught the tricks of survival in combat by old-timers. They would be young, fit, eager, and well trained.

The Normandy battle, however, caused far higher casualties than had been anticipated. From late July on, ETO was short of men, especially riflemen. It would get worse; the 29th suffered 400 percent casualties in its rifle companies. The Army scrambled to make up ETO's 300,000-man shortfall in fighting men. Eisenhower put cooks, drivers, mechanics, clerks, and other rear-echelon personnel into the replacement pipeline for the infantry companies. But it was the home front that had to provide the bulk of the reinforcements. Marshall speeded up training time for youngsters still in the States. He also greatly expanded the immediately available pool by ending the Army Specialized Training Program (ASTP).

The ASTP was a pet of Secretary of War Henry Stimson. The idea was to take 150,000 of the brightest draftees and offer to put them through college if they opted for the Army (the Navy had a smaller but similar program already in place; Stimson wanted to compete). Those given the offer were young men whose test scores indicated they would get cushy rear-echelon jobs with rapid promotions or be sent to Officer Candidate School. Those who accepted had to forgo those opportunities: while they were in ASTP they would remain privates. But the Army would provide their room, board, and tuition, and pay them at a private's rate, $50 per month. They would take regular classes at the colleges and universities, majoring in areas where the Army anticipated specialists would be needed later in the war, such as mathematics, engineering, or foreign languages. Naturally these "whiz kids" were much resented. A popular saying with ordinary infantry had it that ASTP stood for All Safe Till Peace.

Most ASTPers got started on their education in the fall semester of 1943. By the summer semester of 1944, most were gone. In February 1944, in anticipation of manpower needs after the battle became joined, Marshall cut the program from 150,000 to 30,000. Simultaneously General Arnold decided that with air superiority won over Europe, the Air Force wasn't going to need anywhere near as many pilots as it had thought. He released 71,000 aviation cadets for the ground forces.[1] The would-be pilots dubbed themselves "grounded butterflies."

So suddenly there were 190,000 of the best and brightest of the Army's inductees from 1942–43, enough for more than ten divisions, available for assignment. What an asset—at a time when every other combatant was taking conscripts too old, too young, too ill to fight, the U.S. Army was feeding into its fighting force its best young men.

More than half the ASTPers got sent into rifle companies, as replacements. The Army had promised them a free education, then changed its mind and put them into the front lines, where most of them would never have ended up if they had declined the offer to enter the program. There was some bitterness and much bitching, then off to a brief basic training course.

When Pvt. Robert Curtis arrived at Camp McCoy, Wisconsin, fresh from Hope College, he joined other ex-ASTPers in a large room. An officer gave a welcome speech. "With your ability and background," he said, "you are something special, and we are therefore going to give you a *choice*."

"As we moved to the assignment table, the officer looked up at you and inquired, 'What will it be, rifle, machine gun, or mortar.' "[2]

In training camp they merged with another stream of replacements on the way to Europe, the ordinary American kids who turned eighteen years of age in 1944 and who either volunteered so they could select a service or waited to get drafted. Working-class kids, the kind many ASTPers would never have met in civilian life, but the two often hit it off immediately. Kurt Vonnegut had been an ASTPer at Cornell University before joining the 106th Division. He was in a rifle squad, "and those guys were the best guys I ever met."[3]

Roughly half the reinforcements flowed from the States to France—usually Le Havre—organized as divisions, such as the 99th and the 106th. The remainder of the men were not organized at all. They were simply privates on their way into the battle wherever they were needed. They would be assigned as individuals to companies in the line. They were called replacements.

About half the three-million-plus men who served in the U.S. Army in ETO came onto the Continent as replacements. A disproportionate number of them went straight to the rifle companies. Tens of thousands of others came as members of quickly put together high-number infantry divisions composed of units drawn from all over that had not trained together. At the time of the Bulge possibly more than four out of every five infantrymen up front were replacements or men who were members of inadequately trained divisions that were new to combat.

How those reinforcements got from their basic training to a foxhole was the responsibility of the Replacement System. The colonels on the staff felt their first responsibility was to the needs of the front, which they decided meant keeping the flow going at maximum speed without regard for what was going into the flow.

When a ship arrived at Le Havre, a replacement went directly to a "reception" depot, a tent city where he knew no one. Then on to a "stockage" depot, where he received a rifle, lectures in hygiene, and, if lucky, some desperately needed additional training. Some of the replacements had never even held an M-1 or qualified with any weapon.[4] Lt. George Wilson, CO of a rifle company deeply involved in the Bulge, received 100 replacements on December 29: "We discovered that these men had been on the rifle range only once; they had never thrown a grenade or fired a bazooka, mortar, or machine gun."[5]

After two days to a week at the stockage, the replacement went to the 3rd Replacement Depot, or "Repple Depple," which supported the First Army, and later to a forward battalion supporting a corps. Finally he was brought forward to a company CP and led out to a foxhole. He did not know the name of anyone around him.

"Being a replacement is just like being an orphan," one soldier told an Army survey team. "You are away from anybody you know and feel lost and lonesome."[6]

Pvt. Morris Dunn, who ended up with the 84th Division, spent weeks in a Repple Depple. "We were just numbers, we didn't know anybody, and I've never felt so alone and miserable and helpless in my entire life—we'd been herded around like cattle at roundup time. . . . On the ride to the front it was cold and raining with the artillery fire louder every mile, and finally we were dumped out in the middle of a heavily damaged town."[7]

That was how most of the replacements got to the most dangerous place in the world—unknown, unknowing, scared, bewildered, untrained. According to Captain Roland, "only a Kafka could truly describe the depersonalizing effects of the replacement system."[8] Every one of nearly a million men who went through it agreed. Had the Germans been given a free hand to devise a replacement system for ETO, one that would do the Americans the most harm and least good, they could not have done a better job.

The Repple Depple was universally despised and denounced. "When the war is over," one replacement said to another, "I'm going to attend the war crimes trial of the men responsible for this system. I want to watch them shoot the bastards!"[9]

Yet the system had been based on some solid thinking and past experience and of course good intentions. It failed because of unexpected (but predictable) consequences. The Army knew it had problems and did some studies. These led to inconsequential "reforms," such as putting recreational facilities into the Repple Depples and changing the designation from "replacement" to "reinforcement" for its perceived psychological benefit.

One suggestion was on the mark. It was to put the replacements in squads that would stay together from basic training to the foxholes. That would have helped. To have put them into companies would have been even more effective in creating that bond that is critical to combat infantry. Best would have been as battalions, ready to relieve combat-weary units at the front. Better than nothing at all would have been orientation lectures on life at the front, taught by wounded veterans.

These suggestions were not acted on. The Repple Depple system stayed. At the end of the war in Europe, men were still assigned as individuals to combat units. In this the Army failed to look after its own.

The replacements paid the cost. Often more than half became casualties within the first three days on the line. The odds were against a replacement's surviving long enough to gain recognition and experience.[10]

They came in, according to Pvt. Ken Russell of the 82nd Airborne, "all good boys with the strength of a mule and the ignorance of old maids. We pitied the scared, shy eager youngsters who were awe-struck around us old boys [Russell was nineteen]. . . . In the first battle they usually died in heaps."[11]

It was to the obvious benefit of the old boys to help the new kids, but nevertheless most veterans tried to avoid replacements.

For one thing the new men tended to draw fire, because they bunched up (Ken Russell commented that "veterans died separately and not in bunches as replacements often did"), talked too much, or lit cigarettes at night. For another, men just didn't want to make friends with guys whom they expected to die soon. Veterans resented replacements for one overwhelming reason—when replacements came, it meant the division was staying in the line, or attacking.

So most of his first days on the line, the recruit remained alone. If a replacement did get some attention from the veterans, it didn't help his morale. As one old-timer said, "When you bring in a bunch of recruits, the talk gets louder and more boisterous to make an impression." Pvt. Clayton Shepherd found himself with Company K, 332nd Infantry, 84th Division. As he got to the platoon, a patrol came in. "They said, 'This man got his head blowed off, this man his arm blowed off,' and all that. And I thought, Jesus Christ, what am I getting into here? They shouldn't have told us new guys that. They scared the hell out of me before I even got started."[12] Veterans in the 90th Division—themselves replacements just a few days or weeks earlier—told newcomers not to worry about getting killed. "Death can't be all that bad," they pointed out. "No one ever heard a dead man complain."[13]

In February 1945, Capt. Douglas Smith, 94th Division, gathered a bunch of replacements in a cellar just behind the front lines. He wanted to instill some confidence, so he told them they were joining the finest combat outfit in the whole damned Army. After, he asked his sergeant, Jim Morrison, "Did I make sense, or did I sound like I was full of shit?"

"You sounded sincere enough," Morrison replied, "but they know the only reason they're here is because someone else got hit or killed. Otherwise they wouldn't be here."[14]

Replacements usually came up in small groups. They clung to one another, because other recruits were the only ones in the entire U.S. Army with whom they had anything in common. Their first day, they bunched up physically on the front; if they survived the almost certain shelling, they learned not to. Dutch Schultz remembered a time in the Bulge when five replacements were killed by one shell "before they were even assigned to any of the platoons."[15]

In the Repple Depple, the soldiers were merely numbers, with no choice as to where they were going to go. Except once, when

Capt. James Eikner of the Rangers showed up. The Bulge was on and the Rangers had been decimated in the Hurtgen Forest. Eikner was there to pick some recruits. "The Rangers select the people that they want," he explained, "and they have to measure up. They have to be outstanding young men—above average in physical and mental stamina—and we took in no low IQ cases."

Eikner got a few thousand men together in the auditorium at the Repple Depple. He told them "quite frankly who we were and what we were, [that] we would do our best to give them whatever training we could—sort of an on the job training—and that when we left we would go directly into the front line and combat." He asked for volunteers and got hundreds. He selected fifty-three "who seemed to measure up."

He took them by truck back to the Bulge. "Just as we were dumping them out why here comes an enemy artillery barrage and these poor guys, new to combat, the first shell fire they had heard, scattered in all directions. It took us a while to get them all rounded up. Two or three were killed and many wounded."[16]

Replacements exposed themselves senselessly. Pvt. Robert Curtis of the 76th Division remembered his first day on the line. His mortar crew moved to a bluff hanging over a river. "Since everything seemed quiet on the other side of the river," Curtis said, "I stood up to get a better look. There was an almost instant explosion." A mortar shell went off a few yards away.

"Jesus Christ, *Get Down!*" the sergeant screamed. "I've got a wife and kids at home."[17]

In early January, Sergeant Lick of the 1st Division received five replacements for his platoon. One was from the Air Force ground crew, one from the quartermaster, one a mechanic, and two fresh from basic training. The Air Force man got a fever and was sent back. So too for the quartermaster. The mechanic became a machine gunner and survived. As for the two replacements from the States, "they volunteered to go back to battalion H.Q. for rations and on the way both got hit by a shell, killing one and wounding the other. They didn't even get their names on our platoon roster."[18]

Pvt. Jim Graff of the 35th Division was a nineteen-year-old replacement who went into the line at night and never saw his foxhole companion until first light. A month later he was a veteran. His squad leader saw some replacements being dumped in the middle of

INFANTRY DIVISIONS

DIVISION NUMBER	ENTERED COMBAT	DAYS IN COMBAT	CASUALTIES			% OF TURNOVER
			BATTLE	NON-BATTLE	TOTAL	
1	6 June 1944	292	15,003	14,002	29,005	205.9
2	8 June 1944	303	15,066	10,818	25,884	183.7
3	15 August 1944	233	13,101	15,299	28,400	201.6
4	6 June 1944	299	22,454	13,091	35,545	252.3
5	16 July 1944	270	12,475	11,012	23,487	166.7
8	8 July 1944	266	13,458	7,598	21,056	149.4
9	14 June 1944	264	18,631	15,233	33,864	240.4
13	No Combat	0	—	—	—	—
17	25 December 1944	45	3,166	834	4,000	119.6
26	12 October 1944	199	9,956	6,895	16,851	176.3
28	27 July 1944	196	15,904	8,936	24,840	204.2
29	6 June 1944	242	20,111	8,665	28,776	184.8
30	15 June 1944	282	17,691	8,347	26,038	180.9
35	11 July 1944	264	15,406	10,082	25,488	

CASUALTIES

DIVISION NUMBER	ENTERED COMBAT	DAYS IN COMBAT	BATTLE	NON-BATTLE	TOTAL	% OF TURNOVER
36	15 August 1944	227	11,238	14,919	26,157	185.7
42	17 February 1945	106	3,598	2,351	5,949	42.2
44	24 October 1944	230	6,111	7,637	13,748	97.6
45	15 August 1944	230	10,458	15,991	26,449	187.7
63	6 February 1945	119	4,547	3,472	8,019	56.9
65	9 March 1945	55	1,052	1,250	2,302	16.3
66	1 January 1945	91	1,098	849	1,947	13.8
69	11 February 1945	65	1,556	1,791	3,347	23.8
70	3 February 1945	83	3,996	4,235	8,201	58.2
71	6 February 1945	49	788	1,081	1,869	13.3
75	25 December 1944	94	3,954	4,062	8,016	56.9
76	19 January 1945	95	3,126	2,430	5,556	39.4
78	13 December 1944	125	7,890	4,367	12,257	87.0
79	19 June 1944	248	14,875	8,582	23,457	166.5
80	8 August 1944	239	14,460	11,012	25,472	180.8
83	27 June 1944	244	15,248	8,732	23,980	170.2
84	18 November 1944	152	6,561	3,250	9,811	69.6
86	29 March 1945	34	760	473	1,233	8.8

DIVISION NUMBER	ENTERED COMBAT	DAYS IN COMBAT	CASUALTIES			% OF TURNOVER
			BATTLE	NON-BATTLE	TOTAL	
87	13 December 1944	134	5,555	6,032	11,587	82.2
89	12 March 1945	57	1,006	1,074	2,080	14.6
90	10 June 1944	308	18,460	9,157	27,617	196.0
94	17 September 1944	183	5,607	5,203	10,810	76.7
95	20 October 1944	151	6,307	3,834	10,204	72.4
97	1 April 1945	31	934	384	1,318	9.4
99	9 November 1944	151	6,103	5,884	11,987	85.1
100	9 November 1944	163	4,790	7,425	12,215	86.7
102	26 October 1944	173	4,867	3,958	8,825	62.6
103	11 November 1944	147	4,543	4,826	9,369	66.5
104	24 October 1944	178	7,011	6,396	13,407	95.1
106	10 December 1944	63	8,163	2,508	10,671	75.7

ARMORED DIVISIONS

DIVISION NUMBER	ENTERED COMBAT	DAYS IN COMBAT	CASUALTIES			% OF TURNOVER
			BATTLE	NON-BATTLE	TOTAL	
2	2 July 1944	223	6,751	7,116	13,867	95.9
3	9 July 1944	231	10,105	6,017	16,122	111.5
4	28 July 1944	230	5,988	4,508	10,496	98.4
5	2 August 1944	161	3,554	3,592	7,146	67.0
6	28 July 1944	226	5,526	7,290	12,816	120.1
7	14 August 1944	172	6,150	4,352	10,502	98.4
8	23 February 1945	63	1,313	1,141	2,454	23.0
9	16 December 1944	91	3,952	1,459	5,411	50.7
10	2 November 1944	124	4,697	3,684	8,381	78.5
11	23 December 1944	96	3,216	1,921	5,137	48.1
12	7 December 1944	102	3,436	2,540	5,976	56.0
13	10 April 1945	16	493	246	739	6.9
14	20 November 1944	133	2,896	1,400	4,296	40.3
16	5 May 1945	3	12	231	243	2.3
20	24 April 1945	8	76	319	395	3.7

Source: Order of Battle, United States Army in World War II—European Theater of Operations, *Office of the Theater Historian, ETO, December 1945*

a village. He told Graff to pick out an assistant BAR man for himself. "I went out in the streets and this one individual looked lost," Graff recalled. "I asked if he knew anything about a BAR."

"Hell, no," the replacement replied. "I don't know anything, not even about this rifle they just gave me." It was an M-1. Graff figured everyone in the Army had qualified on an M-1 and was astonished. The replacement explained that he had been a mechanic in the artillery for years. He had taken his basic in 1941 when the Army was still using the 1903 Springfield bolt-action rifle. Graff took him anyway.[19]

War is full of surprises. On at least one occasion, the greenness of a replacement officer paid big dividends. During the Bulge, company commander John Colby told a platoon leader, fresh from the States, to capture a house.

"He walked up to it and knocked on the door. Jesus! I had not given him instructions on how to take a house on the outskirts of a village. Instead of heaving in a grenade and having his men kick in the door and rush in firing away, he was standing there waiting for someone to open it."

A German sergeant in his undershirt, suspenders hanging down, answered the knock. The replacement lieutenant said something to him. The German came outside and yelled. Several other Germans rose up from positions behind a fence and barn and put their hands in the air. The sergeant sent a runner to a machine-gun crew with orders to come in and give up. The entire group, American and German, moved into the village. At each house, the German sergeant called on more of his men to give up.

Germans and Americans alike were wearing white sheets. They milled together in the village square. Americans frisked Germans for watches, pistols, and binoculars and, the astonished Colby noted, "some Germans were doing the same to my men."

German sergeants abhorred disorder. This one barked out orders, in English and in German. He ordered Colby's men to line up on one side of the road, the Germans on the other. He called them all to attention. Then he formally surrendered his company to Colby.

Colby commented, "Had our new, green, inexperienced officer taken that first house properly, as I intended, all kinds of shooting would have broken out with lots of casualties. As it was no one got hurt and we took about a hundred prisoners. That's the way to fight a war."[20]

It was bad enough being an untrained infantry replacement; it could be worse going into armor untrained. Yet many did. One tank commander remembered that in the Bulge "I spent long hours in the turret when I was literally showing men how to feed bullets to the gun. Could they shoot straight? They couldn't even hold the gun right! In the midst of the toughest fighting of the Third Army's campaign I was teaching men what I had learned in basic training."[21]

Sgt. Raymond Janus of the 1st Infantry Division got a new three-man crew for his light tank. They were all eighteen years of age. Only one had driven a car, and that only to church on Sundays. He became driver. Neither of the other two had any experience firing a machine gun or a 37mm tank gun. Janus gave them a two-hour demonstration. Then they moved out on a mission.

The tank had hardly proceeded a half kilometer when the driver panicked and rolled the tank down a hill. The crash threw Janus out of the turret and on his head, causing a severe concussion that cost him his hearing.[22]

The replacements paid the price for a criminally wasteful Replacement System that chose to put quantity ahead of quality. Its criteria was the flow of bodies. Whose fault was this?

Eisenhower's first. He was the boss. And Bradley's. And Patton's. They demanded an ever greater flow of replacements while doing precious little to insist on improving the training, and got what they demanded. In no other way did the American high command in ETO show such disengagement as Eisenhower, Bradley, et al. did in failing to look at the source of their replacements and then to force some obvious and relatively easy improvements in the Repple Depples and in the assignment methods. It can only be that Eisenhower, Bradley, et al. had no clear conception of life on the front line. They didn't listen to foxhole GIs often enough. So they threw the eighteen-year-olds and the former ASTPers into the battle, untrained, alone.

The American Army approaching Germany in the fall of 1944

was in part a Children's Crusade. It had hundreds of thousands of eighteen-to-twenty-year-old soldiers, most of them at the cutting edge of the general offensive and almost none of them properly trained for combat. Captain Roland remembered receiving replacements in January, "a number of whom had eaten Christmas dinner at home with their families, who were killed in action before they had an opportunity to learn the names of the soldiers in the foxholes with them."[23]

As noted, Eisenhower said that in war everything is expendable—even generals' lives—in pursuit of victory. If victory required replacements, some of them would have to be expended. One had to be tough. The problem here is that the Replacement System was guilty of the worst sin of all in war, inefficiency. It was paying lives but getting no return. It was just pure waste and the commanders should have done something about it.

Example: In January 1945, Capt. Belton Cooper of the 3rd Armored Division got thirty-five replacements to help crew the seventeen new tanks the division had received. "These men had just unloaded from the boat in Antwerp a few hours earlier," Cooper said. "They had received no previous indoctrination on what they were to do." Not one had any previous experience with tanks. "Most of them had never even been in a tank or even close to one."

Cooper gave them a brief verbal orientation. Then his mechanics took small groups into tanks, where each recruit got to fire the main gun three times. "This was all the training time permitted," Cooper remembered, because the guides came to take the tanks to their assignments to the various units.

The previous night, the thirty-five replacements had been in Antwerp. At 1500 they lumbered off in a convoy of seventeen tanks headed for the front. Two hours later, fifteen of the seventeen were knocked out by German panzers firing 88s.[24]

It often happened that more than half the replacements sent directly into combat became casualties in the first few days.

Green divisions put into the front also suffered needless casualties. In December, the 87th Division replaced the 26th Division in the line. "So there we sat and shivered in the rain and darkness while contact patrols were sent back to try to lead the relieving company up to us," Lieutenant Otts of the 26th remembered. "Finally, just before midnight, they arrived—fresh and green. We had been afraid to talk above a whisper for fear of bringing a mortar or 88 barrage in on us, but they came up talking loudly, wanting to know where their foxholes were, shining flashlights, and making quite a racket."

Otts got his platoon—down to fifteen men—out of there. On the road leading to the rear, the 26th had only dared to use a single jeep driving at full speed, and then only once a day. Now it was bumper to bumper with 87th Division vehicles. "We shrugged it off with a few remarks of 'They'll learn' and forgot about them."[25]

Captain Leinbaugh remembered a platoon, thrown together in the Repple Depple and led by a captain "obviously fresh from the States," that was thrown into the Bulge. They were close-shaven, clear-eyed, and wearing clean uniforms. Their bayonets were fixed. To Leinbaugh, "They seemed totally out of place—an alien cast which had wandered onto the wrong stage."

The new captain led his men out to a blocking position on the line. But rather than working through the wood and flanking the objective, he sent the men straight across a field of deep snow toward a fieldstone hut. The Germans let them get in close. When they opened fire, every one of the GIs was killed.

"We were as mad at the new outfit as we were at the Germans—maybe more so," Leinbaugh remembered. "We kept calling them dumb bastards. Twelve good men were dead. This sort of thing couldn't have happened to us; we knew better."[26]

They should have passed on what they knew. The Army should have set up a system to make sure they passed it on. Little things, that took only minute in the telling, like the German practice of firing machine-gun tracer ammunition high to coax Americans to maneuver beneath it, then firing low without tracers; or how to distinguish the distinctive smell of German infantry with their sweat-stained leather equipment; or that the easiest way to judge how close to danger you were after riding a deuce-and-a-half to the front was how fast the trucks drove away. The only way to learn about combat is to experience it—but surely the Army could have done more to promote passing on information to replacements and to new divisions, from division staffs down to front-line squads.

If a replacement survived the first few days, he had become a combat veteran, but still with a lot to learn. In the good outfits, old-timers took charge. "It came down to a hard core of those remaining who hold the unit together," Capt. Douglas Smith decided. A core "that can accept the replacements, train them, fit them into the squads even when they had passed their own limits of endurance long ago, and so they are able to carry on until they are gone and the process starts all over again."[27]

The 29th Division's saying—we are three divisions, one in the grave, one in the hospital, one at the front—could be applied to more than two dozen U.S. divisions in ETO. And the one at the front consisted of replacements who did not know what to do and war-weary veterans whose fatalistic attitudes suggested that it did not matter what they did. Fortunately, there was that core Captain Smith described who could teach as well as fight. It was critical to the victory, because by the end of the war men who had been Stateside on D-Day made up virtually the whole of the fighting army.

The Army was always learning. After the war it conducted surveys among the ETO veterans, including detailed material on their training, rightly figuring that it was the combat veterans who could best judge its effectiveness. A majority of the men surveyed had their training in 1944 and fought in the last six to eight months of the war. Perhaps half of them had been through Repple Depples.

Every combat veteran I've interviewed, when asked about training, starts with some version of, "Nothing can prepare you for combat." Virtually all the men surveyed agreed. The paratroopers commented that they thought they had been put through a training regime so tough that "combat can't be worse than this," only to discover it was. There was a consensus among the GIs that training should be tougher, with more live ammunition, and that the best way to prepare a soldier for combat was to improve his stamina and physical strength.

The veterans pointed to many additional shortcomings in their training. About 80 percent said they did not know enough about German weapons, how to defend against them or how to attack them. They further felt their knowledge of German tactics was deficient. They wished they had been taught more aircraft identification. Ninety percent were unprepared for mine warfare. No one had said to them one word about trench foot, much less how to prevent it.

No surprise: they felt all those hours spent doing close order drill and learning military courtesy were wasted. They felt their weapons training had been good. But they had not been taught to follow close behind supporting artillery fire, they tended to slow down on making contact, they allowed German indirect fire to pin them down, their noise and light discipline at night was poor, they bunched together when fired on. Those that survived the first few days learned how to do better, but they could have been taught at far less cost back in the States.[28]

Captain Roland remarks, "The marvel is that the draftee divisions were able to generate and maintain any esprit de corps at all. Formed originally by mixing men indiscriminately from throughout the nation, thus severing all personal, social, community, and regional bonds, identified by anonymous numbers and replenished through the notorious Reppel Depples, their only source of morale, other than the shared experience of hazard and hardship, was the character and patriotism of the soldiers. Fortunately, that proved to be sufficient."[29]

In an article in *Army History,* published by the U.S. Army's Center of Military History in 1994, Prof. Francis Steckel indicts the Army for two reasons: "First, the replacement system rushed men into combat without adequate preparation and created an unnecessarily arduous challenge of adjustment on the field of battle. Second, the small number of divisions required units to remain in the front lines without rest and beyond the limits of individual human endurance, thus causing an earlier than necessary breakdown of veterans whose invaluable combat experience and skills were lost prematurely."[30]

I'd add a third indictment: failure to pass on even rudimentary information. It was not the job of the front-line machine gunner or tanker to train replacements. The Army was supposed to do that and it failed.

12

The Air War

BETWEEN JUNE 6, 1944, AND May 6, 1945, an average of 5,000 American soldiers and airmen per day entered the Continent.[1] At the end of 1944, the U.S. Army in the European Theater of Operations numbered 2,700,000 men. Of these, 500,000 were in the Army Air Force. In the ground forces, roughly 300,000 were front-line infantry, with another 300,000 or so in the artillery, armor, or other combat-support roles. Of the Air Force personnel, about half were ground crews and administrative types. The other half, some quarter of a million young Americans, were pilots or air crew in the Eighth and Ninth Air Forces.

They saw plenty of combat but their living conditions were far better than those on the front lines. Airmen had beds, clean sheets, hot food, showers, clean clothes. They had some privacy, if only a footlocker in the bunkhouse. They had regular and easy access to a London in which a pack of cigarettes would pay for a woman and a night's worth of booze. They got medals and promotions faster than the ground soldiers. They were the envy of the men in the foxholes.

But there were moments when airmen envied the infantry. For the crews on the bombers, there was no choice about whether to enter a raging battle, or stay put and out of it, or run away—willy-nilly the bomber crews went in when the plane did. On a B-17 or a B-24, the pilot took (rather than led) his nine crew members into an apparently solid wall of exploding 88mm shells. The men could not move around, hide, duck, run away. The gunners could shoot, but only if a German fighter came at the bomber from the right angle. For those not shooting, flying through flak was an experience similar to an infantryman's getting caught in the open in a shelling. Men were helpless and terrified.

One difference in the combat experience of ground and air warriors was in depth of perception. In interviews, infantry veterans emphasize that their war was twenty meters to the left and twenty meters to the right. Beyond that, they saw little and knew less. Seldom did a foot soldier get to see more than a tiny bit of the U.S. Army in Europe. Airmen saw the war on a continent-wide scale. They were on one of thousands of planes, spread as far as one could see. It frequently happens that infantrymen, asked in an interview what they remember most vividly about the war, will recall a specific incident, while an airman will generalize. As did Lt. Marvin Kraft, a navigator in the Eighth Air Force: "What struck me most was the scope, scale and intensity of the war. Looking back, it seems we were on some kind of giant assembly line. We moved to a grand design."[2]

Kraft *was* part of an assembly line, one that reached from Willow Run, where the B-24s were made at the Ford plant, to Berlin, where bombs made in a munitions plant in Mississippi were dropped. And he was part of a grand design, to destroy Germany's ability to make and move weapons. To that end, the United States invested a considerable portion of her total effort in the bombing campaign. At the pinnacle of the effort were the four-engine bombers in the Eighth Air Force. It is best described by oral historian Gerald Astor in his 1997 book, *The Mighty Eighth: The Air War in Europe as Told by the Men Who Fought It:* "In all likelihood, the world will never see another organization like the Mighty Eighth, which at its zenith nearly blotted out the sky with aircraft."

Astor goes on to note, "Like all great enterprises, particularly when operating under the demands of war, it was hardly a smoothly running machine."[3] The frustration inherent in the air war was very high. The infantry could measure progress by numbers of enemy killed or taken prisoner, and by ground gained. But the airmen seldom saw an enemy fall, never took a prisoner. Far from winning, they seemed in the late fall of 1944 to be in danger of losing, as the Luftwaffe proved exceedingly difficult to kill off. In the summer and fall of 1944, the bombers had gone deep into Germany to strike oil, transportation, and industrial targets. Often there were no German fighters to contest the skies. But by late fall, in time for the Ardennes counteroffensive, the Luftwaffe had made a comeback. It was able to put planes in the air for night bombardment of Bastogne and other towns when conditions permitted. On Christmas Eve the Germans mounted their biggest aerial effort of the entire campaign in Northwest Europe. On New Year's Day some 600 German planes hit British airfields at Eindhoven and Brussels, destroying 180 or more parked planes.

This was discouraging in the extreme. For nearly half a year the Americans had been going after the Luftwaffe's fuel supplies and the factories where the planes were being made, and now there were more enemy planes in the skies than there had been six months earlier. The Germans had dispersed aircraft production from twenty-seven main plants to 729 small ones. The number of single-engine fighters reaching the Luftwaffe rose from 1,016 built in February 1944 to 3,013 in September. (Overall, German armament production rose in November 1944 to 260 percent above the beginning of 1942.)

Still, as a result of the oil campaign, the new planes were rather like the new tanks that went into the Bulge—great weapons but what was the use of them when there was no fuel? And the German pilots entering the battle in late 1944 had insufficient training time to become competent; in most cases, no more than an hour or two in the air a week.

For the Allies, the big worry in late 1944 about the air war was Germany's jet aircraft production. The ME 163 single-engine and ME 262 twin-engine fighters had already been built by the hundreds. The Arado 234 jet bomber was just coming into production. They were capable of 550 miles per hour, about 100 miles per hour faster than the P-51s and P-47s. Not until October 1945 did the Americans expect to have a jet airplane (and in the event, two years after the end of the war, the ME 262 being flown at Wright-Patterson AFB, Dayton, Ohio, was still judged superior to the new USAF P-80 jet fighter).[4]

Going into the year 1945, some Allied airmen feared that if the war lasted until June the jets might yet restore control of German skies to the Luftwaffe. As early as September, Gen. Carl Spaatz, commanding the Eighth Air Force, had given jet production priority among his targets second only to oil. On January 9, 1945, he gave jets first priority. Still they came on. In the air as on the ground, the Germans had demonstrated a resourcefulness and determination that in the wake of the pounding they had taken invited the use of the word "miracle."

The air crews of the American bombers, meanwhile, discovered they had to fly more missions. First it was twenty-five, then it was raised to thirty-five. It kept climbing, as high as seventy in a few cases. There were volunteers who completed 100 missions. Occasionally the missions were so-called milk runs, with no fighter opposition and no flak. More often there would be one or the other. Much too often they faced both fighters and flak. In 1943, before the P-51 provided long-range fighter escort over Germany, only 35 percent of the Eighth Air Force crews survived twenty-five missions. The figure rose to 66 percent after the P-51 came along in 1944.[5]

The crews on the four-engine bombers—nine men, plus the pilot—were like an infantry squad in size but not in rank or function. The four men in the forward section of the plane—pilot, co-pilot, bombardier, navigator—were officers. They were on the offensive. Their job was to deliver bombs on target. Six sergeants* were on the machine guns: one at the nose gun, one in the top turret, two waist gunners, the ball turret gunner crammed into a tiny, rotating Plexiglas sphere that hung below the plane just behind the bomb bay doors, and the tail gunner looking to the rear. They were on the defensive. Their job was to shoot down or ward off attacking German fighters. Rank made little difference in the Army Air Force, at least within a crew, where the officers and sergeants were as close to one another as in an infantry squad. They trained together and fought together.

The B-17 was dubbed the Flying Fortress. It bristled with machine guns, thirteen .50-calibers in all. So did the B-24 Liberator. The idea was that with all those heavy machine guns blazing away a bomber could defend itself from any attack. In fact in 1943 the Army Air Force discovered it could not. Indeed scientists doing studies for airmen recommended getting rid of the machine guns,

---

*When the Air Force leaders learned that the Germans treated sergeants better than privates in POW camps, they made every enlisted man who flew over Germany a sergeant.

the ammunition, and the gunners altogether. Then the bombers could fly higher and faster and would be safer. No way, replied the pilots—we want to shoot back. So the guns and the gunners stayed; the pilots and their crews were all in it together.

The British, meanwhile, had given up on daytime bombing altogether, because of the unacceptable loss rate. So the British bombed by night—huge raids by hundreds of bombers, making no attempt to hit a specific target smaller than a city—while the Americans went in during daylight—huge raids by hundreds of bombers, making every effort to hit a specific target.

The B-17 had a top speed of 287 miles per hour, with a range of 2,000 miles when carrying 6,000 pounds of bombs. A total of 12,731 were built by Boeing, Douglas, and Lockheed during the war. The B-24 could carry up to 8,800 pounds of bombs and had a maximum speed of 300 miles per hour, with a range of just over 2,000 miles. By the end of the war 18,190 had been built.

The American pilots and their crews were astonishingly young to be in control of such huge aircraft. Sgt. Robert Hastings was a ball turret gunner on a B-24. In a 1996 interview, he described his fellow crew members. The oldest was the navigator, who was twenty-five years old. Three men, including the pilot, were twenty-three years old, one was twenty-one, one was twenty, two were nineteen, and two were eighteen. They were civilian soldiers, with no previous flying experience. Before joining the Air Force, the navigator had been in advertising and was a copywriter. "Four were students," Hastings remembered, "including me. One was a farmer, one was a draftsman, there was a truck driver, a grocery clerk, and a milkman. Three were married. And of the ten of us we represented eight different states."[6]

The stress began with wake-up, breakfast, and briefing. In February 1943, Sgt. Andy Rooney, a reporter for *Stars and Stripes,* went on a mission on a B-17. He stumbled with the officers through the predawn darkness to the briefing hut. The briefing officer stood in front of a wall covered with a blanket. He had a long pointer in his hand. When all were seated, he stepped up to the wall, scanned the room, then grasped the lower right-hand corner of the cloth and threw it back. "There was a hush at first as the flyers stared intently at the map. Gradually a murmur developed and then gasps as they

realized it was a large-scale map of a western sector of Germany.
Our destination was—Wilhelmshaven!"[7]

Wilhelmshaven meant flak and terror. Most missions were like
that, and sometimes the briefing left men immobile. One navigator
was paralyzed by the briefing, time after time. His buddies would
carry him to the plane. Once aboard, he was okay. Capt. Robert
Johnson recalled there were three pilots he knew who got a bad case
of "109 jitters" (referring to the ME 109). Two were useless. The
third was trembling and had to be supported as he left the briefing
room. "But he was the bravest guy I ever knew," said Johnson—who
had the second-highest number of aerial victories in Europe. "He
was a Jewish boy and built like the Liberty Bell, narrow shoulders
but a hell of a big butt. He fit the P-47 beautifully. He was absolutely scared to death of flying combat, but he forced himself to
and he did. He flew. He never became an ace but was certainly there
and helped out."[8]

The stress increased on the airfield. The men pulled themselves into the planes through an opening in the side. The officers
moved from the midsection through the bomb bay, walking on a
narrow steel beam with the 500- or 1,000-pound bombs hanging
down on either side. The cockpit in a B-17 was above and immediately ahead of the bomb bay. The top turret gunner was behind the
cockpit. To get to the nose area, the bombardier bent down and
went under the pilot and past the radioman's position. All this had
to be done while wearing heavy coats, gloves, boots. The ball turret
gunner's fighting position was in a Plexiglas bubble, hydraulically
powered, which he moved around with foot pedals. The gunners
had silk gloves with electrically heated gloves on top.

Every man on the plane was cramped. Whether in the pilot's
seat or in the tail gunner's position, once in place a man could
scarcely shift his weight, stretch, scratch, or otherwise give physical
release to his pent-up energy. Nor could he close his eyes, or otherwise rest. He had to remain at full alert for three, four, five, seven, or
more hours. Men took care to drink only one cup of coffee and hold
down on the food at breakfast.

Lt. Chuck Halper had a navigator who needed to go on almost
every mission. "He carried big paper containers with lids. Despite
layers of clothing, parachute harness, Mae West, heated suit,

trousers, long johns, etc. he would make his contribution in the containers, slap the lid on and get dressed. Later, when the bombardier took over on the bomb run, the navigator would hook up to a portable oxygen bottle, pick up the carton and go back and stand in the bomb bay. When the bombs fell free, he would throw the container out. We were all somewhat flak happy and each of us accepted his behavior as perfectly normal. We named his special bomb *flieger scheisse,* German for flying shit."[9]

With his crew settled in and checking the equipment, the pilot started his engines, one by one. The roar of hundreds of engines revving up overwhelmed the senses. Then came the taxi to takeoff position, then the signal to go, then the pilots starting down the runway, one right on the tail of another. Lt. Les Lennox, a B-17 pilot, recalled forty years later, "The people in air traffic control today would be absolutely appalled if they could see our only method of controlling all those bombers. Taking off at thirty-second intervals and climbing through all types of weather, in darkness while maintaining radio silence. When two aircraft have a near miss today it makes national news. We had so many each day we thought nothing of it."[10]

Climbing through cloud cover, trying to maintain formation, flying wingtip to wingtip, made for a high pucker factor. Collisions happened. Lt. J. K. Havener, a B-26 pilot, said, "On numerous occasions a 36-ship formation would join up below the overcast and then bore on up through it in formation." He recalled Lt. Roy Russell, who was flying number two wing position in a flight of six when the clouds got so black with rain he lost sight of the lead ship's right wingtip. He drifted slightly left. His left wingtip hit the vertical stabilizer of the lead plane. That plane, its rudder badly damaged, had to abort. It successfully crash-landed on a farm near the Cliffs of Dover. Russell, meanwhile, despite the loss of his wingtip, flew on and completed the mission. He loved the war, he once told a buddy. "I was young, crazy and looking for glory." He volunteered for a second tour and flew a total of seventy missions.[11]

In 1943 and the first nine months of 1944, when the bombers got above the clouds and headed east they were often set on by German fighters rising up from airfields in France. Following the liberation of France, thankfully, the skies were free of the enemy until the flying armada crossed into German airspace. That meant, however, hours of fighting off boredom and tedium in a cramped position in freezing cold in an unpressurized airplane at 24,000 feet, taking in oxygen from a tank, staying warm with electric heat in the gloves and boots, with nothing to do but watch for the enemy and stay on the tail of the guy in front.

When the bombers approached the target, everyone burst into activity. The 88s on the ground would begin to fire. Their radar told them the bombers' altitude; they set the fuse and then sent the shell up ahead of the formation, where the bombers would fly into the explosion (which sent out shrapnel of considerable size). The Allied countermeasure was to drop chaff to confuse the German radar. The German countermeasure to that was to have a scout plane fly on the edge of the bombers' formation and radio down the altitude.

Spreading out and taking evasive action was the natural reaction to concentrated flak ahead, but it was forbidden for two reasons. First, to achieve the precision results the bomber generals demanded, the flights had to stay close together and drop their bombs when the lead plane did. Second, to provide the concentrated firepower necessary to drive off German fighters, the pilots had to keep their wingtips in a near-touching position. And from the Initial Point (IP) to the target, they had to fly slow and steady, in paradelike formation, no evasive maneuver of any kind allowed. For the pilots, that went against every human instinct. But they were helpless, because from the IP until the bombs were dropped, the bombardier was in command of the plane. It went where he told the pilot to take it.

Sgt. Stan Catterazole, a ball turret gunner, said "the worst part is coming in and the flak is busting out, they would just saturate that area with these 88 shells, just exploding all around you. Now you have to fly right through it, and the ones that didn't hit you, above or below or beside, you could feel the compression waves from the explosion and the whole plane would vibrate. Me being in the ball turret I was scared shitless countless times. My job was to watch the bomb-bay door and when he hollered bomb-bay doors open then I would radio back and tell them that the doors were open. Then I would confirm that the bombs were away. . . . When you got back and saw the holes here and holes there from the shrapnel, you get a sense of how you cheated death every time you went up."[12]

Those holes caused by shrapnel, and the opening of the bomb bay doors, let in a rush of cold air. In the mission Andy Rooney went on, shrapnel clipped off the tip of the plastic nose of the plane, leaving a jagged hole the size of a man's fist. "The bombardier, in a moment of panic, tore off his gloves and tried to stuff them in the gaping hole," Rooney remembered. "Within minutes his hands had frozen and chips of flesh broke off his fingers as they caught on the jagged edges of the plastic."[13] The surgeon of the 95th Bomb Group, Capt. Jack McKittrick, remembered gunners coming home with all the skin torn off their hands. Their guns would jam and in the excitement of battle the men forgot about how cold it was in those planes and shed their gloves to clear the jam and their hands would freeze to the bare metal of the machine guns.[14]

The B-24s could take an amazing amount of punishment and still fly, and the B-17 pilots claimed theirs were the most durable plane ever built. The B-17s were not fast, they were not maneuverable, they didn't carry the heaviest bomb load, but they were as close to indestructible as anything made by man that can fly could be. Thousands of them returned to England with two or three engines gone, hydraulic systems drained, wounded crewmen on board.

Sergeant Catterazole had a fairly typical experience on a mission to Munich. On the bomb run, flak put one engine out of action, then another. "So now we have only two engines and we are coming in and we drop our bombs, but when we turn around we can't stay with the group, not enough power, so we start falling behind." The captain eased her down to 10,000 feet "and we were trying to hold that altitude but we still didn't have enough power so we began throwing everything we could off the plane. Radio sets, anything that would lighten our load. We threw off our guns and then the pilot called back to me and said that I had to drop the turret. This huge turret had to go, so I loosened the four nuts on the yoke, there is a big yoke that holds the turret in place, and we are hanging on and I jump on the turret and kicked it one last time and the damned thing is just hanging there on this one nut and the pilot is yelling at me to release it and I am yelling back that I'm trying."

Catterazole gave it one last kick and it was "turret away!" He looked down "through this huge hole where the turret used to be and there 300 feet below was the Channel, it looked pretty damn close, so I put my Mae West on, I don't swim so good." But the pilot managed to bring her in "at a place the English call the 'wash,' a big long beach where planes would make emergency landings." (In

1996, an eighteen-year-old student asked Catterazole, "Since you were on bomb runs where you were dropping bombs on people you never saw or ever knew, what were your feelings and emotions when you were doing something like that?" Catterazole's answer could not be improved upon: "First of all, I always thought that I don't want to be here.")[15]

Sgt. George Hintz was a ball turret gunner on a B-17. On February 25, 1945, he was at 24,000 feet, eight miles from the target, when the 88 shells began bursting about him. The flak put the number four engine out of action. The plane began to lose altitude. The pilot dropped the bomb load over an unidentified town and turned back toward the French border. Enemy fighters attacked. They shot away a part of the nose and their machine guns made Swiss cheese out of the wings and fuselage. The rear gunner had his guns shot out of his hands.

"Then our number three engine took a hit," Hintz recalled. "The loud hissing of punctured oxygen tanks below the flight deck and the leaking hydraulic tanks just above those oxygen tanks increased the possibility of an explosion." The number two engine caught fire and flames threatened to explode the leaking fuel tanks. The pilot ordered a bailout, "and although we were now at a dangerously low altitude, we all made it, landing near the Swiss-German border, but luckily on the Swiss side.

"Incredibly, our severely damaged and now pilotless B-17 flew on and made a respectable crash landing in a forest clearing."[16]

Navigator Marvin Kraft recalled the time Luftwaffe .50-caliber bullets caused a serious gasoline leak. Fumes were filling the bomb bay. The pilot ordered everyone to get out of the flak jacket, put on a life vest and parachute, and prepare to jump. He dropped the bombs over the North Sea. Kraft was "standing over the open bomb bay, looking down into the cold North Sea far below, with my parachute on my chest, I was terrified. It hurt to move, and I was numb with fear. Fortunately we were able to shut off a valve ahead of the leak and the pilot got us home safely. On such aborts, we did not get credit for a mission."[17]

For all their legendary toughness, the B-17s and B-24s went down in staggering numbers. In the Eighth Air Force, 6,537 B-17s and B-24s were lost, along with 3,337 fighters. The life expectancy of a four-engine bomber that didn't get destroyed by flak or fighters was about the same as for a crew, some thirty-five missions. The record for a single plane, named *Rum Dum,* was 101 missions.

But even when they were war-weary, almost incapable of rising from the ground or being controlled in the air, the generals thought up a use for them. They were stripped down, loaded with 20,000 pounds of explosive, and set out after the toughest targets, submarine pens and V-weapon launching sites. A two-man crew would take the flying bomb to the English coast, where they would bail out over land and a mother ship would take control by radio signals and guide the pilotless bomber over the sea and onto its target. That was the theory; in practice several pilots were killed in this hazardous undertaking, including Joseph Kennedy, Jr., before it was mercifully called off.[18]

For all bomber crews it was distressing in the extreme to watch B-17s or B-24s explode and disintegrate. Or to watch a wounded plane begin to descend, obviously out of control, and to start counting the parachutes as they popped open, hoping to God that the count went up to ten, seldom getting that high. And for the airmen there was no ceremony of burial, no opportunity to say good-bye to a dear friend. But if they could not gather up his body, they did have to gather up his belongings, and that was one tough moment, back at barracks, sorting through the footlocker of the guy you ate breakfast with, making sure there was nothing in his personal effects that would shock his parents and loved ones.

Andy Rooney witnessed a particularly awful death. He was on an air base in England as a flight returned. The radio was crackling as there were half a dozen bombers with dead and dying men aboard. Then there was a frantic call: the ball turret gunner in one B-17 was trapped. The gears that rotated the ball to put the gunner in position to shoot and then returned him to the position that let him climb out and back up into the airplane had been hit and were jammed. He was caught in his plastic cage.

Two engines were out and the plane was losing altitude fast and barely making 135 miles per hour, close to stall-out speed. The pilot ordered the crew to throw out everything. The men started pitching out machine guns, ammunition, oxygen tanks, and every instrument they could tear loose. The pilot opened the petcocks on the fuel tanks to drain them down to the last few gallons. The hydraulic system was spewing fluid. The wheels could not be brought down. A belly landing was inevitable. For eight minutes, the pilot, the tower, and the ball turret gunner talked on the radio. The gunner knew what was coming. Rooney wrote, "We all watched in horror as it happened. We watched as this man's life ended, mashed between the concrete pavement of the runway and the belly of the bomber."[19]

The pilots, mostly in their mid-twenties, were generally admired, respected, obeyed, even loved. A special favorite with all who knew him was Maj. James Stewart, the actor already famous for parts in *The Philadelphia Story* and *Mr. Smith Goes to Washington*. Stewart had enlisted as a private, made his way into pilot training school, earned his wings. The Air Force knew he was a good flyer but didn't want to risk him, so he was assigned to the staff. He insisted on flying. He became a squadron commander. One of his pilots, Lt. Hal Turrell, said of Stewart, "He was a wonderful human being and excelled as a command pilot. He was always relaxed with crews but rarely visited off the base because of his celebrity status and famous face, he would be mobbed by civilians. He never grandstanded by picking missions. If our group led the wing, he flew."[20]

Stewart was one of the sensible pilots, and thus a survivor. As his fellow pilot, Lt. Saul Levine, put it, "Most losses were on the early missions. Survival rates improved with experience. Learning how to fly high-altitude close formation, hoarding your gas supply, being particularly watchful during assemblies, all contributed to better survival chances. Keeping rested and laying off the booze before flights also mattered."[21]

Missions could be soul-searing experiences. Lt. Leo Fenster was a bombardier-navigator in a two-engine B-26. He was part of a crew that had survived five crash landings before its sixty-first mission. Fenster remembered that the last one was the worst one. The crew's mission was to toss chaff out of the plane, which required it to fly ahead of and far below (3,000 feet) the bombers coming on in formation. The German gunners concentrated their fire on Fenster's plane because they knew the purpose of the chaff drop. "Of all the missions," Fenster recalled, "I never incurred the volume and the intensity of ground fire we suffered in this one. The Germans literally threw their entire arsenal of ack-ack. The barrage was so unbelievably intense that for a period of 15 minutes before the dropping of the bombs and 15 minutes after, the noise of the continuous explosions engulfing us was overwhelming. Our plane, for a period of thirty minutes, rocked from side to side and up and down and frankly, I did not believe we would survive.

"If one can have a conversation with God during such an intensive barrage, I did and frankly, I made certain commitments with God which affected the rest of my life in the way I conducted myself."[22]

Lt. Raymond Murray, a B-17 pilot, recalled a mission against an oil refinery. "There was no ducking anything for us in the box barrages of flak. There was nothing you could do but sit there and say Hail Marys as fast as you could. Planes were going down all around us, but I'll always remember the first one. I was looking right at this plane because I was flying on him when it took a direct hit between number 3 and number 4 engines. I saw the wing rise up in the air, the pilot turned his head very slowly and looked out at me with no expression. Then we saw parachutes spilling out, a couple of them bursting into flames as they opened. Then the plane started cartwheeling and spinning. Not too many chutes got out, possibly four or five. Then the aircraft exploded, and that is when I became a very religious man."

Murray was nineteen years old. "I was so young that with the passing years time has erased most of the bad things I'd seen. The only memories that I now have of combat missions are hours and hours of boredom interrupted by moments of sheer terror. But until that last one I felt detached. I didn't have anything to do with it, I was never going to get hit.

"I talked to our flight surgeon, Capt. Jack McKittrick about this one day. He was a very nice guy. He said, 'That's why we give you whiskey, and that's why you're all so young. If you thought about it, you wouldn't fly combat.' "[23]

The combat experiences were different for airmen from the ground troops, but there was a similarity in reaction. After three months, most infantrymen suffered some form of battle fatigue. For the airmen, that happened after twenty-five to thirty missions. Still their commanders kept them in battle.

Flight Surgeon McKittrick treated men who had reached, and sometimes passed, the breaking point. "Men would approach me and say, 'Captain, you can do anything you want, but I just can't fly this next mission. I'm too scared.' " He recalled an incident in 1943, when "one of our good pilots got hysterical on the truck taking us down to the mess hall. He went absolutely berserk."

McKittrick sent such men to a nearby general hospital, "where the doctors would use sodium pentathol injections to get the boys to recount their experiences because a lot of them couldn't express themselves when they were conscious. Getting it out of them was an important form of therapy." In the last week of February 1944, McKittrick's group flew deep penetration raids every day. "The boys were getting exhausted, and they were coming home so terrified they couldn't eat or sleep. And they'd have to get up at 0300 hours and start all over again."

McKittrick and some other flight surgeons sent a letter to Gen. Curtis LeMay, CO of the 3rd Air Division, Eighth Air Force, asking him to ease off before the crews broke from shell shock. When he got the letter, LeMay called every flight surgeon in the division to his headquarters. According to McKittrick, "He reamed us out but good. I can still see him sitting there with a big cigar in his mouth, and he said, 'Gentlemen, I know you are professionals but we are too. I don't want you to interfere with the way we're running the war and we will not appreciate any more letters.' "

McKittrick saw to it that crews got liquor rations after a mission during debriefing. "It was done very methodically," he said, "and it did a great deal to settle them down and it gave them a little more appetite. It helped to relax them slightly from the horrors of a particularly terrifying mission that, all too often, surpassed fiction. And I'll be damned if the Women's Christian Temperance Union didn't try their best to put a stop to that."[24]

The Allies were putting much of their productivity and some of the best of their young men into the air war, paying a tremendous price in treasure, lives, and physical and mental suffering. It was frustrating in the extreme, therefore, to deal with the fact that night area bombing had not destroyed German morale and that daylight precision bombing had not destroyed German production. Frustration added to the stress and led to some desperate measures.

Eighth Air Force headquarters, unhappy with the results of previous forays, attributed the errors to a shortage of time for the lead bombardier to set his Norden bombsight once his plane began its run from the IP to bombs away. So the staff ordered the next mission over Cologne to make its final approach upwind. That would slow the planes and give the bombardiers more time. It also gave the 88s a slower target.

In the event, the lead plane's release mechanism did not function. So the whole formation flew through the flak without dropping a single bomb. The lead swung around for another go at it. The others followed, fearful but obedient. "We expected hell and caught it," navigator Frank Aldrich recalled. "Aircraft were dropping out of formation all over the place, and when the bombs failed to tumble out of the lead aircraft for the second time, we wheeled around to form for a third run." But there were not enough planes left for a run and the lead pilot abandoned the mission. Aldrich's plane, badly shot up, dropped its bombs in a field and made a successful crash landing.[25]

There were many aborted raids, and screwed-up ones. On the afternoon of March 2, 1945, the men of the 323rd Group, Ninth Air Force, set out on a mission to the Sinzig Railroad Bridge. The formation consisted of 216 B-26 Marauders carrying 400 tons of bombs and eleven B-26s bringing chaff along. On the bomb run in to the target, with bomb bay doors open and the bombardiers keyed to trigger their bombs away when the lead aircraft dropped its bombs, the plane flying on the wing of the leader got a hard flak hit. The concussion caused it to release its bombs prematurely. The rest of the formation let loose when the bombardiers saw those bombs dropped. As a consequence, all 400 tons of bombs landed six miles short of the target. The cost to the Americans was one plane shot down, one lost in a crash landing, eight damaged, and another case of almost unbearable frustration.[26]

By the beginning of 1945 most of the Ninth Air Force was stationed in France. To keep the Marauders flying over targets in Germany even in bad weather, the airmen adopted a technique first used by the Germans for night bombing of London during the Blitz. Specially equipped Pathfinder planes would lead the B-26s. The Pathfinder would follow a radio beam that would take it to the target. Along the way various radio signals from other stations in France told the Pathfinder where he was with respect to the drop point. It made fairly accurate bombing possible—when everything worked—but it had disadvantages. As Lt. Ned Grubb explained it,

"The IP was located 25 or 30 miles from the target in order to allow time for the Pathfinder pilot to 'bracket' the beam and nail it down for an accurate run. This resulted in a much longer-than-usual straight flight path to the target, which was most unpopular with the pilots behind as it provided a better-than-usual opportunity for the enemy gunners to set up their flak patterns."

But it also allowed the Marauders to bomb through snow and cloud, so as Grubb pointed out, "The enemy now had to worry about bombing attacks during rotten weather—a time that up to now was a period of relative relaxation, when they could attend to the maintenance of flak guns, aircraft, etc., and possibly get some rest."[27] If everything worked—of course it seldom did—the system was amazingly accurate. The circle of error was only 300 feet.

When the skies were clear enough, the P-47s stationed in France provided fighter escort for the B-26s. Prior to the bomb run, half of the escorting force would orbit above the bomber formation as top cover, while the other half peeled off to dive-bomb the 88mm batteries. At first this was successful, but the Germans adjusted. They held their fire until the bomb run had begun. The P-47s then had no way of knowing the exact location of the 88s, because of smoke, and they couldn't risk getting hit by the falling bombs, so they had to wait until the bombs had hit. Then they would go in again. B-26 pilot J. K. Havener commented, "The courage of these fighter jockeys diving right into the maws of 88s spewing out lethal shells is beyond description."[28]

Fighter pilots were special. They had swagger, bounce, energy. No more than most airmen, perhaps, but these qualities were on display more often—in the air and on the ground. As one example, fighter pilots downplayed the danger from flak. Lt. Wayne Gatlin, a P-51 pilot, remarked that "one of those bomber fellows was saying, 'why the flak was so thick, even the automatic pilots in the bombers were bailing out.'" Gatlin said he hardly noticed the flak, but when pressed confessed that "what's nice about fighters, you can dodge flak easily whereas the bomber boys can't do it very well, especially on the bomb run."[29]

The workhorse P-47s could carry a surprisingly heavy bomb load for a single-engine, single-pilot plane—six five-inch rockets and 2,000 pounds of bombs, plus eight .50-caliber machine guns. But the pilots had to see the targets. To continue to operate in bad weather, General Quesada came up with a radar device that would allow his P-47s to bomb through cloud cover. American radar operators in France would track the flight of a group of P-47s. The pilot of the lead ship would follow a radio beam to the target. The radar controllers back at base would tell the lead pilot when to drop the bombs.

"We hated this," Lt. Philip Wright recalled, "and were furious over the authority given the controllers, safely tucked away from the action. Flying straight and level at 10,000 ft. and 250 miles per hour, we were sitting ducks for the Germans' radar controlled flak, nothing more than lousy bomber pilots."

In mid-February 1945, Quesada flew in a four-plane mission with Wright and two others. On the way to the planes, P-47s armed with two 500-pound bombs and ammunition for the eight .50-caliber machine guns, Quesada said, "Gentlemen, just forget I'm a general." With a grin, he added, "If you can."

As the planes approached the target, the radar started acting up. The pilots peeled off, formed up for another run, and were again frustrated by the malfunctioning radar. After four more tries, Quesada scrubbed the mission. So, in Wright's words, "we opted to dive bomb and strafe a panzer division. It was too good a target to pass up while we still had all our bombs and ammunition. Diving down through a barrage of 20 and 40 mm. flak, I lined up on the target and let fly. My bombs made a great hit, and I hoped Quesada was as impressed with me as I was." He was, and that was the end of the radar-controlled missions.

On another mission, Wright had an unusual experience. He got a radio call from a man who identified himself as the ground controller for an armored division. The controller said German tanks were hiding in such and such a wood and asked the P-47s to go after them. Wright and his buddies flew to the wood, where "the ground and air erupted! Bursts of 88 mm. flak were going off everywhere. We had been suckered into a flak trap! The Germans had located the American radio frequency and had a controller, speaking with a perfect American accent, who had fooled us."[30]

The most famous bombing raid of the war, against Dresden on February 13–14, 1945, has been called the most barbaric, senseless act of the war. During the night RAF Bomber Command carried out a raid with 873 bombers dropping thousands of incendiaries and high-explosive bombs up to four tons. This set the city on fire and started a firestorm as the rising column of intense heat sucked up oxygen and burned it, creating hurricane-like winds and temperatures up to 1,000 degrees Fahrenheit or higher. At noon, 311 B-17s from Eighth Air Force released 771 tons of bombs on the flaming city, with the aim of catching firemen and rescue workers when they were out on the streets. The following day 210 B-17s dropped another 461 tons. The firestorm raged for four days and could be seen for 200 miles. In Dresden people in air raid shelters suffocated or were baked alive. Kurt Vonnegut described the scene in a letter he wrote his parents shortly after the war: "On February 14th the Americans and the R.A.F. came over. Their combined labors killed 250,000 people in twenty-four hours and destroyed all of Dresden—possibly the world's most beautiful city. But not me.

"After that we were put to work carrying corpses from Air-Raid shelters; women, children, old men; dead from concussion, fire or suffocation. Civilians cursed us and threw rocks as we carried bodies to huge funeral pyres in the city." (Vonnegut was eventually liberated by the Soviets, after "their [Soviet] planes strafed and bombed us, killing fourteen, but not me." His POW railroad car had earlier been shot up by Americans. Vonnegut says he is the only man to be shot at by Germans, Americans, and Russians, and bombed by the British and survive).[31]

On the fiftieth anniversary of V-E Day, during a discussion of World War II on television among Joseph Heller, Vonnegut, and me, Vonnegut said, "The bombing of Dresden didn't shorten the war by one second. There is only one person in this world who benefited from that raid, and that's me."

But although Dresden is generally considered to be the most destructive raid in the European war, it was not. Just before Dresden, the Allied bombers had hit Berlin (a 1,000-bomber raid) and Leipzig even harder. Those bombings were feebly protested, if at all. What made Dresden special was its apparent absence of military or industrial targets. People were outraged at the destruction of the heart of a relatively undamaged city known throughout the world for its beauty. Further, the death toll at Dresden was initially wildly inflated, to as high as the 250,000 figure cited by Vonnegut. The Germans later revised the figure to 135,000. Recent disclosures put the figure at 35,000. No one knows for certain, as Dresden had many refugees in the city.

The protest came first from Nazi propaganda, but as soon as the widespread damage in Dresden became known as fact there was an outcry in the Allied world. British critics of area bombing in general raised numerous questions about the necessity for the raid. Even Churchill, who had helped set the Dresden raid in motion by asking RAF Bomber Command to find more means of "harrying the German retreat," backed away. On March 28 he warned his chiefs of staff of the folly of any "bombing of German cities simply for the sake of increasing the terror" and as a result coming into possession "of an utterly ruined land."

Why would the Allies want to bomb a commercial city devoid of genuine targets? There are many answers. The one that makes the most sense to me is that the Allies had just plain run out of targets. The cities along the Rhine-Ruhr in western Germany had been demolished and/or occupied by mid-February. Berlin, Leipzig, and other central German cities were rubble. Dresden was one of the few relatively intact cities left (it is not true that Dresden attracted refugees because it had never been bombed—it had been, twice, although in much smaller raids). When questioned by Secretary of War Henry Stimson about the need for the raid, General Marshall indicated that the Russians had asked the Allies to disrupt German communications (there was a significant railroad marshaling yard in Dresden), seeming to put the blame on them. But the Soviets said they had made no such request. But by this time—mid-1945—the Soviets were already creating what would become Communist East Germany and thus had a political motivation to pretend they were the great friends of the common German people, when the capitalists were destroying their homes and families.

The British, unjustifiably, got most of the blame. Dresden became something of a mark of shame to the British establishment, as it became the symbol of terror bombing. So much so that Gen. Arthur Harris, commander of RAF Bomber Command, was the sole major British wartime leader not honored with a knighthood.

The Americans involved in the raid will have none of that. Lt. Dave Nagel said in an interview, "If you saw London, like I saw it, you wouldn't have any remorse. I don't know anyone who was remorseful. I didn't hate anyone, but near the end we were nervous, up-tight. . . . As time went on, for me a dead German was the best German. To this day, I won't buy German goods, if I can help it. I am prejudiced."[32]

Lt. John Morris declared, "I'm hardly ashamed of having gone to Dresden that day. It was sound strategy to prevent the Wehrmacht from falling back to regroup and be lethal again. So we bombed the hell out of the railroad marshaling yards and road hubs along the Wehrmacht's line of retreat, up and down Germany's eastern border. I don't rejoice at the 35,000 Germans killed there. I doubt there were many Jews in that number. The good burghers of Dresden had shipped them all off to Auschwitz." Morris went on to put the raid in perspective: "It is true that the RAF purposely started a firestorm, causing many of the casualties. It was a tactic they frequently tried. But they, and we, killed more people in other cities, on other days. So did the Russians. So did the Japanese. So did the Germans. Dresden was not unique."[33]

Eighth Air Force prided itself on its pinpoint bombing and all but denied its role in the Dresden bombing. But from a German point of view, in the last few months of the war one could hardly tell if those were British or American planes dropping bombs on their cities. Capt. Dan Villani of the 398th Bomb Group was a pilot of a B-17 who was part of the massive raid on Berlin in mid-February. Decades later, he recalled that "most of the formation spread out to avoid the flak and in so doing ruined the accuracy of the drop. I'm sure many of the pilots didn't give a damn. They just wanted out of a target area as fast as possible. . . . The aiming point was the center of Berlin and I don't think this was bombing a military target. But I personally felt no remorse. They brought Hitler to power and supported him and sealed their fate."[34]

From 1943 onward, after he was thrown on the defensive, Hitler had exhorted the German people to hang on just a bit longer, secret weapons were on the way. Most of that was typical Hitler bombast. The closest he came to a secret weapon that could reverse the situation was the jet airplane, and in a variety of ways he grossly misused it. His biggest mistake was to insist that the ME 262 be built as a bomber rather than a fighter, a mistake compounded by his insistence on continuing to build conventional bombers. Half the planes produced in Germany in 1944 were bombers; in 1945 it was still 40 percent. Meanwhile Germany was losing 82 percent of its effective strength in the air per month, or a loss rate of about 1,200 planes out of an average strength of 1,300.[35] The jets could have cut those losses considerably, but there were never enough of them. Total production was 1,433, but only 200 or so got into combat and never more than twenty-five at a time. These were paltry figures compared to the numbers of Americans in the air—in one March 1945 raid on Berlin there were 1,250 B-17s escorted by almost as many fighters.

The ME 262 and other German jets outclassed all other World War II planes, but they were no more war-winners for Germany in the last year of the war than were the V-weapons. If the P-51s could not match the ME 262s in the air, they could shoot them up on the ground, or drop their bombs on the telltale extra long runways the jets required (by early 1945, the jets were reduced to hiding in the woods and using the autobahn for a runway), or along with the big bombers go after known production sites. Reportedly some 500 jets were destroyed before delivery to the Luftwaffe.

The jets and the V-weapons were cause for worry, and both did considerable damage, but both came too late, in too small numbers, and were so badly mishandled, that they could only postpone and make more costly the Allied victory, not prevent it.

That does not answer the questions, Was strategic bombing critical to the victory? Was it a wise use of resources? It certainly was costly to the enemy: it is estimated that two million people, soldiers and civilians, were engaged either in anti-aircraft defense or in the cleanup and repairs after the bombings.[36]

But it was terribly costly to the Allies, too, in resources and lives. America put some of her best young men in those B-17s and it cannot be said, one way or another, if that was the best utilization of their talents and abilities. As a personal judgment, it is hard to see that the terror bombing of cities had a significant impact on the fighting fronts, or that going after specific factory systems, such as ball-bearing plants, was worth the cost. Where the payoff came, and it was critical, was to force the Germans on the defensive in the air, which freed the Allied armies in Europe from fear of the Luftwaffe, and in the oil campaign, which was such a spectacular success that by the spring of 1945 the Wehrmacht was out of gas. In and of itself, that justified the investment in four-engine bombers. The war could not have been won without them.

13

Medics, Nurses, and Doctors

IT WASN'T ANY DIFFERENT getting killed in World War II than in the Civil War, but if the shrapnel, bullet, or tree limb wounded a GI without killing him, his experience as a casualty was infinitely better than Johnny Reb's or Billy Yank's, beginning with his survival chances. Military medicine had vastly improved in the twentieth century. The medical team, from medics in the field to the nurses and doctors in the tent-city hospitals, compiled a remarkable record. Over 85 percent of the soldiers who underwent emergency operations in a mobile field or evacuation hospital survived. Fewer than 4 percent of all patients admitted to a field hospital died. In the Civil War it had been more like 50 percent.

Wonder drugs and advanced surgical techniques made the improvements possible, but it was people who had to get the wounded into a hospital before it was too late for the nurses and the drugs and the surgeons to do their work. Those people were the medics.

In an infantry battalion of twelve platoons, there were thirty to forty medics. After time on the line, whether a week or a month, most units were down to one medic per platoon. The medics varied as much in motivation as in size and shape, but a common theme was a refusal to kill along with a desire to serve.

One of the heroes at Pointe-du-Hoc on D-Day, Pvt. Ralph "Preacher" Davis of the Rangers, asked in September to be transferred to the Medical Corps, for religious reasons. He was accepted immediately, as volunteers for the Medics were hard to find. On a night patrol, Preacher got hit in the back by a sniper. He was paralyzed below the waist. (After the war he achieved his ambition of becoming an ordained minister, before he died of the wound.) Sgt. Frank South said Preacher was "deeply respected for his courage—proven in battle—and his devotion—also proven."[1]

The combat experience brought forth from Preacher a strong moral reaction. Others had strong responses, too, but sometimes in the opposite direction. Preacher couldn't bring himself to kill anymore; some men who started out as medics because of religious conviction changed on encountering the reality of war—they requested transfer to the line company, meaning they wanted to pick up a rifle and shoot back.

The medics had done all the training an infantryman did, except for weapons. In training camp, the medics had been segregated into their own barracks, kept away from the men they were learning to save, apparently for fear of contamination of the real soldiers. The rifle-carrying enlisted men and the medics developed little camaraderie. One lieutenant confessed that he and his platoon "mildly despised" the men of the Medical Corps because they were conscientious objectors.[2] Their mere presence cast a moral shadow over what the infantrymen were training to do. They were often ridiculed, called names such as "pill pusher,"* and the tourniquets and bandages they put on imagined wounds in field exercises were a joke. So was their only real work, treating blisters and the like.

But in combat, they were loved and admired without stint. "Overseas," Medic Buddy Gianelloni recalled, "it became different. They called you Medic and before you know it, it was Doc. I was nineteen at the time."[3]

On countless occasions, when I've asked a veteran during an interview if he remembered any medics, the old man would say something like, "Bravest man I ever saw. Let me tell you about him . . ." Here is a typical account: Pvt. Mike DeBello got hit by a machine-gun bullet that ripped right through the upper muscle of his right arm. "Doc Mellon was the bravest kid I ever saw. He came running right through the machine-gun fire and put a tourniquet on my arm." Mellon got smashed by the concussion from an 88. His shoul-

---

*Or "shank mechanics" because of the salt tablets they handed out.

der was out of the socket. He should have gone back to the aid station, but as he later explained, he felt "there were just too many wounded guys to work on, so I took some codeine and morphine. I couldn't raise my arm beyond my waist, so here I was trying to work on these wounded guys with one hand."[4]

To preserve their noncombatant status under the Geneva Convention, the War Department did not give medics combat pay (ten dollars extra a month) or the right to wear the combat Infantryman Badge. This was bitterly resented. In some divisions riflemen collected money from their own pay to give their medics the combat bonus. As to their right to wear the badge, five enlisted medics in ETO were awarded the Medal of Honor; hundreds won Silver or Bronze Stars.[5]

Medic Ed Grazcyck of the 4th Division had earned a Bronze Star. Later, when his company underwent a shelling in the Hurtgen Forest, one of the sergeants was killed by shrapnel in the neck and Grazcyck took a large fragment in the back of his head. He was unconscious and looked gone. Beside him, a third man was screaming for a medic. Lt. George Wilson ran to the wounded man and found him "frantically gripping what was left of one arm with his remaining hand. The arm was gone, almost to the shoulder."

As Wilson stared helplessly, Medic Grazcyck came to. He told Wilson to get a tourniquet on the man, handed him some morphine, explained how to use it, then gave verbal instructions as Wilson sprinkled sulfa powder on the gory stump and bandaged the wound. As Wilson completed the job, both the wounded man and Grazcyck passed out. Wilson got a jeep to carry them back to the aid station. They survived.[6]

Medics served in the line companies. They were in the foxholes in static situations. But if the Americans were on the offensive they sometimes had to stay behind with the wounded, feeling lonely and abandoned. On other occasions, when an attack failed and the men fell back, medics had to go between the lines to deliver aid and start the wounded man on his way to the field hospital.

Pvt. Byron Whitmarsh of the 99th Division described what it was like for the medics during a shelling: "There are worse things than being a rifleman in the infantry, not many, but being a medic is one of them. When the shelling and shooting gets heavy it is never long until there is a call for 'MEDIC!' That's when your regular GIs can press themselves to the bottom of their hole and don't need to go out on a mission of mercy."[7]

Once the medic reached the wounded man, he did the briefest examination, put a tourniquet on if necessary, injected a vial of morphine, cleaned up the wound as best he could, sprinkled sulfa powder on it, slapped on a bandage, and dragged or carried the patient toward the rear. Pvt. Robert Phillips, a medic with the 28th Division, came to dread the sound of incoming shells and the invariable "Medic!" cry that forced him to leave his hole. As he worked, shell fragments whittled down the trees and casualties increased. He remembered for the rest of his life the job of examining a wounded man at night, cutting away clothes in the darkness, feeling for the wound: "It was like putting your hand in a bucket of wet liver."[8]

Pvt. Benedict Battista was a medic with the 90th Division who went the whole way from Utah Beach to Central Europe, "trying to save lives." After the war, he reflected, "I don't regret what I did but if I had to do it all over again I wouldn't want to be a medic. I have seen too much blood. I would want to be in a maintenance outfit in the army."[9]

On his initial mission in the field, Sergeant Gianelloni came near to total failure. "The first person that I treated who was wounded happened to be an old rough-and-tough sergeant. He had a piece of shrapnel go through his boot and up there by his toes and it wasn't a serious wound, but to him it was. . . . I sat down alongside of him and he was moaning and groaning, and I said well I have got to cut your shoe off and he said well come on don't talk get me taken care of, so I cut his shoe off and I am getting ready to put the bandage on and I looked down and there is blood all over my hand, so I lean over the side and I have the dry heaves.

"And he is getting more aggravated by the minute this sergeant. He says come on don't do that, he said take care of me. I said I am doing the best I can."

The patient was getting nervous, and he was armed and angry. Gianelloni decided to give him a shot of morphine, not because he needed it but because "I didn't want that son of a gun to get all worked up. So I got a morphine packet out of my pouch and I rolled up his sleeve and I pushed it in his arm there and I am squeezing that thing and squeezing it and he is yelling and I'm squeezing and finally the damn thing broke. I said, oh, I forgot to puncture the needle. I said oh."

Gianelloni threw the packet away. His patient picked up his rifle "and he said, 'you bastard you better take care of me or I am going to shoot you.' I said, 'Just one more time,' so I got another packet and I punctured the needle that time and I gave him a half of a grain of morphine. That got him reeling." It should have—according to Gianelloni one sixteenth of a grain is sufficient to knock a man out for an operation.[10]

If the medic didn't do the job right and fast, he lost the patient. And sometimes he had to deliver his first aid while under aimed enemy fire because occasionally Germans would fire at a medic at work between the lines. Private Phillips was wounded while tending to a wounded man. On Christmas Day, Pvt. Louis Potts of the 26th Division was fired on while attending a wounded soldier. He stayed in the snow-covered field and went to work on another casualty. This time the German sniper got him in the forehead. His sergeant commented, "Potts was small in stature. . . . He did his very best to help the wounded, regardless of personal danger."[11]

I've heard dozens of such stories, from German and American veterans, usually, however, from a man who heard about such a thing as opposed to seeing it himself. Albert Cowdrey of the U.S. Army's Center of Military History insists that they were uncommon. He points out that careful studies demonstrated that "the Germans by and large were following the Geneva Convention." Although men wearing their Red Cross armband were shot, sometimes it was because the red cross had not been seen. The response of the medics is conclusive: it was to make themselves more visible, not less. They began to wear two armbands and paint a red cross in a white square on their helmets. They were confident that most Germans or GIs would respect the symbol if only it could be seen. (Cowdrey contrasts this with the Pacific War, where medics were special targets of the Japanese and responded by taking off the armbands and even dyeing their bandages jungle green.)[12]

Lt. Wenzel Andreas Borgert commanded an antitank unit in the German army in Normandy. He described an American attack in which ten of his fifteen men were wounded. He radioed for an ambulance. "And this much I acknowledge," Borgert said in an interview, "that at the very second that the big Red Cross flag came over the hill behind me, the Americans stopped firing immediately. I can honestly say that made a big impression on me, because there was no such thing as Red Cross on the Russian front."

Both sides tended to their wounded. Borgert noticed an American officer and crossed no-man's-land to talk. The American opened the conversation in German.

"Where did you learn such good German?" Borgert asked.

"My family is German," he said. Then he asked Borgert if he didn't want to surrender, as "Germany has lost the war in any case." No, Borgert replied. He would continue to fight. But he let the American know that as soon as dark came, he intended to pull back from his present position.

"Then I won't attack you till dark," the American replied, and it was done.[13]

Americans sometimes shot medics. Maj. John Cochran of the 90th Division recalled a forward observer who would call for a barrage when he knew the Germans were eating—he had a sixth sense about it, according to Cochran. After calling for a cease fire, he would say, "Get ready to do it again." He explained to Cochran that in five or ten minutes "their medics will come out to treat the casualties and we'll get them, too."[14]

Sgt. Robert Bowen of the 101st recalled that on December 23, in the Bulge, two men from his platoon were wounded. "They lay in the snow, one babbling incoherently and the other screaming." Bowen tried to get to them, but German fire drove him off. Medic Evert Padget said he would try, explaining that the Germans would honor his Red Cross patch. "He went out there. It was one of the bravest acts I had ever witnessed. Enemy bullets were plowing up the snow around him until he reached the wounded men. Then the German fire slackened and he tended the two men—although both were beyond rescue, at least Padget gave them some morphine. Then he returned to the American line and the firing resumed." Bowen confessed, "I thought of the wounded Germans who had lain in the road the day before and our guys had tried to kill whomever went out to help them."[15]

In Normandy, on D-Day Plus Two, Pvt. Ken Webster of the 101st saw a German jeep pop out of some smoke and drive boldly through the village of Vierville. It was flying a large Red Cross flag and carried two wounded Germans on stretchers in back, with a big husky German paratrooper at the wheel. It was so surprising a sight, no one made a move to stop it, until finally when it was almost out of the village an American officer stopped it. Webster described the result: "The jeep was commandeered. The driver, a medic, was shot for carrying a pistol, and the two wounded men were left by the side of the road to die."[16]

Lt. Charles Stockell saw medics fight each other. His diary for July 25 reads, "An American medic and a German medic in No Man's Land treating the wounded get into a fist fight. The war stops for 10 minutes until the American clobbers the Kraut."[17]

On one occasion, a medic inspired a company to seize an objective. Captain Colby's company was on the Our River during the Bulge. Colby told his men to attack across the frozen river. They did but were driven back by a machine gun.

All but one man made it back to the American-held bank of the river. He was a casualty. As Colby related the story, "He lay still in the middle of the frozen river. A medic (I am pretty sure it was Vosburg) left the pitiful concealment on our bank of the river and made his way to the fallen man's side. The machine-gun opened up again. Spurts of snow flew up from the burst, which were falling around the two.

"The medic got to his feet and stepped across the wounded man, thus placing himself between the machine-gun fire and the casualty. Lying in the snow, he began tending his patient.

"With that, the rest of Company E headed across the river to the far side, each man banging off a few shots as he went." The wounded man survived and the attack was a success.[18]

Too often, when the medic arrived the man was dead. In that case it was the medic's responsibility to oversee the retrieving and hauling of the body back to a Graves Registration crew. Bill Mauldin described one such crew. Its personnel, he said, "could have played the gravediggers in Hamlet."[19] They were usually drunk, a necessary condition for their job.

They became callous. Pvt. Kurt Gabel of the 17th Airborne described the day he had participated in the gruesome job of finding and stacking up the dead from his outfit following a failed attack in a snow-covered field. The bodies were frozen. After a morning's work, Gabel and his buddies had a large stack. A Graves Registration crew drove up in a deuce-and-a-half truck. Two guys got in the back of the truck, two others went to the pile.

The two on the ground grabbed a body by shoulders and legs and swung him three times to gain momentum, chanting, "one—two—three—*heave!*" The body flew through the air and landed on the truck with a thump. The men on the truck dragged the corpse to the far end and got ready for the next. They did it again.

Gabel stepped forward. He looked like the combat infantry-man he was. He had his rifle dangling from his shoulder. Touching it lightly, he said in a matter-of-fact voice, "You do that once more and I'll blow your goddamn heads off."

For a moment, no one moved. Then the men on the truck slowly climbed down, and the four-man crew gently lifted the next body and placed it on the truck.[20]

The men killed in action were buried as soon as possible in small temporary cemeteries, later dug up and taken to a division or army cemetery in the rear. This too was temporary. After the war ended, the family had the right to have the body brought home. Many parents or widows decided, however, to leave their loved ones where they fell. Those bodies went into one of the beautifully land-scaped military cemeteries maintained by the American Battle Monuments Commission. The largest are in Normandy and Lux-embourg.

Robert Bradley was an aid man with the 30th Infantry Division. He had been a medical student before the war. A religious man, he preferred to save rather than to kill. He went into Omaha Beach on June 10. He slept along a hedgerow. Starting at dawn, through to the end of the war, he set about saving lives.[21]

His instruments were crude. He tied scissors to one of his wrists with a shoestring in order to have them handy to cut away bloody clothing. He carried extra compresses in his gas mask con-tainer. His raincoat had many patches cut out of the tail, because he had learned to slap a piece of raincoat on a sucking chest wound, then cover it with a compress.

In Normandy, Bradley learned how to get to his patients in a hurry. In basic training he had detested learning to turn somersaults, but he found that the best way to go over a hedgerow was in a dive, headfirst. Then he would dash to the wounded man in the open field, a man who had been abandoned and who was utterly dependent on the medic. Bradley remembered "the unspeakable light of hope in the eyes of the wounded as we popped over a hedgerow."[22]

Sgt. Frank South, a medic in the Rangers, noticed something that also struck other medics: "During training it was not uncommon to hear one say, 'If I lose a leg (arm or whatever) please shoot me. I don't want to go home a cripple.' Never, in combat, did I, or anyone I know, hear this, no matter how bad the wound."[23]

An officer in the 90th Division remarked, "We had so much faith in our medics' ability that we firmly believed we would not die if they got to us in time."[24] Lt. Jack Foley of the 101st Airborne had typical praise for his medic, Pvt. Eugene Roe. "He was there when he was needed, and how he got 'there' you often wondered. . . . He struggled in the snow and the cold, in the many attacks through the open and through the woods."[25]

When the temperature went below the zero mark Fahrenheit, even the medic couldn't help. "What worked against the soldier was shock," Pvt. Richard Roush, a medic in the 84th Division, said. "It didn't really make much difference whether a soldier was barely or severely wounded in that extremely cold weather, he would immediately go into shock. We couldn't do anything for him because we didn't have any means to warm a wounded soldier. We could not save him."[26]

"The medic could do more with less to do with than anyone," Ken Russell of the 82nd Airborne remarked.[27] The medic seldom had much, and often not enough. Morphine was a most important drug, because it would relax the wounded man and help keep him from going into shock. In the Bulge, to keep it from freezing, the medics carried it next to their bodies. One man carried his in his underwear top. Others carried their morphine under their arms.

During the Bulge, Medic Roush kept the life-saving plasma in a metal pan he placed on top of the engine. Since his jeep had no antifreeze, he had to run the engine every half hour anyway, which kept the plasma from freezing. But "after about five days of this I could go no further so I just fell out and went to sleep. When I awoke my jeep was frozen and so was the blood plasma."[28]

Carrying so much morphine around a battlefield proved to be a temptation at least one medic could not resist. Medic Gianelloni related the story. There was a shelling. He heard the cry "Medic!" "I said, 'oh shit,' got up and went in the direction of the call for help."

It took him into the next platoon's area. He asked who was hurt. "Doc, look over there," one of the GIs responded. There was the platoon medic, walking like a zombie, even as shells continued to come in. Gianelloni tackled him and discovered he had given himself morphine when the shelling began. It turned out he had become an addict.[29]

Once the wounded man was behind the main line of foxholes, four litter bearers from the forward aid station, located a few hundred yards to the rear, summoned by radio or telephone, would come forward to evacuate him. That usually took about fifteen minutes. They would haul the soldier to wherever they had parked their jeep—25 meters to 100 meters back—load him into one of the four litter bearers mounted on the jeep, and drive as rapidly as possible to the battalion aid station, a kilometer or so to the rear.[30]

In early August, Lieutenant Stockell of the 2nd Infantry Division was hit badly in the leg—twenty deep shrapnel wounds. A medic got to him, did some patch work, and helped him to the rear. There a jeep awaited. "I am laid across the hood," Stockell wrote in his diary, "like a slaughtered deer."

At the aid station, "it is a blur. I did wake up in a field hospital to find two doctors taking my combat boots off and stealing my Luger pistol. I protest but then the fog closes in again."

In the field hospital, doctors gave Stockell more morphine and plasma and an antitetanus shot. They removed his bandages and cleaned up the wounds, put on fresh bandages, made a tentative diagnosis of his case, and labeled him for evacuation. An ambulance took him to Omaha Beach—he remained unconscious—where he was transferred by landing craft to an LST, then taken to Portsmouth, then by rail to the hospital.

"I next woke up in England." From the time he was wounded until he was in a modern hospital across the Channel took twenty hours. There he recovered, as did more than 99 percent of the men evacuated from Normandy to England.[31]

Corp. Walter Gordon of the 101st was one of them. Outside Bastogne on Christmas Eve, he was hit in the left shoulder by a sniper's bullet. It passed out from the right shoulder. It had brushed his spinal column; he was paralyzed from the neck down. Two buddies hauled him out of his foxhole and dragged him back into the woods—"as a gladiator was dragged from the arena," according to

Gordon—where the medic gave him morphine and plasma. Sgt. Carwood Lipton held the plasma bottle under his arm to keep it flowing. Within minutes, a jeep was taking Gordon to the forward aid station.

An hour after he was wounded, Gordon was in an ambulance headed toward an evacuation hospital in Sedan. There—still the same day—he was marked for air evacuation to England. Once there, the doctors put Crutchfield tongs on him to keep him immobile. For six weeks he lay on his back with no movement. His recovery was not rapid but it was complete. Gordon went on to live a full and successful life.[32]

Air evacuation was more comfortable as well as much faster than going to England by LST. And it was safer. Worldwide, only forty-six of the 1,176,048 patients air-evacuated throughout the war died en route.[33]

The remarkable rate of recovery for wounded GIs was based on mass-production, assembly-line practices. How well it worked, from the medic to the aid station to the field hospital to England, can be judged by the reaction of the men of the front line, who were almost certain to get caught up in the process, with their lives depending on it. As one lieutenant put it, "We were convinced the Army had a regulation against dying in an aid station."[34]

The recovery rate also benefited from the general physical condition of the wounded. First of all the GIs were selective even within their age group. One out of three potential inductees was rejected by the Army doctors for physical reasons—a telling reminder of the effects of the Depression on the American people. Second, they were, generally, in excellent physical condition. Third, they were free from body lice, thanks to DDT, and adequately fed. As against this, they were generally exhausted even before the shock of injury hit them. But if the medic could get to the wounded man in time to stop the bleeding and prevent shock, his chances for recovery were excellent.

Most patients came back to consciousness in the field or evacuation hospital. They were groggy from the morphine. The first sight many of them saw was a nurse from the Army Nurse Corps (ANC). She was harassed, wearing fatigues, exhausted, and busy. But she was an American girl, she had a marvelous smile, a reassuring attitude, and gentle hands. To the wounded soldier, she looked heaven-sent.

The first nurses to enter the Continent came in on June 10 at Omaha. They were members of the 42nd and 45th Field Hospitals and the 91st and 128th Evacuation Hospitals. They were the vanguard of the 17,345 ANC who served in ETO in 1944–45. That was seventeen times as many ANC personnel as existed in the entire Army in 1942. By 1945, total ANC strength was nearly 60,000.

These pioneers had to overcome many obstacles. The first was the act of volunteering. There was a nationwide slander campaign about women in uniform, as vicious as it was false. The jokes were gross. They were told by rear-echelon soldiers and civilians. No one who had ever seen an Army nurse in action in a field hospital, nor any wounded soldier, ever told such jokes. But because they were so widely told by people who didn't know what they were talking about, recruitment slowed down to a trickle. A questionnaire showed that of those nurses who did volunteer, 41 percent had to overcome the opposition of close relatives. Only half said their closest male friends were supportive, whereas 80 percent of their closest female friends had supported their decisions.[35]

Under the circumstances, recruitment was insufficient. To speed it up, the Army made the ANC more attractive. From June 1944 onward, nurses were given officers' commissions, full retirement privileges, dependents' allowances, and equal pay. And the government provided free education to nursing students.

In his January 1945 State of the Union Address, President Roosevelt referred to the critical shortage of nurses in Western Europe and proposed that nurses be drafted. A bill to do so passed the House and came within one vote in the Senate.[36]

One untapped source was African-American nurses. When the war ended there were only 479 black nurses in a corps of 60,000. This was because the Army assigned a quota, not because the black nurses didn't want to serve. But in the America of that day, it was unthinkable that black nurses could care for white American soldiers. (In June 1944 one unit of sixty-three African-American nurses went to a hospital in England, to care for German POWs.)[37]

The continuing shortage of nurses meant that those who served at field or evacuation hospitals were badly overworked. The experiences of the 77th Evacuation Hospital were typical. By mid-1944, the 77th was a veteran outfit. It had been in England in the summer of 1942, then went to Oran in November, on to Constantine in January 1943, Tébessa in February, La Meskiana in March, Tébessa again, Bône in April, Palermo in September, on to Licta in October, and in November back to England to get ready for D-Day. Clearly the battalion-sized team knew how to pick up and move in a hurry.

On July 7, 1944, the 77th entered Normandy at Utah Beach. It set up at Ste.-Mère-Eglise. It was open within a day. During the first twelve hours it treated 1,450 patients, or two per minute. In the first six days the 77th handled 6,304 patients in triage. For the first week, patients came in at a round-the-clock rate of one per minute.

The ambulances coming from the battalion aid stations had to line up, three abreast, in lines reaching up to 200 yards. The six doctors worked as rapidly as possible but were only just able to keep up with the litter bearers carrying patients in from the ambulance and out the back of the receiving tent. Not only were litters coming and going; there was space for 100 litters in the tent and it was nearly always filled. There were litters bearing wounded men in open spaces on the ground outside the tent. Along the sides of the tent sat the walking wounded, clutching their souvenirs. A tag showed whether and how much morphine the casualty had received from the medic. The doctors went from patient to patient, asking questions, scanning each record, lifting the dressing to check each wound.[38]

The nurses changed dressings, administered medications, checked each record, monitored the vital signs, and while they were doing those jobs they rearranged the blankets and gave the soldier a smile. They were too busy to do much more. As Lt. Aileen Hogan described her experiences in Normandy, "I have never worked so hard in my life. I can't call it nursing. The boys get in, get emergency treatment, penicillin and sulfa, and are out again. It is beyond words."[39]

Red Cross volunteers helped meet the need for comfort. The first two Red Cross women to arrive in Normandy were hospital workers, Jean Dockhorn and Jascah Hart. They waded ashore with the first Army nurses on June 10 and went to work. On July 31, Red Cross hospital worker Beatrice Cockram described her activities and emotions: "To walk down a ward virtually made my heart bleed to see how much was to be done just washing faces and giving drinks of water. The nurses are too busy with the vital blood plasma, penicillin and sulfa treatments."[40]

Lt. Aileen Hogan was forty-two years old when she volunteered for the ANC a few days after Pearl Harbor. She was with the 2nd General Hospital Unit in Normandy. She described her duties on the penicillin team. "At seven [1900 hours] all the penicillin needed for the first round is mixed and two technicians and one nurse make the rounds of the hospital giving penicillin to the patients. One loads the syringes and changes needles, the other two give the hypos. At the rate of 60 to a tent, one gets groggy. It is an art to find your way around at night, not a glimmer of light anywhere, no flashlights of course, the tents just a vague silhouette against the darkness, ropes and tent pins a constant menace, syringes and precious medications balanced precariously on one arm."[41]

When the nurses had waded ashore at Omaha or Utah, they had rolled their pants legs up to keep them from getting wet. Such niceties didn't last long. Lt. Mary Eaton told her friends back home that the nurse in France "shows only trousers and shirts, leggings, and boots in her summer wardrobe this year. Headgear is a tin helmet, worn at all times."[42]

After its month at Ste.-Mère-Eglise, the 77th Evacuation Hospital moved forward to St.-Lô, then Le Mans, next Chartres, where it arrived on August 24, close behind the advancing line. One member wrote a vivid description of the countryside in the wake of battle: "Along the sides of the roads, the fields were filled with grain and the farmers were beginning to harvest. An occasional field was dotted with foxholes where the infantry had dug in. All along the road, on each side about forty yards apart, were foxholes, covered and marked by a wisp of straw tied to the top of a pole. These had been dug with military preciseness by a retreating enemy for protection of the drivers, who could leap into them when Allied planes began a strafing attack.

"Just outside Chartres, enemy hangars and barracks had been blasted into heaps of debris. Neighboring fields were pock-marked with bomb craters. Stacks of enemy aerial bombs still piled around the field. Near the barracks a large garden had been planted by enemy airmen and the vegetables were still in the neat, orderly beds."

The hospital set up outside Chartres, in a field that soon became mud up to the hubs of the trucks. The mud clung to shoes in huge clumps. Nevertheless, by evening the pyramidal tents for quarters and many of the hospital tents had been erected, and by early afternoon the next day the hospital was completely set up and ready to receive patients.

Later, outside Verviers during the Bulge, the 77th underwent a heavy artillery bombardment and deliberate strafing from German fighters. Two dozen nurses were wounded. Even as the strafing planes returned, most of the injured nurses were being tended to— they had become patients.

The mission of the 77th at Verviers—which was about twenty kilometers east of Liège—was that of a holding unit, which meant a combination of triage, holding, and evacuation. It was at this point that the patients were sorted out. The doctors made the decision. They sent a few men directly back to duty. Others were tagged for a general hospital in Liège, where they would spend a few days before being returned to duty. Those who would take longer to heal went to Paris. Most of them traveled by rail. A few were tagged for immediate air evacuation to England.

During the Bulge, the hospital was all but overwhelmed. The capacity was supposed to be 750 patients, but more than double that number were in the hospital by late December. Despite the overload, the Red Cross workers and nurses managed to put up some Christmas decorations and provide wrapped Christmas presents to the patients—candy, books, various toilet articles. And the cooks provided a Christmas dinner for all that featured turkey and the works, plus grapes and apples.

Funny stories helped them keep going. One concerned a Red Cross worker, Miss Eisenstadt, who picked up a chart expecting to see where and how the patient was wounded. What she saw astonished her.

"How on earth did you ever get shot with two arrows?" she blurted out.

The full-blooded American Indian on the cot replied with righteous indignation, "That's my name, not my injury!"[43]

In a letter home, nurse Ruth Hess described setting up and opening a field hospital that had moved forward in the wake of the American sweep through France: "We arrived late in the evening and spent all nite getting ready to receive patients. We worked until 3:00 p.m. Then started nite duty, 12 hours at 7:30 p.m. For nine days we never stopped. 880 patients operated; small debridement of gun shot and shrapnel wounds, numerous amputations, fractures galore, perforated guts, livers, spleens, kidneys, lungs, etc. everything imaginable. We cared for almost 1500 patients in those nine days." Then the hospital packed up and moved forward.[44]

Like many of the nurses, Hess found herself weak with admiration for the wounded men. Lt. Frances Slanger of the 45th Field Hospital expressed the feeling in an October letter addressed to *Stars and Stripes* but written to the troops: "You G.I.'s say we nurses rough it. We wade ankle deep in mud. You have to lie in it. We have a stove and coal. . . . In comparison to the way you men are taking it, we can't complain, nor do we feel that bouquets are due us. . . . It is to you we doff our helmets.

"We have learned about our American soldier and the stuff he is made of. The wounded don't cry. Their buddies come first. The patience and determination they show, the courage and fortitude they have is sometimes awesome to behold. It is a privilege to receive you and a great distinction to see you open your eyes and with that swell American grin, say, 'Hi-ya, babe.' "

Slanger was killed the following day by an artillery shell. She was one of seventeen Army nurses killed in combat.[45]

In January 1945, Lt. Marjorie LaPalme was with the 41st Evacuation Hospital in Belgium, caring for the wounded from the Bulge. Her patients, she wrote home, "always have a smile . . . always wanting to talk to us about home and families. Great kids. I love them all! Like my own brothers!

"When I came over here I was just 21—among the youngest— Now these kids are coming in at eighteen."[46]

Whatever their age, the nurses bore their burdens and met their responsibilities and stayed cheerful. "The life of an army nurse," Lt. Hess wrote home. "I love it!"[47]

"Doctors in all military hospitals did a great job," Ken Russell of the 82nd Airborne remarked. He knew; he had been their patient. "The doctor in the forward field hospital was one of the most dedicated people you could meet. He would work long hours without adequate supplies—and the wonderful nurses did the same thing. They did not even have decent lighting. I have heard of them picking shrapnel or a bullet out of a wounded man by flashlight."[48]

Their patients were often mangled beyond imagination. Dr.

William McConahey was a battalion surgeon in the 90th Division in Normandy. "I've never seen such horrible wounds, before or since," he wrote. "Legs off, arms off, faces shot away, eviscerations, chests ripped open and so on. We worked at top speed, hour after hour, until we were too tired to stand up—and then we still kept going."[49]

Dr. Joseph Gosman was an orthopedic surgeon with the 109th Evacuation Hospital. He got to Normandy in time for the St.-Lô battle. "I was floored by the turmoil," he recalled. One patient had been in a jeep when it set off a mine. X-rays showed "undamaged bolts, washers, bushing in the muscle as on a work-bench." Another man had been shot in the side. The bullet entered a large vein and "floated" in the current of the vein into the right ventricle of the heart and then into the left auricle. The X-ray showed it bobbing in the heart chamber. A third soldier was carrying a Swiss Army knife in his pants pocket. Shrapnel had hit it, and bits of knife and shell entered his thigh together. "X-ray picture looked like a table setting with knife, fork and spoon and other stuff." A fourth was crouched beside a manure pile when a shell landed on it, "filling his thigh from knee to buttocks with manure, all tightly packed as into a sausage." These were a few of the almost 200,000 battle-wounded men who were treated in the hospitals in 1944.[50]

Gosman noticed a look among survivors of such wounds. It was "an appearance of naked bankruptcy, the stunned emptiness . . . of men whom death had breathed on and passed by." He was especially struck by a GI lying on his bunk, silent, who looked "like somebody rescued from the ledge of a skyscraper." He read the chart and was astonished to learn that the soldier had been shot in the neck. The bullet had entered on the left, missed the nerves, carotid artery, and jugular vein, drilled a neat hole in the spinal column without touching the spinal cord, and exited. The man needed no surgery; his chief symptom was a sore neck.[51]

In Bastogne, the medical team of the 101st was sorely tried. The aid station became a field hospital, accumulating wounded. There were doctors present, sometimes working twenty-four-hour shifts. When they ran out of plasma they took fresh blood from the lightly wounded and combat exhaustion cases. The surgeons attempted no major operations, concentrating instead on keeping their patients alive until definitive surgery could be done at a general hospital.

Two days before Christmas, a successful airdrop provided penicillin, morphine, litters, and blankets. Still the patients suffered. Infection was spreading in the "wards" (which were generally in cellars) and they stank of gas gangrene. The 101st put out a call for help that was answered by volunteer surgeons who flew into Bastogne by glider and set up their operating theater in a tool room next to a garage.

For all medical teams the Bulge was a huge crisis. Trench foot cases outnumbered gunshot, shrapnel, and wood wounds. Army medical historian Albert Cowdrey comments, "The marvel is that the medical system continued to operate under the burdens imposed simultaneously by weather and war."[52]

Both sides treated the enemy wounded in their hands, as well as they could. Captured medical teams were put to work. Lt. Briand Beudin, a surgeon with the 101st who parachuted into Normandy shortly after midnight, June 6, was taken prisoner at 0300 in the aid station he had set up. The Germans helped carry the American wounded to one of their aid stations, "where we medics were treated as friends by the German medical personnel." The doctors worked together through the night and the following days. Although a prisoner for some weeks, Beudin found his stay at the 91st *Feldlazarett* to be "most interesting." He learned German techniques and taught them American methods.[53]

The German doctors, with a land line of communications, had a supply crisis in France, while the American doctors, with the Atlantic Ocean between them and their supplies, were well supplied. This was due to the Allied air forces, dominating the skies over France. It put the German medical teams in a desperate situation. They made do with what they had. Nurse Ruth Hess wrote home on August 8 to report, "We sent our surgical teams and our men to a German hospital that had been captured to operate and evacuate the patients to us. All the work the Germans did was dirty surgery— every one was covered with pus, gangrene, bed sores, and filth—absolutely skin and bones. . . ."[54]

Her scorn was real but not typical. Usually when the young warriors started comparing living conditions—what's it like on the other side?—the answer often came out, "better." Ex-GIs tell me, vehemently, how much better the German boots were than the

American, but I've heard just the opposite from ex-Wehrmacht. So too for equipment and weapons.

Most of all for food. The Germans envied the Americans their rations—especially the cigarettes and chocolate bars—not only in their quantity, but quality. But whenever GIs overran a storage area for the German field kitchens, they marveled at the wonders they beheld.

A nurse in the 77th Evacuation Hospital remembered the glories of a ration dump outside Chartres (including vegetables ready for harvest outside the barracks). "Delicious sardines and cheese," she wrote. "The cheese was put up in a collapsible tube like toothpaste, and was of the variety which smells so bad but tastes so good. There were eggs and oranges."[55]

The doctors had to be shrinks as well as surgeons. Some of the patients—as many as 25 percent when the fighting was heavy—were uninjured physically but were babbling, crying, shaking, or stunned, unable to hear or to talk. These were the combat exhaustion casualties. It was the doctors' job to get as many as possible back to normalcy—and back to the lines—as soon as possible.

In the field hospitals, the American doctors treated the men as temporarily disabled soldiers rather than mental patients, normally categorizing them with the diagnosis "exhaustion." For the sake of both prevention and cure, the doctors tried to treat such patients as close as possible to the line. Typically the doctors at battalion level kept the exhaustion cases at their aid stations for twenty-four hours of rest, often under sedation. The men got hot food and a change of clothing. In as many as three quarters of the cases, that was sufficient, and the soldier went back to his foxhole.[56]

Good company commanders already knew that to be the case. Captain Winters of the 101st commented that he learned during the Bulge "the miracle that would occur with a man about to crack if you could just get him out of his foxhole and back to the CP for a few hours. Hot food, hot drink, a chance to warm up—that's what he needed to keep going."[57]

Men who needed more than a quick visit to the CP or battalion aid station were sent back to division medical facilities, where the division psychiatrist operated an "exhaustion center" that could hold patients for three days of treatment. The bulk of these men were also returned to the line. Those who had not recovered went on to the neuropsychiatric wards of general hospitals for seven days of therapy and reconditioning. The extreme cases were air-evacuated to the States.[58]

The system worked. Ninety of every hundred men diagnosed as exhaustion cases in ETO were restored to some form of duty—usually on the line. As they had done with the men wounded by bullets and shrapnel, so did the medics, nurses, and doctors do for the exhausted casualties—give them the best possible medical care ever achieved in an army in combat to that date.

14

Jerks, Sad Sacks, Profiteers, and Jim Crow

THE GIs IN ETO were highly selected in age and physical health, somewhat selected in intelligence, well disciplined. The Army's training system added inches to their chests and leg and arm muscles. It also instilled a sense of responsibility, along with a fear of the consequences of disobeying an order, not to mention criminal behavior: nicely summed up in the old drill sergeant's saying, "The Army can't make you do something, but it sure as hell can make you wish you had." It also did a good job of recognizing and promoting talented young men who were capable of standing the stress and leading effectively.

War brings out the best in many men, as the tiny sample of the men of ETO quoted or cited in this book testifies. To generalize, a large majority of the GIs in Northwest Europe in 1944–45 did their best at whatever they did, and in most cases they discovered that they were capable of doing far more than they had ever imagined possible. Thousands of men between twenty and twenty-five years of age responded to the challenge of responsibility magnificently. They matured as they led and, if they survived, they succeeded in their postwar careers. In one way, they were lucky: only in the extremity of total war does a society give so much responsibility for life-and-death decision-making to men so young. Together, the junior officers and NCOs who survived the war were the leaders in building modern America. This was in some part thanks to what they had learned in the Army, primarily how to make decisions and accept responsibility.

The Army was unlike civilian society in most ways, but ETO and the home front were together in their shared sense of "we." It was a "we" generation, as in the popular wartime saying, "We are all in this together." In the Army, this general attitude was greatly reinforced. The social bond within the Army was like an onion. At the core was the squad, where bonding could be almost mystical.

Lt. Glenn Gray (after the war a professor of philosophy) put it well: "Organization for a common and concrete goal in peacetime organizations does not evoke anything like the degree of comradeship commonly known in war. At its height, this sense of comradeship is an ecstasy. Men are true comrades only when each [member of the squad] is ready to give up his life for the other, without reflection and without thought of personal loss."[1]

After the squad came succeeding layers, the platoon, company, on up to division, all covered by the loose outermost layers of corps and army. The sense of belonging meant most GIs wouldn't dream of stealing from or cheating a buddy within the squad or company, or of slacking off on the job, whether as front-line infantry or driving a truck.

But the Army was so big—eight million men at its peak, from a low of 165,000 four years earlier—and put together so quickly, that thousands of sharp operators and sad sacks, criminals and misfits, and some cowards made it through the training process and became soldiers in ETO. Some were junior officers in infantry divisions and the price for their incompetence was casualties. More were rear-echelon soldiers, completely free of a sense of "we," who in one way or another took advantage of the opportunities presented by the war.

Joseph Heller's character Milo Minderbender in *Catch-22* is an exaggeration, but not an invention. The United States was sending to Europe colossal quantities of goods. Given the amounts involved and the constant need for haste, there was a vulnerability that a few soldiers found irresistible. More than a few, really—the figures on stolen goods are staggering. The matériel for the Americans fighting in Italy came in through the port of Naples. It came in day and night—weapons, ammunition, rations, fuel, trucks, electrical equipment, and much more. Every item was eagerly sought on the black market. One-third of all the supplies landed in Naples was stolen. In Italy, once an entire train carrying supplies to the front simply disappeared.

The cornucopia of American goods coming into a Europe that had been at war for five years led to the greatest black market of all time. Most American soldiers participated in it to some extent, if in no other way than by trading cigarettes for perfume, or rations for jewels. A few got rich off it.

At the opposite extreme from the young entrepreneurs were the sad sacks, those guys who could never be found when there was a patrol to run or a job to be done, who had mastered the art of getting lost in the Army so well they became practically invisible. In between were the jerks and assholes, usually men who had been made NCOs or junior officers who exploited their rank in chickenshit ways, but at the head of the list there stood the formidable figure of the general in charge of all supplies in ETO. At the bottom of the list were the cowards, and Jim Crow.

They were all part of the U.S. Army in ETO, and this chapter is a glance at a few of them.

Most GIs did their job, fought well, managed to stay out of serious trouble, and were generally regarded as "good guys." The ones who slipped and became jerks for a night, or a day, or a week, could usually blame it on wine, which was present in almost every cellar in France and Belgium (in sharp contrast to the Pacific Theater, where the men drank homemade stuff, always vile, but with a punch). Paul Fussell, in *Wartime,* catches the situation exactly in his chapter title "Drinking Far Too Much, Copulating Too Little."

When it came to drinking, the men of ETO were just boys. Growing up in the Depression, their experience with alcohol was pretty much limited to a few beers on graduation night, and a lot of beer on Saturday nights in training camp in Georgia or wherever, and in English pubs. This in no way prepared them for the challenge France had to offer.

On December 15 Dutch Schultz, 82nd Airborne, stationed in an old French army barracks, got a pass to Reims, champagne capital of the world. There he ran into three high school buddies from another outfit. The corks popped. "This was my first experience with champagne," Schultz recalled. "I started drinking it like soda pop." He can't recall anything that happened in Reims after the drinking started, but he does remember what happened when he got back to barracks.

"I headed for my bed which was an upper bunk on the second floor of my building. When I got to my bed, I found someone sleeping in it."

Dutch shook the man awake. "What the hell are you doing in my bed?" he roared.

The soldier roared back: "It's my bed, what the hell do you think you are doing? Get the hell out of here!"

They started throwing punches. The lights went on. Every man in the room wanted to kill Schultz. To his consternation, he discovered he was not only at the wrong bed, but also the wrong room, the wrong barracks, the wrong battalion. "I made a hasty retreat."

"Jerk!" the men called out as he fled, using a variety of obscene adjectives to express their feelings.[2]

The guys who were permanent jerks were the usual suspects—officers with too much authority and too few brains, sergeants who had more than a touch of sadist in their characters, far too many quartermasters, some MPs. The types were many in number and widely varied in how they acted out their role, but the GIs had a single word that applied to every one of them: chickenshit.

Fussell defines the term precisely: "Chickenshit refers to behavior that makes military life worse than it need be: petty harassment of the weak by the strong; open scrimmage for power and authority and prestige . . . insistence on the letter rather than the spirit of ordinances. Chickenshit is so called—instead of horse- or bull- or elephant shit—because it is small-minded and ignoble and takes the trivial seriously. Chickenshit can be recognized instantly because it never has anything to do with winning the war."[3]

There were some at the front, not many. In most cases they were visitors who didn't belong there. Captain Colby led an attack down a road in the hedgerow country. His company got hit hard and dove into the ditches. A firefight ensued. After a half hour or so, Colby looked up to see his regimental commander standing above him, "nattily attired in a clean uniform, and his helmet was clean and sported a silver star. He was the picture of coolness."

"You can't lead your men from down there," he snapped.

"Come up here and tell me what happened. Try to set an example of how an officer should behave."

"Come down here, sir, and we can talk about it," Colby replied.

"Come up here," the general replied. "That's an order."

To Colby's relief, a mortar round went off a few meters from the general. "He joined me in the ditch."[4]

Most chickenshits were rear-echelon. There are innumerable stories about them. Sgt. Ed Gianelloni remembered the time in Luneville when his division was temporarily out of the line and the opportunity came to take the first showers in two months. For the officers, there was a public bath, where Frenchwomen bathed them. For the enlisted, there were portable showers in the middle of a muddy field. Everyone undressed, piled up clothes and weapons, and stood around shivering, waiting for the hot water.

"All right, you guys," the engineering sergeant in command barked out, "you got one minute to wet, one minute to soap, and one minute to rinse off and then you get out of here."

A private standing near the weapons pile reached in, grabbed an M-1, pointed it at the sergeant, and inquired politely, "Sergeant, how much time did you say we have?"

The sergeant gulped, then muttered, "I'll tell you what, I am going to take a walk and check on my equipment. When I come back you ought to be done."[5]

General Patton had more than a bit of the chickenshit in him. He was notorious for being a martinet about dress and spit-and-polish in Third Army. He ordered—and sometimes may have gotten—front-line infantry to wear ties and to shave every day. Bill Mauldin did a famous cartoon about it. Willie and Joe are driving a beat-up jeep. A large road sign informs them that "You Are Entering The Third Army!" There follows a list of fines for anyone entering the area: no helmet, $25; no shave $10; no tie $25; and so on. Willie tells Joe, "Radio th' ol' man we'll be late on account of a thousand-mile detour."

But it was no joke. Patton's spit-and-polish obsession sometimes cost dearly. It not only had nothing to do with winning the war, it hurt the war effort.

Twenty-year-old Lt. Bill Leesemann was in a reconnaissance section of the 101st Engineer Combat Battalion, attached to the

26th Division. On December 18, the 26th, along with the 80th and the 4th Armored, got orders to break off the attack in Lorraine, turn from east to north, and smash into the German southern flank of the Bulge. This required frenetic activity. Leesemann's job was to go from division headquarters in Metz to the Third Army Engineer headquarters in Nancy, to pick up maps—no one in the attacking divisions had any maps of Luxembourg. It was a sixty-kilometer drive. Leesemann and his driver took off late on December 19, as the 26th was forming up to head toward Luxembourg. It wouldn't be able to move out until the maps arrived.

It was raining; the road was muddy; troops moving north caused delays. It was full dark by the time Leesemann got to Nancy. He stopped at a crossroads, where "a real spit-and-polish MP was directing traffic." Leesemann asked directions to the Engineers hq. The MP took one look at the dirty, unshaven lieutenant and driver and ordered them to the MP post. He said they could not proceed into Third Army area until they had washed the jeep, shaved, and put on clean uniforms. Leesemann replied that such things were out of the question and explained the urgency of the situation. The MP called his corporal.

Twenty minutes later the corporal arrived. After further interrogation, he called the sergeant. The sergeant came, more talk, finally he called Engineers hq. Permission to come on was granted.

Leesemann drove to the hq, "a large chateau with surrounding gardens. The sentries at the large iron gate entrance gave us the same routine with threats of being arrested; 'No way will we be responsible for admitting you two into the Command area.' "

Another call, another wait. Eventually, but not without further adventures in the maze of Third Army, Leesemann got the maps and returned to 26th Division hq. It was 0500 hours, December 20. The division had been ready to move since 0100 hours. It was waiting for the maps.[6]

The biggest jerk in ETO was Lt. Gen. John C. H. Lee (USMA 1909), commander of Services of Supply (SOS). He had a most difficult job, to be sure. And of course it is in the nature of an army that everyone resents the quartermaster, and Lee was the head quartermaster for the whole of ETO.

Lee was a martinet who had an exalted opinion of himself. He also had a strong religious fervor (Eisenhower compared him to

Cromwell) that struck a wrong note with everyone. He handed out the equipment as if it were a personal gift. He hated waste; once he was walking through a mess hall, reached into the garbage barrel, pulled out a half-eaten loaf of bread, started chomping on it, and gave the cooks hell for throwing away perfectly good food. He had what Bradley politely called "an unfortunate pomposity" and was cordially hated. Officers and men gave him a nickname based on his initials, J.C.H.—Jesus Christ Himself.[7]

Lee's best-known excess came in September, at the height of the supply crisis. Eisenhower had frequently expressed his view that no major headquarters should be located in or near the temptations of a large city, and had specifically reserved the hotels in Paris for the use of combat troops on leave. Lee nevertheless, and without Eisenhower's knowledge, moved his headquarters to Paris. His people requisitioned all the hotels previously occupied by the Germans, and took over schools and other large buildings. More than 8,000 officers and 21,000 men in SOS descended on the city in less than a week, with tens of thousands more to follow. Parisians began to mutter that the U.S. Army demands were in excess of those made by the Germans.

The GIs and their generals were furious. They stated the obvious: at the height of the supply crisis, Lee had spent his precious time organizing the move, then used up precious gasoline, all so that he and his entourage could enjoy the hotels of Paris. It got worse. With 29,000 SOS troops in Paris, the great majority of them involved in some way in the flow of supplies from the beaches and ports to the front, and taking into account what Paris had to sell, from wine and girls to jewels and perfumes, a black market on a grand scale sprang up.

Eisenhower was enraged. He sent a firm order to Lee to stop the entry into Paris of every individual not absolutely essential and to move out of the city every man who was not. He said essential duties "will not include provision of additional facilities, services and recreation for SOS or its Headquarters." He told Lee that he would like to order him out of the city altogether, but could not afford to waste more gasoline in moving SOS again. He said Lee had made an "extremely unwise" decision and told him to correct the situation as soon as possible.[8]

Of course Lee and his headquarters stayed in Paris. And of course there was solid reason for so doing. And of course the combat veterans who got three-day passes into Paris could never get a hotel room, and had to sleep in a barracks-like Red Cross shelter, on cots. The rear-echelon SOS got the beds and private rooms. And their numbers grew rather than shrank. By March 1945, there were 160,000 SOS troops in the Department of the Seine.[9]

The supply troops also got the girls, because they had the money, thanks to the black market. It flourished everywhere. Thousands of gallons of gasoline, tons of food and clothing, millions of cigarettes, were being siphoned off each day. The gasoline pipeline running from the beaches to Chartres was tapped so many times only a trickle came out at the far end.

Most of this was petty thievery. It was done at the expense of the front-line troops. As one example, the most popular brand of cigarettes was Lucky Strike, followed by Camel. In Paris, the SOS troops and their dates smoked Lucky Strikes and Camels; in the foxholes, the men got Pall Malls, Raleighs, or, worse, British cigarettes.*

But a large part of the black market was run by organized crime. Here is a story told to me by a former lieutenant who worked as a criminal investigator for the SHAEF adjutant general's office. There was a colonel from the National Guard, born in Sicily, who was in Transport Command. His administrative job gave him the use of a C-47. On every clear day he flew, with a co-pilot, from London to Paris and back. He took in cartons of cigarettes and brought back jewels and perfumes. His trade flourished but there were a lot of payoffs to make, too many people involved. By mid-December, SHAEF's criminal investigators were ready to arrest him, but he got a tip and fled in his C-47, with a co-pilot and a box stuffed with jewelry.

"Over the Channel," the lieutenant told me, "he shot the co-pilot, then smashed his face beyond recognition. He was a hell of a pilot; he landed on the edge of the water at an extremely low tide near Utah Beach. The plane with the co-pilot's body wasn't found until the next day's low tide—and the colonel had left his dog tags on the dead man. We learned later that a French farm couple had

---

*When Maj. Rolf Pauls was captured, the American lieutenant doing the initial interrogation offered him a Lucky. Pauls offered one of his German cigarettes in return. The lieutenant lit up, inhaled, coughed, and said, "Oh, fields and meadows." "Yes," Pauls replied, "fields and meadows. Your Luckies are much better." (Rolf Pauls interview by Hugh Ambrose, EC.)

watched an American pilot as he stole a donkey and cart, loaded a box onto the cart, slipped into peasant's clothing, and was last seen headed toward Sicily."[10]

The German army had its fair share of jerks. There too they were often quartermasters. Colonel von Luck recalled that in early September, during the retreat through France, he came on a supply depot. His tanks, trucks, and other vehicles needed fuel; his men needed ammunition and food. He demanded it be handed over.

The sergeant in charge gave what Luck called "the typical, impudent reply: 'I can issue nothing without written authority.' When I asked, 'And what will you do if the Americans get here tomorrow, which is highly likely?' the answer was: 'Then in accordance with orders I will blow the depot up.'

"As my men advanced threateningly on the sergeant, weapons at the ready, I replied, 'If I don't have fuel, ammunition, and food within half an hour I can no longer be responsible.' " The sergeant looked at the grim-faced Luck and his men and gave them what they needed.[11]

Similar scenes were enacted a thousand times and more during the retreat. At the other end of the scale, corps commanders in the Wehrmacht could be as crazy as Hitler. Like their leader, they moved long-gone regiments and divisions around on their maps. From the safety of their headquarters, they ordered counterattacks by phantom units. In January 1945 in Belgium, Lt. Col. Gerhard Lemcke of the 12th Panzer Division, a career soldier, had a typical experience. He had his hq in a farmhouse on a hill. From the kitchen window he could see Sherman tanks in the process of surrounding his position. He got orders to attack, which he ignored.

A staff officer drove up. He had been drinking, to bolster his courage—staff officers seldom came to the front, and when they did they were afraid of the combat commanders. In this case, the officer informed Lemcke that he had come to take Lemcke into custody.

"May I ask why?"

"You have not carried out the orders of the Corps commander."

"And what am I to do? Should I tell them to throw rocks? Or maybe snow, there's lots of that—I have nothing else. The artillery battery behind me, they don't shoot anymore because they have no ammunition. But Corps has ordered them to stay and defend us.

How about telling Corps hq to take back their guns and send their personnel up here to become part of my infantry."

"You tell them," the lieutenant replied.

Lemcke got on the radio. Corps repeated the order to attack. Lemcke again refused. Corps then told the lieutenant to arrest that man and bring him in. As the lieutenant made to do so, Lemcke's men surrounded him. "These were soldiers who had been with me since Russia," Lemcke recalled. "A number of them had long since earned the Iron Cross 1st Class. They would not allow this lieutenant to take me anywhere."[12]

Next to Hitler himself, the biggest jerks in Germany were Reichsmarschall Hermann Goering and Reichsfuehrer SS Heinrich Himmler. In November 1944 Himmler was put in command of the eastern bank of the Upper Rhine. Himmler knew a lot about how to terrorize and slaughter civilians, but nothing about military affairs. On January 3, 1945, he ordered Maj. Hannibal von Lüttichau to attack.

"I don't doubt that these orders were developed with the greatest care," Lüttichau told Himmler. "But we must have fuel."

"You don't need to drive," Himmler replied.

"But a dug-in panzer is easily destroyed from the air," Lüttichau explained. "The panzer's strength is to shoot and move. Suddenly pop up and fire and get out of there! Besides, I don't have ammunition. It doesn't matter how much heroism we have, we won't last a day before our soldiers know that we are crazy and stick their hands in the air and give up. What should I do about that?"

Himmler ordered him arrested. He was, but his Iron Cross 1st Class protected him and he survived.[13]

In general, the American press corps covering ETO—whether for the wire services, individual newspapers or magazines, radio, or the GIs' paper, *Stars and Stripes*—did an outstanding job. The names of the top reporters, like the names Eisenhower, Bradley, Patton, Collins, resonate through the ages. The list included Edward R. Murrow and Walter Cronkite, Ernie Pyle and Andy Rooney, Eric Sevareid and A. J. Liebling, Martha Gellhorn and Anne O'Hare McCormick, John P. Marquand and Robert Sherrod, James Agee and William Shirer, among others. Best known of all was Ernest Hemingway, correspondent for *Collier's* magazine. If being a jerk is first of all being self-centered, Papa was one.

When Hemingway sat down to write, he was the only person in view. His dispatches to *Collier's* were about what he saw, did, felt. His biggest moment came when he and his driver, Pvt. Archie Pelkey, hooked up with a Resistance group headed for Paris. It was August 19. The sun rose and "it was a beautiful day that day" and Hemingway got to carry vital information to headquarters. "I had bicycled through this area for many years. It is by riding a bicycle that you learn the contours of a country best, since you have to sweat up the hills and can coast down them."

"Never can I describe to you the emotions I felt," he opened his report from Paris, before going on to three columns about how he felt.

There were many adventures with the Resistance group, and much drinking. As only he could, Hemingway loved these French fighters for their courage, elan, and simplicity. They wanted to have one more drink, one more kiss from the barmaid, and be off for Paris. So did Hemingway. But on the edge of the city they were ordered off the road by an American MP.

That evening it rained very hard but Pelkey and Papa were snug in a bistro, with a bottle of wine and some cheese and bread, looking down on Paris. They talked about their newfound French friends.

"They're a good outfit," Pelkey said. "Best outfit I ever been with. No discipline. Got to admit that. Drinking all the time. Got to admit that. But plenty fighting outfit. Nobody gives a damn if they get killed or not."

"Yeah," Papa replied. Then, he concluded his dispatch, "I couldn't say anything more, because I had a funny choke in my throat and I had to clean my glasses because there now, below us, gray and always beautiful, was spread the city I love best in all the world."[14]

Ernie Pyle didn't see the war that way, which is why he is read a half century later, and Hemingway isn't. In a 1995 two-volume anthology of the best of World War II reporting, done by the Library of America, there are twenty-six dispatches from Pyle, one from Hemingway. Everyone knew that Hemingway was brave, foolish, and sentimental. What they wanted to know was what the GIs and the high command were doing. That was what Pyle and nearly all of the others gave them.

∎

Rumors and wisecracks help men endure the unendurable, which is why they are integral to every war. In ETO, thousands of rumors circulated. Some were frightening ("we're going to jump into Berlin" among the paratroopers, for example), but most were hopeful. They promised an end: Germany is in revolt; the war will be over before Christmas; Hitler is dead; and so on, endlessly. Or the rumors promised reward: every paratrooper (or combat infantry, or artilleryman, or medic, or whatever) was going to get a free car from Henry Ford when the war was won. Others promised relief: our division is being withdrawn from combat and returned to the States to train new troops. In POW camps, it was that an exchange of prisoners is imminent.

Pvt. Harold Snedden of the 28th Division marched through Paris on liberation day. As he paraded down the Champs-Elysées, he heard a rumor, one that spread almost instantly up and down the long columns: "The brass has decided to keep us here to police the city." Sadly, Snedden was quickly disabused.[15]

Pvt. Ed Jabol of the 1st Division had the satisfaction of getting a reward from a rumor he started. In the hedgerow fighting, he and his buddy told one other person each that the local water was contaminated, just to see how long it took to get back to them. The following day, word came down from headquarters to drink only wine until the water could be treated.[16]

Wisecracks and clichés abounded in ETO. Most of them were coarse, sexual, and punctuated by the vilest language. But some were directed to specific complaints and were heard almost as often as the words "GI" or "dogface." They included, "You never had it so good," "You've found a home in the Army," and "What more could you possibly want." Others were teasing: "Too bad you were asleep when the girls came by" or "I hear you are getting promoted." Some were just devilish: "I hear you are going to reenlist."

There were thousands of ordinary criminals in ETO. Hundreds of them were caught, tried by court-martial, and sentenced to the stockade or, in the case of rape or murder, to death by firing squad. Sixty-five men were ordered shot. Eisenhower had to pass the final judgment. In sixteen cases he changed the sentence to life in the stockade; forty-nine men were shot.

Desertion was also punishable by death by firing squad, but the U.S. Army had not carried out such a sentence since 1864. Desertion was a serious problem in ETO, partly because it was relatively easy to do in Europe (there were no desertions on the Pacific islands), partly because of the never-ending nature of the combat, partly because the Army tried to get deserters back to their outfits and give them a second chance, meaning deserters could figure there wouldn't be any punishment if they were caught.

In November 1944, Lieut. Glenn Gray, on counterintelligence duty, found a deserter in a French woods. The lad was from the Pennsylvania mountains, he was accustomed to camping out, he had been there a couple of weeks, living on venison, and intended to stay until the war ended. "All the men I knew and trained with have been killed," the deserter told Gray. "I'm lonely. . . . The shells seem to come closer all the time and I can't stand them."

He begged Gray to leave him. Gray refused, said he would have to turn him in, but promised he would not be punished. The deserter said he knew that; he bitterly predicted "they" would simply put him back into the line again—which was exactly what happened when Gray brought him in.[17]

One deserter only, Pvt. Eddie Slovik, went through the process from confession to court-martial to sentence to execution by firing squad. Slovik got to France as a replacement in August. On the 25th, he spent the night in a village, dug in with some other replacements. There was shelling. In the morning, when they moved out, he stayed behind. That afternoon, he hooked up with some Canadian infantry, with whom he spent the next six weeks. Then he was turned over to American MPs, who escorted him back to the company to which he had been assigned.

Slovik told the CO he was too frightened of the shelling and swore, "If I have to go out there again I'll run away."

He later put that warning in writing, at the end of a written confession of desertion. He wanted to spend the rest of the war in the stockade. Bad luck for him; by the time he came to trial it was November 11, and the strain of the fighting at the Siegfried Line was leading to an increase in desertions. The high command was looking to set an example. Slovik fit perfectly. He was found guilty and sentenced to execution. By the time Eisenhower gave the case its last review, on January 30, the Bulge had made desertion an even greater problem. Eisenhower did not intervene. On January 31, Slovik was executed.[18]

Slovik's case excited comment and controversy. There was a

hue and cry about Army justice. Eisenhower never backed away from his decision. He thought the case about as clear-cut as one could get. But whatever the merits, it helps put the Slovik execution in some perspective to mention that during the course of the eleven-month campaign in Northwest Europe, when Eisenhower had one deserter put to death, Hitler had 50,000 executed for desertion or cowardice.

One of the stressful strains on platoon and company commanders was recognizing and dealing with battle fatigue. The best of them could anticipate the breaking point with an individual before it occurred, and get them some rest. Severe cases went to the rear, for treatment. A few returned to the front line; many more were put on limited duty. The temptation to fake combat exhaustion was there.

One evening in the Hurtgen, Lt. George Wilson welcomed two replacements, radiomen, to his company, and directed them to a foxhole. There was some shelling. In the morning, the smaller of the two replacements dashed over to Wilson's foxhole and dove in.

"He was shaking violently," Wilson remembered, "and tears streamed down his face. His whole frame quivered with the spasms, and he was barely able to tell me between sobs that he couldn't take it. He just had to get the hell out; I had to let him go to the rear. He sobbed like a baby during the entire outburst and beat his head on the ground."

Wilson tried talking to him, to no avail. Wilson tried getting tough: "I told him angrily that I had been in front-line combat for over five months and no one would let me go back. Since he had just arrived, he sure as hell wasn't going back."

That brought on more hysteria. He sobbed that he would desert. Wilson said go ahead—and you'll get shot. Next Wilson told him how ashamed his parents would be. He sobbed that he didn't care. "I'm just a dirty, no-good, yellow, Jewish SOB."

Eventually he calmed down and returned to his foxhole. But later that day his buddy, a big man, came to Wilson and put on a similar performance, but he wasn't as convincing as the first guy. "I blew my top," Wilson wrote, "and shouted at him that the two of them were trying to play me for an idiot, and I'd had it with them.

"Surprisingly, he readily admitted it and even went on to describe how they had spent the night before planning the charade. It seems they had both been actors in college and had had some training."

The following day, another shelling. The bigger of the two replacements went bonkers. Tears streaming down his face, he begged Wilson to send him to the rear. "I turned on him angrily and pointed my rifle at his chest, saying that if I heard one more word out of him I'd shoot. He stopped bawling instantly."

The shelling resumed. The man got a piece of shrapnel in his arm, the million-dollar wound. He was out of there. Wilson never saw him again. Nor the first guy, who took himself to the rear and talked his way into a hospital as a battle fatigue case.[19]

In the popular World War II cartoon strip *The Sad Sack,* the character was a naive, confused, lazy, bumbling private, but happy enough and almost lovable. In real life, a sad sack was a miserable person. Perpetually unhappy himself, he tried to make everyone around him equally miserable. He was filled with hate—for his officers, for the Army, for blacks, Jews, Italians, whoever. Whenever he could get away with it, he was a bully. He was a habitual liar. He disappeared when real work or fighting had to be done. Not only did he fail to carry his weight, he was a constant and serious drain on the Army's efficiency. At his extreme, the sad sack was a mean, vicious son of a bitch, without a redeeming virtue.

The worst sad sack of all was Jim Crow.

The world's greatest democracy fought the world's greatest racist with a segregated Army. It was worse than that: the Army and the society conspired to degrade African-Americans in every way possible, summed up in the name Jim Crow. One little incident from the home front illustrates the tyranny black Americans lived under during the Second World War.

In April 1944 Corp. Rupert Timmingham wrote *Yank* magazine. "Here is a question that each Negro soldier is asking," he began. "What is the Negro soldier fighting for? On whose team are we playing?" He recounted the difficulties he and eight other black soldiers had while traveling through the South—"where Old Jim Crow rules"—for a new assignment. "We could not purchase a cup of coffee," Timmingham noted. Finally the lunchroom manager at a Texas railroad depot said the black GIs could go on around back to the kitchen for a sandwich and coffee. As they did, "about two dozen

German prisoners of war, with two American guards, came to the station. They entered the lunchroom, sat at the tables, had their meals served, talked, smoked, in fact had quite a swell time. I stood on the outside looking on, and I could not help but ask myself why are they treated better than we are? Why are we pushed around like cattle? If we are fighting for the same thing, if we are to die for our country, then why does the Government allow such things to go on? Some of the boys are saying that you will not print this letter. I'm saying that you will."[20]

In ETO, many black soldiers were assigned to prisoner duty. It is the universal testimony of the German POWs interviewed for this book that they got better treatment from black than white guards, to the point that the POWs had a saying, "The best American is a black American."[21]

Old Jim Crow ruled in the Army as much as in the South. Blacks had their own units, mess halls, barracks, bars—State-side, England, France, Belgium, it didn't matter. There were no black infantry units in ETO. There were nine Negro field artillery battalions, a few anti-aircraft battalions, and a half dozen tank and tank destroyer battalions. Some did well, some were average, some were poor.

The 969th Field Artillery Battalion earned praise from Gen. Maxwell Taylor for its supporting fire during the defense of Bastogne. "Our success," Taylor wrote the 969th's commander, "is attributable to the shoulder to shoulder cooperation of all units involved. This Division is proud to have shared the Battlefield with your command." He put the battalion in for a Distinguished Unit Citation, which it received on February 5, the first Negro combat unit to be so honored.[22]

Patton had not been eager to accept black tankers, because he fancied that black men did not have quick enough reflexes to drive tanks in battle.[23] But when at the end of October the 761st Tank Battalion, the first Negro unit committed to combat, showed up assigned to the 26th Division, Third Army, Patton welcomed the black tankers warmly: "Men, you're the first Negro tankers to ever fight in the American Army. . . . I don't care what color you are, so long as you go up there and kill those Kraut sonsabitches. Everyone has their eyes on you and is expecting great things from you. Most of all, your race is looking to you. Don't let them down, don't let me down."[24]

They didn't. The battalion spent 183 days in action. Every commander it fought under sent his commendations. It won one Medal of Honor and many Distinguished Service Crosses.

The Negro 827th Tank Destroyer Battalion, however, had a poor record, so bad that the Army almost disbanded it and many commanders refused to have it. The causes were familiar: untrained, with white officers who were the castoffs of other units, poorly equipped. Shortly after the end of the war Walter Wright, chief historian of the Army, commented that the real trouble was the inferior officers. Blacks had to have the best, Wright insisted, because "American negro troops are ill-educated on the average and often illiterate; they lack self-respect, self-confidence, and initiative; they tend to be very conscious of their low standing in the eyes of the white population and consequently feel very little motive for aggressive fighting."

Why should they, Wright went on, when every black soldier knew "that the color of his skin will automatically disqualify him for reaping the fruits of attainment. No wonder that he sees little point in trying very hard to excel. To me, the most extraordinary thing is that such people continue trying at all."[25]

It wasn't only that the whites wouldn't reward a black soldier who did his job well; those blacks who did strive were ridiculed by their fellows for doing so. Isaac Coleman was the second oldest of fourteen children, raised on a farm in Virginia. He had quit school at age fifteen to work; besides, there was no public high school for blacks in his area. He enlisted in 1941 and moved up rapidly "because I was ambitious and did my job the best I could. I was obedient and accepted responsibilities. Others called me 'Uncle Tom' and worse, and I had a few run-ins with black soldiers, but I was satisfied. I made Master Sergeant when I was twenty-years-old." That meant $140 a month, most of which he sent home.

Sergeant Coleman fought his way through Europe. He got back to Virginia in January 1946. "When I got home there was snow on the ground and a white fellow at the bus station gave me a ride home. My father came out barefoot and picked me off the ground. Daddy cried and we visited and saw everybody that night. Daddy had seven boys in the war, six overseas at once, and we all came home. I wouldn't have minded staying in the Army but my wife was a teacher and didn't want to quit, so I gave in. I bought a farm with the GI Bill."[26]

Most black soldiers never got a chance to fight. For a few, an opportunity came during the replacements crisis at the time of the Bulge. Within General Lee's SOS were thousands of physically fit black soldiers whose jobs could be done by limited-duty personnel. Lee offered them an opportunity to volunteer for the infantry, then be placed in otherwise white units, without regard to a quota but as needed.

When SHAEF Chief of Staff Lt. Gen. Walter B. Smith read a circular Lee had put out, he stormed into Lee's office. Smith had been in charge of "negro policy" for the Army in 1941; he told Lee, "It is inevitable that this circular will get out, and equally inevitable that the result will be that every negro organization, pressure group and newspaper will take the attitude that, while the War Department segregates colored troops into organizations of their own against the desires and pleas of all the negro race, the Army in Europe is perfectly willing to put them in the front lines mixed in units with white soldiers and have them do battle when an emergency arises."

Breathing deeply, Smith went on, "Two years ago I would have considered this the most dangerous thing that I have ever seen in regard to negro relations."

"I can't see that at all," Lee replied. (Whatever his faults, he stood tall on this one.) "I believe it is right that colored and white soldiers should be mixed in the same company."

"I'm not arguing with that, one way or the other," Smith snapped. "But the War Department policy is different."[27]

Smith couldn't persuade Lee, but he did convince Eisenhower to maintain an essential segregation in ETO: the Supreme Commander declared that Negro volunteers would be trained as platoons and put into the line on that basis.

At this point, Catch-22 took over. The Replacement Depots were not prepared to train platoons, only individuals. Individual replacements were badly needed in the all-black artillery and tank battalions, but the depots could train only infantry. There were 4,562 volunteers, many of them NCOs who took a reduction to private to do so. The Replacement Depots were not prepared to handle so many.

On March 1, 1945, the first 2,253 volunteers had completed their training. They were organized into thirty-seven rifle platoons and sent to the front, where they were distributed as needed to the companies. The platoon leader and sergeant were assigned from the company, and of course were white.[28] With some exceptions, the platoons preformed well. A few were outstanding. In general, their performance was so good it led many officers who served with them to reject segregation in the Army of the future. If anything, the judgment was that they were too aggressive. In one case, three black soldiers used a captured panzerfaust to knock out a Tiger tank. They were rewarded with a week in Paris. Thereafter, there were many black soldiers seen stalking the enemy's armored monster with panzerfaust in hand.[29]

Maj. Gen. Edwin Parker, CO of the 78th Division, said of his Negro platoons: "Morale: Excellent. Manner of performance: Superior. Men are very eager to close with the enemy and to destroy him. . . . When given a mission they accept it with enthusiasm, and even when losses to their platoon were inflicted the colored boys pressed on."[30]

Jim Crow was on the run, but not done. In the last month of the war, the worry became: what happens when we move into barracks? It was unthinkable that blacks and whites would share the same barracks. In the event, that worry proved to be misplaced. After two months in an integrated barracks, a battalion commander in the 78th Division said he had no problems of any kind and explained, "White men and colored men are welded together with a deep friendship and respect born of combat and matured by a realization that such an association is not the impossibility that many of us have been led to believe. . . . When men undergo the same privations, face the same dangers before an impartial enemy, there can be no segregation. My men eat, play, work, and sleep as a company of men, with no regard to color."[31]

There were other hopeful signs that the Army would soon be rid of Jim Crow. *Yank* magazine did print Corporal Timmingham's letter. A couple of months later, he wrote again. "To date I've received 287 letters," he said, "and, strange as it may seem, 183 are from white men in the armed service. Another strange feature about these letters is that the most of these people are from the Deep South. They are all proud that they are from the South but ashamed to learn that there are so many of their own people who are playing Hitler's game. Nevertheless, it gives me new hope to realize that there are doubtless thousands of whites who are willing to fight [Jim Crow]." *Yank* noted that it had received thousands of letters from GIs, "almost all of whom were outraged by the treatment given the corporal."[32]

After the experience of World War II, by the end of 1945 the ground had been prepared for Jim Crow's grave. Chief Historian Wright concluded his wartime report on the employment of Negro troops with these words: "My ultimate hope is that in the long run it will be possible to assign individual Negro soldiers and officers to any unit in the Army where they are qualified as individuals to serve efficiently."[33] That was done, under the command and leadership of the colonels, majors, captains, and lieutenants of ETO, who had seen with their own eyes. Within a decade, the Army had changed from being one of the most tightly segregated organizations in the country to the most successfully integrated.

15

Prisoners of War

ONE OF THE MOST dangerous moments in combat in Europe in World War II came the instant a man decided he was no longer willing or able to continue combat. He threw down his weapon and raised his hands, or showed a white flag—sometimes alone, sometimes in a group, sometimes in company strength or even more— and thus exposed himself to an armed enemy soldier he had been trying to kill a moment before, and who was frequently mad with battle lust. His chances of getting shot were high. They stayed high until he was safely in the rear in a POW cage.

Most of the men who stuck to their guns until out of ammunition and about to be overrun, before throwing up their hands and calling Comrade! never made it to POW status. The German trick of sending unarmed men on patrols, so that if caught they could say they were trying to surrender, made it difficult and dangerous for individual Germans to give up, as the GIs shot all Germans found between the lines. The Germans were equally unforgiving.

The SHAEF War Crimes Files are stuffed with incidents: "Case 6-123, Company B, 394th Infantry. Near Losheim on 17 December the Germans surrounded a platoon. The GIs raised a white flag, but German tanks nevertheless overran the position, covering some men with earth and firing into the foxholes. Somehow 22 men managed to surrender. The Germans herded them into a nearby draw and gunned them down. Only the aid man escaped.

"Case 6-156. Witness: Pvt. Andrew S. Protz. At Honsefeld, 5 US soldiers raised a white flag and came forward. The Germans opened fire, killing 4 and wounding 1, whereupon a German tank deliberately ran over the wounded man as he begged for help."[1]

Pvt. Edward Webber of the 47th Infantry Regiment described a gruesome, but hardly unique, incident. He was advancing on a damaged German tank. The crew had ceased firing its machine gun, opened the turret, and were waving a white flag. Webber and his buddies moved forward. The machine gun began firing again— probably by some young fanatic who refused to give up with the rest. Webber's squad fired back. "The crew came pouring out of the bottom escape hatch," Webber said. "They were hollering *'Nicht schiessen! Nicht schiessen!'* But by this time we were in an infuriated rage. The crewmen were lined up on their knees and an angry soldier walked along behind them and shot each in the back of the head. The last to die was a young, blond-headed teenager who was rocking back and forth on his knees, crying and urinating down both trouser legs. He had pictures of his family spread on the ground before him. Nevertheless, he was shot in the back of the head and pitched forth like a sack of potatoes."[2]

Sgt. Zane Schlemmer of the 82nd Airborne treated POWs differently. "We had developed an *intense* hatred for anything and everything German," he wrote in a memoir. "We were particularly unhappy about sending them, as prisoners, to our rear. We had to stay up there and resented anyone going back to shelter and warmth. So, we always cut their belts and, with our jump knives, cut the buttons off their pants, so that they had to hold up their pants in order to keep them. It was humiliating for them, particularly the officers."[3]

Both the American and the German army outlawed the shooting of unarmed prisoners. Both sides did it, frequently, but no courts-martial were ever convened for men charged with shooting prisoners. It is a subject everyone agreed should not be discussed, and no records were kept. Thus all commentary on the subject is anecdotal.

I've interviewed well over 1,000 combat veterans. Only one of them said he shot a prisoner, and he added that while he felt some remorse he would do it again. Perhaps as many as one-third of the veterans I've talked to, however, related incidents in which they saw other GIs shooting unarmed German prisoners who had their hands up. The general attitude was expressed by Lt. Tom Gibson of the 101st Airborne, who told me in graphic detail of the murder of ten German POWs by an American airborne officer—he shot them while they were digging a ditch and were under guard. Gibson commented: "I firmly believe that only a combat soldier has the right to judge another combat soldier. Only he knows how hard it is to retain his sanity, to do his duty and to survive with some semblance of honor. You have to learn to forgive others, and yourself, for some of the things that are done."[4]

For the airmen who had to bail out over Germany the most dangerous moment was when they hit the ground. If local civilians got to them before military officials arrived, they would attack the Americans with rocks, pitchforks, and hunting weapons. Many were killed by noncombatants overwhelmed by anger and hatred.

In the November fighting, Lieutenant Fussell's infantry platoon came on a deep crater in a forest where a squad or two of German soldiers, some fifteen to twenty men, were gathered. "Their visible wish to surrender—most were in tears of terror and despair—was ignored by our men lining the rim," Fussell later wrote. As the Germans held their hands high, Fussell's men, "laughing and howling, hoo-ha-ing and cowboy and good-old-boy yelling, exultantly shot into the crater until every single man down there was dead. . . . If a body twitched or moved at all, it was shot again. The result was deep satisfaction, and the event was transformed into amusing narrative, told and retold over campfires all that winter."[5]

Sgt. Robert Jamison, 90th Infantry Division, recalled an incident during the Bulge: "We stopped a German tank with our bazooka and retrieved two of its crew. One had been very badly wounded in the leg. Some bastard lieutenant queried him about his outfit and he refused to answer. The lieutenant then shoved him out of the door and shot him in the back. That was the closest I came to killing one of our own."[6]

Capt. Charles Stockell was in position near Elsenborn Ridge. "We had a young private, a sweet natured 19 year old kid, who had two brothers killed in Normandy. It turned him into a fiend where Germans were concerned. He killed every one he could including any prisoner. It had become a court martial offense to send a prisoner back with Junior."

During the Bulge, Stockell was standing with the battalion commander outside headquarters. The CO needed to send a note to one of the companies. He called Junior over and gave him the mission. "Junior trotted off down the street. A German who had been hiding in one of the houses for 72 hours appeared at the front gate, bowing, smiling, hands on his head.

"'*Kamerad! Kamerad!*'

"Junior never broke stride, but pulled his pistol and shot the man in the face as he jogged past. The CO swore and dashed his helmet to the ground; Junior had struck again."[7]

Most of the shooting stories are not so cold-blooded; generally, they are about front-line riflemen immediately after a firefight in which they had seen buddies killed. On the American side, almost never did officers give direct orders to shoot prisoners. The word the paratroopers spread among themselves before D-Day was, "No prisoners, per orders of General Gavin [or Ridgway, or Taylor]," but I've not seen any documentary evidence for this "order," and in fact the paratroopers took many prisoners on June 6. There is a written order from Headquarters, 328th Infantry Regiment, dated December 21, which reads: "No SS troops or paratroopers will be taken prisoner but will be shot on sight."[8]

The excuse for that order was the Malmédy massacre. That event occurred on December 17. Battery B, 285th Field Artillery Observation Battalion of the 7th Armored Division, was moving southward toward St.-Vith when Peiper's lead elements ran into the unit outside Malmédy. Peiper drove into the column, shooting and creating complete confusion. GIs abandoned their vehicles in panic and dove for the ditches or tried to run to the nearby forest. Peiper ordered them rounded up and drove on.

Whether Peiper gave a direct order to shoot the prisoners or not, is not clear. It is known that he had been an adjutant of Heinrich Himmler and that as a battalion commander in Russia he burned two villages and killed all the inhabitants. The veteran SS troops he led in the Ardennes had long experience on the Eastern Front where shooting POWs was a commonplace. Hitler had issued a directive that in the Ardennes the German troops should be preceded "by a wave of terror and fright and that no human inhibitions should be shown." This first came to light when Lt. Col. George Mabry, one of the heroes of Utah Beach on D-Day, reported that his battalion had captured a German colonel who had Hitler's written order on him.[9]

Over the first four days of the Bulge, when his panzers were on the move, Peiper's command murdered approximately 350 American POWs and at least 100 unarmed Belgian civilians. But Peiper was not present at Malmédy while the GIs from Battery B were rounded up, about 150 of them. A second panzer column approached. The Germans parked a tank at either end of a snow-covered field near the wood. A command car drew up. The German officer stood up, pulled his pistol, took deliberate aim at an American medical officer in the front rank of the POWs, and shot him. As the doctor fell, the German shot an officer next to him. Then the two tanks opened up with their machine guns on the POWs.

Pvt. Homer Ford was one of the prisoners. He later testified, "They started to spray us with machine-gun fire, pistols, and everything. Everybody hit the ground. Then they came along with pistols and rifles and shot some that were breathing and hit others in the head with rifle butts. I was hit in the arm, and of the four men who escaped with me, one had been shot in the cheek, one was hit in the stomach, and another in the legs."[10] Men took off for the wood, and many made it. Of the 150 POWs, 70 survived.

As a massacre, by World War II standards, that wasn't much. And Hugh Cole's conclusion in his official history of the Bulge is: "So far as can be determined the Peiper killings represent the only organized and directed murder of prisoners of war by either side during the Ardennes battle."[11] But the cold-bloodedness of the Malmédy atrocity sent an electric shock through the U.S. Army. The dead were discovered by a patrol a couple of hours after the deed. Cole remarked that "the speed with which the news of the Malmédy massacre reached the American front-line troops is amazing." By nightfall the word had gone out to the foxholes—over a 100-kilometer front—that the Germans were shooting American POWs. This had two effects: first, many SS troopers who surrendered were shot; second, GIs who were thinking of surrendering changed their minds.[12]

The Malmédy massacre seemed to many Americans to be the perfect example of Nazi brutality. After the war it was the subject of extensive hearings before a U.S. military tribunal at Dachau. Seventy-three former members of Peiper's SS command were tried.

Forty-three were sentenced to death, twenty-two to life imprisonment, including Peiper, and eight to prison terms of ten years. Many of these sentences were commuted; no one served his full sentence.[13]

American retaliation for Malmédy had already been extracted, by the treatment of SS prisoners who fell into the GIs' hands. Pvt. J. Frank Brumbaugh of the 82nd Airborne remembered hiking past the site of the Malmédy massacre. "GIs and some POWs were out in the field. They were digging the solidly frozen bodies of the murdered American soldiers out of the snow, frozen in grotesque positions with arms and legs in all positions."

An hour or so later, he saw some paratroopers who had a bunch of Germans wearing either U.S. jump boots or infantry combat boots, obviously stolen from captive, wounded, or dead Americans. The American paratroopers shot those wearing combat boots out of hand, on the grounds that if they had taken them from wounded or captured GIs, they may have caused injury or death, because the snow was deep, the weather bitter cold.

"Those German captives found wearing U.S. parachute boots were made to remove the boots and socks, roll their trousers above their knees, and march around in the snow until their feet were totally frozen and they could no longer feel a knife prick, nor walk." The prisoners were sent back to field hospitals, where both feet had to be amputated.

Brumbaugh commented, "I suppose it might be called an atrocity, but I felt at the time it was a brutal but effective means of teaching the Germans a valuable and necessary lesson, which was, you don't f——k with paratroopers!"[14]

During the first days of the Bulge, there were many bizarre incidents involving prisoners. Lt. Walter Melford, a former ASTPer who had earned a commission just before going into combat, was German-born. He had immigrated to the United States with his family in the mid-1930s and grown up in Brooklyn. He was in intelligence and he was in great danger from both sides. When his unit was surrounded, and the colonel was about to surrender, Melford got together with four other native-born Germans who had become GIs. They agreed they could not possibly surrender, and took off. When they encountered an American patrol, Melford called out, "Vee are Americans." Hands up! was the reply, and the five men with German accents wearing American uniforms were all arrested. Melford told an MP that he was from Brooklyn. Who plays shortstop for the Dodgers? Melford didn't know. It took him a couple of days to properly identify himself.

Two months later, Melford was with an armored column attacking in the Ruhr industrial area. The American tanks trapped a German battalion in a large factory. The CO turned to Melford. "It would be quicker and easier if you could talk those guys into surrendering," he said. Melford mounted two loudspeakers on a tank and it lumbered forward. *"Ihr seid vollkommen umzingelt . . . "* he called out ("You are completely surrounded . . ."). A couple of hundred Germans came out waving white flags. The CO told Melford to march them into a liberated Russian POW compound. "I had them lined up in columns of four, and sitting up there holding the mike I gave the order, *'Vorwärts marsch!'* and headed them straight into the compound. It was just wonderful."[15]

One unknown German solved the problem of surrendering with a nice bit of imagination and guts. Twenty-year-old Sgt. James Pemberton of the 103rd Division led a night patrol near Mulhausen. He started off with nine men. On the way back, he counted ten. "I had a problem, but I said nothing because I thought I knew what was going on and couldn't do anything about it. As soon as we got back to headquarters and into a lighted room I had my rifle ready and that Kraut started yelling, *'Kamerad, Kamerad!'* No weapons or anything. He'd been on guard duty, heard us, and decided he'd had enough of the war and just joined my squad and became a POW."[16]

The Germans got their first big bag of American POWs in the opening days of the Bulge, some 20,000 (altogether, the Germans took some 30,000 GIs and 26,000 airmen prisoner in Northwest Europe). The largest haul came on December 19, when two regiments of the 106th Division surrendered. At 7,500 men, this was the largest mass surrender in the war against Germany.

Pvt. Ernest Vermont heard his lieutenant call out, "Cease fire," then, "Destroy your weapons." For Vermont, "that was the worst thing I ever did in my life." The Germans rounded his unit up and started marching the GIs to the rear. They would take watches, spit on the Americans, or cuff them across the head. In one village Vermont was stoned by some Hitler Youth. "The humiliation of being taken prisoner was almost more than I could endure."[17]

Vermont used a word that seemed apt to many of the men of the 106th. Private Vonnegut refused to obey the order to surrender. He took off with three others to try to make it back to American lines. Tall, skinny, no overcoat, no weapon, no boots. Shots rang out. The GIs dove into a ditch. After ten minutes, "They crawled into a forest like the big, unlucky mammals they were." Their luck got worse; they were trapped and forced to surrender. But luck returned: they were not shot but marched off to the east. As they hiked, at each road junction another group of GIs joined them. They were going downhill, like water, growing in numbers as they merged on the main highway on the valley floor. Tens of thousands of Americans shuffled eastward, their hands clasped on top of their heads. Vonnegut called it a "river of humiliation."[18]

Corp. Roger Foehringer of the 99th Division was marched into a barracks, where a young German soldier approached him for interrogation. "I gave him 'the glare' and he gave me the finger. He had good English and the first thing he did was shove his Luger into my stomach and pull the dog tags off my neck." Then he got Foehringer going in a conversation on his home life, what he did before the war, where he went to school. "It wasn't a very thorough interrogation," Foehringer felt. The German almost certainly felt otherwise, that he had gotten everything he could. Corporals don't have much information, in any army.

The following day, December 19, Foehringer began a four-day march. The first day, "we were marching by rows and rows of German troops, tanks and half-tracks and horse-drawn artillery, every imaginable type." They bedded down in a straw pile. They were not fed. On the third day, "we ran out into a sugar beet field that had been turned over. I had never seen a sugar beet in my life, but I ran out in the field and grabbed one and the Germans didn't shoot. And lo and behold it was something that gave me energy, sugar, heat and the strength to go on."

Eventually the GI POWs reached railheads, where they were loaded onto French railway cars that the Germans had used as cattle cars. The floors were covered with manure. The GIs were sealed in, from 80 to 100-plus to a car, so tightly packed together there was not room for a man to sit, much less lie down. Even the dead remained standing. There were no waste facilities beyond an occasional tin bucket. The stench was unbearable, except that it had to be borne. Sometimes twice a day, sometimes once, sometimes not at all, the Germans opened the cars and gave the men water. The long, slow freight trains made ideal targets for P-47s, and the American pilots continually raked the unmarked cars with machine-gun fire and hit them with rockets. Many died, German and American.

Pilot Lt. Jim McCubbin was in a boxcar that two P-47s attacked. Watching the bombs leave the wings, he said, "That gave me a feeling of life in the infantry. I was much more scared than I had ever been in the air." He was thankful that the Germans had a flak car that was shooting back. "If it hadn't been for their firing, the P-47s would have made several more passes. I should know. I had done this frequently."[19]

Private Vermont recalled being strafed by machine-gun fire. "The bullets came through the boxcar killing many men. I believe I was the only one left alive. The others had either been killed or were badly wounded."[20] It was the worst experience almost every man who had it ever had.

When they finally arrived at the various camps in central and eastern Germany, the POWs had widely different experiences, depending on which service they came from, their rank, and most of all the camp administration and guards. Goering had a romantic view of the Knights of the Sky and a sense of brotherhood with fellow pilots; the Luftwaffe ran the camps holding downed flyers; except for inadequate rations, the Army Air Force POWs fared relatively well.[21]

But as one prisoner of the Luftwaffe observed, "The German rations were just enough to insure starvation in its most prolonged and unpleasant form."[22] Lieutenant McCubbin, the P-47 pilot, who was shot down and entered a prison camp near Nuremberg on his twenty-fourth birthday, described the conditions: "The good news was that the soup had peas. The bad news was that over half the peas had worms in them. We soon stopped discarding the worst ones, to just squeezing out the worms, to finally just enjoying the protein. We slept on a hard floor in groups to conserve body heat and to share the one blanket. When one person's pain became unbearable, we would all roll to the other side in unison."[23]

To the prisoners, by far the most important provision of the 1929 Geneva Convention on POWs was the one on rations, which required that they be equal to the ration received by the soldiers of the holding power. In the United States, there was more than enough food and the provision was met, even exceeded. In Europe, priorities had to be set and POWs came toward the end of the list. Nowhere outside the United States were POWs adequately fed. GIs who weighed 180 pounds when captured in the Bulge weighed 120 or 100 pounds when liberated. Private Vermont recorded, "I weighed 140 lbs when I went into prison and weighed 92 pounds when I was released."[24] And the GIs had been marginally better fed than Russian POWs or concentration camp inmates.

In general, meals consisted of black bread and thin potato soup, twice a day. Col. Joe Matthews of the 106th Division recalled that he sometimes got "green hornet soup," made of beet tops and horsemeat. It got its name because its surface was covered with maggots stained green from the beet tops. Among the prisoners there were heated arguments over eating the maggots. Matthews, an agricultural chemist, decided they were protein and ate them.[25]

Enlisted infantrymen fared even worse. One sergeant reported that "I went from 135 pounds to 95 pounds in four months of imprisonment. All we were given to eat was a cup of soup and a piece of ersatz bread each day. This was a systematic brutality to keep us dependent on the next meal and too weak to try to escape. I had frozen feet, jaundice, fleas, lice, dysentery, two foot infections and general malnutrition. . . . The only difference between the concentration camps and the Stalag I was in was that we were not killed off with gas or bullets. . . . I do not remember one act of mercy or compassion on the part of the Germans."[26]

There is ample testimony from those who were there that German officers and guards, at some camps, murdered or ill-treated POWs, by forcing them to labor in inhumane conditions, by torturing them and subjecting them to constant, pointless harassment. There is other testimony that indicates the Germans did the best they could in a difficult situation. And there is something ironic about the inhumane conditions under which many prisoners labored—the cause was the Allied air forces. In city after city, following a raid, POWs in camps nearby were brought in to clean up. That's how Private Vonnegut was brought face-to-face with the horror of a major raid (Dresden, February 1945) and came to write Slaughterhouse-Five.

Corporal Foehringer had a similar experience. He was in

Würzburg in March 1945, when the British firebombed the city. Ordered into a cellar, and then out again, he felt "the most tremendous wind you've ever felt and the whole sky and city of Würzburg seemed to be in flames. The incendiary bombs had hit the roofs of the buildings throughout the city and set them on fire." The fires burnt through the roofs, down the floors, the debris falling inward after it, and incinerated the civilians hiding in the cellars. For the next week, Foehringer and his fellow prisoners worked to remove the debris and carry out the dead.[27]

In most cases, being a POW in World War II was about as bad a human experience as one could have. For certain, there was nothing good to be said about being a POW. Which was worse, being a German in Russian hands or a Russian in German hands? An American in Japanese hands or a Pole in German (or Russian) hands? No one can say, but on a scale of horror they all rank ahead of being an American in German hands.*

How the U.S. Army treated its prisoners is a part of the story of its campaign in Northwest Europe. The Americans took their first big bag of German POWs, over 100,000, in Tunisia in May 1943. Eisenhower complained that they had never taught him at West Point what to do with so many prisoners. The War Department made the commonsense decision to bring them to the States. They could be brought over in troop transports returning from North Africa that would otherwise be empty. They could work on America's farms, where the labor shortage was acute.

I saw my first German soldiers in June 1944 in Whitewater, Wisconsin. They were members of the Afrika Corps and they were frightening to an eight-year-old—big, strong, blond, hardworking, well disciplined. Next to them the GI guard, even with his tommy-gun slung over his shoulder, looked puny. I watched the Germans work alongside my mother at the local pea cannery, sorting debris

*For comparison sake, between 34 and 38 percent of Americans held by the Japanese as prisoners died; about two-thirds of Russian prisoners held in Germany appear to have died; and the proportion of Germans captured on the Eastern Front who died has been estimated as high as 80 percent. In the West, .7 percent of Americans held as POWs by the Germans died; 1 percent of the Germans held by the Americans died. For a full discussion, see Albert Cowdrey, "A Question of Numbers," in Günter Bischof and Stephen E. Ambrose, eds., *Eisenhower and the German POWs: Facts Against Falsehood* (Baton Rouge: Louisiana State University Press, 1992).

out of the shelled peas, and that helped take the Superman image away. These were just farm boys doing what farm boys do.

More big bags of prisoners came at Falaise, and in the fall battles, and then during the Bulge. From August through December, the troop ships bringing young Americans to Europe to fight were taking young Germans to America to farm. Some 400,000 each way.

The best place of all to be in the winter of 1944–45 for a German male born between 1910 and 1927 was in a POW camp in the United States. There the German soldiers had security, shelter, and ample sustenance. They had a soft, cushy life—enhanced by hard physical labor in the day, something most Germans love to do—including university classes in subjects ranging from English literature to advanced mathematics; movies; humane guards; a decent camp administration.

Pvt. Josef Bischof was an Austrian captured in December 1944. He was sent to Colorado, where he worked on beet and potato farms. Many of the farmers whose fields he worked were second-generation German-Americans, still speaking the old language and holding to many of the old ways. "They would tell us," Bischof recalled, " 'Now, boys, if you work hard today my wife will have fried chicken for you tonight, with pie and ice cream,' and we would really pitch in." When the war ended, Bischof wanted to stay in the United States. Austria was in a shambles, he had no family, and "in America they let you work as much as you want." Young and healthy, Bischof figured it would only take him a few years to start climbing, owning his own house, running his own business. But in 1946 he and his buddies were sent home.[28]

POW camps were scattered throughout the United States. Generally the prisoners spent their days in the fields, their nights in barracks previously occupied by the young Americans now sailing to Europe or fighting there. Often, the guards were Negro soldiers.

It is one of the war's many ironies that the soldiers of the nation fighting for racial purity and the domination of the world were shocked by the way white Southerners treated blacks. They said indignantly that Germans had treated the blacks better in their pre–World War I African colonies. And the planters proved the point by treating German POWs better than they did the local black laborers. In the cotton fields, for example, the daily quota for black pickers was 250 pounds, for the POWs, 100 pounds.

In a camp in Louisiana, the Germans suffered terribly from the heat and humidity in the cane fields, but they prospered with the community. They went to the Saturday night movies downtown, where they sat downstairs while the blacks sat in the balcony reserved for "colored." They went unescorted (a man would have had to have been some kind of fool—or Nazi, or both—to try to escape and get back to Germany; I know of only one who did so). They attended local dances; there were some romances and even a few marriages.[29]

The system worked to everyone's benefit. The crops got planted, cultivated, harvested. The prisoners were better off than they ever would have been in the Wehrmacht. The U.S. Army in its treatment of POWs compiled a record of decency and efficiency in an area in which all other countries, save Britain and Canada, must today hang their heads in shame.

In April 1945 a rebuilt American division that had more of its former members in German POW camps than any division in the Army, the 106th Infantry, was rushed from Rennes, France, to Germany to deal with a desperate situation, the mass surrender of hundreds of thousands of German soldiers. The 106th was needed to guard and care for the prisoners. At one point the division was responsible for 330,000 men. Despite a shortage of food, medicine, and shelter, the 106th carried out its mission well. The men earned the commendation from their CO, Maj. Gen. D. A. Stroh: "Your superior performance has reflected great credit to all concerned."[30]

Still there was some brutality, considerable hardship, much illness, and a relatively high death rate. As official Army historian Albert Cowdrey reminds us, conditions in the terribly overcrowded American POW camps in Germany in the spring of 1945 "offer a sobering corrective to any remaining illusion that in World War II all the inhumanity was on one side."[31] But with regard to the widely publicized charge that the United States deliberately starved one million POWs to death, it is a monstrous lie.*

*As shown in Bischof and Ambrose, eds., *Eisenhower and the German POWs.*

Part Four

OVERRUNNING GERMANY

At the beginning of the New Year, the GIs once again went on the offensive. They had rough terrain, the Siegfried Line, mighty rivers, and deep ravines to cross, all defended by German soldiers fighting for their homeland. Conditions were miserable; it was one of the worst winters ever in Northwestern Europe. It was fought, in large part, by citizen soldiers who had been college students or high school graduates in 1944 and became frontline infantry in 1945.

16

Winter War

January 1945

ON NEW YEAR'S EVE, 1944, Lt. John Cobb (USMA 1943) was in a ferry, part of a convoy crossing the English Channel. He was a replacement officer for the 82nd Airborne Division, on his way to Elsenborn Ridge. "Notwithstanding blackout and security conditions," he wrote years later, still somewhat startled, "every ship in the Channel sounded whistles or sirens or shot off flares at midnight on New Year's Eve."[1]

That same night, Corp. Paul-Arthur Zeihe of the 11th Panzer Division was on the front line near Trier. "Just before midnight the shooting stopped almost entirely," he remembered. "As the clock struck twelve, the Americans began with their fireworks, sending illuminated rockets into the air. Suddenly, by the light of their rockets, we saw the Americans getting out of their holes, clutching their rifles and pistols, jumping, skipping around, shooting their weapons and lighting up the whole valley. I can still see them before me today, caught against the light of their rockets, prancing around on a background of fresh snow. It did not take long before we were doing the same thing, firing off illuminated rockets, shooting our weapons.

"It lasted about five, maybe six minutes. It slowed, then stopped. We disappeared back into our holes, and so did they. It was

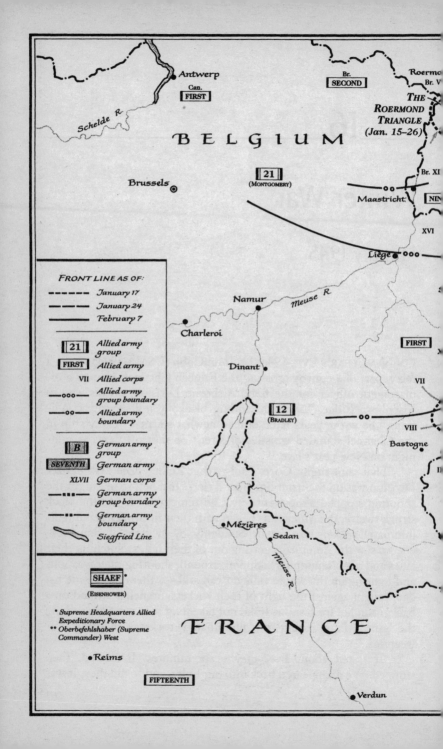

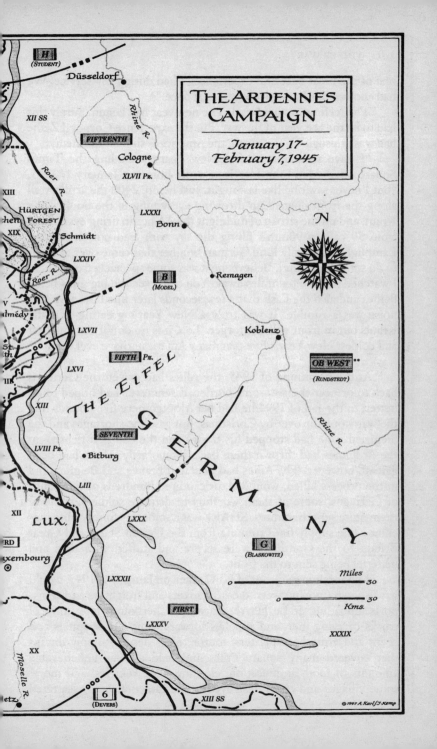

THE ARDENNES CAMPAIGN

*January 17–
February 7, 1945*

H
(STUDENT)

Düsseldorf

XII SS

Rhine R.

FIFTEENTH

Cologne

XLVII Ps.

Roer R.

LXXXI

Bonn

XIII

HÜRTGEN
chen FOREST

XIX

Schmidt

LXXIV

Roer R.

B
(MODEL)

Remagen

N

V

lmédy

LXVII

Koblenz

St
th

LXVI

FIFTH Ps.

THE EIFEL

OB WEST••
(RUNDSTEDT)

IIK

XIII

Rhine R.

LVIII Ps.

SEVENTH

Bitburg

G E R M A N Y

LIII

XII

LUX.

LXXX

RD

xembourg
◎

G
(BLASKOWITZ)

LXXXII

Miles
0 ————————— 30

0 ————————— 30
Kms.

FIRST

LXXXV

XXXIX

XX

Moselle R.

etz

6
(DEVERS)

XIII SS

© 1997 A. Karl / J. Kemp

one of the most beautiful experiences I had during my service. We had allowed our humanity to rise that once."[2]

The feeling was universal. The new year had begun. Surely this had to be the last year of the war. But the experience Corporal Zeihe had was unusual. To the north, the Americans shot at the enemy.

"I have seen quite a few New Years, including the Times Square one," Maj. John Harrison wrote home on January 1, 1945, "but I never saw one like last night. Just before 2400 the artillery all along the front opened up throwing everything in the book at the Kraut, and on the stroke of midnight the AA began firing everything from 50 cals to 90mm's filling the sky with lead poison for any Lamplight Charlie [a lone German bomber that came over at night to do some harassing]. Believe me it was some spectacle from where I watched it some ten miles away. You could see the big guns belch flames and also the flash that a few seconds later filled the sky. The noise was a rumble. It was truly a New Year's greeting that the Krauts out in front will not forget. Too, it is no doubt the loneliest and coldest New Year's Eve that many Americans have ever spent."[3]

At the beginning of 1945, the Allies had driven the Germans back to or near their western border. Eisenhower had hoped to do better; in the fall of 1944 he had bet Montgomery five pounds that the war would be over by Christmas. But gasoline shortages and the Siegfried Line had stopped his troops and the counteroffensive in the Ardennes had thrown them back, temporarily. Much had been gained, however. The Allies had liberated France and Belgium and in the process killed, wounded, or captured hundreds of thousands of Germans, some of them woefully inadequate soldiers, some of them quite superb soldiers. SHAEF was a smoothly functioning machine. The supply lines running from the United States and Great Britain to the Continent were secure and stuffed with men and matériel being sent to the front.

A panoramic snapshot of ETO taken on January 1, 1945, would have shown (moving west to east): tankers and freighters and transports unloading at Le Havre, Antwerp, Cherbourg; long lines of trucks carrying men and supplies forward; tent city hospitals and corps and army headquarters; motor repair depots; supply dumps that covered many square miles and held all but unbelievable amounts of food, ammunition, clothing, fuel, vehicles, and more; some villages and cities destroyed, some intact; airfields scattered across France and Belgium, swarming with activity; a constant movement of tanks, cannon (both self-propelled and towed), jeeps and trucks, all headed east; closer to the German border, the big cannon lined up, the batteries spaced parallel with the front line; aid stations; more cannon; and at the front itself, American troops dug in, cold, hungry, exhausted but victorious.

A panoramic snapshot of Germany, starting in Berlin and going westward, would have shown city after city in ruin, on fire; in rural areas little evidence of war; along the Rhine River the great industrial cities of the Rhine-Ruhr region in ruin; between the Rhine and the Siegfried Line nothing, if the weather was good enough for the Jabos to operate (the most noticeable difference between the two snapshots would have been the complete absence of trucks or trains on the German side); abandoned vehicles, some disabled by the Jabos, some by mechanical problems; no artillery in sight because of camouflage; and at the front itself, German troops dug in, cold, hungry, exhausted, and just defeated in their great offensive gamble.

Two themes dominate the memories of the men who fought the January battles: the cold and American artillery. Every veteran I've ever interviewed, from whatever side, agrees that this was the coldest they had ever been, but disagrees on firepower: each man insists that the other guy had more artillery. GIs can remember shellings that never seemed to have an end; so can the British troops. The GIs and their division, army, and army group commanders complained of a shortage of artillery shells (to which complaint the War Department answered, you are shooting too often), but in fact the Americans had twice as much and more artillery ammunition as the Germans.

This was a triumph of American industry and of the American way of war. This battle was raging along Germany's border. German shells had to travel from a hundred to only a couple of dozen kilometers to reach German guns on the front line. American shells had to travel thousands of kilometers to get there. But such was American productivity, many more American than German shells were arriving. The German attempt to cut Allied supply lines with their submarines had failed; the Allied attempt to cut German supply lines with their Jabos had great success. So the Americans banged away, confident that more shells were on the way. The Germans husbanded their shells, uncertain if any more would ever arrive.

As to the cold, all suffered equally. How cold was it? So cold that if a man didn't do his business in a hurry he risked a frostbitten penis. So cold that Pvt. Don Schoo, an AA gunner attached to the 4th Armored Division, recalled, "I was due on guard and went out to my half track to relieve the man on guard. He couldn't get out of the gun turret. His overcoat was wet when he got in and it froze so he couldn't get out."[4] It was so cold the oil in the engines froze. Weapons froze. Men pissed on them to get them working again, a good temporary solution but one that played hell with the weapon.

Sergeant Schlemmer of the 82nd Airborne wore layers of wool sweaters and overcoats and cut holes in his mummy-type sleeping bag so he could wear that, too. He had modified his wool gloves by slitting the fingers and sewing them together, except for the thumb and trigger finger, thus making them modified mittens. "Even with all this damn clothing, I never was warm," he recalled. Good luck: he acquired a long-haired German dog from a company of German soldiers his platoon had ambushed in a railroad cut. Schlemmer named the dog Adolph. He was Schlemmer's sleeping companion: "We'd curl up against each other wherever we could find a place to sleep."[5]

Nights ranged from zero degrees Fahrenheit to minus ten and lower. Men without shelter—other than a foxhole—or heat either stayed awake, stomping their feet, through the fourteen-hour night, or they froze. Major Harrison had as one of his most vivid memories of that January the sight of GIs pressed against the hot stones of the walls of burning houses, as flames came out of the roof and windows. They were not hiding from Germans; they were trying to get warm for a minute or two.[6]

The GIs, and the Germans opposite them, went through worse physical misery than the men of Valley Forge. Washington's troops had tents, some huts, fires to warm by and provide hot food. They were not involved in continuous battle. By contrast, the conditions in Northwest Europe in January 1945 were as brutal as any in history, including the French and the German retreats from Moscow in midwinter, 1812 and 1941.

But in this battle, the Germans were not retreating. They fought back against the American advance, which could barely move forward anyway in the ice and snow, forcing the Americans to pay the highest price possible for taking back the territory lost in the Bulge. But the generals from Eisenhower down insisted that the AEF go over to the offensive. Eisenhower had under his command seventy-three divisions. Of the total, forty-nine were American, twelve British, three Canadian, one Polish, and eight French. He had forty-nine infantry, twenty armored, and four airborne divisions. As against this, the Germans had seventy-six divisions. Some were second-rate, most traveled by horse or foot, all were understrength, a few were excellent. A SHAEF G-2 summary of January 3 declared, "Special units . . . composed of extremely good type young soldier with high morale and considerable faith in victory. Some adopted view that it was either case of victory or death since nothing left if Germany lost war. . . . Volksgrenadier Divisions rather mixed but generally good. . . . German soldier is fighting with great determination and bravery. Desertions few."[7]

Given the near equality in firepower, the absence of fighter-bomber support on most January days owing to weather, and the brutality of conditions—snowbanks, icy roads, rough terrain—a general winter offensive had little appeal. Nevertheless Eisenhower decided to launch attacks north and south of the Bulge, in an attempt to trap the Germans at its western tip and to regain the ground lost in the second two weeks of December. He felt he had no option. The Allies could not shut down offensive operations while the V-1s and V-2s continued to bombard Antwerp, London, and other cities. They could not stop seeking the earliest possible victory when the Nazis were exhorting the German people: stay with it just a little longer, secret war-winning weapons were on the way. Who knew what they might be? The jet fighter plane and the V-weapons were dangerous enough.

Eisenhower wasn't alone in planning a January offensive. Hitler launched one of his own on New Year's Day—Operation Northwind, an attack in Alsace. The Red Army, meanwhile, was preparing for its biggest offensive ever, set for January 12. January 1945 was to see more fighting than any January in history.

The initial January offensive by the Allies was directed against the German salient. Montgomery had wanted to attack west to east, to drive the Germans out of the Bulge (actually, he thought the weather too severe for offensive operations and didn't want to attack at all, but the pressure on him was irresistible). Eisenhower and

Bradley wanted to attack the base of the salient from the north with U.S. First Army and from the south with U.S. Third Army. But Patton had already put the bulk of his striking power into the relief of Bastogne, and thus had his center of gravity in the middle of the Bulge, not at its southeastern base. And Monty absolutely refused to attack along the northeastern base—the most he would agree to was an attack on the flank. So it was agreed that First and Third Armies would meet at Houffalize, a village some five miles north of Bastogne. When the linkup took place, the Bulge would be cut in half. "The small solution," German generals sniffed.

Eisenhower had wanted Monty to get First Army started on January 1, and thought he had a promise from Montgomery to do just that. But Monty delayed until January 3, which made Eisenhower furious, even though the cold, snow, and overcast on January 1 and 2 so badly hampered Third Army that it had to issue orders to hold in position regiments and divisions that had been alerted to attack.

Montgomery, meanwhile, sent a letter to Eisenhower demanding that he, Montgomery, be given full control of the land battle, now that Eisenhower's strategy had been tried and failed. And of course there should be a single thrust, in the north, with Patton placed in a holding role. Montgomery presented Eisenhower with a directive to those ends for Eisenhower's signature.

Instead of signing, Eisenhower issued his own directive. He returned First Army to Bradley's control and insisted that there would be a broad-front advance into Germany once the Bulge had been eliminated. "The one thing that must now be prevented," he emphasized, "is the stabilization of the enemy salient with infantry, permitting him opportunity to use his Panzers at will on any part of the front. We must regain the initiative, and speed and energy are essential."[8]

In a covering note, Eisenhower was simple, direct, forceful. "I do not agree," Eisenhower said of Montgomery's argument for a single ground commander. He said he had done all he could for Monty and did not want to hear again about placing Bradley under Montgomery's command. "I assure you that in this matter I can go no further." He added, "I have planned an advance" to the Rhine on a broad front and ordered Montgomery to read his directive carefully. All the vagueness of earlier letters and directives to Montgomery was now gone. The "I" stood for the United States.

In conclusion, Eisenhower told Montgomery that he would no longer tolerate debate on the subject of command. "I would deplore the development of such an unbridgeable gulf of convictions between us that we would have to present our differences to the CCS," he said, but if Montgomery went any further that was exactly what he would do.[9]

Montgomery knew who would go if Eisenhower told the CCS it is him or me. He replied with a cable asking Eisenhower to tear up the letter demanding sole command of the ground forces and followed it up with a handwritten letter. "Dear Ike," Monty began, "you can rely on me and all under my command to go all out one hundred percent to implement your plan."[10]

For the front-line infantry, armor, and artillery of U.S. First and Third Armies, that plan put them into one of the most God-awful offensives of this or any other war. All but forgotten today, the battle that raged through January was for the GIs among the worst of the war, if possible even more miserable than Hurtgen or Metz. There was no glamour, little drama, zero maneuver. It was just straight-ahead attack, designed to eliminate the Bulge and then return to the German border. It was fought in conditions so terrible that they can only be marveled at, not really imagined. Only those who were there can know. More than once in interviewing veterans of the January fighting, when I ask them to describe the cold, men have involuntarily shivered.

These were the combat soldiers of ETO. At this time they numbered about 300,000. Perhaps half the enlisted were veterans, including replacements or men in divisions who had come into the battle in November or December and including many who had been wounded once or twice. In the junior officer ranks, the turnover had been even greater, almost three-quarters. Still there was a corps of veterans in most of the divisions, including junior officers who had won battlefield promotions—the highest honor a soldier can receive, and the source of outstanding junior officers—and sergeants, most of whom by this stage were the privates of Normandy, St.-Lô, Falaise, Holland, and the Bulge, survivors who had moved up when the original NCOs were killed or wounded. These newly made lieutenants and sergeants, some of them teenage boys, most of them in their early twenties, provided the core leadership that got the U.S. Army through that terrible January.

There were some unusual junior officers on the front. One was Lt. Ed Gesner of the 4th Infantry Division. He was a forty-year-old who had been transferred out of OSS because he was too old to jump behind enemy lines. He knew survival tricks that he taught his platoon, such as how to create a foxhole in a hurry in frozen ground (he shot eight rounds into the same spot, quickly dug out the loose dirt with his trench knife, placed a half stick of TNT in the hole, lit the fuse, ran back thirty meters, hit the dirt, got up and ran back before the dust settled and dug with his trench shovel; within minutes, a habitable foxhole).

Another officer in Gesner's battalion described him in action that January: "He was all over the place, moving his platoon. I saw him using three different weapons—a carbine, an M-1, and a Thompson .45-cal. He seemed to be firing a lot more than most officers, and instead of stopping to reload he'd trade guns with one of his men or pick up a fallen man's weapon. They all thought he was great. One time when he ran out of ammo at the edge of a trench he jumped in and began to club a German with his rifle butt. The poor German quickly threw his hands up."[11]

The junior officers coming over from the States were another matter. Pink-cheeked youth, they were bewildered by everything around them. Major Winters, himself a private back in 1942, commented that during the Bulge: "I looked at the junior officers and my company commanders and I ground my teeth. Basically we had weak lieutenants. I didn't have faith in them. What the hell can I do about this?" He decided, "In a pinch, talk to your sergeants."*

The sergeants told him who among the replacement officers was weak, who looked like he was going to get men killed, who looked like he might make it. Winters did what he could to get his most experienced NCOs with the weakest officers and scattered the veterans among the lieutenants as best he could. He knew whom to keep an eye on—and the following day he replaced a company commander in the middle of an attack. He also gave battlefield promotions to a number of his sergeants.[12]

In the hundreds of companies stretched along the front, similar

---

*Sgt. Josh Honan of the Canadian Army was addressing a military cadet school in Ireland in 1996. Question: "What would you say is the most important thing a good officer should possess?" "A good sergeant," Honan replied. He added, "Good officers don't arrive ready-made from officer school. Sergeants have to retrain them."

scenes were taking place before and during the great offensive. Lieutenant Otts had a company commander who was uncomfortable at the front. On January 9, the captain told Otts he was going back to battalion CP and Otts should take over. "I told him he was going to have another case of battle fatigue on his hands and lose his last lieutenant if I was left alone in command of the company much longer. He just laughed, told me I would be all right, and took off. I was only a 2nd lieutenant and just twenty-two years old."[13]

When the order to attack got down to the line companies, the men were outraged. "I could not believe it," Sgt. John Martin of the 101st declared. After two weeks of fighting surrounded, "I could not believe that they were going to put us on the attack. I figured, Jesus, they'll take us out of here and give us some clothes or something." Major Winters said, "It pissed me off. I could not believe that after what we had gone through and done, after all the casualties we had suffered, they were putting us into an attack."[14] The GIs of all the divisions who had fought in the Bulge felt the same.

It wasn't just that they figured it was some other guy's turn; it was that they were exhausted, completely drained even before they jumped off. Practically every one of the men had a bad cold and runny nose to add to the misery (pneumonia sent many back to hospitals)[15]—and they were jumping off into conditions that would have taxed them to the breaking point at their peak physical condition. In the woods in the Ardennes, the snow was a foot and more deep, frozen on top, slippery, noisy. To advance, a man had to flounder through the snow, bending and squirming to avoid knocking the snow off the branches and revealing his position. Visibility on the ground was limited to a few meters. An attacker had little contact with the men on his left and right, and he could not see a machine-gun position or a foxhole until he was almost on top of it. There were no roads, houses, or landmarks in the woods. Squads on the attack had to move on compass bearings until they bumped into somebody, friend or enemy.

Attacking along the roads was near impossible, because they were ice-coated on top, with black ice under the snow. German 88s were zeroed in on the roads, which were also mined. But attacking through the cleared grazing fields was equally daunting. There was no concealment and many of the GIs had no camouflage of any kind.

On January 9, an officer from the Criminal Investigation Division of the 26th Division asked Col. Ken Reimers of the 90th Division if he had a Lieutenant Barry in his outfit. Reimers did. The CID officer wanted to arrest Barry; it seemed he had stolen some sheets from a civilian house in the 90th's area and cut holes in the center of them. The CID officer claimed a lot of looting had been going on and that he was going to put a stop to it. But Reimers asked some questions and discovered that Barry had hit on the idea of sheets for camouflage in the snow, and had distributed one to every man in his platoon. When Reimers explained this to the division commander, Gen. Earnest Bixby, Bixby said, "Promote him." Reimers explained that Barry was already a first lieutenant. "Well, give him a Bronze Star then, for his initiative."[16]

Under the sheet, if he was lucky enough to have one, the average infantryman had the pockets of his combat jacket crammed with rations, shaving articles, pictures, cigarettes, candy, dry socks, writing paper and pens, and mess kit with spoon and fork. He had his raincoat folded over the back of his belt or wore it to help keep warm. He carried from two to four Army-issue thin wool blankets and a shelter-half slung over his shoulder. Whenever the GIs had to make a forced march of more than just a few miles the roadside would be strewn with blankets, overcoats, overshoes, and gas masks. A truck would follow along behind, collect the equipment, bring it forward, and reissue it—hopefully before dark.

Pvt. Lester Atwell of the 87th Division described what attacking across the snowy fields was like: "We started out. Then there came the long, wild scream and crash of German artillery, and then the double line, thin-looking without overcoats, indistinct in the swirling snow, wavered and sank down flat, then struggled up and went on, heads bend against the wind. This was 'jumping off,' this cold, plodding, unwilling, ragged double line plunging up to their knees in snow, stumbling, looking back."[17]

Kurt Gabel of the 17th Airborne Division was in the opening attack on January 3, near Mande-St.-Etienne, some ten kilometers north of Bastogne. His platoon moved in a column through a wood, then spread out to cross an open, snow-covered field. "Suddenly the air directly above us was alive with sounds I had not heard before," Gabel wrote. It was the screeching sound of the "screaming meemies," the German *Nebelwerfer*, or multiple rocket.

"The first salvo crashed into our formation as the next rounds already howled above us. The platoon leader spread his arms and yelled, 'Hit it!' I hit the snow, face first, and felt multiple concussions as the rockets pounded down. They howled and burst, and I clawed the ground and whimpered inside, now knowing that this was carefully preregistered concentration, a fire trap that the Germans had waited for us to walk into and lie down in."

Between explosions, Gabel heard a yell, "Move!" It struck him as incongruous. He turned his head as best he could while pressing his body into the ground, and saw to his right "a captain running toward the rifle squad. 'Get up!' he yelled, his face contorted with rage. 'Get up, you stupid bastards. You'll die here. There's no cover. Move! Move!' He grabbed one soldier by the shoulder and kicked another. I had never seen that kind of rage. 'Get 'em up, goddamn it!' he bellowed, thrusting his fist up and down in the signal for double time."

Gabel was more than impressed: "The rockets seemed to lose their terror next to that captain. I did not know who he was and did not care. I jumped up and stumbled forward." Others did the same. The platoon got to the far side of the open field. The men threw themselves down in a drainage ditch, exhausted.

"Fix bayonets!" Gabel felt the shock of the order jerk his body. "Fix bayonets? That's World War I stuff. Bayonets were for opening C-ration cans." Not this day. All around Gabel, "there was the blood-freezing sound of fourteen bayonets drawn from scabbards and clicking home on their studs under the rifle barrels."

"Let's go," the platoon leader called out. All fourteen men jumped out of the ditch, formed into a line of skirmishers, rifles at high port, and moved toward the German position. They began shouting "Geronimo!" Gabel screamed with the others. They got into the German lines. Enemy soldiers tried to lift their hands. Still yelling, troopers thrust their bayonets into the Germans. They took the village; their reward was that they got to spend the night in town.[18]

One thing that kept many of those thrown into these early January attacks going was the thought of where they would spend the night. They had left their overcoats and sleeping bags behind. That day's objective, usually, was the next small village to the east. "It was something to live for," Pvt. Jack Ammons of the 90th Division remembered.[19] If the GIs could drive the Germans from the houses before dark, why then it would be the GIs occupying the cellars, out of the wind, with a bit of heat, a chance to sleep. If the Germans held the town, the GIs would spend the first hours of darkness digging foxholes in frozen ground, in the wood nearest the village, and the remainder of the night stomping in the foxholes, staying awake to keep from freezing—and then have to move out on another attack in the morning.

It sometimes happened that the Germans occupied one set of cellars, the GIs the other. Occasionally they shared the same cellar, unknown to each other until the morning. Private Schoo went into a cellar and found three German soldiers sleeping on the floor. Schoo got a couple of buddies and they woke the Germans up. One could speak English. "We had them get wood for a fire, we heated food and coffee for all—we sat up all night talking, in the morning we took them back to HQ (they were nice guys)."[20]

Another characteristic of the January fighting was the horror created by a high incidence of bodies crushed by tanks. Men slipped, tanks skidded. The wounded couldn't get out of the way. Twenty-year-old Dwayne Burns of the 82nd Airborne saw a fellow paratrooper who had been run over by a tank. "If it hadn't been for the two pair of legs and boots sticking out of all the gore, it would have been hard to tell what it was. I looked away and thought for sure that I was going to vomit. I just wanted to throw my weapon away and tell them I quit. No more, I just can't take no more."[21]

But he had to, because the pressure from above to keep moving was irresistible. The generals wanted results, so the colonels wanted results, so the men kept moving, no matter what. The 3rd Battalion of the 513th Parachute Infantry Regiment, 17th Airborne, provides one example of how the junior officers responded to the pressure and managed to get more out of the men than the men knew they had it in them to give. By afternoon of January 6, the battalion had lost its CO and most of the hq staff to an artillery shell. Two company commanders were out of action. In I Company, Lt. Eugene "Fatboy" Crowley had assumed command.

That evening, orders came from regiment down to battalion to take the village of Flamierge. Battalion didn't get the orders out to Lieutenant Crowley until midnight, and then the plan was a bad one: to attack at 0900. When Crowley gathered his platoon leaders and told them what was expected, Lt. J. Dickson Phillips of the 2nd platoon protested against "the very idea of going in broad daylight over snow-covered, open terrain, completely dominated by an enemy-held ridge, when at least a good part of the attack route could be crossed in darkness." Crowley gave the stock reply: orders were orders.

At 0900 Crowley led the way. At first, a silent advance of 165 or so men spread across the field, which rose up to a ridgeline. When the Americans were half across the 300-meter-wide field, three German tanks appeared on the ridge. They opened fire with their cannons and machine guns. The Americans burrowed into the snow, trying to hide, out of bazooka range (100 meters at best), nothing to fire back with except rifles. After taking casualties for fifteen minutes, Crowley ordered a retreat. Pvt. Don Scott recalled, "we were like jack-in-the-boxes popping up and down all over, trying to dash ten steps and dive into the snow again. For the German tankers it was target practice time with live targets." Fewer than 100 men made it back to the starting line.

Crowley reorganized and regrouped, then ordered another attack. Again he led the way, creeping and crawling, the men following. They got about halfway up the hill again when the tanks reappeared and drove them off, once more with heavy casualties.

Then occurred the bravest action Private Scott saw in the war. A bazooka man and his assistant gunner started crawling up the slope, toward the tanks. About halfway there, they stopped and appeared to have an argument. "Then the assistant turned and started crawling back toward the American lines," Scott recalled. "The bazooka man continued crawling toward the tanks 200 yards away, carrying the load of bazooka shells, still unseen by the enemy. When he got within 100 yards of the tank he took a shot at one. It landed 10 yards short. That caught the Germans' attention and before he could reload (the bazooka is a two-man weapon) the tankers just blew him up with cannon and machine gun fire.

"When the assistant gunner stood up to make his last dash to the baseline foxholes, someone shot him."

Lieutenant Crowley ordered another attack. "This time let's see if we can pick up some bazookas along the way and get those bastards," he barked. "We started creepy-crawling up that damn hill again," Scott remembered. "When we got to 150 yards of the tanks, they fired one last 88 and then withdrew. Just plain turned around, pulled over the crest of the ridge and went away." They had most likely run out of ammunition.

I Company followed. On the downhill slope leading into

Flamierge the Americans were fired on by enemy infantry, "but rifle fire was not all that daunting after the bloodbath from the tanks. We just charged right in and the Germans had to run out the other side of town."[22] At a cost of half his company, Crowley had taken the objective.

Not all company commanders were so willing to follow orders unquestioningly. On at least one occasion, two company commanders simply refused to carry out a direct order to attack. They were Capt. Jay Prophet and Lt. Harold Leinbaugh, commanding Companies A and K of the 333rd Infantry Regiment, 84th Division. The morning after a night spent in a wood, under regular shelling, the battalion commander, a colonel, came to the front and ordered A and K Companies to advance another half mile. Prophet refused. So did Leinbaugh. Prophet protested that all the weapons were frozen, the companies were at half strength, the men exhausted. The colonel threatened a court-martial.

"Colonel," Prophet replied, "there's nothing I'd like more right now than a nice warm court-martial."

The colonel refused to believe the weapons were frozen. Prophet ordered a test. Not one of the weapons could be fired. The colonel began to chew out the captains for their own and their men's appearance. He said it looked like no one had shaved for a week. Leinbaugh said there was no hot water. The colonel, who prided himself on being a product of the old National Guard, gave a tip: "Now if you men would save some of your morning coffee it could be used for shaving." Leinbaugh stepped over to a snowbank, picked up the five-gallon GI coffee can brought up that morning, and shook it in the colonel's face. The frozen coffee produced a thunk. Leinbaugh shook it again.

"That's enough," said the colonel. "Goddammit, I can hear."[23]

In most cases, the colonel's will prevailed. Lt. Col. William DuPuy, CO of a battalion in the 90th Division, came across a squad of mortarmen and some riflemen huddled at the edge of an embankment just short of the village of Doncols. "Who's in charge here?" he barked.

"I'm first sergeant of C Company, Colonel," Sgt. John Peterson answered.

"Well, let's get these men into town. You aren't doing any good out here."

"But they've got a bead on us from those windows up there, sir."

"No buts. Get these men moving. Let's go!"

Peterson pulled his .45 from the holster and yelled, "Okay, follow me, you guys!" He started through an opening in the embankment. As the men struggled to their feet behind him, a bullet got Peterson in the head. He fell dead at Colonel DuPuy's feet. DuPuy was stunned. He just stood there. Then he called out, "Follow me," and started down the embankment, looking for another opening.[24]

For the Germans, their physical misery was exacerbated by the terrible thought that what they were doing was the absolutely worst thing they could do for their country and the German people. It was perfectly obvious to every one of them. As Lt. Walter Rahn of the 11th Panzer Division put it, "Why were we holding up the Americans in the west and allowing the Russians to penetrate Germany? It was senseless what we were doing there, fighting the Americans."[25]

For the sake of their families, their homes, their countries, the German soldiers should have packed it up on the Western Front and gone east to defend against the Red Army. Only Hitler and his Nazis could benefit from continuing to fight the Western Allies. That the tens of thousands of German soldiers in this situation, knowingly fighting against their own best interests, could carry on, effectively and bravely, was a triumph of discipline and dictatorship.

They suffered terribly, from the weather and from the Americans. "We had never seen the way a rich man fights a war," Col. Gerhard Lemcke said, referring to American artillery.[26] Capt. Gerhard Winkler, a tank commander, recalled: "When you're sitting in a tank in a forward position and you're seen, fear that makes your knees shake comes on. It always did when you are helpless and exposed. The Americans, who had more than enough ammunition, covered us with shells for one or two hours. We sat inside the tank, with dry mouths, not saying a lot, smoking one cigarette after another, hoping that the shells will miss you."[27]

Bad as it was to be shelled in a tank, Maj. Helmut Ritgen of Panzer Lehr found his heart went out to the infantry. In a 1995 interview, he said, "The infantry had to hold the Americans back, and retreat on foot, crossing rivers with no bridges and so forth, in midwinter. I'm a tanker, but the infantry was the real miracle arm of

Hitler." Ritgen paused, then added, "I think it would be impossible for the present generation."[28]

When the offensive began on January 3, the U.S. First Army and Third Army were separated by twenty-five miles of rugged hills and gorges, frozen rivers, tortuous icy roads, snow-laden forests, and tens of thousands of battle-hardened German troops who were highly skilled in utilizing terrain features and villages as fortified positions. From the south, the lead units of Third Army—the 26th and 90th Divisions—moved out toward Houffalize. To the north, First Army lurched forward.

The 82nd Airborne was one of First Army's divisions. It was attacking southward from Trois-Ponts. Colonel Vandervoort's battalion of the 505th PIR was in the van. "January 3rd dawned cold and foggy, and more snow expected," the regimental history recounted. "Before moving out everyone left his musette bags, sleeping bag, and overcoat in a pile and fervently hoped that supply sergeants would be able to get them forward before dark." H-Hour was 0830. The men jumped off and initially all went well. Then an open field stretched between them and the village of Fosse, the first objective. Small-arms fire came on them in such volume that it was impossible to advance. Nevertheless company and platoon commanders tried to get the men to follow—only to be shot down themselves before taking a half dozen floundering steps in the two-foot-deep snow. Colonel Vandervoort got artillery on the German position, and sent a couple of Shermans to support the infantry. The barrage forced the Germans to pull out, and the paratroopers moved into Fosse. But they were not allowed to settle down in the cellars; they moved out to a wood where they dug in for the night.

Sgt. William Tucker, waiting for his turn to get patched up at the aid station, saw Lt. Col. Edward Krause, of the division staff, pacing up and down. Krause had come out of I Company; every officer of the company had been killed or wounded that day. Two-thirds of the men were casualties. These men were veterans of North Africa, Sicily, Italy, Normandy, Holland, and the Bulge.

"Well, colonel," Tucker said softly, "a lot of the old boys got it today." Colonel Krause did not reply. He looked away as his eyes filled with tears.

As the temperature dropped and the snow continued to fall, the 505th learned that the trucks couldn't get through the fields to bring on their gear, so there would be no overcoats, packs, or sleeping bags. Water was a problem because the canteens froze solid. The cold and exposure caused old wounds to flare up and, remarkably, triggered many relapses of malaria that had been contracted in the Mediterranean. The regimental history comments, "Although the plight of the men was bad enough, that of the wounded in many cases was tragic. Despite the heroic efforts of the Medics (many of whom became casualties themselves) who labored unceasingly all night long, some of the more seriously wounded died of exposure."

In the morning, January 4, the sleepless men of Companies B and C resumed their attack—really, slogging through the snow, one man breaking trail for two followers, with two tanks in support. They came to an open hill, strongly defended. The tanks rolled forward and began raking the hillside with .50-caliber bullets and 75mm shells. "Everyone opened fire, shooting as fast as they could pull triggers and load clips. In a very short time (probably less than a minute), German soldiers started popping out of holes with their hands in the air." Cease fire! Sgt. Herman Zeitner called out. The firing died down.

"Then an incredible spectacle occurred. From every position on that hill, Germans began climbing out of holes while troopers stood there with their mouths wide open at the sight of approximately 200 Germans milling around." Amazingly, in this encounter the 505th, which had suffered so grievously the previous day, had nary a scratch.

January 5 and 6 were more of the same—a kilometer or so advance each day. The good news on January 6 was that the engineers had bulldozed a road through the fields to the front, so trucks could bring the GIs their cold-weather gear. On January 7, the bad news was that at 0800 hours Colonel Vandervoort was hit by mortar fire. "This stunned the battalion," the regimental history notes, "which had come to believe that its long-time commander was invincible." The wounds were disabling; eventually they ended his Army career prematurely. As Army historian S. L. A. Marshall put it, "The U.S. Army lost a file that was destined for higher command."[29]

The German retreat out of the Bulge was slow, stubborn, and costly to the Americans—but to the Germans also. Hitler, always insistent on holding captured ground, refused to consider pulling out of the Bulge and returning to the Siegfried Line. In order to hold in the Bulge, and thus retain the threat of an offensive thrust westward, Hitler attacked in Alsace with the idea of preventing further American reinforcements moving north to the Ardennes.

Operation Northwind, starting January 1, hit Lt. Gen. Alexander Patch's U.S. Seventh Army. Eventually a total of fifteen U.S. divisions with 250,000 men were involved in the fighting, which took place along a front that ran almost 150 kilometers from Saarbrücken in the north to a point on the west bank of the Rhine south of Strasbourg. This was a natural salient along the bend of the Rhine, so the battle was something of a mirror image of the one going on to the north in the Ardennes.

Behind the salient, the Alsatian Plain stretched westward from the Rhine to the foothills of the Vosges Mountains. It was unsuitable to the defense. The textbook response to the Northwind attack would have been to fall back on the rough country and leave the plain to the Germans. That was what Eisenhower wanted to do, but politics intervened. De Gaulle told the Supreme Commander that if they were cadets at military school he would agree with Eisenhower's opinion, but as the French leader he absolutely could not accept abandoning Strasbourg, not only for reasons of national pride but because of the fearful reprisals the Gestapo was sure to take on the citizens of Strasbourg. Eisenhower reluctantly agreed and the order went out to Seventh Army: hold your ground. As a result, bitter battles were waged through January at Wingen, Philippsbourg, Herrlisheim, Rittershoffen, and elsewhere.

Col. Hans von Luck's 125th Regiment of the 21st Panzer Division had the mission of breaking through the American lines on the northwestern base of the salient, cutting across the eastern foothills of the Vosges and thus severing the American supply line to Strasbourg. That required, of all things, breaking through the Maginot Line. It ran east–west in this area, following the Rhine River bend. The Maginot Line, built at such great expense, had seen no fighting to speak of in 1940—the Germans went around it—but in January 1945 a part of the line was used for the purpose it had been designed for and showed what a superb fortification it was.

On January 7, Luck approached the Line south of Wissembourg, at Rittershoffen. "Suddenly we could make out the first bunker, which received us with heavy fire. Our leading men and the accompanying SPV landed in thick minefields; the artillery stepped up its barrage of fire."[30] The Americans, composed of men from the

Winter 1945

St.-Hubert Forest, Belgium, January 1. Pvt. John Mincek and Pvt. Luther Jack, at their machine gun, protecting Third Army headquarters.

Street fighting in Saarlautern, January 2. The tank is firing at a house with eight snipers and a heavy machine gun.

The cold was intense during the Bulge, often below zero on the Fahrenheit scale, seldom above thirty-five degrees. *Left:* Making foxholes in Belgium, January 2. These men from the 2nd Division have learned one way to deal with frozen ground. *Below: An* unidentified GI from the 35th Infantry Division takes up his position on the newly established front line near Bastogne, January 3.

OPPOSITE:
Top: Belgium, January 5. The men of Company I, 84th Division, head east on the offensive.

Center: Luxembourg, January 5. A German POW helps GIs carry a wounded German soldier. Both Germans were teenagers.

Below: January 5, Belgium. 2nd Infantry Division men get ready for whatever might come.

Left: Chow time in the Hurtgen Forest, January 5. Somehow the quartermasters and cooks managed to get hot food to the front line—sometimes.

Above: The Ardennes, January 6. A GI looks over a frozen German casualty.

Left: Corp. Irvin Kruger, 4th Cavalry Reconnaissance Squadron, Beffe, Belgium, January 7, trying to spot German snipers.

Near Bastogne, January 8. The 4th Armored Division on the attack—on foot.

Men of the 90th Infantry Division wait out a shelling, Wiltz, Luxembourg, January 9.

The snow covered the Ardennes from before Christmas until well into February. *Top:* Pvt. Jesse Kenner, 501st PIR, 101st Airborne, displays his bazooka from his half shelter outside Foy, Belgium, January 11. *Center:* Sgt. Raymone Horner and Pvt. Romaine Mounts, in a new M-24 light tank, January 14. *Below:* Pvt. Roy Jordan digs in for a night in the Ardennes, January 14. Once a man got through the frozen earth, the digging was easier, although never easy.

Left: Supply trucks bring up the chow. Belgium, January.

Below: In the Ardennes, or in any wooded area, GIs supplemented their rations with fresh meat. Here Pvt. Clinton Calvert and Corp. Roy Swisher bring some in. Luxembourg, January 12.

Right: Belgium, January 12. The GIs were on the offensive by this time; they left their bedrolls when they attacked; here Sgts. Nicholas Esposito and Charles Lynch tear loose their frozen sleeping bags, which they will bring forward to the front line, with luck before dark.

Left: A Sherman tank advances in Belgium, January 14. By this time everyone was heartily sick of the snow, no matter how pretty.

Below: Pvts. James Acosta and Kenneth Horgan, 3rd Armored Division, in the Ardennes, January 14, have their bazooka handy in the event of a German armored attack. Clear days with sunshine meant colder nights, but they also meant the U.S. Army Air Force could fly, a blessing to the ground troops.

Battery B, 37th Field Artillery, 2nd Infantry Division, Belgium, January 18.

January 23. GIs from the 78th Division trying to master cross-country skiing. Few GIs had any training in winter war and precious little suitable clothing. These men are wearing bedsheets taken from Belgian houses.

Above: A mortar crew from the 7th Armored Division at work near St.-Vith, January 24.

Right: Pvt. Joe Fink digs his foxhole with a pickax. January 30, Wirtzfeld, Belgium.

Below: February 2, Horsbach, France. Pvt. Vincent Wenge, 70th Division, bails out his foxhole after a temporary thaw.

The Rhine and Victory

Above: Rhineland fighting, February 27. Men from the U.S. Ninth Army move forward.

Right: Kerpen, Germany, February 28. Mortar crews firing in close support of advancing infantry.

Below: Infantry from the 1st Division in Gladbach, Germany, March 1. German attempts to defend the flat Rhineland from troops like these were futile, costly, and senseless.

By March, the U.S. Army in Northwest Europe was made up of relatively few veterans and lots of replacements, many of them 1944 high school graduates. After a few days on the line, the replacements became veterans, capable of a high level of combat effectiveness. *Above:* A 105mm cannon in action outside Erp, Germany, March 6. *Below:* Street fighting in Koblenz, March 18.

These photographs were taken by Capt. William Mustanich of the 254th Field Artillery battalion. On March 12, his company crossed the Rhine River on a pontoon bridge to take up positions on the east bank. On March 17, it had orders to move. A few minutes before 1500, as his vehicles passed under the Ludendorff Bridge, he snapped this shot, saying as he did so, "This damn bridge has made history." Ten minutes later, the bridge collapsed. He turned and got this shot, *below*. *(Two photos courtesy William Mustanich)*

The most welcome sight in the world for these Polish prisoners in Dachau was the appearance of GIs. The Poles ran up a homemade American flag to welcome their liberators, men of the 45th Division.

Corp. Larry Mutinsk, 45th Division, hands out his last pack of cigarettes to prisoners in Dachau.

SS guards at Dachau had been lined up by men of the 45th Division. One of the guards made a break for it, which brought forth a volley of fire from the GIs. All but three of the SS guards fell to the ground, feigning death.

German officers wait along the autobahn near Giessen, Germany, watching vehicles of the U.S. 6th Armored Division move up to the front.

By March 29,1945, the U.S. Army was over the Rhine and pouring into Germany. These German POWs, marching west to their POW camps, were astonished at the number of trucks, tanks, half- tracks, and vehicles of all kinds their enemy possessed. But in the end, what beat the Wehrmacht was not so much equipment as men. The GIs had proven themselves; here was the fruit of their victory.

79th Infantry Division, the 14th Armored Division, and elements of the 42nd Infantry Division, utilized the firing points, trenches, retractable cannon, and other features of the Line to the fullest. They stopped the Germans cold.

Over the next two days, the Germans reinforced the attack, with new 88s and some tanks, along with the 25th Panzer Division. They again assaulted the Line. At one point, they managed to drive the Americans out by getting close enough to throw grenades into the embrasures, but they were immediately driven back by heavy artillery fire.

Still the Germans came on. At times the battle raged inside the bunkers, a nerve-shattering experience made worse by the ear-shattering noise of explosives. Eventually Luck got through. On January 10, he moved his regiment forward for an attack on Rittershoffen, preparatory to assaulting another part of the Maginot Line from the rear (the French defenses were all pointed east), in order to widen the breach. That night, he got into the village, but was not able to drive the Americans out. They held one end, Luck's men held the other. The situation in nearby Hatten village was similar. There then developed a two-week-long battle that Luck, a veteran of Poland, France, Russia, North Africa, and Normandy, characterized as "one of the hardest and most costly battles that ever raged."[31]

Both sides used their artillery nonstop, firing 10,000 rounds per day. The shelling was a curse to both sides, as the lines were never more than one street apart, and sometimes they were on the same side of the street, occasionally in the same house. Pvt. Pat Reilly of the 79th recalled, "It was a weird battle. One time you were surrounded, the next you weren't. Often we took refuge in houses where the Germans were upstairs. We heard them and could see them and vice versa. If they didn't make a move we left and if we didn't make a move they left."[32] Flamethrowers were used to set houses afire. Adding to the horror, the civilian population had hidden when the battle began and now the women, children, and old folks huddled in the cellars. There was no electricity. The pipes had frozen so there was no water. The soldiers, on both sides, did what they could to feed and care for the civilians.

Individual movement by day was dangerous. At night, trucks rolled up, on both sides, bringing ammunition and food, carrying out wounded. The houses, public buildings, and the church were in ruins. The dead, including some 100 civilians, lay in the streets.

There was hand-to-hand fighting with knives, room-to-room fighting with pistols, rifles, and bazookas. Attacks and counterattacks took place regularly.

On January 21, Seventh Army ordered the much depleted 79th and 14th Armored Divisions to retreat from Rittershoffen. The Americans abandoned the Maginot Line and fell back on new positions along the Moder River. Luck only realized they had gone in the morning. He walked around the village, unbelieving. At the church, he crawled through the wreckage to the altar, which lay in ruins. But in its place behind the altar, the organ was undamaged. Luck directed one of his men to tread the bellows, sat down at the organ, and played Bach's chorale *Danket Alle Gott*. The sound resounded through the village. German soldiers and the civilians of Rittershoffen gathered, knelt, prayed, sang.[33]

Fifty years later, I was in Rittershoffen with Luck and a half dozen of his men, along with some American veterans of the battle. The mayor invited Luck to the new church, sat him down at the organ, and once again he played Bach.

Overall, the Northwind offensive was a failure. The Germans never got near Strasbourg, nor could they cut American supply lines. It was costly to both sides: Seventh Army's losses in January were 11,609 battle casualties plus 2,836 cases of trench foot. German losses were around 23,000 killed, wounded, or missing (Seventh Army processed some 5,985 German POWs).[34]

In the Ardennes, K Company, 333rd Regiment, 84th Division, was the spearhead for First Army's drive on Houffalize. One member of the company, Pvt. Fred "Junior" Olson, had come in as a replacement on New Year's Eve. He remembered that no one gave him any advice or information: "It was as if there was no way to explain it, that I would find out for myself in due time." He was comforted when Sgt. "Pop" Teebagy, the old man of the company at thirty-five years, told him "everything will be all right, kid." Teebagy's age, Olson said, "gave his words some credence."

Over the next week, Olson had enough experience to make him a hardened veteran. In his first firefight, a German got behind his foxhole, which was an outpost. Olson was eating "one of those damn chocolate bars out of the K ration" and never noticed. His buddy, Sgt. Paul Zerbel, saw the German when he was ten feet away. Zerbel beat the German to the draw.

After killing the German, Zerbel said it was time to get out of there. He led, Olson followed. "We were going single-file down through the trees," Olson recalled, "and I tripped." As he did, a machine-gun burst cut the limbs off right above his head. "You won't believe it; you know, it was the only time this ever happened to me." His life flashed past him. "It didn't last long, just a matter of seconds. I still know in my own mind that if I hadn't tripped I'd have been killed."

When Zerbel and Olson reached the company lines, Olson was greatly relieved. "I was told it was past midnight and January 7th had been my birthday. For some strange reason I had persuaded myself that if I could live through my nineteenth birthday, I could make it all the rest of the way; that somehow everything was going to be all right. Here it was, January 8th, and I'd made it."[35]

The company continued to attack. On January 13, Lt. Franklin Brewer protested to the company commander, "There is not one man in the company fit to walk another mile, much less fight." But division headquarters said that as the company had just spent a day in a village, where it had "rested and reorganized," it was fit for duty. Translated to English from Army lingo, rested and reorganized meant the men had found the ruins of a house to break the wind, huddled down in frozen overcoats, and fallen into an exhausted sleep. At 0330, it was up for breakfast—tepid coffee and Spam-and-cheese sandwiches—then a march toward Houffalize.

That morning the company had a typical encounter. The lead squad came under fire from the by now familiar log-covered emplacements. The Germans opened fire too soon, permitting the GIs to pull back and take cover without casualties. There appeared to be a platoon in the emplacements. The GIs did what came naturally to them—they called in the artillery. Within minutes, more than a hundred rounds of 105 shells whistled low over their heads, then exploded against the German position. Some of the shells had fuse delays; others were white phosphorus. "As the barrage lifted," the company history records, "we moved forward quickly and built up a firing line within forty yards of the Germans. The small-arms exchange lasted only a few minutes before a white rag on the end of a rifle was waved frantically from a hole. The Germans—eight or ten of them—crawled out of their holes, stretching their arms as high as possible as they trudged apprehensively toward us through the snow.

"We advanced cautiously toward their positions, climbing over felled trees and forcing our way through a network of fallen branches. A dozen dead and wounded Germans sprawled on the ground. The artillery had done a thorough job, a case of overkill. The snow was blackened by huge chunks of frozen earth; several German gun emplacements had received direct hits. White phosphorus fragments smoldered and hissed in the snow. The stench of cordite and clouds of smoke hung over the hollow."

Moving forward, Captain Leinbaugh came across a German major, propped against a tree. His right leg had been cut off at mid-thigh. The German said to Leinbaugh, quietly and in good English, "Please shoot me." Leinbaugh kept on walking. Farther on, one of the sergeants caught up to Leinbaugh and asked if he had seen the guy with his leg cut off.

"Yeah, he asked me to shoot him."

"Yeah, he asked me, too."

"Did you?"

"Hell, you know I couldn't walk off and leave the poor son of a bitch to die like that."[36]

That same day Maj. Roy Creek of the 507th PIR, one of the heroes of D-Day, met two aid men carrying a severely wounded paratrooper back to the aid station. Creek took his hand to give him encouragement. The trooper asked, "Major, did I do OK?"

"You did fine, son." But as they carried him away, Creek noticed for the first time that one of his legs was missing. "I dropped the first tear for him as they disappeared in the trees. Through the fifty years since, I still continue to fight the tears when I've thought of him and so many others like him. Those are the true heroes of the war. I hope and pray that we never fight another one."

About this time, Creek learned that war didn't have to be unrelenting hell. His battalion was linked up with the British 51st Highland Division. He was invited to dinner at division hq mess. He accepted, but when he showed up he was embarrassed by his unkempt appearance. The British CO "was wearing battle dress, brass shined, neatly pressed, boots shined, etc. The mess was located in a small but nice house. In the dining area, the table was covered with a white table cloth, service of flat silver, with glasses and candles. Dinner was served by a mess attendant dressed in a white stiffly starched uniform. It consisted of a delicious fresh beef stew, freshly baked bread, real butter and strawberry jam. I enjoyed it very much and as I finished my glass of vintage burgundy, the small can of cold beans in my pocket—my dinner for that evening, had the British not invited me to dinner—felt big and awkward. As I gave my thanks before excusing myself, I felt a great admiration for the British who truly knew how to minimize the hardships of war."[37]

On January 7, the senior British officer on the Continent, the commander of 21st Army Group, which included the U.S. Ninth Army but no longer the First, held a press conference. Montgomery told the press that on the very first day of the Bulge, "as soon as I saw what was happening I took certain steps myself to ensure that if the Germans got to the Meuse they would certainly not get over the river. And I carried out certain movements so as to provide balanced dispositions to meet the threatened danger . . . i.e., I was thinking ahead." Soon Eisenhower put him in command of the northern flank, and he then brought the British into the fight, and thus saved the Americans. "You have thus the picture of British troops fighting on both sides of American forces who have suffered a hard blow. This is a fine Allied picture." It had been an "interesting" battle, Montgomery said, rather like El Alamein; indeed, "I think possibly one of the most interesting and tricky battles I have ever handled." He added that GIs made great fighting men, when given proper leadership.[38]

Every American in Europe was outraged. As the GIs and their officers saw the battle, they had stopped the Germans before Montgomery came onto the scene. Almost no British forces were even engaged in the Bulge. Far from directing the victory, Montgomery had gotten in everyone's way and botched the counterattack.

But what was especially galling about Montgomery's version of the Bulge was his immense satisfaction with the progress of the counterattack. Although the linkup of First and Third Armies was still a week away, and although the Germans were pulling out in good order, saving much of their equipment and men, Monty was claiming complete victory. Patton ranted and raved to every reporter who would listen, telling them publicly what he had already written privately in his diary—that had it not been for Montgomery, "we could have bagged the whole German army. I wish Ike were more of a gambler, but he is certainly a lion compared to Montgomery, and Bradley is better than Ike as far as nerve is concerned. Monty is a tired little fart. War requires the taking of risks and he won't take them."[39]

On January 14, K Company advanced to within a half mile of First Army's final-phase line. "We were on high ground only a mile from Houffalize. With a cold sun breaking the clouds, with the tanks from 'Hell on Wheels' [the 2nd Armored Division] spread along the ridgeline, and with fighter-bombers patrolling the skies to the east, it had suddenly become a lovely war."[40]

The feeling didn't last long. When the linkup took place the following day, the companies faced east and attacked again, this time to close to and then breach the Siegfried Line. January 15 is generally considered the last day of the Battle of the Bulge, but no one could have convinced the GIs of that. They still had a hard push ahead, to get back to the positions they had held one month earlier.

It was a disheartening experience to have to fight for ground once held. The 4th Infantry Division had come ashore at Utah Beach on D-Day; along with the 1st and 29th Divisions, it had been in continuous combat since June 6, 1944. Lt. George Wilson joined the 4th just before the St.-Lô breakthrough—by which time it had a 60 percent turnover of officers. Now, in the second half of January 1945, he found himself fighting for terrain that was becoming more and more familiar to him. Suddenly, "I realized we were retracing the route we had taken when chasing the Germans over four months before, in September. We learned that our overall mission was to penetrate the Siegfried Line at the exact same spot we'd broken through before." Wilson was struck by the thought that of the thirty-odd officers in his regiment in September, only three remained active. All the others had been killed or wounded; in addition the regiment had lost many replacement officers over those four months.

Wilson remembered that in September, when he had come through the village, "St. Vith had been a very charming little farming town left unmolested by the Germans, who had not tried at all to defend it." He knew that St.-Vith had been the scene of a tank battle on the third day of the Bulge, and that it had been used by the Germans as a headquarters and communications center, and therefore heavily bombed by the Allies, but he was not prepared for what he saw. "From the southern heights we got a clear view of total ruin.

All we could see were the jagged outlines of the shattered walls that had once been buildings. It was like a nightmarish surrealistic painting. Nothing was undamaged; there was no sight of life.

"One could not help reflecting on the battles we had fought in the same area in September, 1944. We also wondered how many lives had been lost for what appeared to be no gain after almost five months of hell."[41]

The total toll of American casualties in the Bulge was 80,987. More than half the killed or wounded came in January. For the period December 16 to January 2, the defensive phase of the battle for the Americans, the figures were 4,138 killed in action, 20,231 wounded in action, and 16,946 missing. For the period January 3 through 28, when the Americans were on the offensive, the losses were 6,138 killed, 27,262 wounded, and 6,272 missing. Thus January 1945 was the costliest month of the campaign in Northwest Europe for the U.S. Army in KIA and wounded. Total German casualties in the Bulge are estimated from 80,000 to 104,000.[42]

The Battle of the Bulge had political consequences of the greatest magnitude. Hitler's decision to strip the Eastern Front of men and weapons in order to seek a decision in the West led to the crushing of the depleted German forces in the East, beginning January 12 with the Red Army offensive. The Red Army overran eastern Germany and Central Europe, which led to a half century of Communist enslavement. The man responsible for this catastrophe was the world's leading anti-Communist, but he chose to sacrifice his nation and his people to the Communists instead of defending against them in the East and allowing the British and Americans to advance in the West.

"The American soldier won the battle." That is the authoritative voice of Russell Weigley. He goes on: "If the victory was less than complete, the fault lay mainly in generalship's failure to seize fully the opportunities created by the valor of the men."[43]

What kept them going? Discipline, to be sure, just as in the German army, and unit cohesion, and training. But for many, it was a sense of having no option and a realization that the only way out of combat was to annihilate the German army. "Such a view was not an impersonal concept imposed by higher authority," Michael Doubler writes, "but a living idea that guided the daily activities of many commanders and soldiers. They instinctively realized that the only way for them to go home was to keep pushing forward."

Doubler goes on to quote Col. James Rudder of the Rangers, who sent an open letter to his troops: "There is only one reason for our being here and that is to eliminate the enemy that has brought the war about. There is only one way to eliminate the enemy and that is to close with him. Let's all get on with the job we were sent here to do in order that we may return home at the earliest possible moment."[44]

At the end of January, the American armies in Northwest Europe were again at the German border. Surely, this time, they would break through and get across the Rhine.

17

Closing to the Rhine

February 1–March 6, 1945

AT THE BEGINNING of February the front lines ran roughly as they had in mid-December, but behind the line the differences were great. On December 15, the Germans had crowded division on top of division in the Eifel, while the Americans in the Ardennes were badly spread out. On February 1, the Americans had division piled on division in the Ardennes, while the Germans in the Eifel were badly spread out. Whatever units the Germans got out of the Bulge they sent off to plug the line somewhere else, because they felt the Americans were not likely to attack into the Eifel, which was heavier forest than the Ardennes. That, however, was exactly what Patton and Bradley wanted to do. With most of First and Third Armies already in the Ardennes, it made sense to them to attack from that area.

Eisenhower did not agree. He needed Third Army divisions to go south, to help Lt. Gen. Jacob Devers's forces eliminate the Colmar Pocket. And he wanted First Army to attack north of the Ardennes, south of Aachen, to get the Roer River dams, so that the U.S. Ninth Army could cross the Roer downstream from the dams, then close to the Rhine. Montgomery's British and Canadian armies could then cross the Lower Rhine with their right flank secured by Ninth Army.

But when one of Eisenhower's staff officers telephoned

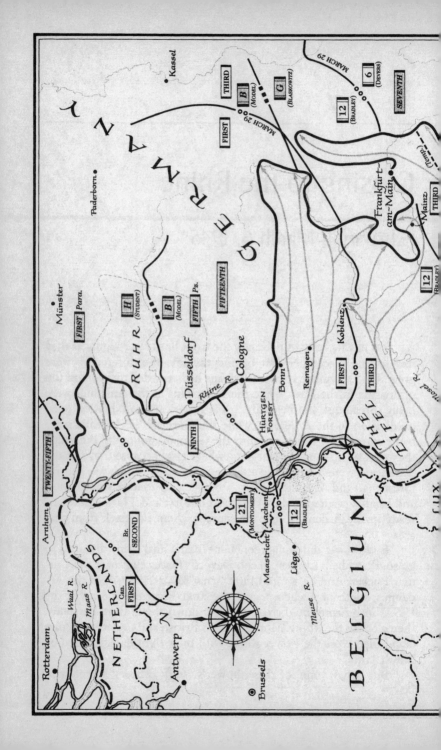

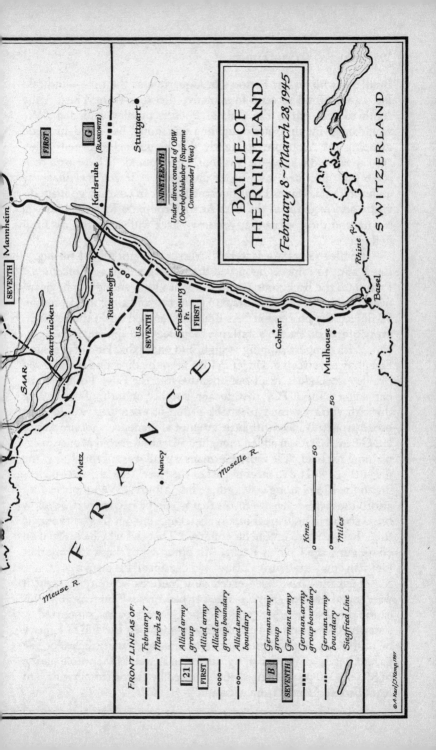

BATTLE OF
THE RHINELAND
February 8 ~ March 28, 1945

NINETEENTH

Under direct control of OBW
(Oberbefehlshaber [Supreme
Commander] West)

SWITZERLAND

Mannheim

SEVENTH

Saarbrücken

SAAR

Metz

Nancy

Moselle R.

Meuse R.

FRANCE

Rittershoffen

U.S.
SEVENTH

Strasbourg
Fr.

FIRST

Colmar

Mulhouse

Rhine R.

Basel

Karlsruhe

G
(BLASKOWITZ)

FIRST

Stuttgart

FRONT LINE AS OF:
February 7
March 28

21   Allied army
group
FIRST Allied army
000   Allied army
group boundary
00   Allied army
boundary

B   German army
group
SEVENTH German army
         German army
         group boundary
         German army
         boundary
         Siegfried Line

Kms.
0   50

Miles
0   50

© A. Karl / J. Kemp, 1997

Bradley—who was at Patton's headquarters at the time—and said Ike wanted Brad to send four or five divisions from Third Army south to help out at the Colmar Pocket, Bradley exploded. "We would be giving up a sure thing for a side show," he roared, his hand gripping the telephone so tightly that his knuckles turned white. "Go ahead and take all the divisions!" he shouted. "There is more at stake than the mere moving of divisions. . . . If you feel that way about it, then as far as I am concerned, you can take any goddam division and/or corps in the 12th Army Group, do with them as you see fit, and those of us that you leave back will sit on our ass until hell freezes."

Bradley's final words were, "I trust you do not think I am angry. But I want to impress upon you that I am *goddam well incensed*." Patton, in the background, said in a voice loud enough to be heard over the telephone, "Tell them to go to hell and all of us will resign. I will lead the procession." As Bradley slammed down the receiver, every officer on Patton's staff rose to his feet and applauded.[1]

With tempers running so high, and under that kind of pressure, Eisenhower retreated. He let Patton keep the divisions and allowed Bradley to conduct an all-out offensive into the Eifel. For the combat soldiers of ETO, that meant another month of struggling through snow or mud to attack a dug-in enemy. It would be a broad-front advance, with little attempt at maneuver. Its aim was to kill Germans. "As an added thought," Eisenhower told Monty in explaining his plan, "the more Germans we kill west of the Rhine, the fewer there will be to meet us east of the river." He insisted on closing to the Rhine along its length, telling Monty, "We simply cannot afford the large defensive forces that would be necessary if we allow the German to hold great bastions sticking into our lines at the same time that we try to invade his country." That was why he insisted on eliminating the Colmar Pocket.[2] In other words, he feared another German counteroffensive that would disrupt all his plans.

That may have been excessively cautious—Monty thought it was; so did Patton—but Eisenhower had cause. One reason for his caution was the fighting quality of the German troops, supported by a steady flow of new and excellent equipment. At the end of January he told Marshall that "there is a noticeable and fanatical zeal on the part of nearly all [German] fighting men as well as the whole nation of 85,000,000 people, successfully united by terror from within and fear of consequences from without."[3]

He had it right and put it perfectly. The Germans knew what they had done as the conquerors and occupiers of Europe, and thus what they could expect when it was their turn to be conquered and occupied. As to terror, deserters could expect to be hanged and their families sent to concentration camps. The Nazi Party was still feared and obeyed. So long as Hitler was alive, it would be. Until then, the Germans would fight.

Eisenhower preferred to fight them west of the Rhine, and to close to the river from the Swiss border to Arnhem. At that point he could pull twenty divisions out of the line to create a reserve force that would then be capable of exploiting any opportunity that came along. "If we jam our head up against a concentrated defense at a selected spot," he said, "we must be able to go forward elsewhere. Flexibility requires reserves."[4] By this stage of the war, flexibility was Eisenhower's outstanding tactical quality. What he had learned in the preceding twenty-eight months of combat was to expect to be surprised and to be ready to seize opportunities.

Conditions in the February fighting were different from January, yet just as miserable in their own way. A battalion surgeon in the 90th Division described them: "It was cold, but not quite cold enough to freeze, this February in 1945. Rain fell continually and things were in a muddy mess. Most of us were mud from head to foot, unshaven, tired and plagued by recurrent epidemic severe diarrhea. . . . It was miserable to have to jump from one's blankets three or four times a night, hastily put on boots, run outside into the cold and rain and wade through the mud in the dark to the straddle pit. As likely as not the enemy would be shelling the area, and that did not help." He noted that the diarrhea was accompanied by severe abdominal cramps, vomiting, and fever.

"As usual, it was the infantrymen who really suffered in the nasty fighting. Cold, wetness, mud and hunger day after day; vicious attack and counterattack; sleepless nights in muddy foxholes; and the unending rain made their life a special hell." They were hungry because, much of the time, supply trucks could not get to them. Between heavy army traffic and the rain, the roads were impassable. The engineers worked feverishly day and night throwing rocks and logs into the morasses, but it was a losing battle.[5]

On February 2 General Patton, plagued by impossible roads, ordered dog sled teams flown in from Labrador. His idea was to use them to evacuate wounded in the snow. By the time the first team arrived, however, the snow had melted, so the dogs were never used.[6]

What was unendurable, the GIs endured. What had been true on June 6, 1944, and every day thereafter was still true—the quickest route to the most desirable place in the world—Home!—led to the east. So they sucked it up and stayed with it and were rightly proud of themselves for so doing. Pvt. Jim Underkofler, a former ASTPer, was in the 104th Division. Its CO was the legendary Gen. Terry Allen; its nickname was the Timberwolf Division; its motto was "Nothing in Hell will stop the Timberwolves."

"That might sound corny," Underkofler said in a 1996 interview, "but it was sort of a symbolic expression of attitude. Morale was extremely important. I mean, man alive, the conditions were often so deplorable that we had nothing else to go on, but your own morale. You know you're sitting there in a foxhole rubbing your buddy's feet, and he's rubbing yours so you don't get trench foot. That's only an example of the kind of relationship and camaraderie we had."[7]

The straight line between Aachen and Cologne ran through Düren, on the east bank of the Roer River. But rather than going directly, Bradley ordered the main effort made with the veterans from Elsenborn Ridge and the Battle of the Bulge, through a corridor some seventeen kilometers wide south of the dreaded Hurtgen Forest. By so doing, the Americans would arrive at the Roer upstream from the dams and thus, once across the river, be free to advance over the Cologne Plain to the Rhine without danger of controlled flooding. The first task was to get through the Siegfried Line, still a formidable obstacle although in many places devoid of troops to utilize it. And every veteran in an ETO combat unit was well aware that this was where the Germans had stopped them in September 1944.

The generals were enthusiastic for this one. Gen. Walter Lauer, commanding the 99th Division, paid a pre-attack call on Sgt. Oakley Honey's C Company, 395th Regiment. Honey recalled that Lauer stood on the hood of a jeep, had the men gather around him, and gave a speech, saying, "We had fought the Krauts in the woods and the mountains and had beaten them. Now we were going to get a chance to fight them in the open." Honey commented, "Whoopee! Everyone was overjoyed." He added sarcastically, "You could tell by the long faces." Lauer went on: "We are in for a lot of new experiences and we are happy—happy because we are, at long last, to go on the offensive." Sgt. Vernon Swanson's comment: "How can a man be happier than that?"[8]

On February 4, C Company pushed off, into the Siegfried Line. Swanson remembered that "our visibility was severely limited because it began snowing and shortly the heavy winds caused the snow storm to reach blizzard proportions. The order then came to fix bayonets." Honey recalls "charging into a snow storm with fixed bayonets and the wind blowing right into our faces. After moving through the initial line of dragon's teeth we began encountering deserted pillboxes. At one command post out came ten Germans with hands in the air offering no resistance."

Pvt. Irv Mark of C Company said, "I remember taking one pill-box, and this stands out in my memory. The Krauts were waiting to surrender and the one in charge seemingly berated us for taking so long to come and get them. He said, '*Nicht etwas zu essen*' (nothing to eat). Strange we didn't feel one bit sorry for them." Swanson noted that "none of our company can recall any direct fire during our advance through the West Wall, although artillery shells dropped on us. We suffered no combat casualties possibly because we were much smarter than we had been six weeks earlier, particularly about booby traps and land mines."[9]

Few companies were that lucky. Sgt. Clinton Riddle of the 82nd Airborne was in Company B, 325th Glider Infantry. At 0200, February 2, he accompanied the company commander on a patrol. "We walked to within sight of the dragon teeth of the Siegfried Line. We walked parallel with the line quite some distance. We could barely make out the pillbox on either side of the road that led through the dragon teeth. The teeth were laid out in five double rows, staggered. The Krauts had emplacements dotting the hillsides, so arranged as to cover each other with cross fire, and all zeroed in on the road where it passed through the teeth."

Returning from the patrol, the captain ordered an attack. "It was cold and the snow was deep," Riddle recalled. A company went first. It was met by small arms and mortar fire and was quickly driven to the ground. "There was more fire from the emplacements than I ever dreamed there could be," Riddle remarked, an indication of how well concealed many German fortifications were. "Men were falling in the snow all around me. That was an attack made on the belly. We crawled through most of the morning." Using standard fire-and-movement tactics, the Americans managed to drive the Germans beyond the ridge and over the road.

"When we reached the road leading through the teeth," Riddle said, "the captain looked back over his shoulder and said, 'Come on, let's go!' Those were the last words he ever said, because the Germans had that road covered and when he was half-way across he got hit right between the eyes. There was only three of us in our company still on our feet that we could account for when it was over."

Another twenty-five men turned up and the new CO, a lieutenant, began employing fire-and-movement to attack the pillboxes on either side of the road. But the Germans had been through enough. After their CO ordered the initial resistance, and then fired the shot that killed the American captain, his men shot him and prepared to surrender. So, Riddle relates, "When we reached the pill boxes, the Germans came out, calling out 'Kamerad.' We should have shot them on the spot. They had their dress uniforms on, with their shining boots. We had been crawling in the snow, wet, cold, hungry, sleepy, tired, mad because they had killed so many of our boys."10 They were through the initial defenses of the Siegfried Line, and that was enough for the moment.

The 90th Division reached the Siegfried Line at exactly the spot where the 106th Division had been hit and decimated on December 16. Pvt. Jack Ammons spent the night of February 5–6, 1945, in a bombed-out building on the edge of the line. "The village was eerie," he remembered. "It looked like a million ghosts of previous campaigns had passed through it." At 0400, February 6, the 359th Regiment of the 90th picked its way undetected through the dragon's teeth, minefields, barbed wire, and pillboxes in the outer ring of the fortifications. Shortly after dawn, pillboxes that had gone unnoticed came to life, pouring fire into the tanks and reinforcements following the infantry, stopping the advance. A week-long fight ensued.

The Germans employed a new tactic to confound the Americans. Captain Colby explained it: "Whole platoons of infantrymen disappeared as a result of the German tactic of giving up a pillbox easily, then subjecting it to pre-sighted artillery and mortar fire, forcing the attackers inside for shelter. Then they covered the doorway with fire, surrounding the pillbox after dark, and blowing it in. The men soon learned it was safer outside the fortifications than inside."[11]

On February 9, regimental chaplain Father Donald Murphy noted a variation of the tactic in his diary: "K Company was in a pillbox. The GI outpost fell asleep and Jerries captured all of them, including Lts. Franklin and Osborne. The pillboxes are really death traps. You are helpless when you get in them."[12]

Patton inspected a command pillbox: "It consisted of a three-story submerged barracks with toilets, shower baths, a hospital, laundry, kitchen, storerooms, and every conceivable convenience plus an enormous telephone installation. Electricity and heat were produced by a pair of diesel engines with generators. Yet the whole offensive capacity of this installation consisted of two machine guns operating from steel cupolas which worked up and down by means of hydraulic lifts. As in all cases, this particular pillbox was taken by a dynamite charge against the back door. We found marks on the cupolas where 90 mm shells, fired at a range of two hundred yards, had simply bounced."

To Patton, this was yet another proof of "the utter futility of fixed defenses. . . . In war, the only sure defense is offense, and the efficiency of offense depends on the warlike souls of those conducting it."[13]

Captain Colby gives a vivid snapshot of American artillery in action: "We were looking at a day's assignment of about a dozen pillboxes. We were on slightly higher ground and could see them plainly. As we studied the prospect with sinking feelings, a self-propelled 155mm gun chugged and clanked up to us. A lieutenant dismounted and walked over.

" 'I hear you could use some fire,' he said.

"We did everything but hug him. We told him to pick out a pillbox and let fly.

"The lieutenant pointed to a pillbox. The gunner lowered the muzzle of the howitzer, opened the gun's breech-block, and peered through the barrel at the target. Satisfied with his aim, he told the loaders to stuff in a round."

A 155mm shell weighed 100 pounds. It took two men to put it on a carrier equipped with handles like a litter, two others to pick up the carrier and hold the shell to the chamber of the gun. A fifth man shoved it in and stuffed in the bags of gunpowder. When the breech was closed and all was ready, the gunner yanked the lanyard.

The tremendous roar was, Colby said, "thrilling to an infantryman." He noted that the .30-caliber bullets he was shooting were 0.3 inch in diameter, while the 155 shell was 6.1 inches.

"The shell struck the pillbox and covered it with a sheet of flame from the explosive charge it carried. A perfect smoke ring popped out of an air vent in the top."

"Scratch one pillbox," the lieutenant said.

"It is still standing," Colby retorted.

"Yep. But there ain't anyone left alive inside. If there is, his brains are scrambled."

Colby felt that having revealed their position, they should take cover before the Germans started their counterfire. "Aw, hell," the lieutenant said, "let's blast some more before the fun starts. You wanta fire one?"

How could Colby resist? After another line-of-sight aim through the open bore, the gun was loaded and Colby gave a jerk on the lanyard. Scratch another pillbox. The lieutenant told Colby to get behind the gun when it next fired, saying he could watch the shell all the way to the target.

"He zeroed in on another pillbox. Sure enough, when the gun fired I could see a black dot arc swiftly toward the target. Again, there was a flash that covered the whole target. They fired a round or two at each pillbox out in front of us, then folded their equipment and clanked away to another scene. When we moved up, we found only dead or dazed men inside the pillboxes."

Colby's final comment was, "No matter how many pillboxes or bunkers there might be, the fact was that man had built them and man was tearing them down. The elaborate system of 'Dragon's Teeth' proved to be worthless and brought from us exclamations of amazement at the labor the Germans had expended."[14]

That point was equally true when applied to the Atlantic Wall. At the Siegfried Line in February, as at the Atlantic Wall in June 1944, the Germans got precious little return on their big investment in poured concrete.

One small German investment paid big dividends. It was the Schu mine. Like the S-mine, the Schu was an invention of the devil.

It was simple, easily made, cheap, and deadly. The Schu mine was a wooden box the size of a box of kitchen matches. It contained a quarter pound of TNT, which looked and felt like laundry soap. When a man stepped on it he forced a nail into a detonator, setting off an explosion that could tear off a foot or do even worse damage. There were thousands of Schu mines buried in the mud, in the fields, and in the towns along the Siegfried Line.

When G Company, 328th Regiment, 26th Division, jumped off to attack that February, along the Saar River south of Luxembourg, it had not gone half a block when four men stepped on mines and had to limp or hobble to the rear. The 1st Platoon set up an observation post in the battered church. Just outside there was the body of an American soldier, but it was impossible to remove the corpse because the Germans had booby-trapped his body and placed a ring of Schu mines around him. "The church was in a shambles," Lieutenant Otts recalled. "The roof was gone and there were great gaping holes in the sides. There was only one opening that we could get to on the side toward the enemy. The street was filled with Schu mines and booby traps, but the heinies knew where they were and would slip out and toss grenades into the church. The building was so large and so strewn with rubble that we could always hit the prone and escape being wounded." Still, Captain Seeley stepped on a Schu mine and was killed.[15]

Lt. John Cobb, 82nd Airborne, had arrived in France on January 1. By the end of January he was a veteran. On February 7, he was traveling with his platoon by truck to the village of Hurtgen; they arrived just before dark. Jumping out, Cobb had the men form up and started marching. They marched until 0100 February 8, when they reached a village, completely destroyed. Cobb found a cellar to put his platoon in, but in an hour orders came down to move out. The task was to accompany a squad of engineers using mine detectors with the mission of clearing a trail across the Kall River valley. The work went slowly and consumed most of the day.

The site had been the scene of a battle in November in which a battalion of the 28th Division had taken a terrible pounding. Cobb's company was the first American unit to move back into the valley, dubbed by the 28th "Death Valley." Cobb described what he saw: "Immobile tanks and trucks and the bodies of dead American soldiers were everywhere. The snow and cold had preserved the dead and they looked so life-like it gave one a very eerie feeling; it was hard to believe they had been dead for three months. It was as if a snap-shot of a deployed combat unit had been taken, with everything as it was at a given moment in the past. The forward elements with tanks and infantry, the command posts, the medical aid station with men still lying on their stretchers, and the destroyed supply trucks were all in their proper places just as if someone had set up a demonstration from the field manual—but the actors were all dead."[16]

By February 8, U.S. Ninth Army, north of Aachen, had gotten through the Siegfried Line and closed to the Roer, but it could not risk an assault across the river so long as the Germans held the upstream dams and thus retained the capability to flood out the Roer Valley. First Army, meanwhile, was working its way through the Line south of Aachen. On the 10th, V Corps won control of the dams, only to discover that the Germans had wrecked the discharge valves the previous evening, thus creating a steady flooding that would halt the Ninth Army until the waters receded.

While they waited, the GIs sent out reconnaissance patrols and practiced new techniques in river crossings. For Company K, in the center of Ninth Army's front, north of Aachen, that meant sending squads at night in rubber boats over the flooding Roer, to locate minefields and gun emplacements and to capture prisoners. Along with the other regiments in the line, engineers worked with the infantry on assault boat training and in experimenting in perfecting assault boat tactics. On February 12 the engineers successfully demonstrated the use of assault boats, pontoons, rafts, and shooting communication wire across the river with rockets and grenade launchers. Smoke generators, first used in September 1944, were an innovation that the front-line troops greatly appreciated.

While they practiced and waited for the river to drop, the men of K Company had the unusual experience of receiving visitors. "With the Roer as a buffer," one of them wrote, "rear-echelon types who normally stayed away from the line paid us a call. First we had a correspondent, and then two colonels from XIII Corps headquarters showed up at the CP to take a look at the crossing area." Lt. George Pope, at the 1st Platoon OP, was the host. "They were middle-aged guys in their thirties," Pope remembered. "I took them up to the second floor of a building that offered a good view up and down the river." They were wearing neckties and had the chin straps buckled on their helmets. "A couple of rounds come in, little stuff, not particularly close, and these sons of bitches hit the goddam floor. You wouldn't believe it. They said, 'Let's get out of here!' I almost broke up."[17]

D-Day was February 23. After dark on the 22nd, tanks drove to the river's edge. Engineers lugged the 400-pound assault boats through deep mud to forward assembly areas. Huge trailer trucks with girders and pontoons for the heavy-duty bridges ground forward to final staging areas. In the 29th Division the men gathered beside the boats. The night "was as cloudy and damp and chill as February weather can be. Many of the men had gotten soaked to the skin in wading through the waist- and neck-deep water of the canals and trenches and along the banks of the flooded river. Equipment and supplies had become soaked and heavy, and in many cases useless. The men had no way to dry themselves and were forced to huddle together in the mud and water, shivering, shaking and praying."[18]

For the 104th Division, the objective was Düren. The obstacles between them and the town were nearly as formidable as the Channel and the Atlantic Wall had been in June 1944. The river was from two to four meters deep, 300 to 400 meters wide, with currents running more than ten kilometers per hour. The nearest cover on the west (American) side was 300 meters inland. On the German side, the riverbanks were heavily mined from the river to the trench system that commanded the river. Antipersonnel mines were in the water, on the concertina wire along the river's edge, and in front of the trenches. Extensive minefields, including Schu and S-mines, were throughout the depth of the German position.

Conditions were similar along the whole stretch of the Roer. A tanker with the 84th Division noted that when the smoke-generator battalion opened the valves on their huge steel canisters, vast gray clouds spread across the river, which was both reassuring and eerie. At midnight three infantry companies "made their way down the slopes toward the river, where they crouched beside their boats. We felt special kinship with these riflemen as they waited in the mud for the order to jump off. Tankers were safe behind their armorplate and most of the support troops were in cellars or holes, but these poor bastards had no place to hide." Their attack orders read, "Pursue the enemy relentlessly to the limit of every man's endurance."[19]

■

At 0245, February 23, the Roer River line, thirty-five kilometers long, burst into a ball of fire. It was one of the heaviest barrages of the war. Big guns, ranging from 75mm to 240mm; heavy and light mortars; rockets; direct fire from tanks; .50-caliber machine guns and 40mm anti-aircraft guns—every weapon the Americans had hurled against the enemy a forty-five-minute deluge of bullets and high explosives designed to stun, kill, or drive him from his position. Men who were there were men who had been through many barrages; their testimony is that this was the biggest one they ever saw. Ninth Army alone had more than 2,000 artillery pieces firing 46,000 tons of ammunition.[20]

"In the middle of it all," a lieutenant in the 84th wrote, "a lone German machine gunner decided he'd had enough. He fired a long burst of tracers at his tormentors. It was his last mistake. Every tank, every antiaircraft gun, every machine gunner within range returned the fire. Waves of tracers and flat-trajectory rounds swept toward the hole, engulfing it in a single continuous explosion. We cheered lustily, and Capt. George Gieszl commented, 'Now that's an awfully dead German.' "[21]

At 0330 the first assault waves shoved their boats into the river. In the 84th, assault companies had several boats overturn, but most of the men swam to the enemy banks, though wet and cold and many without weapons (there were only thirty rifles in one 130-man company). The engineers were able to get only three of the original thirty-four boats back to the west bank for the next load. The assault troops moved inland. Behind them, engineers worked feverishly to build footbridges and to get a cable ferry anchored on the far bank. By 0830 the job was done and ammunition, supporting weapons, and communication wire were ferried across. By 1030 elements of the assault companies had entered Düren.[22]

Altogether six divisions were involved in crossing the river. Their experience varied. Some companies found the river to be the most serious obstacle; others got some small-arms and artillery fire and in some cases were turned back. Generally, however, the crossing went well, thanks to the artillery preparation and the smoke.

By this stage of the war the infantry-artillery coordination was one of the outstanding features of the U.S. Army in ETO. As one example, when the 104th occupied the town of Düren the 3rd Battalion, 413th Infantry, received orders to take the insane asylum that occupied a hill and was the key feature of the area. Here was the telephone conversation between Lt. Col. Edward Shinkle of the 385th Field Artillery Battalion and Lt. Col. William Summers, CO of the 3rd Battalion: "Hello Bill, this is Eddie. When are you going to jump?"

"We'll be ready in about an hour, Eddie. Jump off at 0230."

"OK. Here is what we will do. One barrage across the road, one on each side, and deepen. We will move [the bombardment] east to the end of the line of buildings at a rate of one hundred yards every three minutes. When you reach the end of the buildings we will put all guns on the hill for five minutes. How's that?"

"OK, Eddie."

The guns opened on schedule. Forty-eight rounds landed on the first line and were reported as accurate. The earth shook and great clouds of red and brown dust rose from buildings on that side of town. Sporadic enemy fire ceased in that sector. The infantry moved forward. Summers called the barrage "beautiful and accurate. It went forward exactly as planned and completely neutralized enemy resistance in a vital area."[23]

By the afternoon the engineers had a footbridge over the Roer. By the end of February 24, treadway bridges were in place, allowing the tanks and artillery to join the infantry on the east bank. K Company crossed on a narrow, swaying footbridge that night. It beat swimming but it wasn't easy. The men had thirty or forty pounds of combat gear. Half the duckboards were underwater and there was only a single strand of cable for a handhold. The Germans had the range and were pumping in artillery. The shooting was blind in the smoke and dark, but still close enough to be disconcerting. Sgt. George Lucht recalled his dash across the bridge: "The Germans had regrouped and their artillery was falling on both sides of the river, and I was thinking, Boy, this is just like Hollywood."[24]

Once over the Roer there was open, relatively flat ground between the Americans and the Rhine. It was the most elementary military logic for the Germans to fall back. Why defend a plain that had no fortifications when Germany's biggest river, the Rhine, was at your back? It made no sense. Yet that is what everyone knew Hitler would do—indeed, Eisenhower counted on it. And Hitler did. He ordered his army to stand and fight. As it had neither fixed positions nor a river line for defensive purposes, the men should utilize the villages as strong points. These were German villages inhabited by loyal Germans. When the 5th Division got into one of them, there were signs painted on the walls which said, "See Germany and Die," "Onward Slaves of Moscow," and "Death Will Give You Peace."[25]

Those signs didn't stay up long, because the walls came tumbling down. The GIs used the techniques of street fighting that they had learned in the fall 1944 campaign. "The old hands at the game go through a town keeping inside the houses," one veteran explained. "They use bazookas to knock holes in the dividing walls as they go, and when they come to the end of the block and have to cross the street to the next block they throw out smoke first and cross over under cover of that." The most important things in street fighting were to stay off the streets and "keep dispersed, move fast, and keep on moving whatever happens. . . . Keep your head up and your eyes open and your legs moving, and at all costs keep apart."[26]

The German residents quickly came to appreciate what American firepower could do to their homes. Pvt. Karl Drescher, a teenage German infantryman, remembered a firefight on February 25. A German burgher crawled up to his position and told him to stop shooting, else the Americans would destroy the village. "That tore it for me," Drescher exclaimed. "I told him he better disappear or I'd shoot him. Because we were the ones who had to fight the war that he started, not I! I was a boy when it began, I had not started it." In the next village, a burgher suggested that he go over to such-and-so a hamlet to prepare his positions, as it had already been destroyed. "I told him to get lost, we were fine where we were." The burgher kept complaining. Drescher asked which was his house. When the burgher pointed it out, Drescher set up a mortar next to it and fired five quick rounds, then cleared out just before American artillery blasted the house to pieces.[27]

Replacements coming forward for the Germans were frightfully young or alarmingly old. The old men looked for the best chance to surrender. The boys looked for a fight. Sgt. Ewald Becker of Panzer Grenadier Regiment 111 remembered a squad of youngsters that reported to him. "I told them that the war wasn't just about them but that it also mattered what happened to the men standing to the right and left of them. They had a difficult time understanding that it wasn't an individual effort. At the same time they had all been in the Hitler Youth and believed in the war and our chances of winning."[28]

Private Drescher was one of them. In one village he and his squad found a full platoon down in a cellar. "They all wanted to surrender, to allow the front line to roll over them. We, we wanted to continue the war."[29] So did others. Captain Colby remembered a German counterattack from this period. Although the 6th SS Mountain Division had no artillery support, it launched a particularly vicious assault. "Although our artillery and mortar fire was poured into the ranks of the fanatical SS men, it was ultimately rifle fire that stopped them. Some of the Germans were dropped in their tracks only a dozen feet from the American positions. Bodies of friend and foe were found literally in the same foxholes, so active was the fighting. The Germans were using with extravagance their only remaining source of defense—the bodies of their soldiers."[30]

Through February, Patton attacked, whatever the conditions. He was at his zenith. His nervous energy, his drive, his sense of history, his concentration on details while never losing sight of the larger picture combined to make him the preeminent American army commander of the war. Those qualities, and his professional competence. He was constantly looking for ways to improve. In early February, for example, he ordered all Sherman tanks in his army to have an additional two and a half inches of armor plate, salvaged from wrecked tanks, put on the forward hull or glaces plate of the tanks—and was delighted with the results; for the first time, a Sherman could take a direct hit from an 88 and survive. He also had flamethrowers mounted on the tanks, using the machine-gun aperture—and again was delighted with the results. They were highly effective against pillboxes. Still, nothing could beat the 155mm guns; according to Patton, "At three hundred yards the 155 shell will remove a pillbox for every round fired."[31]

Patton's worst enemy was the weather, and what it did to the roads. On the left flank of Third Army, east of St.-Vith, the local inhabitants watched with dismay as the tanks and trucks tore up their dirt roads—roads they did not use in the winter, by law. The nightly freezes, the daily thaws, the attempt to use them for heavy traffic, combined to make them impassable. Patton at one point in early February was forced to turn to packhorses to supply the front line.

Still he said attack. Bradley wanted him to stop, so that he could shift some divisions from Third to First Army. "On the tenth," Patton remembered, "Bradley called up to ask me how soon

I could go on the defensive. I told him I was the oldest leader in age and in combat experience in the U.S. Army in Europe, and that if I had to go on the defensive I would ask to be relieved. He stated I owed too much to the troops and would have to stay on. I replied that a great deal was owed to me, and unless I could continue attacking I would have to be relieved. I further suggested that it would be a good thing if some of his Staff visited the front to find out how the other half lived."[32]

On February 26 elements of Third Army captured Bitburg. Patton entered the town from the south while the fighting was still going on at the northern edge of town. "In spite of the fact that shells were falling with considerable regularity, I saw five Germans, three women and two men, re-roofing a house. They were not even waiting for Lend-Lease, as would be the case in several other countries I could mention."[33] Dozens of GIs make the same point: in Italy and France, the residents left the rubble in the streets, waiting for someone else to clean it up, while in Germany the residents were cleaning up as soon as the battle passed their villages.

About this time Patton put out an order that Medal of Honor or Distinguished Service Cross winners should be kept out of the front line, because such men usually attempted to outdo themselves and got killed, "whereas, in order to produce a virile race, such men should be kept alive."[34]

Patton was spending six hours a day in an open jeep, inspecting, urging, prodding, demanding. He crossed the Sauer River on a partly submerged footbridge, under a smoke screen (from which emerged another Patton legend, that he had swum the river). On February 19, when First Army to the north was waiting for the Roer to recede, Patton wrote Bradley a letter "saying that all the U.S. troops except the Third Army were doing nothing at all, and that while I was still attacking, I could do better with more divisions. . . . This is the only letter I ever wrote for the record, but I felt very keenly at that time that history would criticize us for not having been more energetic."[35]

History was very much on his mind. In the evenings, he was reading Caesar's *Gallic Wars*. He was especially interested in Trier, at the apex of the Saar-Moselle triangle, on his northern flank. The historic city of the Treveri, according to Caesar, had contained the best cavalry in Gaul. As Russell Weigley puts it, "Patton's passion for retracing the paths of ancient conquerors, whenever doing so could at all plausibly be combined with present strategic or tactical advantage," had caught him up.[36]

He wanted Trier. To take the city, Patton inveigled the 10th Armored Division out of Bradley and sent it to take Trier. Bradley had not intended to let Patton get the division so deeply committed. "The tent maker," said Patton, using his nickname for Omar Bradley, "felt that we should stop attacking, and it took me and all three corps commanders half a day to get permission to continue the attack for another 48 hours." Later he commented, "It always made me mad to have to beg for opportunities to win battles."[37]

Lt. Col. Jack Richardson (USMA 1935) of 10th Armored led a task force named for him in the attack into Trier. When he got to the Moselle River, he saw an intact bridge. He was in the leading vehicle of his battalion of armored infantry when he saw the wires leading to the demolition charges at the far end of the bridge. Jumping out of the vehicle, he raced across the bridge under heavy fire and cut the wires. Patton's comment was, "The acid test of battle brings out the pure metal." (Richardson was killed in April.) Patton also noted that the piers and buttresses of the Kaiserbrücke Bridge dated back to 28 B.C. Driving into the city along Caesar's road, Patton "could smell the sweat of the Legions," imagining them marching before him into the still surviving amphitheater where the Emperor Constantine the Great had thrown his captives to the beasts.

All set up by his triumph, Patton made the most extravagant claim: "Had we been refused permission to continue this attack, the whole history of the war might have been changed, because the capture of Trier was one of the turning points."[38]

Still he could not rest. Third Army had started the February campaign farther from the Rhine than any other army on the Western Front. At last through the Siegfried Line, he still had so far to go to the Rhine that he feared his would be the last army to cross. "We are in a horse race with [Lt. Gen.] Courtney [Hodges]," Patton wrote his wife. "If he beats me [across the Rhine], I shall be ashamed."[39]

By the middle of the first week in March, Ninth and First Armies were closing to the Rhine, threatening to encircle entire divisions. Hitler not only would not give permission to fall back, he ordered counterattacks. As a consequence, thousands of German troops were trapped on the west bank, where they either surrendered or were killed. First Army intelligence declared: "Perhaps it is too early to be optimistic but everyone feels that resistance is on the point of crumbling and that this time we are going to the Rhine quickly without being slowed down." The following day intelligence noted, "The Boche, although not in any sense getting up and surrendering in mass, are fighting a disorganized defensive battle. Stiff resistance where it has been encountered has been centered in the small towns and usually after an hour of so of fighting, the soldiers have come out with their hands up."[40]

The generals were full of drive, push, excitement, anticipation. Gen. William Hoge, CO of Combat Command B, 9th Armored Division, typified the intense energy of the senior commanders. On March 5 he assembled his unit commanders to give them their mission. It was to advance. "Go around resistance, don't get in a fight. . . . Infantry battalions will leapfrog. By-pass towns if possible. . . . Get help from tanks as you can. If no AT guns, shove tanks out in front. Infantry will come on in half-tracks." But this Go! Go! Go! spirit did not reach all the way to the bottom of the command. Sgt. "Speedy" Goodson, A Company, 27th Battalion, groggy from lack of sleep, wandered aimlessly into the open just as some German artillery started coming in. "Get back under cover," his platoon leader yelled.

"Aw, it won't make any difference, Lieutenant. They'll get us sooner or later as long as they keep sticking us out here in front." Combat historian Ken Hechler comments, "that was the mood of most of the men as they slogged forward in the early days of March. It was cold, clammy and rainy. Sweat mixed with grime, and underwear stuck and stank. . . . Nobody's heart was really in the fight. They kept on only because their training had made their actions mechanical, and they were so tired out, they just didn't give a damn. Then along came the needle and the whip, and they moved out again, driving toward the Rhine and a succession of objectives that seemed to stretch to infinity."[41]

The great goal, almost surely impossible, was to get a bridge. So desperate were the Americans that they used a ruse they had earlier executed dozens of Germans for using. The 83rd Division assembled a task force of German-speaking GIs, put them in German uniforms, provided them with tanks and other vehicles disguised and camouflaged to look like German models. The task force set out after dark, March 2, talked its way through the German lines, and at dawn reached the Rhine at Obercassel. A German sentry challenged the column; a firefight broke out; the task force was strong enough to fight its way to the bridge but the noise of battle alarmed the town's air raid warden and he set off the alarm. The German engineers at the bridge took that as the signal to blow it, just as the American tanks were rolling up.[42]

Cologne was a magnet for First Army. The famous cathedral city was the fourth largest in Germany and the biggest on the Rhine. The Germans had never imagined invaders from the west would get that far, so Cologne was defended only by a weak outer ring of defenses, manned by bits and pieces of a hodgepodge of divisions, and a weaker inner ring, manned by police, firemen, and Volkssturm troops. Such forces could not long hold up an American army that was at the peak of its power.

The Americans were pouring through the Siegfried Line. The Germans were standing and fighting as best they could. American columns were advancing fifteen kilometers a day and more, encircling German divisions, forcing a surrender. Meanwhile the artillery was pounding the cities and bridges. Maj. Max Lale, 401st Field Artillery, wrote his wife on March 2, "I have often read that an army on the move is a happier army than one which sits, and now I can believe it. . . . I saw a bed of pansy blooms. . . . Tonight, just at dusk, I stood from a long distance away and watched the plumes of smoke, the flashes of flames, and listened to the long, low rumble that marked the death of one of the oldest cities in Europe."[43]

On March 5, Gen. Maurice Rose's 3rd Armored Division entered the city, followed later that day by Terry Allen's 104th Division. The next day Rose's tanks reached the Hohenzollern Bridge but, predictably, most of the structure was resting in the water, as were the other Cologne bridges over the Rhine.

In Cologne, only the great cathedral stood, damaged but majestic. Like St. Paul's in London, it had been used as an aiming point, but was never knocked down. Critics of the air forces said it survived because it was the target; others claimed it, like St. Paul's, was spared by divine intervention; still others said it was a tribute to the magnificent workmanship of medieval cathedral builders.

It was carnival time. Mardi Gras came on Tuesday, March 7. In Cologne, one of the most Catholic of German cities, the inhabitants did their best to celebrate. Lt. Günter Materne, a German artillery officer, recalled that his men spotted a ship tied to a wharf, investigated, and found it filled with champagne and still wines. They proceeded to have a party. People emerged from their cellars to join in. "And so we had a great time," Materne said. "We got drunk. People came up to me and said, 'Take off your uniform. I'll give you some civilian clothes. The war is already lost.'" But Materne, although drunk, spurned the temptation and the next day, badly hungover, managed to get across the Rhine in a rowboat.[44]

He was one of the last Germans to escape. Hitler's decision to defend the Cologne Plain and the rest of the country between the Siegfried Line and the Rhine had cost Germany heavily. The Americans had taken 250,000 prisoners and killed or wounded almost as many. More than twenty divisions had been effectively destroyed. The Allied air forces were by now taking full advantage of the lengthening days and better weather, blasting every German who moved during daylight hours, flying as many as 11,000 sorties in one day.

Sergeant Becker, in a Tiger tank, knew what that meant. "The Americans attacked from all directions at once. From above, below, sideways."[45]

On the first day of World War II, then Colonel Eisenhower had written his brother Milton: "Hitler should beware the fury of an aroused democracy."[46] Now that fury was making itself manifest on the west bank of the Rhine River. The Allies had brought the war home to Germany. Now it was German villages that lay in ruins as the front lines passed on.

A group of men from the 101st got into Cologne a couple of weeks after the occupation of the city. They were impressed by the extent of the destruction. Every window shattered, every church hit, every side street blocked with rubble. The giant statue of Bismarck on a horse was still standing, but Bismarck's sword, pointing toward France, had been cut off by flying shrapnel. The paratroopers wandered to the river, where they began pointing and laughing at the grotesque ruins of the *Hängebrücke,* or suspension bridge. An elderly German couple stood beside them. The Germans began to cry and shake their heads. All their beautiful bridges had been twisted and mangled, and here were American boys laughing.[47]

Many of the GIs were glad enough to see German villages and cities in ruins. In World War I, Germany had escaped destruction. It was Germany's turn this time. Bring this war home to the Germans and they won't be starting another one anytime soon was the feeling. What bothered them more than German bridges blown up by the German army was the fact that they were there, on the front lines, with hard fighting ahead. In some cases, they had been there since June 6, 1944. It should have been someone else's turn.

Something more bothered them. Pvt. David Webster of the 101st spoke directly to it. On February 15, a buddy had died a particularly gruesome death. Webster wrote, "He wasn't twenty years old. He hadn't begun to live. Shrieking and moaning, he gave up his life on a stretcher. Back in America the standard of living continued to rise. Back in America the race tracks were booming, the night clubs were making record profits, Miami Beach was so crowded you couldn't get a room anywhere. Few people seemed to care. Hell, this was a boom, this was prosperity, this was the way to fight a war. We wondered if the people would ever know what it cost the soldiers in terror, bloodshed, and hideous, agonizing deaths to win the war."[48]

"God, I hate the Germans," Eisenhower once wrote Mamie. In the first years of the war he had hated them for making aggressive war and for all the misery they brought to the countries they overran. By 1945, when most of the Nazi empire had been liberated by the Allies, he hated them for forcing him to destroy their cities and kill their young men, for making him order young Americans into battle, for fighting for a cause that wasn't just hopeless and evil, but directly contrary to the best interest of the German nation. But it had to be done.

18

Crossing the Rhine

March 7–31, 1945

THE RHINE was by far the most formidable of the rivers the GIs had to cross. It rises in the Alps and flows generally north to Arnhem, where it makes a sharp turn to the west. It was between 200 and 500 meters wide, swift and turbulent, with great whirlpools and eddies, two to three meters deep. The Germans on the far bank were disorganized and demoralized, dismayed by their losses in the insanity of trying to fight it out on the Cologne Plain, but still determined and capable of utilizing the natural advantages the Rhine gave them to defend their country.

Those advantages included the scarcity of suitable crossing sites. There were only two or three places from Cologne south that were even possible. Worse, along that stretch there were no major objectives on the east bank or inland for some fifty kilometers and the hinterland was unsuitable for offensive warfare. The terrain was heavily wooded, undulating and broken in many places by narrow valleys.[1] The roads twisted and turned, rose and fell, as in the Ardennes.

North of Cologne, Montgomery's Twenty-first Army Group had many suitable crossing sites, good terrain for a mobile offensive, and major objectives just across the Rhine in the Ruhr Valley. Beyond the Ruhr the north German plain led straight to Berlin. So while Eisenhower's heart was with Bradley, Hodges, and Patton, his mind was up north, with Monty. Gen. Harold "Pinky" Bull, SHAEF G-3, and his planners had decided that up north was the right place for the main crossing. Eisenhower agreed, but warned that "the possibility of failure cannot be overlooked. I am, therefore, making logistic preparations which will enable me to switch my main effort from the north to the south should this be forced upon me."[2]

To the north, Montgomery's armies were closing to the river. As they did, he began to build his supply base for the assault crossing and exploitation that would follow. Altogether he required 250,000 tons of supplies, for the British and Canadian forces and the U.S. Ninth Army and 17th Airborne Division. Ninth Army had been part of Twenty-first Army Group since the preceding fall; the 17th Airborne Division had arrived in Europe in December and had been thrown immediately into the Battle of the Bulge. It had combat experience, but had not made a combat jump and was currently making practice jumps in Belgium.

Montgomery's staff had begun planning for the Rhine crossing back in October 1944, as soon as it was evident that Market-Garden had failed. The final plan was almost as elaborate as for Overlord, the scope almost as big. Eighty thousand men, slightly less than half the number of men who went into France on June 6, 1944, would cross the Rhine by boat or transport airplane on the first day for Operations Plunder (the crossing by boat) and Varsity (the airborne phase), with an immediate follow-up force of 250,000 and an ultimate force of one million.

As usual, Montgomery proceeded with what Weigley has characterized as the majestic deliberation of a pachyderm. He set D-Day for March 24. For the two weeks preceding the assault, he laid down a massive smoke screen that concealed the buildup—and gave the Germans ample warning about where he was going to cross. He gathered 600 rounds of ammunition per artillery piece. Beginning March 11, the air forces pounded the Germans on the east bank, hitting them with 50,000 tons of bombs. Monty invited Churchill and many other dignitaries to join him to watch the big show.

Beginning February 28, Ninth Army had been pushing east toward the Rhine. Progress was slow and costly. Company K, 333rd Regiment, received orders to advance on and take the village of

Hardt, between the Roer and the Rhine. After an all-day march through mud and cold, followed by a few hours' rest, the company formed up an hour before dawn. More than half the company were replacements. Everyone was groggy, exhausted even before the day began. And wary, since they knew their flank was open yet they were pressing on deeper into the German lines.

Sgt. George Pope got delayed in getting his squad to jump off. "And here comes [Capt. George] Gieszl and the battalion commander, right? And the battalion CO says, 'For Christ's sakes, Pope, it's after eight and you haven't . . .' And I stopped the colonel right there and said, 'What's the big fucking rush? Where the fuck you think you are at, Louisiana on maneuvers? This ain't maneuvers, this is real shit, and I'm going out there, not you.' That's what I told the colonel, right? I didn't give a crap about nothing."[3]

The company moved out, got to Hardt, attacked, and got stopped by machine-gun fire and a shower of 88s. Two men were killed. The others hit the ground. Pvt. Mel Cline called on skills he'd not used since basic training. "We were flat, prone on our bellies. This German machine gunner was directly to our front. That was the only time in combat that I fired aimed shots like we did on the range in training. We could see this German come up from his hole, fire, and duck down again. I adjusted my sights, got the range, and squeezed off several clips before I finally hit his gun and put him out of action. When we reached his hole, I found the bullet had glanced off his machine gun and mangled his arm."[4]

Pvt. Leonard Bowditch was in a turnip patch when he was hit with shrapnel in the knee. "They were getting ready to evacuate me, and Lieutenant Leinbaugh was talking to several of us who had been wounded. I told him I wanted him to have my scarf as a good-luck piece, so I gave it to him and he wrapped it around his neck. He told me it couldn't have been too lucky, since I had just been hit. I said it worked just fine for me since I had a million-dollar wound and was going home."[5]

Pope's squad got caught in the open. "We were all pinned down," he remembered, "and I see guys turning their heads, I felt like doing that myself. It was flat as a floor. There wasn't a blade of grass you could hide under. I'm yelling, 'Shoot, you sons of bitches!' That was a tough time."

Lt. Bill Masters took charge. He was in the edge of a wood with half of his platoon. The remainder of his men and the other platoons were getting pounded out in the open flat field. Masters recalled, "The fire was awfully heavy and the casualties were increasing. I decided I had to get these guys moving or a lot more were going to get killed." He ran forward, swearing at the men to get them going as he passed them. "I got up as far as a sugar-beet mound that gave some cover, close enough to toss a grenade at the German machine gunner right in front of me. But I couldn't get the grenade out of my pocket—it was stuck." A German tossed a potato masher at Masters. "It landed right next to me but didn't explode."

The enemies commenced firing at each other. Both missed. Both ran out of ammunition at precisely the same time. Masters knelt on one knee, reloaded, as did the German. Again the enemies looked up at the same time, and fired simultaneously. Masters put a bullet between the machine gunner's eyes. When Masters took off his helmet to wipe his brow, he found a bullet hole through the top.

Masters ran to the first building on the outskirts of town, where he had some cover. "I had this dead-end kid from Chicago I'd made my bodyguard [Pvt. Ray Bocarski]. He came in close behind me, and then a number of men pulled up and we went from building to building cleaning out the place and captured a sizable batch of German paratroopers in those houses." Lt. Paul Leimkuehler gave a more vivid description of Masters's action: "He killed a machine gunner and opened the way into that little town. He was leading, running down the main street like a madman, shooting up everything in his way."[6]

The Germans had two 75s and two 88s presighted on the village. Armor-piercing shells crumbled the walls. Captain Gieszl and the FO called for a counterbarrage. Within minutes, the German guns were out of action. Over the next few days the company advanced toward the Rhine. Sometimes there was resistance, sometimes not. Just before the leading platoon got to the Rhine a German platoon barged into the middle of the company column. A point-blank exchange of rifle fire and grenades lasted several minutes. Four men were wounded, including Masters. Several Germans were killed, the rest surrendered.

By March 7, the company was in Krefeld, on the banks of the Rhine. By some miracle, the men found an undamaged high-rise apartment in which everything worked—electricity, hot water, flush toilets, and telephones with dial tones. They had their first hot baths in four months. They found cigars and bottles of cognac. Private

Bocarski, fluent in German, lit up, sat down in an easy chair, got a befuddled German operator on the phone, and talked his way through to a military headquarters in Berlin. He told the German officer he could expect K Company within the week.[7]

That was not to be. Having reached the river, K Company along with the rest of Ninth Army would stay in place until Montgomery had everything ready for Operation Plunder. The troops badly needed the rest. The night after taking Hardt, Pvt. J. A. "Strawberry" Craft was so totally exhausted that after getting into his foxhole he told the sergeant he was going to sleep that night. The sergeant warned him, "You might wake up dead." Craft replied, "I'll just have to wake up dead." Decades later he still remembered the exchange, and explained, "I needed the sleep, and I got it, too."[8]

Sergeant Pope's reply to his colonel had a counterpart in the 103rd Division. Sgt. Joe Skocz was out on a night patrol. His lead scout was a veteran of sixty-five days of combat and had always done his duty. Suddenly the patrol stopped. Skocz went forward to see what was up. The scout, crouching behind a tree, pointed ahead and said, "There's people out there. They're waiting to nail us."

"They're not moving," Skocz pointed out.

"Neither are we."

Skocz ordered the scout to go forward and see what he could see. And as Skocz remembered it, "He leans up real close to my head and he says, 'Fuck you, Sergeant. You wanta find out, go up yourself.' " Skocz did and discovered there was nothing out there. "When we got back, I told him I never wanted to see him on the front lines again."[9]

Sgt. William Faust of the 1st Division had been in combat in two continents and six countries. By March 1945, he said, "Those of us still remaining of the 'Big Red One' of 1942 had lost the desire to pursue, the enthusiasm we had for this sort of thing in Africa, Sicily, France, Luxembourg and Belgium was no longer with us."[10]

On March 15, former ASTP student Pvt. Martin Duus of the 103rd Division, who had been in combat since the previous December, got hit in the neck. The bullet exited through his right shoulder. "My whole right arm was dead. I couldn't move it. I thought I'd lost it. I couldn't look." He never used it again; it was paralyzed. But his reaction belied the seriousness of the wound, while it spoke eloquently of the state of the old hands: "I was damn glad I was hit and could get out of there. Absolutely. My fear was I'd get well enough to go back."[11]

On March 7, Patton's forces were still fighting west of the Rhine, trying to close to the river from Koblenz south to Mainz and in the process trap further German forces facing the U.S. Seventh Army. Patton was having divisions stolen from him, to dispatch south to help Seventh Army get through the Siegfried Line east of Saarbrücken. That made him furious, but he calmed down when Bradley agreed to move the boundary between Third and Seventh Armies some twenty kilometers south of Mainz. That put the best stretch of river for crossing south of Cologne in his sector. He was thinking of crossing on the run, and hoping he could do it before Montgomery's elephantine operation even got started, and before Hodges, too, if possible.

But his men were exhausted. "Signs of the prolonged strain had begun to appear," one regimental history explained. "Slower reactions in the individual; a marked increase in cases of battle fatigue, and a lower standard of battle efficiency—all showed quite clearly that the limit was fast approaching."[12] Company G, 328th Infantry Regiment, was typical. It consisted of veterans whose bone-weariness was so deep they were indifferent, or on the edge of battle fatigue, plus raw recruits. Still it had the necessary handful of leaders, and superb communications with the artillery, as demonstrated by Lieutenant Otts in the second week in March, during Third Army's drive toward the Rhine. Sgt. G. I. described it in a 1988 letter to Otts: "My last memory of you—and it is a vivid one—is of you standing in a fierce mortar and artillery barrage, totally without protection, calling in enemy coordinates. I know what guts it took to do that. I can still hear those damn things exploding in the trees. I lost one foxhole buddy to shrapnel in that barrage, and then his replacement. I don't know who was looking after me."[13]

Otts established a platoon CP, took off his equipment and both field jackets, and started to dig a hole. "Mortar shells started falling almost as thick as rain drops and we all hit the ground fast," he remembered. "Instead of covering my head, I, like a fool, propped up on my right elbow with my chin resting on my hand, looking around to see what was going on. All of a sudden something hit me on the left side of my jaw that felt like a blow from Jack Dempsey's right. . . . I stuck my hand up to feel the wound and it felt as though half my face was missing." One of his men crawled over to try to put a bandage in place. He looked at Otts and cried, "Oh God, Lieutenant, this is all for me." He had to be evacuated. The company commander came limping over to Otts. He had been hit in the foot and intended to turn the company over to Otts, but he took one look at Otts's face and cried, "My God, no, not you too," turned, and limped back to his foxhole.

Otts got up to start walking back to the aid station when a sniper got him in the shoulder, the bullet exiting from his back without hitting any bone. He was on his way home. For the others, the pounding continued. Lt. Jack Hargrove recalled, "All day men were cracking mentally and I kept dashing around to them but it didn't help. I had to send approximately fifteen back to the rear, crying. Then two squad leaders cracked, one of them badly."[14]

First Army was moving east, all along its front. Hodges had divisions making fifteen kilometers per day, sometimes more. They were taking big bags of prisoners. They were looking forward to getting to the river, where they anticipated good billets in warm, dry cellars and a few days to rest and refit. There was even a chance they could stay longer, as there were no plans for crossing in their sector, where all the bridges were down or soon would be. First Army was, in essence, SHAEF's reserve. Eisenhower counted on it to give him the flexibility to send a number of divisions either north to reinforce Monty or south to reinforce Patton, depending on developments. To free up those divisions, First Army had to close to the river along its whole sector. There would then be no danger of a German counterattack, and large numbers of Americans could be pulled back and put in reserve.

The Germans, meanwhile, were in near full retreat. Although their orders were that no unit could cross to the east bank of the river without authorization from Hitler, individuals were taking matters into their own hands. Maj. Rolf Pauls, who had lost an arm in Russia but continued to serve (he later became West Germany's first ambassador to both Israel and China, and ambassador to the United States), found himself fighting with the river immediately at his back. He ordered his 88s and the few remaining tanks over the last standing bridge in his sector. The high command threatened to court-martial Pauls and called him a coward. He pointed out that he needed his artillery behind the front lines and that the tanks were almost out of fuel, and got away with it.[15]

Seventeen-year-old Pvt. Siegfried Kugler recalled hiding in a wood and watching the Americans marching toward the Rhine. "When we saw everything that was going past, all the artillery, tanks, and trucks, well I've got to say I just flipped. I thought: how can you declare war on such a country?"[16]

On the morning of March 7, Gen. John Millikin, commanding III Corps on First Army's right flank, sent his 9th Armored Division to close to the west bank of the Rhine. The mission of Combat Command B (CCB) of the 9th, commanded by Gen. William Hoge, was to occupy the west bank town of Remagen, where a great railroad bridge spanned the Rhine. It had been built in the midst of World War I, to facilitate the movement of supplies to the Western Front, and named for Gen. Erich Ludendorff. On the east bank, there was an escarpment, the Erpeler Ley. Virtually sheer, rising some 170 meters, it dominated the river valley. The train tracks followed a tunnel through the Erpeler Ley. (A touch of irony: in December 1918, III Corps, First Army, had crossed the Rhine at Remagen as part of the Allied occupation forces. My grandfather, Col. Harry M. Trippe, U.S. Army Corps of Engineers, was one of the men to cross the Ludendorff Bridge.)

It was dank, cold, with clouds down almost to the treetops. That kept the American fighters and bombers on the ground, but not the little Piper Cubs. As CCB moved toward the Rhine, Lt. Harold Larsen of the 9th Division artillery flew ahead in a Piper Cub looking for targets of opportunity. At around 1030 he was approaching Remagen, when to his astonishment he saw the Ludendorff Bridge, its massive superstructure looming out in the fog and mists of the river valley. Larsen radioed the news to General Hoge, who immediately sent orders to the units nearest Remagen to take the bridge. They were the 27th Armored Infantry Battalion and the 14th Tank Battalion. Hoge formed them into a task force under Lt. Col. Leonard Engeman, who put Lt. Emmet "Jim" Burrows's infantry platoon of Company A in the lead. Brushing aside light opposition, Task Force Engeman reached a wood just west of Remagen a little before noon. Burrows emerged from the wood onto a cliff overlooking the Rhine. There was the Ludendorff Bridge, intact. German soldiers were retreating across it.

Burrows called back to Lt. Karl Timmermann, twenty-two years old, who had just assumed command of Company A the previous day. Another irony: Timmermann had been born in Frankfurt am Main, less than 160 kilometers from Remagen. His father had been in the American occupation forces in 1919, had married a German girl, and stayed in the country until 1923, when he returned to his native Nebraska with his wife and son. Timmermann had joined the Army in 1940 and earned his bars at OCS at Fort Benning.

Timmermann took one look and got on the radio to Colonel Engeman, who told him to get into the town with his infantry and tanks. As Timmermann set out, Engeman called Hoge, who set off cross-country in a jeep to get to the scene, weighing as he did the prospects of losing a battalion when the bridge blew up against the possibility of capturing it. In addition, he had just received an order to proceed south on the west bank until he linked up with the left flank of Third Army. To go for the bridge he would have to disobey direct orders, risking a court-martial and disgrace.

At 1500 Hoge arrived, looked, and ordered Engeman to seize the bridge. He figured he would lose only one platoon if the Germans blew it when it came under assault. Timmermann, meanwhile, had fought through scattered resistance and by 1600 was approaching the bridge. Germans on the east bank were firing machine guns and anti-aircraft guns at his company. His battalion commander, Maj. Murray Deevers, joined Timmermann. "Do you think you can get your company across that bridge," he asked.

"Well, we can try it, sir," Timmermann replied.

"Go ahead."

"What if the bridge blows up in my face?" Timmermann asked. Deevers turned and walked away without a word. Timmermann called to his squad leaders, "All right, we're going across."

He could see German engineers working with plungers. There was a huge explosion. It shook Remagen and sent a volcano of stone and earth erupting from the west end of the bridge. The Germans had detonated a cratering charge that gouged a deep hole in the earthen causeway joining the main road and the bridge platform. The crater that resulted made it impossible for vehicles to get onto the bridge—but not infantry.[17]

Timmermann turned to a squad leader: "Now, we're going to cross this bridge before—" At that instant, there was another deaf-

ening rumble and roar. The Germans had set off an emergency demolition two-thirds of the way across the bridge. Awestruck, the
men of A Company watched as the huge structure lifted up, and
steel, timbers, dust, and thick black smoke mixed in the air. Many of
the men threw themselves on the ground.

Ken Hechler, in *The Bridge at Remagen,* one of the best of all
accounts of the U.S. Army in action in World War II, and a model
for all oral history, described what happened next: "Everybody
waited for Timmermann's reaction. 'Thank God, now we won't
have to cross that damned thing,' Sgt. Mike Chinchar said fervently,
trying to reassure himself.

"Pvt. Johnny Ayres fingered the two grenades hooked onto the
rings of his pack suspenders, and nodded his head: 'We wouldn't
have had a chance.'

"But Timmermann, who had been trying to make out what was
left of the bridge through the thick haze, yelled:

" 'Look— she's still standing.'

"Most of the smoke and dust had cleared away, and the men
followed their commander's gaze. The sight of the bridge still span-
ning the Rhine brought no cheers from the men. It was like an un-
welcome specter. The suicide mission was on again."[18]

Timmermann could see German engineers at the east end of
the bridge working frantically to try again to blow the bridge. He
waved his arm overhead in the "Follow me" gesture. Machine-gun
fire from one of the bridge towers made him duck. One of A Company's tanks pulled up to the edge of the crater and blasted the
tower. The German fire let up.

"Get going," Timmermann yelled. Major Deevers called out,
"I'll see you on the other side and we'll all have a chicken dinner."

"Chicken dinner, my foot, I'm all chicken right now," one of
the men of the first platoon protested. Deevers flushed. "Move on
across," he ordered.

"I tell you, I'm not going out there and get blown up," the GI
answered. "No sir, major, you can court-martial and shoot me, but I
ain't going out there on that bridge."

Timmermann was shouting, "Get going, you guys, get going."
He set the example, moving onto the bridge himself. That did it.
The lead platoon followed, crouching, running, dodging, watching
for holes in the bridge planking that covered the railroad tracks (put

down by the Germans so their vehicles could retreat over the bridge) but always moving in the direction of the Germans on the far shore.

Sgt. Joe DeLisio led the first squad. Sgts. Joe Petrencsik and Alex Drabik led the second. In the face of more machine-gun and 20mm anti-aircraft fire they dashed forward. "Get going," Timmermann yelled. The men took up the cry. "Get going," they shouted at one another. "Get going." Engineers were right behind them, searching for demolitions and tearing out electrical wires. The names were Chinchar, Samele, Massie, Wegener, Jensen. They were Italian, Czech, Norwegian, German, Russian. They were children of European immigrants, come back to the old country to liberate and redeem it.

On the far side, at the entrance to the tunnel, they could see a German engineer pushing on a plunger. There was nothing for it but to keep going. And nothing happened—apparently a stray bullet or shell had cut the wire leading to the demolition charges. Halfway across the bridge, three men found four packages of TNT weighing thirty pounds each, tied to I-beams under the decking. Using wire cutters, they worked on the demolitions until they splashed into the river. DeLisio got to the towers, ran up the circular staircase of the one to his right, where the firing was coming from, and on the fourth level found three German machine gunners, firing at the bridge.

"Hände hoch!" DeLisio commanded. They gave up; he picked up the gun they had been using and hurled it out the aperture. Men on the bridge saw it and were greatly encouraged. Drabik came running on at top speed. He passed the towers and got to the east bank. He was the first GI to cross the Rhine. Others were on his heels. They quickly made the German engineers in the tunnel prisoners. Timmermann sent Lieutenant Burrows and his platoon up the Erpeler Ley, saying, "You know, Jim, the old Fort Benning stuff; take the high ground and hold it." Burrows later said, "Taking Remagen and crossing the bridge were a breeze compared with climbing that hill." He took casualties, but he got to the top, where he saw far too many German men and vehicles spread out before him to even contemplate attacking them. He hung on at the edge of the summit. But he had the high ground, and the Americans were over the Rhine.[19]

Sixteen-year-old Pvt. Heinz Schwarz, who came from a village only a short distance upstream on the east bank of the Rhine from Remagen, was in the tunnel. "We were all still kids," he recalled. "The older soldiers in our unit stayed in the tunnel, but the rest of us were curious and went up to the bridge tower to get a better look." He heard the order ring out: "Everybody down! We're blowing the bridge!" He heard the explosion and saw the bridge rise up. "We thought it had been destroyed, and we were saved." But as the smoke cleared, he saw Timmermann and his men coming on. He ran down the circular stairs and got to the entrance to the tunnel just as DeLisio got to the tower. "I knew I had to somehow get myself out through the rear entrance of the tunnel and run home to my mother as fast as I could." He did. Fifteen years later he was a member of the Bundestag. At a ceremony on March 7, 1960, he met DeLisio. They swapped stories.[20]

As the word of Timmermann's toehold spread up the chain of command, to regiment, division, corps, and army, each general responded by ordering men on the scene to get over the bridge, for engineers to repair it, for units in the area to change direction and head for Remagen. Bradley was the most enthusiastic of all. He had been fearful of a secondary role in the final campaign, but with Hodges over the river he decided immediately to get First Army so fully involved that Eisenhower would have to support the bridgehead.

First, however, Bradley had to get by General Bull. The SHAEF G-3 was with Bradley when the word arrived. When Bradley outlined his plan, he related, Bull "looked at me as though I were a heretic. He scoffed: 'You're not going anywhere down there at Remagen. You've got a bridge, but it's in the wrong place. It just doesn't fit the plan.'

"I demanded, 'What in hell do you want us to do, pull back and blow it up?'"

Bradley got on the phone to Eisenhower. When he heard the news, Eisenhower was ecstatic. He said, "Brad, that's wonderful." Bradley said he wanted to push everything across he could. "Sure," Eisenhower responded, "get right on across with everything you've got. It's the best break we've had." Bradley felt it necessary to point out that Bull disagreed. "To hell with the planners," Eisenhower snapped. "Sure, go on, Brad, and I'll give you everything we got to hold that bridgehead. We'll make good use of it even if the terrain isn't too good."[21]

The Germans agreed with Eisenhower and Bradley that the Ludendorff Bridge was suddenly the most critical strategic spot in Europe. So like the Americans, they began rushing troops and vehicles to the site, to constrict and then eliminate the bridgehead, and made the last great commitment of the Luftwaffe to destroy it. Major Pauls, who had almost been court-martialed for sending his tanks and artillery over the bridge at Bonn on the morning of March 7, in the afternoon heard praise from the high command "for having been alert enough to get across when you could." He was ordered to march south immediately, to Remagen, that night, March 7–8.[22]

In the morning, the Luftwaffe attacked. Sgt. Waldemar Führing, one of Major Pauls's men, arrived in time to see the strike: "I lay a half mile from the bridge in some bushes. I could see how our Stukas tried to blow up the bridge. They were brave. They got close. But not a single bomb hit the bridge."[23]

Two great masses of men and weapons were on the move, heading toward Remagen. For the Germans, it was a hellish march through mud, traffic jams, abandoned vehicles, dead horses, dead men. Piper Cubs would spot them and bring down a tremendous shelling from American artillery on the west bank.

For the Americans, it was a hellish march over the bridge. Captain Roland of the 99th Division recalled the sign on one of the west bank towers: "Cross the Rhine with dry feet, courtesy of the 9th Armored Division." As he crossed, the night of March 7–8, "my mind flickered back to the historic episode in which Caesar crossed the same stream at almost the same location to fight the same enemy two thousand years before. My reverie was cut short by the whistle and crash of hostile shells. How exposed and vulnerable I felt on that strip of metal high above the black, swirling waters. Walking forward became extremely difficult. I had the feeling that each projectile was headed directly at my chest. Actually, we who had gained the bridge were relatively safe. The shells were hitting in the approaches to the bridge amid the marching troops who suffered many casualties." On the bridge, one shell hit on or near it every five minutes.[24]

Col. William Westmoreland (USMA 1936), chief of staff of the

9th Infantry, crossed that night lying on his belly on the hood of a jeep, spotting ahead for the driver for holes in the planking. In the morning he set up an anti-aircraft battery on top of the Erpeler Ley. He saw his first jet aircraft that day.[25]

Hitler ordered courts-martial for those responsible for failing to blow the bridge. The American crossing at Remagen cost Field Marshal von Rundstedt his job as commander in the West; on March 8, Hitler relieved him and put Field Marshal Albert Kesselring in his place. Hitler dismissed four other generals and ordered an all-out assault to destroy the bridge, including those jets Westmoreland saw, plus V-2s, plus frogmen to place explosives in the pilings, plus constant artillery bombardment. The Americans hurried anti-aircraft into the area. One observer of a German air strike recalled that when the planes appeared "there was so much firing from our guys that the ground shuddered; it was awesome. The entire valley around Remagen became cloaked in smoke and dust before the Germans left—only three minutes after they first appeared."[26]

The struggle for the bridgehead continued. The Americans poured in the artillery, depending on the Piper Cub FOs to direct the shells to a prime target. Sgt. Oswald Filla, a panzer commander, recalled "the impossible amount of artillery. Their artillery observers in the air were very good. Whenever we went anywhere around the bridgehead to see what could be done, we had, at most, a half hour before the first shells arrived."[27]

As the infantry and armor gradually forced the Germans back, hundreds of engineers worked to repair the bridge even as it was getting pounded, while thousands of other engineers labored to get pontoon bridges across into the bridgehead. The 291st Engineer Combat Battalion, commanded by Lt. Col. David Pergrin, worked with grim resolve despite air and artillery assaults. The engineers also built a series of log and net booms upstream to intercept German explosives carried to the bridge by the current.[28]

Capt. John Barnes (USMA 1942) of the 51st ECB was involved in building a twenty-five-ton heavy pontoon bridge. His description of how it was done illustrates how good the American engineers had become at this business. Construction began at 1600 hours, March 10, with the building of approach ramps on both shores two kilometers upstream (south) of the bridge. Smoke pots hid the engineers from German snipers, but "unobserved enemy artillery fire harassed the bridge site. Several engineers were wounded and six were killed. The Germans even fired several V-2 rockets from launchers in Holland, the only time they ever fired on German soil."

Construction continued through the night. "The bridge was built in parts, with four groups working simultaneously on 4-boat rafts, mostly by feel in the dark. By 0400 the next morning, fourteen 4-boat rafts had been completed and were ready to be assembled together as a bridge. When the rafts were in place they were reinforced with pneumatic floats between the steel pontoons so the bridge could take the weight of 36-ton Sherman tanks."

The engineers used triple anchors to hold the rafts in place, but as the bridge extended out to midstream the anchors couldn't hold, despite help from the motorboats. "At about this time we discovered that the Navy had some LCVPs in the area and we requested their assistance. Ten came to the rescue. They were able to hold the bridge against the current until we could install a 1" steel cable across the Rhine immediately upstream of the bridge, to which the anchors for each pontoon were attached. This solved the problem of holding the bridge against the current. The remaining 4-boat rafts were connected to the anchor cable, eased into position and connected to the ever extending bridge until the far shore was reached.

"Finally [sic!], at 1900 March 11, 27 hours after starting construction, the 969-ft heavy pontoon bridge was completed. It was the longest floating bridge ever constructed by the Corps of Engineers under fire. Traffic started at 2300, with one vehicle crossing every two minutes. During the first seven days, 2,500 vehicles, including tanks, crossed the bridge."[29]

On March 17 the great structure of the Ludendorff, pounded unmercifully by first the Americans and then the Germans, finally sagged abruptly and then fell apart with a roar, killing twenty-eight and injuring ninety-three of the engineers working on it. But by then the Americans had six pontoon bridges over the river, and nine divisions on the far side. They were in a position to head east, then north to meet Ninth Army, which would be crossing the Rhine north of Düsseldorf. When First and Ninth Armies met, they would have the German Fifteenth Army in the Ruhr Valley encircled. It took First Army ten days of fighting through deep gullies and dense woods against fierce opposition to reach the autobahn, only eleven kilometers east of Remagen. But once there, it had good roads leading north.

■

Michael Doubler rightly judges that everything came together at Remagen. All that General Marshall had worked for and hoped for and built for in creating this citizen-army, happened. It was one of the great victories in the Army's history. The credit goes to the men—Timmermann, DeLisio, Drabik, through to Hoge, Bradley, and Ike—and to the system the U.S. Army had developed in Europe, which bound these men together into a team that featured initiative at the bottom and a cold-blooded determination and competency at the top.[30]

Up north, Montgomery's preparations continued. Down south, Patton's Third Army cleared the Saarland and the Palatinate in a spectacular campaign. As his divisions approached the Rhine, Patton had 500 assault boats, plus LCVPs and DUKWs, brought forward, along with 7,500 engineers, but with no fanfare, no fuss, no publicity, in deliberate contrast to Montgomery and so as to not alert the Germans. On the night of March 22–23, the 5th Division began to cross the river at Oppenheim, south of Mainz. The Germans were unprepared; by midnight the entire 11th Regiment had crossed by boat with only twenty casualties. Well before dawn the whole of the 5th and a part of the 90th Divisions were across. The Germans launched a counterattack against the 5th Division, using students from an officer candidate school at nearby Wiesbaden. They were good soldiers, and managed to infiltrate the American positions, but after a busy night and part of the next morning they were dead or prisoners.

At dawn, German artillery began to fire, and the Luftwaffe sent twelve planes to bomb and strafe. The Americans pushed east anyway. By the afternoon the whole of the 90th Division was on the far side, along with the 4th Armored. Patton called Bradley: "Brad, don't tell anyone but I'm across."

"Well, I'll be damned—you mean across the Rhine?"

"Sure am, I sneaked a division over last night."

A little later, at the Twelfth Army Group morning briefing, the Third Army reported: "Without benefit of aerial bombing, ground smoke, artillery preparation, and airborne assistance, the Third Army at 2200 hours, March 22, crossed the Rhine River."[31]

The following day Patton walked across a pontoon bridge built by his engineers. He stopped in the middle. While every GI in the immediate area who had a camera took his picture, he urinated into the Rhine—a long, high, steady stream. As he buttoned up, Patton said, "I've waited a long time to do that. I didn't even piss this morning when I got up so I would have a really full load. Yes, sir, the pause that refreshes." When he reached the east bank, he faked a fall, rose with two hands of German soil and remarked, "Thus William the Conqueror."[32]

That night, March 23–24, Montgomery put his operation in motion. Generals Eisenhower and Simpson climbed to a church tower to watch Ninth Army do its part. More than 2,000 American guns opened fire at 0100, March 24. For an hour, more than a thousand American shells a minute ranged across the Rhine, 65,261 rounds in all. Meanwhile 1,406 B-17s unloaded on Luftwaffe bases just east of the river. At 0200 the assault boats, powered by fifty-five-horsepower motors and carrying seven men with a crew of two, pushed off. Not until the first boats were almost touching the far shore did the American artillery lift its fire and begin plastering targets farther to the east. The enemy was so battered that only a few mortar shells landed among the first wave. Things went so well that before daylight, the 79th and 30th Divisions were fully across the river, at a cost of only thirty-one casualties. They set off, headed east.

At airfields in Britain, France, and Belgium, meanwhile, the paratroopers and gliderborne troops from the British 6th and the American 17th Airborne Divisions began to load up in their C-47s, C-46s, or gliders. This was an airborne operation on a scale comparable with D-Day; on June 6, 1944, 21,000 British and American airborne troops had gone in, while on March 24, 1945, it was 21,680 British and American. Altogether there were 1,696 transport planes and 1,348 gliders involved (British Horsa and Hamicar gliders, and American Wacos; all of them made of canvas and wood). They would be guarded on the way to the drop zone and landing zone (DZ and LZ) by more than 900 fighter escorts, with another 900 fighters providing cover and patrol over the DZ. To the east, 1,250 additional P-47s would guard against German movement to the DZ, while 240 B-24s would drop supplies to the men in the DZ. Counting the B-17s that saturated the DZ with bombs, there were some 9,503 Allied planes involved.[33]

The airborne troopers' objectives were wooded high ground

affording observation of the river crossing sites, exits from Wesel, and crossings of nearby streams. Churchill, Eisenhower, Brooke, and many other dignitaries, plus the press, were present to watch. A couple of B-17s were loaded with cameramen and assigned to fly around the DZ to take pictures. What concerned them was the flak; the Ruhr Valley and environs, Germany's industrial heartland, was the most heavily defended in the country. German artillery and anti-aircraft gunners had years of experience in fighting off the air raids over the Ruhr, and the transports and gliders would be coming in low and slow (500 feet at 120 knots per hour), beginning just after 1000 hours. The tow planes had two gliders each, instead of one as on D-Day and in Market-Garden, a hazardous undertaking even on an exercise.

The DZ was just north and east of Wesel. It took the air armada two and a half hours to cross the Rhine. Lt. Ellis Scripture was the navigator on the lead plane, a B-17. It was a new experience for him to fly in a B-17 at 500 feet and 120 knots—that was perilously close to stall-out speed. Still, he recalled, "It was a beautiful spring morning and it was a tremendous thrill for us as we led the C-47s to the middle of the Rhine. Hundreds and hundreds of aircraft came flying over. . . . The thrill was the climax of the entire war as we poured tens of thousands of troops across the final barrier to the Fatherland."[34]

Reporter Richard C. Hottelet was on one of the B-17s carrying cameras to record the event. "The sky above was pale blue," he wrote. "Below us, golden soil and bright green meadows were cut by long morning shadows. Flying at a few hundred feet, banking steeply to let the cameramen get their shots, we saw the solid phalanxes of olive-green troop carriers and tow planes and gliders nose to tail. . . . It was a mighty olive-green river that surged steadily and inevitably over Germany."

Once across the river, on the edge of the DZ where the big bombers and fighters had just dropped their bombs, the scene changed: "Here there was no sunlight; here in the center of green and fertile land was a clearly marked area of death. The smoke seemed a shroud." The German anti-aircraft guns sprang to life. Hottelet's plane was hit; he had to bail out, but fortunately not until the plane had crossed back to the west bank of the river, where he landed safely among friends.[35]

Earlier that morning, before the flights took off, over the radio

"Axis Sally" had told the men of the 17th Airborne to leave their parachutes home, because they would be able to walk down on the flak. She had not lied. The flak and ground fire were the most intense of any airborne operation of the war. One American officer, a veteran from the Normandy drop, said there "was no comparison," while an equally experienced British officer said that "this drop made Arnhem look like a Sunday picnic."[36]

Sgt. Valentin Klopsch, in command of a platoon of German engineers in a cow stable about ten kilometers north of Wesel, described the action from his point of view. First there was the air bombardment, then the artillery, all of which put the fifteen- and sixteen-year-olds in his platoon into panic. When the shooting stopped, they were amazed to find themselves still alive, even though badly shaken. They got up, began looking around, and started congratulating each other for surviving. Klopsch and a couple of other old hands told them to get down, because the enemy was coming.

"And now, listen," Klopsch said. "Coming from across the Rhine there was a roaring and booming in the air. In waves aircraft were approaching at different heights. And then the paratroopers were jumping, the chutes were opening like mushrooms. It looked like lines of pearls loosening from the planes." The Luftwaffe flak gunners, who had thought their day was over when the bombers passed by, went back to work. The flak was heavy, "but what a superiority of the enemy in weapons, in men, in equipment. The sky was full of paratroopers, and then new waves came in. And always the terrible roaring of the low flying planes. All around us was turning like a whirl." The Americans formed into squads and platoons, set up their mortars, and went to work themselves. They attacked Klopsch's cowshed. His platoon fired until out of ammunition, when Klopsch put up a white flag. "And then the Americans approached, chewing gum, hair dressed like Cherokees, but Colts at the belt." He and the surviving members of his platoon were marched to a POW cage on a farm and ordered to sit and not move. Decades later, he recalled "What a wonderful rest after all the bombardments and the terrible barrage."[37]

The C-46s took a pounding from the flak. This was the first time they had been used to carry paratroopers. The plane had a door on each side of the fuselage, which permitted a faster exit for the troopers, a big advantage over the single door on the C-47s. But what was not known until too late was that the C-46's fuel system was highly vulnerable to enemy fire. Fourteen of the seventy-two C-46s burst into flames as soon as they were hit. Eight others went down; in each case the paratroopers got out, but the crews did not.

For the gliders, it was terrifying. The sky was full of air bursts and tracers. Machine-gun bullets ripped through the canvas. The pilots—all lieutenants, most of them not yet eligible to vote—could not take evasive action. They fixed their eyes on the spot they had chosen to land and tried to block out everything else. Over half the gliders were badly hit and nearly all made crash landings amid heavy small-arms fire.

Pvt. Wallace Thompson, a medic in the paratroopers, was assigned a jeep and rode in the driver's seat behind the pilots of a Waco. He was very unhappy about this. Through the flight he kept telling the pilots, Lts. John Heffner and Bruce Merryman, that he would much prefer to jump into combat. They ignored his complaints. As they crossed the river, the pilots told Thompson to start his engine, so that as soon as they landed they could release the nose latches and he could drive out.

Over the target, just a few meters above the ground, an 88 shell burst just behind Thompson's jeep. The concussion broke the latches of the nose section, which flipped up and locked, throwing the pilots out. The blast cut the ropes that held the jeep, which leaped out ahead of the glider, engine running, flying through the air at high speed, Thompson gripping the steering wheel with all his might. He made a perfect four-wheel landing and beat the glider to the ground, thus becoming the first man in history to solo in a jeep.

The glider crashed and tipped, ending up in a vertical position, rear end up. Lieutenants Merryman and Heffner somehow survived their flying exit, but were immediately hit by machine-gun bullets, Heffner by one in the hand and Merryman by two in the leg. They crawled into a ditch. Thompson drove over to them.

"What the hell happened?" he demanded, but just then a bullet creased his helmet. He scrambled out of the jeep and into the ditch, where he berated the pilots and the entire glider program. "His last word," Merryman recalled, "was that he had just taken his last glider ride, they could shoot him and put him in one, but that would be the only way." Then Thompson treated their wounds and after treating other wounded in the area, drove Merryman and Heffner to an aid station.[38]

Varsity featured not only a flying jeep; it also provided a unique event in U.S. Army Air Force history. The glider pilots bringing in the 194th Glider Infantry were told two weeks before the operation that one more infantry company was necessary to the 194th's mission, and that they would be it. There were nearly 200 of them. They had received a quick briefing in infantry tactics and weapons. They landed under heavy ground fire and took substantial casualties among the infantry and pilots, but despite continuing machine-gun fire and exploding mortars, they got organized and did their job. Later that day they were attacked by 200 German infantrymen, a tank, and two flak guns, but managed to drive them off. Lt. Elbert Jella damaged the tank with his bazooka. The retreating tank ran over one of the flak guns; the other was captured by the glider pilots. Overall the Air Force officers fighting as an infantry company suffered thirty-one casualties. They got written up in *Stars and Stripes*.[39]

At the aid station, Lieutenants Merryman and Heffner met the crew of a B-24 that had been shot down and successfully crashlanded. The Air Force guys told their story: when they started to dash out of their burning plane, the first man was shot, so the rest came out with hands up. The Germans took them to the cellar of a farmhouse, gave them some cognac, and held them "while the Germans decided who was winning. A little later the Germans realized they were losing and surrendered their weapons and selves to the bomber crew. The Germans were turned over to the airborne and the bomber crew went to the aid station." This was perhaps the only time a bomber crew took German infantry prisoners.[40]

The German gunners, all in the Luftwaffe, wanted no part of ground fighting. When the airborne troops began to form up and move to their objectives, the Germans tended to give up. It helped the men of the 17th Airborne considerably that they had just been issued the new 57mm recoilless rifle, which weighed only forty-five pounds, was fired from the shoulder, and was more deadly than the bazooka.[41] Before the end of the day the airborne troops had all their objectives, and over the next couple of days the linkup with the infantry was complete. Twenty-first Army Group was over the Rhine and headed east.

By the first week of spring 1945 Eisenhower's armies had done what he had been planning for since the beginning of the year—

close to the Rhine along its length, with a major crossing north of Düsseldorf—and what he had dared to hope for and was prepared to support, additional crossings by First Army in the center and Third Army to the south. The time for exploitation had arrived. Some of the Allied infantry and armored divisions faced stiff resistance, others only sporadic resistance, others none at all. Whatever was in front of them—rough terrain, enemy strong points, more rivers to cross—their generals were as one in taking up the phrase Lieutenant Timmermann had used at the Remagen bridge—"Get going!"

The 90th Division, on Patton's left flank, headed east toward Hanau on the Main River. It crossed in assault boats on the night of March 28. Maj. John Cochran's battalion ran into a battalion of Hitler Youth officer candidates, teenage Germans who were eager to fight. They set up a roadblock in a village. As Cochran's men advanced toward it, the German boys let go with their machine gun, killing one American. Cochran put some artillery fire on the roadblock and destroyed it, killing three. "One youth, perhaps aged 16, held up his hands," Cochran recalled. "I was very emotional over the loss of a good soldier and I grabbed the kid and took off my cartridge belt.

"I asked him if there were more like him in the town. He gave me a stare and said, 'I'd rather die than tell you anything.' I told him to pray, because he was going to die. I hit him across the face with my thick, heavy belt. I was about to strike him again when I was grabbed from behind by Chaplain Kerns. He said, 'Don't!' Then he took that crying child away. The Chaplain had intervened not only to save a life but to prevent me from committing a murder. Had it not been for the Chaplain, I would have."[42]

From the crossing of the Rhine to the end of the war, every man who died, died needlessly. It was that feeling that almost turned Major Cochran into a murderer. On the last day of March, Sergeant Schlemmer of the 82nd had a particularly gruesome experience that almost broke him. His squad was advancing, supported by a tank. Six troopers were riding on the tank, while he and five others were following in its tracks, which freed them from worry about mines. A hidden 88 fired. The shell hit the gun turret, blowing off the troopers, killing two and wounding the other four. "The force of the blast blew them to the rear of the tank near me," Schlemmer recalled. "They lay as they fell. A second round then came screaming in, this time to ricochet off the front of the tank. The tank reversed gears and backed up over three of our wounded, crushing them to death. I could only sit down and bawl, whether out of frustration of being unable to help them, whether from the futility of the whole damn war, or whether from hatred of the Germans for causing it all, I've never been able to understand."[43]

That same day, Corp. James Pemberton, a 1942 high school graduate who went into ASTP and then to the 103rd Division as a replacement, was also following a tank. "My guys started wandering and drifting a bit, and I yelled at them to get in the tank tracks to avoid the mines. They did and we followed. The tank was rolling over Schu mines like crazy. I could see them popping left and right like popcorn." Pemberton had an eighteen-year-old replacement in the squad; he told him to hop up and ride on the tank, thinking he would be out of the way up there. An 88 fired. The replacement fell off. The tank went into reverse and backed over him, crushing him from the waist down. "There was one scream, and some mortars hit the Kraut 88 and our tank went forward again. To me, it was one of the worst things I went through. This poor bastard had graduated from high school in June, was drafted, took basic training, shipped overseas, had thirty seconds of combat, and was killed."

Pemberton's unit kept advancing. "The Krauts always shot up all their ammo and then surrendered," he remembered. Hoping to avoid such nonsense, in one village the CO sent a Jewish private who spoke German forward with a white flag, calling out to the German boys to surrender. "They shot him up so bad that after it was over the medics had to slide a blanket under his body to take him away." Then the Germans started waving their own white flag. Single file, eight of them emerged from a building, hands up. "They were very cocky. They were about 20 feet from me when I saw the leader suddenly realize he still had a pistol in his shoulder holster. He reached into his jacket with two fingers to pull it out and throw it away.

"One of our guys yelled, 'Watch it! He's got a gun!' and came running up shooting and there were eight Krauts on the ground shot up but not dead. They wanted water but no one gave them any. I never felt bad about it although I'm sure civilians would be horrified. But these guys asked for it. If we had not been so tired and frustrated and keyed up and mad about our boys they shot up, it never would have happened. But a lot of things happen in war and both sides know the penalties."[44]

Hitler and the Nazis had poisoned the minds of the boys Germany was throwing into the battle. Capt. F. W. Norris of the 90th Division ran into a roadblock. His company took some casualties, then blasted away, wounding many. "The most seriously wounded was a young SS sergeant who looked just like one of Hitler's supermen. He had led the attack. He was bleeding copiously and badly needed some plasma." One of Norris's medics started giving him a transfusion. The wounded German, who spoke excellent English, demanded to know if there was any Jewish blood in the plasma. The medic said damned if he knew, in the United States people didn't make such a distinction. The German said if he couldn't have a guarantee that there was no Jewish blood he would refuse treatment.

"I had been listening and had heard enough," Norris remembered. "I turned to this SS guy and in very positive terms I told him I really didn't care whether he lived or not, but if he did not take the plasma he would certainly die. He looked at me calmly and said, 'I would rather die than have any Jewish blood in me.'

"So he died."[45]

By March 28, First Army had broken out of the Remagen bridgehead. General Rose's 3rd Armored Division led the way, headed for Paderborn and the linkup with Ninth Army to complete the encirclement of the German army in the Ruhr. That day, Rose raced ahead, covering 150 kilometers, the longest gain on any single day of the war for any American unit. By March 31, he was attacking a German tank training center outside Paderborn. Rose was at the head of a column in his jeep. Turning a corner, his driver ran smack into the rear of a Tiger tank. The German tank commander, about eighteen years old, opened his turret hatch and leveled his burp gun at Rose, yelling at him to surrender.

Rose, his driver, and his aide got out of the jeep and put their hands up. For some reason, the tank commander became extremely agitated—later, it was rumored in the American army that the German knew Rose was Jewish, but that almost certainly was not true—and kept pointing to Rose and hollering at him while gesturing toward Rose's pistol. Rose lowered his right arm to release his web belt and thus drop his hip holster to the ground. Apparently, the German boy thought he was going to draw his pistol; in a screaming rage, he fired his machine pistol straight into Rose's head, killing him instantly. The driver and the aide managed to flee and lived to tell the story. Maurice Rose was the first and only division commander killed in ETO.[46]

The tank school at Paderborn had brand-new Tigers. They could be deadly. Ten of them caught a column of Shermans in the open. The Tigers destroyed seventeen Shermans and a dozen half-tracks, but they paid a price of their own. One advantage of the Sherman was that it could traverse its turret much faster than the Tiger. In the right circumstances, an American tank commander could get in the first shot. In this action, one 3rd Armored tanker used that advantage well. Knowing that the Sherman's 75mm cannon could not penetrate the Tiger's armor, he had his gunner load a white phosphorus round. As a Tiger turned on him, he fired. The shell struck the glaces plate of the Tiger right above the driver's compartment with a blazing crescendo of flames and smoke. Captain Cooper, who saw the fight, reported that "the whole face plate in front of the turret was covered with burning particles of white phosphorous which stuck to the sides of the Tiger. The smoke engulfed the tank and the fan in the engine compartment sucked the smoke inside the fighting compartment. The German crew thought the tank was on fire and immediately abandoned it even though the tank actually suffered very little damage."

The American tanker turned his turret and fired another white phosphorus shell at a second Tiger, again hitting the front glaces plate with similar results. Cooper commented, "Thus the brave ingenious tank commander knocked out two Tigers without ever getting a penetration."[47]

Such resistance was rare. In most cases the retreating Germans did not stop to fight. Generally they passed right through the villages, rather than use them as roadblocks or strong points. This was fortunate for the villages, because the American practice was to demolish any buildings that were defended, but if white flags were waving from the windows and no German troops were in sight, they let it be.

First and Third Armies were advancing in mostly rural areas, untouched by the war. The GIs were spending their nights in houses. They would give the inhabitants five minutes or so to clear out. The German families were indignant. The GIs were insistent. As Lt. Max Lale put it in a March 30 letter home, "None of us have any sympathy for them, because we all have been taught to accept the consequences of our actions—these people apparently feel they are the victims of something they had no hand in planning, and they seem to feel they are being mistreated." The stock joke had it that every German had a cousin in Milwaukee.[48]

The rural German homes had creature comforts—electricity, hot water, flush toilets, soft white toilet paper—such as most people thought existed in 1945 only in America. On his first night in a house, Pvt. Joe Burns spent five minutes in a hot shower. Fifty-one years later he declared it to be "the most exquisite five minutes in my life. Never before or since have I had such pure pleasure."[49] Pvt. David Webster recalled washing his hands at the sink and deciding "This was where we belonged. A small, sociable group, a clean, well-lighted house [behind blackout curtains], a cup of coffee—paradise."[50]

Things were looking up, even though there was still a lot of Germany to overrun.

19

Victory

April 1–May 7, 1945

EASTER CAME on April 1 in 1945. In many cases the celebration of the Resurrection brought the GIs and German civilians together. Sgt. Lindy Sawyers of the 99th Division and his squad had moved into a house that was big enough to allow the frau and her two small girls to remain. He remembered that on the day before Easter, "I entered the house and heard a wail from the mom and kids." He asked what was wrong and was told that some of his men had found and stolen the family Easter cake. Sawyers investigated and caught two recruits who had done the deed. He returned the cake to its rightful owners. "There was great rejoicing and I felt virtuous, for a second at least.

"Easter Sunday morning a lot of us went to services in the church in town. There we sat, with weapons, for the service in the church of the conquered whose goods we were systematically looting."

Pvt. Joe Bombach was a professional musician in the 99th. He liberated a violin and went to the service with a buddy who was a pianist. The church had an organ. They began playing. The church was full and the Germans asked for more. They played for three hours. "The Germans loved it. I thought it was one of the most memorable happenings we had. It brought us all together for a day."

Sgt. Oakley Honey in the same outfit recalled that as his squad left the house they had slept in, "the old lady was handing something to each guy as we left. As I got to the woman, I could see tears in her eyes as she placed a decorated Easter Egg in my hand. We had treated them well and not disturbed the main part of the house. For this they were thankful. There was an unwritten code. If you had to fight for a town, anything in it was yours. If we were allowed to walk in unopposed, we treated the population much better."[1]

For artilleryman Max Lale, "it was a bit like Easter at home," he wrote his wife on April 2. "The German children were out searching for brightly colored eggs as our own youngsters do. Most of the families in town gave Easter eggs to our soldiers."[2]

On Easter Sunday 1944, the U.S. Army had had no troops or vehicles of any kind on the European Continent north of Rome. The American airmen had been a powerful presence in the skies over Germany, but on the ground the only Americans in Germany were POWs. One year later, there were over one million GIs in Germany, most of whom had been civilians in 1943, many of them in 1944. Tens of thousands of American vehicles, two-and-a-half-ton trucks, jeeps, DUKWs, armored personnel carriers, self-propelled artillery, towed artillery, towed LCVPs, and more rolled down the autobahns and secondary roads, covered by thousands of airplanes ranging in size from Piper Cubs to B-17s and B-24s—most of them built in 1943 or 1944, some of them in 1945.

Captain Lale described the scene: "Day after day we roll down German roads, going ever deeper into the interior of the country. Now they are country trails, and now they are autobahns, but always they are alive with army vehicles rolling forward. You get the feeling that the army is an immense flood pouring over the countryside, tipped with violence at the crest and depositing flotsam in the backwaters. You move with the tide, and it carries you along in an almost effortless fashion."[3]

In the villages and small towns in central Germany, civilians stood on the sidewalks, awestruck by this display of mobility and firepower. Few of them had any illusions about how the war was going to end. Churchill once commented that "the Hun is always either at your throat or at your feet." The GIs agreed. The older German civilians they met told the Americans they had never been Nazis, had never trusted Hitler, and had no desire other than to be done with the war so that they could get on with their lives. They

DRIVE TO THE ELBE
April 4 – May 7, 1945

FRONT LINE AS OF:
- - - - April 4
· · · · April 21
——— May 7

21	Allied army group
FIRST	Allied army
◦◦◦	Allied army group boundary
◦◦	Allied army boundary
⤳	Siegfried Line

NETHERLANDS

GERMANY

Kiel
Lübeck
Wismar
Schwerin
Hamburg
Bremen
Elbe R.
Hanover
Magdeburg
Dessau
Torgau
Berlin
Elbe R.
Dresden
Liepzig
Colditz
Weimar
Nordhausen
Kassel
Paderborn
Münster
Dortmund
Düsseldorf
Cologne

RUHR POCKET (April 4)
RUHR

Can. FIRST
Br. SECOND
21 (MONTGOMERY)
12 (BRADLEY)
NINTH
FIRST
FIFTEENTH

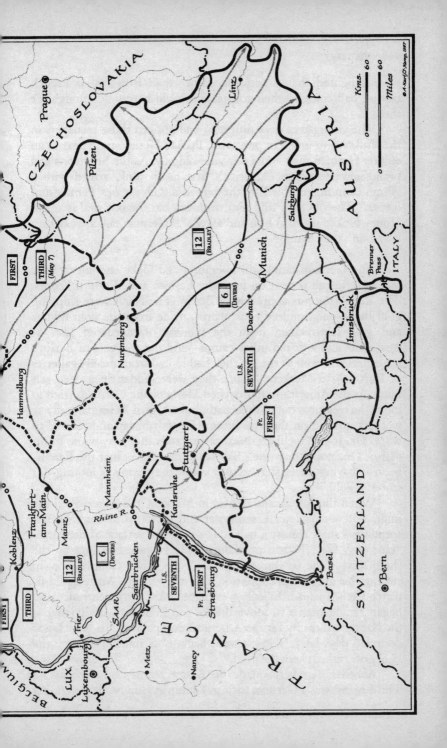

were delighted that Americans, rather than Russians or French troops, had come to their towns, and could hardly do enough for them.

The youngsters were different, and not just those teenagers in the Volksstrum units. In one town, Private Honey stood next to an elderly German man and a ten-year-old boy. As the Shermans and brand-new Pershings (America's first heavy tank, armed with a 90mm cannon) rumbled by the boy said, *"Deutsches Panzer lind besser."* The old man told him to shush, but the boy said it again. Honey looked down at him and asked, "If German tanks are better, why aren't they here?"[4]

The German tanks still operating and lucky enough to have fuel were in full retreat on both the Eastern and Western Fronts. The Red Army was approaching Berlin. The Nazis were shipping gold bars—one hundred tons' worth, made from the gold fillings and gold teeth taken from the mouths of murdered Jews at Auschwitz and a dozen other camps—and the contents of Berlin's art galleries as well as the art they had looted from the art galleries of Europe—to Merkers. There they were hidden in a deep salt mine. As the Americans approached Merkers, the Germans tried to move the treasures out of their path, but on April 1 German railway workers insisted on their traditional Easter holiday and refused to work. Dr. Josef Goebbels, Nazi propaganda minister, wrote in his diary, "One could tear one's hair when one thinks that the Reichsbahn is having an Easter holiday while the enemy is looting our stores of gold."[5]

When the Americans arrived in Merkers, they discovered the mine. A few days later Eisenhower and Patton paid it a visit, descending a shaft almost a half mile under the surface of the earth. "Hot dog, Ike!" Patton proclaimed. He proposed sealing up the shaft, leaving the treasures in place. Then, when Congress began cutting the Army's appropriation after the war, the Army could finance itself. Instead, Eisenhower placed MPs at the entrance and began arrangements to move the loot to Frankfurt, designated as the headquarters city for the American occupation zone, which was done ten days later. The art went back to its rightful owners; the U.S. government kept the gold.[6]

Another discovery, made on Easter Sunday by elements of Third Army, was a German toxic gas dump at Hundstadt containing some 50,000 gas-filled shells ready to be fired. Other gas dumps were found later, including five barges on the Danube loaded with 2,500 gas-filled bombs.[7] The Americans had their own stocks, just in case. The Germans had inaugurated gas warfare in the trenches of World War I, a criminally stupid mistake because the prevailing winds in Europe blow west to east. Consequently German generals in World War II wanted no part of gas. But of course they could not make a final decision, only Hitler could. But even in early April 1945, when he was at his most desperate and most crazed, he never ordered gas warfare. Apparently this was because he had been gassed in World War I. So it was not true that Hitler would stop at nothing; he drew the line at gas warfare.

The GIs were surprised to find how much they liked the Germans. Clean, hardworking, disciplined, cute kids, educated, middle-class in their tastes and life-styles—the Germans seemed to many American soldiers to be "just like us." Private Webster of the 101st hated the Nazis and wished more of the German villages would be destroyed, so that the Germans would suffer as the French and Belgians and Italians had suffered, and thus learn not to start wars. But despite himself, Webster was drawn to the people. "The Germans I have seen so far have impressed me as clean, efficient, law-abiding people," he wrote his parents on April 14. They were regular churchgoers. "In Germany everybody goes out and works. They are cleaner, more progressive, and more ambitious than either the English or the French."[8]

With a growing area of western and central Germany under American occupation, the high command ordered a policy of non-fraternization. GIs were told they could not talk to *any* German, even small children, except on official business. This absurd order, which flew in the face of human nature in so obvious a way, was impossible to enforce. Still some tried. Webster recalled a replacement lieutenant who "became such a fiend on the non-fraternization policy that he ordered all butts field-stripped [torn apart and scattered] so that the Germans might derive no pleasure from American tobacco."[9]

In some cases the GIs mistreated the civilian population, and they engaged in widespread looting, especially of wine, jewelry, Nazi memorabilia, and other portable items. Combat veterans insist that the worst of this sort of thing was carried out by replacements who had arrived too late to see any action. These American teenagers could be especially brutal in their treatment of German POWs. There were some rapes, not many because the Army's policy was to identify, try, and, if found guilty, execute rapists (forty-nine GIs were shot for rape or murder). Overall, it is simple fact to state that the American and British occupying armies, in comparison to the other conquering armies in World War II, acted correctly and honorably. As a single example, a German woman in Königsberg when it was occupied by the Red Army recalled how, after she and her friends had been repeatedly raped, "we often asked the soldiers to shoot us, but they always answered: 'Russian soldiers do not shoot women, only German soldiers do that.' "[10]

So the Germans in areas occupied by the Americans were lucky, and they knew it. They did their best, most of them, to please the Americans, with considerable success. There was something approaching mutual admiration. That caused the GIs to wonder about what they had heard about the Germans. Glenn Gray spoke to the point: "The enemy could not have changed so quickly from a beast to a likable human being. Thus, the conclusion is nearly forced upon the GIs that they have been previously blinded by fear and hatred and the propaganda of their own government."[11] The theme of German-American relations in the first week of April 1945 was harmony.

Corp. Roger Foehringer was an ASTP student who went into the 106th Division. He was captured along with four buddies. On Easter Sunday, their guards began marching them east, to flee the oncoming American Army. Foehringer and his men dropped out of the line, hid in a wood, and thus escaped. They started moving west. Near the village of Versbach someone shot at them. They ran. Up on a hill they saw two elderly gentlemen waving their arms, motioning for the GIs to come their way. They did. The Germans showed them a cave and indicated they should stay put. They spent the night. They could hear and see the German army heading east.

In the morning, Foehringer related, "two young boys came into the cave and brought with them black bread, lard and ersatz coffee. Hot!!!! We couldn't communicate with them, but they let us know we should stay put. This continued through April 5. Late in the afternoon of the 6th, the boys came running up to the cave yelling, 'Amerikaners komme, Amerikaners komme!' So we and the boys raced down the hill toward Versbach. The whole little village was surrounding a jeep in the center of the square and on top of the hood of the jeep was an American sergeant waving a 45 around in the air."

It turned out the sergeant was a mechanic with a tank destroyer outfit from the rear who had got to drinking and decided he was going to the front to see what it was like. So he stole a jeep and took off. He had no idea where he was and hoped Foehringer did. For his part, before risking an attempt to pass through the front line from the German side, Foehringer wanted to thank those who had helped him. "Every jeep in the world had a foot locker with all kinds of stuff," he remembered: "Candy bars, rations, bandages and medical supplies. So we opened the foot locker and threw everything to the people." Then all five GIs scrambled onto the jeep. "There wasn't much to us," Foehringer explained. "I was down to 100 pounds, so were the others. So we were only about 500 pounds."

The sergeant drove west, toward Würzburg. Foehringer saw "burning German half-tracks, tanks, trucks, dead soldiers laying alongside the road, but no sign of troops, ours or theirs." Near Würzburg they came into the lines of the 42nd Division, safe and sound. They were able to report that there was no German front line.*

On Easter Sunday, Twenty-first Army Group and Twelfth Army Group linked up near Paderborn, completing the encirclement of the Ruhr. Some 400,000 German soldiers were trapped, while the remainder of Nazi Germany was cut off from its weapons and ammunition supply. Eisenhower issued a proclamation to the German troops and people, in leaflet form and via radio, urging the soldiers to surrender and the people to begin planting crops. He described the hopelessness of their situation and warned them that future resistance would only add to their future miseries.[12]

Most Germans heartily agreed. Thousands of soldiers threw

*Thirty years later Foehringer, with his family, returned to Versbach. He had never gotten the names of the boys who helped him, but through inquiry he got the names of two brothers of about the right age. He went to one brother's home and was greeted by the frau, who took one look and yelled back at her husband, *"Mein Gott,* it's the American!" He came running. The two men recognized each other immediately and embraced. The other brother was summoned. The families celebrated. Foehringer hosted a grand dinner at the local restaurant. (Roger Foehringer memoir, EC.)

down their arms, took off their uniforms, put on civilian clothes, and headed home. Farmers began plowing, even if they had to use human rather than horse power. But a core of fighting men remained, including SS, Hitler Youth, officer candidates. Many of them were fanatics; nearly all of them were mere boys. They didn't know much about making war, but they were such daredevils and so well armed they could cause considerable harm. Twenty-year-old Pvt. Erich Womelsdorf of the 11th Panzer Division, who had fought in Russia and France, described what he saw. "Two trucks from Berlin arrived, crowded with boys of fifteen and sixteen. Each of them had a brand-new panzerfaust. They went out hunting, climbing a switchback road up into the Harz Mountains, hiding, waiting for the next tank to come along. When it came, they hit it from the side, then ran away, to play the game again. They could not be pinned down. It held the Americans up, some, but it really did not accomplish much. My division commander refused to deploy them. He said, 'I never want to carry that responsibility.' "[13]

Thousands of ordinary German soldiers also carried on the battle. Many were at the front involuntarily—their fear of the Gestapo was greater than their fear of the GIs—but an impressive percentage were there because they felt it was their duty. Like most of those who continued the struggle, Maj. Hannibal von Lüttichau had conflicting motivations. "I hoped the Americans would hurry up and get it over because we expected nothing good from the Russians," he said in a 1995 interview. But still he continued to fight the Americans, because "We needed to hold out as long as possible in order to maintain a good conscience; we could not betray the Fatherland. This is something every soldier knew."[14]

There was another motivation. Lt. Wenzel Andreas Borgert put it this way: "The Allies' insistence on unconditional surrender made us fight longer. If they had said, get rid of the Nazis, none of us would have objected to that. But none of the Allies said that."

The German troops lived in a special hell. Borgert spent the last eight weeks of the war without once getting out of his uniform. "Always on the front," he recalled in 1995. "Hunger, lice, exhaustion, cold—you can never understand. Day after day of anxiety and casualties. My friend was shot in the head, one of his eyes was gone, but I could feel no more. I saw hundreds of wounded, and I could do nothing. I still have fragments in my head. Every soldier curses war."[15] Still he continued to make war.

∎

Because Borgert and so many others continued to fight, the GIs continued to take casualties. One of them was Lt. Will Rogers, Jr., of the 7th Armored Division. He had been in the campaign since August, at the front. He saw things from the bright side. "High times," he had called it when his jeep led the column into Chartres—after giving the order, on his own initiative, to spare the cathedral tower. At Verdun, his outfit had run out of gas. He used the opportunity to take his platoon to the American cemetery at St.-Mihiel. With fresh fuel the following day, he took his reconnaissance vehicles on patrol through the maze of World War I trenches. Rogers got on the radio and began explaining to his platoon the details of the battle of Verdun. "A million soldiers fell," he said. Suddenly over the radio came the sharp bark of his task force commander: "Lieutenant Rogers—let's fight one war at a time!"

Rogers won a Bronze Star in the Battle of the Bulge. He crossed the Rhine at Remagen. On Easter Sunday 1945 he was as usual in the lead jeep. He rounded a corner and a panzerfaust got him—shrapnel in the hip. "Wounded in the Ruhr (rear) pocket," he explained. He didn't regard it as a million-dollar wound. "Evacuated to England," he complained. "Never did get to meet the Russians."[16]

Eisenhower was free to send his armies wherever he chose. Montgomery wanted him to give First Army to Twenty-first Army Group and let it join Ninth Army for a drive on to Berlin—under his command. Hodges wanted Berlin, as did Simpson, Patton, Brooke, and Churchill. But Bradley didn't and neither did Eisenhower. Partly their reason was political. At the Yalta conference the Big Three had agreed to divide Germany into zones of occupation, and Berlin into sectors. In central Germany, the Elbe River was the boundary. If Simpson's Ninth or Hodges's First Army fought its way across the Elbe and on to Berlin, they would be taking territory that would have to be turned over to the Soviet occupation forces; if they fought their way into Berlin they would have to give up more than half the city to the Red Army. Eisenhower asked Bradley for an estimate on the cost of taking Berlin. About 100,000 casualties, Bradley replied, and added that was "a pretty stiff price to pay for a prestige objective, especially when we've got to fall back and let the other fellow take over."[17]

Further, Eisenhower believed that if the Americans tried to race the Russians to Berlin, they would lose. Ninth and First Armies were 400 kilometers from Berlin; the Red Army was on the banks of the Oder River, less than 100 kilometers from the city. And the Red Army was there in great strength—more than 1,250,000 troops.

Another consideration: Eisenhower's goal was to win the war and thus end the carnage as quickly as possible. Every day that the war went on meant more death for the concentration camp inmates, for the millions of slave laborers in Germany, for the Allied POWs. If he concentrated on Berlin, the Germans in Bavaria and Austria, where many of the POW and slave labor camps were located, would be able to hold out for who knew how long.

There is a parallel here with the end of the American Civil War. Just before Appomattox, some of Robert E. Lee's staff suggested to him that he disband the Army of Northern Virginia and instruct the troops to scatter into the West Virginia mountains, where as small groups they could carry on guerrilla warfare. Lee was appalled by the suggestion. He said there could be nothing worse for the South than having armed bands roaming the countryside without discipline or direction.

But Hitler was no Lee. And the SS and Hitler Youth were not only fanatics, but were armed with the most modern weapons, which gave small groups of them a firepower greater than that of the Army of Northern Virginia at its peak. Even after the surrender of the Ruhr, the Germans never ran out of guns or ammunition. These boys could get all the panzerfausts, potato mashers, machine guns, burp guns, rifles, Schu mines they could carry. If they were lucky enough to have fuel, they could have Tiger tanks, 88s, and more heavy stuff. This combination of fanatic boys and plenty of weapons and ammunition created a nightmare situation.

After the mid-April surrender of 325,000 troops (plus thirty generals) in the Ruhr pocket, the Wehrmacht packed it in. Lt. Günter Materne was a German artilleryman caught in the pocket ("where everything was a complete mess"). Out of ammunition and fuel, he destroyed his self-propelled cannon. "At the command post, the CO of our artillery regiment, holding back his tears, told us that we had lost the war, all the victims died in vain. The code word 'werewolf' had been sent out by Hitler's command post. This meant that we were all supposed to divide up into small groups and head east." Not many did, Materne observed. The veterans sat down and awaited their American captors.[18] There was no attempt by the regular army to maintain a front line.

The Volkssturm, the Waffen SS, and the Hitler Youth were another matter. They fought fiercely and inflicted great damage. The GIs never knew, when the lead jeep rounded a corner, what was ahead. If inexperienced boys were there, they would fire—most often a panzerfaust shell at the jeep. The Americans would proceed to smash the village. "I'm not going to be the last man killed in this war" was the feeling, so when some teenage boy fired on them, they brought down a tremendous amount of shells. It was chaos and catastrophe, brought on for no reason—except that Hitler had raised these boys for just this moment. The fanatics were forcing the Americans to do to the German civilians and cities what Hitler wanted to do to them, because they had shown themselves to be unworthy of him.

The Allied fear was that Hitler would be able to encourage these armed bands to continue the struggle, over the radio. His voice was his weapon. If he could get to the Austrian Alps he might be able to surround himself with SS troops and use the radio to put that voice into action.

Exactly that was happening, according to OSS agents in Switzerland. SHAEF G-2 agreed. As early as March 11, G-2 had declared, "The main trend of German defence policy does seem directly primarily to the safeguarding of the Alpine Zone. This area is practically impenetrable. . . . Evidence indicates that considerable numbers of SS and specially chosen units are being systematically withdrawn to Austria. . . . Here, defended by nature the powers that have hitherto guided Germany will survive to reorganize her resurrection. . . . Here a specially selected corps of young men will be trained in guerrilla warfare, so that a whole underground army can be fitted and directed to liberate Germany."[19]

In September 1944, SHAEF intelligence had declared the German army dead. In mid-December 1944, SHAEF intelligence had missed altogether the gathering of the largest army the Germans ever put together on the Western Front. Having paid so heavily for its complacency in December, SHAEF intelligence went the other direction in March 1945 when it gave Eisenhower a report that was grossly exaggerated ("armaments will be manufactured in bomb-proof factories, food and equipment will be stored in vast underground caverns, with the most efficient secret weapons yet invented") and alarmist. Yet there was a core of truth to it. If the factories and underground storage facilities were imaginative, the threat of Hitler and a radio was not. He could ask his fanatics to hold on and hold out, until the Western Allies and the Soviet Union went to war.

There was a receptive audience to that line. Capt. John Cobb of the 82nd Airborne remembered an incident on the day of the surrender of the Ruhr pocket. He was in charge of a temporary prisoner compound. "The German who was the ranking officer made a request to see me. I received him, expecting some complaint about living conditions or treatment. Instead, he requested that he be allowed to join us with German volunteers when we began our attack against the Russians. He was incredulous when I informed him that we had no intentions of fighting the Russians."[20]

Corp. Friedrich Bertenrath recalled how the war ended for him: "There were still about 150 of us, and forty vehicles. The Americans came up. They searched us but we did not hold up our hands. After a bit, a bottle of schnapps was passed around. Each took a sip. An American said, 'You are all prisoners.' Someone from our side said, 'Forget about taking us prisoners, let us join you to go fight the Russians.'

" 'Forget that,' one of the Americans replied. They were decent men. We were allowed to get into our vehicles—they gave us some gas—and we drove with them through the area as if it were peacetime. There was an American jeep in front and one behind us, and in between twenty German tanks and APCs. It was a beautiful spring day. There were no more planes, no more Jabos above us."[21]

Sgt. Bruce Egger remembered a lieutenant who surrendered to him. The lieutenant spoke perfect English "and was as blond, sharp, and arrogant as a Hollywood version of a Nazi officer. He gave us a lecture about why the Americans should not have waged war on Germany; we should have joined them fighting the true enemy, which was Russia, and that it was not too late. We laughed at him, but as the Cold War developed, I often thought of his words."[22]

Eisenhower's mission was to get a sharp, clean, quick end to the war. The Russians were going to take Berlin anyway. There were more German divisions in southern Germany than to the north. The best way to carry out the mission was to overrun Bavaria and

Austria before the Germans could set up their Alpine Redoubt. Eisenhower ordered Ninth Army to halt at the Elbe, First Army to push on to Dresden on the Elbe and then halt, and Third Army and Seventh Army, plus the French army, to overrun Bavaria and Austria.

Put another way, he refused to race the Russians to Berlin. He was much criticized for this. It remains his most controversial decision of the war. It has been much written about, including by me. I have nothing to add to the debate, except this: in thirty years of interviewing GIs, reading their books and unpublished memoirs, corresponding with them, I have not yet heard one of them say that he wanted to charge into Berlin. For the GIs, what stood out about Eisenhower's decision was that he put them first. If the Russians wanted to get into the ultimate street fight, that was their business.*

American POWs were a major concern. The Germans held 90,000 U.S. airmen and soldiers in stalags scattered across central and southern Germany. They were in a ghastly condition that would only get worse as the Third Reich disintegrated. Liberating them became a primary goal.

For Patton, one POW camp was mesmerizing. It was in Hammelburg, on the road to Leipzig. He was obsessed with it because his son-in-law, Lt. Col. John Waters, was a prisoner there. So although Hammelburg was some forty kilometers behind the front, at the end of March Patton ordered a rescue mission. General Hoge, who had moved up to command the 4th Armored Division, got the assignment. He was dead set against it; rescue missions had no military purpose, he told Patton, and were likely to produce nothing but dead Americans on both sides of the barbed wire. Patton told him to get moving. So Hoge reluctantly created Task Force Baum (Capt. Abraham Baum commanding), but he kept it small because of his fears. Task Force Baum consisted of 307 officers and men in sixteen

---

*Gregori Arbatov was a rifle company commander in the Red Army in the Battle of Berlin. He took terrible casualties. Some of them were men he had led in the Battle of Moscow, and so many others. Fifty years later, he still shook with fury at the thought of Stalin's insistence on taking the city. Arbatov said any sane man would have surrounded Berlin, pounded it with artillery, and waited for the inevitable capitulation. "But not that son of a bitch Stalin. He sent us into the city, with all those crazy Nazi kids, and we bled." The estimated casualty cost was 100,000.[23]

tanks, twenty-seven half-tracks, seven jeeps, three self-propelled 105mm guns, and a cargo carrier. It shot its way through German resistance and got to the stalag on the second day.

Lt. Marvin Shelley of the 103rd Division was a POW in Hammelburg when Task Force Baum arrived. "The tanks knocked down our fences and shot the place up," he recalled. "We rushed out to greet them, and they were not all that enthused. The task force had information that there were 250 American officers in Hammelburg. Actually, it was more like 2,500. Lieutenant Colonel Waters was so happy to be liberated, he was running up and down the company street with this little American flag, and he got hit. By American shells. It didn't kill him, but it ruined his leg.

"The task force couldn't believe it. They had no way to get all of us out of there. They told us we could do whatever we wanted to—go back to the prison, take off on our own, or stay with them. A lot of the prisoners went back inside. I decided to stay with the tanks. You'd be surprised how many men can get on a tank—30 or 40. When the tanks would turn, guys would slide off and then they'd run and you'd help them back on. The lead tank got hit by a panzerfaust. Bodies went flying, and that stopped the convoy real quick." They had run into a Waffen SS ambush.

Outgunned, outnumbered, surrounded, Task Force Baum broke up. A number of the soldiers were killed, others wounded, the remainder taken prisoner. The original POWs returned to the stalag. Lieutenant Shelley was one of them. "There was the German general in charge of the camp, real nice English-speaking general, and he's smiling as we get to the warehouse, standing there like he's greeting all of us. 'Good seeing you, ha ha, we meet again,' things like that."[24] The camp was finally liberated in mid-April.

For a few days after this debacle, Patton seemed subdued, not so much because he recognized what a fool he had been as because he feared another newspaper furor. But the news didn't leak until April 12, the day President Roosevelt died. When Bradley's aide Maj. Chet Hansen saw him the following morning, "he was robust again. 'What the hell,' he said, 'with the President's death you could execute buggery in the streets and get no farther than the fourth page.' "[25]

When the camps were liberated during the regular course of operations, the GIs usually found the guards gone, the POWs awaiting them. The sight of an American or British soldier was a signal for an outburst of joy. Capt. Pat Reid of the British army was in Colditz prison. It was a castle in a rural area of central Germany. The prisoners were Allied officers, "bad boys" to the Germans because they had escaped from other stalags. Colditz was supposed to be escape proof, but these incorrigibles kept escaping (one via what may have been the world's first hang glider), although few made it to Switzerland. When I visited Colditz in 1987 with Reid and two American officers, the place had been turned into an anti-Nazi museum. Reid and the Americans showed the East German guide hiding places and tunnels he had not discovered in a decade of working there.

Reid described the moment on April 15, a day after the guards took off, when a single American soldier stood at the gate, "his belt and straps festooned with ammunition clips and grenades, submachine gun in hand." An Allied officer cautiously advanced toward him with outstretched hand. The GI took it, grinned, and said cheerfully, "Any doughboys here?"

"Suddenly, a mob was rushing toward him, shouting and cheering and struggling madly to reach him, to make sure that he was alive, to touch him, and from the touch to know again the miracle of living, to be men in their own right, freed from bondage, outcast no more, liberated, their faith in God's mercy justified, the nobility of mankind vindicated, justice at last accomplished and tyranny once more overcome. Men wept, unable to restrain themselves. Men with tears streaming down their faces kissed the GI on both cheeks—the salute of brothers."[26]

At Moosburg, Allied POWs who had been marched away from the oncoming Russians, under horrible conditions and at great risk, were gathered—some 110,000 of them, including 10,000 Americans. There was no place their guards could take them by this time, so the guards took off. Maj. Elliott Viney of the British army was among the POWs. He kept a diary. April 29, 1945: "AMERICANS HERE! Three jeeps in the camp and all national flags hoisted. The boys brought in cigars, matches, lettuce and flour. The scenes have been almost indescribable. Wireless blaring everywhere, wire coming down, [POWs] wearing Goon bayonets and caps. The SS put a panzerfaust through the guard company's barracks when they refused to fight."[27]

■

To most German soldiers, the sight of a GI or Tommy standing in front of them was almost as welcome an event as it was for the Allied POWs. Those who surrendered safely thought themselves among the luckiest men alive. In mid-April, Sergeant Egger recalled, "I fired at a deer in the evening while hunting but missed, and five German soldiers came out of the woods with their hands up. I bet they thought we had excellent vision."[28]

Egger went hunting for sport; Lt. Charles Stockell did it for food. On April 14 he recorded in his diary, "We have taken so many prisoners we are on half rations. I have become the battalion hunter. Each day I go out with a jeep and a ¾ ton truck and shoot it full of deer, pheasants and hare to feed the men. They love it. We are taking 2,000 prisoners and 200 guns per day now."[29]

On the east–west autobahns, German troops marched west on the median while Americans on tanks, trucks, and jeeps rolled east on the road. Sgt. Gordon Carson of the 101st—which was headed toward Salzburg—recalled that "as far as you could see in the median were German prisoners, fully armed. No one would stop to take their surrender. We just waved." Private Webster couldn't get over the sight of "the Germans, who only a short time ago had been so difficult to capture, coming in from the hills like sheep to surrender." He recalled "the unbelievable spectacle of two GIs keeping watch on some 2,500 enemy."

Occasionally the 101st ran into opposition, especially at river crossings, where SS troops would fire from the far side to hold the Americans back until the bridge could be blown. Every single bridge in the path of the 101st was destroyed by German engineers as the Allies approached. Major Winters was struck by the German fanaticism: "They were destroying their own bridges when the uselessness of the destruction was clear to any idiot."[30]

The 101st was riding in DUKWs. Most GIs were riding on vehicles of every description, always heading east. A few infantry, however, were still slogging forward the same way they had crossed France and Belgium and the Rhineland, by foot. "We walked another twenty-five miles today," Sergeant Egger recorded on April 20. "Training in the States, where a twenty-five-mile hike had only been a monthly occurrence, had not been this tough. Naturally the men were complaining, but I always preferred walking to fighting."[31]

Sometimes they had to fight. On April 27, G Company came to Deggendorf, northeast of Munich. There were some Hitler Youth in the town of 15,000. They had no artillery or even mortar support, no tanks, no skills at making war. But they had machine guns and panzerfausts and they let go. "The bullets sounded like angry bees overhead," Egger wrote. American artillery destroyed the hive. Later, in the by then destroyed town, one of his buddies said to him, "Wouldn't it be a hell of a note to go through all this and then check out so close to the end? The thought of being killed by some fanatical thirteen-year-old scares the hell out of me. After coming this far I don't want to die now."[32]

Lieutenant Leinbaugh described a typical incident in the drive east from the Rhine. Company K was riding in deuce-and-a-halfs. "As our miles-long convoy passed a line of hills, several rifle shots cracked overhead and we saw puffs of smoke from positions near a hill-top. Our trucks braked to a quick stop and a thousand M1s returned the fire. In a minute, a white handkerchief waved vigorously from a foxhole, and two bedraggled Germans, hands in the air, came stumbling and running down the hill to appreciative cheers. We drove on, leaving the two standing forlornly in a ditch."[33]

As the Tommies and GIs moved deeper into Germany, they made discoveries that brought on a great change in attitude toward Germany and its people. On April 11, the 3rd Armored Division got into Nordhausen, on the southern side of the Harz Mountains in central Germany. Capt. Belton Cooper was near the van as the GIs worked their way into town. Suddenly, "a strange apparition emerged from the side of one of the buildings. A tall frail-looking creature with striped pants and naked from the waist up. It appeared to be a human skeleton with little signs of flesh, if any. The skin appeared to be like a translucent plastic stretched over the rib cage and sucked with a powerful vacuum until it impinged to the backbone in the rear. I could not tell whether it was male or female. There was no face, merely a gaunt human skull staring out. The teeth were exposed in a broad grin and in place of eyes were merely dark sockets. I did not see how it was humanly possible for this pathetic creature to have enough strength to walk. As we proceeded down the road, we encountered more and more of these gaunt figures standing or sitting but most of them were sprawled on the road where they had collapsed. In their last struggle to survive, they had attempted to walk as far away from their tormentors as possible."

Cooper came to a warehouse, where German civilians, old men, women, and children, were plundering. "The crowd was ravenous; they were pushing and shoving. They paid absolutely no attention to the poor pitiful wretches lying in the streets." Further on, "we passed three large stacks of what appeared to be wastepaper and garbage piled in rows six feet high and 400 feet long. The stench was overwhelming and as I looked I noticed that parts of the stack were moving. To my absolute horror, it dawned on me that these stacks contained the bodies of naked human beings. A few were still alive and they were writhing in the excrement and human waste."

General Collins ordered that every civilian in Nordhausen had to work around the clock until the bodies were buried. Bulldozers came forward to dig a mass grave. Later, Cooper discovered the V-2 underground rocket factory, where the slave laborers worked—until they starved. East of Nordhausen the following day, he came across a schoolhouse with some trees around it. On closer examination it turned out to be a rocket assembly plant. The trees were aluminum fuel tanks piled on each other and covered with camouflage nets.[34]

Lt. Hugh Carey, who became governor of New York in the 1980s, was at Nordhausen on April 11. Thirty years later he wrote, "I stood with other American soldiers before Nordhausen. I inhaled the stench of death, and the barbaric, calculated cruelty. I made a vow as I stood there that as long as I live, I will fight for peace, for the rights of mankind and against any form of hate, bias and prejudice."[35]

Eisenhower saw his first slave labor camp on April 13. It was Ohrdruf Nord, near the town of Gotha. He later called what he saw the shock of his life. He had never seen such degradation, had never imagined the bestiality man was capable of committing.

"Up to that time I had known about [Nazi crimes] only generally or through secondary sources," he wrote. Like so many men of his age, he was deeply suspicious of wartime propaganda as a result of having learned after World War I that his government had grossly exaggerated its descriptions of supposed German atrocities. So he had discounted the stories he had heard about the camps. The reality was far worse than the stories and all but overwhelmed him.

"I visited every nook and cranny of the camp because I felt it my duty to be in a position from then on to testify at first hand about these things in case there ever grew up at home the belief or assumption that the stories of Nazi brutality were just propaganda." That night, he sent communications to both Washington and London, urging the two governments to send newspaper editors, photographers, congressmen, and members of Parliament to visit the camp and make a record. That was done.[36]

Day after day over the next couple of weeks, more camps were discovered. On April 15 the British got into Belsen. That day Edward R. Murrow went to Buchenwald, just north of Weimar. Like Eisenhower and every GI who saw one of the camps, Murrow feared that no one could believe what he saw. He gave a description on his CBS radio program. In his conclusion, he said, "I pray you to believe what I have said about Buchenwald. I have reported what I saw, but only part of it. For most of it I have no words. . . . If I've offended you by this rather mild account of Buchenwald, I'm not in the least sorry. I was there."[37]

Martha Gellhorn of the *New York Times* visited the main camp at Dachau. Then she flew out on a C-47 carrying liberated POWs to France. She talked to them about Dachau, which they had just seen.

"No one will believe us," one soldier said. They all agreed. "We got to talk about it, see? We got to talk about it if anyone believes us or not."

Marguerite Higgins of the rival *New York Herald Tribune* was also there. She reported, "The liberation was a frenzied scene. Inmates of the camp hugged and embraced the American troops, kissed the ground before them and carried them shoulder high around the place."[38]

On April 27, the 12th Armored Division approached Landsberg-am-Lech, west of Munich. There was a Wehrmacht unit and a Waffen SS unit in the town. The Wehrmacht commander decided to withdraw across the Lech River. The SS commander wanted to fight. The regular officer told him to do as he wished, but the Wehrmacht troops were getting out of there. When the civilians saw the soldiers leaving, they hung out white sheets. The sight infuriated the SS. "In their rage," Lt. Julius Bernstein related, "they went from house to house and dragged outside whomever they found and hanged them from the nearest tree or lamp post. As we rode into Landsberg, we found German civilians hanging from trees like ripe fruit."

Later that day an awful black, acrid smoke appeared. It came from one of the outlying camps of the Dachau system. When the Americans approached, the SS officer in charge had ordered the remaining 4,000 slave laborers destroyed. The guards had nailed shut the doors and windows of the wooden barracks, hosed down the buildings with gasoline, and set them on fire. The prisoners had been cremated alive. Later, Bernstein helped load civilians from Landsberg into trucks to take them to see the atrocity. "Would you believe that no one admitted any knowledge of the camp?" he later wrote. "They told us they thought it was a secret war factory, so they didn't ask questions. They all defended Hitler, saying, 'The Führer knew nothing of this!' They blamed Goering, Goebbels and Himmler, but not their dear Führer."[39]

Major Winters was one of the first to arrive at Landsberg. "The memory of starved, dazed men," he related, "who dropped their eyes and heads when we looked at them through the chain-link fence, in the same manner that a beaten, mistreated dog would cringe, leaves feelings that cannot be described and will never be forgotten. The impact of seeing those people behind that fence left me saying, only to myself, 'Now I know why I am here!' "[40]

On April 25, at Torgau on the Elbe River, Lt. William Robertson, 69th Division, First Army, met a Red Army soldier. Germany was divided. A spontaneous celebration ensued. Hundreds of Red Army soldiers found rowboats and rafts and came over to the American side. The factory in Torgau produced harmonicas and accordions, so there was music and dancing. Pvt. Andy Rooney was there for *Stars and Stripes*. So was combat historian Sgt. Forrest Pogue, who as usual was at the front, interviewing the GIs. They danced with female soldiers—reportedly the best snipers in the Red Army.

To the south, Third Army was penetrating Czechoslovakia (already assigned to the Russians for occupation) while Seventh Army raced eastward past Munich and down into Austria (where no boundary lines had yet been set). Eisenhower urged the GIs to get as far into Austria as possible.

There wasn't much resistance. Eighteen-year-old Herbert

Mittelstadt, a member of a German anti-aircraft unit, was in the province of Vorarlberg, in western Austria. He recalled his last day as a soldier: "On May 1st, our lieutenant approached the twenty-five of us, and gravely announced, 'I no longer believe that there is any way possible for us to win this war. I am going to discharge you, and whoever wants to, can continue to fight with me as a Werewolf.' Only one guy raised his hand. His family was in East Prussia, and the possibility of his ever returning was extremely slim anyway. Since the lieutenant had only a single ally, he said, 'The whole thing is not worth it. I'm going to discharge myself as well!' "41

Eisenhower had stayed away from Berlin in part because the political division of Germany into zones of occupation had already been agreed to by the Big Three. Denmark, overrun by the Germans in 1940, was another matter. The Danes expected to be liberated and freed, not occupied. The British and Americans had that as their policy. The Soviets, however, had a different goal. In early April, SHAEF learned via Ultra that the Red Army was advancing toward Denmark even as Stalin denied any intention of doing so. The Japanese ambassador in Sweden reported to Tokyo (the message was intercepted and decoded by the Allies) that if the Red Army got into Denmark, Stalin intended to bring the country "into the Soviet sphere of influence and thus secure an outlet from the Baltic into the North Sea."42 To prevent that from happening, Eisenhower ordered Montgomery to get to Lübeck and Wismar as soon as possible. Monty thought that was attacking in the wrong direction; he wanted to go south for Berlin, not north toward the Baltic Sea. Eisenhower insisted.

The U.S. Ninth Army led the way, with the 82nd Airborne in the van. The operation involved crossing the Elbe River. It began on April 29. Dutch Schultz was there. The boats were wood and canvas. No life jackets. "This was to be our first river crossing," he complained. "We knew nothing about crossing rivers in the middle of the night. The river was 400 meters wide and swift. We knew the war was winding down. This raised our anxiety level. The longer we were exposed to combat, the more we felt like fugitives from the law of averages. In addition to all of the other combat risks, we now faced the possibility of drowning.

"Twelve men to a boat, not unlike putting sardines in a can. Our leader was urging us to paddle faster. He sounded like a coxswain counting cadence for one of the Ivy League rowing teams.

At mid-river, it started snowing and at the same time we collided with another boat which led to a shouting match about who had the right of way. It was unbelievable. But nothing happened."

Once across, Schultz headed east. He got caught in a barrage of 20mm shells. He jumped into a ditch, where he "saw a German soldier, who wasn't much more than fifteen years of age. We were about ten feet apart, with both of our weapons aimed at each other. He dropped his rifle and raised his hands over his head."

That afternoon, a German machine gun opened up from a nearby wood. "For the sake of glory, I decided to go after it with hand grenades. After running into the woods and crawling about fifty feet in the general direction of the machine gun, I suddenly thought, Why in hell am I doing this?

"Without so much as a second thought, I retraced my steps and rejoined my platoon. This abortive attempt to be a hero ended my combat career in the European Theater of Operations."[43] The 82nd got to Wismar and the Red Army never got to Denmark.

As individuals, squads, companies, regiments, divisions, corps, as entire armies, the Germans were surrendering. The crazies were still fighting, like chickens with their heads cut off, even though Hitler had shot himself on April 30. But most of the shooting was over. The dominant thought in every GI's head was home. On May 6, Don Williams of *Stars and Stripes* wrote an article that gave them the bad news. Williams wrote, "No man or woman, no matter how long he or she has been in service, overseas or in combat, will be released from the Army if his or her services are required in the war against Japan." There would be a point system for demobilization; so many points for length of service, time already spent overseas, combat decorations (which suddenly became very valuable; earlier they had been ignored), and the number of dependent children in the States. Soldiers under eighteen years old got extra points. Soldiers deemed essential for war duties and those with insufficient points (the majority) would either stay on as occupation troops or ship out for the invasion of Japan. "In the meantime," Williams wrote, "don't write home and tell your mother or sweetheart that you'll be home next week or next month. For most of you, it just ain't so."[44]

∎

On May 7, the campaign of the U.S. Army in Northwest Europe came to an end. That morning, at SHAEF headquarters in Reims, German delegates signed the unconditional surrender. The Russians insisted that there be a second signing, in Berlin, which took place on May 8.

Men reacted differently. Sgt. Ewald Becker of Panzer Grenadier Regiment 111 was near his home in Kassel. "We went out onto the streets to surrender. The first vehicle to come was an American jeep and as I raised my hands he waved and grinned at me and continued to drive. Then another jeep with four men. They stopped and gave me chocolate. They said something I didn't understand and drove on. Then a German vehicle came with a white flag. I asked him what was going on and he said the war has been over for two hours. I went back to the village and we tapped the first available keg. Within two hours, I can say with confidence, the entire village was drunk."[45]

Sergeant Pogue was in Pilsen, Czechoslovakia. What he remembered most vividly was, "The lights went on." He realized he had not seen a light shining anywhere in Europe, except Switzerland, since he went ashore at Omaha Beach on June 7, 1944.[46]

Corp. James Pemberton had been in ASTP at Oklahoma State in 1943. He ended up in the 103rd Division and by the end of the war he had been in combat for 147 days. "The night of May 8, 1945 I was looking down from our cabin on the mountain at the Inn River Valley in Austria. It was black. And then the lights in Innsbruck went on. If you have not lived in darkness for months, shielding even a match light deep in a foxhole, you can't imagine the feeling."[47]

Lieutenant Stockell was with Forrest Pogue in Pilsen. In his diary entry for May 8, he wrote: "Germans pouring into Pilsen by the thousands to get away from the Russians in Prague. Later at the receptions I get to meet Edvard Beneš [president of Czechoslovakia] and Jan Masaryk [foreign minister]. A friend sneaked me into the first banquet between the Russians and the Americans. [Soviet General Vasili] Chuikov* proposed a toast with a full glass of vodka. Bottoms up! General [Clarence] Heubner said if he drank like that, he'd

*Chuikov was the hero of Stalingrad and had commanded the assault on Berlin.

be under the table. Chuikov first got angry but when Heubner's remark was translated, he turned to Heubner and said in English while pointing under the table, 'Meet your friends!!' "[48]

Many units had a ceremony of some sort. In the 357th Combat Team, 90th Division, the CO had all the officers assemble on the grassy slopes of a hill, under a flagpole flying the Stars and Stripes. The regimental CO spoke, as did the division commander. "I can't remember their words," Lt. Col. Ken Reimers said, but he remembered counting the costs. "We had taken some terrible losses—our infantry suffered over 250 per cent casualties. There was not a single company commander present who left England with us, and there were only a half dozen officers in the whole regiment who landed on Utah Beach."[49]

The 90th Division had been in combat for 308 days—the record in ETO—but other divisions had taken almost as many casualties. The junior officers and NCOs suffered most. Some of America's best young men went down leading their troops in battle. Dutch Schultz paid his officers and NCOs a fine tribute: "Men like Captains Anthony Stefanich, Jack Tallerday; Lieutenants Gus Sanders, Gerald Johnson; and Sergeants Herman R. Zeitner, Sylvester Meigs, and Elmo Bell, to name only a few were largely responsible for my transformation to a combat infantryman able to do his job. They taught me to overcome my fears and self-doubts.

"Not only were these men superb leaders both in and out of combat, but, more importantly, they took seriously the responsibility of first placing the welfare of their men above their own needs."[50]

There is no typical GI among the millions who served in Northwest Europe, but Bruce Egger surely was representative. He was a mountain man from central Idaho. At the end of 1943 he was in ASTP at Kansas State. When the ASTP program was cut, he got assigned to Fort Leonard Wood for training. In October 1944 he arrived in France and went into a Repple Depple. On November 6, he went on the line with G Company, 328th regiment, 26th Division. He served out the war in almost continuous front-line action. He never missed a day of duty. He had his close calls, most notably a piece of shrapnel stopped by the New Testament in the breast pocket of his field jacket, but was never wounded. In this he was unusually lucky. G Company had arrived on Utah Beach on September 8, 1944, with a full complement of 187 enlisted men and six officers. By May 8, 1945, a total of 625 men had served in its ranks. Fifty-seven men of G company were killed in action, 183 were wounded, 116 got trench foot, and 51 frostbite.

Egger rose from private to staff sergeant. After the war, he got a degree in forestry in 1951 and served in the U.S. Forest Service for twenty-nine years.

In his memoir of the war, Egger spoke for all GIs: "More than four decades have passed since those terrible months when we endured the mud of Lorraine, the bitter cold of the Ardennes, the dank cellars of Saarlautern. . . . We were miserable and cold and exhausted most of the time, we were all scared to death. . . . But we were young and strong then, possessed of the marvelous resilience of youth, and for all the misery and fear and the hating every moment of it the war was a great, if always terrifying, adventure. Not a man among us would want to go through it again, but we are all proud of having been so severely tested and found adequate. The only regret is for those of our friends who never returned."[51]

The GIs
and Modern America

AT THE BEGINNING of World War II my father, a small-town doctor in central Illinois, joined the Navy. My mother, brothers, and I followed him to the Great Lakes, then to Pensacola. When he shipped out to the Pacific in 1943, we moved to Whitewater, Wisconsin, to live with my grandmother. Consequently, I didn't see many GIs during the war. But in 1946, when Dad got out of the Navy and began to set up a practice in Whitewater, we had what amounted to a squad of ex-GIs for neighbors. They lived in a boardinghouse while attending the local college (today the University of Wisconsin-Whitewater) on the GI Bill.

Dad put up a basketball backboard and goal over our garage. The GIs taught me and my brothers to play the game. We were shirts and skins. I don't know that I ever knew their last names—they were Bill and Harry, Joe and Stan, Fred and Ducky—but I've never forgotten their scars. Stan had three, one on his arm, another on his shoulder, a third on his hand. Fred and Ducky had two, the others had one.

We didn't play all that often, because these guys were taking eighteen or twenty-one credits per semester. "Making up for lost time," they told us. Their chief recreation came in the fall, when they would drive up to northern Wisconsin for the opening week-end of deer season. Beginning in 1947, when I was twelve years old, I was allowed to go with them.

We slept in the living room of a small farmhouse, side by side in sleeping bags on the floor. There was some drinking, not much, as we would get up at 4 A.M. ("0400" to the ex-GIs, which mystified me), but enough to loosen their tongues. In addition, their rifles came from around the world—Czech, British, Russian, American, Japanese, French—and each man had a story about how he acquired his rifle. It was there that I heard my first war stories. I've been listening ever since. I thought then that these guys were giants. I still do.

Stan was the senior NCO in the bunch. He took charge. No one voted, there was no discussion, it was just taken for granted that he was our leader. In the morning, he got us organized. This was cultivated land, hilly, interspersed with woods of twenty or so acres each. Stan would study a wood with his binoculars, then bark out the assignments. Two men would go to the far end of the wood, two others would post up along the sides, two more would stand on the edge of the near end. The other six would march through the wood, shouting to drive the deer out so the posted men could get a clear shot. After they got their deer, they became the drivers and the others were put on post. We all got our deer.

They don't hunt that way in northern Wisconsin today. Hunters go out as individuals, most often building a platform in a tree for their stand (deer never look up for danger). A couple of weeks before opening day, they set out bait—apples or cabbages—around the tree. They too usually get their deer, but that kind of hunting has no appeal for me and I no longer participate.

By the time I went to Madison for my own college education, the ex-GIs had graduated and were off making their livings. Over the next four years I developed my fair share of academic snobbery, encouraged by my professors. They put me to reading such books as Sloan Wilson's The Man in the Gray Flannel Suit (1955), David Riesman's The Lonely Crowd (1951), and William Whyte's The Organization Man (1956). These books, like the professors, deplored the conformity of the 1950s. They charged that the young executives and corporate men of the 1950s marched in step, dressed alike, seldom questioned authority, did as they were told, worked always, were frighteningly materialistic, devoid of culture and individualism. By the time I became a graduate student, I was full of scorn for them and, I must confess, for their leader, President Eisenhower—the bland leading the bland.

But in fact these were the men who built modern America. They had learned to work together in the armed services in World War II. They had seen enough destruction; they wanted to construct. They built the Interstate Highway system, the St. Lawrence Seaway, the suburbs (so scorned by the sociologists, so successful with the people), and more. They had seen enough killing; they wanted to save lives. They licked polio and made other revolutionary advances in medicine. They had learned in the army the virtues of a solid organization and teamwork, and the value of individual initiative, inventiveness, and responsibility. They developed the modern corporation while inaugurating revolutionary advances in science and technology, education and public policy.

The ex-GIs had seen enough war; they wanted peace. But they had also seen the evil of dictatorship; they wanted freedom. They had learned in their youth that the way to prevent war was to deter through military strength, and to reject isolationism for full involvement in the world. So they supported NATO and the United Nations and the Department of Defense. They had stopped Hitler and Tojo; in the 1950s they stopped Stalin and Khrushchev.

In his inaugural address, President John F. Kennedy described the men and women of his generation: "The torch has been passed to a new generation of Americans—born in this century, tempered by war, disciplined by a hard and bitter peace, proud of our ancient heritage—and unwilling to witness or permit the slow undoing of those human rights to which this nation has always been committed."

The "we" generation of World War II (as in "We are all in this together") was a special breed of men and women who did great things for America and the world. When the GIs sailed for Europe, they were coming to the continent not as conquerors but liberators. In his Order of the Day on June 6, 1944, Eisenhower had told them their mission was: "The destruction of the German war machine, the elimination of Nazi tyranny over the oppressed peoples of Europe, and security for ourselves in a free world." They accomplished that mission.

In the process they liberated the Germans (or at least the Germans living west of the Elbe River). In Normandy, in July 1944,

Wehrmacht Pvt. Walter Zittats was guarding some American prisoners. One of them spoke German. Zittats asked him, " 'Why are you making war against us?' I'll always remember his exact words: 'We are fighting to free you from the fantastic idea that you are a master race.' "[1] In June 1945 Eisenhower told his staff, "The success of this occupation can only be judged fifty years from now. If the Germans at that time have a stable, prosperous democracy, then we shall have succeeded." That mission, too, was accomplished.

In the fall semester of 1996 I was a visiting professor at the University of Wisconsin-Madison. I taught a course on World War II to some 350 students. They were dumbstruck by descriptions of what it was like to be on the front lines. They were even more amazed by the responsibilities carried by junior officers and NCOs who were as young as they. Like all of us who have never been in combat, they wondered if they could have done it—and even more, they wondered how anyone could have done it.

There is a vast literature on the latter question. In general, in assessing the motivation of the GIs, there is agreement that patriotism or any other form of idealism had little if anything to do with it. The GIs fought because they had to. What held them together was not country and flag, but unit cohesion. It has been my experience, through four decades of interviewing ex-GIs, that such generalizations are true enough.

And yet there is something more. Although the GIs were and are embarrassed to talk or write about the cause they fought for, in marked contrast to their great-grandfathers who fought in the Civil War, they were the children of democracy and they did more to help spread democracy around the world than any other generation in history.

At the core, the American citizen soldiers knew the difference between right and wrong, and they didn't want to live in a world in which wrong prevailed. So they fought, and won, and we all of us, living and yet to be born, must be forever profoundly grateful.

_____Afterword_____

ONE OF THE best things that comes from having a best-seller is the incoming mail. On this book it has been staggering and rewarding, far beyond anything my previous books have generated, by a factor of at least ten. Flattering reviews in prestigious publications are obviously welcome, but they can't compare to letters from men who were there. One of my favorites, dated March 15, 1998, handwritten, follows:

"Dear Sir: I had to write and compliment you on the book _Citizen Soldiers_. It was well written and very factual. I should know. I was there, from the first day on Utah Beach. It brought back so many special memories—so long ago. I was in the 90th Division, 357th Infantry. John Colby was my company commander and I was a platoon sgt. I put John on a jeep stretcher the first time he got hit in the hip. The first company commander you wrote about as running away with shell shock [see p. 46] I went and got him, carried him out of a mine field, and took him to Doc McConahey in the aid station. I was one of the ones mentioned that walked into Doc McConahey's for help (I was 18 at the time) with my bottom jaw shot off [see p. 327]. Here is what happened. I was in a prison compound, the advancing U.S. Army was going to overrun the prison camp, so the Krauts, they lined us up and shot the 60 of us—machine gun and then through the back of the head with a pistol.

"You wrote that [Pvt. Gus] Schroeder came in with about 100 German prisoners [see p. 268]. He did. I was with him. He had about four rounds in his Tommy gun. I had used all I had, and had a German Walther 9mm pistol with three shots in it. The reason we had no trouble was that most of those German POWs were actually Russians that had been captured by the Krauts, and put in the German Army—against their will—or get executed—they wanted to give up. They would be better off than we were in that miserable rain, snow and mud.

"My wife and I went back after the 50th anniversary of D-Day. I got an original battle map from John Colby and used it, starting with my feet in the water at Utah, climbed the sand dune, and then followed the map across France in the biggest Mercedes I could rent. Best trip I ever took. Enough of the memories your book stirred up—it gave me a much broader view of what was going on. My part was very small, not knowing anything but what was going on in our company. Thanks for the memories.

"Sgt. Donald L. Foye, 31423833, Co. E, 357th Infy, 90th Division."

Another heart-warmer came from Wallace Berger, who was "a scared, lonely 19-year-old replacement brought to the lines during the winter of 1944 with the 26th Division. . . . I felt again the cold, the fear of tree-bursts, the closeness with my fox-hole buddy Pat Healy (we slept in each other's arms for warmth) and at times the sense that we would never get out of there alive.

"So thank you for writing a book about my war. I think that in a way it gave me a feeling of a certain kind of peacefulness, as if something has been put to rest by the telling."

Pvt. Edward Schiff of San Diego wrote that reading the book "brought old memories flooding back; some surprisingly vivid, and some I wish I could forget, a few pleasant ones, such as the day my company was chosen to lead an attack, and we started out riding on the backs of tanks. As we roared past our front lines, all the men in foxholes stood up and cheered.

"I returned home on a hospital ship, after being wounded on Christmas Day, attacking toward Bastogne. As we sailed into Charleston Harbor, there was a huge sign on the dock with just two words, 'WELL DONE!'

"Other memories are much darker. The misery of the cold and wet and mud; the terror of going into an attack; the shock when almost everyone I knew was killed or wounded, some right next to me. The worst was the time I fired my machine gun into a German patrol that was so close I could see their faces. I never found out what happened to them, which lets me think there are some old men in Germany today, sitting around telling their grandchildren of the American machine gunner who scared them to death. At other times I realize the chances are good that I killed at least some of the men in that patrol. They were probably teenagers, as I was, with their whole lives ahead of them, until I squeezed that trigger. All had relatives and sweethearts whose lives were shattered and who may be grieving even now."

In a handwritten letter, Pvt. James Howley recalled, "I am one of the soldiers you wrote about." He was drafted in 1943, trained in Texas, shipped over to Scotland in the spring of 1944, across the English Channel on D-Day plus ten, and assigned to the 9th Infantry Division. "I was trained as a wire man and sent over as a rifleman with no infantry training, then put on an antitank gun that I never had seen until then. My job became digging holes. We crossed the Rhine at night before the bridge collapsed and got a half track full of Schnapps—about eight or ten cases. For a few days we didn't care whether it rained or snowed. One of the guys we called 'mole' because he could always find a hole to jump into at the slightest sound. After we got that Schnapps he went out on a .50 caliber MG when a Jerry plane came over and fired up at it. The plane turned on him and in its strafing run killed him and a radio man."

The letters contain a fair amount of complaints, a principal one being that I left out this or that division, which is fair enough, but I can't do anything about it now, and, anyway, the book was not intended to be a comprehensive history. One veteran's criticism was that my only mention of the National Guard was in the story about the Sicilian-born colonel (p. 338). Guilty. My only excuse is that I just figured everyone knows that the 29th Division (242 days in combat, 204 percent turnover), which plays a major role in my account, was a National Guard division (the "Blue and Gray," from Virginia, Maryland, and Delaware) and one of the best outfits in the Army.

Another unhappy veteran complained about my remarking that the colonel was from Sicily. He accused me of succumbing to and feeding prejudices against Sicilians, and pointed to the impressive combat record of Italian-Americans in the war. He told me I ought to be ashamed. I can only reply that my source for the story stressed the colonel's Sicilian origin, and it is his story, not mine. So too with the three complaints about my keeping in the word "Jewish" in a quote from Lt. George Wilson (p. 344).

Nearly every letter points out a typo or two. We get them corrected in the next printing. Many point to errors of fact, and thus are extremely embarrassing to me. Three facts that I'll never ever get wrong again are: the German Panther tank carried a .75mm cannon, not an 88; in Michigan, at its Willow Run plant, the Ford Motor Company made B-24s, not B-17s; during training, medics were called chancre mechanics, not shank mechanics.

On a more positive note, a goodly number of veterans have written that the book caused them to reflect on what they had learned in the Army, especially responsibility. Private Berger concluded his letter, "I have known for a long time that my life was changed by that experience, and maybe I understand it a little better now."

Many veterans have written about the way the Army made it possible for them to know far more about their fellow citizens. Cpl. William Schaufele described his experience. He turned eighteen years of age on December 7, 1941. He was a student at Yale and managed to finish the year, then went into the 10th Armored Division and was in Bastogne for the Battle of the Bulge. He wrote, "One impression I took away from combat was that, in many, if not all, cases enlisted men knew better what to do in actual combat than their officers. Heterogeneity didn't seem to play a role. I served with people who had *no* high school education, worked at menial jobs, came from small rural villages or working-class neighborhoods, and many were better soldiers than I. Some were promoted to sergeant and busted two or three times in training, but, by the time we entered combat, they were back as tank commanders—and rightly so."

Some of the stories are funny. Jim Betts, who went on to serve in Korea, was an eighteen-year-old freshman at the University of Georgia in the fall of 1946. Some three thousand of his fellow freshmen were GIs, three, four, or five years older than he, attending the university on the GI Bill. On the first day, the student body president, "a small obviously 4F kid with a high voice, told us that all freshmen would wear the school beanie all year. From way up in the balcony came a voice that was so powerful you could feel the vibration: 'I'll be goddamned!' This brought a roar from the veterans. I learned that the man had been a Marine sergeant in the Pacific. No one wore a beanie."

I get a lot of specific stories or anecdotes that are riveting but frustrating, because if I had known them they certainly would have been in the book. Sometimes they confirm another guy's story. For example, the one about the forward observer who saw a moving haystack and called in artillery fire on it (p. 253) prompted one of the gunners on the 105s that did the shooting to write. He said the gun crew thought it was all a joke and for the remainder of the war, and at postwar reunions, they would get a laugh from remembering the time they shot at a moving haystack. Not until fifty-three years later did they discover there really was a target and they had knocked out a German tank.

Pvt. Jack Crawford provided another confirmation when he wrote about the story on page 341. Crawford went ashore at Utah Beach on D-Day plus twelve with the 4th Division. He fought in the hedgerows, at Mortain, and in the Hurtgen Forest, was wounded three times, and awarded a battlefield commission. He went AWOL from a hospital to rejoin his outfit in the Hurtgen. When he arrived at Bradley's headquarters, in Spa, he went into a bar "and sitting there was Ernest Hemingway and Colonel Buck Lanham, C.O. of the 22nd Infantry, 4th Division. Lanham asked me to come over and I was very pleased to talk to Hemingway as I had read some of his books. As we drank and talked, I felt he was full of it and this really wasn't his war. He was telling tales of hijinks in Paris. I finally got pissed off and said he should come up to my battalion with me in the Hurtgen to see what the war was really like instead of sitting back thirty miles from the front lines. The Colonel jumped on me and said I was out of line, so I stood up, saluted the Colonel, said 'F—— you, Hemingway,' and walked out."

I've had dozens of letters from front-line veterans who say they never saw a colonel, much less a general, where they were. But I've had a couple of GIs write to say that this colonel or that general made it to the front lines in their sector.

Wyatt Barnes sat down to write me a "two or three page letter, at most," but it ended up as a twelve-page single-spaced memoir, one of the best I've ever read. Some highlights: Barnes started off as an ASTP student at Brooklyn College in mid-1943. Then it was off to Fort Polk, Louisiana, where "we were all miserable. Especially, we detested our new comrades, who were mostly from Appalachia and the deep South, with a few from Idaho and Montana. They were rural and spoke in funny accents; we despised their ignorant ways. In turn, they disparaged our elitism and urban mores. I flaunted my subscription to the *New York Times,* thus inviting their special loathing. In time we adjusted to them and they to us."

Barnes shipped over to England in August 1944, then on to France in mid-October and into the line with the 80th Division as a replacement. "Five of us were admitted to the 1st squad, 1st platoon. We five knew each other slightly from our replacement trek, bonding among us came later." In late November, Barnes was in an offensive against the Maginot Line in Lorraine. He got caught in a shelling. An 88 came down right next to him, but it was a dud.

In mid-December, the 80th packed up and headed north, toward the southern shoulder of the Bulge, part of the Third Army counterattack. "We were in 2¹/₂ ton trucks for the trek north. This was a new torment in the bitter cold and interminable night. No rations. There were frequent stops because of the clogged roads, occasions we used for piss-calls. This task was an ordeal. Cramped and frozen, we eased ourselves off the back end into the furious wind and performed the needed function. The weather was utterly appalling."

On Christmas Day, the 80th joined the 4th Armored for the final push to break through to Bastogne. "We formed a skirmish line. Not a word was spoken. Then we began to move, 8 or 10 feet separating the men. Soon the rounds started coming, their tiny sonic booms causing distinct snaps as they passed close by. A tracer round struck the frozen ground in front of me and described an arc over my head. Then, after about 100 yards, I felt the slug strike just below my right collar bone. After the impact, and this still seems incredible, I could actually feel the bullet piercing the tissues and organs within, clipping through each in sequence. Time, almost literally, must have stood still as my whole being concentrated on this devastating physical assault. The bullet exited down, just to the left of my right shoulder blade.

"I fell forward, and the instant I hit the ground I intoned 'two months' to myself. This was the million dollar wound! Two months would give me relief from the line and get me through the worst of the winter." Actually, the wound was worse than Barnes thought; his right lung had been pierced and there was serious internal bleeding. For him, the war was over. Barnes recounted in some detail his evacuation from the snow-covered field back to a jeep, then to an aid station, then the 39th Evacuation Hospital, next Paris by train, and finally a flight to England to the 160th General Hospital near Cheltenham. He concluded, "Your tribute to the medical people in the ETO was richly deserved."

American Heritage printed the chapter on medics, nurses, and docs (my own favorite chapter, as lives are being saved, not destroyed) and got a big mail in response, the letters telling this or that story about being saved by a medic and how wonderful the medics and nurses and doctors were. It almost breaks your heart to read some of them. We now have the letters in the archives of the Eisenhower Center, available to scholars and visitors, and I hope someday someone does a book on U.S. Army medicine in World War II.

The *American Heritage* article produced another story that has to be told. It comes from A. Bruce Campbell of the 11th Regiment, 5th Division, who wrote it up at the time, and who described it as "probably the most remarkable piece of battlefield surgery in World War II."

November 10, 1944, the 5th Division was attacking at Metz. Pvt. Henry Roon of B Company, 2nd Regiment, caught a mortar shell fragment in his throat. He fell prostrate in the mud with a perforating wound of the neck, with the wound exit over the tracheal area and a fracture of the trachea. Pvt. Duane Kinman, a nineteen-year-old medic with two years of high school education, finished binding up a chest wound and rushed over to help. "He saw Roon turning blue in the face, gasping and suffocating to death. Kinman whipped out his jackknife. Roon made protesting motions which Kinman overruled, saying, 'I don't like to do this, but it's the only way you're going to live.'

"Then, without wasting any more time in deliberation and with perfect presence of mind and recollection of two lectures given him a year previous in basic training, Kinman prepared to perform an operation which is delicate in the best of surgical conditions. He knew he had to open up the windpipe and he knew he had to have a tube or edge to insert to keep it open. He saw a fountain pen in Roon's pocket and seized that.

"With machine guns chattering all around, with mortar shells still landing, with a muddy field for an operating table, a gray sky for light, and his jackknife for a scalpel and without benefit of any anesthetic or drug, Kinman cut into Roon's throat, carefully avoiding the jugular, made a longitudinal one and a half inch incision in Roon's windpipe, cleanly and safely. Then he slipped the rounded end of Roon's fountain pen into the incision to keep the cut open and told Roon, 'Now keep that pen in your windpipe and you'll be okay.' "

Kinman helped Roon get to the rear and walk to an aid station. The battalion surgeon found nothing to improve upon. Two other tracheotomies performed by surgeons there the same day were unsuccessful.

Pvt. Eldon McDermeit was an ASTP student who went to the front line with the 70th Infantry Division: "On our third night on the line, two of our guys were bayoneted in their foxholes. They had obviously been asleep. The next day all of the 70th Division infantry had to exchange our sleeping bags for two blankets. It was much harder to stay warm with blankets so we stayed awake. We seldom got hot meals on the front line. We ate K-rations almost exclusively. Our first hot meal was after six weeks on the line. Our next hot meal was five weeks later."

I learn a lot from the veterans. Lt. Sidney Lowery was a field artillery liaison pilot. He said he and his friends flew the Piper Cubs without wearing a parachute, which would have been useless at the altitudes they flew anyway; besides "it was safer to stay in the Piper Cub when hit because of its aeronautical characteristics, which often enabled the pilot to make an emergency landing." (See the photo in the insert "The Air War.") Lowery added that "our greatest danger was friendly fire. Each of us was flying missions to direct fire by our own division artillery, but at the same time, and further back, Corps artillery were conducting their own missions, with larger caliber weapons, totally unaware of what we were doing. So as we were directing our own unit's fire while flying over the front line, we frequently felt a sort of 'whoosh' and a bump, as the Corps artillery shell passed by. I had more than one chum who was shot down by our own artillery."

The trench foot mail (p. 259) has been heavy. The theme is summed up by one letter: "For five decades I've carried around a sense of shame at being evacuated for trenchfoot. The Army (but not the nurses and doctors) made me feel I had let down the side. Your account has helped me get over those bad feelings."

Pvt. Norman Redlich of the 100th Division remembered that "in late November, 1944, after spending another night in a cold wet foxhole, and after following as best I could the instructions to remove our boots at night and dry our socks, I awoke and found that I could no longer fit into my boots because my feet had swollen like balloons. Barely able to walk, I was removed to a field hospital and told that I would be back on the line in a matter of days. But the pain intensified, and my feet started to turn white, and then purple. The pain became so excruciating that I was given a shot of morphine. It was so bad that I could not place a sheet over my toes and had to sleep with the blankets and sheets turned back."

Redlich was shipped back to the States on the *Queen Elizabeth I,* which had been converted into a hospital ship. He recalled, "virtually the entire contingent of passengers had trenchfoot, many of them with toes and legs amputated. I felt both lucky and guilty. In many respects, I still do."

Redlich's blunt honesty is typical of the GIs I've interviewed or corresponded with over the years. Shakespeare wrote that old men remember, with advantages, the deeds they did as warriors. With a few exceptions, I've always found the opposite. Many times in group interviews I've heard something like this exchange: "I'm no hero. He's the hero."

"No, not me. You want to hear about a real hero, let me tell you about so-and-so."

One letter came from a man who identified himself as a Jewish slave laborer in a German factory making panzerfaust shells. He said he and his fellow slaves had discovered that if they mixed sand in with the sulfur they could render the explosive inoperable, and that they could do it when the German inspectors' heads were turned. He said only German soldiers put on the final touch, the trigger mechanism. But those German soldiers liked to take a break. When they did, the slaves speeded up their output but in the process screwed up the mechanism. The German soldiers were glad to have a higher output and never inspected the shells that had been produced while they were on break. That, he said proudly, was his contribution, and he was glad to see from the story about German duds in this book (pp. 65–66) that the GIs had noticed and lives had been saved.

Lt. Bryce Stevens was a combat engineer with the 87th Division. He said the book "brought back memories of events, sights and even smells of that time and place that I hadn't thought of in a long time." One of those memories was of his first shower after three months of continuous combat: "The procedure was to strip off, put your dirty clothes (except for boots) in a pile, run buck-naked across duckboards to the next tent where the showers were. There they turned on the water long enough to get wet, then turned it off while you soaped up. The water then came on again to rinse off. Back to the dressing tent where clean clothes were issued. All this in freezing weather. I don't remember how we managed to get clothes that fit."

Richard Meier wrote that his uncle, Gordon Meier, was in the Losheimergraben railroad station fight (p. 195) and Pvt. Herbert Meier, a German soldier quoted in the book who was also in that fight, was a cousin of his uncle. "It makes the Bulge almost like Gettysburg—cousins across the lines from each other."

Gordon Meier wrote, "I remember that railroad station very well. We came under artillery shelling. We got under the freight tracks (4 inches of concrete). The Germans came marching right down the railroad tracks. You could hear their steel-heeled boots. We killed lots of them. The shelling started again and we pulled back 500 yards. I remember the Germans had long overcoats and they would tuck them up around the waist so they could run easier. We got one young German officer for interrogation but he was dying. He had two pieces of bread with jelly on them."

Robert Kettler's father was in the 80th Division, wounded and captured near Nancy on September 22, 1944. He died in Stalag 4G on October 1. Kettler was four years old when the telegram came: "I still remember the emotional storm that swirled through our house that day. Standing by a blue chair where Mother sat weeping while family and friends gathered to console her in a ritual that was by then all too familiar, even in our small Indiana town, I knew that something monumental had happened to us." In 1995, Kettler, his daughter, and his mother paid their first visit to his father's grave, in the American Cemetery and memorial near Liège, Belgium.

At the graveside, Kettler wrote, "I touched Mother's arm. 'It's a beautiful place,' I said."

"Yes, it is," she replied. "And I'm so grateful I could be here with you. But it's a long way from Shelbyville, Indiana."

As they drove away from the cemetery, Kettler continued, "we talked quietly in the car, our voices filled with relief and release. We had stood at my father's grave. Now we could go home."

Kettler described his experience in the Summer 1996 edition of

Traces, published by the Indiana Historical Society. I've received dozens of other articles, privately printed books, memoirs, and documents of all types, including company- or battalion-level oral histories gathered and printed by someone from the unit. This is wonderful. I'm delighted to be able to put them into the archives at the Eisenhower Center at the University of New Orleans, where they will be available to future scholars and descendants.* I only wish they had been available when I wrote this book.

I'm learning all the time. Here's one that I didn't know. In January 1945, Pvt. Richard Lockhart of the ill-fated 106th Division was a POW in Stalag IXB, Bad Orb, Germany. It was a smallish, primitive camp, housing several thousand Russian, Serbian, and French soldiers—all privates. There were no medical facilities, no sanitary services, no heat, and not much grass soup. When Lockhart and his fellow American POWs arrived, the guards held a roll call. They ordered all Jews to step forward. A dozen did. The guards separated them and sent them off to a slave-labor camp, over the vehement protests of Lockhart and others. Many of the Jewish POWs died. What prompted them to step forward? Lockhart wondered. He conjectured that it may have been an affirmation of their culture and religion, or it could have been out of naïveté, a sense that the U.S. Army uniform they were wearing would protect them.

I know one Jewish soldier who rightly feared capture, so when it was imminent he switched dog tags with a dead buddy. It worked for him, but not for his folks, who got a telegram from the War Department telling them he had been killed in action.

My mentor, Dr. T. Harry Williams, taught me to let my characters speak for themselves. "They always say it better than you ever could," he insisted. The paragraph that follows proves his point. It was written by Lt. Charles Jordan, 9th Division.

"I have read of fearless people, I even had a runner for a short time who I think was pretty close to fearless (he got killed), but I was not fearless. My worst fear was of screwing up or showing my fear to those around me. A distant second was fear of death. In my earliest days this included the fear of being wounded but this rapidly trans-

---

* The Eisenhower Center's address is 923 Magazine St., New Orleans, LA 70130. Director Douglas Brinkley continues actively to seek memoirs, documents, oral histories, and other material from veterans of ETO; although I'm retired, this is the project closest to my heart, and I urge all veterans to deposit copies of their material in the archives.

formed into a desire. The absolute worst period of fear came as we were organizing for an attack. We never knew what to expect or when to expect it, and the longer the wait the greater the fear. The fear of death came openly when I was lying in a ditch, or a hole, or on the ground and artillery or mortar shells were exploding around me. There was absolutely nothing positive to do about these situations except lay there and pray. Since the days when I lived with fear constantly, I have found that fear for yourself cannot hold a candle to the fear engendered by the serious illness of your wife or children. I'd rather be shot at every day of the week and all day Sunday than face that situation."

Sgt. Milt Lamm was a student at Indiana University in the fall of 1942 who went on active duty in February 1943. Then it was off to ASTP, and when that folded into the infantry. He was a replacement in the 84th Division from the end of November 1944 until the following April. He won a Silver Star and a Bronze Star. He provides some vivid images. Two examples:

"I began my combat life all by myself in a foxhole half full of water in front of a German pill box at Lindern, Germany. For the next several days, all I did was cringe at the bottom of the foxhole while the 88's pounded us. I had no idea what was going on.

"The German entrenching tool was vastly superior to our pick and shovel. In the American Army you had to have a pick and your buddy a shovel. The German pick and shovel were one and the same. You simply converted the pick into a shovel and vice versa by changing the handle angle. So, we all carried a German entrenching tool."

One of the best comments came in a beer-drinking bull session with some veterans. We were talking about what it all meant. I never caught the name of the man who gave us the following image, but I'll never forget what he said: "Imagine this. In the spring of 1945, around the world, the sight of a twelve-man squad of teenage boys, armed and in uniform, brought terror to people's hearts. Whether it was a Red Army squad in Berlin, Leipzig, or Warsaw, or a German squad in Holland, or a Japanese squad in Manila, Seoul, or Beijing, that squad meant rape, pillage, looting, wanton destruction, senseless killing. But there was an exception: a squad of GIs, a sight that brought the biggest smiles you ever saw to people's lips, and joy to their hearts.

"Around the world this was true, even in Germany, even—after

September 1945—in Japan. This was because GIs meant candy, cigarettes, C-rations, and freedom. America had sent the best of her young men around the world, not to conquer but to liberate, not to terrorize but to help. This was a great moment in our history."

Another bright image came from a veteran who said that he felt he had done his part in helping to change the twentieth century from one of darkness into one of light. I think that was the great achievement of the generation who fought World War II on the Allied side. As of 1945—the year in which more people were killed violently, more buildings destroyed, more homes burned than any other year in history—it was impossible to believe in human progress. World Wars I and II had made a mockery of the nineteenth-century idea of progress, the notion that things were getting better and would continue to do so. In 1945 one had to believe that the final outcome of the scientific and technological revolution that had inspired the idea of progress would be a world destroyed.

But slowly, surely, the spirit of those GIs handing out candy and helping bring democracy to their former enemies spread, and today it is the democracies—not the totalitarians—who are on the march. Today, one can again believe in progress, as things really are getting better. This is thanks to the GIs—along with the millions of others who helped liberate Germany and Japan from their evil rulers, then stood up to Stalin and his successors. That generation has done more to spread freedom—and prosperity—around the globe than any previous generation.

John Lydon, a thirty-four-year-old attorney in Chicago, wrote me in 1998 that his father had served in SHAEF. "Most of my young life," Lydon confessed, "I never really understood my father. I blamed him and his generation for everything from McCarthyism to the Vietnam War to Watergate. I never gave them credit for the Interstate Highway System, IBM, NASA, the Civil Rights Act of 1965, the fall of Communism, or any of it. Then I read your book. You have helped me understand my father. When my son is old enough, I will give him your book so he can get to know his grandfather."

Sgt. Henry Halsted, who won a Bronze Star, participated after the war in some experimental programs that brought together college-age German and American veterans in England, and a similar one in France. The idea was to teach through contact and example. In 1997, Halsted got a Christmas card from a German participant living in Munich: "I think often of our meetings and mutual ideals. Indeed, the 1948 program and everything connected with it was the most important, decisive event for me. Influenced my life deeply!"

And a French participant wrote, "In 1950 France was in ruins. I saw only a world marked by war, by destruction, by the shadow of war, and by fear. I believed that it was not finished, that there would be a next war. I did not think it would be possible to build a life, to have a family. Then came the group of young Americans, attractive, idealistic, optimistic, protected, believing and acting as though anything was possible. It was a transforming experience for me."

That spirit—we can do it, we can rebuild Europe and hold back the Red Army and avoid World War III—was the great gift of the New World to the Old World in the twentieth century. America paid for that gift with the lives of some of its best young men. When I read the letters from the veterans I'm almost always impressed by their brief accounts of what they did with their lives after the war. They had successful careers, they were good citizens and family men, and many of them made great contributions to their society, their country, and the world. Then I think about those who didn't make it, especially all those junior officers and NCOs who got killed in such appalling numbers.

These men were natural leaders. They died one by one. Of each of them, I wonder, What life was cut off here? A genius? It is impossible to imagine what he might have invented; we do know that his loss was our loss. A budding politician? Where might he have led us? A builder? A teacher? A scholar? A novelist? A musician? I sometimes think the biggest price we pay for war is what might have been.

Lt. Waverly Wray comes to mind. So do Capt. Anthony Stefanich and Lt. Col. Robert Cole and so many others, gone long before their time, their deaths depriving us of the gift of their lives. When they tolled the bell for Wray, Stefanich, Cole, and the hundreds of their buddies who went down, that bell tolled for all of us.

My son, Hugh Ambrose, conducted, translated, and edited all of the German interviews, and here he describes some of the veterans' impressions of the American GI.

Dedicated to the memory of our honored friend,
Col. Hans von Luck

THE GERMAN veterans who agreed to be interviewed for this book offered some important insights into the character of the American GI and the war on the Western Front.* The Germans themselves, while not a representative sampling of their entire army, were of varying service grades and almost all of them had seen action on two or more fronts. The terms they used to describe the U.S. Army would, if misunderstood, anger many American veterans. Voicing the verdict of the Wehrmacht, Maj. Gerhard Lemcke of the 12th Panzer Division said that when one went to the Western Front, one learned "the way a rich man fights a war." But if American veterans listen carefully to what these German veterans said, they will not feel themselves slighted. The German veterans were actually praising the GIs who, having won their war in Europe without hate, left none in their wake.

As described by Maj. Helmut Ritgen, the rich Americans kept a businesslike schedule. "Normally, the Americans were very aggressive in the morning, but at night they were tired and they stopped fighting. From 7 pm at night till morning, there was absolute

* All of the German oral histories quoted here come from the Ambrose Collection at the Eisenhower Center in New Orleans.

peace." Once begun, the day's campaign featured the U.S. air force and artillery. As far as the Germans were concerned, Allied air superiority won the war in the West. Unchallenged in the air, Allied planes made pass after pass over their enemies' columns and fortified positions, bombing and strafing. Like many of the troops sent to repel the Normandy invasion, Walter Jungmichel never made it to the battlefield; a Jabo came screaming down upon him and "put so many holes in my car that I could see through it."

Air supremacy also meant that the American artillery observer circled slowly over the battlefield in a small plane, banking his wings to and fro as he maneuvered for a good look at the action. The German army lived in fear of him. "It was suicide," remembered Capt. Walter Schäfer-Kehnert, "to fire at anything if you were in sight of an artillery observation plane." Once spotted, the Germans figured "we had, at most, a half an hour before the first shells arrived." Worse, the Americans had so many shells that they seemed "to fire at individual soldiers." The combination of Jabos, carpet bombings, and artillery, in the opinion of Captain Schäfer-Kehnert, left the German army "more or less paralyzed."

In short, the Germans asserted that the GIs let the high explosives do the hard work. "[The American] infantry did not attack," said Maj. Rolf Pauls of the Wehrmacht's 363rd Infantry Division, "until [it] could be sure that the positions [it was] attacking were more than half destroyed, which makes sense if you can afford to do it." Nor did the American troops press the attack with reckless abandon. According to their adversary, the GIs "fought bravely, but if things weren't going well, they'd back off, bomb, and try again the next day." For contrast, one German artillery captain recalled that "when [the Russian infantry] got fire from our artillery, they did not go down like the Americans . . . no, the Russians were running under the artillery. You sat there with your pistol and your gun because they were coming." The Russians had a lot in the way of visceral motivation and little in the way of weaponry. With the Americans, the situation was reversed. Given the GIs' dramatic strategic advantage, the Germans concluded, it was simply "not necessary for Americans to throw themselves at solid resistance."

Nor did the Americans find it necessary to wage a ruthless campaign. As has been mentioned previously, both sides respected the Red Cross. The Americans and the Germans trusted one another to stop shooting while the dead and wounded were hauled away. They trusted the other's medical corps to treat all of the wounded. That trust, which led to many strange episodes out on the battlefield, meant everything to the soldiers. No German veteran ever discussed the Western Front without talking about the Red Cross at length. The Eastern Front, once again, provided the contrast. In Russia, said the Germans, "[our] wounded were either taken with us or they were shot."

With both the Eastern and Western Fronts disintegrating in the early months of 1945, the difference between them loomed ever larger in the minds of German soldiers. From the west came their opponents, the Americans, who—while irrevocably set upon the destruction of the Nazi regime—saw themselves as liberators. Although an implacable foe, the GI was, in the end, on someone else's soil liberating someone else's family. From the east came Germany's enemy, the Russian army, imbued with ancient and ethnic hatreds, and armed with a passion for revenge. Shuddering at the thought of the Russians exacting retribution from their homeland, German soldiers in the west found that fighting against the Americans "did not sit well with us." Explaining their anxiety, Walter Jungmichel remembered how he and his comrades "had to fight [the GIs] earnestly . . . and put up resistance, when all the time we were hoping that the Americans would push far into Germany." They were so concerned, in fact, that many Germans tried to persuade the American troops to join them in a war against the Red Army. The suggestion, however fantastic, underscored their faith in the U.S. Army, which had always balanced the goal of unconditional surrender with a respect for human life.

Although the Germans had come to respect their opponents' manner of waging war, the GIs' attitude took some getting used to. Lt. Walter Rahn recalled the day that he was captured while attacking an American position. The GIs threw him in their scout car and proceeded to press their counterattack. "The interpreter asked me from time to time—while they attacked my men—if I would call for their surrender. I was so shocked—I had never experienced anything like this during my long years of war—that I could think of nothing to say."

Other German soldiers were struck not so much by the Americans' cavalier attitude as their magnanimity. After years of grueling combat, Sgt. Ewald Becker remembered the day that he and his comrades decided they had to give up. "We went out into the streets to surrender. The first vehicle to come was an American jeep. I raised my hands. He waved at me and continued to drive. The second was a slightly larger American vehicle with four men. They stopped and gave me chocolate. They said something I didn't understand and drove on." Eventually, other GIs arrived to take away the weapons of Becker and his men, place them under a nominal guard, and walk them to the nearest POW camp.

As for the condition of the Allied camps, few veterans had any complaints. When Gustav Spreckels, a sergeant with the Panzer Lehr Division, became a POW, the guards told him "to throw everything away. America is rich and you will get everything new." More important than food and clothing, however, was the soldier's desire to be recognized as such. The German veterans interviewed for this book believed that they had been neither Nazis nor criminals; they had been soldiers. And they all praised the Americans for drawing this distinction between the two. "When I went into prison camp, I said I was with the 116th Panzer Division. And the U.S. Army said, 'OK, good division.' We were well known and there was no ill will toward us."

In the POW camp in which Lt. Walter Padberg found himself, the authority to release prisoners rested in the hands of a young American doctor. "One day [the doctor] asked me," recalled Padberg, " 'Do you know of any young ladies in the area? Because, damn it, I'm probably going to be here for months.' 'Yes,' [Padberg] said, 'I'll look around.'

"Nearby there was a release camp for the women who had helped out in the news media. They had worn a uniform and were therefore now interned." Padberg got to know some of the women there. After a time he "found a beautiful young woman from Königsberg. She had already heard that her parents were dead. She was alone and did not know where to go." When Padberg asked her if she'd like to meet his friend she exclaimed, "Yes! An American doctor. Excellent!" "She went back [to the States] with him," Padberg happily concluded. "They got married and wrote me several nice letters to the effect that I had made a good match."

In the years since the war, the relationship between the German and American veterans has flourished. On several occasions, the American and German veterans associations have held joint ceremonies to honor their fallen comrades. But more often individuals have met by chance on some former battlefield. During the ensuing conversation—which usually begins with "What outfit were you with?"—they find that they have a lot in common. Both the American veterans and the former soldiers of the Wehrmacht enjoy celebrating their postwar accomplishments. Like all grandparents, both take great pride in having created a prosperous and safe country for their children and grandchildren. They also enjoy talking to others who were there. Only somebody who was there understands that a front-line soldier's war amounted to looking out after your friends while "trying to get out of this dirty business alive."

Their mutual understanding has led to some startling conversations. Cpl. Hans Herbst had obviously had one such conversation about his entry into Belgium in late October 1944. "I was in my armored personnel carrier about 17 or 18 vehicles behind the lead tank on a small dirt track through the forest." The convoy came to a bridge. "There were two American anti-tank positions built there. We saw them. The first of our tanks opened fire. My friend Murray Shapiro, one of the Americans in the position across from us, told me [later] that that first shot killed all but one of his men in the first two positions. The survivors returned fire upon us, blowing up four of the Panther tanks headed down the narrow track. We pulled back."

When I think about how much a soldier's comrades meant to him, I wonder how the veterans can ever put the past behind them. But Herbst's story reveals more than just two men swapping tales. It is the conversation of two men who have learned to forgive. The American soldier can take a great deal of credit for making that conversation possible. He fought hard to win the war. But every step of the way, he strove to create peace. Such a tribute is perhaps as fine as any old soldier could wish, especially when it comes from his former opponent. "I only want to add," said Herbst with a chuckle, "that today when I am with Americans, we are friends. They tell me I am lucky to be alive. I tell them I'm lucky that they are such poor shots."

Notes

PROLOGUE

1. The B. H. Vandervoort memoirs at the Eisenhower Center (EC), University of New Orleans, contain Vandervoort's testimonial to Wray, along with his recommendation for the Medal of Honor. Wray's story is also told in Wills, *Put on Your Boots and Parachutes!*, 86–87.

2. Honoré de Balzac, as quoted in Weigley, *Eisenhower's Lieutenants*, 127.

3. Colby, *War from the Ground Up*, 37.

4. Adolf Rogosch interview by Hugh Ambrose, EC.

5. English, *A Perspective on Infantry*, 169.

CHAPTER 1: EXPANDING THE BEACHHEAD

1. Henderson, "D-Day + 1, Omaha Beach," in Roush, *World War II Reminiscences*, 95–100.

2. Wills, *Put on Your Boots and Parachutes!*, 212.

3. Otis Sampson memoir, EC.

4. Frank Woosley memoir, James Coyle memoir, Sam Applebee memoir, and Otis Sampson memoir, EC.

5. Otis Sampson memoir, EC.

6. Wills, *Put on Your Boots and Parachutes!*, 91.

7. Balkoski, *Beyond the Beachhead*, 170.

8. Friedrich Bertenrath interview by Hugh Ambrose, EC.

9. Balkoski, *Beyond the Beachhead*, 178–79.

10. Ibid., 177.

11. Sidney Salomon memoir, EC.

12. Edward Gianelloni oral history, EC.

13. Jim Finn memoir and newspaper clipping, *The Hackensack (N.J.) Record*, June 3, 1994, in EC.

14. Charles Stockell memoir, EC.

15. Fred Hall oral history, EC.

16. Robert Miller oral history, EC.

17. Balkoski, *Beyond the Beachhead*, 154.

18. Ibid., 148.

19. Ibid., 155–56.

20. Weigley, *Eisenhower's Lieutenants*, 127.

21. Murphy, *Heroes of WWII*, 206–9.

22. Colby, *War from the Ground Up*, 41, 42, 45.

23. Arthur Schultz memoir, EC.

24. Otis Sampson memoir, EC.

25. Günter Behr interview by Hugh Ambrose, EC.

26. Helmut Hesse interview by Hugh Ambrose, EC.

27. James Delong oral history, EC.

28. Friedrich Bertenrath interview by Hugh Ambrose, EC.

29. Moench, *Marauder Men*, 203.

493

30. Friedrich Bertenrath interview by Hugh Ambrose, EC.
31. Ambrose, *Eisenhower*, Vol. I, *Soldier, General of the Army*, 315–17.
32. OSS report of June 14, 1944, EC.
33. Doubler, *Closing with the Enemy*, 43–47.
34. Ruppenthal, *Logistical Support of the Armies*, Vol. I, 420–22.
35. Pogue, *The Supreme Command*, 543.
36. Chandler, ed., *The D-Day Encyclopedia*, 141.
37. Fraser, *Knight's Cross*, 503–5.

CHAPTER 2: HEDGEROW FIGHTING

1. Hastings, *Overlord*, 248.
2. James Delong oral history, EC.
3. Ambrose, *Eisenhower*, Vol. I, *Soldier, General of the Army*, 317.
4. Ibid., 319.
5. Pogue, *Supreme Command*, 188.
6. English, *A Perspective on Infantry*, 184.
7. Ambrose, *Eisenhower*, Vol. I, *Soldier, General of the Army*, 321.
8. Hastings, *Overlord*, 156.
9. Ambrose, *Band of Brothers*, 110.
10. Hastings, *Overlord*, 155.
11. William Craft oral history, EC.
12. Ellis, *On the Front Lines*, 94.
13. Hastings, *Overlord*, 187–88.
14. Ibid., 190.
15. Fussell, *Wartime*, 268.
16. Belton Cooper memoir, EC.
17. Ibid.
18. Wilson, *If You Survive*, 35.
19. Balkoski, *Beyond the Beachhead*, 212.
20. Moench, *Marauder Men*, 223.
21. English, *A Perspective on Infantry*, 180.
22. Doubler, *Closing with the Enemy*, 45–46.
23. Ibid., 58.
24. Weiss, *Enemy North*.
25. Doubler, *Closing with the Enemy*, 49–51.
26. Walter Padberg interview by Hugh Ambrose, EC.
27. Fraser, *Knight's Cross*, 509–10.
28. Rolf Pauls interview by Hugh Ambrose, EC.
29. Adolf Rogosch interview by Hugh Ambrose, EC.
30. Hastings, *Overlord*, 183.
31. Frederick Ruge interview by Stephen Ambrose, EC.
32. Doubler, *Closing with the Enemy*, 66.
33. Gerhard Lemcke interview by Hugh Ambrose, EC.
34. Hastings, *Overlord*, 181–82.
35. Ibid., 206.
36. Balkoski, *Beyond the Beachhead*, 253–54.
37. Ibid., 254.
38. Hastings, *Overlord*, 218.
39. Edward Gianelloni oral history, EC.
40. Colby, *War from the Ground Up*, 161.
41. Balkoski, *Beyond the Beachhead*, 264.

42. Belton Cooper memoir, EC.
43. Balkoski, *Beyond the Beachhead,* 274–77.

CHAPTER 3: BREAKOUT AND ENCIRCLEMENT

1. Hastings, *Overlord,* 273.
2. Bradley, *A Soldier's Story,* chapter 17.
3. Ambrose, *Eisenhower: Soldier and President,* 149.
4. Pyle, *Ernie's War,* 332.
5. James Delong oral history, EC.
6. Belton Cooper memoir, EC.
7. MacDonald, *The Mighty Endeavor,* 305.
8. Weigley, *Eisenhower's Lieutenants,* 153.
9. Pyle, *Ernie's War,* 336.
10. Edward Gianelloni oral history, EC.
11. Belton Cooper memoir, EC.
12. Herbert Meier interview by Hugh Ambrose, EC.
13. Joachim Barth interview by Hugh Ambrose, EC.
14. Bradley, *A Soldier's Story,* 358.
15. Weigley, *Eisenhower's Lieutenants,* 153.
16. Hastings, *Overlord,* 255.
17. Joachim Barth interview by Hugh Ambrose, EC.
18. Belton Cooper memoir, EC.
19. Günter Feldmann interview by Hugh Ambrose, EC.
20. Weigley, *Eisenhower's Lieutenants,* 154.
21. Hastings, *Overlord,* 256.
22. Ibid., 258.
23. Weigley, *Eisenhower's Lieutenants,* 157, 166.
24. Hastings, *Overlord,* 259–60.
25. Belton Cooper memoir, EC.
26. Weigley, *Eisenhower's Lieutenants,* 160.
27. Friedrich Bertenrath interview by Hugh Ambrose, EC.
28. Walter Padberg interview by Hugh Ambrose, EC.
29. Ambrose, *Eisenhower,* Vol. I, *Soldier, General of the Army,* 82.
30. Weigley, *Eisenhower's Lieutenants,* 177.
31. Ibid., 175.
32. Ibid., 185.
33. Heinz-Günter Guderian interview by Hugh Ambrose, EC.
34. Weiss, *Enemy North.*
35. Ibid.
36. Ibid.
37. Baldridge, *Victory Road,* 101.
38. Weigley, *Eisenhower's Lieutenants,* 216–17.
39. Robert Weiss memoir, EC.
40. Heinz-Günter Guderian interview by Hugh Ambrose, EC.
41. Weiss, *Enemy North.*
42. Helmut Ritgen interview by Hugh Ambrose, EC.
43. Colby, *War from the Ground Up,* 195.
44. Charles Stockell memoir, EC.
45. Ambrose, *Eisenhower,* Vol. I, *Soldier, General of the Army,* 331.
46. Ibid., 332.
47. Ibid., 331.

48. Herbert Meier interview by Hugh Ambrose, EC.
49. Günter Materne interview by Hugh Ambrose, EC.
50. Walter Padberg interview by Hugh Ambrose, EC.
51. Herbert Meier interview by Hugh Ambrose, EC.
52. Friedrich Bertenrath interview by Hugh Ambrose, EC.
53. Colby, *War from the Ground Up*, 241.
54. Wilson, *If You Survive*, 70.
55. Walter Padberg interview by Hugh Ambrose, EC.
56. Walter Kaspers interview by Hugh Ambrose, EC.
57. Hans-Heinrich Dibbern interview by Hugh Ambrose, EC.
58. Colby, *War from the Ground Up*, 232.
59. Ambrose, *Eisenhower*, Vol. I, *Soldier, General of the Army*, 336.
60. Hastings, *Overlord*, 313.

CHAPTER 4: TO THE SIEGFRIED LINE

1. Ambrose, *Eisenhower*, Vol. I, *Soldier, General of the Army*, 337.
2. Paul-Alfred Stoob interview by Hugh Ambrose, EC.
3. Günter Mollenhoff interview by Hugh Ambrose, EC.
4. Belton Cooper memoir, EC.
5. Province, *Patton's Third Army*, 36, 42.
6. Edward Gianelloni oral history, EC.
7. Wilson, *If You Survive*, 68.
8. *Move Out*, copy in EC.
9. Ibid.
10. Wilson, *If You Survive*, 82–83.
11. Hatch, *4th Infantry "Ivy" Division*, 31.
12. Doubler, *Closing with the Enemy*, 153.
13. Fred Hall memoir, EC; *New York Sun*, October 24, 1944.
14. Weigley, *Eisenhower's Lieutenants*, 301.
15. The classic account of Market-Garden is Ryan, *A Bridge Too Far*.
16. Ambrose, *Band of Brothers*, 117–18.
17. Otis Sampson memoir, EC.
18. Arthur Schultz memoir, EC.
19. Otis Sampson memoir, EC.
20. Arthur Schultz memoir, EC.
21. Wills, *Put on Your Boots and Parachutes!*, 139.
22. D. Zane Schlemmer memoir, EC.
23. Otis Sampson memoir, EC.
24. Arthur Schultz memoir, EC.
25. Murphy, *Heroes of WWII*, 209.
26. Wills, *Put on Your Boots and Parachutes!*, 130.
27. Booth and Duncan, *Paratrooper*, 227–30.
28. Otis Sampson memoir, EC; Wills, *Put on Your Boots and Parachutes!*, 141–43.
29. Booth and Duncan, *Paratrooper*, 236.
30. Weigley, *Eisenhower's Lieutenants*, 314.
31. Booth and Duncan, *Paratrooper*, 235–36.
32. Weigley, *Eisenhower's Lieutenants*, 315.
33. Will, *Put on Your Boots and Parachutes!*, 154.
34. Clinton Riddle memoir, EC.
35. Arthur Schultz memoir, EC.

CHAPTER 5: THE SIEGFRIED LINE

1. Ambrose, *The Supreme Commander*, 529.
2. Doubler, *Closing with the Enemy*, 128–29; Cole, *The Lorraine Campaign*, 28–29.
3. Cole, *The Lorraine Campaign*, 29.
4. Weigley, *Eisenhower's Lieutenants*, 386.
5. Cole, *The Lorraine Campaign*, 266.
6. Ibid., 145.
7. Ibid., 272–73.
8. Weigley, *Eisenhower's Lieutenants*, 387.
9. *New York Sun*, October 24, 1944.
10. Fred Hall memoir, EC.
11. Ambrose, *Eisenhower*, Vol. I, *Soldier, General of the Army*, 354–55.
12. Ibid., 357.
13. Wilson, *If You Survive*, 11–18.
14. Belton Cooper memoir, EC.
15. Doubler, *Closing with the Enemy*, 102.
16. Wenzel Andreas Borgert interview by Hugh Ambrose, EC.
17. Friedrich Bertenrath interview by Hugh Ambrose, EC.
18. Doubler, *Closing with the Enemy*, 97.
19. Friedrich Bertenrath interview by Hugh Ambrose, EC.
20. Belton Cooper memoir, EC.
21. Doubler, *Closing with the Enemy*, 123–25.
22. Ibid., 97–98.
23. *New York Sun*, October 24, 1944.
24. Fred Hall memoir, EC.
25. Ibid.
26. Doubler, *Closing with the Enemy*, 100.
27. *New York Sun*, October 25–27, 1944.
28. *Reporting World War II*, Vol. II, 274.
29. *Life*, November 6, 1944.
30. John C. Harrison papers, EC.

CHAPTER 6: METZ AND THE HURTGEN FOREST

1. Leinbaugh and Campbell, *The Men of Company K*, 89.
2. Fussell, *Doing Battle*, 27.
3. Leinbaugh and Campbell, *The Men of Company K*, 21.
4. Ibid., 33.
5. Ibid, 41.
6. Ibid., 45.
7. Ibid., 46.
8. Weigley, *Eisenhower's Lieutenants*, 389.
9. Doubler, *Closing with the Enemy*, 134–35.
10. Egger and Otts, *G Company's War*, 33.
11. Ibid., 35.
12. Ibid., 52.
13. Cole, *The Lorraine Campaign*, 440–43; Doubler, *Closing with the Enemy*, 138.
14. Doubler, *Closing with the Enemy*, 140.
15. Ibid., 72.
16. Forrest Pogue oral history, EC.
17. Miller, *A Dark and Bloody Ground*, 1.

18. Ibid., 33.
19. Ibid., 28.
20. Ibid., 45.
21. Ibid., 60.
22. Chernitsky, *Voices from the Foxholes*, 62–63.
23. Miller, *A Dark and Bloody Ground*, 79.
24. Ellis, *On the Front Lines*, 220.
25. Wilson, *If You Survive*, 132, 145–47.
26. Doubler, *Closing with the Enemy*, 188–89.
27. Wilson, *If You Survive*, 183.
28. Ellis, *On the Front Lines*, 78.
29. Miller, *A Dark and Bloody Ground*, 150–52.
30. Ibid., 162.
31. Salomon, *2nd U.S. Ranger Infantry Battalion*, 25.
32. James Eikner memoir, EC.
33. Len Lomell memoir, EC.
34. James Eikner memoir, EC.
35. Miller, *A Dark and Bloody Ground*, 168.
36. Gerald Heaney papers, EC.
37. Miller, *A Dark and Bloody Ground*, 169.
38. R. Potratz memoir, EC.
39. George Williams interview by Forrest Pogue, EC.
40. Miller, *A Dark and Bloody Ground*, 171.
41. George Williams interview by Forrest Pogue, EC.
42. Len Lomell memoir, EC.
43. George Williams interview by Forrest Pogue, EC.
44. Miller, *A Dark and Bloody Ground*, 169.
45. Ibid., 203.
46. Leinbaugh and Campbell, *The Men of Company K*, 73.
47. Len Lomell memoir, EC.
48. James Eikner memoir, EC.

CHAPTER 7: THE ARDENNES, DECEMBER 16–19

1. John Eisenhower, *The Bitter Woods*, 81.
2. Robert Merriman memoir, EC.
3. Jack Barensfeld memoir, EC.
4. Franklin Anderson memoir, EC.
5. Eisenhower to Marshall, January 10, 1945, Eisenhower Library, Abilene, Texas.
6. John Eisenhower, *The Bitter Woods*, 113–19.
7. Cole, *The Ardennes*, 675.
8. Heinz-Günter Guderian interview by Hugh Ambrose, EC.
9. James Madison oral history, EC.
10. Swanson, *Upfront with Charlie Company*.
11. Charles Roland memoir, EC.
12. John Eisenhower, *The Bitter Woods*, 179.
13. Jochen Peiper interview by Ken Hechler, EC.
14. Heinz Kokott interview by Ken Hechler, EC.
15. Jochen Peiper interview by Ken Hechler, EC.
16. Ibid.
17. Günter Materne interview by Hugh Ambrose, EC.
18. Heinz Kokott interview by Hugh Ambrose, EC.

19. Friedrich Bertenrath interview by Hugh Ambrose, EC.
20. Heinz Kokott interview by Hugh Ambrose, EC.
21. Charles Roland memoir, EC.
22. Swanson, *Upfront with Charlie Company,* 8.
23. Dettor's memoir is in *The Bulge Bugle,* Vol. 13, No. 4 (November 1994), a publication of the Veterans of the Battle of the Bulge, copy in EC.
24. John Eisenhower tells the Bouck story in greater detail in *The Bitter Woods,* 184–94.
25. Ibid., 192.
26. Charles Roland memoir, EC.
27. Roger Foehringer memoir, EC.
28. Hasso von Manteuffel interview by Ken Hechler, EC.
29. MacDonald, *A Time for Trumpets,* 144–45.
30. Heinz Kokott memoir, EC.
31. Heinz-Günter Guderian interview by Hugh Ambrose, EC.
32. Jochen Peiper interview by Ken Hechler, EC.
33. Karl Drescher interview by Hugh Ambrose, EC.
34. Ambrose, *Eisenhower: Soldier and President,* 170–71.
35. Ibid., 172.
36. Kenneth Delaney memoir, EC.
37. Jack Barensfeld memoir, EC.
38. Herbert Meier interview by Hugh Ambrose, EC.
39. Friedrich Bertenrath interview by Hugh Ambrose, EC.
40. Jochen Peiper interview by Ken Hechler, EC.
41. Mocnik's memoir is in *The Pekan,* newsletter of the 526th Armored Infantry Battalion, Vol. 15, No. 1, copy in EC.
42. John Eisenhower, *The Bitter Woods,* 231.
43. Richard Winters interview, EC.
44. Walter Gordon interview, EC.
45. Ralph Hill memoir and letters, EC.
46. Jack Belden, "Retreat in Belgium," *Reporting World War II,* 596–99.
47. Kurt Vonnegut interview, EC.
48. Ambrose, *Eisenhower: Soldier and President,* 172–73.
49. Cunningham, "Battle of the Bulge," *Reporting World War II,* 575.
50. Charles Roland to Stephen Ambrose, January 17, 1995, EC.

CHAPTER 8: THE ARDENNES, DECEMBER 20–23

1. Swanson, *Upfront with Charlie Company.*
2. Charles Roland memoir, EC.
3. Doubler, *Closing with the Enemy,* 208–10.
4. Ibid., 203.
5. Arnold Parish memoir, EC.
6. Benjamin Vandervoort memoir, EC.
7. Jochen Peiper interview by Ken Hechler, EC.
8. Gavin to Vandervoort, October 6, 1979, EC.
9. Ambrose, *Eisenhower: Soldier and President,* 173–74.
10. Ed Cunningham, "Battle of the Bulge," *Reporting World War II,* 590.
11. Howard Randall oral history (with a copy of his "Indentification" card), EC.
12. Leinbaugh and Campbell, *The Men of Company K,* 133.
13. Ambrose, *Eisenhower: Soldier and President,* 175.
14. John Harrison collection, EC.
15. Gordon Carson oral history, EC.

16. Rapport and Northwood, *Rendezvous with Destiny*, 586.
17. Doubler, *Closing with the Enemy*, 217.
18. Robert Bowen memoir, EC.
19. Helmuth Henke interview by Hugh Ambrose, EC.
20. Gottfried Kischkel interview by Hugh Ambrose, EC.
21. Gerd von Fallois interview by Hugh Ambrose, EC.
22. Ibid.
23. Jochen Peiper interview by Ken Hechler, EC.
24. Heinz-Günter Guderian interview by Hugh Ambrose, EC.
25. Jochen Peiper interview by Ken Hechler, EC.
26. Günter Brückner interview by Hugh Ambrose, EC.
27. Jack Barensfeld memoir, EC.
28. Cole, *The Ardennes*, 667.

CHAPTER 9: THE HOLIDAY SEASON

1. Egger and Otts, *G Company's War*, 115.
2. Ibid., 99.
3. Donald Chumley oral history, EC.
4. *Memorable Bulge Incidents*, 26.
5. Swanson, *Upfront with Charlie Company*, 11.
6. Herbert Meier interview by Hugh Ambrose, EC.
7. Swanson, *Upfront with Charlie Company*, 5.
8. Günter Materne interview by Hugh Ambrose, EC.
9. Leinbaugh and Campbell, *The Men of Company K*, 115–18.
10. Ibid., 112–13.
11. Clair Galdonik oral history, EC.
12. Gottfried Kischkel interview by Hugh Ambrose, EC.
13. Egger and Otts, *G Company's War*, 73.
14. *Memorable Bulge Incidents*, 63–64.
15. Ambrose, *Band of Brothers*, 193.
16. Egger and Otts, *G Company's War*, 110.
17. D. Zane Schlemmer memoir, EC.
18. *The B Battery Story:* The 116th AAA Gun Battalion history, copy in EC; Mac-Donald, *A Time for Trumpets*, 540, 555.
19. Phillip Stark memoir, EC.
20. Belton Cooper memoir, EC.
21. *Memorable Bulge Incidents*, 54.
22. *Memorable Bulge Incidents*, 10; Kurt Vonnegut interview by Stephen Ambrose, EC.
23. Colby, *War from the Ground Up*, 463.
24. Henry Andersen oral history, EC; Bill Everhard memoir, EC.
25. Leo Zarnosky memoir, EC.
26. I'm indebted to Bill Everhard and John Goetz for written memories of this incident; they are in EC.
27. Quoted in Bill Everhard's memoir, EC.
28. Charles Stockell memoir, EC.
29. John Eisenhower, *The Bitter Woods*, 342–43.
30. Ibid., 343–45.

CHAPTER 10: NIGHT ON THE LINE

1. William Craft oral history, Lynn Sims collection, EC.
2. Leinbaugh and Campbell, *The Men of Company K*, 83.

3. Egger and Otts, *G Company's War*, 209.
4. Leinbaugh and Campbell, *The Men of Company K*, 115.
5. Balkoski, *Beyond the Beachhead*, 185–87.
6. Gabel, *The Making of a Paratrooper*, 153–54.
7. *The Bulge Bugle*, Vol. 13, No. 4 (November 1994), 17.
8. Leo Lick memoir, EC.
9. Richard Jepsen memoir, EC.
10. Egger and Otts, *G Company's War*, 139.
11. Doubler, *Closing with the Enemy*, 222.
12. Gabel, *The Making of a Paratrooper*, 163.
13. Ingersoll, *Top Secret*, 111.
14. Cowdrey, *Fighting for Life*, 259.
15. Ibid., 266.
16. Colby, *War from the Ground Up*, 344.
17. Leo Lick memoir, EC.
18. Cowdrey, *Fighting for Life*, 267.
19. Egger and Otts, *G Company's War*, 212.
20. Ibid., 223.
21. Leinbaugh and Campbell, *The Men of Company K*, 53.
22. Charles Roland memoir, EC.
23. Clair Galdonik oral history, EC.
24. *Memorable Bulge Incidents*, 30.
25. Arthur Schultz memoir, EC.
26. Leinbaugh and Campbell, *The Men of Company K*, 189.
27. Donald Schoo memoir, EC.
28. Colby, *War from the Ground Up*, 377.
29. Ken Russell memoir, EC.
30. Gray, *The Warriors*, 119.
31. Swanson, *Upfront with Charlie Company*, 3.
32. Egger and Otts, *G Company's War*, 210–11.
33. Ibid., 63.
34. Ambrose, *Band of Brothers*, 186.
35. Balkoski, *Beyond the Beachhead*, 220.
36. Leinbaugh and Campbell, *The Men of Company K*, 111–12.
37. Arnold Parish memoir, EC.
38. Stanley Kalberer memoir, EC.
39. Vonnegut, *Slaughterhouse-Five*, 101.
40. Egger and Otts, *G Company's War*, 135.
41. Fred Claesson oral history, EC.
42. Ambrose, *Band of Brothers*, 186.
43. Egger and Otts, *G Company's War*, 118.
44. Leinbaugh and Campbell, *The Men of Company K*, 52.
45. Ambrose, *Band of Brothers*, 186.
46. Gabel, *The Making of a Paratrooper*, 164.
47. Egger and Otts, *G Company's War*, 209.
48. Leinbaugh and Campbell, *The Men of Company K*, 156.
49. Colby, *War from the Ground Up*, 240.
50. Ibid., 63.
51. Ibid., 537.
52. Leinbaugh and Campbell, *The Men of Company K*.
53. Ambrose, *Band of Brothers*, 241.
54. Dwayne Burns memoir, EC.

55. Swanson, *Upfront with Charlie Company,* 15.
56. Ambrose, *Band of Brothers,* 110; Colby, *War from the Ground Up,* 44.
57. Carwood Lipton interview and memoir, EC.
58. Leinbaugh and Campbell, *The Men of Company K,* 279.

CHAPTER 11: REPLACEMENTS AND REINFORCEMENTS

1. Perret, *There's a War to Be Won,* 373–74.
2. Robert Curtis memoir, EC.
3. Kurt Vonnegut interview, EC.
4. Steckel, "Morale Problems in Combat," 2.
5. Wilson, *If You Survive,* 214.
6. Miller, *A Dark and Bloody Ground,* 135.
7. Leinbaugh and Campbell, *The Men of Company K,* 63.
8. Charles Roland memoir, EC.
9. Perret, *There's a War to Be Won,* 376.
10. Steckel, "Morale Problems in Combat," 3.
11. Ken Russell memoir, EC.
12. Leinbaugh and Campbell, *The Men of Company K,* 91.
13. Colby, *War from the Ground Up,* 74.
14. Douglas Smith memoir, EC.
15. Arthur Schultz memoir, EC.
16. James Eikner memoir, EC.
17. Robert Curtis memoir, EC.
18. Leo Lick memoir, EC.
19. *Memorable Bulge Incidents,* 81.
20. Colby, *War from the Ground Up,* 393–94.
21. Ellis, *On the Front Lines,* 306.
22. Steckel, "Morale Problems in Combat," 4.
23. Charles Roland memoir, EC.
24. Belton Cooper memoir, EC.
25. Egger and Otts, *G Company's War,* 87.
26. Leinbaugh and Campbell, *The Men of Company K,* 153.
27. Douglas Smith memoir, EC.
28. Doubler, *Closing with the Enemy,* 249–50.
29. Charles Roland memoir, EC.
30. Steckel, "Morale Problems in Combat," 6.

CHAPTER 12: THE AIR WAR

1. Doubler, *Closing with the Enemy,* 266.
2. Roush, *World War II Reminiscences,* 174.
3. Astor, *The Mighty Eighth,* 434.
4. Weigley, *Eisenhower's Lieutenants,* 573; Moench, *Marauder Men,* 272.
5. Astor, *The Mighty Eighth,* 419.
6. Robert Hastings interview by Adam Dayan, Wisconsin Veterans Museum, Madison.
7. Rooney, *My War,* 119.
8. Astor, *The Mighty Eighth,* 426.
9. Ibid., 341.
10. Hawkins, *B-17s Over Berlin,* 212.
11. Havener, *The Martin B-26 Marauder,* 191.
12. Stan Catterazole oral history, Wisconsin Veterans Museum, Madison.

13. Rooney, *My War*, 125.
14. Hawkins, *B-17s Over Berlin*, 260.
15. Stan Catterazole oral history, Wisconsin Veterans Museum, Madison.
16. Hawkins, *B-17s Over Berlin*, 263.
17. Roush, *World War II Reminiscences*, 177.
18. Hawkins, *B-17s Over Berlin*, 215.
19. Rooney, *My War*, 95.
20. Astor, *The Mighty Eighth*, 428.
21. Ibid., 377.
22. Leo Fenster memoir, EC.
23. Hawkins, *B-17s Over Berlin*, 256.
24. Ibid., 260.
25. Astor, *The Mighty Eighth*, 382.
26. Moench, *Marauder Men*, 351.
27. Havener, *The Martin B-26 Marauder*, 234–37.
28. Ibid., 187–88.
29. Astor, *The Mighty Eighth*, 341.
30. Philip Wright memoir, EC.
31. The Vonnegut wartime letters are printed in *Traces of Indiana and Midwestern History*.
32. Astor, *The Mighty Eighth*, 397.
33. Ibid.
34. Ibid., 398.
35. Memo to President Eisenhower from Ralph Williams, April 6, 1960, Eisenhower Library.
36. Astor, *The Mighty Eighth*, 420.

CHAPTER 13: MEDICS, NURSES, AND DOCTORS

1. Frank South memoir, EC.
2. Colby, *War from the Ground Up*, 73–75.
3. Edward Gianelloni oral history, EC.
4. Leinbaugh and Campbell, *The Men of Company K*, 228.
5. Cosmos and Cowdrey, *Medical Service in the European Theater of Operations*, 363.
6. Wilson, *If You Survive*, 99–100.
7. Swanson, *Upfront with Charlie Company*, 3.
8. Cowdrey, *Fighting for Life*, 261.
9. Colby, *War from the Ground Up*, 82.
10. Edward Gianelloni oral history, EC.
11. Egger and Otts, *G Company's War*, 110.
12. Cowdrey, *Fighting for Life*, 251–52.
13. Wenzel Andreas Borgert interview by Hugh Ambrose, EC.
14. Colby, *War from the Ground Up*, 73.
15. Robert Bowen memoir, EC.
16. Webster, *Parachute Infantry*, 41.
17. Charles Stockell memoir, EC.
18. Colby, *War from the Ground Up*, 82.
19. Mauldin, *The Brass Ring*, 232.
20. Gabel, *The Making of a Paratrooper*, 209.
21. Bradley tells his story in *Aid Man!*, now out of print and rare. Cowdrey, *Fighting for Life*, 252–55, summarizes it.
22. Cowdrey, *Fighting for Life*, 253.

23. Frank South memoir, EC.
24. Colby, *War from the Ground Up*, 70.
25. Ambrose, *Band of Brothers*, 184.
26. *Memorable Bulge Incidents*, 29.
27. Ken Russell memoir, EC.
28. *Memorable Bulge Incidents*, 28.
29. Edward Gianelloni oral history, EC.
30. Perret, *There's a War to Be Won*, 488.
31. Cowdrey, *Fighting for Life*, 255.
32. Ambrose, *Band of Brothers*, 197–98.
33. Center for Military History, *The Army Nurse Corps*, 15.
34. Colby, *War from the Ground Up*, 73.
35. Campbell, "Servicewomen of World War II," 254.
36. Center for Military History, *The Army Nurse Corps*, 8.
37. Ibid., 9.
38. Allen, *Medicine Under Canvas*, 118.
39. Litoff and Smith, "Today We Have Lived History," 20.
40. Litoff and Smith, "This Is War," 9.
41. Litoff and Smith, *We're in This War, Too*, 164.
42. Ibid., 161.
43. Allen, *Medicine Under Canvas*, 140.
44. Litoff and Smith, *We're in This War, Too*, 153.
45. Ibid., 169.
46. Ibid., 175.
47. Ibid., 160.
48. Ken Russell memoir, EC.
49. Colby, *War from the Ground Up*, 73–75.
50. Cowdrey, *Fighting for Life*, 262.
51. Ibid., 262–63.
52. Ibid., 267.
53. Briand Beudin oral history, EC.
54. Litoff and Smith, *We're in This War, Too*, 159.
55. Allen, *Medicine Under Canvas*, 130.
56. Cosmos and Cowdrey, *Medical Service in the European Theater of Operations*, 385.
57. Richard Winters interview, EC.
58. Cosmos and Cowdrey, *Medical Service in the European Theater of Operations*, 385–86.

CHAPTER 14: JERKS, SAD SACKS, PROFITEERS, AND JIM CROW

1. Gray, *The Warriors*, 43.
2. Arthur Schultz memoir, EC.
3. Fussell, *Wartime*, 80.
4. Colby, *War from the Ground Up*, 61.
5. Edward Gianelloni oral history, EC.
6. William Leesemann memoir, EC.
7. Bradley, *A Soldier's Story*, 405.
8. Ambrose, *The Supreme Commander*, 488–89.
9. Pogue, *The Supreme Command*, 323.
10. The informant insists on remaining anonymous.
11. Luck, *Panzer Commander*, 210.
12. Gerhard Lemcke interview by Hugh Ambrose, EC.

13. Hannibal von Luttichgau interview by Hugh Ambrose, EC.
14. Ernest Hemingway, "How We Came to Paris," *Collier's*, October 7, 1944.
15. Chernitsky, *Voices from the Foxholes*, 70.
16. Ed Jabol oral history, EC.
17. Gray, *The Warriors*, 17-18.
18. Huie, *The Execution of Private Slovik*, 131.
19. Wilson, *If You Survive*, 155–57, 168–69.
20. *Yank*, April 28, 1944.
21. Walter Kaspers interview by Hugh Ambrose, EC.
22. Lee, *The Employment of Negro Troops*, 652.
23. Weigley, *Eisenhower's Lieutenants*, 660.
24. Lee, *The Employment of Negro Troops*, 661.
25. Ibid., 704.
26. Sims, "They Have Seen the Elephant," Isaac Coleman memoir.
27. Lee, *The Employment of Negro Troops*, 689–93.
28. Ibid., 693–95.
29. Weigley, *Eisenhower's Lieutenants*, 661.
30. Lee, *The Employment of Negro Troops*, 697.
31. Ibid., 702.
32. *Yank*, July 28, 1944.
33. Lee, *Employment of Negro Troops*, 705.

CHAPTER 15: PRISONERS OF WAR

1. SHAEF War Crimes Files, copy in EC.
2. Edward Webber memoir, EC.
3. D. Zane Schlemmer memoir, EC.
4. Ambrose, *Band of Brothers*, 210.
5. Fussell, *Doing Battle*, 124.
6. Colby, *War from the Ground Up*, 532.
7. Charles Stockell memoir, EC.
8. Cole, *The Ardennes*, 264.
9. Ibid., 261–62.
10. Ed Cunningham, "The Battle of the Bulge," in *Reporting World War II*, Vol. II, 582.
11. Cole, *The Ardennes*, 262.
12. Ibid., 263.
13. John Eisenhower, *The Bitter Woods*, 237.
14. J. Frank Brumbaugh memoir, EC.
15. Walter Melford memoir, EC.
16. James Pemberton memoir, EC.
17. Ernest Vermont memoir, EC.
18. Vonnegut, *Slaughterhouse-Five*, 37, 61–62, with thanks to the author for permission to quote.
19. Astor, *The Mighty Eighth*, 414.
20. Ernest Vermont memoir, EC.
21. Durand, *Stalag Luft III*, 358–59.
22. Ibid., 158.
23. Astor, *The Mighty Eighth*, 415.
24. Ernest Vermont memoir, EC.
25. Whiting, *Death of a Division*, 117.
26. Durand, *Stalag Luft III*, 358.
27. Roger Foehringer memoir, EC.

28. Josef Bischof interview by Stephen Ambrose, EC.
29. Schott, "Prisoners Like Us."
30. Bischof and Ambrose, *Eisenhower and the German POWs*, 234.
31. Cowdrey, "A Question of Numbers," 92.

CHAPTER 16: WINTER WAR

1. John Cobb memoir, EC.
2. Paul-Arthur Zeihe interview by Hugh Ambrose, EC.
3. John Harrison letters, EC.
4. Don Schoo memoir, EC.
5. D. Zane Schlemmer memoir, EC.
6. John Harrison memoir, EC.
7. Weigley, *Eisenhower's Lieutenants*, 572.
8. Ambrose, *Eisenhower: Soldier and President*, 179.
9. Ibid.
10. Ibid., 180.
11. Wilson, *If You Survive*, 238.
12. Ambrose, *Band of Brothers*, 209.
13. Egger and Otts, *G Company's War*, 129.
14. Ambrose, *Band of Brothers*, 208, 218.
15. Colby, *War from the Ground Up*, 389.
16. Ibid., 381.
17. Ellis, *On the Front Lines*, 97.
18. Gabel, *The Making of a Paratrooper*, 172–75.
19. Colby, *War from the Ground Up*, 373.
20. Don Schoo memoir, EC.
21. Dwayne Burns memoir, EC.
22. Don Scott memoir, EC.
23. Leinbaugh and Campbell, *The Men of Company K*, 167–68.
24. Colby, *War from the Ground Up*, 378.
25. Walter Rahn interview by Hugh Ambrose, EC.
26. Gerhard Lemcke interview by Hugh Ambrose, EC.
27. Gerhard Winkler interview by Hugh Ambrose, EC.
28. Helmut Ritgen interview by Hugh Ambrose, EC.
29. Langdon, "Ready," 112–13.
30. Hans von Luck oral history, EC.
31. Ibid.
32. Colley, "Operation Northwind," 15.
33. Hans von Luck oral history, EC.
34. Colley, "Operation Northwind," 16.
35. Leinbaugh and Campbell, *The Men of Company K*, 157, 161–62.
36. Ibid., 177–82.
37. Roy Creek memoir, EC.
38. Ambrose, *Eisenhower: Soldier and President*, 180.
39. Ibid., 180–81.
40. Leinbaugh and Campbell, *The Men of Company K*, 190.
41. Wilson, *If You Survive*, 234–35.
42. Weigley, *Eisenhower's Lieutenants*, 574.
43. Ibid.
44. Doubler, *Closing with the Enemy*, 228.

CHAPTER 17: CLOSING TO THE RHINE

1. Ambrose, *Eisenhower*, Vol. I, *Soldier, General of the Army*, 380.
2. Weigley, *Eisenhower's Lieutenants*, 578.
3. Ambrose, *Eisenhower*, Vol. I, *Soldier, General of the Army*, 381.
4. Ibid., 382.
5. Colby, *War from the Ground Up*, 414–15.
6. Province, *Patton's Third Army*, 169, 174.
7. Jim Underkofler interview, Wisconsin Veterans Museum, Madison.
8. Swanson, *Upfront with Charlie Company*, 16.
9. Ibid., 14.
10. Clinton Riddle memoir, EC.
11. Colby, *War from the Ground Up*, 407.
12. Ibid., 403.
13. Patton, *War as I Knew It*, 251.
14. Colby, *War from the Ground Up*, 409–10.
15. Egger and Otts, *G Company's War*, 175–76.
16. John Cobb memoir, EC.
17. Leinbaugh and Campbell, *The Men of Company K*, 217.
18. Ellis, *On the Front Lines*, 66.
19. Leinbaugh and Campbell, *The Men of Company K*, 218.
20. Weigley, *Eisenhower's Lieutenants*, 607.
21. Leinbaugh and Campbell, *The Men of Company K*, 219.
22. Hoegh and Doyle, *Timberwolf Tracks*, 229.
23. Ibid., 23–31.
24. Leinbaugh and Campbell, *The Men of Company K*, 220.
25. Egger and Otts, *G Company's War*, 228.
26. Ellis, *On the Front Lines*, 92.
27. Karl Drescher interview by Hugh Ambrose, EC.
28. Ewald Becker interview by Hugh Ambrose, EC.
29. Karl Drescher interview by Hugh Ambrose, EC.
30. Colby, *War from the Ground Up*, 426.
31. Patton, *War as I Knew It*, 243.
32. Ibid., 240.
33. Ibid., 248.
34. Ibid., 246.
35. Ibid., 243.
36. Weigley, *Eisenhower's Lieutenants*, 589.
37. Ibid., 593–95.
38. Patton, *War as I Knew It*, 250, 247.
39. Weigley, *Eisenhower's Lieutenants*, 595.
40. Ibid., 617.
41. Hechler, *The Bridge at Remagen*, 35.
42. Ibid., 16–17.
43. Max Lale's wartime letters are reprinted in the *East Texas Historical Journal*.
44. Günter Materne interview by Hugh Ambrose, EC.
45. Ibid.
46. D. Eisenhower to Milton Eisenhower, Sept. 1, 1939, Eisenhower Library, Abilene, Texas.
47. Ambrose, *Band of Brothers*, 265.
48. Ibid., 239.

CHAPTER 18: CROSSING THE RHINE

1. Weigley, *Eisenhower's Lieutenants*, 625.
2. Ibid.
3. Leinbaugh and Campbell, *The Men of Company K*, 224.
4. Ibid., 231.
5. Ibid.
6. Ibid., 232.
7. Ibid., 257.
8. Ibid., 234.
9. Stannard, *Infantry*, 81.
10. William Faust memoir, EC.
11. Stannard, *Infantry*, 182.
12. Ellis, *On the Front Lines*, 205.
13. Egger and Otts, *G Company's War*, 217.
14. Ibid., 216–23.
15. Rolf Pauls interview by Hugh Ambrose, EC.
16. Steinhoff, *Voices from the Third Reich*, 413.
17. Doubler, *Closing with the Enemy*, 161–63; Weigley, *Eisenhower's Lieutenants*, 626–27.
18. Hechler, *The Bridge at Remagen*, 115.
19. Ibid., 115–21.
20. Steinhoff, *Voices from the Third Reich*, 410–11.
21. Bradley, *A General's Life*, 406.
22. Rolf Pauls interview by Hugh Ambrose, EC.
23. Waldemar Führing interview by Hugh Ambrose, EC.
24. Charles Roland memoir, EC.
25. William Westmoreland interview, EC.
26. Doubler, *Closing with the Enemy*, 164.
27. Oswald Filla interview by Hugh Ambrose, EC.
28. Doubler, *Closing with the Enemy*, 165.
29. Roush, *World War II Reminiscences*, 218–19.
30. Doubler, *Closing with the Enemy*, 167.
31. Weigley, *Eisenhower's Lieutenants*, 643.
32. Province, *Patton's Third Army*, 226.
33. Weigley, *Eisenhower's Lieutenants*, 648.
34. Hawkins, *B-17s Over Berlin*, 267.
35. Richard Hottelet, "Airborne Assault," *Reporting World War II*, Vol. II, 649–59.
36. Gabel, *The Making of a Paratrooper*, 263.
37. Valentin Klopsch memoir, in the 513th PIR remembrance binder, EC.
38. Arthur Tappan memoir, EC.
39. Frisbee, "Operation Varsity."
40. Arthur Tappan memoir, EC.
41. Weigley, *Eisenhower's Lieutenants*, 648.
42. Colby, *War from the Ground Up*, 447.
43. D. Zane Schlemmer memoir, EC.
44. James Pemberton memoir, EC.
45. Colby, *War from the Ground Up*, 462.
46. Belton Cooper memoir, EC.
47. Ibid.
48. Lale, "My War," 15.

49. Joe Burns oral history, EC.
50. David Webster memoir, EC.

CHAPTER 19: VICTORY

1. Swanson, *Upfront with Charlie Company*, 28.
2. Lale, "My War," 15.
3. Ibid., 17.
4. Swanson, *Upfront with Charlie Company*, 29.
5. Gilbert, *The Day the War Ended*, 7–8.
6. Dwight Eisenhower interview, EC.
7. Province, *Patton's Third Army*, 238, 270.
8. Ambrose, *Band of Brothers*, 257.
9. Ibid.
10. Gilbert, *The Day the War Ended*, 5.
11. Gray, *The Warriors*, 152.
12. Dwight Eisenhower, *Crusade in Europe*, 405.
13. Erich Womelsdorf interview by Hugh Ambrose, EC.
14. Hannibal von Lüttichgau interview by Hugh Ambrose, EC.
15. Wenzel Andreas Borgert interview by Hugh Ambrose, EC.
16. Calvin Boykin memoir, EC.
17. Ambrose, *Eisenhower and Berlin, 1945*, 89.
18. Günter Materne interview by Hugh Ambrose, EC.
19. Ambrose, *Eisenhower and Berlin, 1945*, 75.
20. John Cobb memoir, EC.
21. Friedrich Bertenrath interview by Hugh Ambrose, EC.
22. Egger and Otts, *G Company's War*, 250.
23. Gregori Arbatov interview by Stephen Ambrose, EC.
24. Stannard, *Infantry*, 36–38.
25. Weigley, *Eisenhower's Lieutenants*, 710.
26. Reid, *The Latter Days at Colditz*, 226.
27. Gilbert, *The Day the War Ended*, 37.
28. Egger and Otts, *G Company's War*, 242.
29. Charles Stockell memoir, EC.
30. Ambrose, *Band of Brothers*, 269.
31. Egger and Otts, *G Company's War*, 242.
32. Ibid., 247.
33. Leinbaugh and Campbell, *The Men of Company K*, 259.
34. Belton Cooper memoir, EC.
35. Gilbert, *The Day the War Ended*, 11.
36. Dwight Eisenhower, *Crusade in Europe*, 408–9.
37. *Reporting World War II*, Vol. II, 685.
38. Ibid., 720, 724.
39. Roush, *World War II Reminiscences*, 166–67.
40. Ambrose, *Band of Brothers*, 270.
41. Steinhoff, *Voices from the Third Reich*, 490.
42. Gilbert, *The Day the War Ended*, 12.
43. Arthur Schultz memoir, EC.
44. *Stars and Stripes*, May 6, 1945.
45. Ewald Becker interview by Hugh Ambrose, EC.
46. Forrest Pogue interview, EC.
47. James Pemberton memoir, EC.

48. Charles Stockell memoir, EC.
49. Colby, *War from the Ground Up*, 471.
50. Arthur Schultz memoir, EC.
51. Egger and Otts, *G Company's War*, 252–53.

EPILOGUE

1. Walter Zittats interview by Hugh Ambrose, EC.

Bibliography

Allen, Max. *Medicine Under Canvas: A War Journal of the 77th Evacuation Hospital.* Kansas City, Mo.: The Sosland Press, 1949.

Ambrose, Stephen E. *Band of Brothers: E Company, 506th Regiment, 101st Airborne, from Normandy to Hitler's Eagle's Nest.* New York: Simon & Schuster, 1990.

———. *Eisenhower.* Vol. I, *Soldier, General of the Army, President-Elect, 1890–1952.* New York: Simon & Schuster, 1983.

———. *Eisenhower and Berlin, 1945: The Decision to Halt at the Elbe.* New York: W. W. Norton, 1967.

———. *Eisenhower: Soldier and President.* New York: Simon & Schuster, 1990.

———. *The Supreme Commander: The War Years of General Dwight D. Eisenhower.* Garden City, N.Y.: Doubleday, 1970.

Astor, Gerald. *The Mighty Eighth: The Air War in Europe as Told by the Men Who Fought It.* New York: Donald Fine Books, 1997.

Baldridge, Robert C. *Victory Road.* Bennington, Vt.: Merriam Press, 1995.

Balkoski, Joseph. *Beyond the Beachhead: The 29th Infantry Division in Normandy.* Harrisburg, Pa.: Stackpole Books, 1989.

Bischof, Gunter, and Stephen Ambrose, eds., *Eisenhower and the German POWs: Facts Against Falsehood.* Baton Rouge: Louisiana State University Press, 1992.

Booth, Michael T., and Spencer Duncan. *Paratrooper: The Life of Gen. James M. Gavin.* New York: Simon & Schuster, 1994.

Boritt, Gabor, ed. *War Comes Again: Comparative Vistas on the Civil War and World War II.* New York: Oxford University Press, 1995.

Bradley, Omar. *A General's Life.* New York: Simon & Schuster, 1983.

———. *A Soldier's Story.* New York: Henry Holt, 1951.

Bradley, Robert. *Aid Man!* New York: Praeger, 1970.

Campbell, D'Ann. "Servicewomen of World War II." *Armed Forces and Society,* Vol. 16, No. 2 (winter 1990).

Center for Military History. *The Army Nurse Corps.* Washington, D.C.: GPO, CMH Publication 72-14, 1993.

Chandler, David, ed. *The D-Day Encyclopedia.* New York: Simon & Schuster, 1994.

Chernitsky, Dorothy. *Voices from the Foxholes, by the Men of the 110th Infantry.* Published by Dorothy Chernitsky, 18 Country Club Blvd., Uniontown, PA 15401, 1991.

Colby, John. *War from the Ground Up: The 90th Division in WWII.* Austin, Tex.: Nortex Press, 1991.

Cole, Hugh M. *The Ardennes: The Battle of the Bulge.* Washington, D.C.: Office of the Chief of Military History, 1965.

———. *The Lorraine Campaign.* A volume in the *United States Army in World War II: The European Theater of Operations* series. Washington, D.C: Department of the Army, 1950.

Colley, David. "Operation Northwind: Greatest Defensive Battle." *VFW Magazine*, January 1995.

Cosmos, Graham, and Albert Cowdrey. *Medical Service in the European Theater of Operations*. Washington, D.C.: Center for Military History, 1992.

Cowdrey, Albert. *Fighting for Life: American Military Medicine in World War II*. New York: The Free Press, 1994.

———. "A Question of Numbers," in Bischof and Ambrose, *Eisenhower and the German POWs*.

Doubler, Michael D. *Closing with the Enemy: How GIs Fought the War in Europe, 1944–1945*. Lawrence: University of Kansas Press, 1994.

Durand, Arthur. *Stalag Luft III: The Secret Story*. Baton Rouge: Louisiana State University Press, 1988.

Egger, Bruce E., and Lee M. Otts. *G Company's War: Two Personal Accounts of the Campaigns in Europe, 1944–1945*. Tuscaloosa: University of Alabama Press, 1992.

Eisenhower, Dwight D. *Crusade in Europe*. Garden City, N.Y.: Doubleday, 1948.

Eisenhower, John. *The Bitter Woods: The Battle of the Bulge*. New York: G. P. Putnam's Sons, 1969.

———. *Strictly Personal*. Garden City, N.Y.: Doubleday, 1974.

Ellis, John. *On the Front Lines: The Experience of War Through the Eyes of the Allied Soldiers in World War II*. New York: John Wiley & Sons, 1980.

English, John A. *A Perspective on Infantry*. New York: Praeger Special Studies, 1988.

Fraser, David. *Knight's Cross: A Life of Field Marshal Erwin Rommel*. New York: HarperCollins, 1993.

Frisbee, John. "Operation Varsity." *Air Force Magazine*, March 1996.

Fussell, Paul. *Doing Battle: The Making of a Skeptic*. Boston: Little, Brown, 1996.

———. *Wartime: Understanding Behavior in the Second World War*. New York: Oxford University Press, 1989.

Gabel, Kurt. *The Making of a Paratrooper: Airborne Training and Combat in World War II*. Lawrence: University of Kansas Press, 1990.

Gilbert, Martin. *The Day the War Ended: May 8, 1945—Victory in Europe*. New York: Henry Holt, 1995.

Gray, Glenn. *The Warriors: Reflections on Men in Battle*. New York: Harper & Row, 1959.

Hastings, Max. *Overlord: D-Day and the Battle for Normandy*. New York: Simon & Schuster, 1984.

Hatch, Gardner, ed. *4th Infantry "Ivy" Division: Steadfast and Loyal*. Paducah, Ky.: Turner Publishing, 1987.

Havener, J. K. *The Martin B-26 Marauder*. Blue Ridge Summit, Pa.: Tab Books, 1988.

Hawkins, Ian L., ed. *B-17s Over Berlin: Personal Stories from the 95th Bomb Group*. Washington, D.C.: Brassey's, 1990.

Hechler, Ken. *The Bridge at Remagen*. Missoula, Mont.: Pictorial Histories Publishing Company, 1993.

Hemingway, Ernest. "How We Came to Paris." *Collier's*, October 7, 1944.

Hoegh, Leo, and Howard Doyle. *Timberwolf Tracks: The History of the 104th Infantry Division*. Washington, D.C.: Infantry Journal Press, 1946.

Huie, William Bradford. *The Execution of Private Slovik*. New York: Duell, Sloan and Pearce, 1954.

Hynes, Samuel, et al., eds. *Reporting World War II: American Journalism 1938–1946*, 2 vols. New York: Library of America, 1995.

Ingersoll, Ralph. *Top Secret*. New York: Harcourt Brace, 1946.

Lale, Max. "My War." *East Texas Historical Journal*, Vol. 32 (1994).

Langdon, Allen. *"Ready": The History of the 505th*: 82nd Airborne Division, 1986.

Lee, Ulysses. *The Employment of Negro Troops*. Washington, D.C.: Office of the Chief of Military History, 1966.

Leinbaugh, Harold P., and John D. Campbell. *The Men of Company K: The Autobiography of a World War II Rifle Company*. New York: William Morrow, 1985.

Litoff, Judy, and David Smith. " 'This Is War and I Guess I Can Take It:' The World War II Letters of American Red Cross Women Overseas." Paper given at annual meeting of the American Red Cross Overseas Association, July 2, 1994.

———. " 'Today We Have Lived History:' The D-Day Letters of U.S. Women." Paper given at the Eisenhower Center, May 16, 1994.

———. *We're in This War, Too: World War II Letters from American Women in Uniform*. New York: Oxford University Press, 1994.

Luck, Hans von. *Panzer Commander*. New York: Praeger, 1989.

MacDonald, Charles. *The Mighty Endeavor: American Armed Forces in the European Theater in World War II*. New York: Oxford University Press, 1969.

———. *A Time for Trumpets*. New York: William Morrow, 1984.

Mauldin, Bill. *The Brass Ring*. New York: Norton, 1971.

Memorable Bulge Incidents: Living Legends. Published by Veterans of the Battle of the Bulge, P.O. Box 11129, Arlington, VA 22210.

Miller, Edward G. *A Dark and Bloody Ground: The Hurtgen Forest and the Roer River Dams, 1944–1945*. College Station: Texas A&M University Press, 1995.

Moench, John O. *Marauder Men: An Account of the Martin B-26 Marauder*. Longwood, Fla.: Maalia Enterprises, 1989.

Move Out: The Combat Story of the 743rd Tank Battalion. n.p., n.d. Copy in Eisenhower Center, University of New Orleans.

Murphy, Edward F. *Heroes of WWII*. New York: Ballantine, 1991.

New York Sun, October 24–27, 1944.

Patton, George S. *War as I Knew It*. Boston: Houghton Mifflin, 1947.

Perret, Geoffrey. *There's a War to Be Won: The United States Army in World War II*. New York: Random House, 1991.

Pogue, Forrest C. *The Supreme Command*. A volume in the *United States Army in World War II: The European Theater of Operations* series. Washington, D.C.: Office of the Chief of Military History, 1954.

Province, Charles M. *Patton's Third Army: A Daily Combat Diary*. New York: Hippocrene Books, 1992.

Pyle, Ernie. *Ernie's War: The Best of Ernie Pyle's World War II Dispatches*. New York: Touchstone/Simon & Schuster, 1986.

Rapport, Leonard, and Arthur Northwood. *Rendezvous with Destiny: A History of the 101st Airborne Division*. Greenville, Tex.: 101st Airborne Division Association, 1965.

Reid, Pat. *The Latter Days at Colditz*. London: Hodder and Stoughton, 1952.

Rooney, Andy. *My War*. Holbrook, Mass: Adams Media Corp., 1995.

Roush, John H., ed. *World War II Reminiscences*. Reserve Officers Association of California, P.O. Box 4950, San Rafael, CA 94913, 1995.

Ruppenthal, Roland. *Logistical Support of the Armies*. Two volumes. A volume in the *United States Army in World War II: The European Theater of Opera-*

tions series. Washington, D.C.: Office of the Chief of Military History, 1953.

Ryan, Cornelius. *A Bridge Too Far*. New York: Simon & Schuster, 1974.

Salomon, Sidney. *2nd U.S. Ranger Infantry Battalion*. Doylestown, Pa.: Birchwood Books, 1991.

Schott, Matthew. "Prisoners Like Us: German POWs Encounter Louisiana's African-Americans." *Louisiana History,* Vol. 36, No. 3 (Summer 1995).

Sims, Lynn. "They Have Seen the Elephant." Veterans' Remembrances from World War II for the 40th Anniversary of V-E Day. Ft. Lee, Va., 1985.

Stannard, Richard M. *Infantry: An Oral History of a World War II American Infantry Battalion*. New York: Twayne, 1993.

Steckel, Francis C. "Morale Problems in Combat: American Soldiers in Europe in World War II." *Army History,* Summer 1994.

Steinhoff, Johannes, and Peter Pechel and Dennis Showalter, eds. *Voices from the Third Reich: An Oral History*. New York: Da Capo Press, 1994.

Swanson, Vernon, ed. *Upfront with Charlie Company: A Combat History of Company C, 395th Infantry Regiment, 99th Infantry Division*. North Royalton, Ohio: 1995.

Vonnegut, Kurt, Jr. "Memoirs." *Traces of Indiana and Midwestern History,* Vol. 3, No. 4 (Special Issue, Fall 1991).

———. *Slaughterhouse-Five, or The Children's Crusade*. New York: Delacorte Press, 1994 edition.

Wandrey, June. *Bedpan Commando: The Story of a Combat Nurse During WWII*. Elmore, Ohio: Elmore Publishing, 1989.

Webster, David Kenyon. *Parachute Infantry: An American Paratrooper's Memoir of D-Day and the Fall of the Third Reich*. Baton Rouge: Louisiana State University Press, 1994.

Weigley, Russell. *Eisenhower's Lieutenants: The Campaigns of France and Germany, 1944–1945*. Bloomington: Indiana University Press, 1981.

Weiss, Robert. *Enemy North, South, East, West*. Portland, Ore.: Strawberry Hill Press, 1998.

Whiting, Charles. *Death of a Division*. New York: Stein and Day, 1980.

Wills, Deryk. *Put on Your Boots and Parachutes! Personal Stories of the Veterans of the U.S. 82nd Airborne Division*. Published 1992 by Deryk Wills, 70 Hidcote Road, Oadby, Leicester LE2 5PF, England.

Wilson, George. *If You Survive*. New York: Ballantine, 1987.

Oral Histories, Memoirs, Letters

U.S. VETERANS

Henry Andersen
Franklin Anderson
Jack Barensfeld
Briand Beudin
Robert Bowen
Calvin Boykin
J. Frank Brumbaugh
Dwayne Burns
Joe Burns
Donald Chumley
Gordon Carson

Fred Claesson
John Cobb
Isaac Coleman
Belton Cooper
James Coyle
William Craft
Roy Creek
Robert Curtis
Kenneth Delaney
James Delong
James Eikner

Dwight D. Eisenhower
Bill Everhard
William Faust
Leo Fenster
Jim Finn
Roger Foehringer
Clair Galdonik
Edward "Buddy" Gianelloni
Ed Gilleran
John Goetz
Walter Gordon
Fred Hall
John Harrison
Joseph Heller
Ralph Hill
Ed Jabol
Richard Jepsen
Stanley Kalberer
William Leesemann
Leo Lick
Carwood Lipton
Len Lomell
Walter Melford
Robert Merriman
Arnold Parish
James Pemberton

Forrest Pogue
Clinton Riddle
Charles Roland
Andy Rooney
Ken Russell
Sidney Salomon
Otis Sampson
D. Zane Schlemmer
Donald Schoo
Arthur "Dutch" Schultz
Don Scott
Douglas Smith
Frank South
Phillip Stark
Charles Stockell
Arthur Tappan
James Underkofler (Wisconsin Veterans Museum)
Benjamin Vandervoort
Ernest Vermont
Kurt Vonnegut
Edward Webber
David Webster
William Westmoreland
Richard Winters
Frank Woosley

GERMAN VETERANS

Bernhard Backer
Joachim Barth
Ewald Becker
Günter Behr
Herbert Berger
Friedrich Bertenrath
Josef Bischof
Wenzel Andreas Borgert
Günter Brückner
Hans-Heinrich Dibbern
Friederich Dittmer
Karl Drescher
Gerd von Fallois
Günter Feldmann
Oswald Filla
Waldemar Führing
Günter Gaida
Reinhold Gerbig
Helmut Gohlke
Klaus Groeger
Heinz-Günter Guderian
Kuno Heilmann
Helmuth Henke
Hans Herbst

Kurt Hering
Helmut Hesse
Günter Hölting
Karl-Heinz Jahn
Walter Jungmichel
Walter Kaspers
Gottfried Kischkel
Valentin Klopsch
Heinz Kokutt
Gerhard Lemcke
Hans von Luck
Hannibal von Lüttichgau
Hasso von Manteuffel
Günter Materne
Herbert Meier
Günter Möllenhoff
Walter Padberg
Rolf Pauls
Jochen Peiper
Johannes Puppe
Walter Rahn
Helmut Ritgen
Adolf Rogosch
Frederick Ruge

Walter Schäfer-Kehnert
Gustav Spreckels
Paul-Alfred Stoob
Franz Terwelp
Franz Thelen
Karl Thieme

Erwin Vogel
Gerhard Vogtländer
Gerhard Winkler
Erich Womelsdorf
Paul-Arthur Zeihe
Walter Zittats

Index

**POCKET
BOOKS**

BAND OF BROTHERS

Stephen E. Ambrose

The *Sunday Times* #1 bestseller and a major BBC series
produced by Tom Hanks and Steven Spielberg.

In BAND OF BROTHERS, Stephen E.
Ambrose pays tribute to the men of Easy
Company, a crack rifle company in the US
Army. From their rigorous training in
Georgia in 1942 to the dangerous parachute
landings on D-Day and their triumphant
capture of Hitler's 'Eagle's Nest' in
Berchtesgarden, Ambrose tells the story of
this remarkable company. Repeatedly sent
on the toughest missions, these brave men
fought, went hungry, froze and died in the
service of their country.

'Superb . . . his scholarly writing style seems
to know that heroism needs no cheap
embellishment. Gripping and humbling'
GLASGOW HERALD

PRICE £6.99
ISBN 0 7434 2990 7

**POCKET
BOOKS**

D-DAY

JUNE 6, 1944

Stephen E. Ambrose

D-DAY is the brilliant telling of the battles of
Omaha and Utah beaches. Hailed as the premier
American narrative and military historian, Ambrose
relives the epic victory of democracy on the most
important day of the twentieth century.

'Definitive . . . His evidence is overwhelming'
Wall Street Journal

'*D-Day* is mostly about people, but goes even
further in evoking the horror, the endurance,
the daring and, indeed, the human failings in
Omaha Beach . . . Outstanding'
The New York Times Book Review

'Reading this history, you can understand why for
so many of its participants, despite all the death
surrounding them, life revealed itself in that
moment at that place'
The New York Times

PRICE £8.99
ISBN 0 7434 5015 9